EXPLORING THE PSALMS

VOLUME TWO
Psalms 89 -150

EXPLORING
THE
PSALMS

VOLUME TWO
Psalms 89 -150

JOHN PHILLIPS

LOIZEAUX BROTHERS
Neptune, New Jersey

First Two-Volume Edition, July 1988

Library of Congress Cataloging-in-Publication Data

Phillips, John, 1927 –
Exploring the Psalms / John Phillips.
Contents: v. 1. Psalms 1-88 — v. 2. Psalms 89-150.
ISBN 0-87213-653-1
1. Bible. O.T. Psalms—Commentaries. I. Title.
BS1430.3.P46 1988
223'.207—dc19   88-12938

ISBN 0-87213-653-1 set
ISBN 0-87213-678-7 v.1
ISBN 0-87213-679-5 v.2

Printed in the United States of America

10 9 8 7 6 5 4 3

CONTENTS

Psalm 89

THE DAVIDIC COVENANT

I. THE ACTUAL SIGNIFICANCE OF THE COVENANT (89:1-4)
  A. The Principles Involved (89:1-2)
  B. The Person Involved (87:3)
  C. The Promise Involved (87:4)
II. THE ABSOLUTE SECURITY OF THE COVENANT (89:5-18)
  A. God's Power in Heaven (89:5-8)
    1. The Heavenly Court (89:5-6)
    2. The Heavenly Chorus (89:7-8)
  B. God's Power in History (89:9-18)
    1. The Revelation of that Power (89:9-13)
      a. Revealed in Conquest (89:9-10)
      b. Revealed in Creation (89:11-13)
    2. The Response to that Power (89:14-18)
       He Praises God for:
      a. His Righteous Principles (89:14)
      b. His Redeemed People (89:15-16)
      c. His Royal Protection (89:17-18)
III. THE AMAZING SPLENDOR OF THE COVENANT (89:19-37)
  A. Made with David Personally (89:19-28)
    1. It Was Majestic in Expression (89:12-23)
      a. The Divine Initiative (89:19-20)
      b. The Divine Incentive (89:21-23)
    2. It Was Merciful in Execution (89:24)
    3. It Was Messianic in Expectation (89:25-28)
      a. The Messiah's Dominion (89:25)
      b. The Messiah's Deity (89:26-27)
      c. The Messiah's Durability (89:28)
  B. Made with David Perpetually (89:29-37)
    1. The Breadth of the Contract (89:29)
    2. The Betrayal of the Contract (89:30-32)
    3. The Blessings of the Contract (89:33-37)
IV. THE APPARENT SUSPENSION OF THE COVENANT (89:38-51)
  A. The Protest (89:38-45)
  B. The Prayer (89:46-52)
    1. O Lord, Remember My Condition (89:46-48)
    2. O Lord, Remember Your Covenant (89:49-51)

THIS PSALM is entitled *"Maschil* of Ethan the Ezrahite."* It is the twelfth of thirteen *maschil* psalms especially written for instruction. Ethan the Ezrahite was one of the wise men of the east, so renowned for wisdom that Solomon's sagacity is compared with his. He is often identified with Jeduthun, and it is at least possible that he is Ethan the singer, a Levite of the family of Merari, appointed by David as one of the leaders of the temple music. On the surface, identifying the psalm with Ethan would place it back in the very early days of the kingdom. The fact that it is a song of the Davidic covenant would seem, again on the surface, to date it in David's reign. But, as we shall see, it is a song which mourns the apparent collapse of that covenant. Some have speculated that Ethan outlived Solomon long enough to witness the disruption of the kingdom and that this song is an impassioned appeal to the Lord to remember His promise and pledge to David.

Most seem to feel, however, that the psalm relates to the exile when the Davidic covenant seemed to be torn to shreds by a God whose patience was exhausted by the wickedness of the later kings of David's line. If this is so, some unknown author might have picked up a previous hymn by Ethan, adapted it to the times, perhaps added to it, and republished it under Ethan's name. Or, it could be that Ethan was a prophet as well as a singer and a sage. He may have written this psalm foreseeing where the idolatries Solomon had introduced into his kingdom would eventually end.

The tone of the psalm, however, suggests that the final breakup of the monarchy was fresh in the mind of the author. So probably, with an early manuscript in front of him, this unknown author or editor elaborated on a previous poem by Ethan, adapting it to the uncertainties of the hour. Some have suggested that the psalm was written by the youthful Jehoiachin during his exile in Babylon. For thirty-six years he languished in prison, but after the death of Nebuchadnezzar he was released and kindly treated by Evil-Merodach, the next Babylonian king.

It was of this godless man, Jehoiachin, that the prophet Jeremiah wrote: "Write ye this man childless"; that is, childless as far as the throne was concerned. The royal dynasty of David through Solomon came to an abrupt end in this man. No further son of David's line through Solomon and through Jehoiachin would be allowed to sit upon the throne of David. It hardly seems possible that Jehoiachin could have written this great psalm of the covenant—unless his prison experiences taught him wisdom.

All of which still leaves us with our question unanswered: who wrote this psalm? If it was written during the captivity, as so many seem to feel, then perhaps it was written by Daniel.

Daniel was of royal blood. He was a captive in Babylon and had been there since the time of the first deportation in the fourth year of Jehoiakim. The final breakup of the monarchy must have touched Daniel deeply. First the boy king Jehoiachin arrived in Babylon to be flung unceremoniously into prison. Then Zedekiah came, his eyes blinded, tales of his treachery common knowledge throughout the city. Daniel's visions of the coming dominance of the Gentiles must have added to his sense of shame at the wretched failure of Israel to fulfill its national destiny of bearing witness to the world of the goodness and grace of God. Many a time, especially in his early years in Babylon—before later visions brought things more clearly into focus—he must have prayed just such a prayer as this prayer of "Ethan the Ezrahite." It is quite possible this psalm found its way into our Bible by way of Daniel's very able pen. Who can tell?

It is in four parts, and it is a long psalm, so we shall simply sketch its highlights. However, a detailed analysis is given so that its symmetrical structure can be appreciated and all its parts can be more fully explored.

I. The Actual Significance of the Covenant (89:1-4)

God has entered into contractual agreement *only* with the nation of Israel. The constitution of other nations may indeed acknowledge God, but no other nation has God as its guarantor and committed ally. This amazing political situation is Israel's alone. God's covenant with Israel is unique.

A. The Principles Involved (89:1-2)

"I will sing of the mercies of the LORD forever: with my mouth will I make known Thy faithfulness to all generations. For I have said, Mercy shall be built up forever: Thy faithfulness shalt Thou establish in the very heavens." Mercy! Faithfulness! These are the underlying principles of the Davidic covenant.

"I will sing . . . for I have said. . . ." Everything around this singer is dark. His nation lies in ruins, but he lays hold of two divine principles and these fill his soul with song. He lays hold of God's mercy. (The word is the usual word in the psalms—lovingkindness—that marvelous characteristic of God whereby He shows us not just His kindness, but His superlative kindness—His lovingkindness.) He uses the word seven times. God's mercy takes the psalmist *back*—all Israel's *history* has been one long exposition of God's lovingkindness.

He lays hold on God's faithfulness, and he uses this word seven times also. This word, faithfulness, points the psalmist *on*—all Israel's *hopes* are wrapped up in that word. No matter what failure there may be in Israel, God cannot fail. He is faithful to His Word and faithful to His own character. These are the principles involved.

B. The Person Involved (89:3)

"I have made a covenant with My chosen, I have sworn unto David, My servant." The covenant was not made with wicked Jehoiakim or with weak Jehoiachin or with wretched Zedekiah. The covenant was made with David. The psalmist goes back to the original agreement. The Lord could not tear up a covenant with David, no matter how full of faults and failures his successors had been. After all, a contract was a contract.

C. The Promise Involved (89:4)

"Thy seed will I establish for ever, and build up thy throne to all generations. Selah." Verses three and four sum up the promise of the Davidic covenant and are taken almost word for word from the actual contract itself. It is as though the psalmist has a copy of the agreement in his hand, as though he waved it before the Lord and with a resounding "selah" cried, "There, what do you think of that? Here it is, in writing, part of Your own inspired Word. You have promised to establish David's throne forever."

It is true that when God entered into contract along similar lines with Solomon a conditional clause was added, but no such conditional clauses were in the original Davidic covenant. There was a provision that if David's heirs sinned they would be punished, but nothing could annul the wide scope of the original covenant. Indeed, behind the Davidic covenant was an older and equally irrevocable, unconditional, divine agreement—the Abrahamic covenant. That was the significance of the covenant with David and that is how the psalmist begins.

II. THE ABSOLUTE SECURITY OF THE COVENANT (89:5-18)

The psalmist elaborates on it, rehearsing before the Lord some of his own observations about God's promise to David. He looks at this contract in the light of God's power in Heaven and in the light of God's power in history.

A. God's Power in Heaven (89:5-8)

The psalmist climbs up Jacob's ladder, as it were, for a better view of things. The Davidic throne on earth, after all, was but an extension of the divine throne in Heaven. David was God's regent on earth.

1. The Heavenly Court (89:5-6)

"And the heavens shall praise Thy wonders, O LORD: Thy faithfulness also in the congregation of the saints." The word for "heavens" comes from a verb meaning "to beat." The word embodies the idea of the heavens as a "beaten out" place, beaten out as a metal that is fashioned into a plate. If God could so beat out the heavens, so form and fashion the canopy of the skies, then He was quite able to beat out the nations into submission to Himself.

But more: up there in glory, the psalmist saw the congregation of the saints, the assembly of the holy ones. Perhaps he saw the four-and-twenty elders and the four living creatures, supernatural beings who, being holy themselves, can best appreciate the holiness of God.

He tells something else about that court: "For who in the heaven can be compared unto the LORD? Who among the sons of the mighty can be likened unto the LORD?" The "sons of the mighty" are the sons of Elohim; they are the angelic beings. The psalmist saw the holy ones and the angelic beings in Heaven, and he saw these mighty creatures subservient to the mighty Lord who underwrote the covenant with David and the consequent well-being of Israel. He saw God's court.

2. The Heavenly Chorus (89:7-8)

He describes the anthem that awakes the echoes of the everlasting hills. He hears the thunder of God's praise as the celestial choirs proclaim the sanctity and strength of the living God. The sound reverberates around the throne. God is to be feared in the secret conclaves of Heaven; He has no equal among the lofty ones on high. His is an unswerving integrity, and He is able to subdue the raging of the sea. The hosts of Heaven sing of these things. All this assures the psalmist that God cannot break the Davidic covenant. Whatever would the angels say! Their songs would trail off to nothing.

Sometimes in my study I play records while I work. If I'm in a hurry when I leave, instead of taking the needle off the record and properly shutting off the phonograph, I simply switch it off. The music then ceases with a drawn-out wail. The psalmist tries to imagine such an impossible situation in Heaven. He conjures up a vision of the angels in full song, celebrating the glorious faithfulness of a God who is utterly dependable. But then they see Him breaking His promise to David and their songs trail off to nothing. . . . Impossible!

B. God's Power in History (89:9-18)

1. The Revelation of that Power (89:9-18)

That power is revealed in God's *conquest* (89:9-10). As in so many of the psalms, the singer goes back to that greatest of all events in Hebrew history—the exodus from Egypt and the overthrow of "Rahab" (a poetic name for Egypt). One mighty sweep of God's arm and the armies of Egypt were no more.

But more significantly, that power is revealed in God's *creation* (89:11-13). The psalmist looks around the earth and pictures to himself the two most prominent features of his native land, Tabor and Hermon. Mount Tabor towered above the monotonous plain beneath, clothed almost to the top with trees. It was a notable landmark. God had made it!

This was the God who had pledged Himself to David. The Davidic covenant certainly could not fall apart because God was too weak to enforce it, or because some petty pagan princeling thought to challenge it. Thrilled with his contemplation of this revelation of God's power in conquest and creation, the psalmist hurries on.

2. The Response to that Power (89:14-18)

He begins to praise God! The circumstances were dark, never in all of Hebrew history had they been blacker and more ominous. The throne of David was gone, the monarchy was in ruins, the surviving kings languished in exile, the people were scattered.

He praises God for *His righteous principles* (89:14). "Justice and judgment are the habitation of Thy throne: mercy and truth shall go before Thy face." He praises God for *His redeemed people:* "Blessed is the People that know the joyful sound. . . . In Thy righteousness shall they be exalted" (89:15-16). God could not let His people down! The psalmist praises God for *His royal protection:* "For Thou art the glory of their strength. . . . The Lord is our defence; and the Holy One of Israel is our King" (89:17-18).

With magnificent faith the psalmist came to the conclusion that since God is so *great* in conquest and creation, He is unique; since God is so *good* that He cannot break His spoken word, why then, Israel could afford to sing because all was well. God is still on the throne. He sang because of the absolute security of the covenant, a security which temporary shiftings of the sands of time could not erase. The rock of God's dynamic and dependability may be covered up for a moment as the seas of fortune surge, but it cannot be removed.

III. THE AMAZING SPLENDOR OF THE COVENANT (89:19-37)

From soaring in the heavens, from traveling back in time, the psalmist comes back and once again picks up his copy of the covenant. He reads it through again and is astonished at the fresh wonders which shine out upon him from its peerless paragraphs. He sings again of the wonder of it all—that God should commit Himself so irrevocably, so irreversibly to David, and through David to Israel. He reminds himself of the unique features of the covenant.

A. Made with David Personally (89:19-28)

1. It Was Majestic in Expression (89:19-23)

We could well linger here over each delighted expression of the psalmist. Note that *the divine initiative* is underlined by the singer: "Then Thou spakest in vision to Thy holy one. . . . I have found David My servant; with My holy oil have I anointed him" (89:19-20). In those early days before he sinned with Bathsheba, David had indeed been the ideal servant of the Lord. In the camp, in the court, and in the cave, as a fugitive who carried with him everywhere the fragrance of the anointing oil poured upon him by Samuel, David was all that God could want in a servant. The eye of God rested on David in satisfaction down there in Hebron when he was anointed afresh to be king by the tribe of Judah and also up there in Jerusalem when he was anointed king over all Israel. He was "a man after God's own heart." Taking all the initiative, God came to His servant and treated him as the anointed of God.

Note, too, *the divine incentive* (89:21-23). God promised to deliver David from two things: from *subversion by the conspiritor* (89:21-22) and from *subjection to the conqueror* (89:23). Neither the foe within nor the foe without would ever succeed. The whole story of David, as the psalmist very well knew, was proof that God kept His word. Not even Absalom's formidable conspiracy succeeded, and certainly no foreign foe ever successfully fought against David.

This covenant was majestic in its expression.

2. It Was Merciful in Execution (89:24)

"But My faithfulness and My mercy shall be with him: and in My name shall his horn be exalted." God knew that David was only human. He failed. He fell as badly as any man has ever fallen. Yet God had mercy upon him; God was faithful to His promise despite David's unfaithfulness in the matter of Bathsheba and Uriah.

This encouraged the psalmist. If God was faithful to David *then,* He would be faithful to David *now!*

3. It Was Messianic in Expectation (89:25-28)

With a bold leap into the future, the psalmist picks up one of the more notable features of the Davidic covenant and runs with it through the ages to the end of time. God's promises to David were, after all, to be "yea and amen" in Christ, in great David's greater Son. He mentions three aspects of the Messiah.

The dominion of the Messiah: "I will set his hand also in the sea, and his right hand in the rivers" (89:25). There is a reference here to the eastern and western boundaries of the promised land, to the Mediterranean Sea in the west and the river Euphrates in the east. But in its fullest messianic sense this verse embraces the whole world.

The deity of the Messiah: "He shall cry unto Me, Thou art my father, my GOD, and the rock of my salvation. Also I will make him My firstborn, higher than the kings of the earth" (89:26-27). This is one of the few places in the Old Testament where God is referred to as a father. It was a name for God often on the lips of Jesus. His first recorded utterance shows us how, from the very beginning, He claimed God as His Father: "Wist ye not I must be about My Father's business?" His Father's business was not the craft of a carpenter; it was the dark and dreadful business of the cross. He went into death with the same name upon His lips: "Father, forgive them, they know not what they do." And after the terrible hours of darkness He called upon God as His Father once more: "Father, into Thy hands I commend My spirit." It was on His lips again after the resurrection; it was His characteristic name for God; He was uniquely God's Son.

The durability of the Messiah: "My mercy will I keep for him for evermore, and My covenant shall stand fast with him" (89:28). That mercy was shown in sending the angels to sustain Him in Gethsemane, in forbidding profane hands to touch Him once He was dead, and in flinging wide the portals of death before Him. In Christ the Davidic covenant will find its fullest and most glorious fulfillment when, in a coming day, He comes back to reign and is made "higher than the kings of the earth." The psalmist exults, then, in the fact that the covenant was made with David personally.

B. Made with David Perpetually (89:29-37)

1. The Breadth of the Contract (89:29)

"His seed also will I make to endure forever, and his throne as the days of heaven." Again the psalmist focuses on the messianic aspect of the covenant. The "seed of David" was Christ, of course. No wonder there was such breadth in the covenant! No wonder it could guarantee everlasting blessing!

2. The Betrayal of the Contract (89:30-32)

"If his children forsake My law . . . then will I visit their transgression with the rod, and their iniquity with stripes." This was the warning to Solomon. The psalmist could look back over the tragic history of the monarchy and see how terribly necessary this clause had been. The Babylonian captivity itself was the final blow of the rod. The crimes of so many of Judah's kings fill many a dark page of Old Testament history. Manasseh especially, Judah's longest reigning king, turned his kingdom into a veritable Sodom and Gomorrah. Allowing Jeconiah to be childless so far as the throne was concerned was an act of justice, too. We learn from the New Testament that

God went back and redrew the messianic line, starting with Nathan, another of David's sons; that line ran down the annals of history until it ended with the virgin Mary and in Jesus, her Son. Joseph, the lineal descendant through Solomon, was only the foster father of Jesus.

3. The Blessings of the Contract (89:33-37)

The psalmist recalls the promise: "Nevertheless My lovingkindness will I not utterly take from him." It is an *unconditional pledge* (89:33-35). Pardon and permanence are again the themes. The psalmist reiterates God's unconditional pledge: "My covenant will I not break, nor alter the thing that is gone out of My lips. Once have I sworn by My holiness that I will not lie unto David" (89:34). According to Hebraists, the word for "alter" means "to fold" or "to double." The Septuagint renders it "to make void." If we were to put it in our vernacular, God promises that He will not double-cross His covenant. He will not alter it in the slightest. After all, when He made the covenant with David, He knew what kinds of people would sit on David's throne. He was not taken by surprise by Solomon's excesses, Rehoboam's folly, the stupidity of Ahaz, or the unspeakable vileness of Manasseh.

The psalmist follows this unconditional pledge with a word about the *unconquerable power* of the God who made it: "His throne [shall be established] as the sun before Me, it shall be established for ever as the moon" (89:36-37). He adds a resounding *selah*. You Babylonians! You Gentile nations! Go and blot out the sun, pull down the moon if you think you can keep a son of David off David's throne forever!

Thus ends the great euology of the Davidic covenant. But the psalmist has not finished. There is a wail of anguish in his next word: "But!" All of a sudden, it seems, he folds up his copy of the contract, puts it away, looks at the disarray of the kingdom, weeps, and speaks of things as they were before His eyes.

IV. The Apparent Suspension of the Covenant (89:38-51)

While it was impossible that the covenant could be canceled, it had certainly been suspended.

A. The Protest (89:38-45)

He rehearses seven things which were all too evident as he looks around at the triumphant Babylonians and at the uprooted and castoff nation of Israel.

He speaks of the displeasure of the Lord, of the disruption of the covenant, of the destruction of the nation, of the delight of the foe, of the defeat of the army, of the dishonor of the throne, of the dismay of the king.

He thinks particularly of Zedekiah in all his abysmal wretchedness: "Thou hast covered him with shame. Selah." Almost defiantly he writes it down: Selah! "There, what do you think of that?" In view of all the exceeding great and precious promises to David—what about it? Then, hastily, as if he had been too daring, he falls on his knees.

B. The Prayer (89:46-51)

His prayer is in two parts.

1. O Lord, Remember My Condition (89:46-48)

He himself, it would seem, was in captivity and deeply conscious of it. He tells the Lord that *His displeasure seems unending*: "How long, LORD? wilt Thou hide Thyself for ever?" (89:46) He uses the covenant name for God.

He tells the Lord that *his days seem uncertain* (89: 47-48). "Remember how short my time is: wherefore hast Thou made all men in vain? What man is he that liveth, and shall not see death? Shall he deliver his soul from the hand of the grave? Selah" (89:47-48). Even a saint like Daniel, who lived to be a very old man in Babylon and who rose to great power in the land under both the Babylonians and the Persians, never knew when death would claim him. Certainly, he must have known how precarious was his hold on life. The psalmist longs to see the disruption of the Davidic covenant end in his own lifetime.

If Daniel did write this psalm, he lived to see the end of the captivity but not the resumption of the Davidic covenant. That would have to wait until the coming of Christ.

2. O Lord, Remember Your Covenant (89:49-51)

He thinks of *the fame previously assured*: "LORD, where are Thy former lovingkindnesses, which Thou swarest unto David in Thy truth?" (89:49). Again and again God had made Himself famous for His mercy, love, and grace. Had that changed? Had God changed? If then, why not now? He thinks of *the shame presently allowed*: "Remember, LORD, the reproach of Thy servants. . . . Wherewith Thine enemies have reproached, O LORD . . . they have reproached the footsteps of Thine Anointed" (89:50-51). The words may have been inspired by the thought of the actual insults offered to wretched Zedekiah as he was led blind and desolate through the streets of Babylon on his way to prison. Insults offered to God's servants, fallen as they were, were insults offered to the Lord's anointed and to God Himself.

The psalm ends with a doxology which in turn ends the third
book of Psalms: "Blessed be the LORD for evermore. Amen, and
Amen." Thus the psalmist brings his soul to rest. All is well; the
Davidic covenant is secure. It is not in his hands, but in God's hands.
In this, Israel's darkest hour, he will worship God for whatever
shadows may be cast upon the nation; they are only shadows after
all. As the hymn writer puts it:

> Behind a frowning providence
> God hides a smiling face.

Psalm 90

LIFE AT ITS BEST IS VERY BRIEF

I. THE RIGHT PERSPECTIVE (90:1-6)
  A. The Sovereignty of God (90:1-2)
    1. He Is a Tremendous God
    2. He Is a Tender God
    3. He Is a Timeless God
  B. The Sympathy of God (90:3-4)
    1. He Knows the Tyranny the Tomb Has over Us (90:3)
    2. He Knows the Tyranny that Time Has over Us (90:4)
  C. The Severity of God (90:5-6)
II. THE REAL PROBLEM (90:7-12)
  A. Our Lives Are so Sinful (90:7-8)
  B. Our Lives Are so Short (90:9-10)
  C. Our Lives Are so Serious (90:11-12)
III. THE RESULTING PRAYER (90:13-17)
  A. A Fresh Evidence of the Moving of God (90:13)
  B. A Fresh Enduement of the Mercy of God (90:14-15)
  C. A Fresh Expression of the Might of God (90:16)
  D. A Fresh Effulgence of the Majesty of God (90:17)

NEXT TO THE BOOK OF JOB, Psalm 90 is most likely the oldest piece of writing in the Bible. This psalm and probably the anonymous one which follows were written by Moses in the wilderness on the way from Egypt to Canaan. It is of interest to recall that Genesis had not yet been published. Moses may well have already written Genesis, together with Exodus, Leviticus, and parts of Numbers, but these works were not yet in circulation. Thus, Psalm 90 stands in grand isolation as the oldest psalm in history, one of the grandest psalms ever penned, and the first great masterpiece of the Hebrew hymnbook.

Those who collected the various psalms, arranged them, and put them into their proper order placed this psalm strategically. They divided their hymnbook into five lesser books, each of which corresponds with one of the books of Moses. The fourth book of psalms begins with Psalm 90, and its songs are songs of the wilderness. It corresponds in tone and teaching with the book of Numbers.

Israel had come up to Kadesh-barnea. The spies had been sent into Canaan, and ten had brought back a negative report. The land, they said, was a dreadful place, full of great, fenced cities and inhabited by giants, the dreadful sons of the Anakim. Two men brought in a minority report. It is a good land, they said, a land flowing with milk and honey. As for the foe: once get your eye on God, who cares for giants? The majority ruled, fear drove out faith, the tribes elected not even to attempt to conquer Canaan, and God allowed them to suffer the consequences of their choice. Everyone over twenty years of age would perish in the wilderness. The terror by night, the arrow by day, the pestilence in the darkness, the destruction at noonday, the lion, and the adder would all take their toll. It was the sentence of death on a whole generation. The wilderness *way* gave place to the wilderness *wanderings*. Instead of the promised land, it would be the desert sand. Instead of the conquest of Canaan, there would be woe in the wilderness.

From then on Israel marched, but she marched without point or purpose. The Israelites simply moved from place to place, leaving behind them a trail of bones in desolate graves hollowed in the sand. They wandered thus for forty years, a year for every day the spies were in Canaan. God held over the unbelieving people a sandglass of forty years during which every man and woman of the older generation would perish.

It was as the Israelites turned gloomily back to the burning sands of Sinai that the stately stanzas of this song were written by Moses, "the man of God." Only eight people in the Bible are called that directly and by name—Moses (Deuteronomy 33:1); Samuel (1 Samuel 9:6-10); David (Nehemiah 12: 24); Elijah (1 Kings 17:18); Elisha (2 Kings 4:7); Shemaiah (2 Chronicles 11:2); Igdaliah (Jeremiah 35:4) in the Old Testament; Timothy (1 Timothy 6:11) in the New Testament. Two are complete strangers to us: Shemaiah and Igdaliah. But then, many of God's notables are not readily recognized on earth.

I. THE RIGHT PERSPECTIVE (90:1-6)

A. The Sovereignty of God (90:1-2)

1. A Tremendous God

The psalm begins with the name of God, Adonai, "the Sovereign Lord." The name speaks of God in His government, God in His sovereign relationship to earth. What a tremendous God we have! He controls all the factors of space and time. Nothing can slip by Him. Let us keep that perspective in mind.

2. A Tender God

"LORD, Thou hast been our dwelling place." The word translated "dwelling place" literally means "den." God is our den! In most houses I'd rather be invited into the den than into the living room. Often the living room is cold and formal, whereas the den is warm and cozy. Moses, when he thought of God, thought of a den. He thought of God as a tender God, One in whose loving arms a person could really be at home.

3. A Timeless God

"Thou hast been our dwelling place in all generations. Before the mountains were brought forth, or ever Thou hadst formed the earth and the world, even from everlasting to everlasting." Life indeed is very brief. But not so God. He is from everlasting to everlasting, from eternity to eternity.

Let us keep these perspectives in mind. God is a sovereign God, tremendous, tender, and timeless. But He is not so great and vast that He is remote and cold. He invites us to come and find our den in Him!

Moses moves on to develop this thought.

B. The Sympathy of God (90:3-4)

God's great eternal loving heart goes out to man in sympathy.

1. God Knows the Tyranny the Tomb Has over Us (90:3)

"Thou turnest man to destruction, and sayest, Return ye children of men." Rotherham renders that: "Thou causest man to return even unto atoms [to be pulverized as the dust] and [then] Thou sayest, Return! ye sons of men." There is the sympathy of God. He returns man to the dust, and then He returns the dust back to man! Death is a dark and dreadful reality, but for the believer there is something beyond—resurrection! God's sympathy sees the tyranny the tomb has over us, but it is a conquered tomb. Moses did not have as much light upon that subject as we who stand on the resurrection side of Calvary.

We creep toward the sepulcher in the gloom of that Saturday night. There they are, the ironclad soldiers of Rome, pacing up and down before the solid stone that seals a rich man's tomb. Upon that tomb is the seal of empire. Who would dare tamper with that seal? Who could brave those marching men, the merest tip of mighty Caesar's finger?

Suddenly the tough troopers stand still in their tracks. All about them is the stillness of the night. The first faint blush of dawn is in the sky and there is the merest glint of light upon the tomb. Then, of its own accord and without touch of human hand, the Caesar's seal cracks wide. Then slowly, eerily, and likewise of its own accord, the great stone begins to roll. First it shows but a crack, then firmly and forever back it rolls. The hair stands up on the soldiers' necks. They stare in horror. The tomb is empty.

But wait, what's this? Into the growing morning twilight comes a shining one, his face ablaze with the glory of God and his garments shining with the light of another world. It is an angel come down from Heaven to take charge of that empty tomb. With one wild yell of terror, the keepers fling down spear, shield, and sword and flee headlong from the scene.

"This thing, O King Agrippa" said Paul, "was not done in a corner." The tomb is empty! Christ is risen! Death is conquered! If we are numbered indeed among those who must return to the dust, we are numbered too among those who will return from the dust.

So Moses speaks of the sympathy of God for those who know the tyranny of the tomb.

2. God Knows the Tyranny that Time Has over Us (90:4)

"For a thousand years in Thy sight are but as yesterday when it is past, and as a watch in the night."

A thousand years—how long a time it seems to us. The United States does not have a quarter that much history. A thousand years ago in England William the Conqueror had not yet landed his Norman adventurers on Britain's shores. To God a thousand years is but an evening gone, a mere watch in the night—the third part of a single night.

God sees us hurrying through our little span of life, our threescore years and ten. His sympathy goes out to us because of the tyranny time has over us. He has engineered us for eternity, yet we are prisoners of time. We keep in mind, then, the perspective of the sovereignty of God and the perspective of the sympathy of God.

C. The Severity of God (90:5-6)

This is another perspective we must not forget. Moses brings God's judgment sharply into focus. That judgment is fresh in Moses' mind, for he has just heard God pass righteous sentence on a whole generation. It was a generation which had been purchased by blood and saved by a strong hand and an outstretched arm. It was a generation which had experienced nothing but the grace, goodness, and greatness of God all the way from bondage in Egypt to the borders of Canaan. Yet it was a generation which did nothing every step of the way but criticize and complain, doubt and disobey. Now, the patience of God exhausted, the righteous sentence has gone forth and the judgment of God has fallen. Moses cannot forget that. It is a perspective to keep in mind.

Drawing upon his recent memories of Kadesh-barnea, Moses underlies in this hymn the fact that God's judgments are *swift, sure,* and *solemn:* "Thou carriest them away as a flood; they are as a sleep: in the morning they are like grass which groweth up. In the morning it flourisheth, and groweth up; in the evening it is cut down, and withereth." The grass that grows in the Jordan Valley and in the Dead Sea basin is just like that. It seldom grows into a turf. It shoots up in the early spring with great promise and then just as swiftly seeds and dies, leaving no trace of its existence for the rest of the year except for a few straggling sun-scorched stems. God is not to be trifled with. It is a perspective to keep in mind.

It may seem to us that His judgments are delayed. That is because we are creatures of the day. But to a God who writes off a thousand years of our time as a mere watch in the night, what are twenty or fifty years?

Some time ago I saw a television program on the development of radar. On an observation screen in an airport control tower was a tiny dot which represented a plane flying from Denver to Seattle. I sat watching the small television screen, but the dot scarcely seemed to move. In fact, although I watched as hard as I could, I could not detect the slightest change of position. The screen was too small to register any change. But that plane was streaking toward its destination at two or three hundred miles an hour. My perspective was too limited to register the movement.

It is just so with God's judgments. They are thundering down upon the world today, hurtling into the lives of godless, rebellious men, women, and young people, but we are far too circumscribed in our perspective to be able to detect the speed with which God's judgments are approaching. Moses wants us, however, to keep the perspective in mind. God's judgments are swift, sure, and solemn. God is loving, but He is not lax. Moses urges upon us the right perspective.

II. The Real Problem (90:7-12)

Moses drops the use of the third person and picks up the first person, and now he casts his verbs in the past tense. He is speaking now of things taken right out of recent history, things with which the people who first sang this song were all too sadly familiar. In this section he harps on two notes—*man's sin* and *God's sentence.*

A. Our Lives Are so Sinful (90:7-8)

"For we are consumed by Thine anger, and by Thy wrath are we troubled. Thou hast set our iniquities before Thee, our secret sins in the light of Thy countenance." There is no such thing as secret sin. God sees what we do, hears what we say, and puts what we fondly imagine to be our secret sins right out in the open.

Some years ago I knew a preacher whose constant theme was sin and hell. He thundered away at it each time I heard him speak. One day as he warmed up to his usual theme—sin and judgment— suddenly a woman stood up and accosted him. The preacher turned white. The woman had been saved recently and had been accepted into the fellowship in which this man was preaching. What a story she had to tell of secret sin with that very man in her unconverted days. It all came out publicly, shamefully. The man was ruined. For years he had carried his guilty secret with him, never thinking that one day it would find him out in such a dreadful way.

God sets our secret sins in the light of His countenance. They stare Him in the face; they cry aloud for exposure and punishment. And judged they will be—either in this life or in the life to come.

B. Our Lives Are so Short (90:9-10)

"For all our days are passed away in Thy wrath: we spend our years as a tale that is told. The days of our years are threescore years and ten; and if by reason of strength they be fourscore years, yet is their strength labour and sorrow; for it is soon cut off, and we fly away." There were 603,000 men of war in Israel, men of twenty years old and upward, when the nation played the coward at Kadesh-barnea. That vast army was under the sentence of death. If a man was twenty, he died by the time he was sixty; if he was thirty, he died by the time he was seventy; if he was forty, he died by the time he was eighty—fourscore years.

The vast host tramped from place to place through the wilderness. Alongside them marched death. Not a man knew when or where he would strike. The whole adult nation lived on death row. Every man marched with a ghost by his side. And, one by one, they fell and were buried in the shifting sand—and the camp moved relentlessly on and on. The wilderness became one vast graveyard.

"Life is so short!" said Moses. He himself, and Aaron his brother, Israel's high priest, were both under the same sentence of death. They were men living in the past. Their tale was told, they had no future. They could think about their redemption from Egypt, but they could never look forward to life in Canaan. They had sinned once too often, and for them the grace of God had been replaced by the government of God.

C. Our Lives Are so Serious (90:11-12)

"Who knoweth the power of Thine anger? Even according to Thy fear, so is Thy wrath. So teach us to number our days, that we may apply our hearts unto wisdom." With every living soul there comes a built-in time fuse. Some fuses burn slowly, others more quickly. Every birth signals the beginning of a countdown which, without variation, zeroes on a forced exit from this scene. Yet daily we shrug our indifference, and each night we roll over and go to sleep, while our fuse burns forever down. Life on earth in a space-time dimension is a one-way, dead-end street. Every day about four hundred thousand new people arrive on this planet, four or five every second. Every day hundreds of thousands of people leave it for eternity, their time fuse burned out.

One night in the cold Atlantic there was a grim countdown. The mighty *Titanic* hit an iceberg and plunged into the icy depths of the sea, carrying with it many of those who were on board—some drinking, some debating, some despairing, according to their various dispositions. Our planet is but a larger *Titanic,* carrying its enormous passenger list to the chill waters of the grave.

With the children of Israel in the wilderness the maximum number of years was known (Numbers 13–14). With us it is not known. No wonder the Spirit of God urges us to number our days and apply our hearts unto wisdom.

For every unsaved person, of course, the first act of sanity is to accept Christ as Saviour and make sure that the proper destination is reached when the exodus occurs. The unsaved person should get the great white throne in perspective. For the believer, the first act of sanity is to get this life's priorities adjusted in the light of the judgment seat of Christ.

John Beekman, a graduate of Moody Bible Institute, was given a death sentence by his doctor. He had a serious heart condition, and it was unlikely he would live. He had one chance, a very slim one. They could insert a little plastic valve in his heart. At that time only two other people had survived the operation. He might, if he was careful, become "survivor number three." Moody Institute of Science made a film of John Beekman's story which was called just that: "Survivor Number Three."

Once the plastic valve was inserted, John Beekman counted his days and applied his heart unto wisdom. Instead of slowing life down to a careful pace and hoarding his days like a miser, he threw himself into pioneer missionary work amongst the Chol Indians in the tropical jungles of southern Mexico. His story became one of determination and courage, of a life spent prodigally, with one eye fixed firmly on the zero hour announced by his doctors and the other fixed on eternity.

He and his wife Elaine ignored all the doctors' warnings. They plunged through steaming jungles; they lived in primitive conditions; they reduced the Chol language to writing; they translated the Bible into that Indian tongue; they taught the Chols to read, led them to Christ, and saw a new civilization emerge where once there had been only savagery, paganism, and despair.

When I saw the Beekman story I thought of Epaphroditus. Paul said of this courageous warrior, who came to Rome to visit him in prison and who did not spare himself even though he was sick unto death: "For the work of Christ he was nigh unto death, not regarding his life" (Philippians 2:30). Handley Moule translates that like this: "On account of Christ's work he was at death's very door, playing as it were the gambler with his life."

Life is a sinful thing, a short thing, a serious thing. Let us pay heed to the unknown length of fuse each one of us still has left.

III. THE RESULTING PRAYER (90:13-17)

Life which has its perspectives right, which has its greatest problems solved, will be occupied in a definite direction, which is clearly seen in Moses' prayer.

A. A Fresh Evidence of the Moving of God (90:13)

"Return, O LORD, how long? And let it repent Thee concerning Thy servants." This prayer in its original context grew right out of the circumstances in which Moses and the children of Israel found themselves there in the wilderness. Upon their refusal to go in and possess their possessions in Canaan, in spite of all the marvelous, miraculous proofs that God had given of His wisdom, love, and power, God's wrath overflowed. "How long," He demanded of Moses, "will this people provoke Me? and how long will it be ere they believe Me, for all the signs which I have shewed among them? I will smite them with the pestilence, and disinherit them, and will make of thee a greater nation and mightier than they" (Numbers 14:11-12). The Lord was about to turn loose upon the people the same avenging angel who had shortly before smitten the Egyptians.

Then Moses became an intercessor. He pleaded for God to return and for Him to repent of the righteous wrath and judgment He was preparing to send. At once there was fresh evidence of the moving of God both in judgment and in mercy. The Lord did return; He did shepherd the next generation into the promised land. How we need to pray today for a fresh evidence of the moving of God.

B. A Fresh Enduement of the Mercy of God (90:14-15)

"O satisfy us early with Thy mercy: that we may rejoice and be glad all our days. Make us glad according to the days wherein Thou has afflicted us, and the years wherein we have seen evil." Rotherham has a resounding version of that: "Satisfy us in the morning with Thy kindness that we may ring out our joy and be glad all our days."

Yes, the sandglass is there, the sands of time are sinking, but we must not be morbidly occupied with death. We still have today. We must look forward to tomorrow. Above all, we must so know the mercy of God in our lives that each morning will hear us ringing out our joy in the Lord! God's disciplines with us are not intended to flatten us in despair. They are designed to lead us on to such experiences of His lovingkindness, mercy, and grace as will make us sing even in the midst of the fruits of our follies.

C. A Fresh Expression of the Might of God (90:16)

"Let Thy work appear unto Thy servants, and Thy glory unto their children." The future of Israel after Kadesh-barnea lay with the children. It always does. The children are the ones who have to step into our shoes and carry on the purposes of God. God is intensely interested in our children. We need to see God's mighty arm made bare in their lives. We need to pray that He will do His work in them. They need to see His glory for themselves.

As they look at us they see failure. Our failures have brought us where we are, but God can overrule even our failures and show His glory through them. Let us plead for a fresh expression of the might of God, for a work pointed by God directly into the hearts of our children and young people. In Israel every child up to the age of nineteen was destined for the promised land in the sovereign purpose of God. Let us lay hold of something like that for our children.

D. A Fresh Effulgence of the Majesty of God (90:17)

"And let the beauty of the LORD our God be upon us: and establish Thou the work of our hands upon us; yea, the work of our hands establish Thou it."

We go back in thought to a certain slave hut on the Nile. The Hebrew people are herded there in that Goshen ghetto under harsh conditions of slavery. We creep into one of those huts. Perhaps this very day Amram, the father of the little family which lives in this hut, has been whipped and lashed by an Egyptian guard. There is a woman in this house, a dear, godly woman, the mother of three children. Her name is Jochebed; it means "God my glory." She shines in that slave hut like the Shekinah glory in the tabernacle. She transforms that hut into a holy place, bringing a little of Heaven with her into that home. No wonder that out of that home comes a Miriam, an Aaron, and a Moses! That is what Moses is thinking of here: "Let the beauty of the LORD our God be upon us!" He could pray that every tent in Israel might have a woman like Jochebed in it to bless the husband and father and be a benediction to the children. Thus, indeed, would God establish the work of His people's hands so that the rising generation would not repeat the sins and follies of the older, dying generation but would march boldly in to take possession of the promised land.

Let us borrow that prayer: "Let the beauty of the LORD our God be upon us: and establish Thou the work of our hands." Let us neither live nor labor in vain.

Psalm 91

THE HIDING PLACE

THIS IS ONE of the "orphan psalms." We do not know who wrote it. Was it Moses, David, Hezekiah, Nathan the seer, or Isaiah the prophet? Is it clearly intended to be an appendix to the previous psalm, the great "prayer of Moses, the man of God"? Had someone read that great wilderness song and decided that it needed a friend to stand beside it in the hymnbook of the Hebrew people? We do not know. It has simply taken its place at the beginning of the collection of songs which make up the fourth book of the Psalms to stand shoulder to shoulder with the previous masterpiece.

While people are divided as to the actual human author of this psalm, one interesting suggestion is that Moses wrote both Psalms 90 and 91, and that both are an exposition of Deuteronomy 33:27. "The eternal God is thy refuge"—that is the theme of Psalm 90. It is the psalm of the wilderness, the great psalm which contrasts the permanence of God with the mortal frailty of man. The sentence of death had been passed on Israel at Kadesh-barnea. Their sandglass of forty years was running out, but the eternal God was their refuge. "Underneath are the everlasting arms"—that is the theme of Psalm 91.

One of the most interesting things about this psalm is that Satan knew it, memorized it, no doubt hated it, but employed it (in the

27

usual distorted and devious way he ever handles the Word of truth) to try to tempt the Christ of God from the path of obedience to His God.

The devil is a great student of Scripture. I know a man who works for a businessman, a friend of mine holding a good position in the company. When he first went to work for my friend, this man said to himself: "To get on in the company I must learn to think like the boss thinks." He decided to study my friend to find out how he thought. He soon discovered that his employer believed the Bible and spoke to his employees about Christ. Accordingly, in order to think like the boss so that he could get on in the company, this man began to read the Bible. Unlike the management journals, trade publications, technical writings, and legal documents which he had easily mastered in his upward climb, he found he couldn't understand the Bible! He could talk like his boss when it came to trucks and trailers, engines and torques, shipments and accounts, computer printouts and government regulations, miles per gallon and profits in relation to capital investment, but he couldn't talk like his employer when it came to the Bible. He tried, and he made a mess of it. It annoyed him because he saw this as a key to future promotion.

One day my friend offered to send his employees, at his own expense, to a Bill Gothard Seminar. The recently hired man decided that this was his chance. He'd go! He'd get some insight into this mysterious book, the Bible. Then maybe he could talk his employer's language and improve his own chances of success within the corporation. So he went—and was soundly saved as a result! He now understands the Bible, knows why he could not understand it before, and smiles at his former ignorance.

The devil studies the Bible just like that man studied it. He studies it for his own twisted ends. And he is a very diligent student of the Bible, far more diligent than we. His use of this psalm shows us how well he had mastered God's Word.

This lovely psalm was first written in Hebrew, but before the coming of the Lord Jesus into this world the whole Hebrew Bible (our Old Testament) was translated into Greek. In that translation, the Greek Septuagint version, verse 12 has an addition: "He shall give His angels charge over thee ... they shall bear thee up in their hands, lest thou dash thy foot against a stone." Then the words "at any time" are added. They do not appear in the Hebrew Bible, but have been added in the Greek translation. That addition suited Satan perfectly. When he quoted from Psalm 91 in the temptation of our Lord he did not quote the Hebrew, but the Greek. That's how good a student he is of the Bible. He found a version which suited his purpose and quoted from that one. The Lord Jesus refused to fight Satan over which version should be used. He sidestepped that issue by countering Satan's quotation with another and so disarmed the evil one entirely.

We approach this psalm with the knowledge that the human authorship is uncertain, but we are equally sure that God wrote it. We know it contains truth and that it works. So then, let us examine this short but potent psalm.

We call this psalm "the hiding place," for it is a good place to run when things get hot.

I. In Times of Trial (91:1-4)

Whomever was the human author of this psalm, he had found in God such a hiding place in time of trial that he wanted the world to know something about it.

A. His Fortress (91:1-2)

confidence in the Lord

"He that dwelleth in the secret place of the Most High shall abide under the shadow of the Almighty. I will say of the Lord, He is my refuge and my fortress: my God; in Him will I trust." The psalmist uses four names for God in this one statement: Elyon, Shaddai, Jehovah, Elohim. What a great collection of divine names, each having its own special meaning of promise or of power.

1. Elyon, "The Most High": Possession

He is "the possessor of Heaven and earth"—that is the thought connected with this name. He owns everything. The thought is that of *possession*. There's a hiding place for us! We have a God who owns everything! Thirty-six times in the Bible God calls Himself by this name. How about that for a hiding place!

2. Shaddai, "The Almighty": Provision

Someone might say: "It's all very well to know God owns everything. But what does that mean to me?" Two men were passing a bank in a big city. One man said to the other: "They put five million dollars in cold cash in that bank yesterday. I watched the armored truck pull up and saw the money going in." The other man was not at all impressed. The first man had left off two important words— "for you!"

God is Elyon, the possessor of everything, but He is also Shaddai. The thought behind that name, embedded right into its Hebrew structure, is that God is not just a *living* God, but a *giving* God. He is the one who supplies all our needs. The thought is that of *provision*. How about that for a hiding place!

3. Jehovah, "The Lord": Promise

This was the greatest name for God among the Hebrew people. He is the God who exists because He exists, the I AM, the eternal, immutable, unchangeable One. Especially, He is God in covenant-relation with His own. The thought here is that of *promise.* He is the God who has pledged Himself to do certain exceeding great and wonderful things for His own, things which cannot be thwarted by any demon in hell, any adversary on earth, or any failure in us. How about that for a hiding place!

4. Elohim, "God the Creator": Power

The word always occurs in a plural form accompanied by a singular verb—something which would be very bad grammar in connection with anyone but God. If I said, "We is going back to Atlanta," I would be using poor English. God can say: "We is" because He exists in three persons and yet is one God. The word Elohim in the singular would simply not be full enough to convey all that is meant in the revelation of God. Elohim occurs twenty-seven hundred times in the Bible. Its first occurance links it with creation. Thus, Elohim is God as creator. The thought is that of *power.* How about that for a hiding place!

Possession, Provision, Promise, Power—such is our fortress, our refuge, our hiding place! Surely we owe this psalmist a vote of thanks for giving us such a great thought of God. Thus, the psalmist shows us his fortress.

B. His Foes (91:3)

He sees trials arising from two sources: first from a person, then from a pestilence. He says: "Surely He shall deliver thee from the snare of the fowler, and from the noisome pestilence."

In the last chapter of his fascinating book, *Fifty Years in the Church of Rome,* Father Chiniquy tells how God delivered him again and again from the snare of the fowler after his break with the church, which for so long had commanded his loyalty and love. Twenty-three times he was stoned publicly, often by furious mobs intent on killing him. When his enemies saw that he was a hard man to kill, they tried to ruin his character. For much of eighteen years they kept him in the hands of sheriffs, under bail, a prisoner awaiting suits brought against him by enemies who swore to the most outrageous lies as truth. Thirty-two times his name was called before magistrates in various cities of Illinois and French Canada. No less than seventy-two false witnesses were brought forward by his former colleagues to support their false accusations. "But God be thanked," he wrote, "every time, from the lips of the perjured witnesses, we got the proof that they were swearing falsely at the instigation of their confessors." God delivered him over and over again from the snare of the fowler.

We are in a wicked world. Its forces of wickedness are led by the father of lies. We never know from moment to moment what snares are being set for our feet, but we have a God who can deliver us from the snare of the fowler. If we trust Him He will keep us.

So the psalmist confessed how much he owed to God: "As for me, my feet had well-nigh slipped," he says in Psalm 73:2. The traps were there, they were cunningly concealed, baited, and ready to be sprung.

C. His Faith (91:4)

"He shall cover thee with His feathers, and under His wings shalt thou trust: His truth shall be thy shield and buckler." Once, not far from a mission station in the heart of Africa, a forest fire swept through the bush leaving death and desolation in its wake. After the fierce flames had subsided, a missionary took a walk down one of the trails looking at the havoc wrought on every hand by the fire. He noticed a nest by the side of the way. Enthroned on the nest he saw the charred remains of a mother hen. Idly he kicked the poor heap with his foot and, to his astonishment, out from under the burned and blackened carcass there ran some baby chicks. Mother love had taught that hen to give her life for her brood. They had found refuge from the flames beneath her feathers.

Interestingly enough, on one occasion the Lord Jesus likened Himself to a hen. Like that mother hen in the Angolan forest, the Lord Jesus spreads His pinions over His own. He deliberately gave Himself up to the fierce heat, the blazing wrath of God at Calvary. We, sheltering beneath His wings, find an eternal refuge from the flames.

Here the psalmist's faith, like ours, comes home to rest. "He shall cover thee with His feathers, and under His wings shalt thou trust." No enemy can get at us there. He is our hiding place in times of trial.

II. IN TIMES OF TERROR (91:5-10)

This world is a planet under siege. Satan holds it in an iron grip. It is a world where terror and atrocity are commonplace, especially in lands where the gospel has never brought its blessings or where God's Word has been set aside. There are countries in the world today where naked terror is the order of the day. For people living in such lands Psalm 91 must be a constant court of appeal. It is a psalm which will come into its own, in full fruit and flower, during the great tribulation. It anticipates the needs of the small believing minority in Israel during that coming reign of terror.

Already the world is preparing itself for the coming of the great beast out of the sea. Observers of contemporary culture believe that we have already entered what is called "the age of terror." In the United States alone the FBI estimates that some fifteen thousand people are members of clandestine terrorist organizations. They tell us that the relative quiet is really a deceptive calm and that before long we can expect a major outbreak of terror in this country. There are estimated to be between fifty and one hundred terrorist organizations mobilized around the world. Water supplies of the major cities and nuclear power plants are targets scheduled for attack. Terrorists are acquiring increasingly sophisticated weapons and some say they will even use homemade atomic bombs.

The psalmist lived in a violent age, too. If the writer was Moses, we know that he and his people had just escaped the concentration camps of the Nile. History's attempt at genocide, the extermination of a race, had been foiled only by divine intervention.

If the psalmist was Hezekiah or the prophet Isaiah, he lived under the threat of terror. The oppressor of that day was another great northern power—the empire of Assyria. The Assyrians were international gangsters who backed their campaigns of terror with a formidable war machine. The world trembled whenever Assyrian kings felt the need to prove themselves on the battlefield. Any city which resisted demands that it surrender was made a public example. Leading citizens were skinned alive or impaled on sharpened stakes to scream out their closing hours in unspeakable torment. The balance of the population, young and old alike, were deported to some far-off land and thoroughly dispersed in order to destroy whatever national unity they might still have. The Assyrians made as much use of terror as they did of troops to enforce their will on the world. The Assyrian nightmare haunted the ancient world for centuries.

"Thou shalt not be afraid for the terror by night," said the psalmist. It might be terror of darkness, of defeat, of disease, of destruction at high noon—no matter! There is a hiding place: "A thousand shall fall at thy side, and ten thousand at thy right hand; but it shall not come nigh thee."

We need always to remember when interpreting these wonderful psalms that they are part of the Hebrew hymnbook. These are not gospel songs, written for those who have put their trust in Christ since Calvary. They are old Hebrew hymns and belong primarily and essentially to the nation of Israel. We need to exercise spiritual discernment before claiming such promises as blanket guarantees of well-being today.

The Old Testament blessing for Israel included national prosperity and divine protection. So long as Israel walked in step with God there was not a nation that could defeat her in battle or successfully invade her land. The godly Jew could legitimately claim the promises of Psalm 91 in an hour of danger and could expect that, although people fell all around by the thousands, neither the flying arrow nor the sinister pestilence would come near him.

But we are not Old Testament Hebrews. We are New Testament Christians. For us God's blessings are essentially spiritual rather than national and temporal. We have no unconditional guarantee from God that, so long as we live godly lives, we shall escape the ordinary terrors of life. As a boy, with the other children in school, I was issued a gas mask, just like everyone else at the beginning of World War II. My father taped up all our windows as protection from flying glass, should the bombs fall on our street. One did— within fifty yards of our house. We had an air-raid shelter in our garden, and many a night we cowered there as searchlights probed the night sky, bombs came screaming down, and shrapnel from antiaircraft guns fell like rain. We had no immunity from the perils of war just because we were Christians. We lost loved ones and Christian friends.

Think of Corrie Ten Boom's story. She, her sister, and her father made their home a refuge for the persecuted Jews in town. Surely God would protect them! Surely "the terror that cometh by night" would never come near them! Surely they had earned that, at least, and the blessing of God for those who bless Abraham's seed would be theirs. But no! One night that dreaded knocking at the door came to their house. The interrogation followed, as did the beatings, the indignities, the nightmare ride packed like cattle in a boxcar, and the final dreaded destination, Ravensbruck. Exposure, starvation, slavery, torment, and atrocities all took place. They did not escape the barbed wire, the threats, the ever present roll calls. The yawning mass grave at the far end of the camp claimed Corrie's sister.

What about Psalm 91 when all this was happening? Its interpretation belongs to an Old Testament people in an Old Testament place walking in Old Testament piety. God has not promised us immunity from persecution, but He has promised to go with us through fire and flood and fear: "Lo, I am with you always."

Corrie Ten Boom did escape from Ravensbruck and became a missionary whose testimony captured the imagination of the world. Her sister was a martyr.

But do we have no hiding place from the terror? Indeed we do! God does not keep us *from* terror; He keeps us *in* the terror.

So the psalmist talks of a hiding place in times of trial and of terror.

III. In Times of Temptation (91:11-16)

Now comes the dragon, that old serpent, the adder. Three chapters in from the beginning of our Bible we meet that serpent for the first time; three chapters from the end of the Bible we meet that serpent for the last time. He does not appear often in person on the sacred page. He speaks only three times in all the verses of Holy Writ. But his influence is everywhere. In this world, a sworn enemy of grace, we can expect temptation. The enemy will not leave us alone. He will even quote Scripture to lead us astray. Or rather, he will misquote it—deleting something here, adding something there, giving it a cunning twist, a subtle inference. God has anticipated all that.

A. A Triumphant Path (91:11-13)

"For He shall give His angels charge over thee, to keep thee in all thy ways. They shall bear thee up in their hands, lest thou dash thy foot against a stone. Thou shalt tread upon the lion and adder; the young lion and the dragon shalt thou trample under feet."

God has promised us an escort home. That does not mean that we can make daring experiments with God and do foolish, unscriptural things on the assumption that no matter what we do nothing can go wrong. That was what the devil wanted Jesus to do. He urged Him to throw Himself down from the temple heights, to do some spectacular, eye-catching thing because God had promised to keep Him from harm. No! That is not what it means. God, however, promises us an angel escort home. Angels, says the writer of Hebrews (1:14), are "ministering spirits sent forth to minister to those who shall be heirs of salvation." We shall not know until we get to Heaven how much we owe to these mighty ministers who attend us on the homeward way.

One striking example comes from the life of David Brainard, missionary to the Susquehanna Indians. One day he cast himself down beside a stream to rest as the evening shadows began to steal across the sky. He watched some beavers build a dam across the stream, but other eyes were watching him. A party of warriors sent out to kill him were watching him and biding their time.

Presently they drew near. The paleface was on his knees talking to the Great Spirit in the sky. As he prayed they saw a rattlesnake glide alongside him and lift its ugly head to strike, its fork tongue flickering near his face. Brainard, deep in prayer, was unaware of it. Then, without apparent reason, the rattler glided away and disappeared in the underbrush. "The Great Spirit is with him," said the Indians and they too stole away. The next morning when Brainard entered the Indian settlement the whole tribe came out to meet him and gave him a prophet's welcome to their midst.

It was just one incident—one of the few revealed instances of our angel escort home. Perhaps if we spent more time in prayer as Brainard did we would know more about these things.

So then, before us there is a triumphant path. And at the end of it, a great trampling on the dragon when the Lord comes back with His own.

B. A Tremendous Promise (91:14-16)

Not just one promise, but a triple promise—one of those threefold cords of Scripture which are not easily broken. It sets before us *a reciprocal kind of love.* "Because he hath set his love upon Me, therefore I will deliver him: I will set him on high, because he hath known My name" (91:14).

It sets before us *a reassuring kind of liberty*. "He shall call upon Me, and I will answer him: I will be with him in trouble: I will deliver him, and honor him" (91:15).

It sets before us *a rewarding kind of life*. "With long life will I satisfy him, and shew him My salvation" (91:16).

Such is the ministry of temptation. The devil tempts to bring out the worst in us; God permits it so that it might bring out the best. And with every victory gained another step is taken toward the victor's crown.

Let us borrow the language of another poet:

> And I said to the man who stood at the
>   gate of the year:
> "Give me a light, that I may tread safely into
>   the unknown!"
> And he replied:
> "Go out into the darkness and put your hand
>   into the hand of God.
> That shall be to you better than light and
>   safer than a known way."
> So I went forth and finding the hand of God
>   trod gladly into the night.
> And he led me toward the hills and the
>   breaking of the day in the lone East.

"He that dwelleth in the secret place of the Most High shall abide under the shadow of the Almighty."

Psalm 92

PRAISE THE SAVIOUR,
YE WHO KNOW HIM

I. The Excellence of Praise (92:1)
II. The Exercise of Praise (92:2)
   A. We Should Rest the Day with Him
   B. We Should Review the Day with Him
III. The Exuberance of Praise (92:3)
   A. Praise Can Be Blissful
   B. Praise Must Be Balanced
IV. The Exhaustlessness of Praise (92:4-5)
   A. The Things His Hands Have Performed (92:4-5a)
   B. The Things His Heart Has Planned (92:5b)
V. The Exception to Praise (92:6-7)
   A. The Insensitive Man (92:6)
   B. The Iniquitous Man (92:7)
VI. The Explosion of Praise (92:8)
VII. The Expectation of Praise (92:9-11)
   A. The Lord's Triumph Shown to the Psalmist (92:9)
   B. The Lord's Triumph Shared by the Psalmist (92:10-11)
VIII. The Expression of Praise (92:12-15)
   A. How Happy Are the Lord's People (92:12-14)
      1. The Fruitfulness of the Palm
      2. The Fragrance of the Cedar
   B. How Holy Is the Lord's Person (92:15)

THIS PSALM is a song of the Sabbath. The title reads: "A Psalm or Song for the sabbath day." It is closely followed by five other psalms without titles, which has led commentators to believe that they were deliberately arranged by the compilers of the Hebrew hymnbook to form one continuous song service for the Sabbath.

We do not know when or why the psalm was written. One suggestion is that the song has special reference to the first desecration of the Sabbath by a Hebrew. We recall the occasion. Israel had come up to Kadesh-barnea. They had sent in the spies into Canaan. The majority report had been depressingly negative, and the people wished themselves dead. God granted that which they requested by sentencing everyone over twenty to death in the wilderness. The first recorded death after that was of the man who profaned the Sabbath. He was caught picking up sticks without any regard to the fact that the Sabbath had been given to Israel as a special day of rest. This worldly-minded man was sentenced to death and executed. Thus, God gave Israel a lesson on the sanctity of the Sabbath day (Numbers 15:36).

Immediately afterward, God told the Hebrew people to wear a fringe of blue, the heavenly color, on the borders of their garments—the part of their garment which came in closest contact with the world. It was to remind them that they were a people separate from the world by the will of heaven.

If ever there were a border of blue to be woven and worn as a heavenly fringe about the heart to remind us of the sanctity of the Lord's day it is this little Hebrew hymn.

We do not know if that is what inspired this psalm, however. The psalm seems to have been used in the second temple, rebuilt after the Babylonian captivity as a special song for the Sabbath. According to the Jews, it was sung as an accompaniment to the drink offering when the first lamb was offered at the Sabbath burnt offering.

It is a song of praise. Indeed, its theme can be summed up in the well-known line of our hymn: "Praise the Saviour, ye who know Him."

I. The Excellence of Praise (92:1)

"It is a good thing to give thanks unto the LORD, and to sing praises unto Thy name, O MOST HIGH."

That is the highest of all occupations. The sinless sons of light who stand before the throne of God in glory do that. The four living creatures of the Apocalypse do that. They stand there, at the very center of things, and lift their voices to sing the praise of Him who sits upon the throne. These are the cherubim, highest of all created intelligences. Lucifer, son of the morning, was once numbered in their ranks and led the worship of the angels. There is nothing an intelligent creature can do that is more fitting to his intellectual, emotional, and volitional capacities than offer praise to God.

This aspect of the psalms, the repeated exhortation by God that people should praise Him, was a great source of perplexity for C. S. Lewis at one point in his life. Like so many others, he despised the man who was constantly looking for praise. Around every dictator and every celebrity, can be found those who are only too willing to flatter and praise in the hope of getting something in return.

Yet we are told that "it is a good thing to give thanks unto the Lord and to sing praises" to the name of God Most High. How are we to account for that? Why does God so often demand that we praise Him?

C. S. Lewis thought his way out of the problem by beginning with inanimate objects which can have no inherent personal rights. In St. Paul's Cathedral, along one of the main aisles there hangs a famous picture by Holman Hunt entitled *The Light of the World.* It is a picture in rich color of Christ standing outside the closed and weed-entangled door of the human heart. That picture demands that we admire it! Why? Because admiration is the appropriate response to such a work of art. The person who does not pause to admire such a picture is insensible to greatness; he lacks the ability to enjoy a rewarding experience.

C. S. Lewis says the idea of God demanding worship as some vain woman wants compliments on her appearance is absurd. Even if such a deity were to exist it is not likely that He would come to us for admiration. We are the lowest of creatures upon whom He has endowed intelligence. As Lewis points out: "I don't want my dog to bark approval of my books." God demands praise because, as the catechism puts it, man's chief end is "to glorify God and enjoy Him forever." To praise God is the intelligent, emotional, volitional thing for a creature to do when brought into the presence of One so glorious, so holy, so loving, so worthy of wonder and worship as God. Not to praise Him proves us lacking in something. To praise Him, spontaneously, delightedly, is proof we are alive to all that He is.

So then, the psalmist begins with the excellence of praise. It is a good thing to give thanks to the Lord and to sing praises unto His name. It is the appropriate response to One who combines in Himself the fact that He is Lord (Jehovah) and that He is Most High (Elyon, supreme Governor of the world).

II. The Exercise of Praise (92:2)

There are two times of the day when it is especially appropriate to be taken up with God.

A. We Should Rest the Day with Him

"To show forth Thy lovingkindness in the morning"—that's a sensible thing to do. Put the day into His gracious, loving hands. We do not know what a day may bring forth. There might be some great tragedy just around the corner, or some sudden temptation, or some unexpected opportunity. It is wise to put the day into His care and keeping, to rest the day with Him. Then, whatever lies ahead, we shall face it with Him.

B. We Should Review the Day with Him

"And Thy faithfulness every night." There is something appropriate about linking the morning with a consideration of God's lovingkindness and the evening with a consideration of His faithfulness. At the end of the day, looking back over its crowded events— at that accident in the kitchen, at that little word of testimony, at that loss of a job or promotion at work or at that tough exam—we can thank God for His faithfulness. We thank Him not, perhaps, for giving us what we sought, but for giving us what was best.

III. THE EXUBERANCE OF PRAISE (92:3)

There are times when praise will not be denied, times when it wells up like a floodtide in the soul, when like Jordan at harvest time it overflows its banks. It demands expression. There are times when, like the hymnwriter, we cry:

> Oh for a thousand tongues to sing
> My great Redeemer's praise.

A. Praise Can Be Blissful

"Upon an instrument of ten strings, and upon the psaltery." Bring on the music! Strike up the orchestra! Pull out the stops! Music is a great aid to praise. There are times when the emotions are too full for words—when the heart takes over and the only way we can express ourselves is with an instrument. What is in the soul has to come out at the feet and the fingers. Most of us are too staid in our public worship to clap our hands! The orientals had no such inhibitions. If they wanted to praise they summoned the orchestra and made a joyful noise. Praise can be blissful.

But, the psalmist delivers a warning.

B. Praise Must Be Balanced

"Upon the harp with a solemn sound." The word for "a solemn sound" is *higgayon*, a word used in three psalms (9:16; 19:14; and here in 92:3). The word actually denotes a soliloquy or a meditation. We must not get carried away with music; we must balance it with meditation.

I was once shocked to hear the pastor of a church call upon his people to give Jesus a good clap. And the people gave Him a round of applause as though He were some pop star. That is excess. A sense of balance would remind us that He is the One before whom the shining seraphim hide their faces because of His burning holiness.

The psalmist is calling here for "meditative music on the harp."

The music is only the vehicle; the meditation, the words are the important thing. Let us never become flippant and irreverent in our emotional excitement. It is only a short step from uncontrolled bliss to blasphemy.

IV. THE EXHAUSTLESSNESS OF PRAISE (92:4-5)

The fact that we have so many hymnbooks is proof enough that, when it comes to praising the Lord, there is no end of ways in which we can express ourselves. The psalmist suggests two great themes.

A. The Things His Hands Have Performed (92:4-5a)

"For Thou, LORD, hast made me glad through Thy work: I will triumph in the works of Thy hands. O LORD, how great are Thy works!"

We should praise Him for His work in *creation*. Think, for instance, of how many factors were necessary before life as we know it could exist on earth. A few are listed here.

1. The earth rotates at about one thousand miles per hour. If it turned at one hundred miles per hour our days and nights would be ten times as long. The sun would burn up all vegetation in the daytime, and frost would kill anything remaining at night.
2. If the sun were twice as hot as it is, or half as hot as it is, the earth would be a red hot cinder or else a sphere of eternal ice.
3. Suppose the earth were much closer to the sun than it is, or much farther away; again, life would be impossible because of the forbidding temperature.
4. The proportion of sea to land is about three-quarter sea to one-quarter land. If the proportion had been reversed there would be neither sufficient evaporation or rainfall, and the world would become a desert.

We could go on and on. God has carefully balanced all the factors which make life possible on our planet. We should praise Him for His work in creation.

We should praise Him for His work in *providence*. If this psalm was composed by one of the repatriated Jews just returned from Babylon, what an example he had before him of the providential dealings of God with men. Who would have believed, despite the optimistic and undaunted predictions of the prophets, that God would so work in the heart of a pagan conqueror that he would voluntarily let the Jewish people go free to repopulate their ancestral land and rebuild their ancient temple!

History is filled with examples of God's hand in history and His heart planning for His people and for the general well-being of mankind—so much so that one definition of history is that it is *His*-story.

We should praise Him for His work in *redemption*. "I will triumph in the works of Thy hands," sings this unknown songster from the past. How much more should we? Those lovely hands of His that fashioned Adam's clay, that were placed upon the heads of little children, that broke the bread beside the sea, that touched the leper, now bear the scars of Calvary. That was the ultimate work of those hands—to blaze a trail for us from the dark paths of sin right into the glorious presence of God.

We can praise Him then, for the things His hands have performed.

B. The Things His Heart Has Planned (92:5b)

"And Thy thoughts are very deep." Of course they are! Sometimes we are asked to explain a deeper mystery of the faith. How can God be sovereign and at the same time give us power of choice? If God is omnipotent and overflowing with lovingkindness, why does He permit so much suffering? The best we can say to some of these questions is that God's thoughts are very deep. If we understood everything then we should be omniscient.

It should not trouble us that some issues are too profound for us. It gives us an opportunity to trust Him. It allows us to praise Him because He is so much wiser than we are.

V. The Exception to Praise (92:6-7)

He takes a look at two kinds of men who find it impossible to praise God.

A. The Insensitive Man (92:6)

"A brutish man knoweth not; neither doth a fool understand this." There are some men who are so wrapped up in their own conceited thoughts that they cannot discern spiritual things, nor are they always the dullest and densest of men in matters of intellect. Some of the world's most brilliant people have been insensitive to the things of God.

One of the greatest minds of all time belonged to Albert Einstein. His theory of relativity gave us the atomic age. He reduced the complexity of the universe to the deceptively simple formula $E=MC^2$. Popular books have been written to explain the mysteries of relativity. The theory, however, is not simple; its mathematics are decipherable by only a small elite of the scientific community. Once asked if it were true that only three people really understood the subject, Eddington jokingly replied, "I'm trying to think who the third person is."

Yet Einstein was insensitive to spiritual truth. Asked by a rabbi if he believed in God, Einstein replied, "I believe in Spinoza's God who reveals himself in the orderly harmony of all that exists, not in the God who concerns himself with fates and the actions of human beings." *(Time,* February 1979, p. 76). In other words, he believed in a conveniently remote and removed God not likely to interfere in his own personal life. "The universe," he declared, "could not operate on chance." Often he would make such statements as "God does not play dice." But Einstein did not know God. He was annoyed at the new theories of an expanding universe. He wrote: "To admit such possibilities seems senseless." Jastrow says: "This is curiously emotional language for a discussion of some mathematical formulas. I suppose the idea of a beginning in time annoyed Einstein because of its theological implications." Einstein did not believe in the God of creation.

So, for all his brilliance, he missed the most important facts of all, the greatest truths discoverable. He never knew what it was to praise a personal, living, loving God. In the last analysis, he was spiritually insensitive because, like all the rest of us, he needed to be born again and, like so many, apparently never was.

B. The Iniquitous Man (92:7)

"When the wicked spring as the grass, and when all the workers of iniquity do flourish; it is that they shall be destroyed for ever." The psalmist looks at the rapid growth of evil and its equally rapid ruin. God has a way of allowing wickedness to flourish in the life of a person and of cutting it down when it has come to full flower and fruit. We are living in a time when wickedness is flourishing. There is no thought of God, still less of praising God in the lives of those who promote perversion and pornography. How could there be? The two things could never coexist in a regenerate human heart. God allows such men to have their way in the world just as we allow weeds to grow in our garden—until the time is ripe to cut them down.

VI. The Explosion of Praise (92:8)

"But Thou, LORD, art most high for evermore." For every other statement the psalmist has needed at least two lines. For this one he needs but a single line. It is an exclamation, an explosion. He has been looking at the insensitive and iniquitous man in whose life there is no room for praising God. Now he turns back, looks full into the face of the Eternal, and says: "They shall be destroyed for ever: But Thou, LORD, art most high for evermore."

According to Graham Scroggie, this psalm has a symmetric structure. He sees it as having five paragraphs. The psalm is a psalm for the Sabbath day (the seventh day); therefore, the middle paragraph has seven lines. The other four paragraphs—the two that lead up to the middle one, and the two that lead away from the middle one— each have six lines. And in the center of the middle paragraph, which has seven lines, is this verse. It is an explosion of praise at the heart of the psalm.

Thoughts of God, especially when God is seen in contrast with the wickedness of the world, sometimes do that. They produce a burst of praise. That is why the Lord in His wisdom wanted the Jews to have a Sabbath—so that they could have a day for undistracted praise of God. That is why we set aside the first day of the week—so that we, too, can have time to give expression individually and collectively to worship and praise.

VII. THE EXPECTATION OF PRAISE (92:9-11)

God *is* going to be universally praised! Of that there can be not the slightest doubt. There is no future at all for the Lord's enemies—those who insult Him and ignore Him. They have denied the purpose of their being. They have become like the little girl who came home from school distressed because she had lost her birth certificate, required at school. She wept out her loss to her mother, "I've lost my excuse for being born," she said.

The psalmist now emphasizes the triumph of the Lord.

A. The Triumph Shown to the Psalmist (92:9)

"For, lo, Thine enemies, O LORD, for, lo, Thine enemies shall perish; all the workers of iniquity shall be scattered." That word "lo" suggests that he had just witnessed some such overthrow of the forces of wickedness. Wickedness comes on strong but it is deceptive, for the forces that bind evil men together in an enterprise are all-destructive and self-defeating in the end.

When the builders of Babel set to work, the Holy Spirit knowingly observed that "slime had they for mortar." They were building not with stone but with brick, with dried mud; and their bonding agent was slime. Nothing permanent can be built with slime and mud, especially when it is built in defiance of God. Sooner or later God simply knocks it down, and the whole thing disintegrates by reason of its inherent instability.

B. The Triumph Shared by the Psalmist (92:10-11)

"But my horn shalt Thou exalt like the horn of an unicorn [the wild ox]: I shall be anointed with fresh oil. Mine eye also shall see my desire on mine enemies, and mine ears shall hear my desire of the wicked that rise up against me." The Lord's enemies were his enemies; his enemies were the Lord's enemies. Those who attacked him also attacked the living God. He was on the way up; they were on the way down.

The wild ox was noted as a strong and untameable beast, like the wild buffalo of the African veldt. As the wild ox tossed its horn in triumph, so the psalmist expected to triumph. It was a theme for praise! How could he possibly lose? No matter how many or how strong his foes, no matter how dark and ominous his circumstances—he was on the winning side! Praise the Lord!

VIII. THE EXPRESSION OF PRAISE (92:12-15)

The psalm ends with praise being brought into a final focus. The singer looks first at the Lord's people, then at the Lord's person.

A. How Happy Are the Lord's People (92:12-14)

He sees them as verdant, virtuous, and venerable. "The righteous shall flourish like the palm tree: he shall grow like a cedar in Lebanon. Those that be planted in the house of the LORD shall flourish in the courts of our God. They shall still bring forth fruit in old age; they shall be fat and flourishing."

What a contrast with the fleeting existence of the lost.

1. The Fruitfulness of the Palm

The palm has a tap root. It stands straight and tall and its roots go down through the barren soil to be watered in the depths. It is an evergreen, noted for its variety of fruit. He sees the righteous flourishing like the palm as they enter old age. One traveler in the East reports seeing palms standing ninety feet tall and bearing fruit after two hundred years.

2. The Fragrance of the Cedar

In contrast with the palm, the cedar flourishes in the snows and storms of the mountains and spreads its roots out, entwining them around the rocks. It, too, is an evergreen, glorious in its foilage. Its wood is incorruptible, fragrant, and richly grained.

The psalmist says: "How happy are the Lord's people to be like that as they approach old age!"

B. How Holy Is the Lord's Person (92:15)

"To show that the LORD is upright: He is my rock, and there is no unrighteousness in Him." God is to be praised because of the kind of God He is. His character is such that it should draw us out in worship. Worship is the ascription of "worthship" to God. It would be very difficult to worship a god who could lie or lust as did the gods of the heathen. It is easy to worship a God marked by complete *rectitude, reliability,* and *righteousness,* such as our God. So then, let us praise the Lord.

Psalm 93

HE WHO STILLS THE STORM

THERE IS NO title to this psalm, which has led some to link it with Psalm 92. Actually, it is the first of a series of remarkable *theocratic* psalms (the others are Psalms 95 through 100). These are psalms which magnify Israel's theocracy.

We are familiar with the standard forms of government we have on earth. We have *autocratic* government (governments headed by a strong man or a dictator); we have *monarchic* government (headed by a king with more or less absolute power); we have *democratic* governments (governments in which the people rule). In all the history of the world only Israel has had a true *theocratic* form of government—a government in which there is no man-appointed or self-appointed ruler but rather a government directed by God.

From the beginning of its history until the time of Samuel this was Israel's sole form of government. It failed, not because God failed, but because Israel failed. When the people demanded of Samuel that he give them a king so that they might be like the other nations round about, he wept. God said to him: "Hearken unto the voice of the people in all that they say unto thee: for they have not rejected thee, but they have rejected Me, that I should not reign over them" (I Samuel 8:7).

There is, of course, a sense in which the monarchy, as it existed under Israel's constitution, was still essentially theocratic in character. The ideal king viewed the throne of David as the Lord's throne;

the king was merely God's temporary vice-regent. His character and calling were to be that of a shepherd, pastoring the people of God. Certainly David viewed the throne in that way. The nation was not a private preserve upon which the king could prey, but a pasture to be kept and cultivated for the flock of God.

Even in the northern kingdom of Israel, long after it had severed all ties with Jerusalem and the throne of David, in days when one of its weakest and most wicked kings reigned, King Ahab could not do what he liked with impunity. He wanted his neighbor's vineyard. He was prepared to buy it and to pay generously. When Naboth refused to sell because it was not his to sell—it was his family's inheritance in the land, given them of God, and he could not dispose of property which did not belong to him—Ahab did not dare to take it from him by force. Jezebel, his pagan wife, had no such scruples. She was astonished that her husband, the king, had these limitations to his power. She had no such concepts of sovereignty. She arranged for the stubborn subject to be murdered and presented the king with the coveted vineyard as a gift. Shutting his eyes to the crime, Ahab went down to inspect his ill-gotten gains, only to be met by Elijah, who told him he had just sealed his own death warrant.

The theocracy in Israel was but a shadow of what God intended for His people. It has been shelved for the time being, but God is not through with it. He intends to restore the theocracy during the millennial reign when the Lord Jesus, the second person of the Godhead, will reign directly over Israel and through Israel over all the earth.

This psalm anticipates that day. It is theocratic in character and content and it is prophetic.

It is in that light we are going to examine it. Short as it is, it pulsates with tremendous truth. The Jewish people will sing just such a psalm when Jesus comes to rescue beleaguered Israel from the beast and the massed might of the world.

Yet it is not without a historical context. These theocratic psalms seem to have been born out of a restoration of the theocratic-type kingdom at the end of the Babylonian captivity. There was not, of course, a complete restoration of the theocracy, because the reborn nation was under Gentile control; but it was a partial restoration. The excitement of the Jews who came back to reclaim the promised land in the name of God no doubt gave rise to this outburst of praise.

The psalm is in three parts.

I. The Times Are Held by Him (93:1-2)

We can understand how a Jew of the restoration would believe that. There had been a two-fold miracle. There had been a *providential miracle.* A great world power had arisen on the international scene. It had overthrown Babylon, the nation which had deported the Jews into captivity. Then, contrary to what everyone might have expected, the new regime proved itself astonishingly liberal, especially to the Jewish people. Its king, flushed with victory, magnanimously signed a mandate for their return to Palestine and backed it with the arm of imperial power.

There had been a *prophetic miracle*—an even greater wonder. All this had been prophesied. Isaiah, well over a century before, had actually named this great liberator. And Jeremiah had given the date when it all would happen. So no wonder this singer could see that the times were in God's hand.

We are going to carry the psalm forward to its fulfillment in the reestablishment of the theocratic kingdom at the coming of Christ. The Jews, such as are left of them at the end of the great tribulation, will see both the providential and the prophetic in their miraculous deliverance by a King greater far than Cyrus, the Persian.

A. An Expression of the Full Sovereignty of God (93:1a)

"The LORD reigneth, He is clothed with majesty; the LORD is clothed with strength, wherewith He hath girded Himself." The Revised Version puts it like this: "Jehovah hath proclaimed Himself king; He hath robed Himself with majesty." The verbs are in the perfect tense, expressing not just a fact, but an act. God has visibly stepped down into the arena of human affairs in the person of the Lord Jesus and deliberately taken the administration of earth's affairs into His own hands.

Self-coronation is rare. It is an expression of self-created and self-manifested power. There is one arrogant example of it in European history. In 1799 Napoleon abolished what was left of the government of France derived from the French Revolution. He set up a new government of three members, called the Consulate, and had himself proclaimed First Consul. Not satisfied with that, he began to undermine all governmental powers which did not lie in his own hand. In 1804 the French Senate voted him the title of emperor. "When I see an empty throne," he said, "I feel the urge to sit on it."

For his coronation, the new emperor chose Notre Dame Cathedral in Paris. He summoned the Pope to come and perform the honors. At the last moment, just as the pope was about to place the crown on Napoleon's head, the fat little dictator seized it from him and crowned himself—just to show that he personally had won the right to wear it and that he owed nothing to Rome. Then he turned around and crowned Josephine empress.

But Napoleon was only a tyrant, for all his military genius and statesmanship. In the end, England defeated him at sea and joined with a few others to tear him from his European throne. Napoleon proclaimed himself king, robed himself with majesty, and died a lonely exile on St. Helena—never out of sight of the British warships which had halted his ambitions and which now patrolled his prison.

But one of these days Jesus is coming again. He is going to overthrow what is left of the great world revolution and its monstrous tyrant, the beast; by sovereign right, He will proclaim Himself King and robe Himself with majesty. He will do that because He owes His world empire to nobody but Himself, and because no human authority can be set over Him to crown Him. He will crown Himself and robe Himself, then turn to His beloved, the Church, and invest her with the rank and robes of royalty, as well.

B. An Examination of the Fresh Stability of Earth (93:1b)

"The LORD reigneth . . . the world also is established, that it cannot be moved." Moral order, in such chaos on earth, is now restored, for Jesus will reign with a rod of iron and a firm, unfaltering hand. The tiny remnant of Jews and Gentiles who will enter into the millennial kingdom will heave a sigh of relief. At last—there is a strong, stable government on earth!

There is very little stability in the governments of men. Democracies were seen by Nebuchadnezzar in his vision of world government to be partly iron, partly clay. What more fitting symbol could there be than iron and clay? By nature, they refuse to mingle, a mixture of strength and weakness which marks the western democracies. Dictatorships fare no better, for eventually they end in rebellion or war.

Jesus will bring fresh stability to earth. He will found an empire which will stretch from pole to pole and from sea to sea; it will last unchallenged for a thousand years—a thousand years of peace and prosperity and progress.

C. An Exposure of the False Suppositions of Men (93:2)

"Thy throne is established of old: Thou art from everlasting." The communists have marched for years under the slogan, "Time is on our side." They are wrong, for time is on God's side. He has all time at His disposal. He works to His own faultless timetable. He is never in a hurry. He has outlived other empires; He will outlive the Russian empire, too.

God has driven His ploughshare through all the great empires which have arisen on earth to defy Him. The Egyptian empire waxed and waned in history for hundreds upon hundreds of years. Its beginnings are lost in the mists of time. When Abraham, the founding father of the Hebrew race, went down to Egypt and saw the great pyramid, he was looking at a monument built up to a thousand years before his time. Imhotep, the architect of the first pyramid, was as removed from Abraham as Nero is from us. Where is the Egypt of the pharoahs today? We can find bits and pieces of it in the British Museum and the Cairo Museum, and other scraps in collections around the world. That is all.

What about the Assyrian empire, the Babylonian, the Persian, the Greek and Roman empires? They are all gone. Where is the British empire I knew as a boy? Gone! The ghost of it still haunts the world in the British Commonwealth of Nations, but the empire is no more.

God's empire, however, is older than the stars. The universe is thought to be about twenty billion years old. When we go back to that cataclysmic moment in time, when the universe was born and the galaxies began their awesome rush through space, we find that God was there then. Time is on His side; His throne is forever.

II. The Tempest Is Hushed by Him (93:3-4)

The psalmist looks toward the end of the age.

A. The Awesome Power of the Nations (93:3)

"The floods have lifted up, O LORD, the floods have lifted up their voice; the floods lift up their waves." He sees the nations rise, hears them roar, watches them rage. He sees the nations as they have been throughout the long reach of history, but particularly as they will be at the end of the age.

Just prior to the time of Christ's return, the nations will rise in one final, seething cauldron of hate—hatred of each other, hatred of Israel, hatred of God. The beast's global empire will begin to disintegrate. The armies of the East will mobilize against him, march westward to destroy Babylon, cross the Euphrates, and move toward Megiddo. The armies of the West will mobilize as well. Like the frustrated Antiochus Epiphanes of old, the Antichrist of tomorrow will seize Jerusalem and begin a systematic program to exterminate the Jews before marching on to Megiddo to settle accounts with the East. Not even an impending crisis in his affairs will stop him from this last act of anti-Semitic hate.

The nations will rise like the storm-tossed sea. There is a reason why Israel is seen as the land in the symbolism of Scripture and the nations as the troubled sea. There is a reason why Isaiah said: "Woe to the multitude of many people, which make a noise like the noise of the seas; and to the rushing of the nations, that make a rushing like the rushing of mighty waters" (Isaiah 17:12).

Poet and psalmist see it alike. They see the final rising of the Gentile seas against the headland of Israel in one last, furious attempt to swamp and submerge God's ancient people forever.

But it is all in vain! The nations, in single waves or in one vast heaving tide, can no more swamp Israel than the ocean waves can triumph over the rocky cliffs of the shore.

B. The Actual Paralysis of the Nations (93:4)

"The LORD on high is mightier than the noise of many waters, yea, than the mighty waves of the sea." It does not always look that way. It often seems that God has lost control. In actual fact, He is working to a plan—a plan revealed to us in the Bible. It is there that we find the blueprints of the great Architect for the final well-being of mankind. Man, in his blindness, refuses to look at the plans and accuses God of being a blunderer.

At one time I was engaged in a discussion with an agnostic. He took the usual approach, holding up to ridicule the moral chaos of the world. His final thrust was: "If your God made the world, He did a very poor job of it."

I said to him: "Suppose you bought a complex piece of machinery. When it was installed you were given an operator's manual and warned to read it and follow instructions carefully because the manufacturer's liability and warranty would be voided if you did not do as instructed. Instead of heeding the manual, however, you threw it away, saying you were not going to be told how to run this equipment. So, you went ahead, you did it your way, and you ruined the machine. Then you blamed the manufacturer for making such a poor job of that piece of expensive, intricate equipment.

"That is just what you have been doing. When God made the world He sent along some instructions as to how things should be done. Like so many others, you will not read God's manual, the Bible. Things are very evidently in terrible shape in this world, but don't blame God. Blame yourself."

God certainly has not mixed up His plans. He is marching down the ages of history in giant strides toward Megiddo and the millennium. Since today is the age of grace, God is not answering back to men for their insults. But when He finally does, "the Lord is mightier than the noise of many waters, yea, than the mighty waves of the sea."

The psalmist has almost finished. He turns his eyes away from the threatening nations to the house of God which, in his day, had probably just been rebuilt.

III. THE TEMPLE IS HOME TO HIM (93:5)

There it stood in Jerusalem, a shadow of the once magnificent building erected by Solomon. But, just the same, there it stood. The psalmist has two words to say to his own heart, to the Hebrew people, to the heathen nations round about, to all peoples on earth.

A. Trust! The Law Is There (93:5a)

"Thy testimonies are very sure." The Bible often speaks of God's law as "His testimonies," because it was the function of the law to bear witness to God's demands and to man's duties. In Solomon's temple, those testimonies were kept in the sacred ark in the holy of holies. Copies of those testimonies were in circulation so that the people might know just what it was that God expected of them.

Nehemiah tells us that when he was temporary governor of Jerusalem Ezra the scribe read that law to the assembled people in Jerusalem. The reading of that law produced a revival. The people wept because of their national sins which had left them a mere dependency, a tiny and insignificant province in the mighty empire of Persia. They "separated themselves . . . unto the law of God," was the way Nehemiah put it (Nehemiah 10:28).

That was the first thing then; it should be the first thing now. It will be the first thing in a coming millennial day when Ezekiel's temple is built and the nations of the earth are constituted "one nation under God with liberty and justice for all." The American dream will become a reality for all the nations of mankind. All will be ruled by the testimonies of the Lord. People learn to trust those testimonies because they point to paths of happiness for the children of men.

B. Tremble! The Lord Is There (93:5b)

"Holiness becometh Thine house, O Lord, for ever." The temple was *His* house! Let it never be forgotten that while God is love, He is also holy.

The Lord has returned! He has taken up residence in His house! Neither the temple nor the land will be defiled again. His holiness will ensure that.

Thus ends this anonymous little hymn. It begins with His *royal highness;* it ends with His *impeccable holiness.*

When the Jews set up the liturgy for their new temple in Jerusalem, they selected a special psalm to be sung each day of the week. One of the seven was this one, Psalm 93. They selected this psalm to be sung on Friday, the day before the Sabbath. The Talmud explains why. "It was on the sixth day that the Lord finished the work of creation. After that He entered upon His Sabbath rest, and began His reign over the earth." So then, this little psalm is truly a prelude to the millennium itself.

The God who intends to set up His millennial Sabbath of rest on this planet wants to set up a miniature millennium in our hearts. He would like us to acknowledge Him as His royal majesty and let Him still the storms of rebellion and sin. Let Him come into His house, these bodies in which we live, so that He might make them His temple. He would like us then to acknowledge His impeccable holiness as the continuing law of our lives.

Psalm 94

THE AVENGER

I. THE SUPPLICATION (94:1-7)
 A. Hearken, Lord! (94:1-2)
  1. Vengeance Is Your Right (94:1)
  2. Vengeance Is Your Responsibility (94:2)
 B. Hasten, Lord! (94:3-7)
  1. The Heathen Demonstrate Their Power (94:3)
  2. The Heathen Declare Their Prowess (94:4)
  3. The Heathen Destroy Thy People (94:5-6)
  4. The Heathen Defame Thy Person (94:7)
II. THE SERMON (94:8-11)
 A. The Approach (94:8)
 B. The Appeal (94:9-10)
  1. God as Creator (94:9)
  2. God as Corrector (94:10a)
  3. God as Counselor (94:10b)
 C. The Application (94:11)
III. THE SOLILOQUY (94:12-23)
 A. The Psalmist Explores the Principles of God's Dealings (94:12-15)
  1. A Parental Aspect to God's Ways (94:12a)
  2. A Pedagogical Aspect to God's Ways (94:12b)
  3. A Providential Aspect to God's Ways (94:13-14)
   a. God Provides a Period of Relief (94:13a)
   b. God Plans a Place of Retribution (94:13b)
   c. God Pursues a Policy of Reinstatement (94:14)
  4. A Practical Aspect to God's Ways (94:15)
 B. The Psalmist Experiences the Pleasure of God's Deliverance (94:16-19)
  1. His Case (94:16-17)
  2. His Cry (94:18)
  3. His Comfort (94:19)
 C. The Psalmist Examines the Potential of God's Decisions (94:20-23)
  1. The Outraging of the Majesty of God (94:20-21)
  2. The Outpouring of the Mercy of God (94:22)
  3. The Outworking of the Morality of God (94:23)

WE DO NOT KNOW when this psalm was written, nor by whom, nor under what specific circumstances. It is a cry for vengeance. Its position in the Hebrew hymnbook has been questioned because it seems to interrupt the flow of the seven theocratic psalms (Psalms 93, and 95–100). But while the psalm does not actually state that God is on the throne, it certainly assumes that He is.

We do not know to which enemies the singer refers, although it is generally accepted that this is one of the post-exilic psalms, that is, a song of the returned remnant. Certainly, in those difficult pioneer days described so vividly in Ezra and Nehemiah, there were plenty of foes, and not all the governors of Persia, under whose jurisdiction the little nation of Judah fell, were beyond being influenced by the struggling nation's nearer and more vocal foes; nor, for that matter, were all the kings of Persia as magnanimous as Cyrus. Ahasuerus, the Xerxes of secular history, was quite willing to put his name to a document calling for the wholesale massacre of Jews throughout the length and breadth of the empire.

In its prophetic context, the psalm looks ahead to the days of the Antichrist and to Israel's future sufferings in the great tribulation. Then certainly, the cry for an avenger will be raised loudly and legitimately in the will of God.

The psalm is heralded because of its treatment of God's moral government of the earth. Jews and Gentiles alike, the chosen people and the nations and empires of earth, are reminded that God overrules in man's affairs. The psalmist tells them that God has His own infallible means of educating the children of men.

In the second temple, this psalm was sung every Wednesday, the middle day of the week. It is often the middle sections of life which give us the most trouble.

I. THE SUPPLICATION (94:1-7)

The psalm opens with prayer. Beset with doubts and difficulties, with fears within and fightings without, the psalmist sensibly turns his thoughts toward God.

A. Hearken, Lord! (94:1-2)

What he wants is vengeance. The concept of vengeance is not at all uncommon in the Old Testament. The Mosaic Law not only made provision for it but demanded it. There was a person in the Old Testament called "the avenger of blood." If someone committed an act of willful murder it was the duty of the next of kin to hunt down the murderer and slay him. The six cities of refuge, scattered up and down the promised land, three on each side of the Jordan River, existed solely because the avenger was abroad. If a man was guilty of involuntary manslaughter, he fled to one of these cities where he was safe, once his case had been reviewed by the high priest. However, if a deliberate murderer sought sanctuary in one of these cities, he was formally expelled and could be killed by the avenger of blood.

The psalmist tells the Lord that, given the prevailing injustice and oppression, He must act in accordance with His own law. He Himself must become the avenger of blood.

1. Vengeance Is Your Right (94:1)

"O LORD GOD, to Whom vengeance belongeth; O GOD, to Whom vengeance belongeth, show Thyself." It reads stronger than that in revised texts: "God of vengeance, Jehovah. God of vengeance, shine forth." The word "vengeance," moreover, is in the plural to underline the completeness of the retribution the psalmist has in mind.

We can see how fitting such a prayer will be in the dark and dreadful days of the beast. Apart from those specific instances legislated under the Mosaic Law, it is always best to leave vengeance in God's hands. The psalmist understood that. Vengeance is your right, Lord, he said.

2. Vengeance Is Your Responsibility (94:2)

"Lift up Thyself, Thou judge of the earth: render a reward to the proud." If we are to forego revenge and leave vengeance with God, then righteous retribution becomes His responsibility. As God is judge of the earth, there are wrongs that need to be righted, atrocities that need to be repaid, pride that needs to be abased. So the psalmist cries: "Hearken, Lord!"

But that is not all.

B. Hasten, Lord! (94:3-7)

The psalmist points out to the Lord how the foe has been behaving. Simply spelling it out should be enough to get the Lord to act!

1. The Heathen Demonstrate Their Power (94:3)

"LORD, how long shall the wicked, how long shall the wicked triumph?" This is an age-old problem, one we meet repeatedly in the psalms, one we find stirring the hearts of the prophets. It puzzles us, and it hardens skeptics and agnostics in their unbelief. Why do the wicked triumph? Seemingly they do. One of the significant things that Daniel tells us about the coming Antichrist is that he will "make craft to prosper."

2. The Heathen Declare Their Prowess (94:4)

"How long shall they utter and speak hard things? And all the workers of iniquity boast themselves?" The word translated "utter" is stronger than that. It occurs eleven times in the Old Testament, always in the poetical books, and literally means "to belch out."

The picture we conjure up is that of an active volcano erupting and spewing out the sulphuric fumes, deadly lava, and ash which seethe from the depths. When Mount St. Helens in Washington erupted it threw a cubic mile of dirt sixty thousand feet into the air. Gigantic mud slides composed of melted snow mixed with volcanic ash and, driven by waves of super-heated gas, erupted out of the crater. Clouds of hot ash made up of pulverized rock were belched twelve miles into the sky to fall back like dirty snow all over the eastern part of the state of Washington and in neighboring states. Schools, factories, stores, offices, highways, and airports were closed because of near zero visibility. The psalmist reminds the Lord that his enemies, the enemies of His people, are doing that. They are belching out poisonous boasts and blasphemies.

3. The Heathen Destroy God's People (94:5-6)

"They break in pieces Thy people, O Lord, and afflict Thy heritage. They slay the widow and the stranger, and murder the fatherless." They do not hesitate to murder the weak, the defenseless, and even the stranger. From very earliest times among the peoples of the Middle East hospitality to the stranger was regarded as a solemn and sacred duty. The guest was sacrosanct. With total disregard for code or custom, the ungodly were preying on the orphan, the widow, the alien—all those least able to defend themselves.

4. The Heathen Defame God's Person (94:7)

"Yet they say, THE LORD shall not see, neither shall the God of Jacob regard it." That was the ultimate. They had degraded the true and living God, Israel's God, the God of Jacob, to the status of a petty tribal deity, like the idols of the nations round about. As the graven images of the heathen were empty, powerless things, so was Jah.

No wonder the psalmist says, "Hasten, Lord! It is not so much that Your people are being ravished—You are being ridiculed. Surely, You are not going to sit idly by and tolerate that!"

II. THE SERMON (94:8-11)

He turns from pleading with God to pleading with his fellow countrymen. Many of them had given up, not having the spiritual discernment to see that the present circumstances were only temporary, that God was still on the throne. All too often when our situation seems beyond us we think it is beyond God—especially when our pleas "Lord, hearken! Lord, hasten!" seemingly fall upon deaf ears.

A. The Approach (94:8)

"Understand, ye brutish among the People: and ye fools, when will ye be wise?" This is certainly not the Dale Carnegie approach! Evidently the psalmist does not know "how to win friends and influence people." He has never heard of "the power of positive thinking." He comes out punching. He will certainly get the attention of his hearers, even if he makes them fighting mad in return.

B. The Appeal (94:9-10)

The psalmist sets God before them in a three-fold light.

1. God as Creator (94:9)

"He that planted the ear, shall He not hear? He that formed the eye, shall He not see?" What a simple, but sublime approach! The psalmist would have been even more forceful if he had known as much about the eye and the ear as we do today. But the Holy Spirit, who guided his hand as he wrote, certainly knew!

Think of the omniscient genius of a God who can create an eye! The eye contains tens of millions of electrical connections. It can handle one and a half million messages at once. About eighty percent of all the knowledge we absorb comes through the eye. When we look at an object, light passes through the lens of the eye and is brought into correct focus on the retina. Covering less than the space of an inch, the retina contains one hundred thirty-seven million light-sensitive receptor cells—one hundred thirty million rods for black and white vision and seven million cones for full color vision. These rods and cones are part of an extremely complex system. The tiny eye muscles move about one hundred thousand times a day to bring objects into focus. A man would have to walk fifty miles a day to give his legs similar exercise!

Only an omniscient, omnipotent God could create an eye, an ear, or any other of the awesomely intricate human organs.

Of course, the unknown singer of this psalm could not possibly know what we know about the eye and the ear. He knew enough, however, to attribute their creation to God. And he was wise enough to make the logical connection. Surely the God of such creative genius—the God who could invent and engineer the human ear and eye—surely such a God can hear and see! Of course He can! That is the first point in the appeal.

2. God as Corrector (94:10a)

"He that chastiseth the heathen, shall not He correct?" The word "correct" means to reprove, rebuke, call to account. Kirkpatrick reminds us that this passage stands almost alone in the Old Testament in its explicit assertion of the fact that God corrects, disciplines, and educates the nations, just as much as He does Israel. God loves heathen peoples as much as He loves the Hebrew people. God never leaves Himself without a witness. The heathen nations might not know God in the full sense that those blessed with an open Bible know Him, but He loves and corrects them just the same.

3. God as Counselor (94:10b)

"He that teacheth man knowledge, shall not He know?" Of course He knows! How foolish it is for us to imagine for a moment that God does not know what is going on. He is *God*! The psalmist simply extrapolates from the human to the divine. Since man can see and hear, since man is a moral, intelligent being—how foolish to imagine that God is anything less. Indeed, He is infinitely more. This, then, is the appeal.

C. The Application (94:11)

"The LORD knoweth the thoughts of man, that they are vanity." The word for "thoughts" is literally "fabrications" or "plaitings." Men twist and twine their thoughts like a woman plaits her hair, but no matter how tortuous and twisted the thinking of men, God can unravel it all. Even our most secret thoughts are as plain as print to Him.

He calls them "vanity." The word is "breath," or, as we would say today—so much hot air! Paul picks up this very verse in explaining to the sophisticated Corinthian believers the emptiness of human wisdom (I Corinthians 3:20).

The supplication gave way to the sermon. The sermon now gives way to the soliloquy.

III. THE SOLILOQUY (94:12-23)

In this section of the psalm, the singer talks to himself.

A. The Psalmist Explores the Principles of God's Dealings (94:12-15)

He comes to a fourfold conclusion about God's ways in the world.

1. A Parental Aspect to God's Ways (94:12a)

"Blessed is the man whom Thou chastenest, O LORD." That's quite a concept. The word rendered "blessed" is the usual word in the psalms for "happy." As a father disciplines his child, so God disciplines His people. Just as a father loves his child and wants the best for him, so also does God. The writer of Hebrews tells us that one proof we are in the family of God is seen in God's chastening of us. The psalmist saw the truth of that. He recognized the parental aspect in God's dealings with the nation of Israel.

2. A Pedagogical Aspect to God's Ways (94:12b)

"Blessed is the man whom Thou chastenest, O LORD, and teachest him out of Thy law." Some lessons can only be enforced by hard experience. They are there, written by God in His Word for our education, but we are so unteachable that God has to take the rod and drive them home by force of bitter circumstance.

3. A Providential Aspect to God's Ways (94:13-14)

"That Thou mayest give him rest from the days of adversity, until the pit be digged for the wicked. For the LORD will not cast off His People, neither will He forsake His inheritance." There are some deep truths in that little statement.

The thoughtful singer sees God *provide a period of relief* (94:13a). He provides rest from the days of adversity. He tempers the wind to the shorn lamb. He does not suffer us to be tempted above what we are able to bear. He sees God *plan a place of retribution* (94:13b). The pit of the wicked is being digged. It may be some little thing, some insignificant item the tyrant has overlooked, but God is at work. His ways are oftentimes hidden, but He is at work. He sees God *pursue a policy of reinstatement* (94:14). The Lord will not cast off His inheritance. God's inheritance in Old Testament times was the nation of Israel. The reinstatement of a small contingent of faithful pioneers in the promised land was proof enough to this singer that God's purposes operated on a very much larger time scale than ours.

The psalmist's words really leap the centuries. Present-day Israel, regathered in part back to the land, is proof that God's policy of reinstatement is still at work. The prophetic Scriptures assure us what the future will be like for Israel. Not even the dark days of the great tribulation will hinder God from bringing His purposes to a successful conclusion. The psalmist, then, lays hold of this providential aspect in God's ways.

4. A Practical Aspect to God's Ways (94:15)

"But judgment shall return unto righteousness: and all the upright in heart shall follow it." Ultimately God will dispossess the wicked and bring righteous judgment back as the supreme principle of government in human affairs.

So then, the psalmist has explored for himself the principles of God's dealings.

B. The Psalmist Experiences the Pleasure of God's Deliverance (94:16-19)

He returns from philosophical meditations to his own case. What it was we are not told, but evidently it had much to do with the writing of this psalm.

1. His Case (94:16-17)

On the surface, it looked as though there were no help and no hope for him. "Who will rise up for me against the evildoers? Or who will stand up for me against the workers of iniquity? Unless the LORD had been my help, my soul had almost dwelt in silence." Apparently there was nobody to stand up for him among men, but he had no doubt that God was on his side.

2. His Cry (94:18)

"When I said, 'my foot slippeth'; Thy mercy, O LORD, held me up." The tenses in the text suggest that this courageous singer had already given himself up for lost. But God had hold of him all the time. We can picture a little boy walking with his dad. His father is holding his hand when suddenly the little fellow slips. Down he would go, except for one thing—daddy had him by the hand. God's mercy was God's hand securing the psalmist in his difficult circumstances.

3. His Comfort (94:19)

"In the multitude of my thoughts within me Thy comforts delight my soul." The word for "thoughts" is rendered "doubts" in the margin of the Revised Version. Another authority suggests the rendering "wandering thoughts." The psalmist was troubled by distracting thoughts. We do not have to go far from our own prayer chambers to realize what wandering thoughts can do for us. Sometimes we find it almost impossible to concentrate in prayer, even when we desperately need to pray. The psalmist found comfort in the fact that God Himself understands and consoles.

That is why in the New Testament we have been given that other Comforter. He is the Paraclete, the One called alongside to help, the One who, as Paul says, "helpeth our infirmities." The word Paul used was the same word that Martha used when she asked the Lord to tell Mary to come and help her in the kitchen. It was practical, immediate, down-to-earth help she wanted. That is the kind of help God gives.

C. The Psalmist Examines the Potential of God's Decisions (94:20-23)

He turns aside from his own troubles to the larger troubles of his people.

1. The Outraging of the Majesty of God (94:20-21)

"Shall the throne of iniquity have fellowship with Thee, which frameth mischief by a law? They gather themselves together against the soul of the righteous, and condemn the innocent blood." It is a practice all too common today. New laws are passed which legalize practices our fathers wrote down as sin, but God is not the ally of those who sin in high places and who do wrong under the shelter of legal forms. Nor is He impressed with modern laws which legalize perversion, pornography, and lust.

2. The Outpouring of the Mercy of God (94:22)

"But the LORD is my defence; and my God is the rock of my refuge." The singer is quite safe! He is sheltered in the cleft of the rock. His enemies must remove that rock to get to him!

3. The Outworking of the Morality of God (94:23)

"And He shall bring upon them their own iniquity, and shall cut them off in their own wickedness; yea, the LORD our God shall cut them off." In the end, morality and right will triumph. The psalm thus ends with a preview of the return of Christ at the end of the tribulation to set up His righteous kingdom on earth. The returning Lord will make short work of His foes, cutting them off in their wickedness as they stand at Megiddo, weapons in hand, to oppose His coming again.

Psalm 95

LEST HISTORY REPEAT ITSELF

I. PRAISING GOD (95:1-7)
   A. We Are Invited to Acclaim Him (95:1)
      1. His Name
      2. His Fame
   B. We Are Invited to Approach Him (95:2-5)
      1. In an Uninhibited Way (95:2)
         a. Gratefully
         b. Gladly
      2. In an Understanding Way (95:3-5)
         a. Mindful of God's Majesty (95:3)
         b. Mindful of God's Might (95:4-5)
   C. We Are Invited to Adore Him (95:6-7)
      1. Instinctively (95:6)
      2. Intelligently (95:7a)
      3. Instantly (95:7b)
II. PROVOKING GOD (95:8-11)
   A. The Sudden Crisis in Israel (95:8-9)
   B. The Settled Character of Israel (95:10)
   C. The Sad Consequence for Israel (95:11)

PSALMS 95–100 are a group within a group. Psalms 93 and 95–100 are *theocratic psalms*. Psalms 95–100 are also *coronation psalms*. They were written or adapted for the dedication of the second temple. The overthrow of Babylon and the regathering of Israel were marvelous events in history. Scarcely a stir was made on earth, but it was an hour which chimed out loudly in heaven. It meant that God had again begun to actively work in history on behalf of His people.

The entire movement culminated in the rebuilding of the temple in Jerusalem. It was an occasion for rejoicing, but if it carried with it the soaring notes of song, it also carried the sober note of suggestion. The people had been gathered into the promised land, but that suggested a notable parallel; they had been gathered into the land

61

once before and had been thrown back out again because of their sin. What if that should happen again?

In looking for a sermon-song to convey that idea, the godly compiler hit on the poem we now know as Psalm 95. It is included in the Hebrew hymnbook as an anonymous psalm, but in Hebrews 4:7 it is quoted as a psalm of David. Commentators have speculated about that, but it need not pose a problem. This psalm could easily have come from the pen of David and been included in the selection of inspired songs because of its obvious suitability to the occasion. If the Holy Spirit quotes the psalm as being Davidic, that should be enough. So, let us leave the *authorship* with David and the *adaption* with some anonymous compiler, led by the Spirit of God to include this long-forgotten poem of David in this particular collection. The compiler himself might not even have been sure that David was the original author of the poem he found so perfectly suitable to his purpose and, for that reason, might have left it anonymous. But the Holy Spirit later tells us it was David's.

Given the Davidic authorship of the psalm and the suggestion that this is the first of half a dozen coronation psalms, another aspect of its suitability can be seen. David was Israel's greatest king; he was the ideal king, the shepherd-king, the divinely-chosen one. All the kings of the house of Judah are compared with David for better or for worse, just as all the kings of the house of Israel are compared with "Jeroboam, the son of Nebat, who made Israel to sin."

As king, David was the first man in the nation to be crowned as God's choice for the throne. He was crowned three times—at least, he was anointed three times which in Israel amounted to the same thing. He was anointed by Samuel, by the house of Judah, and by all Israel. He had *a secret anointing* on the Bethlehem farm. In the power of that anointing he overthrew Goliath of Gath and secured for himself a place in the affections of all but the most carnal of the people of God. He had *a selective anointing* by the men of Judah after the death of Saul. In the power of that anointing he could sit back and watch the Ishbosheth faction in Israel wear itself out. He had *a supreme anointing* when, in a great wave of joy and popular enthusiasm, the people finally gave him his place as sovereign of all the tribes. In the power of that anointing he went out to thrash the nation's foes, put its internal affairs in order, lead a great revival of spiritual life, make provision for the building of the temple, and write half the Hebrew hymnbook.

Thus it is with our Lord. First, we must crown Him Lord of all in our lives. This is a private affair. Then we must crown Him corporately as supreme Head of His people, in the world where He is still rejected by the vast majority. Finally, we shall one day rejoice to see the whole world crown Him Lord of all.

Let us look at our psalm.

It is clearly divided into two parts. In verses 1-7 the theme is *prais-*

ing God. In verses 8-11 the theme is *provoking God.* The first section is worship, the second is warning. Praise and peril go hand in hand.

I. PRAISING GOD (95:1-7)

We begin with a threefold invitation to "worship the King all glorious above, to gratefully sing His power and His love."

A. We Are Invited to Acclaim Him (95:1)

"O come, let us sing unto the LORD: let us make a joyful noise to the rock of our salvation." "Let us!" That phrase is worth studying in both the Old and the New Testaments.

The first time that it occurs is in Genesis 1:26. The eternal God says, "Let Us make man in Our image, after Our likeness." And so He did. The wondering angelic hosts saw Him do something He had not done before. The rest of creation was brought into being by divine decree. The birds and beasts, the creatures of the sea, all came into being by creative command, but not by man! God Himself stooped down to fashion Adam's clay. He Himself breathed into Adam's nostrils the breath of life. Adam became a living soul. He was endowed with the capacity to know and love and worship God. That is the first "Let us." It sweeps away the entire fabric of evolution which says that man is descended from the beasts.

The second "Let us" in Scripture is found in Genesis 11. Adam's fall came to fruition in the flood, and God began again with a second Adam. But, before long, Noah's descendents mobilized in another racial attempt to dethrone God from human affairs. Three times they said, "Let us." They planned a federation of nations, a united nations organization, a world society from which God was to be excluded. They were to have a political, religious, cultural order based on humanism and a one-world government headed by a supreme dictator. Then God said, "Let Us go down. . . . " He answered their "Let us" with His own.

So, it is refreshing as we open this psalm, to see that the phrase "Let us" can be used by man in a different way. "O come, let us sing unto the Lord. . . . " We are to acclaim *His name!* "The Lord!" Jehovah! The God of Covenant! The God who always keeps His Word! The pledged Word of God by the pen of Jeremiah that the captivity would last for just seventy years had been gloriously kept. The prophetic Word of God by the pen of Isaiah that the captivity would be ended by a man named Cyrus had been kept to the letter! "O come, let us sing unto the Lord!" Surely we can enter into that! Has He not kept His Word with us in countless ways? Of course He has.

We are to acclaim *His fame.* "O come . . . let us make a joyful noise to the rock of our salvation." They were not only saved, they were safe! No countermanding decree of any Persian potentate, no obstructionist tactics by the surrounding petty princedoms could reverse what God was doing in history. Did not the history of Babylon demonstrate that even the mightiest of world powers could easily be swept away like markings on the desert sand? Israel was safe. Their trust was in God, and God was the rock of their salvation.

What a wonderful name for God! "The rock of our salvation." Such is His fame! Well might we sing:

> Oh safe to the Rock that is higher than I,
> My soul in its conflicts and sorrows would fly;
> So sinful, so weary, Thine, Thine would I be:
> Thou blest "Rock of Ages" I'm hiding in Thee.

B. We Are Invited to Approach Him (95:2-5)

How wonderful that we have an approachable God. It is one of the wonders of the universe that the great, eternal, uncreated, self-existing God should not only be approachable but also desires us to draw near to Him.

The psalmist tells us how we are to approach Him.

1. In an Uninhibited Way (95:2)

"Let us come before His presence with thanksgiving, and make a joyful noise unto Him with psalms." We are to approach Him *gratefully*. We are to come into His presence with thanksgiving. "His presence" is the usual way of describing an audience with royalty. One comes into the presence. In Eastern lands, people approached the presence with their faces on the floor, groveling in the dust, quaking with fear. God does not want us to grovel, but He certainly wants us to be grateful. The apostle Paul lists ingratitude as one of the cardinal sins and includes it with a host of hideous offences in that dreadful catalog of crime he uses as part of God's indictment of the human race (Romans 1).

We are to approach Him *gladly*. "Make a joyful noise unto Him with psalms." We are to approach Him in an uninhibited way, with a spring in our step and a song in our soul. All too often our meetings are stiff, joyless affairs with everything draped in formality. God would have us enjoy Him.

2. In an Understanding Way (95:3-5)

The fact that we are to approach Him with joy does not mean that we are to be flippant and irreverent. Truth is always balanced. We must not forget the awesome majesty of God, or else we might be tempted to undue familiarity. We are to be:

a. Mindful of God's Majesty (95:3)

"For the LORD is a great GOD, and a great King above all gods" (95:3). The Hebrew word for "gods" here is the word *elohim,* the usual word for God. But, in this connection, it refers to the spirit beings who lurk behind the idols and images of the heathen. These fallen creatures give the inspiration to idolatry and make it possible for graven images to exert such a fearful fascination. We need not wonder that men are held in thrall to sticks and stones when behind them are demons. It is part of Satan's master plan of deception, and effective it is. All idolatrous religious systems have this power to enslave their devotees.

But great as is the power of these false gods to hold men in spiritual blindness and bondage, that power will melt before the power of God, *El,* as the psalmist names Him, emphasizing the concentration of His power. Well the demons know it.

b. Mindful of God's Might (95:4-5)

The psalmist turns from the mystical to the material, from the spirit world to the physical world. He reminds us that the God, into whose august presence we are invited to come, is indeed the great creator of the universe. God's might is everywhere displayed. The psalmist tells us to plumb the depths, to dig deep, for: "In His hand are the deep places of the earth."

He invites us to climb the heights, to scale the lofty mountains, to plant our feet on higher ground. When at last our feet stand on the virgin snows of the age-old hills, "the strength of the hills is His also."

He invites us to sail the sea, to weigh anchor, to shove off from shore, to spread our sails, to venture out beyond sight of land, to learn that "the sea is His, He made it"—all two hundred million square miles of it.

He invites us to explore the earth, the forests and the plains, the deserts and the downs, the pampas and the prairies. "His hands formed the dry land."

So we are to praise Him by acclaiming Him and by approaching Him.

C. We Are Invited to Adore Him (95:6-7)

1. Let Us Adore Instinctively (95:6)

"O come, let us worship and bow down: let us kneel before the LORD our maker." We are not told to say anything, for there are times when words are redundant, when we are overwhelmed by the goodness and greatness of God. All we can do is come in reverence and awe to adore Him. The thoughts roll over us like the billows of the sea. Our hearts are strangely moved; they burn within us. There comes to mind the verse of a hymn: "How great Thou art!" which says it all. Praising Him is all we can do. For the rest, we are lost in wonder and love, in unexpressed, unspoken praise. At such times we worship Him instinctively.

2. Let Us Adore Intelligently (95:7a)

Presently, the full wonder of it surfaces and the conscious mind takes over. "For He is our God!" The wonder of it! Better still, "And we are the People of His pasture, and the sheep of His hand."

No wonder the Holy Spirit reminds us in the New Testament that this is a psalm of David. Who else among the singers of Hebrews could speak so rapturously of the Shepherd and His sheep? The psalmist's mind goes back to his shepherding days. He thinks of the sheep he led from pasture to pasture, how he had *foraged* for them, *fended* for them, *fought* for them, how he had named them and numbered them. He knew them all, each and every one. "We are the People of His pasture, and the sheep of His hand." David would think when putting them into the fold at night, how he would pass each one under his hand, carefully searching for thorns and bruises. So we are to adore God intelligently, with full appreciation of what it means to have a God like Him, and what it means to be His!

3. Let Us Adore Instantly (95:7b)

"To day, if ye will hear His voice." Modern versions have a tendency to break this exclamation off and join it onto the following verses. But it stands well where it is. The psalmist is saying: Adore Him! Do it now! Instantly! Don't put it off! This takes priority and precedence over all else. This is life's highest duty, life's supremest moment. Let nothing come between—not even a flickering moment of time. The moment we allow something to get in between, the mystic moment passes and mundane things intrude. Then life's secular tides sweep us away and, if that is allowed to happen too often, we shall find ourselves swept out to sea, adrift on the heaving billows of life and in deadly spiritual peril.

That is why, at this point, there is such an abrupt change in the psalm. The contrast is startling! Up to now we have been praising God. Now comes a word of warning.

II. Provoking God (95:8-11)

From its setting in the psalms, it seems clear that this song, like its immediate fellows, was added to the Hebrew hymnbook at the time that the second temple was built. The Hebrews have been delivered from the Babylonian captivity. Once before they had been delivered from the Egyptian captivity. That thought reminds the compiler that, in their newfound freedom, the Israelites had rebelled against God in the wilderness. What if they should do it again? In searching for a way to warn he remembers these words of David. How suitable they are!

The psalmist is impressed with the fact that there is a great danger of history repeating itself.

A. The Sudden Crisis in Israel (95:8-9)

"Harden not your heart, as in the provocation, and as in the day of temptation in the wilderness, when your fathers tempted Me, proved Me, and saw My work."

Underline those words "in the provocation" and the word "temptation." These words are Meribah and Massah in the Hebrew. They have been translated in the King James Version following the Septuagint and other ancient versions. Many scholars feel they should have been left to stand untranslated. In the Revised Version, for instance, the verse reads: "Harden not your hearts as at Meribah, as in the day of Massah in the wilderness."

The names Meribah and Massah take us back to the story of the exodus. We turn first to Exodus 17:1-7. There we read of Israel at Rephidim. Pharaoh's hosts had been swept away in the waters of the Red Sea, and Israel was on the march. The people came to Rephidim, but they were desperate because they were thirsty and there was no water. Already they had forgotten the mighty miracles which had liberated them from Egypt. Was God going to allow them now to die of thirst? Of course not! But the unbelieving people rose up in revolt against Moses: "Give us water that we may drink. . . Wherefore is this that thou hast brought us up out of Egypt, to kill us and our children and our cattle with thirst?" They were so infuriated they were ready to stone Moses. Then God told him to smite the rock in Horeb, and from that smitten rock the living waters flowed. Moses, however, "called the name of the place Massah, and Meribah, because of the chiding of the children of Israel, and because they tempted the LORD, saying, 'Is the LORD among us, or not?' " That was at the beginning of the wilderness journey.

The same thing happened again toward the end of the wilderness wanderings, some forty years later. The older generation was dead and their carcasses littered the wilderness. Now a new generation was infuriated with Moses. They were now at fateful Kadesh, on the frontiers of the promised land. We read of it in Numbers 20:1-13. "And there was no water for the congregation: and they gathered themselves together against Moses and against Aaron." This time God told Moses to speak to the rock, but Moses, exasperated by the constant unbelief and rebellion of the people, lost his temper and smote the rock. The water flowed, but "the LORD spake unto Moses and Aaron, 'Because ye believed Me not, to sanctify Me in the eyes of the children of Israel, therefore ye shall not bring this congregation into the land which I have given them.' This is the water of Meribah [adds the Holy Spirit]: because the children of Israel strove with the LORD, and He was sanctified in them."

That was the sudden crisis in Israel. And it happened twice—twice before they even so much as entered the promised land. History certainly does repeat itself.

The psalmist is not through.

B. The Settled Character of Israel (95:10)

"Forty years long was I grieved with this generation, and said, 'It is a People that do err in their heart, and they have not known My ways.' " It was a settled character of chronic disbelief. They saw God's works, but they did not know God's ways. They could not help but know God's works for they were all about them, miracle after miracle, from the time Moses flung his rod on the ground and it became a serpent until the time he made a serpent of brass and set it on a pole so that the serpent-bitten people might look, believe, and live. They saw His works, but they knew not His ways. The character of Israel was one of worldliness and carnality. It persisted all through the forty years in the wilderness. It was a fact well-known to David. It persisted all through the years in the promised land.

There was one more fact to be considered.

C. The Sad Consequence for Israel (95:11)

"Unto whom I sware in My wrath that they should not enter into My rest." Thus, at the beginning of the wilderness journey, the persistent hardness and unbelief of Israel, which came to a climax at Kadesh-barnea, brought down God's sentence on them. Except for Joshua and Caleb, not one of the adults who had experienced the exodus entered into Canaan.

Thus, at the end of the wilderness wanderings, the provocation of Moses and Aaron in smiting the rock when told to speak to it brought down God's sentence. They also were excluded from Canaan.

God's promised rest was lost to an entire generation. The word the psalmist uses for "rest" is the word used in Ruth 1:9 for the rest of marriage. What a tragedy to believe God in bringing them out of Egypt, but not to believe Him in bringing them into Canaan; to trust Him for redemption, but not to trust Him for rest. That was the provocation.

This entire passage is picked up and quoted almost verbatim in the New Testament. It is used by the writer of Hebrews as part of his second warning. Israel's failure to enter into *Canaan rest* is used by him to illustrate the sad possibility of our failure to enter into *Calvary rest*. The result will be spiritually the same: a frustrated, fearful, second-class life and temporal loss. Let us make sure history does not repeat itself in our lives.

Psalm 96

LET US SING

I. ALL GLORY BELONGS TO GOD (96:1-6)
  A. What We Should Sing (96:1-2)
    1. We Should Sing a New Song
    2. It Is a Necessary Song
  B. Where We Should Sing (96:3)
  C. Why We Should Sing (96:4-6)
    Because of:
    1. The Fear of the Lord (96:4)
    2. The Fact of the Lord (96:5)
    3. The Fame of the Lord (96:6)
II. ALL GIFTS BELONG TO GOD (96:7-9)
  We should give of:
  A. Our Wonder (96:7-8a)
  B. Our Wealth (96:8b)
  C. Our Worship (96:9)
III. ALL GOVERNMENT BELONGS TO GOD (96:10-13)
  A. The Principles of the Coming Government (96:10)
    1. Absolute Sovereignty
    2. Absolute Security
    3. Absolute Sanctity
  B. The Prospect of the Coming Government (96:11-13)
    1. For All Nature (96:11-13a)
    2. For All Nations (96:13b)

SING! SING! SING! That is how this psalm begins. It calls us to joyful worship because all *glory* belongs to Him. Give! Give! Give! That is how the psalm continues. It calls us to joyful worship because all *gifts* belong to Him. Let! Let! Let! That is how the psalm ends. It calls us to joyful worship because all *government* belongs to Him.

This is one of the great Hebrew hymns that celebrates the coming reign of Christ. It is another of the theocratic and coronation psalms. Like others in this particular collection, it seems to have been written or chosen especially to celebrate the emancipation of Israel from the Babylonian captivity and the opening of the new

temple in Jerusalem. The repatriated Hebrews saw in this stirring
event evidence of God's sovereignty over the nations and assurance
that one day He would establish on earth a kingdom stretching from
pole to pole and from sea to sea, from the river to the ends of the
earth.

One interesting sidelight of this psalm is that it contains the center
verse of the Bible. "Let the heavens rejoice, and let the earth be
glad; let the sea roar, and the fulness thereof." There is something
fitting in that. At the very heart of the Bible is a call for this planet to
lift its voice in joyful song. This is what God plans in the crowning
day that is yet to come.

The psalm divides into three parts. We learn that all glory belongs
to Him, all gifts belong to Him, and all government belongs to Him.
The psalm was probably sung in the temple by two groups of Levites
and the full choir. It seems likely it was sung in this manner:

Singers	Verse
Levites A	1
Levites B	2
Choir	3
Levites A	4
Levites B	5
Choir	6
Levites A	7
Levites B	8
Choir	9
Levites A	10
Levites B	11-12
Choir	13

I. ALL GLORY BELONGS TO GOD (96:1-6)

The psalm begins with a threefold invitation to the Lord's people
to sing. God wants His people to be happy. We do not have a gloomy
God; we have a glorious God who fills the high halls of Heaven with
anthems and songs of praise. He would have us tune our harps to
sing His praise and join our voices with those celestial choirs who
harmonize in joyful song.

A. What We Should Sing (96:1-2)

The psalmist has no dearth of ideas about what we should sing.

1. We Should Sing a New Song

"O sing unto the LORD a new song: sing unto the LORD, all the earth." The angels sang a song when they watched their mighty maker create the universe. What a sight that must have been! First, there was nothing—just a black void in the limitless expanse of space. Then, with a prodigious, inconceivable, almighty burst of energy, the whole thing exploded into being. Stars and suns and whirling satellites, galaxies and constellations, hydrogen and helium, all hurtling headlong into the vast emptiness until that emptiness was alive with dancing worlds ablaze with light, burning with energy, poised and balanced and governed by inflexible laws and rejoicing to do His will. No wonder the seraphim sang!

Israel sang another song while at the sea. They sang the song of Moses! Pharaoh and his hosts had been drowned in the depths and swept away. The Israelites stood at last, free of Egypt, faces toward the promised land, hearts overflowing with joy. Redeemed by blood, baptized unto Moses in the cloud and in the sea, soon to be gathered around the table in the wilderness, and heading for home! No wonder they sang.

The redeemed are to sing a new song in glory. One of these days the Lord Jesus will step into the spotlight of eternity, take the seven-sealed scroll from Him that sits upon the throne, and be recognized at the seat of power as the only One fit to govern the earth. The moment He takes that scroll the joybells ring in Heaven and they sing a new song. It is the song of the Lamb: "Thou art worthy . . . for Thou wast slain, and hast redeemed us to God by Thy blood" (Revelation 5:9).

This new song is a song for the millennial earth. This is the song the redeemed remnant of Israel and nations will sing as they march away from the valley of Jehoshaphat to take possession of a renewed and replenished planet. It is the full expression and expansion of the new song raised by the little band of repatriated Jews gathered in their rebuilt temple amid the ruins and rubble of Jerusalem. It is a song of hope. It is a song unto the Lord, Jehovah, the covenant-keeping God. It is a song to the Lord of all the earth, and all the earth is invited to harmonize the hymn. The curse of Babel removed, a universal hymn of praise to the true and living God will fill the world with song.

2. It Is a Necessary Song

"Sing unto the LORD, bless His name; show forth His salvation from day to day. Declare His glory among the heathen, His wonders among all people."

No wonder so many of the commentators remind us that this is essentially a missionary hymn. If we had no other verse in the Bible but this one to teach us our duty to the lost in pagan lands, this would be enough. How can we who sit bathed in the full light of the gospel—ransomed, restored, forgiven, Heaven-born, and Heaven-bound—be content to sit in our pews and sing our songs when millions lie in darkness under the shadow of death with never so much as a verse of Scripture in their native tongue? When countless millions live and die in darkness and disease, wrapped in delusion and deception, how can we ignore the missionary implications of the faith?

This is a necessary song. It is to be taught to the tribes of earth who know not the Lord or who have heard of Him only distortedly and distantly. In the millennial age the knowledge of the true and living God will be taught to the tribes of earth as the first great order of business on that new day. In this present age God holds us accountable for the untold millions still untold.

B. Where We Should Sing (96:3)

"Declare His glory among the heathen, His wonders among all people." The people of this world need to know that all glory belongs to God.

We mass our choirs, have song-fests, publish hymnbooks to provide new phrases and melodies for our services of worship and praise—not that we should not do that. But how can we do that week after week without a thought for those who have no song at all? God in heaven could not stand it! With heaven's halls ringing and echoing with the anthems of the angels, God looked upon this poor world of ours, sunk in ruin, sin, and misery, hurrying on to endless pain. "Who will go and teach *them* how to sing?" He said. And Jesus said, "Here am I; send Me."

C. Why We Should Sing (96:4-6)

The psalmist lists three motives for song.

1. The Fear of the Lord (96:4)

"For the LORD is great, and greatly to be praised: He is to be feared above all gods." After all, "The fear of the Lord is the beginning of wisdom." When we get to know Him better we love Him, but a healthy fear of the Lord is where it often begins. That is why the very first work of the Holy Spirit in a human heart is the work of conviction. The Lord Jesus said, "When He, the Spirit of truth is come, He will convince the world of sin, of righteousness and of judgment to come." He convicts of the *nature* of sin, the *need* for righteousness, and the *nearness* of judgment.

The heathen fear their false gods. They grovel in abject terror before most of them, and well they might, for grim and gory they are. The Lord does not want that; He does not want us to grovel. He wants respect born of a conscious knowledge of His wisdom, love, and power.

2. The Fact of the Lord (96:5)

"For all the gods of the nations are idols: but the LORD made the heavens." The word the psalmist uses here for "gods" is derived from the usual word for God, *El*, but it employs the negative participle. The word literally means "good for nothing" or, even more specifically, "nothings." The gods of the nations are good for nothing, they are "nothings," they are nonentities, they are really nonexistent except in the enslaved imaginations of those who worship them.

In contrast, the Lord made the heavens. Here is a motive for song! We are in touch with reality, with the true and living God, with the God whose omnipotent power created the heavens themselves.

3. The Fame of the Lord (96:6)

"Honour and majesty are before Him: strength and beauty are in His sanctuary." Honor! Majesty! Strength! Beauty! The psalmist was thinking perhaps of the restored temple in Jerusalem. When the temple was built, many of the older Jewish repatriates wept because its glory and magnificence were so inferior to that which Solomon had built and which the Babylonians had put to the torch. But they should not weep. The prophet Haggai had a word for them: "Who is left among you that saw this house in her first glory? And how do ye see it now? Is it not in your eyes in comparison of it as nothing? Yet now be strong. . . . Yet once, it is a little while, and I will shake the heavens, and the earth, and the sea, and the dry land; and I will shake all nations, and the desire of all nations shall come: and I will fill this house with glory, saith the LORD of hosts" (Haggai 2:3-7).

As always, there is a mingling of future events in this great prophecy. The desire of all nations did come! His name was Jesus. He came to this temple; He graced it with a glory not of this world. He was not recognized or known, nor was His glory recognized and understood; but He is coming back! When He does: "Honour and majesty are before Him: strength and beauty are in His sanctuary." His glory will be unveiled at last—not to just a Peter, a James, or a John on some lonely holy mount, but to all mankind. What a theme for song!

So then, the psalm begins with the thrice-repeated call: "Let us sing! Let us sing! Let us sing!" We should sing because of the glory that belongs to our Lord. Our song should be such that its echoes are heard to earth's remotest bounds and until, from all of mankind's scattered tribes, there arises to God the worship and praise due to His name. In some degree, already it does. On the Lord's day the praise begins in eastern lands, it follows the sun on its swift journey westward, and it does not cease throughout the day to sound out from land to land.

The psalmist now changes his theme.

II. All Gifts Belong to God (96:7-9)

Give! Give! Give! If we cannot go, we can give! We can give three things.

A. Our Wonder (96:7-8a)

"Give unto the Lord, O ye kindreds of the people, give unto the Lord glory and strength. Give unto the Lord the glory due unto His name."

In ancient times when a subject approached his sovereign he brought a present as token of his submission. How can we do anything less for our Lord? The first thing He wants from us, however, is the glory due to His name. He wants us to acknowledge Him for who and what He is. That comes first.

I was interested to read of the grooming Lady Diana, now the Princess of Wales, has received to prepare her for the role she must play as Britain's future queen. Her refreshing giggle, for instance, had to be schooled into its proper place. Nor can she accept the familiar "Di" as a form of address from any except her husband and the queen. Lady Diana must henceforth live with constant dignity. People expect a monarchy to be larger than life, to be something removed from the banalities of ordinary existence. If one is to be a king or a queen, then one must do it in the proper style.

How much more, then, God demands of us our tribute of wonder and awe. The majesty which surrounds Him is no tinsel trapping of a faded human monarchy. It is the awesome majesty of One whose brightness is above that of the noonday sun.

B. Our Wealth (96:8b)

"Bring an offering, and come into His courts." Giving is part of the life of faith. God expects that we shall honor Him with our substance, with sacrificial offerings—not because He needs it, but because He graciously makes it possible for us to express, in a tangible way, something of the gratitude of our hearts.

In the Old Testament the children of Israel were required to bring sacrifices and offerings, and they were also expected to tithe. The tithe was a form of religious tax, a mandatory ten percent of all income, required by law to support the work of the priests and the Levites. The tithe, extracted from the law, is not one of the principles which govern us in this church age. God, however, expects from us proportionate giving ("according as the Lord hath prospered"). Certainly we cannot give less under grace than was demanded under law. Probably we should give a great deal more. We need to remember that, under law, a tenth was required plus sacrifices and offerings of various kinds.

C. Our Worship (96:9)

"O worship the LORD in the beauty of holiness: fear before Him, all the earth." One thinks of the gorgeous interior of the temple and tabernacle, of the holy place and the holy of holies where all was beauty. The inner linen walls of the tabernacle were gorgeous reds, blues, and purples. The veil was the same. All the furnishings and fittings were of gleaming gold. The place was a holy and beautiful place. God planned it so. The priest in the holy place worshiped in the beauty of holiness. God deliberately joined the two thoughts together. True holiness will always produce beauty. We have all met people whose personal holiness of life has resulted in the transfiguration of their very countenance.

III. ALL GOVERNMENT BELONGS TO GOD (96:10-13)

"Let! Let! Let!" When the Holy Spirit throws His omnipotent power behind such urging then there is no power on earth, in the heavens, or in hell itself that can prevent its coming to pass.

A. The Principles of the Coming Government (96:10)

"Say among the heathen that the LORD reigneth." We note in this verse a threefold principle of the coming millennial kingdom.

1. Absolute Sovereignty

"Say among the heathen [the nations] that the LORD reigneth." God's ideal form of government is not a democratic or a republican form of government. It is not government of the people, by the people, for the people. It is an absolute monarchy with all power concentrated in the capable hands of His dear Son. That is the first principle.

2. Absolute Security

"The world also shall be established that it shall not be moved." There will be no wars, no rebellions, no uprisings, no crime syndicates flourishing in the underworld. It will be a reign of just, holy, impartial, universal law. The foundations of society in the millennial kingdom will be so secure that nothing will be able to challenge them. Satan will be bound, the saints will reign with Christ, sinners will be unable to express their disruptive ambitions and lusts.

3. Absolute Sanctity

"He shall judge the people righteously." There will be no corruption of the legal process. There will be no partiality, no injustice, no biased laws. These are the principles of government.

B. The Prospect of the Coming Government (96:11-3)

He would have us note what and whom it will affect.

1. All Nature (96:11-13a)

"Let the heavens rejoice, and let the earth be glad; let the sea roar, and the fulness thereof." This is what Paul had in mind, surely, when in Romans 8 he speaks of the whole creation "standing on tip-toe" (J. B. Phillips), waiting with earnest expectation for the day when the sons of God will come into their own. Dumb nature will find a mighty voice.

In pointing out that verse 11 is the middle verse of the Bible, Hull says: "In this verse there are seven words in Hebrew, and thirty letters, but it is interesting that fourteen different letters are used, and the initial letters of the words are JHVHJHU which spell Jehovah Jahu, which means 'the Lord, He is God.' "

That, after all, is what makes the prospect of this coming government so joyous!

2. All Nations (96:13b)

"For He cometh to judge the earth: He shall judge the world with righteousness, and the people with His truth." Thus, this great song rises to its ringing climax.

So often when we think of the Lord's coming in judgment, we paint the terrors of the day of the Lord. Terrors there will be, enough and to spare, but the goal of it all is gladness.

The predominant thought behind the word "judgment" here is not punishment, but peace and praise and perfect government. So, while the day still tarries, let Him establish that kind of government in our hearts and lives.

Psalm 97

THE CROWNING DAY THAT'S COMING

PSALM 97 is another of the great coronation psalms that blaze like supernovas in the starry firmament of the Hebrew hymnbook. Like the others, it anticipates the great crowning day that is coming when our Beloved will return to reign upon this planet Earth. And, like all the psalms in the series, it can be best understood in the prophetic context of the coming millennial reign.

The psalm divides into two major parts. We see the Lord celebrated first as the reigning One (97:1-9) and then as the righteous One (97:10-12). The two are inseparable. That is what will make the millennial reign the golden age of earth's history. At last there will rule over the sons of men One who will not only reign with invincible power, but with absolute integrity.

I. THE REIGNING ONE (97:1-9)

The psalmist sees the coming King in two ways.

A. The Ruler of All Nature (97:1-5)

1. His Majesty's Soverign Domains (97:1)

"The LORD reigneth; let the earth rejoice; let the multitude of the isles be glad thereof." The word translated "isles" is the usual one for coastlines and islands. It refers generally to the seagirt lands beyond the shores of Israel, to the lands of the Mediterranean, that vast landlocked sea that bounded much of the Bible world. But, in a larger context, the psalmist is referring to the Gentile nations as a whole. He sees crowds filled with joy at the thought that at last the true King has come to reign.

In 1945, after six seemingly endless years of war, the armies of the Third Reich finally surrendered. There had been the blackout, the bombs, and the stringent rationing. There had been trainloads of wounded, and endless lists of the dead. Suddenly that all stopped. The lights went on again all over the world. The troops came home. The horror camps were emptied. There was world-wide jubilation. War criminals were rounded up and forced to answer for the atrocities they had committed against mankind.

Great though that victory was, it was the mere turning of a page of history compared with the worldwide jubilation which will follow the second coming of Christ. The great tribulation will cease. Armageddon will have put an end to all organized resistance on this planet. Satan will be bound and imprisoned, the beast and the false prophet will be cast headlong into hell, and at last there will be peace! The world will shout: "The Lord reigneth; let the earth rejoice; let the multitude of isles be glad thereof."

2. His Majesty's Secret Dwelling (97:2)

"Clouds and darkness are round about Him: righteousness and judgment are the habitation of His throne." He dwells in the hidden place, in the clouds and in the darkness, in the holy place, where righteous judgment sits enthroned. Mystery and majesty are associated with His throne.

This verse acknowledges the mystery which surrounds God's ways. The deep darkness (literally "thick" darkness) which hides Him from us today and which shrouds His ways upon the earth with such impenetrable mystery should not cause us to doubt. His government can never depart from righteousness, from that which is right. We can take courage in that. There may be times when His secret dwelling is completely obscured to us, when the circumstances of life seem to close in on us as they did on Job, when He remains silent to our cries, when He is seemingly indifferent to our situation; but all the time He is at work.

"All these things are against me," cried Jacob in an hour of deep despair, and indeed, it seemed like it; but already Joseph was making things work together for good, seated at the right hand of power in Egypt.

One day the clouds and darkness will roll away. His secret dwelling will be secret no more.

3. His Majesty's Strong Divisions (97:3-5)

"A fire goeth before Him, and burneth up His enemies round about. His lightnings enlightened the world: the earth saw, and trembled. The hills melted like wax at the presence of the LORD . . . of the whole earth."

Return for a moment to World War II. The western powers won the war and lost the peace. Nazi aggression has been replaced by communist aggression. Nothing improved at all.

Britain emerged from World War II exhausted, impoverished, and virtually bankrupt. She lost her empire, as did France, Holland, and Belgium. Worse! As the imperialist powers one by one surrendered their strategic bases around the world, Russia moved in. The United States picked up the mantle of world power and has spent herself into virtual bankruptcy trying to bolster halfhearted allies and pay the price of peace, propping up the economy of the world.

Nothing has changed—or rather everything has changed and it is for the worse. The world now faces a far more powerful and implacable foe than before. It is horrified by the vision of a superpower armed with apocalyptic weapons, fired by fierce fanaticism, determined to take over the world, and cloaked in a mantle of guile. So much for human efforts to bring in peace.

It will not be like that, however, when Jesus comes. His Majesty's strong divisions cannot be overthrown. All nature stands instant at His command. He can summon fire from the sky, turn solid rock into molten lava, command the fury of the storm. Man's puny weapons are nothing to Him. For the nations to go up against Him with intercontinental ballistic missiles armed with multiple nuclear warheads would be like trying to fight the Russians with a toasting fork; He is the ruler of all nature.

B. The Ruler of All Nations (97:6-9)

All nations are going to acknowledge His coming.

1. The Heathen Peoples (97:6-7)

The psalmist tells us two things that will mark the beginning of the millennial reign.

First, he tells us *how the truth will be revealed.* "The heavens declare His righteousness, and all the people [literally, peoples] see His glory" (97:6). God will begin with the witness of the heavens, with what has well been called "His oldest testament"—the heavens.

The heavens are an untiring witness to the precision, utility, and balance of the laws of God. Each time we stand and gaze at the velvet blackness of the night ablaze with flaming worlds and burning suns, all hurrying on their fantastic journeys in obedience to the Creator's command, we see evidence of this witness.

The God who planned the orbits of the planets, who mapped out the circuits of the stars, who keeps the glowing galaxies moving with awesome precision on predestined paths—this same God rules in the affairs of men (and with the same inflexible laws). Even though we may not be able to declare all His ways, He reveals Himself to all mankind in His majestic creative works—and especially His works in the heavens.

At the Lord's coming there will be astonishing signs in the sky. The heavens will be the heralds of His coming. There will be signs in the sun, in the moon, and in the stars. Even before He cleaves the sky and comes back with the hosts of Heaven behind Him, the Lord's coming will be signaled to earth from on high.

The psalmist goes on. He tells *how the truth will be received:* "Confounded be all they that serve graven images, that boast themselves of idols: worship Him, all ye gods" (97:7). We met this word "gods" in the previous psalm. The "gods" of the heathen are "nothings." Their graven images, their idols are senseless sticks and stones.

Behind them, however, are the fallen *elohim*, the hosts of Satan. The Lord's coming will be the downfall of all such gods. The demons that lurk behind them will suddenly become "nothings" themselves. When the Lord returns He will make an utter end of paganism. The dark superstitions of Hinduism and Buddhism, the idolatries of animist tribes, the thinly veiled paganism of much of Christendom, will be cast swiftly down from their thrones in the imaginations of men.

2. The Hebrew People (97:8-9)

"Zion heard, and was glad; and the daughters of Judah rejoiced because of Thy judgments, O Lord. For Thou, Lord, art High [most high] above all the earth: Thou art exalted far above all gods." The Jews came back from Babylon cured of idolatry. In its place they enthroned formalism, skepticism, and hypocrisy—traits already evident in Malachi's day. All came to full flower in the rejection of Christ.

For nearly two thousand long years the Jewish people have persisted in unbelief. The scales will fall from their eyes at the sight of the returning Christ of God. They will look on Him whom they pierced and they will own Him Saviour, Lord, and King. Thus, the millennial age will dawn. The Hebrews will herald the tidings of the Messiah to earth's remotest bounds and will become, at last, a priestly nation to all the nations of mankind.

The Lord, then, is first seen in this psalm as the reigning One.

II. THE RIGHTEOUS ONE (97:10-12)

The messianic glories of the Lord Jesus should be displayed in the lives of His own redeemed people in all ages.

A. What the Lord Demands of His People (97:10)

"Ye that love the LORD, hate evil: He preserveth the souls of His saints; He delivereth them out of the hand of the wicked." We should take our character from Him. He hates evil, so we should hate evil. We should take sides with Him against the evil so prevalent in our society. Every genuine revival has produced a crusade to clean up society: to oppose evil, no matter how deeply entrenched, no matter when or where or in what way it manifests itself.

Spiritual revival cleans up evil in our own hearts first. It produces an abhorrence of evil which, in turn, takes action against the evil in the land. The worst forms of immorality, impurity, impiety, and injustice in society are attacked, and it is done by a renewal of the moral conscience of a people.

The wake of the Welsh revival swept across the Atlantic and made its impact felt in America. G. Campbell Morgan came to the Northfield Conference, founded years before by D. L. Moody, and brought the news of what was happening in Wales. He had been there and seen it for himself.

Contrition and confession were manifested in those meetings. The awakening spread to conference after conference throughout the United States. In Atlanta, far from the vortex of the awakening, newspapers reported the unusual quickening. On November 2, 1904 a thousand businessmen had a united meeting to seek a moving of the Holy Spirit there. The supreme court of Georgia adjourned; even bars and places of amusement closed down. People poured to the prayer meetings, turning the weekday into a veritable Sabbath. In Gloversville, New York, a typical small town, special meetings were held. The converts included infidels, drunkards, moralists, white and black, Americans, Italians, Swedes, fathers, mothers, young men and women. The tidal wave of revival swept this land. Churches were filled. Gambling dens were closed. Society was purged.

The Methodist Review (1906) reported: "We find evidence of a revival of righteousness in the popular and pulpit protest against the 'sharp practice' and 'double-dealing' of insurance managers; the indignation against rate swindling, oppressive corporations, dishonest officials of banks and trust companies; the public wrath against political scoundrels and the successful overthrow of many such; and the elevation to power of fearless, honest, competent men in many states and cities."

The Lord is righteous. He demands righteousness of His people. Righteousness in His people will result in a cleansing of society at large.

B. What the Lord Does for His People (97:11-12)

"Light is sown for the righteous, and gladness for the upright in heart. Rejoice in the LORD, ye righteous; and give thanks at the remembrance of His holiness." He fills His people with light and laughter! The most astonishing and sweeping spiritual awakenings are, after all, but foretastes of what is going to happen when the Son of righteousness Himself arises with healing in His wings. Then the Lord's people will rejoice "with joy unspeakable and full of glory."

Psalm 98

THE MAGNIFICAT OF THE
OLD TESTAMENT

I. THE LORD'S MIGHT (98:1-2)
   A. The Song of the Lord (98:1-2)
   B. The Strength of the Lord (98:1b)
   C. The Salvation of the Lord (98:2)
II. THE LORD'S MERCY (98:3-6)
   A. The Remembrance of that Mercy (98:3)
   B. The Result of that Mercy (98:4-6)
III. THE LORD'S MAJESTY (98:7-9)
   A. The Jubilation of the Earth (98:7-9a)
   B. The Judgment of the Earth (98:9b)
     1. The Lord Will Rule Faithfully
     2. The Lord Will Rule Fairly

BEFORE WE BEGIN a study of this psalm we must look into the New Testament. The angel Gabriel has been sent from the high halls of heaven to earth with a message. He is to seek out a young, unmarried virgin in the hill country of Galilee, living in the despised provincial town of Nazareth. Although not yet married, the young woman is betrothed to the local carpenter. She is a pure-minded woman with a soul steeped in the Scriptures. She is of humble birth but possesses a royal pedigree, being directly descended from David, Israel's greatest and most glorious king.

The angel finds the young woman, greets her by name, and tells her that she is to become the mother of the long-awaited Messiah. Her son is to be the very Son of God. In answer to her questions Gabriel tells her just how this will happen. He then returns to the realms of bliss, leaving behind him a most astonished and perplexed young woman.

Mary does what one would expect. She has to tell someone, but who? Not Joseph—at least, not yet. Gabriel has already given her a hint by making mention of Elizabeth, her aged relative in Jerusalem. Mary goes to Jerusalem, eager to get Elizabeth's reaction. No sooner does Elizabeth hear the news than she bursts into song, and Mary joins her. That wonderful song of hers, recorded for us in Luke 1:46-55, is called the Magnificat. It is a haunting echo of Psalm 98. We read this psalm, then we read Mary's magnificent hymn, and we can trace all the way through her song the underlying themes of this psalm. It is as though Mary had been meditating on this psalm all the way up to Jerusalem. Elizabeth's song invoked Mary's new song, one right out of this old song which had been in the Hebrew hymnbook for approximately five hundred years.

Psalm 98 is one of the coronation psalms. Like the others in the series, it was included in the Psalter to commemorate the return from Babylon and to anticipate the coming kingdom of Christ. It deals with three magnificent themes.

I. The Lord's Might (98:1-2)

A. The Song of the Lord (98:1a)

"O sing unto the Lord a new song; for He hath done marvellous things: His right hand, and His holy arm, hath gotten Him the victory."

God wants His people to sing. He wants someone to sit down and compose a poem of praise, to create a melody. For this is to be a *new* song.

The psalmist calls for a new song, then he sits down and writes it himself! It was so good that the Holy Spirit put it into the Word of God, where it will outlast the sun.

This is the second time in this series of psalms that we are called upon to sing a new song. The old song was the song of Moses, sung by Israel at the Red Sea when Pharaoh's cavalry was swept away in the returning flood. The new song is the song of the repatriates from Babylon, those who had just experienced a second exodus and had been delivered from a second Egypt. The old song and the new song suggest two other songs. There was the old song of creation, sung by the angelic hosts on high as they saw galaxies spring out of the void of nothingness to turn the black velvet of eternal night into a banner of blazing light. And there is the new song of redemption that now awakens the echoes of the everlasting hills: "Worthy is the Lamb that was slain!"

The poet, then, makes mention of a song for the Lord.

B. The Strength of the Lord (98:1b)

"His right hand, and His holy arm, hath gotten Him the victory." The Lord needed no help to overthrow Babylon and raise up Persia. The epochal, history-making, time-changing events which had resulted in a transfer of world power were breathtaking to these Hebrews who stood at last on the soil of the promised land, right on time, exactly as foretold by the prophets. Men might interpret world events in terms of Persian military power; these people viewed events in terms of God.

That is always a good way to look at the passing events of time. God is in control. Events might be great or small, of merely personal interest or of international significance, but behind them all are God's hand and God's arm.

How often, as we look at our history books, we are forced to admit, "I can see God's hand in that." Consider one event of the Second World War. On June 22, 1941, Hitler hurled three million men, together with the munitions and machines of a blitzkrieg, along a vast front reaching all the way from Poland to the Black Sea at the heart of Russia. He called it Operation Barbarossa. It nearly succeeded. It was panzer warfare in the grand style: columns of tanks and armor racing forward, entrapping whole armies, sweeping all before it. The invading tide reached to the outskirts of Moscow in the north and Stalingrad in the south. There it stopped, overcome by exhaustion, resistance, and mud—then cold and ice and snow. The icy winds from Siberia, "the breath of death," blew in from the steppes. It was colder than the Germans had ever imagined—four times colder than a meat freezer. The tidal wave of German aggression was stopped.

Looking back, historians are awed at how close Hitler came to winning that war. If only Hitler had started Barbarossa fourteen days sooner; if only the rains had held off two weeks longer; if only Hitler had left Mussolini on his own in the Balkans and had attacked Russia when originally planned, in May instead of June. If! If! If! But it was not to be. We see God's hand in that. We can open our maps and draw the very line that God had drawn on His map: the high-tide mark of Nazi aggression from which the invading hordes began to recede, never to return.

Observe God's right hand, and behind that hand, His holy arm! Behind that holy arm stand all the resources and resolve of absolute Deity.

That's something to sing about. And that same right hand and that same holy arm are just as involved in the little affairs of our everyday lives.

C. The Salvation of the Lord (98:2)

"The LORD hath made known His salvation; His righteousness hath He openly shewed in the sight of the heathen." Known! Shown! The heart of the matter, so far as this psalmist is concerned, is the salvation which God arranges for men. It is an amazing fact that God desires our salvation. We cannot produce that salvation, so he has provided it—fully, freely. Even the heathen are forced to admit that Israel's God is mighty to save.

The testimony of H. M. Stanley is very much to the point. In

1869, the *New York Herald* sent him out to Africa to find David Livingstone who, having won the heart of the world, had disappeared in the dark continent. Stanley plunged into the interior of Africa after him and eventually found him near Lake Tanganyika. He was the only other white man within hundreds upon hundreds of miles. Stanley's greeting has gone down in history as the most casual on record: "Dr. Livingstone, I presume." Livingstone refused to return to civilization with Stanley, so Stanley gave him some supplies and remained with him for about five months. Here is his testimony:

"In 1871 I went to him as prejudiced as the biggest atheist in London. To a reporter and correspondent such as I, who had only to deal with wars and mass meetings and political gatherings, sentimental matters were entirely out of my province. But there came for me a long time for reflection. I was out there away from a worldly world. I saw this solitary old man there, and asked myself, 'How on earth does he stop here—is he cracked, or what? What is it that inspires him?' For months after we met I simply found myself listening to him, wondering at the old man carrying out all that was said in the Bible: 'Leave all things and follow me.' But little by little his sympathy for others became contagious; my sympathy was aroused; seeing his piety, his gentleness, his zeal, his earnestness, and how he went quietly about his business, *I was converted by him although he had not tried to do it*" (*Dawn*, December 16, 1929).

Known! Shown! That is what David Livingstone did for Stanley. By his words and actions he won a tough, hardened reporter to Christ and into a knowledge of the salvation that God, in His love and kindness, offers to all mankind. Like Israel of old, Stanley discovered that the Lord is mighty to save.

The psalmist, then, begins with the Lord's might.

II. The Lord's Mercy (98:3-6)

Here the psalmist makes mention of two things.

A. The Remembrance of that Mercy (98:3)

"He hath remembered His mercy and His truth toward the house of Israel: All the ends of the earth have seen the salvation of our God." "This thing was not done in a corner," was Paul's pointed word to King Agrippa as he testified to him of the great salvation Jesus had procured for men by His death and resurrection (Acts 26:26).

The salvation God had just wrought for Israel was without precedent in history. That a mighty, all-conquering world power should deliberately open its hand and let its captives go home, give them financial help and every promise of protection on the way, was unique. God had remembered His mercy. Now Israel must remember it, too. Even heathen nations could not help but take note of what God had done.

It is often thus in the first flush of salvation. We are so grateful, we think we will never forget. How wonderful that, even though we forget Him He does not forget us.

B. The Result of that Mercy (98:4-6)

"Make a joyful noise unto the Lord, all the earth: make a loud noise, and rejoice, and sing praise. Sing unto the Lord with the harp; with the harp, and the voice of a psalm. With trumpets and sound of cornet make a joyful noise before the Lord, the King."

It is the crowning day! The King has come, he has ascended to His throne, all the earth is summoned before Him, the people are invited to participate in His joy. The world is to ring with the noise of music and with the sounds of praise. Instruments of music are brought to add to the ever growing volume of sound. The scene anticipates the millennial reign which will begin with a burst of heartfelt gratitude to God that at last the King has come.

III. THE LORD'S MAJESTY (98:7-9)

He is not only King of the Jews, not only King of kings and Lord of lords over all the Gentile lands, but all creation owns His sway. It was so when He was here the first time; it will be so again.

When He was here before, He could walk calmly on the waves or just as simply hush them to sleep. He could ride an unbroken colt through cheering, shouting, palm-waving crowds. He could command the fish of the sea to fling themselves into Simon Peter's net, or he could summon a single fish to rise to Peter's line. He could command the cock to crow. Water blushed into wine at His word; loaves and fish multiplied in His hands, graves gave up their dead, demons and disease fled before Him, creation's rocks shook beneath Him, the very sun in the sky extinguished its light. All creation owned that its mighty Maker had come. And now, as the psalmist looks down the centuries, he sees that He has come again. Creation goes delirious with delight.

A. The Jubilation of the Earth (98:7-9a)

"Let the sea roar, and the fulness thereof; the world and they that dwell therein. Let the floods clap their hands: let the hills be joyful together before the Lord."

The rivers and the sea, the mountains and the earth all join in exultation. Too often when the sea has roared it has been to destroy, when the rivers have risen to flood it has been to drown, when the hills have moved it has been to devour the cities of men. The coming of the King will change all that. The prophets excel in describing the revolutionary changes to take place in nature when the King comes back, for nature will be redeemed. No longer will the wild beast roar and kill, no longer will the scorpion sting. The lion and the lamb will lie down together. Nature's wildness will be tamed.

Wildness, after all, is a direct result of the fall of the first man. God placed dominion over all things into Adam's hands in paradise but the fall changed all that. There is evidence from biology that thorns are aborted branches and leaves, and that the unpleasant character of thistles results from an aborted state of the calyx. Paul tells us that the whole creation groans and travails in sorrow at the present time. When Jesus comes, however, nature will be tamed. As the second man, the last Adam, He will take dominion over the forces of nature, over the beasts of the earth, over the resources of the planet and will graciously restore them all to their pristine splendor. The curse will be removed; paradise will be restored. In the great restoration that will follow His return, the King will restore to plants and animals their original nature and splendor. Thus, jubilation will fill the earth. Even nature itself will join in the universal hymn of praise—a new song indeed.

B. The Judgment of the Earth (98:9b)

This is not judgment in a terrifying sense; that is, all over and done with at Megiddo and in the valley of Jehoshaphat. But rather, this is judgment in the glorious sense of a King reigning who is an absolute stranger to bribery and corruption, to injustice and unfairness.

1. The Lord Will Rule Faithfully

"For He cometh to judge the earth: with righteousness shall He judge the world." Righteousness is the quality of always doing what is right. Think of it! A King who never makes a mistake, with whom there is no miscarriage of justice! A King who knows not only the word or the deed, but the heart and the motive, as well!

We have all smiled happily at the godlike wisdom of Solomon when faced with two harlots and a little babe. Both the women claimed the child as her own. Solomon called for a sword and proposed dividing the babe between the two of them—and at once the true mother was revealed! The Lord Jesus could say when He lived on earth, "A greater than Solomon is here!" And so He is! What brilliant decisions will be handed down from His throne during the millennium! He will make Solomon's wisdom look like that of a toddler in the kindergarten.

2. The Lord Will Reign Fairly

"With righteousness shall He judge the world, and the people with equity." No bias! No favoritism! Equity!

In western Canada there is a very popular lawn game known as bowls. It is played on a smooth, velvety lawn known as a green. A white, earthenware ball is rolled down the green a distance of twenty-five yards or more. Then the players, in turn, roll much larger balls down the green. The object of the game is to see who can bring his ball closest to the white one, blocking or knocking out opponent's balls in the process.

It all sounds very straightforward. However, it is a game of great skill; the larger balls that are bowled down the green are not quite what they seem. They are made with a bias—that is, one side of the ball is larger than the other. As a result, when it is bowled down the green, unless it is delivered with great speed, it will curve as it rolls. A slow rolling ball will curve as much as six feet from a straight line. Even a fast ball, when it reaches the end of its momentum, has a tendency to turn off from the straight line. The skill of the game is in learning to overcome the bias.

That is what is wrong with every one of us. We have bias; we have an innate tendency to run off the straight line. And, even with the best will in the world, our natural tendencies are so great as to overcome our better judgment. Often even our better judgment is afflicted with bias.

But not Jesus! He was born free of sin, free of bias. That is what sets Him apart from all other men. There was no innate tendency to error and sin in Him. Never once did He depart from the straight line. His whole life was directed to coming alongside the white ball of the known will of God. And when He comes back that is how He will reign. He will reign with equity. No bias, no favoritism, no off-center judgment. No wonder the psalmist urges us to sing a new song.

Psalm 99

THE LAMB UPON HIS THRONE

THIS IS ANOTHER of the theocratic psalms, the coronation psalms which ring with earth's hallelujahs because, at long last, the King has come. This psalm looks first at the future, then at the present, then at the past. It views the Lord as the One who is to come, as the One who is, and as the One who was—the One who occupies all the tenses of time. This is the One that sits upon the throne, eternal, almighty.

The psalm easily divides into three parts. It shows us that the One who sits upon the throne is prophet, priest, and king. In Israel men were anointed for each of these ministries. Jesus is the Christ, the Messiah, the anointed One.

I. THE IDEAL PRINCE (99:1-4)

As so often in these coronation psalms, the King's majesty is paramount.

A. The Lord's Majesty (99:1-3)

This is what one can expect when dealing with the coronation of a king.

1. The Lord is Exalted upon an Eternal Throne (99:1)

"The LORD reigneth; let the people tremble: He sitteth between the cherubims; let the earth be moved." The word translated "tremble" literally means "to shake with fear" or "to be violently agitated emotionally." Well might the peoples of the earth fear at the advent of this King! Well might the earth be moved!

The King who has come back has the marks of Calvary upon Him. The feet that rend Olivet are feet once pierced by Roman nails. He is seen sitting between or upon the cherubim. John describes Him thus in the Apocalypse, "in the midst of the four living creatures." That is, He is in the midst of the *zoan,* the cherubim. The position is full of significance.

In their appearance, the cherubim are astonishing. One displays the face of a lion, another the face of a calf, a third the face of a man, and the fourth that of a flying eagle. They represent the various creatures that live on earth. They are associated with four aspects of God's ways.

a. The Goodness of God

The cherubim appear first in connection with the goodness of God at the gate of the garden of Eden. Adam and Eve, having eaten of the tree of life, have been driven from paradise. When they turned to look back at the portals of their lost Eden they saw a fearful sentinel there, a cherub with a flaming sword. His mission was to keep them from the tree of life.

Suppose Adam, in his lost estate, had crept back into the garden. Suppose he had eaten of the tree of life and had thus circumvented the sentence of death which had been passed upon him. He would have lived forever in his sins, and salvation would have been impossible. He would have become like the fallen angels—deathless in his sins. He would have perpetuated himself in sin without hope of a Saviour. God, in His goodness, made this unforgivable sin impossible. The cherub stood there to make sure that fallen man did not steal eternal life. So the cherubim are connected with the goodness of God.

b. The Grace of God

The cherubim are connected with the grace of God. The likeness of the cherubim was woven into the white, blue, scarlet, and purple tapestries that hung in the holy place and in the most holy place. They were woven, too, into the hanging veil. Within the holy of holies itself, figures of the cherubim, fashioned of purest gold and made out of one piece with the mercy seat, were connected with the sacred ark. In that ark was a copy of the unbroken law of Sinai, a pot of manna, and Aaron's miraculously budding rod. That mercy seat, covering the ark, was God's throne. It was there that the Shekinah glory cloud came to rest. The wings of the cherubim were outstretched to overshadow the mercy seat and their faces gazed inward and downward. They did not gaze outward to keep watch upon whomever might enter, as did the cherub at the gate of Eden.

What did they see? They saw blood. They saw the blood of the goat, slain on the day of atonement, as that blood was sprinkled on the mercy seat. Throughout all the ages that God dwelt thus in the midst of His people, He did so because that blood was sprinkled there. The cherubim were occupied with that. They are associated with the grace of God to man.

c. The Government of God

The cherubim are connected with the government of God. That is how Ezekiel saw them in the opening visions which are such a marked feature of his book. The prophet was impressed by the cherubim, overwhelmed by them; they were terrible to behold. He tells us of their chariots, of the vast interlocking wheels rushing to and fro, wheels within wheels. He tells us of the eyes—so many of them, looking everywhere, missing nothing. The entire vision was one government, a vision of God's vast and complex government of the earth which, in its movements and operations, is often so strange and mysterious to men.

Ezekiel saw the cherubim as creatures linked to earth, yet above and beyond the earth. He saw what few have seen: a fleeting glimpse of the vast machinery whereby God's sovereign will is carried out in heaven above and enforced on earth beneath. Down from on high in great, sweeping arcs to touch the earth, they soared. Up they soared again, back up on high. Down again, up again, never ceasing in their tireless revolutions. Their work was to see that God's will was done on earth, as it is in heaven. They are connected with the government of God over man.

d. The Glory of God

Finally, the cherubim appear in connection with the glory of God. That is how John saw them in the Apocalypse. He saw them before the throne, gazing on the Lord in glory. They summon up the resources of their intellects, the throbbing passions of their hearts, the dynamic of their mighty wills—and they worship! "Holy! Holy! Holy!" they cry as they awake the echoes of the everlasting hills. They do not cease to chant His awesome praise. Their measured tribute is as ceaseless as the movement of the stars. "Holy! Holy! Holy!" And the echo of that cry can be heard ringing throughout Psalm 99: "Holy is He! Holy is He! The Lord our God is holy!"

The singer sees the Lord seated on His exalted throne between the cherubim. They are there to witness the goodness of God, the grace of God, the government of God, and the glory of God. Every time we meet them in Scripture, they are connected with the throne rights of the Lord.

2. The Lord Is Exalted above All Earthly Thrones (99:2-3)

Napoleon, Hitler, the communists—all have torn down thrones. Not many thrones are now left on earth. But Christ, when He comes, will tear down all thrones, all dominions, all ruling powers, all branches of human government—legislative, executive, and judicial.

The psalmist notes *how high* the Lord's throne is: "The LORD is great in Zion; and He is high above all the people [peoples]" (99:2). It has always been God's intention to make Zion the political capital of the world and to make Israel the head of the nations. When God called Israel to be a nation he gave her political ascendancy and spiritual ascendancy over all other nations. He took away Israel's political ascendancy because of her repeated unfaithfulness, and He handed that political ascendancy to the Gentiles, in the person of Nebuchadnezzar. A new period in human history began, called by the Lord Jesus "the times of the Gentiles."

Spiritual ascendancy, however, still remained with Israel. If God had anything to say, He still said it through a Jew. Then, when Israel rejected the Messiah and crucified Christ, God took away her spiritual ascendancy over the nations and invested it in the Church. There began another period in human history called "the fullness of the Gentiles."

At the rapture of the Church, God will again begin dealing with the Jewish people, and spiritual ascendancy will be restored to the Hebrew people. The witnesses in the tribulation age will be Jewish witnesses. At the ultimate return of Christ, "the times of the Gentiles" will end, and God will restore political ascendancy to Israel. Zion will come into its own.

The psalmist anticipates that day. Zion is to be great. The Lord is to be high above all peoples. All nations will acknowledge the authority of Christ, the administration of the Jews, and the ascendancy of Zion. Zion will be the capital of a new world order. All nations will own the supremacy and sovereignty of Christ, exalted over all, on His throne in Zion.

The psalmist notes, too, *how holy* the Lord's throne is: "Let them praise Thy great and terrible name; for it is holy" (99:3). The translators often render that last clause: "Holy is He!" Earth and Heaven are in accord at last! Man on earth responds with the hierarchy of heaven to proclaim the holiness of our Saviour, Lord, and King.

B. The Lord's Morality (99:4)

The basis of the Lord's government is one of the strictest morality. We hear a lot these days about relative morality, a moral standard which varies according to the situation. The Lord knows nothing about such a flexible standard of morality. When the Lord comes He will found His empire on absolute morality.

1. He Embraces Morality

"The king's strength also loveth judgment." The word for "judgment" can be rendered "justice." Observe that the Lord embraces morality in the hour of His strength, the very time when many who rise to power go wrong. As Lord Acton so ably said: "All power corrupts; absolute power corrupts absolutely." History proves these words to be only too true.

Two remarkable examples of this are found in the history of Israel. We read of David that, after a series of outstanding military successes, he "reigned over all Israel, and executed judgment and justice" (1 Chronicles 18:14). So far, so good. It was the high water mark of David's career. The next chapter, however, records the outbreak of war with the Ammonites. In the book of kings we learn that during that war, while his troops were on the front line, David betrayed his own standards of morality and in his strength sinned with Bathsheba. He then used his strength to murder her husband, Uriah. It was the abuse of power.

It was the same with Solomon. Page after page relates Solomon's successes—his wisdom, his wealth, his works. He went from triumph to triumph. The crowning triumph was the visit of the queen of Sheba who, awed and amazed at Solomon's magnificence, broke into a tremendous eulogy: "Blessed be the LORD thy God . . . because the LORD loved Israel for ever, therefore made He thee king, to do judgment and justice" (1 Kings 10:9). Like David, Solomon loved justice. It was the high-water mark in Solomon's career. The very next chapter begins with an ominous "but": "But king Solomon loved many strange women." Solomon undermined his own standards of morality. In his strength he sinned with a high hand against the same Mosaic Law he had copied with his own hand and, in so doing, he laid the foundations of national disaster. It was the abuse of power.

The Lord Jesus, when He comes, will reign first as David, to put down all His foes; then as Solomon, to display to the world the manifold wisdom of God. But never will He, in His strength, depart from justice. He embraces morality. "The king's strength loveth justice."

2. He Establishes Morality

"The king's strength also loveth judgment; Thou dost establish equity." There will be no bias, no deviation from the path of absolute justice, equity, and integrity.

3. He Enforces Morality

"Thou executest judgment and righteousness in Jacob." The word "Thou" is emphatic; it is the word to be emphasized in the sentence. The character of the kingdom reflects the character of the king: He does what He does because He is what He is. He will be the ideal prince.

II. THE IDEAL PRIEST (99:5-6)

In these verses we move from the palace to the temple. The robes of a priest are added to the robes of a king. In any other person that would be alarming. It makes good sense to separate church and state and to keep these two great power bases apart. Nothing can be worse than priestly power backed by the secular arm. Such a mixing of fiery cordials is too strong a drink for man; it goes straight to the head and intoxicates. It leads to excess and tyranny. God kept the two apart under the Mosaic Law in Israel.

But here comes One who can wear both the mitre and the crown. He is not only the ideal prince, He is the ideal priest. That the two thoughts should be linked in one psalm speaks volumes for the inspiration of the Holy Spirit, for no Hebrew would have brought the two offices together in a single person apart from such divine inspiration.

A. Worship Belongs to Him (99:5)

"Exalt ye the LORD our God, and worship at His footstool; for He is holy [holy is He]." This King-Priest sits upon a throne and the peoples of the world come before Him, are given audience by Him, and worship at His feet.

That reminds us of Mary of Bethany. Every time we see Mary of Bethany in the Gospels she is at Jesus' feet. We meet her in life's most *tranquil* hour (Luke 10:39). The Lord had come for a visit to that loved Bethany home. Martha was in the kitchen; Mary was at Jesus' feet. We meet her in life's most *tragic* hour (John 11:32). Lazarus was dead and buried, and sorrow had invaded that home. Jesus had come, but He had come too late, despite the urgent message

sent when Lazarus was so sick. Mary threw herself, not into Jesus'
arms (no woman ever did that), but at His feet. We meet her in life's
most *triumphant* hour (John 12:3). Lazarus was alive from the dead,
and Mary brought her ointment of spikenard, most costly, and was
there at Jesus' feet, pouring it all out in worship. That was when He
came to earth the first time. Mary seemed to understand what it
meant to take one's place at Jesus' feet. When He comes again the
whole world will understand. Worship belongs to Him.

B. Worship Brought to Him (99:6)

"Moses and Aaron among His priests, and Samuel among them
that call upon His name; they called upon the Lord, and He answered them." This is an unusual combination. Strictly, the only one
of these who was a priest according to Levitical Law was Aaron.
Moses was Aaron's younger brother. He was the great lawgiver of
Israel, the great emancipator of the Hebrews, a second father to the
nation. We learn from Exodus 24:6-8 that he exercised priestly
functions in Israel before Aaron did. Indeed, it was he who consecrated Aaron to the priesthood but he was never ordained to be a
priest. He is included here, however, as a priest.

It is the same with Samuel. He was not a priest, though he was a
Levite, but he exercised the priestly office in Israel after the apostasy
of the constitutional priesthood. It had failed in Eli and had been
apostatized in Hophni and Phinehas. So, contrary to normal practice, this godly Levite took the priestly function upon himself—and
with God's fullest approval. He did so because he was a prophet. In
Israel the prophet often assumed authority greater than that vested
in either king or priest.

Moses, Aaron, and Samuel were men greatly used of God in an intercessory capacity. The psalmist saw God raising up such men in
those early days of the restored temple—godly men like Ezra and
Nehemiah, Zechariah and Haggai, men greatly burdened on behalf
of God's people. The inspired poet saw the intercessory ministry
being restored to Israel, but it was a priesthood no longer restricted
to its strict legal forms. His vision thus soars on to a future age when
all priesthood will be vested in Jesus who came, as the writer of Hebrews reminds us, from a tribe with no God-given priestly function.

The Lord Jesus, then, is the ideal priest, yea and more than a
priest, for worship belongs to Him. It will be brought to Him. "For
He is holy!" That's the key to it! He is the "holy One of Israel": all
worship is centered in Him, no matter how irregular that might
seem according to Old Testament convention.

III. The Ideal Prophet (99:7-9)

The great work of the prophet in the Bible was to speak for God
under direct inspiration of the Holy Spirit. The Lord Jesus is proph-

et, priest, and king. It is fitting that this unknown singer of old should grasp this three-dimensional truth.

A. The Prophet's Message (99:7)

"He spake unto them in the cloudy pillar: they kept His testimonies, and the ordinance that He gave them." The message was in the law. The prophets of the Old Testament were all called to minister in times of national apostasy when the law was set aside by Israel. The statement "they kept his testimonies" is extraordinary, for if there was one thing Israel did not do, that was it. Their history was one of continual rebellion against the law of God. Even after the Babylonian captivity, when idolatry had been purged out of Israel's national soul, the leaders of Israel idolatrously put the law in the place of God and began that system of exegesis and commentary which made the law ineffectual, as the Gospels show.

How then could it be said that "they kept His testimonies"? They kept them only inasmuch as those testimonies were kept by Christ, who was the embodiment of all Israel's national ideals. Of whom else could it be said that "He spake unto them in the cloudy pillar"? That One who trod the dusty trails of Sinai with Israel was the same One who, incarnate among them in the days of His flesh, kept the testimonies and ordinances of the law. He was the ideal prophet— the law-giver and the law-liver!

B. The Prophet's Mercy (99:8)

"Thou answeredst them, O LORD our God: Thou wast a GOD That forgavest them, though Thou tookest vengeance of their inventions." We see Him pardoning and punishing at the same time. This is typical of the prophetic ministry of Scripture. When Nathan came to David and David fell down in contrition before God, the *crime* he had committed was removed by God's grace. The *consequences,* however, remained as part of God's governmental dealings with him. David had decreed: "The man shall pay fourfold," when he pronounced sentence on the man in Nathan's parable. Thus it was that the sword struck four times at David's own sons. As the consequences of his behavior pursued him down the years they were used of God, not as a *punative* measure, but as a *purifying* one. God used them not just to *chastise* but to *change* the character of the penitent.

C. The Prophet's Ministry (99:9)

"Exalt the LORD our God, and worship at His holy hill; for the LORD our God is holy." The entire prophetic ministry in Israel was intended to get the people to properly worship the Lord their God—because of His holiness. The prophetic ministry of the Lord

Jesus was the same. When Satan tempted Him, His answer was a brusque: "Thou shalt worship the Lord thy God and Him only shalt thou serve." When the woman at the well tried to evade his convicting statements by engaging Him in religious controversy, He said: "God is a spirit: and they that worship Him must worship Him in spirit and in truth." He Himself accepted worship, but as prophet He directed worship to the Father.

This, then, is the ideal prophet. His message, mercy, and ministry are designed to a single end: to draw out our hearts in worship of the living God.

In this priceless little psalm we have a *prophet to reveal,* a *priest to redeem,* and a *prince to rule.* What more could we ask than that? Especially, when this prophet, priest, and king fulfills every ideal of Holy Writ itself.

Psalm 100

A UNIVERSAL HYMN OF PRAISE

I. APPROACHING GOD (100:1-2)
   A. Unrivaled Harmony (100:1)
   B. Unrestrained Happiness (100:2)
II. APPREHENDING GOD (100:3)
   A. His Person
   B. His Power
   C. His Purpose
III. APPRECIATING GOD (100:4-5)
   A. Coming to Him—Thankfully (100:4)
      1. Arriving at the Temple
      2. Arriving at the Truth
   B. Communing with Him—Thoughtfully (100:5)
      1. An Essential Fact (God's Goodness)
      2. An Eternal Fact (God's Mercy)
      3. An Enduring Fact (God's Truth)

THE TITLE OF THIS PSALM reads, "A Psalm of praise." Rotherham renders that, "Psalm—For a Thank-offering (or for Thanksgiving)." It was used in the second temple in connection with the sacrifices of thanksgiving. The thanksgiving offering was the "peace" offering. It was offered in gratitude for special mercies received from the Lord. In giving us the various laws of the offerings in Leviticus, the Holy Spirit places this offering last (Leviticus 7:11-34). This is probably because true expressions of thanksgiving flow from an appreciation of all that God has done in Christ. Not until we are done with our sins and ourselves can we truly worship as we ought.

The psalm concludes the theocratic and coronation psalms which have been sounding one note of joy after another for the anticipated advent of the Messiah as King. Hence the psalm is prophetic and anticipates the day when Jesus will reign from sea to sea and shore to shore.

Many of the Lord's people have become familiar with this psalm in its metric version. There are two renderings of this psalm in English meter, the best known being affectionately called "Old One

99

Hundredth." It was composed by William Kethe, a Scot and a friend
of John Knox. When Mary Tudor, a fanatical Roman Catholic, became queen of England many Protestants in the British Isles had to
flee the country. William Kethe was one of them. He joined the exiles in Geneva in 1556. His metric version of Psalm 100 first appeared in a Psalter published in London in 1561. It reads:

> All people that on earth do dwell
>   Sing to the Lord with cheerful voice;
> Him serve with fear, His praise foretell,
>   Come ye before Him and rejoice.
>
> Know that the Lord is God indeed,
>   Without our aid He did us make;
> We are His folk, He doth us feed
>   And for His sheep he doth us take.

I. Approaching God (100:1-2)

The settting is millennial, the place is Jerusalem, the scene is the
temple, the occasion is the coronation of Jesus as priest-king of the
earth. The gates of the city are flung open to all mankind. The middle wall of partition, long since broken down in the Church, is now
broken down in the kingdom. The courts of the sanctuary are open
now to "all people that on earth do dwell." Now anyone can come—
Jew or Gentile, Greek or barbarian, Egyptian or Assyrian. The
psalmist describes the coming reign of the king.

A. Unrivaled Harmony (100:1)

"Make a joyful noise unto the LORD, all ye lands. Serve the LORD
with gladness." Or, as Rotherham translates it: "Shout ye unto Jehovah, all the earth." What the psalmist sees and hears is the shout of
the people at the crowning of a popular king. One can well imagine
with what a sigh of relief the remnant of the Gentile nations (the
"sheep" of Matthew 24) realize that the nightmare is over. The beast
is dead, the false prophet is dead, Satan has been incarcerated in the
abyss, war has been abolished at last. The deserts and droughts are
to be no more. Lawlessness, rebellion, and corruption will never
again be tolerated as a means of getting things done. Crime is gone
from the earth. There will be no more need for doctors, nurses, and
morticians. A man will be a mere boy at a hundred! All because of
this wonderful King with the nail-scarred hands! Well might the
psalmist hear a universal shout of praise. The nations are in harmony at last.

Think of the spokes of a wheel radiating from a common hub.
The closer any point might be to the center on any of the spokes, the
closer that point will be to any other as it draws near the center. The
farther away such points are from the hub, the farther those points

will be from each other. What is wrong with the world today is that it has no center. It has no powerful, magnetic force to draw the far-flung nations together in harmony and peace. Each one is going its own way and pursuing its own interests. Often the nations become entangled because, not only is there no center, there is no limiting circumference to draw the boundary line around them all.

When Jesus comes the nations will have just such a center and circumference. As a result, there will be a harmony which will be celebrated by a universal shout of acclamation for the King. He will be the gathering center of the nations, and His law will set their bounds. So we see the nations approaching Him and, consequently, drawing closer and closer to one another in the process. There will be unrivaled harmony.

B. Unrestrained Happiness (100:2)

"Serve the LORD with gladness: come before His presence with singing." The word "presence" can be rendered "face." The essence of all true worship is to come into the presence of the Lord and to appear before His face in adoration.

At best, the Old Testament Hebrew could do this only from a distance, the Gentile from an even greater distance. People were given access to God, but only limited access. Between the sinner and a holy God a number of barriers were erected. There was a gate to the tabernacle, giving entrance to the outer court. Once the gate had been passed, the seeking sinner was confronted with an altar and a laver to teach him that he needed a *radical* and a *recurrent* cleansing. Even when he had been accepted at the altar, unless he were a priest, he could approach no further. He remained in the outer court.

If he were a priest, he could pass the door, enter the holy place, and enjoy the benefits of the table, the lampstand, and the golden altar. But he could go no further than that—unless he was the high priest. He alone, after elaborate ritual preparation once a year, could lift the final veil, pass the last barrier, and come haltingly into the presence of God.

Calvary has changed all that. In the Church we have access right into the presence of God through Christ. Access! The story is told of a little boy who went up to London to visit the king. But he could not get into the palace; the gates were closed against him and a soldier stood on guard. Several policemen were walking up and down to move people along. "But I came to see the king!" the boy explained. "Can't help that, sonny!" said the policeman. "You're not allowed in there." About that time a well-dressed gentleman came along and overheard the conversation, "What's the matter, boy?" he asked. "I want to see the king," the little boy replied. "Well, you just come with me," said the gentleman. He held out his hand and the boy took it. To his surprise the policeman made no attempt to stop him, nor did the guard. Indeed, the guard sprang to attention and presented arms while the policeman unlocked the gate. In they went, along the corridors and right into the presence of the king. The little boy had taken hold of the hand of the prince of Wales, the king's own son. That gave him access.

Such is the birthright of every believer today. He has taken hold of the hand of the Lord Jesus Christ, the Son of God. That assures him of access to the presence of the Father. In a coming day access will be available to all: "Come before His presence with singing." It is an open invitation to all mankind. It will be a day of harmony and happiness for all.

II. Apprehending Him (100:3)

The psalmist has a threefold grasp of the truth concerning the king.

A. His Person

"Know ye that the Lord He is God." "Jehovah, He is Elohim" says the psalmist. That is a truth concerning His person. That is who He is. In accenting the various words of the Bible that call for emphasis, Rotherham makes it clear that the word for emphasis here is the word "Jehovah." The margin of *The Companion Bible* puts it as "Jehovah self." He is God.

That is the first great millennial lesson for the nations, many of whom through the long ages of their history have been steeped in idolatry and false religion. They are to learn from God's sovereign dealings with Israel and in the rebirth and restoration of Israel that Jehovah is the one true and living God. That is a basic truth. Unless we have learned that truth, all other truth will be held in imbalance and out of proportion.

The foundational truth, the basic, bedrock truth is that Jehovah is Elohim. It is simple and elementary, but everything begins with that. This truth, of course, takes on a new dimension of meaning when it is realized that the Jehovah of the Old Testament is the Jesus of the New Testament. Know ye that Jesus, He is God. All other lessons stem from that. Apart from that, all other learning is empty and vain. Throughout the entire church age people have been coming to Christ and getting to know Him better. Throughout the coming kingdom age people will be drawn to the Lord and will come to know Him better. They will apprehend more and more of His person. And what a wonderful person He is!

B. His Power

"It is He that hath made us, and not we ourselves." Primarily, the reference is to Israel as a nation. The Lord made that nation. He began with a single individual named Abraham; He gave that individual a son, then a grandson; He gave that grandson twelve sons and so expanded the individual into a family. Those twelve sons became the patriarchs of the twelve tribes which, in turn, multiplied into a great people. He found those people in slavery, set them free, brought them into Canaan, and made a nation of them.

At the time this psalm was written these events had repeated themselves—the tribes had been uprooted and scattered. But God had made the nation a second time, and it would again prosper and take deep root in the land.

In recent years He has made that nation for a third time. Israel is back in the land—this time to stay. The nation is only in its embryonic form as yet. The great tribulation has to come and purge out the dross; the remaining exiles have to be gathered home. But, as the millennial age dawns, the Hebrew people will bear this testimony to the world: "It is He That hath made us, and not we ourselves." They will have learned that lesson by then, but they haven't learned it yet. They are still putting their trust in their alliances, in their armed forces, in their political and economic influence in world capitals, in their financial genius, and in their natural ability. All these things will fail them, and they will be driven at last into the arms of Jesus, as Joseph's brothers were driven into his. Their testimony will be: "It is He That hath made us, and not we ourselves." Or, as some translators prefer to render it: "He made us and His we are." They have not acknowledged that yet, but they will. They will apprehend Him at last when His power is manifested on their behalf at Megiddo.

C. His Purpose

"We are His People, and the sheep of His pasture." David recognized that fact on the personal level in Psalm 23; it was a comforting truth. The Lord Jesus has declared Himself to be that great Shepherd of the sheep who so gladdened David's heart.

The Lord Jesus is the Shepherd both of Israel and the Church but there is a difference. As the Lord's sheep, Christians are characterized by the word "flock." In John 10:16 the Lord says: "There shall be one flock and one shepherd." It is a pity that the King James Version translators rendered the Greek word *piomne* as "fold." It should be "flock." It occurs only four times in the New Testament. We find it in Matthew 26:31 where, quoting Zechariah 13:7, the Lord Jesus spoke of the scattering of His disciples at Calvary: "I will smite the shepherd, and the sheep of the flock shall be scattered." It is used in Luke 2:8 where the shepherds are described on the night of the Lord's birth: "There were in the same country shepherds, abiding in the field, keeping watch over their flock by night." We also find the word in 1 Corinthians 9:7 where Paul speaks of his right, as a minister of the gospel, to be financially supported in the work: "Or who feedeth a flock, and eateth not of the milk of the flock?" It is the same word Jesus used. "There shall be one flock and one shepherd." He was referring to the Church. A flock is marked by a *center.* The Lord Jesus is the gathering center of the flock. He is still gathering to Himself all those who are to be thus associated with Himself: His sheep, gathered around Himself, who is their center. The Lord Jesus is the only center we have. Since He is in Heaven, our center is in Heaven.

Israel, on the other hand, is characterized by the word "fold." In the same verse in John 10, the Lord Jesus said, "Other sheep I have, which are not of this fold: them also I must bring." That is a different word. It is *aule,* signifying a place. Usually, it was a place in the open air, often enclosed by a circle of stones with an entrance in which the shepherd placed himself as "the door." A flock is characterized by a center; a fold is characterized by a *circumference.* This is evident from the first verse of John 10: the Lord, in describing the Jewish fold, spoke of the thieves and the robbers who refused and rejected Him, seeking access by some other way.

There is nothing as vulnerable and defenseless as a sheep. It is not strong, nor swift, nor smart. It has little defense against its foes. It can easily be scattered, and it then becomes an easy prey to its enemies. Israel's sheepfold was the promised land. It was there that God intended to preserve and protect them. He Himself would be the great door to keep out the wolves. He Himself would see to it that no marauding nation broke in.

Israel, scattered among the nations because of its sins, has been a continuing prey. The Jews have been driven from land to land. Whenever they have found what they thought might be a fold, the walls have given way. They have been plundered, persecuted, preyed upon, and driven from country to country. Out of the land, Israel is like a sheep without a shepherd and without a fold. It is God's purpose to again gather the lost sheep of the house of Israel back into the land. Then He will be to them all the Shepherd they need. "We are His People, and the sheep of His pasture," they will say. Never again will faraway fields look green.

It is inevitable that the psalm ends the way it does. The person found apprehending will be able to appreciate.

III. Appreciating God (100:4-5)

A. Coming to Him—Thankfully (100:4)

1. Arriving at the Temple (100:4a)

"Enter into His gates with thanksgiving, and into His courts with praise." The prevailing thought throughout this psalm is that Jesus is crowned on earth at last. He has been acclaimed the world's rightful king. We are not merely following the plea of a godly Levite for the reunification of the tribes. This psalm goes far beyond that.

Here we have the fulfillment of Isaiah's vision of a millennial earth, of Jerusalem as the world's capital, of Israel as head of the nations, of the Hebrew people as administrators of the new covenant, and of the Lord reigning in person as king. Isaiah envisioned the temple in Jerusalem as "a house of prayer for all peoples" (Isaiah 56:7). He foresaw the day when the Lord would "gather together all nations and tongues to come and see His glory," the day when "all flesh shall come in and bow down before Me, saith the Lord" (Isaiah 66:18,23). As Rotherham says: "Unless we are prepared to turn the whole Old Testament into allegory, a hundred texts are at hand to shew that there will be such a center in the final theocracy."

Under the Old Covenant, Israel had to gather in assembly two or three times a year to keep the great annual feasts. Our Lord's first glimpse of the holy city and the temple, so far as we know, was when, as a boy of twelve, He accompanied His parents to Jerusalem to keep one of those feasts. God did not want His people to forsake this periodic assembling of themselves together, for the feasts were not only to be joyous occasions for fellowship; they were also to be times of heart-searching and times of spiritual exercise. They were intended to teach and instruct the people in God's plans for the ages.

During the millennium the gatherings in Jerusalem will be joyous pilgrimages for all mankind. There will be so much to see, so much to learn. Jerusalem and the temple will be the fountainhead of everything. Jesus will be there. The twelve apostles will be there, sitting on twelve thrones and judging the twelve tribes of Israel.

The people of the millennial earth not only arrive at the temple, but also at the truth.

2. Arriving at the Truth (100:4b)

"Be thankful unto Him, and bless His name!" The ultimate truth will come home to the Hebrew people at last. They will praise the name of Jesus. The truth concerning that blessed name, which Israel has missed through so much of her long, sad history will be known and appreciated at last.

B. Communing with Him—Thoughtfully (100:5)

"For the LORD is good; His mercy is everlasting; and His truth endureth to all generations." The psalm begins with the word "all" and ends with the word "all." It begins with a reference to "all lands" and ends with a reference to "all generations." We see all generations henceforth occupied with the goodness, the mercy, and the truth of God. The phrase, "to all generations," can be rendered, "unto generation after generation." The millennial reign of Christ will last for a thousand years—about twenty five normal generations today.

Generation after generation, born and added to the growing millennial population, will need to learn the truths set before them: "The Lord is good *(an essential fact);* His mercy is everlasting *(an eternal fact);* and His truth endureth to all generations" *(an enduring fact).* What a psalm this is!

Psalm 101

A KING'S RESOLVES

I. THE KING AND HIS CHARACTER (101:1-2)
   A. His Delight (101:1)
   B. His Decision (101:2a)
   C. His Desire (101:2b)
   D. His Dwelling (101:2c)
II. THE KING AND HIS COUNTRYMEN (101:3-5)
   A. Holiness through Sanctification (101:3)
   B. Holiness through Separation (101:4)
   C. Holiness through Severity (101:5)
III. THE KING AND HIS COURTIERS (101:6-8)
   A. The Counselors He Wants (101:6)
      1. Men to Reside with Him
      2. Men to Reign with Him
   B. The Convictions He Wants (101:7-8)
      1. His Personal Resolve (101:7)
      2. His Public Resolve (101:8)

THIS PSALM OF DAVID is a fitting sequel to the coronation and theocratic psalms which precede it. The Holy Spirit must have treasured this little Davidic gem for hundreds of years so that it might be put just here to blaze alongside the other crown jewels of the kingdom. For there is little doubt that this is one of David's poems. It seems to have been written, along with Psalms 15 and 24, to celebrate the bringing up of the ark to Jerusalem. It records David's resolutions and pledges to Jehovah as to the kind of king he would be if only God would come and take up His abode in the capital.

The psalm is a fitting composition for all who rule, all who sit in the seat of justice charged with the responsibility of enforcing the law. It is said that Ernest the Pious, Duke of Saxe-Gotha, sent an unfaithful minister a copy of this psalm. It became a proverb in the land that when a minister of state was guilty of misconduct, "He would soon get the prince's psalm to read."

In its fullest expression this psalm is millennial. The kinds of re-

107

solve made in this psalm are autocratic. The kinds of condition they envision do not exist today, and David himself could only espouse them in the sense that he was the divine representative on the theocratic throne of Israel. The language of the psalm is severe, for when Jesus does reign it will be with a "rod of iron." If *divine mercy* founds the millennial kingdom, *divine morality* will fashion it.

It is a psalm of royal resolve. This is indicated by the nine uses of the word "will" and the six uses of the word "shall." "I will" is the key. David's heart and mind for God are backed by his will. He is determined to be the kind of person and prince God wants him to be.

I. THE KING AND HIS CHARACTER (101:1-2)

Sometime before, David had attempted to bring the ark to Jerusalem, but he had gone about this good work in a wrong way by placing it on a new cart. That was no way to carry the ark of the presence. The Levitical Law made it clear how that sacred and symbolic piece of furniture was to be handled when moved.

We recall that in the days of Moses the princes of Israel presented Moses with six covered wagons and a dozen oxen. Moses accepted the gift "to do the service of the tabernacle" (Numbers 7:5) but then had to decide how to divide the wagons between the three Levitical families responsible for transporting the tabernacle during Israel's wilderness marches. One would have thought he would have given each of the three families two of the wagons and four of the oxen. Instead he gave the family of Gershon two wagons and four oxen and the family of Merari the remaining four wagons and eight oxen. To the family of Kohath he gave none (Numbers 7:9).

The explanation for this seemingly lopsided division of the transportation equipment is given: "Because the service of the sanctuary belonging unto them was that [which] they should bear upon their shoulders." The most sacred objects in the tabernacle, including the ark, were to be personally carried by the Kohathites. The sacred ark was not to be bumped and dragged along on a cart by oxen but was to be carried by hand on the shoulders of this specially privileged family. The best work for God is not accomplished by machinery, however efficient and useful—it is done by hand. David should have known that, since as king he had his own copy of the Levitical Law.

It is not surprising, therefore, that David's first attempt to bring the ark up to Jerusalem ended in disaster. The ark was bumped and jolted along, until at one point it was in peril of falling off the cart altogether. A man named Uzzah put out his hand to steady it—again a worthy intention, surely? Not in the sight of God. Doing a right thing a wrong way brings down God's displeasure, not His blessing. Uzzah died on the spot. In terror, David exclaimed, "How shall the ark of Jehovah come unto me?" The whole project was set aside, and David returned to Jerusalem leaving the ark in the house of Obed-edom.

He was ready to try again, but this time he would do things God's way. Before he even started, however, he told the Lord just what kind of a person he would be if the Lord would only come and dwell in Jerusalem; yes, and what kind of a place he would make Jerusalem, so that it might be worthy of such an august guest.

The psalm enshrines his resolves. It begins with the king himself as David tells the Lord what kind of character he himself will cultivate.

A. His Delight (101:1)

"I will sing of mercy [lovingkindness] and judgment: unto Thee, O LORD, will I sing." Nothing this side of heaven can make a person happier than knowing that he is in fellowship with God. David tells the Lord that his cup of joy would overflow if only He could welcome Him as a guest into Jerusalem. God's gracious lovingkindness would be his constant theme; His unfailing and impartial justice would be ever before his heart. What more can a man want than the conscious knowledge that he and God are neighbors!

How David would have thrilled could he have known that "togetherness" which is such a marked feature of the Christian era (Ephesians 2:5-6). How this unique togetherness should set the joybells ringing in our souls!

B. His Decision (101:2a)

"I will behave myself wisely in a perfect way." Nothing in his own personal behavior would create a situation where he would be out of fellowship with God: "I will behave myself wisely." We go back in David's life to those early days when he had returned, flushed with victory, from the overthrow of Goliath. The women of Israel had scalded the soul of Saul by singing too loudly the praises of David. So popular was David that Saul was afraid of him and sought to kill him. Again and again, the Holy Spirit records of David that he "behaved himself wisely." Throughout 1 Samuel 18 it appears like a refrain until, at the end, the Holy Spirit says: "David behaved himself more wisely than all the servants of Saul: so that his name was much set by".

On the throne, David again resolved to behave himself wisely. There are perils in *prosperity* as well as in *persecution*. Indeed, the perils of advancement are often more subtle and seductive than the perils of adversity. David knew that. He promised the Lord that he would behave himself wisely, and since "the fear of the Lord is the beginning of wisdom" he was really promising the Lord that he would never allow familiarity with holy things to breed presumption in his soul.

C. His Desire (101:2b)

"O when wilt thou come unto me?" he cries. "How shall the ark of Jehovah come to me?" he cried in despair after the death of Uzzah (2 Samuel 6:9). Terror is now changed to earnest longing. There was nothing he wanted more than to know that the Lord, the covenant-keeping God of Israel, would bless and sanctify his capital with His own majestic presence.

There is no greater desire that can possess a human heart than the desire to have God as a guest. We have something David never dreamed of having. We have God as a permanent guest, not just in our neighborhood, but in our hearts.

D. His Dwelling (101:2c)

"I will walk within my house with a perfect heart." What goes on in many homes will not bear inspection. The recesses of an Eastern palace especially were usually places where passion, lust, and excess were given full reign. There a monarch could indulge his every whim. Caprice and carnality were allowed unbridled indulgence.

David invites the Lord to come and inspect his home; he promises that his would be a model home, one into which the Lord could come at any time. There would be no pictures which would have to be hastily hidden. There would be no unseemly quarrels for which he would have to apologize or hope had not been overheard. "I will walk within my house with a perfect heart." The word perfect means "without blemish." As the high priest examined with meticulous care an animal brought to the altar for sacrifice to ensure that it was without blemish, so David assures the Lord that if He would come and be his near neighbor then He could come freely into his home at any time. David would see to it that his heart was as unblemished as a sacrificial lamb.

What a resolve! What homes would we have if we would all make this our daily resolve. "I will walk within my house with an unblemished heart." This was the character of the king. He begins with himself.

II. The King and His Countrymen (101:3-5)

If the living God were to become a permanent resident of Jerusalem, then nothing could be tolerated in the country which would be an offense to Him. David wanted to make sure that nothing in the land would offend his noble guest. To insure that his divine guest would feel at home in Jerusalem, David pledged to maintain a rule of holiness.

A. Holiness through Sanctification (101:3)

"I will set no wicked thing before mine eyes: I hate the work of them that turn aside; it shall not cleave to me." He would separate himself from unholy things, from what he describes as a "wicked thing." The word he uses means "thing of Belial," or "an affair of the abandoned one." Some things have their origin in the very soul of Satan. David would allow no such thing in his country. Idolatry, of course, would be a thing of Belial. David pledges that his kingdom would be set apart in sanctification from the idolatrous practices.

He adds: "The work of them that turn aside I hate." This could be translated: "I hate the practice of depravities." Some forms of behavior are depraved. Our own society tolerates them. David realized that no society could host both deity and depravity. God would not make Himself at home where such practices are condoned.

David says, "It shall not cleave to me." If, perchance, some such thing should fasten itself upon him unawares he would shake it off with the speed and horror of a man upon whose hand a serpent had fastened. He would not knowingly harbor such moral horrors in his heart, his home, or his realm.

B. Holiness through Separation (101:4)

"A froward [perverse] heart shall depart from me: I will not know a wicked person." The word for "wicked" carries the idea of moral depravity. Its Greek equivalent is *ponoros* from which we get our word pornography. David knew God well enough to know that He would not make Himself at home in a pornographic culture.

What a word that is for the United States today! This country was founded by men who crossed the ocean looking for religious freedom. They wrote their faith in God into the constitution of their country, stamped it on the coin of the realm, and founded their institutes of higher learning on biblical principles. There is not a country like it in the world. Where else can a pollster report that fifty percent of the population claims to have some sort of religious experience which they would describe as being "born again"? Yet, at the same time, the United States is drowning in filth. According to one report, five Empire State Buildings filled to overflowing could not contain all the pornographic literature sold in a single year in the United States. Religious life in America today is certainly not the result of a Holy Ghost revival. If it were, the porn shops would be out of business, and homosexuality would be outlawed. Genuine revival is always followed by a return to biblical morality. God does not make Himself at home in a society which thinks that faith and filth can coexist.

David knows better. He promises the Lord that all the weight and authority of the throne and all the inspiration of his own personal example would be behind a drive to clean up the moral character of the nation. That, he realized, was prerequisite for a nation to know anything at all of the presence of God. Separation from sin is essential to national spiritual health.

C. Holiness through Severity (101:5)

"Whoso privily [secretly] slandereth his neighbour, him will I cut off: him that hath an high look and a proud heart will not I suffer." A high look is the visible expression of a proud heart. The word rendered "proud" here is *rechab* which means "broad." The thought is "broadness of heart" or, as we would put it in our vernacular, "broad-mindedness." There are few things more destructive to the life of God's people than narrow-mindedness. It shrinks and shrivels fellowship. It takes bigoted stands on issues. It refuses to see the other person's point of view. It promotes the idea that one person has a monopoly on truth and that if anyone wants to know God he must sign on some particular dotted line. Narrow-mindedness promotes sourness of soul and suspicion of mind.

On the other hand, few things are more destructive of the life of God's people than broad-mindedness. There are some who have great catholicity of interest. They have traveled widely and have exchanged ideas in the marketplace of politics, religion, and philosophy with people from all parts of the ideological world. They have a great capacity for seeing the other person's point of view and a great sympathy with it, too. The danger is that this can dilute one's own personal convictions. Issues no longer seem to be sharply defined; they become blurred.

This country is suffering from largeness of heart. There never was a country like America for largeness of heart, for openhanded generosity, for tolerance, for being willing to see the best in the other person, for giving even the enemy the benefit of the doubt. David knew that broad-mindedness was as bad as bigotry when setting a course for the ship of state.

III. THE KING AND HIS COURTIERS (101:6-8)

A. The Counselors He Wants (101:6)

David tells us the kinds of people he wants to dwell with him and the kinds of people he wants to administer the affairs of the kingdom with him. Look at the men David wanted to *reside with him:* "Mine eyes shall be upon the faithful of the land, that they may dwell with me." We know from the story of Mephibosheth that David had the habit of sitting people at his table. After the Absalom rebellion he did his best to get old Barzillai to come and join that group of privileged courtiers who feasted with him in Jerusalem. Barzillai was just the kind of man David coveted as a close companion. It must have been a lasting disappointment to him that the Gilead clansman pleaded his age as an excuse for declining David's pressing invitation. Happy is the land whose ruler opens his home to people of that calibre.

Look at the men David wanted to *reign with him:* "He that walketh in a perfect way, he shall serve me." That is just how he described his own conduct in verse two. Remember that the word "perfect" means "blameless." David wanted men of integrity to associate with him in the administration of his kingdom.

B. The Convictions He Wants (101:7-8)

He once again begins with himself. He reiterates *his personal resolve:* "He that worketh deceit shall not dwell within my house: he that telleth lies shall not tarry in my sight" (101:7). In contrast, the essence of modern politics and diplomacy is deception. How often we hear that a branch of government has denied a report—only to learn shortly afterward that the report was true all the time. Official lying has become an accepted way of conducting the public business. David made up his mind that such "diplomacy" was not for him. Anyone in his court who wanted to make a policy of lying would find themselves out of office before the day was out.

In concluding, David formulates *his public resolve* (101:8). He resolves to rid the country and the capital of evil men: "I will early destroy all the wicked of the land; that I may cut off all wicked doers from the city of the LORD." The revised text reads: "Morning by morning will I destroy all the wicked of the land." Day by day the first order of business in David's court would be to keep the land and especially Jerusalem purged of the wicked, for Jerusalem was to be the city of God. David was determined that severe sentences would be handed down against evil men.

David's personal and public resolve was that so long as he sat on the throne, Jerusalem was to be a place where God could feel at home. What a pity David forgot that when he caught sight of Bathsheba and involved himself in adultery and murder. For David's idealism broke down in practice. Thus, the psalm's lofty sentiments and resolutions still await a coming day when great David's greater Son will make them a reality during His millennial reign.

Psalm 102
AMIDST THE ENCIRCLING GLOOM

I. A Really Gloomy Situation (102:1-11)
   A. The Psalmist's Cry (102:1-2)
   B. The Psalmist's Condition (102:3-11)
      1. His Endurance Is Gone (102:3-5)
         a. His Days Are Consumed by Fire (102:3)
         b. His Desire Is Consumed by Fasts (102:4-5)
      2. His Environment Is Wrong (102:6-7)
      3. His Enemy Is Strong (102:8-11)
         a. The Greatness of Their Scorn (102:8)
         b. The Grounds for Their Scorn (102:9-11)
II. A Remarkably Golden Sunbeam (102:12-22)
   A. A Dawning Hope (102:12-17)
      1. God Will Remember Zion (102:12-14)
         a. The Truth Factor (102:12)
         b. The Time Factor (102:13)
         c. The Testimony Factor (102:14)
      2. God Will Rebuild Zion (102:15-17)
         a. The Reality of It (102:15-16)
         b. The Reason for It (102:17)
   B. A Distant Hope (102:18-22)
      1. A Future People (102:18-20)
      2. A Future Prospect (102:21-22)
III. A Returning Gray Sky (102:23-28)
   A. His Remaining Fear (102:23-24a)
   B. His Rising Faith (102:24b-28)
      1. You Are a Timeless God (102:24b)
      2. You Are a Tremendous God (102:25-27)
         a. Immeasurable in Power (102:25)
         b. Immutable in Person (102:26-27)
      3. You Are a Trustworthy God (102:28)

THIS IS ONE of the penitential psalms (also Psalms 6; 32; 38; 51; 130; 143), but it is unlike the others. The psalmist does not seem to have any personal guilt to confess. If there is penitence

114

in the psalm, it is more of a national than a personal character. The psalmist is primarily lamenting the condition of the nation of Israel.

The psalm is recognized as messianic because the closing verses (102:25-26) are directly related to Christ in Hebrews 1:10-12. Moreover, the entire psalm can be viewed in the light of the great tribulation and the millennial age to follow.

The psalm has a title: "A Prayer of the afflicted, when he is overwhelmed, and poureth out his complaint before the LORD." The title relates more to the *purpose* of the psalm than the *period* of the psalm, which shows that it is intended for devotional use by those suffering affliction.

The structure of the psalm is almost self-evident. It begins with a strongly autobiographical stanza in which we have the constant use of personal pronouns (102:1-11). Then these are dropped, and the poet thinks of the nation of Israel, its fallen condition and its promised restoration to glory (102:12-22). The psalmist returns to the use of the personal pronoun as the shadows close in. His despair, however, is tempered by hope (102:23-28). The middle verses are indeed, as Scroggie says, "a burst of sunshine in a very gray day, to be followed by more cloud, interpenetrated, it is true, with light."

There is considerable difference of opinion as to who wrote the psalm. Most are agreed that it belongs to the closing days of the Babylonian exile. Rotherham thinks that four people had a hand in composing it. The first stanza he ascribes to Hezekiah, pointing out its close parallel with Hezekiah's prayer in Isaiah 38. Time passes and, during the closing days of the Babylonian exile, another composer adds another stanza (102:12-17). Seeing the close parallel between the afflicted Hezekiah and the afflicted nations, he adopts the psalm and adapts it to the new situation. Still more time passes and the return itself is accomplished. The glowing hopes of the second stanza were fulfilled in only the barest and feeblest way, so another stanza is added applying the hopes to a future generation (102:18-22). Finally, Ezra picks up the composition and writes a closing stanza (102:23-28) before adding the completed poem to the Hebrew hymnbook.

That seems a somewhat complicated history for the psalm. The whole psalm could have been composed toward the end of the Babylonian captivity. The hand that composed it could have been the prophet Daniel's, and he could have composed it in stages. Who, like Daniel, so identified himself with Israel in her fallen fortunes in penitential prayer? Who, like Daniel, had the breadth of prophetic vision to take in the march of the ages and Israel's future, both near and far? As to the fact that the psalmist seems to lament the apparent premature end of his days and that he appears to be describing some debilitating sickness from which he was suffering, we do know that Daniel's life was often in danger. Moreover, we know nothing about Daniel's physical condition between the time he disappeared out of sight in the latter days of Nebuchadnezzar and the time he reappeared as an old man in the days of Belshazzar. There may well have been times when Daniel suffered severe illness. So Daniel could have written this psalm, but we cannot say so for sure. Since it will be helpful to relate the psalm to the life of an individual, we are going to stay with our suggestion that Daniel wrote it.

I. A REALLY GLOOMY SITUATION (102:1-11)

The psalmist is in trouble. It would seem that he is sick, even unto death.

A. The Psalmist's Cry (102:1-2)

He calls upon the Lord to hear him and to help him. "Hear my prayer, O LORD, and let my cry come unto Thee. Hide not Thy face from me in the day when I am in trouble; incline Thine ear unto me: in the day when I call answer me speedily."

Kirkpatrick says that this psalm is full of echoes. In these first two verses we have either quotations from, or allusions to, Psalm 39:12; 18:6, 27:9; 59:16; 31:2; 56:9; and 69:17. The psalmist, whomever he was (and who better than Daniel?), was a man who had soaked his soul in the psalms. When he turns to prayer in an hour of personal need, he goes for help to the book of Psalms. It was thus with our Lord in those dark hours that terminated His life. We find His thoughts roaming through the psalm country. Even in that dread hour of darkness, that mysterious midday-midnight, we find Him voicing His cries in the language of the psalms: "My God, my God, why hast Thou forsaken me?" Have we not often found it so ourselves? Again and again we have discovered ourselves turning back to familiar passages in the psalms when facing a time of sickness, sorrow, or an overwhelming catastrophe.

B. The Psalmist's Condition (102:3-11)

Having pulled out his Hebrew hymnbook and culled from it some half-dozen expressions to employ himself in voicing his cry, the psalmist tells the Lord his troubles. He tells the Lord three things.

1. His Endurance Is Gone (102:3-5)

In the first place, *his days are consumed by fire:* "For my days are consumed like smoke, and my bones are burned as an hearth" (102:3). He compares himself to a piece of charred wood. If he was ill when he wrote this part of the psalm, then it is a fitting description of a man consumed by a high fever.

But there is more. *His desire is consumed by facts:* "My heart is smitten, and withered like grass; so that I forget to eat my bread. By reason of the voice of my groaning my bones cleave to my skin" (102:4-5). He has lost his appetite for food and is wasting away to nothing.

After the vision of the ram and the he-goat, given to Daniel in the third year of the reign of Belshazzar, and after the subsequent explanation by his heavenly visitor, Daniel says: "And I Daniel fainted and was sick certain days; afterward I rose up, and did the king's business" (Daniel 8:27). Something similar had happened to him a year or two earlier when he had received the vision of the four beasts (Daniel 7:15,28).

We cannot identify these spells of sickness with the sickness mentioned in this psalm. Probably the psalm was written much earlier than that, at least the autobiographical parts of it, for the psalmist feels that God is cutting short his days. However, when he had the visions of chapters 7 and 8, Daniel was getting on in years. In any case, we have evidence from the book of Daniel that the great man of God was subject to spells of sickness brought on by spiritual sorrow and sensitivity.

2. His Environment Is Wrong (102:6-7)

"I am like a pelican of the wilderness: I am like an owl of the desert. I watch, and am as a sparrow alone upon the house top." The pelican is not a bird of the wilderness at all; it is a specialized water bird and its natural habitats are located in the Danube Delta where it breeds and in the great lakes of Uganda where it winters. It migrates across the land of Israel.

The owl of the desert is not so easy to identify. The word used has always been a problem for the translator. The King James Version uses the word "owl" sixteen times to render five different Hebrew words. The Hebrew word here is *kekos*, "like an owl," from the word *kos*. Professor Driver renders this word as "tawny owl"; the Revised Version suggests "little owl." The little owl, naturalists tell us, is about 8½" long and breeds in most regions except the desert. If it is the tawny owl, then its natural habitat is the forest. To find an owl of this species in the desert would be to find it in the wrong natural environment.

The sparrow, likewise, is mentioned in an unusual setting—"a sparrow alone upon the house top." This is something of a contradiction because the house sparrow, like nearly all sparrows, is a communal bird seldom found alone. However, when one has lost its mate it will sit on a housetop alone and lament its loss.

Each of these three birds is in the wrong environment. The psalmist is thus lamenting to the Lord that his environment is wrong.

If the author was Daniel, we know that he was snatched away from his homeland in his youth and transported to Babylon. There he was selected as one of the young Hebrews most likely to succeed and was deliberately placed by Nebuchadnezzar in an environment where he would forget his nationality as soon as possible and become a young Babylonian. Even his name was changed to Belteshazzar in honor of one of the local gods. All his life Daniel resisted these efforts to have himself assimilated into the Babylonian culture. Even though he rose to high position in Babylon, he never forgot that he did not belong there. It was not his native environment.

What a lesson for us! This world is not our home; we too, must resist all its efforts to swallow us up. We must constantly remind ourselves, in the presence of God, that our environment is wrong. We are born and bred for another land. We are citizens of Heaven, not earth.

3. His Enemy Is Strong (102:8-11)

He mentions *the greatness of their scorn:* "Mine enemies reproach me all the day; and they that are mad against me are sworn against me" (102:8). We can think of instances in the recorded history of Daniel where this was so. Early in the Persian reign, the leaders of Babylonian society conspired to trap Daniel in the matter of his faith and to have him thrown into the den of lions.

He tells the Lord of *the grounds for their scorn:* "For I have eaten ashes like bread, and mingled my drink with weeping, because of Thine indignation and Thy wrath; for Thou hast lifted me up and cast me down. My days are like a shadow that declineth" (102:9-11). Daniel's great visions of the future, his grasp of the coming rise and fall of empires, his certain knowledge that his beloved people Israel would be tossed between one world power and another for centuries to come, and his deep sense of shame at Israel's past failures and present growing contentment with exile must have saddened Daniel. He saw his countrymen adapting themselves to life in Babylon, adopting the land of their exile as though it were the land of promise, and it made him weep. The spiritual burdens he carried must have made him a misfit in Babylonian social circles, just as his high position made him the object of envy and hate. People could not stand to have a man like Daniel in their midst. They would see him as a spoilsport, forever occupied with the need for separation and with his mystical visions. Saints do not fit well in worldly settings, and Daniel was one of God's rarest saints. Thus ends the first major section of the psalm.

II. A REMARKABLY GOLDEN SUNBEAM (102:12-22)

The psalmist turns from his personal preoccupation with the conditions of his exile in a pagan, idolatrous culture to the plans and purposes of God for the chosen people.

A. A Dawning Hope (102:12-17)

The exiled singer picks up his harp from the willows and strikes a note of hope and promise. He remembers the prophecies of old, the promises of God.

1. God Will Remember Zion (102:12-14)

He weighs three great factors: a truth factor, a time factor, and a testimony factor in a glorious equation of hope.

He weighs first *the truth factor:* "But Thou, O Lord, shalt endure for ever: and Thy remembrance unto all generations" (102:12). That is worth recalling. God is eternal, and God is enthroned! Nobody can overthrow a throne which has its pillars established in eternity. The changing seas of time may roar about the massive headland rocks of such a truth, but to no avail. They fall back, dashed to pieces, and the rock still rears its massive head supreme and sovereign over all. Let the waves come marching in from the mighty deep, rank after endless rank, and the result will always be the same. It is the nature of rock to hurl back the sea. That is the great truth factor. No passing empire of time can overthrow the eternal purposes of God. In His person and in His purposes God is sovereign.

He weighs *the time factor:* "Thou shalt arise, and have mercy upon Zion: for the time to favour her, yea, the set time, is come" (102:13). Daniel, of all men, could sing a song like that. He it was who "understood by books the number of the years" (Daniel 9:2). He it was who, pouring over the prophecies of Jeremiah, realized the time had come for the prophetic clock to strike the hour for the rebirth of the state of Israel. He it was who gave himself to passionate prayer, confessing the sins of Israel as though they were his very own. He it was who, having believed the prophecy of the seventy years, received the prophecy of the seventy weeks. Of all men who ever lived, Daniel knew how to weigh the time factor. Other godly men in exile may have done the same; we know Daniel did.

He weighs *the testimony factor:* "For Thy servants take pleasure in her [Zion's] stones, and favour the dust thereof " (102:14). Even the rubble and ruins of Jerusalem were a delight to Daniel. The existence of such devastation meant that no other nation had tried to have possession of a land and cities deeded by God to Israel. Even in their desolation and neglect the ruins were a testimony to the faithfulness of God. They would rise again in God's good time—in a time that was fast approaching.

2. God Will Rebuild Zion (102:15-17)

The psalmist states his conviction concerning this in two ways. He knows that God will rebuild Zion because both His *name* and *fame* are at stake: "So the heathen shall fear the name of the Lord, and all the kings of the earth Thy glory. . . . He will regard the prayer of the destitute, and not despise their prayer." The return from Babylon would be a thing of such triumph, such an evident token of God's faithfulness to His word, such a glorious event, that even the heathen would acknowledge it. The prayers of the people of God would be answered. They had to be answered.

Thus, the psalmist sees a remarkably golden sunbeam. He seizes hold of a dawning hope. Then, all of a sudden, his song leaps over the ages.

B. A Distant Hope (102:18-22)

We know what happened. The empire changed hands as Babylon fell and Persia strode on stage. The hour had struck on God's great, prophetic clock. Cyrus ascended the throne of the world, issued his great decree of emancipation, and the Jews were free to go back to the promised land.

But what happened? Only a handful went. The rest were quite willing to give financial and moral support, but not for them the difficulties and dangers of pioneering in Palestine! They had experienced a life of ease in Babylon. That must have been a bitter blow to a man like Daniel. He, himself, would have gone in a flash had he not been tethered to Babylon by extreme old age. He had suspected, perhaps, that something like this would happen as he saw his countrymen settling down comfortably in the land of their exile. Be that as it may, the psalmist now switches to the distant hope

1. A Future People (102:18-20)

His thoughts soar to the end of the age and he thinks of praises which one day would rise to God. He underlines the thought and theme of that praise: "This shall be written for the generation to come: and the People which shall be created shall praise THE LORD [*Jah*]. For He hath looked down from the height of His sanctuary; from heaven did the LORD behold the earth; to hear the groaning of the prisoner; to loose those that are appointed to death." Daniel had learned from God about the coming great tribulation in the end times. The psalmist now transfers all his hopes for the ultimate fulfillment of prophecy to the end of the age. He sees the Lord delivering an unborn generation from worse perils than any yet experienced by his people. The Assyrian and Babylonian invasions and captivities would be as nothing to this future crisis from which the Lord Himself would deliver Israel. The prophet-poet sees this future people.

2. A Future Prospect (102:21-22)

"To declare the name of the LORD in Zion, and His praise in Jerusalem; when the people are gathered together, and the kingdoms, to serve the Lord." This did not happen at the return from Babylon. The prophet therefore anticipates the distant end of the age when, during the millennium, the nations will join with Israel and resort annually to Jerusalem to share in the great festivities and to unitedly worship the Lord.

III. A RETURNING GRAY SKY (102:23-28)

It is all very well to dwell in ecstasy on the distant scene where the sunbeams paint the clouds with splendor. It is all very well to anticipate the day when gold will be found at the foot of the rainbow. But what about the present? The psalmist returns somewhat gloomily to his own personal prospects.

A. His Remaining Fear (102:23-24a)

"He weakened my strength in the way; He shortened my days. I said, 'O my GOD [*El*], take me not away in the midst of my days.' " If the author of this psalm was Daniel, and if he wrote this portion in his old age when he had been able to assess the paucity of the response by the Jews to the magnanimous proclamation of emancipation of Cyrus, then the verse as it stands creates a problem. Rotherham points out, however, that the Septuagint version reads quite differently: "He answered him in the way of his strength: tell me the shortness of my days. Do not take me away." If Daniel did write this psalm and if this alternate reading is acceptable, the prophet is now comparing the brevity of his own life (even though he was probably in his eighties) with the eternity of days which belong to God. Also, one can well imagine that the aged prophet, though troubled by the worldliness of so many of his countrymen, was keenly interested in all that was happening. He himself was quite willing to stay on in high office so that he could lend his support. The times were so fascinating, so full of soul-stirring events, he dreaded lest he die before seeing how everything would work out.

B. His Rising Faith (102:24b-28)

He stakes his all in God. He closes with three great facts about God.

1. You Are a Timeless God (102:24b)

"Thy years are throughout all generations." So, even if he cannot stay on, helping to steer the ship of state through the momentous years of the return, the future of Israel is in more capable hands than his. It is in the hands of a God who watches human generations come and go, a God that time can never touch, a God well able to superintend the fortunes of Israel, a God never frustrated by mortality and a sense of the shortness of life.

2. You Are a Tremendous God (102:25-27)

He sees God as *immeasurable in power:* "Of old hast Thou laid the foundation of the earth: and the heavens are the work of Thy hands" (102:25). Go back to the beginning of the earth, to the vast upheavals which laid down the bedrock granite of the planet; you see God at work. Go back even farther to that astonishing moment when a hundred million galaxies sprang instantly into being to begin their headlong journeys into the infinite vastness of space; you see God at work. See yonder the angelic hosts shouting for joy! God is a tremendous God—immeasurable in His power, well able to shepherd little Israel struggling for national survival and seeming to exist only at the vacillating whim of capricious Gentile kings.

He sees God as *immutable in person:* "They [the stars and the heavens] shall perish, but Thou shalt endure: yea, all of them shall wax old like a garment; as a vesture shalt Thou change them, and they shall be changed: but Thou art the same, and Thy years shall have no end" (102:26-27). Astronomers now know how accurate those words are. The vast reaches of space are littered with the debris of outworn stars, stars which have waxed old, expanded, burned themselves out and collapsed or torn themselves apart. They suspect, too, that when their present impetus is spent, the galaxies will come crashing back together again—only to explode once more into a new heaven. But above and beyond them all, impassive, impervious to change, imperial in His sovereignty, is the eternal, uncreated, self-existing God—the God who has bound Himself in covenant relationship with His people. This classic passage is picked up by the Holy Spirit in Hebrews 1:10-12 and applied directly to Christ.

3. You Are a Trustworthy God (102:28)

"The children of Thy servants shall continue, and their seed shall be established before Thee." After all, the future of Israel did not depend on the influence at court of a saintly sage by the name of Daniel. It did not depend on the good graces of a heathen king. It did not depend on the skill and wisdom of a Zerubbabel, a Joshua, or an Ezra nor on the power, personality, and persuasiveness of a cupbearer named Nehemiah. It did not depend on the vigor and vision of a Haggai or a Zechariah, nor on the exhortations of a Malachi. The future of Israel is in the hands of a God who is powerful enough to create the universe, ageless enough to be eternal, faithful enough to keep His Word to His chosen people. The poet realizes that he will never live to see the fulfillment of all that the prophets had spoken. But fulfilled they will be because they are in the keeping of a God who can never break His Word.

Such was Daniel's God! And such is our God.

Psalm 103
THE SONG OF A SOUL SET FREE

THIS IS DAVID'S "Hallelujah Chorus." It is a psalm of singular beauty, with a rhythmic quality all its own. It contains twenty-two verses—the same number of verses as there are letters in the Hebrew alphabet. The covenant title "Lord" (Jehovah) occurs just half that number of times. It is what we call an envelope psalm—it ends in exactly the same way as it begins—the subject matter being thus enclosed or enveloped between the opening and closing words: "Bless the Lord, O my soul." In the original text the verses are all of uniform length and all contain two lines each.

Any time we have trouble praising the Lord we should turn to this psalm, get down before the Lord, and recite it back to Him. It is a paean of perfect praise.

I. GOD'S MAN (103:1-7)

Thoughts of God's grace parade before the soul of the singer. He is God's man! His thoughts soar Godward as he thinks of the benediction he owes to God and of the benefits he receives from God: "Bless the Lord, O my soul: and all that is within me, bless His holy name. Bless the Lord, O my soul, and forget not all His benefits"

123

(103:1-2). There is not much we can bring to God. Can we offer Him our money? He can create galaxies of gold at a word if He wills. Can we offer Him our service? He has ministers of state far greater and more gifted than we to attend His throne. What can we offer Him? We can bring Him thanksgiving and praise. David counts off on his fingers, as it were, five attributes for which the believer can offer praise as he or she comes before the Lord.

A. The Penitent (103:3)

"He forgiveth all thine iniquities." The word "iniquities" is a strong one. It does not mean "mistakes." What if the Bible said Christ died for our mistakes? God forgives our iniquities, all our in-grained perversity, all the bentness of our being. Now, there is an item for praise!

One of the titles of Satan is "the accuser of the brethren." Satan hates God's people and looks for opportunities to accuse us before God's throne. He sifts our souls, tells tales about us. He does not come into the presence of God to tell lies about us. He is far too clever for that. A lie spoken in the presence of God would recoil like a thunderbolt on his own head. He does not have to tell lies about us; all he needs to do is tell the truth about us: "Let me tell you what this one said; let me tell you what that one did; let me describe this other one's secret lusts." What happens when he arrives in God's presence as our accuser? He is stopped at once. He comes as the *adversary,* but there stands our *Advocate,* the Lord Jesus. He raises His pierced hands. "We do know what you are talking about," He says. "There are no such sins. You are talking about a child of God. All is forgiven! All is forgotten!" In both Old and New Testaments the idea behind the word forgiveness is "to take away and put somewhere else." This is just what God has done with our sins. He has taken them away and put them on Jesus; He has taken them away and put them in the sea of God's forgetfulness.

> God will not payment twice demand,
>   First at my Saviour's pierced hand
> And then again at mine.

Bless God for that! David sees the believer as a forgiven pentinent. "He forgiveth all our iniquities."

B. The Patient (103:3)

He comes out of the prison and goes into the hospital: "Who healeth all thy diseases." This verse does not refer to the healing of the body, but to the healing of the soul. That is evident from the grammatical construction of the sentence. Pronouns are nouns which stand for another noun. In this verse the pronoun "thy" stands for the noun "soul." Notice carefully what David is saying. He is saying: "Bless the LORD, *O my soul* . . . who healeth all *thy* [the soul's] diseases." Psalm 107:20 tells how He does it: "He sent His Word and healed them." His own Word is the medicine. It heals the soul's diseases. The infirmary in view here is for the soul, not for the body.

The soul does indeed have its diseases, just like the body. Guilt, fear, doubt, depression, anger, lust, hate, jealousy, spite, and greed are some of them. Psychiatrists and physicians are now telling us that these things can kill us. They can be linked directly to certain diseases and disorders of the body which they cause and aggravate.

C. The Pauper (103:4a)

"Who redeemeth thy life from destruction"; or, as it can be rendered, "He redeems your life from going to waste." The psalmist now takes us into the pawnshop. Here comes a wretched man, utterly destitute. Over the years he has had one prized possession, a ring perhaps, or a necklace. Through all of life's hardships he has managed to keep it because of the memories it holds, memories of better days. But now he has come to an end of all other resources and needs money. There is only one thing to do if he does not want to sell it. He must pawn it. Then perhaps he can get it back along with his self-respect when better times come. So the destitute man goes into the pawnshop and offers the ring to the broker who appraises it in his mind as a very valuable item indeed. Assuring himself he can buy it back, the pauper makes a deal. He gets a pittance for his ring and a ticket to certify the transaction. Up to the date on the ticket he can buy the ring back for the amount of the loan plus interest.

The date for the redemption of the ring draws near, but the pauper has been foolishly optimistic. The date arrives. He goes into the pawnshop, pleading for more time. He pleads for better terms, baring his soul and weeping. He tells the pawnbroker of the happy days when he first received that ring. He pours out all his good intentions. But the pawnbroker has heard such stories before—too many of them. He eyes the plaintiff in contempt: his ruin of rags, his drink-sodden face, his unwashed body, his unkempt hair, his broken old shoes, and he refuses to modify the original terms. The next day the derelict passes the pawnshop and he sees his ring in the window gleaming under bright lights on a background of black velvet. It has a different price tag now, one which represents its real worth, a hundred times the pittance for which it was pawned. He has thrown away his ring the same way he has thrown away his life. It is lost beyond recall. It can be redeemed, but at what a cost, and certainly not by him.

That is the way it is with us. Sin had made paupers of us all. Our lives had been scarred and ruined, pawned for a pittance, but Jesus came into the pawnshop of life, and at Calvary He paid the redemption price. How great a price it was! "Ye know the grace of our Lord Jesus Christ, that though He was rich yet for your sakes He became poor that ye through His poverty might be made rich!" At Calvary He not only redeemed our souls from hell, He redeemed our lives from destruction. We can bless God for that!

D. The Prince (103:4b)

"Who crowneth thee with lovingkindness and tender mercies." He now takes us into the palace. How like our God! He brings us into the palace, along its splendid corridors and into the throne room itself. He is going to crown us the way He does everything else— superlatively. Think of the morning of creation. When God commanded the seas to swarm with fish, did He say: "Let the waters bring forth fish"? No! He used a superlative. He said: "Let the waters bring forth fish abundantly." Think of Moses and Miriam and the children of Israel raising the Bible's first anthem of song on the sands of Sinai. The Egyptian army had been swept away, and how did Moses put it? "The Lord has triumphed"? No! He used a superlative. He said: "The Lord has triumphed gloriously." So God is going to crown us. What with? Just with kindness and mercy? No! He is going to do it in the superlative: "Who crowneth thee with lovingkindness and tender mercies."

E. The Pensioner (103:5)

"Who satisfieth thy mouth with good things; so that thy youth is renewed like the eagle's." Rotherham tells us that the word translated "mouth" can be rendered "old age." "He satisfieth thine old age with good things so that thy youth is renewed like the eagle's." How wonderful to be one of God's happy old people. The devil has no happy old people. He does not have what it takes to make people happy, especially old people, and he would not make people happy even if he could. Howard Hughes was probably the wealthiest man in the world in his day. He died at the age of seventy with fame and fortune, with all the world has to offer. His estate was probated at approximately two and a half billion dollars. He was rarely seen in public for the last twenty years of his life. He spent his final years mostly in pyjamas, living on fudge and cake. He weighed only ninety pounds at death and was suffering from malnutrition! Does that sound like a happy old man?

So David, in his advancing years, raises this poem of praise to God: "Bless the LORD, O my soul, and all that is within me, bless His holy name. Bless the LORD, O my soul, and forget not all His benefits." He was God's man; he was God's old man; he was God's happy old man.

II. God's Mercy (103:8-18)

A. God Manifests His Mercy (103:8-10)

"The Lord is merciful and gracious, slow to anger, and plenteous in mercy. He will not always chide: neither will He keep His anger for ever. He hath not dealt with us after our sins; nor rewarded us according to our iniquities." What a wonderful God we have!

There is an interesting story about Elizabeth I, England's most famous queen. She had a special favorite among her noble courtiers, the Earl of Essex. One day Elizabeth gave him her ring as an indicator of her affection and promised him that if ever he were accused of a crime, he had only to send that ring to her, and she would at once grant him audience so that he might himself plead his case before her. The day came when he needed that ring, for he was accused of conspiracy and high treason. He was executed, for the ring Elizabeth had given him was never presented to her, so she allowed her favorite to die.

The years passed. Then one day the Countess of Nottingham, a relative but certainly no friend of the earl, lay dying herself. She sent a message to Elizabeth asking the queen to come to her. She had a confession which must be made if she were to die in peace. Elizabeth duly arrived at the deathbed and the countess produced the ring the queen had once given to Essex, her favorite. It seems that Essex had given the ring to the countess with the urgent request that it be taken straight to Elizabeth, but the Countess had betrayed his trust. Now, in her last moments, she entreated Elizabeth's forgiveness. At the sight of the ring Elizabeth was livid with rage. She seized the dying countess in her bed and shook her until her teeth rattled. "God may forgive you," she screamed, "God may forgive you, madam, but I never shall."

Thank God for His grace! He holds no grudges, harbors no resentments. There is no sin he will not forgive in this glorious age of grace in which we live, if only we will ask Him in repentance and remorse.

B. God Measures His Mercy (103:11-12)

"For as the heaven is high above the earth, so great is His mercy toward them that fear Him." That is the *vertical measure.* We take a point on this planet and we draw a line upward. We extend that line beyond the clouds, up beyond the remotest planet, up beyond the highest star. Up! That is the vertical measure.

"As far as the east is from the west, so far hath He removed our transgressions from us." That is the *horizontal measure.* We take a point on this planet and we draw a line horizontally, but we must be careful. We must not draw the line from north to south because that is a finite distance. Light travels from pole to pole fourteen times a second. The north-south measure is finite, not so the east-west measure. If we travel north from a given point, sooner or later we will reach the north pole, a definite point; then we travel south to the south pole, another definite point. East and west are a different matter. We can start to travel east and there is no point, so long as we continue in that direction, at which we start to travel west; or we can start to travel west and, no matter how long we continue, there is no point at which we start to travel east. West is always west; east is always east.

So we take a point on earth and draw a line vertically into infinity. We also draw a line horizontally into infinity—"so far hath He removed our sins from us." There is a point on this planet where those two infinite lines intersect: the vertical line and the horizontal line. The point is Calvary! We draw all our lines from the cross. The upright of the cross, driven like a stake into the ground, is where we begin our vertical line. We extend it up into infinity. The crossbar of the tree, flung wide as though to embrace the world, is where we begin our horizontal line into infinity. That is how the Lord measures His mercy—in terms of the cross.

C. God Multiplies His Mercy (103:13-16)

The psalmist has measured God's mercy in terms of distance. He tells us now how God maintains it in terms of time. As his *dimensional illustration* runs at once to the infinite so his *durational illustration* runs to the eternal. God's mercy is from everlasting to everlasting. It is the kind of mercy the Lord enjoined on Peter. Peter, with unheard of magnanimity, thought that if he forgave his brother seven times he would have done his duty to perfection. "Seven times!" said the Lord. "Forgive him until seventy times seven."

The "seventy times seven" concept occurs in only one other place in the Bible: in Daniel's vision of the seventy weeks. Daniel learned toward the end of the seventy years captivity, that God had marked off a span of time—seventy weeks (seventy sevens) of years—during which period of seventy times seven God would be patient, sparing, and forgiving with His people. He would forgive and forgive and forgive until seventy time seven of years. Into that long span of time He has since inserted, as a parenthesis, another special age, known as the church age, which has lasted now for nearly two thousand years. After sixty-nine of the seventy sevens had run their course, God stopped the clock and inserted our age.

D. God Maintains His Mercy (103:17-18)

When the church age is over God will again start the prophetic clock and the last of the sevens will run its course, making up the sum of "seventy times seven" during which time God forgives and forgives and forgives. So that significant expression "seventy times seven" speaks of God's grace. But it is a finite number; it has a beginning and an ending. We add the church age of two thousand years, and it is still a finite number; it still has a beginning and an ending. We add the millennial age of another thousand years, and it is still a finite number. A millennium plus a millennium plus half a millennium plus a millennium more, but it is still a finite number! David throws all calculations aside with one grand stroke of the pen: "From everlasting to everlasting." That is how God maintains His mercy.

"The mercy of the LORD is from everlasting to everlasting."

III. GOD'S MIGHT (103:19-22)

The psalm ends with an acknowledgement of God's might.

A. The Heavenly Throne (103:19)

"The LORD hath prepared His throne in the heavens; and His kingdom ruleth over all." It was the sight of this throne that filled Lucifer with such unholy ambition. It was the sight of this throne, high and lifted up, that led to Isaiah's consecration to the cause of God. This is the throne that fills John's vision in Revelation 4 and 5. Seventeen times in those two short chapters he mentions it. It is the sight of this throne, so stable and sure, which enables the aged apostle to walk calmly through the devastating scenes which follow in the Apocalypse.

B. The Heavenly Throng (103:20-22)

"Bless the LORD, ye His angels, that excel in strength, that do His commandments, hearkening unto the voice of His word. Bless ye the LORD, all ye His hosts; ye ministers of His, that do His pleasure." They excel in strength! They excel in service! They excel in song! There are ten thousand times ten thousand of them, and thousands of thousands of them. They hang upon His words and rush to do His bidding.

The psalmist now comes back to earth. He returns to the beginning: "Bless the LORD, O my soul." At this point his soul might still raise the question, "How?" Just go on reading. "Bless the LORD, O my soul, and all that is within me, bless His holy name. Bless the LORD, O my soul, and forget not all His benefits: Who forgiveth all thine iniquities. . . ."

Sometimes we sing choruses which can be sung as a round. This psalm may be read like that. It locks us into an unending circle of praise. We get to the end; it becomes a new beginning. We get to the end again; it becomes a new beginning again. Such will be our praise in an endless eternity.

Psalm 104
A POEM OF CREATION

I. THE GLORY OF GOD'S PERSON (104:1)
   A. An Instinctive Word of Worship (104:1a)
   B. An Intelligent Word of Worship (104:1b)
II. THE GLORY OF GOD'S POWER (104:2-31)
   A. The Foundation Work of Creation (104:2-9)
      1. The Realm of the Skies above Us (104:2-4)
        a. The Astral Heavens (104:2)
        b. The Atmospheric Heavens (104:3)
        c. The Angelic Heavens (104:4)
      2. The Realm of the Seas around Us (104:5-9)
        a. Setting the Boundaries of the Sea's Reach (104:5-8)
        b. Setting the Boundaries of the Seas Rage (104:9)
   B. The Further Works of Creation (104:10-30)
      1. A Beautiful Scene (104:10-18)
        a. The Running Waters (104:10-13)
        b. The Rolling Hills (104:14-17)
        c. The Rising Peaks (104:18)
      2. A Benevolent Sun (104:19-23)
        a. Its Faithfulness (104:19)
        b. Its Function (104:20-23)
      3. A Bountiful Sea (104:24-30)
        a. The Fullness of the Deep (104:24-25)
        b. The Face of the Deep (104:26a)
        c. The Fearsomeness of the Deep (104:26b)
        d. The Fortunes of the Deep (104:27-30)
   C. The Finished Work of Creation (104:31)
III. THE GLORY OF GOD'S PURPOSE (104:32-35)
   A. A Word about Greatness (104:32)
   B. A Word about Gladness (104:33-34)
   C. A Word about Government (104:35)

THIS PSALM is a true neighbor to Psalm 103. The two go together; some think they have the same author. Psalm 103 celebrates God as the God of circumstance; Psalm 104 celebrates Him as the God of creation. Psalm 103 magnifies God's grace; Psalm 104 magnifies God's glory. Psalm 103 deals with God's mercy; Psalm 104 deals with God's might. The author of Psalm 104 has been called "the Wordsworth of the ancients." He is evidently a man in love with nature and in love with nature's Author and Creator. The poem follows the same plan as Genesis 1. We have days one and two in verses 1-4, the first half of day three in verses 5-9, the second half of day three in verses 10-18, days four, five, and six in verses 19-30, and day seven in verses 31-35.

This is another "envelope" psalm, a fact even more apparent if we assign the final phrase, "Praise ye THE LORD," to the beginning of Psalm 105 as some suggest. The psalm begins and ends with the words "Bless the LORD, O my soul." The use of the "envelope" technique is a poetic way of reminding us that we shall never be done with this theme. It is as eternal as God Himself.

I. The Glory of God's Person (104:1)

A. An Instinctive Word of Worship (104:1a)

"Bless the LORD, O my soul," an expression identical with the opening exclamation of the previous psalm. "Lord" here is the usual word for Jehovah, the God of the covenant, but with the additional meaning "Jehovah Himself." The hymn was inspired by thoughts of Jehovah. So often, when we think of God, we think in terms of our own needs and benefits. It is not often we think solely of God Himself. That, however, is the essence of all true worship; it is to be taken up with what God is in and of Himself. There is no higher or holier occupation which can engage a rational mind.

B. An Intelligent Word of Worship (104:1b)

"O LORD my God, Thou art very great: Thou art clothed with honour and majesty." God's robes of state are honor and majesty. These are His imperial garments, the insignia of His royalty. As the psalmist sees it, in the creation of the world God has clothed Himself with a robe of splendor, fashioned to the form of One who is infinite. Creation shows forth God's eternal power and His Godhead in such a way that no man has any excuse for not believing in Him (Romans 1:20). He Himself may be invisible, but His imperial garments are in abundant evidence everywhere. It is not that men cannot see them; it is, rather, that they refuse to see them. And as our old English proverb puts it: There is none so blind as he who will not see. A contemplation of God's creation will draw out both an instinctive and an intelligent word of worship—instinctive because it

wells up from the heart, and intelligent because it engages the facilities of the mind.

II. THE GLORY OF GOD'S POWER (104:2-31)

The psalmist now begins a sweeping description of creation, not
as seen by the scientist or the historian but as seen by the poet. He
organizes his material around three great focal points.

A. The Foundation Work of Creation (104:2-9)

The psalmist looks first at two great realms: the realm of the skies
above us and the realm of the seas around us.

1. The Realm of the Skies above Us (104:2-4)

He divides the realm of the skies above into three. His poetic eye
takes in each of them and his flowing pen notes down the crowning
wonders of each. He looks first at *the astral heavens:* "Who coverest
Thyself with light as with a garment: who stretchest out the heavens
like a curtain" (104:2). The first thing God created was light, one of
the most mysterious entities in the universe. We know what light
does, but we still do not know what light is. We know that the speed
of light is always constant, and that both time and matter are, in mysterious ways, connected with light. Einstein's famous formula, $E =
MC^2$ (energy equals mass multiplied by the speed of light squared),
ushered in the atomic age. God has clothed Himself with light as
with a garment. Light reveals and conceals at the same time. The
psalmist sees the wide-flung canopy of the sky as a gorgeous curtain
spangled with points of light, each a blazing ball of fire. The word he
uses for "curtain" occurs fifty-three times in the Bible, forty-seven of
them having to do with the tabernacle. God spread the vast canopy
of the astral heavens as easily as a man pitches a tent. The Hebrew
poet is not concerned with the mysteries and mathematics of astron-
omy, but with the awesome power of a Creator who can spread out
the stars as easily as a man might spread a sheet, who can robe Himself in light as gloriously and majestically as a king arrays himself in
purple and scarlet.

The psalmist contemplates *the atmospheric heavens:* "Who layeth
the beams of His chambers in the waters: who maketh the clouds His
chariot; who walketh upon the wings of the wind" (104:3). The engineering marvels of evaporation and precipitation which excited the
wonder of Solomon (Ecclesiastes 1:7) now become the theme of poetic song. The psalmist sees God constructing His penthouse on
high. Only God lays the foundation of His abode on filmy clouds.
The stormclouds and the tempest are chariots. He rides
magnificently down the skies.

The psalmist looks next at *the angelic heavens:* "Who maketh His angels spirits; His ministers a flaming fire" (104:4). Behind the forces of nature are angelic powers. The Apocalypse, particularly, draws the veil to show us angels, good and bad, involved in the control of wind and weather. Angels are assigned to take care of little children and the saints of the Most High. Peter and Paul were both ministered to directly by angels. The Lord Jesus, in His humanity, both at His temptation and after His agony in the garden, was cared for by angels. The angelic heavens, where these mighty beings live, may be in a different dimension than that of our world and subject to different laws. Yet angels were present at creation's morn. Job calls them "the sons of God" and tells us they burst into praise when they saw God displaying His wisdom and power in creating the universe. The psalmist, then, looks at the realm of the skies above us.

2. The Realm of the Seas around Us (104:5-9)

He sees God, first, *setting the boundaries of the sea's reach:* "Who laid the foundations of the earth, that it should not be removed for ever. Thou coverest it with the deep as with a garment: the waters stood above the mountains" (104:5-8). In the early stages of creation the waters covered the earth more than once, but again and again God raised up the mountains until finally He raised them up for the last time and bade them stand fast. All the massive geological movements of past ages were part of God's plan to store the earth with all the riches and resources needed for man's life upon the earth. When the storehouses of the earth were full, God finally decreed an end and set bounds to the sea.

Next, the psalmist sees God *setting the boundaries of the sea's rage:* "Thou hast set a bound that they may not pass over; that they turn not again to cover the earth" (104:9). He has drawn the line in the sand and said to the heaving waves: "Here shall thy proud waves be stayed." For the tides obey God's mighty voice. They know just where and when to stop, at what unseen mark on rocky crag or sandy shore they must cease their march and retreat back whence they came. Even in its fiercest rage the sea acknowledges its bounds.

B. The Further Works of Creation (104:10-30)

The psalmist gathers his anthem around three great movements.

1. A Beautiful Scene (104:10-18)

He looks across the far reaches of the land and exults in the manifest evidences of God's majesty and might, His goodness, and His grace. He looks first at *the running waters* (104:10-13), pausing to consider the rivers, at their source and in their course: "He sendeth the springs into the valleys, which run among the hills" (104:10-12).

He sees the domesticated beasts of the field and the wild beasts of the earth refreshing themselves at the babbling brooks and running streams. He looks also at the rain: "He watereth the hills from His chambers: the earth is satisfied with the fruit of Thy works" (104:13). Every time we experience a prolonged period of drought we are reminded afresh of our utter dependence on the providential goodness of God in sending us rain. Rain was frequently withheld from Israel in times of apostasy. The great prophet Elijah prayed earnestly that it might not rain, and it rained not for the space of three years and six months (a symbolic period pointing to the great tribulation period when God will withdraw His blessing and leave men to their own devices).

The psalmist looks next at *the rolling hills* (104:14-17). His glance takes in first the farm lands: "He causeth the grass to grow for the cattle, and herb for the service of man: that He may bring forth food out of the earth: and wine that makes glad the heart of man, and oil to make his face to shine, and bread which strengtheneth man's heart" (104:14-15). Corn, oil, and wine were commodities for which Palestine was famous. I shall never forget the time when, as a young man in the British Army, I was posted from Egypt to Palestine. I boarded a train in Egypt late one night and watched as the train rolled away across the desolate sands. When I awoke the next morning the train had crossed into Palestine. Instead of flat endless deserts there were rolling hills, and instead of sand there was grass. It was a beautiful scene.

The psalmist glances also at *the forest lands*: "The trees of the LORD are full of sap; the cedars of Lebanon which He hath planted; where the birds make their nests: as for the stork, the fir trees are her house" (104:16-17). When I first went to Palestine in 1948 the hills were mostly rock-strewn areas of desolation. Years of mismanagement under various conquerors and particularly under the Turks had denuded the hills of their forests. The Jews have since replanted many of the great forests which once clothed their hills, so that they may bloom again. Millions of trees now flourish in the forest of Martyrs, the great Balfour Forest, and in other areas. Tourists to Israel can leave a perpetual memorial behind them by planting a tree in one of the new, developing forests so that the countryside is once more beginning to look as it did in the days of this singer of old.

He next turns his eyes to *the rising peaks*: "The high hills are a refuge for the wild goats; and the rocks for the conies" (104:18). A coney has smooth feet and makes its dwelling in the rocks. The psalmist sees that even the high hills have their place in the ecology of the planet and he glorifies God for that, too.

2. A Benevolent Sun (104:19-23)

From the tops of the high hills and mountains his eye naturally rises higher to where the sun blazes in the sky. He thinks first of *its faithfulness:* "He appointed the moon for seasons: the sun knoweth his going down" (104:19). The sun's companion and its compass pay tribute to God. He thinks how faithfully the sun sheds its light abroad, how faithfully the moon catches its beams and reflects them back to the earth. From pole to pole, from sea to sea, from shore to shore, from season to season the world basks in the light of the sun. Day after day the sun "knoweth his going down." It faithfully walks the path ordained for it by God.

He thinks of *its function:* "Thou makest darkness, and it is night. . . . The sun ariseth. . ." (104:20-23). The singer sees the sun departing and darkness comes. The night creatures emerge and the forests ring with the lion's roar. He sees the sun dawning and day-light comes. The nocturnal animals creep away to their dens, and man arises from his bed going forth to work. The psalmist touches each note on his harp with wonder and awe, running up and down the scale of God's benovolent dealings with the earth by means of the sun.

We know much more about the sun today than did the psalmist. It is the source of light and life upon this planet. Were it only a little hotter, it would scorch the globe and turn it into a vast desert. Were it but a little colder, it would allow the arctic to march in triumph from the poles to the equator and turn the earth into a giant block of ice. To maintain the earth at its proper mean temperature, the sun consumes 4,200,000 tons of its weight every second. Yet this prodi-gious output of energy is so controlled and regulated that the thin margin of temperature necessary for life to exist is maintained from age to age. No wonder primitive peoples worshiped the sun.

The psalmist does not make that mistake. He worships the sun's mighty Maker, the One he describes as "the Lord my God."

So the psalmist's gaze takes in the sun, and his thoughts range far and wide as he thinks how much this earth owes to its parent star and how much, in consequence, it owes to the One who brought it into being. But still his wandering eyes rove across the works of God in creation.

3. A Bountiful Sea (104:24-30)

The Hebrews were not a maritime people, despite the coastal land included in their country. They were neighbors to the Phoeni-cians, the greatest maritime people of the ancient world. Tyre and Sidon, the great seaports of these ocean-going explorers, were only a few miles from their native Palestine. At times, as under Solomon, the Hebrews themselves had ventured out to sea in ships.

The psalmist speaks of *the fullness of the deep:* " O Lord, how mani-fold are Thy works! In wisdom hast Thou made them all: the earth is full of Thy riches. So is this great and wide sea" (104:24-25). Perhaps he had stood on the shores of the Mediterranean Sea (his people called it "the Great Sea") and gazed out to where the setting sun dyed its blue waters crimson. As far as his eye could see, stretching toward the west, was the boundless shore of the sea. He would talk to mariners from Tyre who would tell of long weeks spent with sails set to speed them farther and farther to the west. Always the horizon receded before them, opening up distant boundaries of sea they could never reach. They would tell of venturing out beyond the farthest reach of the Great Sea and of creeping northward along new coastlines. They would tell of the dreadful storms they encountered and of the Tin Islands to the north. And always, to the west, where even they did not dare to venture, was the endless expanse of the sea. No man could plumb its depths. A few leagues off shore and no sounding line they had could touch its bottom. The thought of it all filled the psalmist with awe: "This great and wide sea," he exclaims.

He speaks of *the face of the deep:* "There go the ships" (104:26). Perhaps he has seen them, the great Tarshish ships of the Phoenicians, vessels made by men to dare the oceans themselves. Those ships were a source of amazement to the Hebrew landsmen. They would watch their sails spread like wings and breast the billows in search of other lands and the treasures of exotic places far away.

He speaks of *the fearsomeness of the deep:* "There is that leviathan, whom Thou hast made to play therein" (104:26b). Perhaps he had seen the crocodiles of the Nile, only to be told by the mariners that out in the depths of the sea itself were monsters a thousand times more to be feared. One can almost sense the feeling of awe with which the Hebrew poet speaks of these things. If he were one of the later poets, he would think of the story of Jonah and the whale. The deep was a fearful place. Those mighty monsters, which lurked in its gloomy depths, were only at play in an environment his God had made expressly for them.

He speaks of *the fortunes of the deep:* "These wait all upon Thee.... Thou openest Thine hand, they are filled with good. Thou hidest Thy face, they are troubled: Thou takest away their breath, they die" (104:27-30). The psalmist thinks of the continuing *bounty* of what we call nature and of the continuing *balance* of nature. Even death itself was part of the scheme of things, and over it all God rules in perfect wisdom, love, and power. "Thou sendest forth Thy spirit, they are created: and Thou renewest the face of the earth." In the ecological system of nature we see God continually at work. He did not just create the world and leave it to its fate. He is continually sustaining every part of His creation. Every new life that emerges on this earth comes from God. The concept strikes at the very roots of the theory of evolution, which sees all earthly life as the end result of a random working of the forces of chance.

"Nonsense!" says the psalmist. All life comes from God, and He actively concerns Himself with what we call ecology.

C. The Finished Work of Creation (104:31)

"The glory of the LORD shall endure for ever. The LORD shall rejoice in all His works"; or, as some have rendered that last statement: "Let Jehovah rejoice in His works." It is a bold statement. The psalmist is so impressed with the astonishing wonders of creation that he actually calls upon God to rejoice in what He Himself had done! He is carried away. It is almost as though he is afraid God might be robbed of some of the glory which is His due. The psalmist, soaring on the wings of his emotions, borne on the pinions of the vastness of nature, urges God to take delight in that which has awed and delighted him! God's Sabbath rest has been broken; we live in a fallen world, the mark and taint of sin everywhere, but it is still a marvelous, wonderful world.

The psalmist has almost finished his poem, but there is something with which he has to deal before he can put down his pen, something he has hinted at. He must deal with the sad fact of sin in the universe, sin with its accompanying bitterness and blight. He has spoken of the glory of God's person and the glory of God's power. He now turns his thoughts to the purposes of God.

III. THE GLORY OF GOD'S PURPOSE (104:32-35)

He has a threefold closing word.

A. A Word about Greatness (104:32)

"He looketh on the earth, and it trembleth: he toucheth the hills, and they smoke." A look, a touch is enough to remind the earth of the awesome power of the Creator. It is as simple for God to consume the earth as to create it. And now that sin has raised its head in the universe, that is exactly what He intends to do. He will detonate the heavens and the earth, consume them in a fiery holocaust, and then create new ones in which His perpetual purpose in glory will be maintained.

B. A Word about Gladness (104:33-34)

"I will sing unto the LORD as long as I live: I will sing praise to my God while I have my being. My meditation of Him shall be sweet: I will be glad in the LORD." The word "sweet" is usually rendered "pledge" or "surety" and carries the idea of a mortgage. The psalmist's thoughts turn to certain eternal verities, with promises, pledges, and guarantees for which God Himself has given surety. The thought of that is sweet. No wonder he can sing, even though the discordant note of sin still has to be faced.

C. A Word about Government (104:35)

"Let the sinners be consumed out of the earth, and let the wicked be no more." There! He has come out with it at last. There is a discordant note in nature, and man is the cause of it—man and his sin. Sin is a personal thing, and it cannot be judged in its *process* without being judged in the *person*. It is man's perverted will which has spoiled the whole thing. But that is only a temporary state of affairs, for God will one day put an end to that. "Bless thou the LORD, O my soul!" cries the singer as he invites us to go back to the beginning of the psalm and to begin again to worship and praise our Creator.

Psalm 105

HOW GOOD IS THE
GOD WE ADORE

I. Israel's Exhortation (105:1-6)
   A. A Call to Rejoice (105:1-2)
   B. A Call to Return (105:3-4)
   C. A Call to Remember (105:5-6)
II. Israel's Expectation (105:7-15)
   A. How God Decreed the Provisions of the Covenant (105:7-11)
      1. How Sovereign God Is (105:7)
      2. How Sincere God Is (105:8)
      3. How Selective God Is (105:9-10)
      4. How Specific God Is (105:11)
   B. How God Delivered the People of the Covenant (105:12-15)
      1. A Paltry People (105:12)
      2. A Pilgrim People (105:13)
      3. A Protected People (105:14-15)
III. Israel's Exile (105:16-25)
   A. Joseph in Egypt (105:16-25)
      1. The Divine Purpose (105:16)
      2. The Divine Process (105:17-22)
   B. Jacob in Egypt (105:23-25)
      1. Jacob's Descent into Egypt (105:23)
      2. Jacob's Descendants in Egypt (105:24-25)
IV. Israel's Exodus (105:26-38)
   A. The Men Involved (105:26)
   B. The Miracles Involved (105:27-36)
      1. Their Purpose (105:27)
      2. Their Particulars (105:28-36)
         a. Plagues that Filled the Egyptians with Doubt (105:28-29)
         b. Plagues that Filled the Egyptians with Disgust (105:3-31)
         c. Plagues that Filled the Egyptians with Dread (105:32-33)

139

       d. Plagues that Filled the Egyptians with Dismay
          (105:34-35)
       e. Plagues that Filled the Egyptians with Despair
          (105:36)
    C. The Mandate Involved (105:37-38)
  V. Israel's Experiences (105:39-41)
    A. How God Led His People (105:39)
    B. How God Fed His People (105:40-41)
 VI. Israel's Exaltation (105:42-45)
    A. The Lord Was Gracious to Israel (105:42-43)
      1. He Remembered His Promise (105:42)
      2. He Redeemed His Promise (105:43)
    B. The Land Was Given to Israel (105:44-45)
      1. The Remarkable Provision (105:44)
      2. The Real Purpose (105:45)

THIS PSALM and the next one stand shoulder to shoulder and close the fourth book of Psalms. Although Psalm 105 is anonymous, it is generally thought that it was written after the return from Babylon. Like its companion psalm, it is a historical psalm written to commemorate God's goodness to His people and the faithfulness of His dealings. The word "hallelujah," which closes Psalm 104, probably belongs as the opening note of Psalm 105, making it another envelope psalm and tying it even closer to Psalm 106.

The historical psalms (there are three of them of some length in the Hebrew hymnbook: Psalms 78; 105; 106) served a special purpose among the Hebrew people. Books were rare, expensive, and beyond the reach of ordinary people. Hence, if history were to be remembered it must be remembered by rote in the memories of the people. What better way to enshrine it than by turning it into verse and setting it to a tune? Think how much theology we have imbibed that way from our own hymnbooks!

When the pioneer missionary Robert Moffat went out to Africa, one of his first concerns was to reduce the language of the Bechuanaland people to writing. Then he had to teach the natives their alphabet. His pupils were men trained in the wilds, schooled in the lore of the jungle, wise in the ways of the bush, intelligent and educated to suit their own way of life, but the alphabet was beyond them. Why should A be A? And why should B follow A? The missionary was baffled. He was about to give up when one of his pupils suggested he teach them to sing it! At first the idea sounded absurd. After all, there are some things we don't sing! We don't sing the Declaration of Independence or the entries in a bankbook! However, Moffat decided to give it a try. But to what tune? He was a Scot and the tune that came to his mind was one familiar from boyhood days:

Auld Lang Syne! And it worked! The whole village soon rang with the alphabet to the strains of *Auld Lang Syne!*

The Hebrews had thought of this years before. They set their history to music and here, in Psalm 105 and again in Psalm 106, we have a memorable example of this effective way to learn history.

I. ISRAEL'S EXHORTATION (105:1-6)

The psalmist begins with a threefold call to his people.

A. A Call to Rejoice (105:1-2)

"O give thanks unto the LORD; call upon His name: make known His deeds among the people [peoples]. Sing unto Him, sing psalms unto Him: talk ye of all His wondrous works." This is a call to *praise His name* and a call to *proclaim His fame*. Israel's great mission in the world was to proclaim to the nations the faithfulness of the living God. The return from the Babylonian captivity could have provided Israel with a marvelous new chapter and a new text from which to tell the nations of the goodness and unfailing faithfulness of God. Little enough have the nations of the world learned to give thanks and praise to the true and living God. Lands like Britain and America which once were bathed in gospel light are now turning away from God with such determined purpose that some have labeled our era post-Christian. Countless millions of people live in lands where atheism sits enthroned in the seat of power. Other millions find themselves held in the religious fantasies of Hinduism, Buddism, and Islam. Israel, scattered among the nations, is no testimony of the reality of a living God. Indeed, in many Western lands, Jews themselves are in the forefront of the battle to keep the Bible out of the schools, and communism, the most virile and vicious form of atheism ever conceived, was born in the mind of a Jew.

Still, in the psalmist's day, the token return of a remnant of Jews to the promised land, to drive in their stakes and hold the land for the coming of the Messiah, was somewhat of a testimony to the world. The return of the Jews to the land today, although in unbelief, is likewise a testimony to the world—one which is largely unheeded.

B. A Call to Return (105:3-4)

"Glory ye in His holy name: let the heart of them rejoice that seek the LORD. Seek the LORD, and His strength: and seek His face evermore." That should be the great goal of the nations: to return from their wandering and going astray in order to seek the Lord. This is what has always happened in times of revival. The tragedy is that no such national awakenings have ever been permanent. One can wander the valleys of Wales today and find little or nothing left of the great awakening that took place at the turn of the century. The psalmist pleads for such a return which will awaken the nations.

C. A Call to Remember (105:5-6)

"Remember His marvellous works that He hath done; His wonders and the judgments of His mouth; O ye seed of Abraham His servant, ye children of Jacob His chosen." This is an echo from the book of Deuteronomy, a book we could well rename, "the book of remembrance." All down its stately stanzas the words ring: "Thou shalt remember" or "beware lest ye forget." Israel's history has been one long record of forgetfulness. The psalmist hopes that this return will result in a quickening of memory so that never again will the people forget what it owes to the Lord.

When Bunyan wrote *Pilgrim's Progress,* he traced the adventures of Christian and later those of his wife Christiana and her children. On the way to glory Christiana and her children were joined by Greatheart, who became their friend and protector. In due course they came to the Valley of Humiliation, and Greatheart pointed out to the boys where it was that Christian had his great battle with Apollyon: "Your father had that battle with Apollyon at the place yonder, before us," he said, "in a narrow passage just beyond Forgetful Green. Indeed that place is the most dangerous place in all these parts. For, if at any time the pilgrims meet with any fall it is when they forget what favours they have received."

Forgetful Green! The Hebrew people are still wandering in that dangerous place. Britain and America are in danger of losing their spiritual heritage there, as well. Many a Christian has lost his reward and testimony on Forgetful Green.

So then we have Israel's exhortation: to rejoice, to return, to remember. The psalmist now wants to remind Israel of all that it owes to God as a nation.

II. Israel's Expectation (105:7-15)

He begins with the great Abrahamic covenant—the covenant which God drew up between Himself and the founding father of the Jewish race. He has drawn up no such contract with any other nation.

A. How God Decreed the Provisions of the Covenant (105:7-11)

The psalmist has four things to say about the Abrahamic covenant.

1. How Sovereign God Is (105:7)

"He is the Lord our God: His judgments are in all the earth." The One who entered into this unique relationship with the nation of

Israel is "Jehovah our God," the God of covenant and the God of creation, the One whose almighty power was so significantly celebrated in the previous psalm. When God entered into this treaty relationship with Israel He did so as a sovereign power. He was sovereign in making it.

2. How Sincere God Is (105:8)

"He hath remembered His covenant for ever, the word which He commanded to a thousand generations." A thousand generations! From the time Israel was driven out of the land by the Romans until our own day when at long last they have begun to return is only about sixty generations. Israel has not even been a nation for a thousand generations. A thousand generations would take us back before the landing of the Normans on England's shores, before the birth of Christ, before the conquests of Alexander, before the rise of the Persian empire, before the founding of the Hebrew monarchy, before the flood, before the beginnings of the human race. A thousand generations! So sincere is God in keeping His treaty obligations with the nation of Israel that the divinely ordained pact is hewn out of the same stuff as eternity.

3. How Selective God Is (105:9-10)

"Which covenant He made with Abraham, and His oath unto Isaac; and confirmed the same unto Jacob for a law, and to Israel for an everlasting covenant." The promise made to Abraham was renewed to Isaac and then to Jacob. In their persons the divine treaty was narrowed down selectively and specifically to just one nation: Israel. Other nations came from Abraham's fertile loins, such as the Edomite nation and the Arab nations, too—rich and powerful as they have become in modern times. But not with these has God drawn up His treaty. Palestine does not belong to the Arabs. It was deeded by God to Israel, and no vote of the United Nations Organization, no decision of the world powers, and no Arab rage is going to alter that.

4. How Specific God Is (105:11)

"Saying, 'Unto thee will I give the land of Canaan, the lot of your inheritance.' " What could be more specific than that? Three times God has brought this people into the promised land and settled them there despite their adversaries. The first time He placed them there they gave the world the Bible; the second time He restored them the Saviour; this time He plans to give the world the millennium.

So the psalmist recounts how God decreed the provisions of the covenant.

B. How God Delivered the People of the Covenant (105:12-15)

He looks now at the history of the chosen people in the patriarchal age when they wandered as landless clansmen from country to country in Canaan.

1. A Paltry People (105:12)

"When they were but few men in number; yea, very few, and strangers in it [Canaan]." When the nation went down to Egypt they numbered only seventy people, and during the lifetime of Abraham and Isaac they numbered far less than that. They looked so vulnerable. They were like the mighty Amazon at its source—just the tiny trickle of a stream one could dam up with one's foot.

2. A Pilgrim People (105:13)

"When they went from one nation to another, from one kingdom to another people." They migrated from place to place—now they were in the territory of some Canaanite king, now in Philistine country, now in Egypt, now back in Canaan. We see Abraham pitching his tent at Bethel; we see him in Pharaoh's court; then he's back at Bethel, at the place where his tent and his altar were at the beginning. Now Isaac is at Gerar, now at Rehoboth, now at Beersheba. Now Jacob is at Padan-aram, now at the Jabbok, now at Shechem, now at Bethel, now at Ephrath, now at Hebron. And all the while they maintained their pilgrim character, and the symbols of their sojourn were a tent, an altar, a well, and a staff.

3. A Protected People (105:14-15)

"He suffered no man to do them wrong; yea, He reproved kings for their sakes; saying, 'Touch not Mine anointed, and do My prophets no harm.' " Abraham in Egypt, Isaac before Abimelech, Jacob in Padan-aram and before Esau—ever vulnerable but always under the blanket of divine protection.

Israel's great expectation was the full enactment of the Abrahamic covenant. The writer of Hebrews reminds us that the pilgrim patriarchs only saw the promises afar off. They staked their all upon them, however, as though the complete terms of the divine contract were already in full and evident force.

III. ISRAEL'S EXILE (105:16-25)

Still following the general outline of the book of Genesis, the poet now traces the events which led to the exile of the patriarchal family from the promised land and their settlement in Egypt.

A. Joseph in Egypt (105:16-22)

1. The Divine Purpose (105:16)

"Moreover He called for a famine upon the land: He brake the whole staff of bread." There are thirteen famines mentioned in the Bible, and all are significant, for God's hand was in them all. God uses the forces of nature to fashion the destiny of men and nations. The mighty famine which gripped Egypt and Canaan in the days of Joseph was divinely foretold, and its purpose was to drive the chosen people down into Egypt. God's plan was that they might quietly grow into a populous and mighty nation in Egypt during the time the iniquity of the Amorites in Canaan was becoming full.

2. The Divine Process (105:17-22)

He tells the story of Joseph in Egypt. He shows us Joseph *friendless* (105:17), *fettered* (105:18), *forgotten* (105:19), and finally *freed* (105:20). Joseph was a link in the chain of divine providence. The poet tells us one thing about Joseph that is missing from the historical narrative in Genesis. He tells us that his feet were hurt with fetters. He also tells us that the iron entered into Joseph's soul (the word "he" in verse 18 is *nephesh* and can be rendered "his soul"). Joseph was about eighteen when he was sold into Egypt as a slave by his jealous brothers. He was thirty when he made to stand before Pharaoh. How many of those years he spent in prison, falsely accused of molesting his master's wife, we do not know. It was evidently a considerable time. The only hope he had of ever being released was when he befriended Pharoah's chief butler in prison. When the man was released and restored to Pharoah's favor Joseph pleaded that he not be forgotten. But the butler did forget him. Joseph could only cast all upon God. In the end, Joseph was not released for good behavior, though never a prison warden had a more model prisoner; he was not released by influence at court. He was released in the providence of God when the time was ripe for him to be raised to the highest office in Egypt.

Having sketched Joseph's *trials* (105:17-20), the poet goes on to sketch in briefly Joseph's *triumphs:* "He [Pharaoh] made him lord of his house, and ruler of his substance: to bind his princes at his pleasure; and teach his senators wisdom" (105:21-22). He was invested with supreme power, second only to that of the Pharaoh himself. Never has man known such a swift change in his circumstances from *severe adversity* to *supreme advancement.* And it was all part of the divine process whereby the chosen people might find a safe refuge in Egypt and there develop into a nation. They entered Egypt a family; they left it a nation whose very numbers frightened the Egyptians.

B. Jacob in Egypt (105:23-25)

The poet now describes how the whole family was settled in Egypt which was to be their home for four hundred years. It seems like a long time to us—almost twice as long as the United States has been a nation—yet it was but a passing moment of time with God.

1. Jacob's Descent into Egypt (105:23)

"Israel also came into Egypt; and Jacob sojourned in the land of Ham." The Table of Nations shows that the Egyptians (*Mizraim,* "The Two Masters," because Egypt was two countries in one— lower and upper Egypt) were descended from Ham (Genesis 10). So Jacob, the pilgrim patriarch, who was also Israel, the father of the budding tribes, descended into Egypt after determining that this was God's will for him.

2. Jacob's Descendants in Egypt (105:24-25)

He mentions both their *swelling population* and their *subsequent persecution.* They became "stronger than their enemies." Egyptian mistrust and doubt about the Hebrews, who were settled in their midst in the land of Goshen, evidently began at a very early date. Doubtless there were many in the country in high places deeply jealous of Joseph. Joseph was the first of those "court Jews" who appear so often in history with great influence in high places. In the Middle Ages and later such Jews wielded enormous power in the courts of Europe. There needed only to be a change in the dynasty and the coming of a king "who knew not Joseph" for Hebrew fortunes in Egypt to change rapidly for the worse. This later Pharaoh, Egypt's Adolf Hitler, decided that genocide was the best way to deal with "the Jewish question." He turned Goshen into a concentration camp and planned for the systematic extermination of the entire Hebrew race within a generation.

IV. Israel's Exodus (105:26-38)

Now the psalmist stirs the racial memory of his people at its most thrilling point. Never before or since has the world witnessed anything like it. Some three million people living in abject poverty and slavery were gloriously emancipated—not by reform or revolution but by redemption. Throughout the Bible, Hebrew apologists come back again and again to this manifest evidence of God's power and faithfulness. As the resurrection of Christ is the great evidence to which the Church appeals, so the Exodus was the great evidence to which Israel appealed.

A. The Men Involved (105:26)

"He sent Moses His servant; and Aaron whom He had chosen." What a remarkable family Amram and Jochebed raised in that slave hut on the banks of the Nile! Out of it came a Moses, a mighty prince with God, Aaron, a ministering priest for God, and Miriam, a memorable prophetess for God.

B. The Miracles Involved (105:27-36)

1. Their Purpose (105:27)

"They shewed His signs among them, and wonders in the land of Ham." The miracles performed by Moses and Aaron were mighty demonstrations of divine power, the credentials which authenticated their mission at the court of Pharaoh. The Egyptian wizards were able to duplicate one or two of the early miracles by their black magic, but they soon gave up and acknowledged that a greater power than they knew was at work in Egypt.

2. Their Particulars (105:28-36)

The psalmist does not list the miracles in the order they occurred, nor does he list them all. He omits the fifth and sixth miracles. The ones he does mention are out of chronological order, thus: 9, 1, 2, 4, 3, 7, 8, 10. The third and fourth miracles are placed in inverted order (there seems to be no apparent reason for this) and the ninth plague is given first place because that was the plague (darkness) which particularly awed the Egyptians.

We summarize here the plagues as they are listed by the psalmist.

a. Plagues that Filled the Egyptians with Doubt (105:28-29)

The plague of darkness filled the Egyptians with doubt about Pharaoh's deity (105:28). Pharaph was supposed to be the incarnation of Ra, the sun god, the supreme deity in the Egyptian pantheon. The darkness which filled Egypt showed up the falsity of Pharaoh's claims—especially since all the land of Goshen, where the Hebrews lived, was unaffected by this judgment.

The plague of blood filled them with doubt about Pharaoh's decisions (105:29). It was an ominous warning to all Egypt that Pharaoh's intransigence would lead to a bloodbath in Egypt. The nation had planned to exterminate the Hebrew people; God would answer in blood unless there was an immediate change of policy.

b. Plagues that Filled the Egyptians with Disgust (105:30-31)

To find frogs everywhere—in the streets, in the homes, in the kitchen utensils, in their beds, in the beggar's shanty, and in the Pharaoh's palace must have been a disgusting thing. When the plague was removed, their rotting corpses made the whole land stink.

Flies abounded everywhere. This proliferation of annoying and disease-carrying pests must have been just as repulsive as the plague of frogs.

c. Plagues that Filled the Egyptians with Dread (105:32-33)

"Hail for rain!" is the psalmist's expressive way of putting in words this awesome plague. The book of Exodus links "thunderings" to the other two visitations under this plague. Indeed, it was the thunderings which shook Pharaoh. "Intreat the Lord (for it is enough) that there be no more mighty thunderings and hail," he pleaded (Exodus 9:28). The word used for "mighty thunderings" literally means "voices of Jehovah," a strong superlative. The hail, too, was devastating both to crops and cattle.

d. Plagues that Filled the Egyptians with Dismay (105:34-35)

Even before the dread plague fell, that of locusts and caterpillars "and that without number," Pharaoh's servants warned him: "Knowest thou not yet that Egypt is destroyed?" (Exodus 10:7).

e. Plagues that Filled the Egyptians with Despair (105:36)

"He smote also the firstborn in their land, the chief of all their strength." It was this final visitation which convinced even Pharaoh that he could not win this uneven contest. With dead people in almost every home, the horror and fear throughout Egypt must have been beyond description.

These were the miracles. The world has never seen their like and will not until the days of the Apocalypse, when God will again pour out His wrath under the vials.

The psalmist concludes this section of his song by mentioning the mandate given by God.

C. The Mandate Involved (105:37-38)

It was a mandate of emancipation. The Egyptians loaded the Hebrews with their wealth—back pay for countless years of slavery. Then they hurried them out of the land. The psalmist's voice is raised in triumph: "He brought them forth also with silver and gold: and there was not one feeble person among their tribes. Egypt was glad when they departed: for the fear of them fell upon them." They set them free *thoroughly* and *thankfully*. The Egyptians finally bowed to the original mandate of God: "Let my people go."

One day Russia, with millions of Jews forcibly detained and subjected to discrimination and persecution, will meet a fate such as God dealt out to Egypt.

V. Israel's Experiences (105:39-41)

Of all the many incidents which befell Israel on the way to Canaan, that pack the pages of Exodus, Leviticus, and Numbers, the psalmist selects two. Both of these illustrate the faithfulness of God. He has nothing to say about Israel's sins and shortcomings, for that is not his purpose in this psalm. That will be lamented in the next one.

A. How God Led His People (105:39)

"He spread a cloud for a covering; and fire to give light in the night." The Shekinah glory cloud marched ahead of the Hebrews to lead them step by step all the way from Egypt to Canaan. The pillar of fire shed light upon their path by night, the pillar of cloud shaded the camp from the sun's fierce heat by day. Such is the kindness of God! He led His people through terrifying terrain, but He led them in such a way that the worst of their discomforts were alleviated.

B. How God Fed His People (105:40-41)

"The People asked, and He brought quails, and satisfied them with the bread of heaven. He opened the rock, and the waters gushed out; they ran in the dry places like a river." Since there were no means of sustenance in the Sinai desert, God miraculously provided both food and drink for His people and did so unfailingly all the forty years they spent in the wilderness. Imagine what it took to feed all those people three times a day! It was nothing for God to spread a table in the wilderness!

The psalmist is almost finished, but before closing his song he has one more word.

VI. Israel's Exaltation (105:42-45)

A. The Lord Was Gracious to Israel (105:42-43)

1. He Remembered His Promise (105:42)

"For He remembered His holy promise, and Abraham His servant." Abraham had been dead for centuries, but God does not have a short memory. He had told Abraham that He must wait for the cup of Amorite iniquity to be full before He could cleanse the promised land and give it to Abraham's descendants. One can almost picture God in heaven saying to Abraham: "And now Abraham, watch this! I am going to keep My promise."

2. He Redeemed His Promise (105:43)

"And He brought forth His People with joy, and His chosen with gladness." Stand for a moment with Israel on the shores of the Red Sea. What do you hear? You hear the people sing! The Egyptian army has been swept away, and never again will Egypt hold Israel captive. "Thus the LORD saved Israel. . . . Then sang Moses and the children of Israel" (Exodus 14; 15).

B. The Land Was Given to Israel (105:44-45)

1. The Remarkable Provision (105:44)

"And gave them the lands of the heathen; and they inherited the labour of the people." They reaped and gathered where they had not sown. They took possession of houses they had not built and of farms they had not worked. It was a remarkable provision.

2. The Real Purpose (105:45)

"That they might observe His statutes, and keep His laws. Praise ye THE LORD." He had been faithful to them; they must now be faithful to Him. All God wanted in return was their acknowledgement in word and deed that they owed it all to Him. That is exactly what He wants from us.

Psalm 106

NATIONAL CONFESSION

I. A Sound Heart (106:1-6)
  A. An Exciting Note of Praise (106:1-3)
    1. Remembering the Lord's Person (106:1a)
    2. Remembering the Lord's Pity (106:1b)
    3. Remembering the Lord's Power (106:2)
    4. Remembering the Lord's People (106:3)
  B. An Explicit Need for Prayer (106:4-6)
    1. The Psalmist's Concern (106:4-5)
    2. The Psalmist's Confession (106:6)
II. A Sad History (106:7-46)
  A. Natural Blindness in the Place of Bondage—Egypt (106:7-12)
    1. Ungrateful Grumbling (106:7)
    2. Unstinted Grace (106:8-11)
    3. Unrestrained Gladness (106:12)
  B. Negative Behavior in the Place of Barrenness—the Wilderness (106:13-33)
    1. Their Lustful Desires (106:13-15)
    2. Their Lawless Demands (106:16-18)
    3. Their Lying Dogmas (106:19-27)
      a. Unbelief Regarding the Lord (106:19-23)
      b. Unbelief Regarding the Land (106:24-27)
    4. Their Loathsome Deeds (106:28-31)
    5. Their Lasting Distrust (106:32-33)
  C. Near Blasphemy in the Place of Blessing—the Land (106:34-36)
    1. The Fatal Seed (106:34)
    2. The Fearful Weed (106:35-39)
      a. The Deeds of the Heathen Acclaimed (106:35)
      b. The Creeds of the Heathen Accepted (106:35-39)
    3. The Final Need (106:40-46)
III. A Sure Hope (106:47-48)
  A. The Blessing (106:47)
    1. May God End Their Exile (106:47a)
    2. May God Ensure Their Exaltation (106:47b)
  B. The Benediction (106:48)

WE DO NOT KNOW who wrote this psalm. From the pleas of verse 47 it would seem it was written during the captivity in Babylon. Daniel was a man who knew how to pray the kind of confessional prayer we have in this psalm. Perhaps he wrote it about the time he poured out his heart before God as recorded in Daniel 9. If so, it was written by him when he was an old man of about eighty-seven. The Babylonian empire had fallen. The times were pregnant with portents, for old prophecies must now be fulfilled. Yet, there was still no sign of this happening. The exiles were settling down at ease in Babylon, making the best of their new home, and fast forgetting their history and their national destiny. Perhaps at such a time this psalm was penned.

It is clearly a companion to the previous psalm. The two stand shoulder to shoulder. Psalm 105 tells us how God treated Israel; Psalm 106 tells us how Israel treated God. One psalm deals with the faithfulness of God, the other with the faithlessness of Israel.

This psalm is another of the envelope psalms. It begins and ends with the same words: "Praise ye the Lord," so that the close of the psalm is an invitation to go back and commence it all over again. Also, this psalm closes the fourth book of Psalms, and does so with the characteristic doxology which marks the close of the other four books. The psalm looks forward prophetically to the end time, immediately prior to the return of the Lord at the end of the great tribulation.

I. A SOUND HEART (106:1-6)

The opening stanza is personal. The psalmist uses the personal pronouns "I" and "me" to exhort his people to tune harp and voice in praise to the living God. He strikes two notes.

A. An Exciting Note of Praise (106:1-3)

The first word he writes down is a ringing, resounding hallelujah! "Praise ye the Lord!"

1. Remembering the Lord's Person (106:1a)

"Praise ye THE LORD. O give thanks unto the LORD; for He is good." The first "Lord" here is *Jah*, a name which has a special connotation. It underlines for us the fact God never forgets His *compassion*. It speaks of Jehovah as the One who has become our salvation. The first occurrence of the word is in Exodus 15:2 where God is seen as the One who has just saved Israel from the Egyptian army at the Red Sea. The second "Lord" is *Jehovah*, a name which underlines *commitment*. It speaks of God in covenant relation with those He has created and called. It is one of the three great primary names for God in the Old Testament. The psalmist, then, would have us think of the Lord's person. He is a person who never forgets His people.

2. Remembering the Lord's Pity (106:1b)

"For His mercy endureth for ever." As is usually the case in the psalms, the word for mercy means "lovingkindness" or "grace." Our God remembers we are but dust. Israel's sins could not exhaust the lovingkindness of God. Neither can ours. Though we forget Him, He does not forget us; though we turn to our own ways and leave Him out in the cold, His lovingkindness pursues us. He is the love which "will not let me go," the love that the many waters cannot quench, the love that conquers death.

3. Remembering the Lord's Power (106:2)

"Who can utter the mighty acts of the LORD? Who can shew forth all His praise." It is not in us as forgetful humans to worship the Lord as He really deserves. We are so taken up with the passing affairs of the moment.

The story of John Newton reminds us of man's forgetful ingratitude. Newton, in his unregenerate days, sailed the seas as a slaver and sank so low as to become himself the slave of a slave. Then the Lord met him, saved him, raised him up, and put him in the ministry. Even so, he found his treacherous heart so full of ingratitude—as we do ours. He wept over this and described the remedy in one of his great hymns:

> Weak is the effort of our heart,
> And cold our warmest thought;
> But when we see Thee as Thou art,
> We'll praise Thee as we ought.

So the psalmist would have us remember the Lord's power, especially His power in redemption.

4. Remembering the Lord's People (106:3)

"Blessed are they that keep judgment, and he that doeth righteousness at all times." If the singer is still in Babylon awaiting the end of the exile, then he is singling out for a special mention those he feels will not be found wanting when the time comes and the captivity ends. All too often we allow our thoughts to be taken up with those of the Lord's people who have faults and failings. The Holy Spirit would have us be taken up with those who walk consistently in His ways. Surely that is a more profitable theme for our thoughts.

B. An Explicit Need for Prayer (106:4-6)

He is still using the first person singular, still looking at his own needs and at his own heart.

1. The Psalmist's Concern (106:4-5)

"Remember me, O LORD, with the favour that Thou bearest unto Thy People. O visit me with Thy salvation; that I may see the good of Thy chosen, that I may rejoice in the gladness of Thy nation, that I may glory with Thine inheritance." He has three names for God's Old Testament people. They are His chosen, His nation, and His inheritance. The singer wants to see God acting on their behalf by bringing them into the good of His pledged word. He had promised they would stay in Babylon for just seventy years. The psalmist wants to live long enough to see God step back into the arena of human affairs and fulfill His own prophecies.

2. The Psalmist's Confession (106:6)

Here, he changes suddenly from the first person singular to the first person plural, for now he intends to identify himself with the nation in its sins, and he is going to confess those sins. "We have sinned with our fathers, we have committed iniquity, we have done wickedly."

The psalmist uses three great words for sin. The word for "sinned" means to miss the mark, to stumble, to fall, to come morally short. It suggests *sin by practice.* The word for "committed iniquity" means to be bent, crooked, perverse. It suggests *sin by nature.* The word for "done wickedly" expresses the idea of lawlessness, that restless activity of fallen man which reveals itself in restlessness. It suggests *sin by choice.* The nation needs to confess all three: sin by practice, by nature, and by choice. By linking the sin of the exiled Jews in Babylon with the sins of "our fathers" the psalmist expresses a deep sense of national continuity. That is one reason why the study of history is so important. We are where we are today as a nation because we did what we did yesterday. So then, the psalm begins with a sound heart. The psalmist, himself a sound man, identifies himself with the unsoundness of the nation of which he was a part.

II. A SAD HISTORY (106:7-46)

Now begins a long confession of national sin and disgrace. It was the Babylonian captivity which brought home to exercised hearts in Israel the depth, dimensions, and dreadfulness of the national disgrace. There had been other invasions of Israel and other deportations, but the Babylonian deportation was different. The deported Jews left behind a smoking heap of rubble which was once Jerusalem, the place where God had put His name, and they left behind the charred embers of what had once been the temple of the living

God. Moreover, the promised land itself was brought under the heel of the Gentile with no sign of any change in that. Daniel's remarkable visions foretold the opposite. The "times of the Gentiles," which would run on until the end times, had begun with Nebuchadnezzar and would last until the coming of the beast, the last Gentile ruler, and the second coming of Christ.

The psalmist now begins to catalog the nation's sins. This is something unique for the nation of Israel. What other nation is so exercised before God about its national shortcomings, failures, and iniquities? What other nation makes a national anthem out of its national disgrace? Can we imagine London or Paris, Washington, or Moscow calling upon the nation to repent in dust and ashes while its apostasies and iniquities are publicly recited?

In reciting the sad history of failure, the singer divides the story into three parts: one part deals with Israel in Egypt, one with Israel in the wilderness, and one with Israel in the land.

A. Natural Blindness in the Place of Bondage (106:7-12)

He takes the people back to their first exile in the land of Egypt.

1. Ungrateful Grumbling (106:7)

"Our fathers understood not Thy wonders in Egypt; they remembered not the multitude of Thy mercies; but provoked Him . . . at the Red sea." Think of all God had done for them! He had trained Moses to be His ambassador in the court of Pharaoh and had sent him back to Egypt armed with unlimited power. He had laid proud Egypt in the dust. Never before, in all its long and illustrious history, reaching back to the dawn of recorded time, had this nation been so humiliated. God had marched His people out like a conquering army, laden down with spoil.

But at the Red Sea, at the first sign of danger, as soon as the people heard that Pharaoh had mobilized his army and that his chariots were thundering down upon them, they began to grumble. We remember their bitter sarcasm. "Because there were no graves in Egypt, hast thou taken us away to die in the wilderness?" they demanded of Moses (Exodus 14:11). No graves in Egypt! Egypt was a land of graves and tombs! Guilding them and stocking them with treasure against the day of death was a major Egyptian occupation. Egypt was nothing but one vast graveyard; from the pyramids to the lowliest caves, it was a land of graves. "No graves in Egypt" indeed! It was a sarcastic jibe. The singer notes their ungrateful grumbling.

2. Unstinted Grace (106:8-11)

"Nevertheless He saved them." God overlooked their faults (106:8), overcame their fears (106:9), and overthrew their foes (106:10-11). He parted the sea before them, then summoned it back to sweep into oblivion the renowned chariot divisions of Egypt. That was unstinting grace!

3. Unrestrained Gladness (106:12)

"Then believed they His words; they sang His praise." And so they did! What a pity they had to wait until the danger was over before they could trust and triumph thus.

How often God must be grieved with us, too, for our persistent unbelief in the face of all He has done for us. Just let a crisis or a difficulty arise, and back we go to our unbelief. It is well enough for us to sing once the difficulty has passed, but why can we not sing and praise God, looking to Him in the midst of difficulty, knowing that it is but another opportunity for us to see Him at work?

B. Negative Behavior in the Place of Barrenness (106:13-33)

Israel is now in the wilderness in the mind's eye of the singer. He can think of one occasion after another when the nation exhibited gross unbelief and ingratitude.

1. Their Lustful Desires (106:13-15)

"They soon forgat," he says. One would have thought that after the victory at the Red Sea memory would have marched with them. Not so! They had gone only three days' journey into the wilderness when, at Rephidim, they murmured for water. Six weeks later they were complaining again, criticizing the manna and lusting after the flesh: "He gave them their request; but sent leanness into their souls."

How often that happens to us. Finally God gives us what we demand in our carnality and then lets us pay the penalty in resulting spiritual malnutrition.

What a blessing that we do not always get what we pray for! What a tragedy to insist on getting our own way only to find we have chosen far less than God's best.

The psalmist thinks next of their lawless demands.

2. Their Lawless Demands (106:16-18)

"They envied Moses also in the camp, and Aaron the saint of the Lord." The psalmist is referring to the time when Korah, Dathan, and Abiram led a rebellion against the spiritual leadership of Moses (Numbers 16). Korah was a first cousin of Moses and Aaron; Dathan and Abiram were members of the tribe of Reuben, a tribe which had lost its birthright of spiritual leadership to Levi. Korah was a member of the Kohathite Levitical clan. The Kohathites and the Reubenites all camped together on the south side of the tabernacle.

These men were jealous of Moses and Aaron and claimed that they were just as holy as God's anointed leaders. The Lord soon proved the emptiness of their claim and visited them with summary judgment. It is always a serious thing to attack the God-appointed spiritual leadership of the Lord's people.

3. Their Lying Dogmas (106:19-27)

The psalmist underlines two forms of unbelief.

a. Unbelief Regarding the Lord (106:19-23)

The psalmist now refers to the incident of the golden calf. He underlines their *iniquity,* their *ingratitude,* and their *intercessor.* Indeed, had it not been for Moses, God would have made an end of them all then and there. "They made a calf in Horeb," says the psalmist. Horeb—at the very mount where God gave the law and manifested Himself in quaking earth and flaming fire. Horeb—where Moses went yonder into the presence of God receiving from God's hands the Law which set Israel apart from all other nations.

We are given here a glimpse of what God thinks of idolatry. The Hebrews had seen Apis, the sacred bull of Egypt. They had watched the Egyptians, for all their magnificent art, science, and engineering, groveling before animals—bulls and beetles, cats, crocodiles, and cows. Now they wanted to do the same. They had the audacity to make a molten image like a calf. They took their invisible God and cast Him in the likeness of an ox that eats grass. Such is the fine touch of sarcasm with which the psalmist looks back upon this folly; nor was it the end. The Jews were in Babylon now, and had been for nearly two generations, because for hundreds of years they had persisted in the grossest idolatry.

b. Unbelief Regarding the Land (106:24-27)

"Yea, they despised the pleasant land, they believed not His word: but murmured in their tents. . . . Therefore He lifted up His hand against them." The spies had come back with their report, but only two gave a favorable response; the rest were filled with gloomy foreboding. All they could talk about were the difficulties and dangers that lay ahead. They spoke of cities walled up to heaven and of the sons of Anak, a giant race that possessed the land. "Would God we had died in the wilderness." This they did—every one of them except Joshua and Caleb, who had turned in the minority report.

4. Their Loathsome Deeds (106:28-31)

"They joined themselves also unto Baal-peor, and ate the sacrifices of the dead. . . . And the plague brake in upon them. Then stood up Phinehas, and executed judgment. . . ." The place was Peor; the sin was that of becoming devotees of Baal of the Moabites. They joined a sacrificial communion service with the Moabites in the worship of their dead gods. Along with the idolatry went the accompanying immorality. A plague from the Lord swept through the camp, carrying twenty-four thousand people into eternity and was only stayed when Phinehas, the son of Eleazor the son of Aaron the high priest, took a vigorous stand against the apostasy.

5. Their Lasting Distrust (106:32-33)

"They angered him also at the waters of strife, so that it went ill with Moses for their sakes: because they provoked his spirit, so that he spake unadvisedly with his lips." This sin at Meribah (Numbers 20) is placed as the climax by the psalmist because it involved Moses. He was told to speak to the rock, but he lost his temper and smote it, his patience exhausted at last. When Moses was first called of God, he had pleaded, "I cannot speak." Now he was to be kept out of the promised land because he spoke too much. Thus, their distrust and unbelief galled their Maker (106:32) and goaded their mediator (106:33).

What a catalog of persistent rebellion, unbelief, faultfinding, and backbiting! The psalmist turns now to their sad history in the land.

C. Near Blasphemy in the Place of Blessing (106:34-36)

He summarizes the history of Israel in the land in three steps.

1. The Fatal Seed (106:34)

"They did not destroy the nations, concerning whom the Lord commanded them." The command to exterminate the Canaanites was based on the highest wisdom. The land was polluted by the presence of the *nephilim,* the same species of hybrid giant which existed before the flood. Moreover, the religion of the Canaanites was utterly vile, and the morals of the people an open sewer. The Canaanites were so corrupt that the only way to remove their putrifying sore on the body of the human race was surgery. When Israel failed to obey God in this matter, they themselves became infected from the same sore.

2. The Fearful Weed (106:35-39)

Like some noxious and vigorous growth, the sins of the Canaanites became the sins of God's people.

a. The Deeds of the Heathen Acclaimed (106:35)

"[They] were mingled among the heathen and learned their works." It was not long before the Hebrews were as bad as the people they had been told to exterminate.

Wickedness is infectious. Just let us expose ourselves to the wrong kind of books, the wrong kind of TV programs, and soon we will find ourselves lowering our standards to those of the world. We will accept the world's morals and philosophies and "learn their works" as surely as Israel learned the works of the accursed Canaanites.

b. The Creeds of the Heathen Accepted (106:36-39)

There was a threefold downward path into religious apostasy. The first had to do with the *graven images* of the pagans: "And they served their idols: which were a snare unto them" (106:36). God has never allowed His people to look kindly on the worship of idols. The Law, given by God to Moses, mandated against it.

Idolatry is the height of folly, yet there is something about it which is strangely fascinating to mankind. One only has to think of the gross idolatry of Hinduism, Buddhism, and Roman Catholicism to see how many millions of otherwise enlightened people in the world to this day are held in its grip. Nothing could be a greater act of folly than to make an idol out of clay, stone, or metal, and then to fall down and worship the thing as though it were an almighty and living god. The Hebrews grew to a nation in Egypt, a land which abased itself in the grossest polytheism and idolatry. The plagues of Egypt were all aimed at the Egyptian idols. Apologists for idolatry say that the worshipers are not worshiping the idol, but that which the idol represents. The Mosaic Law forbade not only the worshiping and the serving of idols, but even the making of them. So, the first downward step into apostasy for Israel was in having religious intercourse with graven images.

The second downward step had to do with *gruesome immolation:* "Yea, they sacrificed their sons and their daughters unto devils, and shed innocent blood, even the blood of their sons and of their daughters, whom they sacrificed unto the idols of Canaan" (106:37-38). "They sacrificed . . . unto devils . . . unto the idols of Canaan." This explains the fascination which idolatry has over the unregenerate mind. Behind the graven images lurk evil spirits. When a person bows to a graven image, he bows to the demon which lurks behind it. He becomes a prey to that demon which fastens upon his heart, mind, and will. In the grossest forms of idolatry, human sacrifices are demanded: little children are placed on the red hot lap of Moloch; millions of victims are sacrificed to the fierce gods of the Aztecs. The horrible demons which lurk behind such religious systems gloat on human suffering. The devotees of idolatry think that the sacrifices, so costly, of their innocent and helpless children and babes are pleasing to their gods. The gods of the heathen are devils.

That was the second downward step for Israel—becoming so enslaved to the idols they worshiped that no sacrifice was considered too great to propitiate and please them.

The final downward step had to do with *gross immorality:* "Thus were they defiled with their own works, and went a whoring with their own inventions" (106:39). Idolatry and immorality often go hand in hand. The religious worship of the Canaanites involved the vilest forms of sexual immorality. Pornographic symbols were set up all over the country. Worship was consummated with a male or female prostitute. "To go a whoring" was far more than poetic figure of speech; it was at the heart of Canaanite religion.

This was the fearful weed which took root in Israel until it flourished from one end of the land to the other, and its results were sobering.

3. The Final Need (106:40-46)

"Therefore was the wrath of the Lord kindled against His People. . . . He gave them into the hand of the heathen." The psalmist recites the sad story so characteristic of the days of the judges and of the later kings. Israel was *detested* by the Lord (106:40), *discarded* by the Lord (106:41-42), and *delivered* by the Lord (106:43-46) over and over again. For even in His discipline He remembered the people with pity. Indeed, He even made them to be pitied of those who carried them captive. That was the sad history. The psalmist has almost finished. But he cannot finish on a note like that.

III. A Sure Hope (106:47-48)

He turns to the Lord in prayer. Confession is over, petition can now begin.

A. The Blessing (106:47)

He asks God to *end their exile:* "Save us, O Lord our God, and gather us from among the heathen, to give thanks unto Thy holy name" (106:47a). With true spiritual insight the psalmist recognizes that God's own good name is bound up in the complete regathering of Israel. The return from Babylon was only a partial one; the regathering we are witnessing today is only a partial one. One of these days God will end Israel's exile.

He asks God to *ensure their exaltation:* "And to triumph in Thy praise" (106:47b). Once more, gathered back to the land, not partially, but completely, Israel will be able to fulfill at last its national destiny. That awaits the final return of Christ when Israel will triumph in His praise.

B. The Benediction (106:48)

"Blessed be the Lord God of Israel from everlasting to everlasting: and let all the People say, 'Amen.' Praise ye THE LORD." Amen! Hallelujah! Not just a sterile mental assent to incontrovertible historical and theological facts, but a response from the heart.

Thus ends the fourth book of Psalms. And thus ends this psalm, too—with a *Hallelujah* designed to take the singer back to the beginning again. It is as though the Holy Spirit would say, "Go over it again and again and again and again, until its solemn truths have become a part of your soul."

THE SONG OF A SOUL SET FREE

I. How God Regathered the Scattered and Rejected People of Israel (107:1-3)
 A. What the Lord Deserves (107:1)
 B. What the Lord Did (107:2-3)
II. How God Regarded the Spiritual and Real Plight of Israel (107:4-32)
 Israel was like:
 A. A Person Lost in the Desert (107:4-9)
 B. A Person Locked in a Dungeon (107:10-16)
 C. A Person Lying on a Deathbed (107:17-22)
 D. A Person Lashed on the Deep (107:23-32)
III. How God Restored the Scarred and Ruined Property of Israel (107:33-38)
 A. The Land Made Barren (107:33-34)
 B. The Land Made Beautiful (107:35-38)
IV. How God Revived the Social and Religious Prosperity of Israel (107:39-43)
 A. The Sadness of Israel's Judgment (107:39-40)
 B. The Success of Israel's Judgment (107:41-43)

T HE CHIMES OF GOD'S great clock struck the hour in Heaven, and at once God set in motion the decree of Cyrus the Persian. Now free, the Babylonian captives could go home. Their exile was over, the prophecy of Jeremiah fulfilled, the prayer of Daniel answered.

The majority of Jews, many of them born in Babylon since the 70-year exile began, simply yawned in the face of God. Not for them the rigors of a four-month march across a pitiless desert. Not for them the hardships of pioneering in Palestine. They had made the world their home, satisfied with worldly prospects. So, like Demas in New Testament times, having chosen this present evil world, they stayed on in Babylon.

Of the exiled Jews only 42,360 returned, taking with them about 7,000 slaves, of whom some 200 were trained singers. There were 4,000 priests—but from only four of the 24 priestly "courses" into which their order had been divided since Davidic times. It says much about Jewish backsliding in Babylon that, of the whole tribe of Levi, only 74 Levites decided to return to the promised land.

The first contingent to return was led back by Zerubbabel, a prince of the house of David, the only person of royal blood to heed the mighty moving of the Spirit of God. Zerubbabel was accompanied by a priest named Joshua. It was not until 78 years later that Ezra the Scribe led back a second group.

The little band of pioneers, descending at last on the promised land, found it strewn with the debris of former wars. There was no temple; Jerusalem was a heap of rubble. The Edomites had seized much of the land, and the entire central portion of the country was in the hands of men of mixed blood known as Samaritans. It was a discouraging start.

But the hour had struck in the counsels of God. The time was one of fulfilled prophecy and of immense potential. The returned remnant, acutely aware of the sins of the nation that had brought about the captivity, determined to "put first things first." They began by building an altar for God and reinstituting the sacrifices. They began at the heart of things. They put *Calvary*, so to speak, into the center of the picture, since without a proper view of sin and redemption no nation can prosper.

Then they laid the foundation of the temple. That was in their second year, in 535 B.C. The foundation was laid amid the nation's mingled songs and sobs. The musical services instituted by David were restored. Shouts of joy rang out over Jerusalem's ruined walls and desolate streets, and the sobs of the old men added a note of pathos—the old men who remembered the glories of Solomon's temple, now gone forever.

Psalm 107 seems to be one of the psalms centering around these events. It is a psalm we can associate with the laying of the foundation of that temple into the courts of which one day the Messiah Himself would come.

This psalm begins the last of the five books of psalms, sometimes called "The Deuteronomy Book." Just as the last book of Moses is concerned with *the Law* and with *the land,* so are the psalms that make up this book. Psalms 107 through 119 were probably all sung in connection with the laying of the foundation of the new temple.

The stately stanzas of Psalm 107 are not concerned simply with the people gathered back from exile. The psalm has a strong prophetic strain. Behind the obvious allusions to the recent ingathering of exiles, we see the remote shadows of Israel being gathered again in the last days—regathered to be scattered no more. The psalm prefigures the return that has begun in our day, but is (like the return from Babylon) far from complete.

Since this is a long psalm we will simply highlight its main features. Since the psalm is national in character, we will pick up only a few of its verses for personal application.

The psalm divides into four parts. The second section is the major one, punctuated four times with the cry: "Oh that men would praise the LORD for His goodness, and for His wonderful works to the children of men." The angels in the realms of glory must look on in astonishment at the deadness and dullness of the human soul—and with even greater astonishment at the lack of praise of those who claim to have been redeemed by the precious blood of Heaven's Beloved.

I. HOW GOD REGATHERED THE SCATTERED AND REJECTED PEOPLE OF ISRAEL (107:1-3)

A. What the Lord Deserves (107:1)

"O give thanks unto the LORD, for He is good: for His mercy endureth for ever."

The Lord deserves our praise.

There is not much we can give to God. He does not need our money. He will use it if we give it to Him and will reward us in Heaven for our faithful stewardship, but He does not *need* money. He could create gold out of black sand if He wished. He does not need our service. He has countless angels far stronger, swifter, and superior to us. What He wants is our *praise* and our *thanks.* In other words, He wants our *worship.*

B. What the Lord Did (107:2-3)

It is what the Lord did that made Him worthy of thanks. "Let the redeemed of the LORD say so, whom He hath delivered from the hand [the Hebrew word is "clutch"] of the enemy; and gathered them out of the lands . . ."

The repatriated Jews, standing around the foundation of that new temple, were partakers in a miracle. The greatest world power on earth had deliberately opened its hand and let them go.

One wonders why. Probably we shall never really understand the events of that second exodus—the marvelous miracle of a nation reborn when all the laws of history were set in defiance of such a thing ever happening—unless we see standing in the shadows of Babylon, near the throne and close to the heart of

God, the towering figure of a man named Daniel. One suspects it was Daniel who drew Cyrus's attention to the ancient prophecy of Isaiah in which the conqueror was mentioned by name some 220 years before his time (Isaiah 44:28). One suspects it was Daniel who drew Cyrus's attention to the prophecy of Jeremiah about the length of the captivity.

But, whatever the reason, a miracle had transpired. The Persian bear, first seen in prophecy with three ribs in its mouth symbolizing the kingdoms it had destroyed, released its captives. God had come down and, like David of old, had taken the lamb out of the maw of the bear.

"Let the redeemed of the LORD say so, whom He hath delivered from the hand of the enemy." If that injunction was meant to stir up the souls of the Jews, gathered back from exile, how much more it should stir up our hearts to sing. "Let the redeemed of the LORD say so." We have so much for which to be eternally thankful. The Lord has delivered us from the clutches of an enemy greater and fiercer than any human foe. And we should never cease singing. "If the redeemed of the LORD" do not "say so," who will? Let us never allow the testings and troubles of life to rob us of the *joy* of our salvation and of a heart full of gratitude to God.

II. How God Regarded the Spiritual and Real Plight of Israel (107:4-32)

This is the major section of the psalm. It is punctuated by the fourfold repetition of that cry, "Oh that men would praise the LORD for His goodness, and for His wonderful works to the children of men!" Again and again the psalmist will remind us: we have a lot for which to be thankful. Because there are so many ungrateful people in the world, let us be sure that *we* remember to return thanks to God.

The psalmist looks back over Israel's years of exile. The nation had been uprooted and deported, its throne humbled in the dust, its temple committed to the flames, its youth slain or carried away in chains . . . but now nearly 50,000 people had come back to claim the land afresh in view of the coming of the Messiah. The psalmist describes the desolate years. Four pictures rise up before his mind's eye, which He then paints for us with a skillful hand.

A. Israel Was like a Person Lost in the Desert (107:4-9)

The psalmist describes Israel's *desperate condition*. He makes a *dismal confession*, he comes to a *dramatic conclusion*, and he ends with a *determined conviction:* "They wandered in the wilderness in a solitary way [a desert way, a trackless waste] . . . Hungry and thirsty, their soul fainted in them." Such is life when it is out of touch with God. "Then they cried . . . and He delivered . . ."

For three months I lived in Egypt in a large military transit camp on the Suez Canal. Along the canal there was an occasional palm tree, but little else—it was an eerie experience to see a ship sailing down the canal. We could see the ships from our camp, but we couldn't see the canal. It looked as though the ships were moving down the sand. Looking away from the canal in the other direction, the Sahara Desert rolled on toward the west. It was one vast rolling hill of sand after another. There were no paths, no tracks, no signposts, no shelter, no food, no water, no hope for anyone who wandered too far away. That is what the psalmist described—a place where there were *no signposts:* "they wandered in the wilderness"; where there were *no settlements:* "they found no city to dwell in"; and *no supplies:* "hungry and thirsty their soul fainted." That is what life is like out of the will of God.

Israel was like a person lost in the desert, but God had found them and led them back home. "Oh that men would praise the LORD . . . for His wonderful works to the children of men! For He satisfieth the longing soul, and filleth the hungry soul with goodness."

B. Israel Was like a Person Locked in a Dungeon (107:10-16)

We find here the same four characteristics: a desperate condition, a dismal confession, a dramatic conclusion, and a determined conviction.

The psalmist describes Israel's condition. They were a people "such as sit in darkness and in the shadow of death, being bound in affliction and iron; because they rebelled against the words of God . . . Then they cried . . . and He saved them . . . He brought them out of darkness and the shadow of death, and brake their bands in sunder."

God had judged the nation, having found it guilty of the most horrible crimes. The most dreadful sins had stalked the streets unashamed. So sentence had been passed, the prisoner led away, the iron gates slammed shut. Darkness had closed in, and dreary days had dragged by on leaden feet. The horror was always there.

Death haunted the shadows, but God had come and opened the prison doors: "Oh that men would praise the LORD for His goodness, and for His wonderful works to the children of men! For He hath broken the gates of brass, and cut the bars of iron in sunder." Thank God, who can open prison doors.

C. Israel Was like a Person Lying on a Deathbed (107:17-22)

Again we have that fourfold analysis: a desperate condition, a dismal confession, a dramatic conclusion, and a determined conviction.

"Fools [the perverse, those who depend on their own wisdom which is foolishness with God] because of their trangression, and because of their iniquities, are afflicted. Their soul abhorreth all manner of meat; and they draw near unto the gates of death . . . Then they cry unto the Lord . . . He saveth . . . He sent His Word, and healed them."

Sin had brought the nation to its deathbed. The economic physicians, the political and social and religious physicians, the liberal and conservative and scholastic physicians, all tried their hand at doctoring the patient (just as they are all trying their hand at doctoring the ills of the world today), but the nation's case grew steadily worse. Sin was at the root of the trouble, and none of those doctors could diagnose or prescribe for that.

The nation was brought near to extinction. Indeed, it had already been pronounced dead by the watching world powers. But then God stepped in with new life: "Oh that men would praise the LORD for His goodness, and for His wonderful works to the children of men! And let them sacrifice the sacrifices of thanksgiving, and declare His works with rejoicing." How was it done? He "sent His Word, and healed them." It was brought about by a spiritual awakening—one with messianic implications. Here we have a prophetic anticipation of the Lord Jesus, the living Word of God sent forth to heal human sicknesses and the soul's diseases.

The psalmist has one more illustration for those celebrating the revival of the nation.

D. Israel Was like a Person Lashed on the Deep (107:23-32)

For the fourth and final time the psalmist underlines that dreadful condition, dismal confession, dramatic conclusion, and determined conviction.

This time he sees a storm at sea. A cockleshell of a ship is tossed like a cork on mountainous waves. The seasoned sailors have ventured too far from land, the winds have arisen, and the navigation lights are lost. The little vessel is at the mercy of the raging deep, and all hope is lost.

"They that go down to the sea in ships, that do business in great waters; these see the works of the LORD, and His wonders in the deep. For He commandeth, and raiseth the stormy wind, which lifteth up the waves thereof. They mount up to the heaven, they go down again to the depths: their soul is melted because of trouble. They reel to and fro, and stagger like a drunken man, and are at their wits' end."

I was once on a ship which was thrown around like that in the Bay of Biscay. The waves were as high as the bridge and any step the passengers took was a peril. We staggered as if drunken, but our ship was like a Rock of Gibraltar compared with the flimsy boats that sailed the Great Sea in the psalmist's day.

He sees the nation in its peril. The Gentile seas had risen at God's command and had all but sunk Israel completely and forever. Again God had intervened, however: "He maketh the storm a calm . . . He bringeth them unto their desired haven. Oh that men would praise the LORD for His goodness, and for His wonderful works to the children of men! Let them exalt Him also in the congregation of the people, and praise Him in the assembly of the elders."

So for the fourth time the psalmist reminds Israel of the dreadful peril through which the nation had just passed, pointing to both its *cause* and its *cure*.

What does that have to say to us today? Let us make it personal.

A. Do we feel as if we are *lost in a spiritual desert?* This question is not addressed to unsaved people; it goes without saying that they are lost. It is addressed to the Lord's people. Do we find ourselves looking this way and that in our circumstances, without the slightest idea which is the right way to turn or what is the right step to take? Every step seems to be the wrong one. Then this psalm is for us.

B. Do we find ourselves *locked in a spiritual dungeon?* We feel circumstances have hemmed us in. We seem to be bound and chained and, like a prisoner in a death cell, we find ourselves driven to desperation? This psalm is for us.

C. Do we find ourselves *lying on a spiritual deathbed?* Our souls are sick unto death; we are knotted up inside and our situations seem hopeless. We find we have lost our appetites, life has lost its charm. Things we once enjoyed are a dead weight on our hearts. This psalm is for us.

D. Do we find ourselves *lashed on the spiritual deep?* We are overwhelmed because the circumstances through which we are passing are ominous and frightening. We are like a drunken person. We are at the mercy of our circumstances. We seem to stagger from one hopeless effort to another. This psalm is for us.

First, we must remember there is a *cause.* We must search our hearts, go back over our lives, allow the Spirit of God to show us why these things have happened. If sin and forgetfulness of God are at the bottom of the problem, we must confess that and get right with God.

Second, we must remember there is a *cure.* God has *not* abandoned us. He is going to work as great a miracle for us as He did for Israel. He will bring us right through our problems if we will let Him. We will yet praise Him for His goodness and wonderful works.

III. How God Restored the Scarred and Ruined Property of Israel (107:33-38)

We must come back to that little band of repatriated Jews standing around the foundation of the new temple in Jerusalem.

A. The Land Made Barren (107:33-34)

"He turneth rivers into a wilderness, and the watersprings into dry ground; a fruitful land into barrenness, for the wickedness of them that dwell therein."

All around them the Jews could see the harvest of hundreds of years of rebellion and apostasy. Ruined cities. Barren fields. Desolation. This was the land that once had flowed with milk and honey. This was God's "paid in full" for generation after generation of life in defiance of His Word. Israel had ignored His laws and replaced His truths with the religious follies of the pagans.

The psalmist did not have to turn far for illustrations. Everywhere the land was barren. Yet at that point his faith soars.

B. The Land Made Beautiful (107:35-38)

He foresees a great increase in *precipitation:* "He turneth the wilderness into a standing water, and dry ground into watersprings." He foresees a great increase in *population:* "And there He maketh the hungry to dwell, that they may prepare a city for habitation." He foresees a great increase both in crops and in cattle, in *productivity:* "And sow the fields, and plant vineyards, which may yield fruits of increase."

In other words, all the signs of God's displeasure simply vanish away. The scarred and ruined property of Israel is restored.

God transforms barrenness into beauty, sobs into songs. When He has accomplished His purpose in the difficulties of our lives, overnight He can restore all to beauty.

IV. How God Revived the Social and Religious Prosperity of Israel (107:39-43)

A. The Sadness of Israel's Judgment (107:39-40)

That this people, God's people, had to be so dreadfully scourged and scattered before they would listen to Him is inexpressibly sad. The psalmist tells how God diminished and brought the people low, pouring contempt on their princes—those haughty princes of Judah who thought they could do as they pleased.

In closing, however, the psalmist mentions the Lord's restitution.

B. The Success of Israel's Judgment (107:41-43)

All turned out well: "Yet setteth He the poor on high from affliction, and maketh him families like a flock. The righteous shall see it, and rejoice: and all iniquity shall stop her mouth."

The singer beamed on the little flock gathered back from the wilderness of the world. "Whoso is wise, and will observe these things, even they shall understand the lovingkindness of the LORD," he said. God is too wise to make mistakes, too loving to be unkind, too powerful to be thwarted in His ultimate purposes for His own. We can take heart in that.

No matter what we are facing in our lives, let us remember that God is working out a plan, a plan dictated by His lovingkindness and His power.

> How good is the God we adore,
>   Our faithful, unchangeable friend—
> Whose love is as great as His power
>   And knows neither measure nor end!

Psalm 108

TELL ME THE OLD, OLD STORY

I. MUSIC (108:1-3)
   A. The Inspiration of Praise (108:1)
   B. The Instruments of Praise (108:2a)
   C. The Insistence of Praise (108:2b)
   D. The Infectiousness of Praise (108:3)
II. MAJESTY (108:4-6)
   God is:
   A. Majestic in His Government (108:4)
   B. Majestic in His Glory (108:5)
   C. Majestic in His Grace (108:6)
III. MIGHT (108:7-11)
   A. The Basic Facts (108:7-8)
      1. "These are My plans"
        I will . . . I will . . .
      2. "These are My people"
        Mine . . . Mine . . .
      3. "These are My prerogatives"
        Ephraim is . . . Judah is . . .
   B. The Beaten Foes (108:9)
   C. The Beloved Friend (108:10-11)
      1. An Impossible Task (108:10)
      2. An Important Truth (108:11)
IV. MERCY (108:12-13)
   A. A Realistic Assessment (108:12)
   B. A Real Assurance (108:13)

IF YOU HAVE READ thoughtfully through the psalms you will say to yourself when you come to Psalm 108, "I've read all this before." And so you have. The first five verses are taken right out of the last half of Psalm 57, and the last eight verses are taken right out of the last half of Psalm 60. In other words, this is a composite psalm. Two of David's psalms have been commandeered, rearranged, and put down as a new psalm with one or two minor changes.

Why would the Spirit of God lead someone to do that? As Spurgeon once said, "The Holy Spirit is not so short of expressions that He needs to repeat Himself." But we know that the Spirit of God often repeats Himself, and so did Jesus. In Gethsemane the Lord Jesus prayed three times "using the same words." Paul repeated himself. He said to the Philippians, "To write the same things to you, to me indeed is not grievous, but for you it is safe" (Philippians 3). To the Galatians he said, "As we said before, so say I now again" (Galatians 1:9).

Repetition is a sound pedagogical principle. All of the book of Mark except for 55 verses is found in Matthew. Some of us can remember the old-fashioned way of teaching by rote. It was dull, but effective. The whole class would intone the multiplication tables, repeating them out loud in unison day after day: "Twice nine is eighteen; three times nine is twenty-seven; four times nine is thirty-six . . ."

But truth is varied even when it is the same. We have all used a kaleidoscope, an instrument containing loose bits of colored glass between two flat plates and with two plane mirrors so placed that changes of position of the bits of glass are reflected in an endless variety of patterns. With one eye shut, the viewer squints into the kaleidoscope and admires the delightful geometric figure inside. When the rotating head of the kaleidoscope is turned slightly, the same pieces rearrange themselves completely.

That is a metaphor of what the Holy Spirit does here. He takes pieces from two of the psalms and arranges them in a different way, not because He has run out of ideas, but because He wants to bring particular truths before us in a fresh way for a second time.

It is generally thought that Psalm 108 was written after the Babylonian captivity. Some unknown scribe, acting under the inspiration of the Spirit of God, took portions from two of David's earlier compositions and put them together as we have them here, as a new choir piece for the chief musician. The historical situation in David's day and the situation at the time this new psalm was compiled were quite different. Centuries had come and gone, the monarchy had been swept away, the greater part of the tribes had been scattered only to vanish among the nations of the earth. Only a tiny remnant now held the land for the Messiah, and even that remnant was subject to the control of foreign powers. Yet the old words of David are picked up to express the hopes, fears, joys, and sorrows of a new age, a new generation, a new time of need. David's words were still up to date then, and they still are today.

The unknown compiler picked up the *triumphant* parts of

Psalms 57 and 60 to give us this new one, so essentially it is a victory psalm. There may be difficulties, disappointments, and duress, but with God we cannot fail to have victory.

The psalm revolves around four words: *music, majesty, might,* and *mercy.* It shows the end of God's ways with men. That is perhaps one reason why the ends of the two earlier psalms are cut off from the trials and troubles with which they were originally associated and are put together in a new form. The end of God's ways with men is always one of triumph for God and for those who put their trust in Him.

I. MUSIC (108:1-3)

A redeemed people should be a rejoicing people. The first song in Scripture brings that out. We read in Exodus 14:30 and 15:1, "Thus the LORD saved Israel . . . then sang Moses." By Moses' day, there were no songs in Egypt, only sobs and sighs. Similarly, there had been no songs in Babylon. The Jews there had hung their harps on the weeping willow trees and refused to sing the songs of Zion to their pagan captors. But a redeemed people should be a rejoicing people.

A. The Inspiration of Praise (108:1)

"O God," cries the psalmist, "my heart is fixed; I will sing and give praise, even with my glory." As long as we are looking at our own hearts, our fears and frustrations, our follies and failings, we will not be able to sing. As long as we are looking at our circumstances, we tend to be gloomy instead of glad. Let us get our eyes fixed on the Lord, and then we will be able to sing. That is the inspiration of praise—a sense of the greatness, glory, and grace of our Lord.

Consider the experience of William Cowper, one of the great hymn-writers of the Church, the man who wrote:

> God moves in a mysterious way
> His wonders to perform,
> He plants His footsteps in the sea
> And rides upon the storm.

Cowper wrote 64 hymns, many of which have passed into the musical literature of the Church, a priceless treasure.

Yet Cowper himself was for many years a lunatic, locked up in a private asylum. One day, however, this frail, frightened man got his eyes fixed on the Lord. And when he did, his horrors were changed into hymns. He wrote:

> Ye saints of God, fresh courage take,
> Those clouds ye so much dread

> Are big with mercy and will break,
> In blessings on your head.

One of Cowper's biographers tells us how Huntingdon, where the unhappy man lived, "seemed a paradise" after his conversion. From that day his soul was filled with song.

B. The Instruments of Praise (108:2a)

"Awake, psaltery and harp." If we had been living in those days we would have played the harp rather than the piano, and we would have plucked a psaltery instead of a guitar. If we were going to translate culturally from those ancient times to the times in which we live, we would say, "Awake, piano and organ!" "Pull out all those stops. Pound on those pedals. Make those fingers fly."

The ability to take a man-made instrument and make it ring out to the glory of God is a tremendous thing. Many times I have been held almost spellbound by a well-executed musical accompaniment to our hymns. I thank God for it and feel sorry for those who think it sinful to use instruments to accompany the songs of the Church.

C. The Insistence of Praise (108:2b)

"I myself will awake early." An old spiritual says, "My soul is so happy that I can't lay down!" That was how the psalmist felt. He bounded from his bed with a song on his lips. The Hebrew original is graphic. It reads, "Let me awake the dawn." The story is told of a barnyard rooster who assured the admiring hens that the sun got up every morning just to hear him crow.

This psalmist's soul was so filled with song that he wanted to get up, wake the dawn, and wake everyone else too.

Some time ago my wife dreamed she was dying. Her dream was so vivid she thought for a few moments that Heaven was opening up before her and angels were escorting her into the presence of the Saviour. In that mysterious, in-between state between the experience of a vivid dream and the actual moment of awakening, there often occurs a second or so of confusion. The haunting memories of the dream still linger and are as real as life itself, but already the soul is back to everyday realities. In that in-between state, coming back from her vivid dream of going to Heaven, my wife actually woke herself up singing. The lyrics she was singing were a mixture of the ridiculous and the sublime!

> Hey, ho, demario!
> I'm going to see the Lord.

Something like that happened to this psalmist. Even when asleep, his joy in the Lord was so real he couldn't wait to wake up. He wanted to wake up the dawn with his song. In him we see the insistence of praise.

D. The Infectiousness of Praise (108:3)

"I will praise Thee, O LORD, among the people: and I will sing praises unto Thee among the nations." The psalmist wanted to give the whole world a song. That is what is so great about a *happy* believer. He or she infuses a spirit of praise and worship into other people. The praising person is the prevailing person. Such individuals are irrepressible; there is something wonderfully attractive about them and their faith.

II. MAJESTY (108:4-6)

The psalmist's thoughts turn instinctively to the wonderful God upon whom his heart is fixed and who has so filled his soul with song.

He thrills to the fact that our God is:

A. Majestic in His Government (108:4)

"For Thy mercy is great above the heavens: and Thy truth reacheth unto the clouds." Mercy and truth are the cornerstones of God's government. Not just mercy. Not just truth. If God's government were marked by mercy, but not by truth, it would be insipid. If it were marked by truth, but not by mercy, it would be insensitive. So, thank God! "Grace *and* truth came by Jesus Christ." In Him, both are blended in perfection. He knows the worst about us and loves us nonetheless.

The psalmist catches a glimpse of the vastness of God's government. It reaches beyond the heavens, beyond the clouds. He sees the stars marching through space in obedience to the laws of God. He sees a God who is able to take countless stars and their satellites, toss them into prodigious orbits, and keep them whirling and plunging at inconceivable velocities throughout space, with such mathematical precision that we can tell the occasion of an eclipse or the visit of a comet years in advance. Not a speck of dust moves throughout the reach of space but that He knows precisely where it is, why it is there, and what its history has been since the dawn of time. Such a God can be trusted with our lives.

God is also:

B. Majestic in His Glory (108:5)

"Be Thou exalted, O God, above the heavens: and Thy glory above all the earth." One translator renders that, "Up, O God, high over heaven. Up with Thy glory over all the earth."

In ancient Rome when a gladiator in the arena vanquished a foe he looked up at the tiered seats of spectators for a verdict. Should the man be slain or spared? More often than not, the answer was given in an expressive and insistent downward turning of the thumb. "Down with him!" they shouted.

That is what men did when God in Christ veiled His glory and stepped out of eternity into time, wrapped in the flesh of a human being. He went about doing good, placing his hands on the heads of children, touching a loathsome leper, flooding blinded eyes with light. But, in the end, men turned their thumbs down. "Away with this fellow from the earth!" they cried. "Down with Him!"

But men did not have the last word. God said, "Up with Him." "Up, O God, high above the heavens. Up with Thy glory over all the earth." That is what God has done with His glory and what He intends to do with it. Moreover, He wants to exalt His glory here and now in our hearts and circumstances. Then He wants to make His glory ring out eternally in our lives on high.

God is also:

C. Majestic in His Grace (108:6)

"That Thy beloved may be delivered: save with Thy right hand, and answer me." Who is His beloved? Why, *we* are, of course. Since God is God, no power in heaven, earth, or hell can prevent Him from delivering His beloved from whatever troubles him or her—in His own perfect time and way. He is majestic in His grace. He will save with His right hand, the hand of power.

III. Might (108:7-11)

The psalmist continues to develop his theme. Music leads to a consideration of God's majesty and that in turn leads to a consideration of His might. Now let us take these verses that point to Israel's *military past* and to Israel's *millennial future* in order to see if we cannot get something for our own souls out of them.

A. The Basic Facts (108:7-8)

"God hath spoken in His holiness; I will rejoice, I will divide Shechem, and mete out the valley of Succoth. Gilead is Mine; Manasseh is Mine; Ephraim also *is* the strength of Mine head; Judah is My lawgiver."

1. God says, "I will." He says, "These are My *plans*." No power exists that can prevent God from accomplishing His plans.

2. Then God says, "Mine. Mine." He says, "These are My *people*." No power exists that can rob God of His people.

3. God says, "Ephraim is . . . Judah is." He says, "These are My *prerogatives*." No power can say, "No, they are not."

Let us get these basic facts fixed in our minds. Nothing can hinder God from doing what He intends with His *plans*, His *people*, and His *prerogatives*. Consider the first of the three: "I will divide Shechem, and mete out the valley of Succoth."

Both these places figure in the life of Jacob, one after the other. It was at Succoth that Jacob built shelters for his cattle and a house for himself. That was right after his meeting with Esau, a traumatic experience filled with potential for great danger, but one that ended well. It left Jacob emotionally exhausted, however. It had come after years of rootlessness and restlessness, years filled with bickering with his Uncle Laban. With his nerves stretched to the breaking point, Jacob craved only peace and quiet. So he built a house at Succoth. He decided to settle down, give up his pilgrim character, stop being forever on the march. He decided to carve out a small but permanent niche for himself in Canaan and have a home like everyone else.

That was a mistake, since Jacob was settling down out of the will of God. True, God wanted him to settle down—but at Bethel, not at Succoth. Succoth, therefore, represents those times and places in life that tempt us to settle for something less than God's best.

As a rule, the results are disastrous. They were for Jacob. Succoth was followed by Shechem. The piece of property Jacob purchased on which to build his house was sold to him by people from Shechem. Not long after that, Jacob's daughter met a young man from Shechem who got her into serious trouble. She came home pregnant, and although the young man was willing to marry her, the fact remained that he was not a believer. To make matters worse, her brothers took the law into their own hands and aggravated the situation by their vindictive attack on the young man and his family. Poor old Jacob put his head in his hands and wept in despair.

Most of us have found ourselves at "Succoth" and at "Shechem." Somewhere along the line we have settled for something that, while not sinful in itself, is still less than God's best for us. Many of us have lived to reap the fruit of that in our lives and in the lives of those around us.

But notice this. God says, "I will divide Shechem, and mete out the valley of Succoth." In other words, God says, "*These are My plans*—I will give you in My own good, acceptable, and perfect will just what you want. I will give you the *tranquility* you sought at Succoth without the *trouble* you found at Shechem." Those are God's plans. Let us enter into the good of them, only let us make sure we do it at His time and in His way.

B. The Beaten Foes (108:9)

"Moab is My washpot; over Edom will I cast out My shoe; over Philistia will I triumph." There they are: three ancient enemies of Israel. *Moab* was an accursed race, descended from the oldest son of Lot, conceived in a night of drunkenness and incest, the fruit of the flesh, ever seeking ways to hinder and harm the child of God. *Edom* was the unblessed and powerful foe of Israel, conspicuous because it produced at last a Herod to try to murder the infant Christ. *Philistia* was the non-Semitic, Gentile race entrenched in the promised land and always at war with Israel—strong and powerful, able to blind Samson and lay him in the dust, but powerless before David.

As Israel had three powerful enemies, so do we. Israel had the Philistine along with Moab, and Edom; we have the world, the flesh, and the devil, their spiritual counterparts. As Israel's foes were beaten foes, so are ours. What is it that opposes us right now in our hearts, homes, and hopes? Is it the world? The flesh? Satan? Remember, our foes are *beaten foes.*

C. The Beloved Friend (108:10-11)

"Who will bring me into the strong city? Who will lead me into Edom? Wilt not Thou, O God, who hast cast us off? And wilt not Thou, O God, go forth with our hosts?"

1. The psalmist was contemplating here an *Impossible Task* (108:10). The strong city was Edom, with its impregnable rocky fortress of Petra. Petra was protected by an almost impassable approach down a precipitous, narrow gorge. It was hewn out of the beetling (or overhanging) sandstone crags of the mountainside. To subdue that city seemed impossible. The strength of the Edomite city was a byword among men.

It may be that right now some readers are facing a seemingly impossible task. If so, claim this psalm. We simply cannot handle some situations in life. The enemy is too strong, he is already too deeply entrenched, and we have no idea how to get him out.

2. Well, look! This impossible task is balanced by an *Important Truth:* "Who will bring me into the strong city? . . . Wilt not Thou, O God? . . . Wilt not Thou go forth with our hosts?" (108:11). God is still our Beloved Friend. He is *Elohim,* the God of creation. A God who can fling stars into space is certainly able to take a strong city, no matter who holds it in defiance of Him.

Look then at the facts. God's *plans* cannot be *defeated;* God's

people cannot be *divorced;* God's *prerogatives* cannot be *denied.*
Look at the beaten foes. Look at the Beloved Friend. Then
sing.

IV. MERCY (108:12-13)

"Wilt not Thou, O God?" the psalmist pleads. Notice how he
closes the psalm. He rests in the quenchless mercy of God who
takes care of us in spite of our failures and faults.

A. A Realistic Assessment (108:12)

"Give us help from trouble: for vain is the help of man." It is
part of the genius of this psalm that not only do we not know
who wrote or compiled it, but we do not know with certainty
when it was compiled. Nor do we know what special trouble in
the psalmist's life prompted him to put it together. Those troubles may have been national, domestic, or personal. They are
anonymous troubles.

So we can bring *our* troubles along and fit them right into this
psalm. No matter what they are, we can fit them in if we will.
The stanza lies open ready to receive them: "Give us help from
trouble."

"Vain is the help of man." Have we come to that point in life
yet? Have we come up against something we cannot handle, and
nobody else can handle either? Jacob's predicament at Succoth
and Shechem was like that. He was in trouble way over his
head. Friends can sympathize and pray, they can lend support
and understanding, they can offer counsel and love, but, when
all is said and done, the problem remains.

B. A Real Assurance (108:13)

"Through God we shall do valiantly: for He it is that shall
tread down our enemies." *We. He.* Both of us, working together.
Not just *me,* not just *He,* but both of us. God is going to join you
in a holy partnership and bring you through to complete victory. Hopeless extremity is His opportunity.

"There," says the compiler, "send that to the chief musician."
That is certainly something to sing about.

These lines, also by William Cowper, reflecting his assurance
in God's faithfulness, sum up this psalm:

> Deep in unfathomable mines
>   Of never-failing skill
> He treasures up His bright designs
>   And works His sovereign will.
>
> Judge not the Lord by feeble sense,
>   But trust Him for His grace,
> Behind a frowning providence
>   He hides a smiling face.

Psalm 109

LET HIM BE ACCURSED

I. DAVID'S FAITH EXERCISED (109:1-5)
   A. The Divine Attention He Sought (109:1)
   B. The Deadly Attack He Fought (109:2-3)
   C. The Devout Attitude He Taught (109:4-5)
II. DAVID'S FOES EXPOSED (109:6-19)
   A. An Appalling Curse (109:6-15)
      That David might be the victim of:
      1. Spiritual Infamy (109:6)
      2. Social Injustice (109:7a)
      3. Startling Iniquity (109:7b)
      4. Serious Injury (109:8-9)
      5. Stifling Insolvency (109:10-11)
      6. Sordid Inhumanity (109:12)
      7. Sudden Infertility (109:13)
      8. Solemn Invective (109:14-15)
   B. An Appended Claim (109:16-19)
      David, supposedly, was:
      1. Addicted to Cruelty (109:16)
      2. Addicted to Cursing (109:17-19)
III. DAVID'S FEARS EXPRESSED (109:20-31)
   A. O Lord, Remember My Cursers (109:20)
   B. O Lord, Remember My Condition (109:21-25)
      1. Please Be Mindful of Your Mercy (109:21)
      2. Please Be Mindful of My Misery (109:22-25)
   C. O Lord, Remember My Cause (109:26-31)
      1. Let My Assurance Be Vindicated (109:26-27)
      2. Let My Assailants Be Vanquished (109:28-31)

THIS IS THE LAST and most vehement of the imprecatory psalms. It breathes a spirit of vengeance without equal in the Word of God. It calls down the direst curses on the head of an offending individual and does so with passion, persistence, and pointedness. This psalm has caused Christians a

179

great deal of difficulty. All kinds of suggestions have been made for toning down the vindictiveness displayed.

We are reminded by some interpreters that, in the Old Testament, law and not grace prevailed, and that therefore the Old Testament era was plainly inferior to the New Testament era. We are invited by others to render some of the verbs in the future tense, so that we might regard the curses as prophetic of the certain doom of all wicked people. It is suggested that the psalm is not personal, but national, and is quite in keeping with Israel's position. After all, didn't God promise to curse those who cursed Abraham and his seed? The sentence of the law was, "As he hath done, so shall it be done to him" (Leviticus 24:19). "Let me see Thy vengeance on them" is the kind of prayer the persecuted prophet Jeremiah could pray (Jeremiah 11:20). The wise man of Israel could write: "Whoso rewardeth evil for good, evil shall not depart from his house" (Proverbs 17:13).

We are reminded too that the Old Testament does not differentiate between the sinner and his sin as does the New Testament. To include a man's family in his judgment was part of the Decalog and was based on the fact that the Mosaic Law viewed the family as the basic unit of society. We are told that the psalmist cursed like this because he did not know that God had appointed a day in which He would judge the world, and therefore the Old Testament saints expected retribution in this life for any wrongdoing.

Others have seen the passage as entirely prophetic. It has been assigned to Judas, and with some justification, because Peter quotes from it in the upper room after the suicide of that traitor. The psalm may logically be assigned to the Jewish people, who might with every justification thus curse their enemies during the great tribulation.

But having said that, the curses remain—vicious, vindictive, vehement. It is this that has driven some of our best commentators to a totally different conclusion. Rotherham produces half a dozen reasons for thinking that the curse itself (109:6-19) is not that of David at all (J. B. Rotherham, *Studies in the Psalms*, London: H. R. Allenson Ltd.). It is true, no doubt, that this is a psalm of David, as the title suggests. But David did not *curse* in this psalm. What he does is describe in detail the curses being heaped on him by his foes. With that view G. Campbell Morgan agrees. This is the view we are going to adopt here.

The psalm probably belongs to the period when David was forced to flee from Absalom. It is not likely that David would curse his beloved (though wicked) son, nor that Absalom, abandoned as he was, would curse his father.

But two other men might well have voiced the terrible imprecations found in the psalm. One was Shimei, who cursed David as he made his woeful way from Jerusalem. With his own bitter memories of Bathsheba and Uriah to haunt him, David allowed Shimei to curse to his heart's content. The other man who might have been the author of these curses was Ahithophel, David's favorite counselor and one-time best friend, the brains behind the Absalom conspiracy, and a man who stands out clearly in the Old Testament as one of the great types of Judas Iscariot.

The psalm divides into three parts.

I. DAVID'S FAITH EXERCISED (109:1-5)

David turns to God in the face of the dreadful things being said about him.

A. The Divine Attention He Sought (109:1)

"Hold not Thy peace, O God of my praise."

David was puzzled that God was holding His peace when a vehement attack was being made on His anointed. It caused him to urge God to speak out. But, desperate as his situation was, David had not lost his sense of balance. He could still call God the God of his praise or "the God whom I praise." It is marvelous to be able to praise God in the midst of life's adversities. David had learned a lesson not learned by many, even in our marvelous age of grace—he had learned to praise God no matter what.

B. The Deadly Attack He Fought (109:2-3)

"For the mouth of the wicked and the mouth of the deceitful are opened against me: they have spoken against me with a lying tongue. They compassed me about also with words of hatred; and fought against me without a cause."

The Hebrew word for "the wicked" denotes the rebellious and lawless. The lying propaganda of David's enemies was being spread throughout the land. The people had to be given plausible reasons for the palace coup which had driven the king from the throne. The twentieth century has brought lying propaganda to a fine art, but our age has no monopoly on such psychological warfare. Shimei, with his own personal vindictiveness, was no doubt a little more frenzied and foolhardy than most when he went out of his way to hurl his curses into David's face, but probably the whole country was inundated with false stories about David. Much of the propaganda undoubtedly stemmed from the fertile but soured mind of Ahithophel.

C. The Devout Attitude He Taught (109:4-5)

"For my love they are my adversaries: but I give myself unto prayer. And they have rewarded me evil for good, and hatred for my love." David could think back to the love he had personally shown the people who were now execrating his memory and name.

Nothing is worse than when someone we have loved, trusted, helped, and honored turns against us. We are reminded of Shakespeare's *Julius Caesar,* when Mark Antony told the crowds who attended the funeral of the murdered Caesar, pointing to the place where the well-beloved Brutus had stabbed him: "This was the most unkindest cut of all." To be stabbed in the back by a trusted friend is the harshest betrayal. So David thought.

In the face of terrible outward circumstance, then, David exercised faith.

II. DAVID'S FOES EXPOSED (109:6-19)

At this point in the psalm, there is a sudden and dramatic change from plural to singular. The singular form continues throughout this section (6-19) and at verse 20 changes back to the plural. All the way through we have "him," "he," "his," which adds force to the view that the curse now beginning is not really David's, but the curse of his enemies. The more we examine the curse the more likely such an interpretation seems. The passage breathes a spirit alien to David, who had a forgiving spirit. It is more likely that this is the language of David's foes rather than the language of one of God's choicest saints.

The long imprecation is in two parts.

A. An Appalling Curse (109:6-15)

The reviler seems to have left nothing about David uncovered and uncontaminated. He spews volcanic ash from the burning cauldrons of his seething and erupting soul. He hurls dire curses on God's chosen king.

1. Spiritual Infamy (109:6)

The reviler hoped that David would fall under the power of an evil man and that Satan himself would have access to him: "Set thou a wicked man over him: and let Satan stand at his right hand." The margins of some Bibles change the word *Satan* to "adversary," but how better for a malignant man to begin than by wishing that the adversary himself, Satan in person, might be permitted to take his place at David's right hand? Imagine the dreadful state of a man forced to live in constant company with the prince of darkness, to have Satan seeking his destruction at every step, always at hand to whisper dreadful things into his ear, personally opposing every spiritual aspiration, every attempt to please God.

Satan is our adversary. Think of him paying constant attention to a single person, setting aside all his other nefarious affairs to torment one lonely individual. Think, too, of this person not only in constant battle with Satan, but also enslaved by a wicked man, one of Satan's human agents on this sin-cursed planet. What could be worse than this opening statement, a baleful wish for the spiritual infamy of David? With all his faults and failings, sins and shortcomings, David was nevertheless one of God's beloved.

2. Social Injustice (109:7a)

The reviler prayed: "When he shall be judged, let him be condemned." David was a just man. He had done his best to see that all people in his realm were treated equably. David had sought out Mephibosheth, the grandson of Saul, and, instead of having him executed lest he become a threat to the throne, brought him to Jerusalem to show him "the kindness of God." David's tender conscience led him to break off his vendetta against the malicious Nabal at the urgent pleading of Abigail. It was David who, when told that story of injustice by Nathan, swore that the rich man who stole the poor man's lamb should pay back fourfold and, moreover, forfeit his life, and it was David who just as quickly acknowledged his guilt in bitter tears when the point of the parable was made plain.

This bitter reviler hoped that David would become the victim of social injustice. The only man in all Israel who might have had grounds for such a curse was Ahithophel, once David's friend, now Absalom's most astute adviser—and the outraged grandfather of Bathsheba.

The curse continues.

3. Startling Iniquity (109:7b)

"And let his prayer become sin," he said. It is usual to minimize this part of the curse. Some commentators dilute it to the position of a man vainly pleading for clemency before a human judge. But the word used for prayer here is never used of requests made to human beings. On the contrary, this invective voices the hope that when David appeals to God for redress, God will not only refuse to listen to the petition, not only refuse to help the petitioner, but will actually count the prayer itself as an additional aggravation of his sin.

What could be a worse state of soul than to find that one's prayers to God have actually become sin? Such was this malig-

nant man's wish for David. And similar statements were being
coined and passed for verbal currency in Israel to slander David
and justify the takeover of his throne.

4. Serious Injury (109:8-9)

The reviler hoped to see David *broken:* "Let his days be few
. . ." That is, let his life come to a premature end. That was
exactly what Absalom was planning for his father and what
Ahithophel was advising. This sinister man was urging quicker
action than even Absalom was ready for. All the forces of the
new administration were being harnessed to bring a swift end to
David's life.

The reviler hoped also to see David *beggared:* "And let another take his office." With the Absalom rebellion in full force,
this curse was already an accomplished fact. But, as long as
David was alive and surrounded by his personal bodyguard—
those "mighty men," headed by tough old Joab—there was still
a chance David might make a comeback.

The prayer that David might be forever beggared, bereft of
his office, was a hopeless curse, of course. The holy anointing oil
had been poured on David's head, and no Shimei or Ahithophel
or even Absalom was going to change that. (Peter later applied
this part of the curse to Judas.)

Then, too, the reviler hoped to see David *buried:* "Let his
children be fatherless, and his wife a widow." He wanted the
curse to fall not only on David, but also on his family. Back in
Jerusalem, Ahithophel had not gone so far as to advise Absalom
to make a clean sweep of all of David's wives and children. The
rebellion, although strong, was not yet strong enough for that,
but he did advise Absalom to "pollute" all of David's concubines.

Ahithophel wanted two things: revenge for the murder of
Uriah, which is why he advised immediate action to insure
David's death, and revenge for the seduction of Bathsheba,
which is why he urged Absalom to seduce David's concubines.
Doubtless, what he really wanted was the wholesale massacre of
all of David's dependents, and, had the rebellion succeeded,
doubtless he would have advised that course to Absalom as the
only safe policy.

No matter how we look at it, it is a frightful curse—to wish ill
on a man's wife and children. What a revelation of the depths of
Satan in a human soul.

5. Stifling Insolvency (109:10-11)

The reviler said: "Let his children be continually vagabonds,
and beg: let them seek their bread also out of their desolate

places. Let the extortioner catch all that he hath; and let the strangers spoil his labor." He wanted to see David's family destitute and his fortune devoured. The word *catch* is graphic, suggesting the crafty schemes of an unscrupulous creditor who is plotting to get hold of someone's property.

It is bad enough when an unsuspecting person falls into the hands of a financial scoundrel. How much worse to pray that such a thing will happen, to watch eagerly for it to happen, to rub one's hands with glee at the sight of a man's widow and children being driven out into the street.

6. Sordid Inhumanity (109:12)

"Let there be none to extend mercy unto him: neither let there be any to favor his fatherless children." Such are the depths of wickedness of which a human heart is capable: to call down a curse on orphans. If this curse was authored by Ahithophel it is no wonder he went out and hanged himself when he discovered that he had lost credit at court and that David's ultimate triumph was assured.

The most pitiable sight on earth is the sight of a destitute orphan. To curse an orphan betrays a heart and exposes a soul set on fire by hell.

So, it is not David's soul that is exposed by this curse. It is the soul of an enemy in the retinue of Absalom. That Absalom could countenance such a man in his court speaks volumes about his own spiritual condition. Certainly Absalom never sat at David's feet and learned, even in the years he was David's friend, to sing the great psalms of David's early years when, in every sense of the word, David was "a man after God's own heart."

7. Sudden Infertility (109:13)

The reviler said: "Let his posterity be cut off; and in the generation following let their name be blotted out." He wanted to see the extinction of all of David's house by invoking a curse of the Mosaic Law. In that Law, God had warned He would visit the iniquities of the fathers on the children to the third and fourth generation of those who hated Him. The Hebrew, with his strong sense of the family unit, expected to live on in his descendants. To have his genealogy blotted out was the most terrible calamity that could happen to anyone. To pray for such a thing to happen was, in the thinking of a Hebrew, to invoke a curse of fearful magnitude.

All the way through the Old Testament we have a sense of family continuity. It shows up again and again in the long lists of names, meaningless to Westerners but full of significance to the devout Hebrew. To be able to trace one's ancestry back to the tribal head, to Judah or Levi or Ephraim; then back to Abraham and to Noah and through him to Adam—what a sense of continuing history. Then to be the man after whom that long and glorious line was brought to a sudden stop—that was the height of tragedy. Not to have a descendant on the earth in the days of the Messiah. To be cut off. To wish such a tragedy on a man was unspeakably cruel.

8. Solemn Invective (109:14-15)

The reviler prayed for two terrible things.

a. That his family might be accursed in the land (109:14)

He called down a *perpetual blight on David's pedigree:* "Let the iniquity of his fathers be remembered." Think of that. He wanted to go back and rake up the past, dredge up the sins of David's forebears and have them perpetually remembered. Is there any bottom to the depths of degradation in this man's soul? Not content with an all-round curse on David, he wanted to go back through David's family tree and curse Jesse and Boaz and all the others in his long and honored line.

He then called down a *perpetual blot on David's parent:* "And let not the sin of his mother be blotted out." We do not know who David's mother was. We know he cared for her, because when Saul's spite against him was reaching its crescendo, David had escorted both his father and mother to Moab to be out of harm's way. It must have hurt David deeply to hear that this enemy was calling down such an invective on his mother. But worse was yet to come.

b. That his family might be accursed by the Lord (109:15)

"Let them be before the Lord continually, that He may cut off the memory of them from the earth." The reviler wanted David's family not only to be extinguished on the earth, he wanted the memory of that family to be forever obliterated. He invoked the Lord to that effect. He began his curse by calling on Satan; he ended it by calling on the Lord.

There is nothing like this appalling curse elsewhere in the Bible, not even the dreadful curses of the Mosaic Law. They are national, this is personal; they are in the nature of divine retribution for apostasy, this is sheer malice and spite.

But the curser is not yet through.

B. An Appended Claim (109:16-19)

He gives two reasons for calling down this curse. Both are false. He says that David was:

1. Addicted to Cruelty (109:16)

"Because that he remembered not to show mercy, but persecuted the poor and needy man, that he might even slay the broken in heart." Except in the matter of Uriah, no more merciful man than David ever lived in those rough-and-tumble Old Testament times. Even after the horrendous crimes of Absalom, David was willing to forgive. He was willing to forgive foul-mouthed Shimei.

But propaganda cares little for truth. The theory behind today's massive communist propaganda offensive against the free world is the theory of the Big Lie: Tell a lie big enough and often enough and people will believe it. This ancient propagandist accused David of having pity neither for the destitute nor for the despairing.

He says not only that David was addicted to cruelty, he says that David was:

2. Addicted to Cursing (109:17-19)

"As he loved cursing, so let it come unto him: as he delighted not in blessing, so let it be far from him. As he clothed himself in cursing like as with his garment, so let it come into his bowels like water. . . ." He claimed that cursing was the habit of David's mind, that he cursed as naturally as he put on his clothes. Therefore let it cling to him. Thus ends this terrible litany.

The psalm now returns to David, who is still a fugitive from Absalom.

III. DAVID'S FEARS EXPRESSED (109:20-31)

David now offers a threefold prayer in the light of this fearful malediction which he has recorded. It is natural that he should begin by seeking justice from the Lord for what was said.

A. O Lord, Remember My Cursers (109:20)

"Let this be the reward of mine adversaries from the LORD, and of them that speak evil against my soul." David does not have the Christian spirit. How could he, living a thousand years before the Christian era? But he is careful in what he says. He doesn't answer curse with curse. Rather, he refers the whole matter to the Lord.

When Moses was maligned, his habit was to fall on his face before the Lord, leaving his accusers face to face with God. David did the same. He simply tells the Lord that this is a case for the exercise of His justice.

B. O Lord, Remember My Condition (109:21-25)

David asks the Lord to keep two things in mind.

1. Please Be Mindful of Your Mercy (109:21)

"But do Thou for me, O GOD the Lord, for Thy name's sake: because Thy mercy is good, deliver Thou me." David appeals to God by two of His names: Jehovah, the God of Promise; and Adonai (Sovereign Lord), the God of Power. He appeals to Him on the grounds that He is both *willing* and *able* to save him.

2. Please Be Mindful of My Misery (109:22-25)

David reminds the Lord of his *sorrow*, his *sickness*, and his *scorners*. "For I am poor and needy, and my heart is wounded within me." The rebellion of Absalom broke David's heart. We have only to listen to the cry of desolation that burst from David's soul when he heard the news that Absalom was dead. Was there ever such a cry of anguish?

In this psalm, David says, "I am gone like the shadow when it declineth: I am tossed up and down as the locust. My knees are weak through fasting; and my flesh faileth of fatness." We know from several of the psalms that, after his sin with Bathsheba, David was afflicted with a dreadful sickness. He says here he totally lost his appetite. Thus it was a frail and feeble David who headed for the hills with his life in peril.

"I became also a reproach unto them: when they looked upon me they shaked their heads," David says. Even those who might still have been loyal to him in heart looked on this tottering old man in astonishment. This was not the David they had known. That David could fight giants. One can imagine with what malicious delight a man like Shimei would look on the weakened king. So David prays, "Lord, remember my condition."

C. O Lord, Remember My Cause (109:26-31)

David is by no means through. He is still the king, still the Lord's anointed. And God has already assured him that He has put away his sin.

1. Let My Assurance Be Vindicated (109:26-27)

"Help me, O LORD my God: O save me according to Thy mercy: that they may know that this is Thy hand; that Thou, LORD, hast done it." The situation in the early days of the Absalom rebellion was desperate. "The conspiracy was strong," the historian says. Absalom had the bulk of the nation with him, the armed forces (except for David's old guard), and the cleverest man in the kingdom as his counselor.

Victory therefore for David would have to come from God, and David set all his hope in God. He looked to God to vindicate his assurance.

2. Let My Assailants Be Vanquished (109:28-31)

David wants his assailants vanquished for two reasons: First, in order to have *the proof he desires.* "Let them curse, but bless Thou: when they arise, let them be ashamed; but let Thy servant rejoice. Let mine adversaries be clothed with shame . . ." And so they were. We can still see Shimei cowering before David as he returned at last in triumph to Jerusalem. We can still see the monument built to Absalom at which every wayfarer threw a stone in contempt.

David wanted this victory, not so much that he might triumph over his foes, but that his faith might be vindicated, that he might have this additional proof that the Lord his God was a God to be trusted at all times—even in the most desperate times.

David wanted the assailants vanquished for a second reason: that the Lord might have *the praise He deserved.* "I will greatly praise the LORD with my mouth; yea, I will praise Him among the multitude. For He shall stand at the right hand of the poor, to save him from those that condemn his soul." The curse began with the desire that Satan would stand at the right hand of David. David, who has just described himself as poor and needy, wants it to be evident to all that *God Himself* has been standing at his right hand.

Indeed, our God graciously takes His place at the right hand of all those who acknowledge their deep and desperate need of Him.

Psalm 110

THE MELCHIZEDEK PSALM

NO QUESTION ARISES about the authorship of this remarkable little psalm. It was written by David; Jesus said so. The Lord quoted this psalm to silence His critics, challenging them to explain how, since the Christ was to be David's *Son*, David, in the Spirit, could call Him *Lord*. Had there been any doubt about David's authorship or about the messianic interpretation of the psalm, we can be quite sure that the Pharisees, Herodians, Sadducees, and scribes would instantly have pounced on it.

We cannot be sure, however, when David wrote it. Some think it was at the time the kingdom was confirmed to him and his seed was assured the throne-rights of Israel until the coming of the Christ. Others think it was written when he took the ark up to Jerusalem. One thing is certain about that occasion. David laid aside his royal robes and donned a priestly garment. The historian tells us that "David danced before the Lord with all his might" and was "girded with a linen ephod" (2 Samuel 6:14).

A linen ephod was worn by Aaron, by the boy-prophet Samuel, and by David on that notable occasion. Evidently David felt that there was something of a priestly character about this particular service. A linen ephod—worn by a priest (Aaron), worn by a prophet (Samuel), and worn by a king (David)—anticipates the day when Jesus will combine all three offices in His own Person. The psalm is clearly messianic, quoted or referred to seven times in the New Testament and used with great significance on three occasions.

We find it quoted in Matthew 22:41-46 to *confound*. The political-religious spectrum of Hebrew unbelief had focused on Christ in order to trap Him into saying something incriminating. The Herodians tried to catch Him with a loaded political question, the Sadducees with a thorny religious question, and the Pharisees with a difficult moral question. He turned the tables on them, however, by asking a question based on the opening verse of Psalm 110, quoting it to confound, to silence those who were trying to trap Him in His speaking.

We find it quoted in Acts 2:34-35 to *convict*. At the end of his lengthy Pentecostal sermon, Peter drove home the damning charge (that the Jews had murdered their Messiah) by quoting from Psalm 110. The Holy Spirit used the quotation and its application to bring about conviction of sin and immediate repentance in the lives of many of those present.

We find it quoted in Hebrews 1:13 to *confirm*. The author of this epistle has made the point that Christ is far superior to the angels, and to clinch the argument he falls back on Psalm 110. "To which of the angels said He at any time, Sit on My right hand, until I make Thine enemies Thy footstool?"

We see, then, that this is an important psalm. No psalm is referred to more often in the entire New Testament. We can be sure that Jesus loved all the "sure word of prophecy" in the Old Testament, but in a special way He must have reveled in the messianic psalms. As we read these verses we remember that He read them, memorized them, pondered them, and used them— and that therefore endows them with special sanctity for us.

I. THE MESSIANIC PRINCE (110:1-3)

When David composed this song, three themes about the coming Prince sprang to his mind.

A. The Remarkable Position of This Prince (110:1)

"The LORD said unto my Lord, Sit Thou at my right hand, until I make Thine enemies Thy footstool." The LORD said unto *my* Lord. David is in the middle. On one side he sees the LORD, Jehovah; on the other side he sees the Lord, Adonai. Jehovah is speaking to Adonai, his (David's) Adonai. We can see David stare in perplexity at what he has written.

Since New Testament light now shines on that page, let us unravel the problem for him. First, look at the word LORD (*Jehovah*). It is one of the primary names for God in the Old Testament. It is sometimes used as a name for God the Father, sometimes as a name for God the Son, and sometimes as a name for God the Holy Spirit. The context determines in each case to which Person in the Trinity reference is being made. Here in Psalm 110, Jehovah is God the Father.

The word *Adonai* (Lord) refers to God the Son. He was to be David's son, but David calls Him "my Lord." "The LORD said unto my Lord." In other words, Jehovah was speaking to Jesus.

Now look at the word *said* in this remarkable statement. It literally means "oracle" and is usually used of a direct utterance of God—seldom of the word of a prophet. It occurs, for instance, in connection with the four inspired utterances of that hireling prophet Balaam. He came to curse Israel on behalf of Balak, king of Moab, but each time he tried to speak his curse, the Spirit of God seized his tongue and pronounced a divine oracle. Four times we read: "And Balaam took up his parable and said . . ." Each time he spoke something quite contrary to what was in his mind. He voiced a direct prophetic utterance of God.

"The LORD said unto my Lord." We could render that: "The oracle of Jehovah, the Eternal, to my Adonai, my Ruler" as Graham Scroggie does. Amazingly, David was recording a conversation between Jehovah and Adonai.

He knew already that his dynasty was to be singularly blessed of God. That knowledge, dimly apprehended by David, is here made startlingly plain. He was to have a son who would be his Lord and he, David, would acknowledge Him as Lord.

But how could such a thing be? When Nathan first came to David with the promise of a magnificent dynasty, he expressly told him that the Messiah would not come in his lifetime: "And when thy days be fulfilled, and thou shalt sleep with thy fathers, I will set up thy seed after thee, which shall proceed out of thy bowels, and I will establish His kingdom . . . and thy house and thy kingdom shall be established for ever . . ." (2 Samuel 7:12, 16).

So, it was to happen after his death. But a dead father cannot render allegiance to a living son, and a living son cannot exercise lordship over a dead father. Yet here was Jehovah talking to Adonai, with David calling Adonai "my Adonai, my Ruler." Adonai was to be David's Son *and* David's Sovereign, but David himself was to be dead! Here we surely have one of those prophetic utterances of which the apostle Peter spoke when he said that the prophets "searched diligently what, or what manner of time the Spirit of Christ which was in them did signify . . ." (1 Peter 1:11-12).

We can see David scratching his head in bewilderment over that statement, but the solution is simple to us. If David, being dead, was to have a Son who would at the same time be acknowledged by him as his Lord, then David must live again. The first oracle of this psalm, its opening prophetic announcement, carried David over to resurrection ground.

He had barely grasped that astounding fact, if indeed he grasped it at all, before the words flowed again from his Spirit-enlightened mind: "The LORD said unto my Lord, Sit Thou on My right hand, until I make Thine enemies Thy footstool." That was to be the *remarkable position* of the coming Prince. The statement represents a tremendous advance in the Old Testament concept of the coming Messiah.

David knew that the promised Messiah would sit on his throne: Nathan had told him so, but here was something new. The coming Messiah, that One who was to be his Son, would actually sit with Jehovah on *His* throne. Only One who was *God Himself* could ever sit there. David's Son, therefore, was to be David's *God*.

No wonder the enemies of Christ did not dare argue further with Jesus when He confronted them with this Old Testament verse. "What think ye of Christ? Whose Son is He?" He said. They replied: "The Son of David." "How then doth David in spirit call him Lord [Adonai] saying, The LORD said unto my Lord, Sit Thou at my right hand till I make Thine enemies Thy footstool?" Jesus' enemies were before Him. They acknowledged Messiah to be the son of David, but David acknowledged Him also to be the Son of God.

Jesus today is where David envisioned Him—on God's throne in heaven. Where are His enemies? Those who confronted Him in Jerusalem long ago were either saved after Pentecost or they are dead and damned.

B. The Resistless Power of This Prince (110:2)

"The LORD shall send the rod of Thy strength out of Zion: rule Thou in the midst of Thine enemies." Rotherham renders "rod" as "scepter"—"Thy scepter of strength" or, taking into account the Hebrew idiom, "Thy strong scepter." This is the "rod of iron" seen in the second psalm.

The rod was first seen by Israel in the hand of Moses. (The

same Hebrew word is used in the description of those events.)
That rod became a serpent before Pharaoh, a serpent which
swallowed up the serpents into which Pharaoh's magicians
turned their rods. The sign was remarkably relevant because
Pharaoh wore a serpent insignia on his brow: God's man confronted Pharaoh with a sign that needed no explanation. Moses
had in his hand a symbol of power that could swallow up all the
power of Egypt. The same rod divided the Red Sea. When held
up over the battlefield, it enabled Israel to smite Amalek with
the edge of the sword. It is the rod of which David sang in
Psalm 23; the rod that would comfort him in the chill valley of
the shadow of death.

That rod, or at least all that it stood for, is in the hand of
Christ. All power is now held by His pierced hand.

Let us think of an illustration. Come with me to the Tower of
London. Take a look at the crown jewels of England. Among
the regalia, kept in the Tower for the coronation of an English
king or queen, are two scepters. One is the royal scepter with
the cross, and one is the sovereign's scepter with the dove.

The royal scepter with the cross is a golden rod with a jewel-
encrusted handle at one end and a magnificent jeweled setting
at the other. It is held in the sovereign's right hand as the
symbol of imperial power. The end extended toward the ruler's
subjects is surmounted by a diamond-encrusted cross with an
emerald in the center. Below the cross is a magnificent amethyst
and below that is what is believed to be the largest cut diamond
in the world, a brilliant, pear-shaped gem known as the Star of
Africa.

In the left hand, the monarch carries another scepter, a long,
slender, golden wand likewise encrusted with precious stones. It
is tipped with a golden cross which in turn supports a white
enameled dove. This is the scepter of mercy.

The pomp and power of English royalty has shrunk significantly in today's world. Once, a quarter of the world's population acknowledged the sway of those two scepters. Now they are
the embroidery and decorations of a monarch who has little
power. But one day David's son, David's sovereign, will set up
His throne in Zion. His scepter will sway over Israel and Judah,
over the nations of the world and the islands of the sea, from
north to south, east to west, from pole to pole.

His power will be resistless power. "The LORD shall send the
rod of Thy strength out of Zion: Rule Thou in the midst of
Thine enemies." In His hand will be the rod, the scepter of
God. He will not need diamonds, amethysts, rubies, or sap-
phires to encrust that scepter. He will wield a scepter of iron, a
fitting symbol of power unexcelled.

C. The Redeemed People of This Prince (110:3)

"Thy people shall be willing in the day of Thy power, in the beauties of holiness from the womb of the morning: Thou hast the dew of Thy youth."

This verse is full of wonders. The scene is the last great battle before the millennium. The enemies of the Lord are about to be made His footstool. The youthful warriors of beleaguered Israel flock with eagerness to the royal standard of the coming Christ. They are clad in priestly vestments. They are volunteers, "willing in the day of Thy power," not mercenaries. They spring to their feet eagerly at the call to war from on high. The word for "willing" is the usual word for a freewill offering.

The word is used in Exodus 35:29 to describe the money that poured in without stint for the building of the tabernacle—so much so that Moses had to put a stop to the offerings. The word is used for the money that poured into the royal treasury in David's day when he opened the subscription list for the gold, silver, and precious stones needed for the building of the temple (1 Chronicles 29:9, 14-17). The word is used of the money given by the exiled Jews in Persia to speed the pioneers on their way when they returned in the days of Ezra to rebuild the promised land (Ezra 3:5; 8:28).

That is how these young people will volunteer. Only then it will not be freewill offerings of *money*, but of *men* ready for battle. O that today we might see such willingness among the youth of our churches and assemblies. "Here am I, send me!" It is easy enough to get *money*. What we need is *men*.

These volunteers, flocking to the standards of the coming King, will be arrayed as priests. The translators have trouble with the phrase "the beauties of holiness." Scroggie renders it "holy garments." Rotherham renders it "holy adorning." The psalmist has in mind the gorgeous robe "for glory and for beauty" worn by Israel's priests (Exodus 28:2); this war is to be won, not with carnal but spiritual weapons.

God's volunteers are going to battle as priests. David sees them coming like dew from the womb of the morning. Just as the dew shines in countless sparkling drops when the sun rises, so does this army of volunteers. That dew, plentiful and precious in hot Eastern lands, is the chosen symbol of these soldiers of the King. They are born out of the foregoing night. They start forth suddenly, ready to lay down their lives, willing volunteers.

That is what the King will be looking for in the day of His coming. That is what He is looking for today, volunteers.

On the playing-fields of Eton there was once a young man by

the name of C. T. Studd. He had already made a name for himself as captain of the cricket team. After Eton he went to Cambridge University. There, too, he enjoyed the plaudits of his peers as he excelled on the playing-fields. The world was at his feet.

Then came D. L. Moody, an unschooled, brash, shoe salesman from America, but one whose life had been set ablaze by the fires of God. Moody preached and Sankey sang, and C. T. Studd and six others leapt to their feet to become not only converts, but volunteers. They have gone down in the history of the Christian Church as "The Cambridge Seven."

They offered themselves to Hudson Taylor for missionary work in China, offending British imperial sensibilities by donning Chinese garb, eating Chinese food, substituting Chinese ways for English ways. Studd gave up fame and fortune. He labored in China, in India. He blazed a trail through Africa, one of his ambitions being to open up Africa from the Niger to the Nile. He is quoted as saying,

> Some wish to live within the sound
> Of church or chapel bell,
> I want to run a rescue shop
> Within a yard of Hell.

He was one of God's priestly volunteers, going into battle not with the worldly armor of the age, but with those spiritual weapons which are mighty through God for the pulling down of strongholds.

II. THE MELCHIZEDEK PRIEST (110:4)

What a priest Melchizedek is. We look back at the Old Testament to see the need for such an individual. Think of the only human priesthood ever ordained by God, the priesthood of Aaron. It dominates the Old Testament age. Everything about the Aaronic priesthood was significant: the priestly *robes, rituals,* and *restrictions.* Everywhere we are confronted with symbolism and types.

Aaron, his sons, and his heirs had a monopoly on that restricted priesthood: the only way to become a priest was to be born a priest. No amount of wishing, wealth, wisdom, or work, no amount of well-doing would make a man a priest unless he was born into the family of Aaron.

Further, *restrictions* hedged the way and walled up the path of even the most godly of Israel's priests. None but the high priest, for instance, could enter the holy of holies. He could enter but once a year, and then only after the most elaborate ritual precautions. Nor could he linger there. Ordinary priests could not go in at all. These priests were ordained by God. God knew nothing of pagan priests, just as He knows nothing of Roman or Mormon priests today. The only priesthood He ever ordained He restrained with solemn bonds and bars.

As a man intensely interested in the work of the priests, David knew that. It was he who divided them into the 24 courses so that each would have an opportunity to serve.

We can imagine, then, the surprise with which he recorded the words that take up the second great theme of this psalm. What God had to say about the Melchizedek priest struck at the roots of the sacerdotal system in Israel, a system sanctioned by God and already made venerable in David's day by five centuries of practice.

"The LORD hath sworn, and will not repent, Thou art a priest for ever after the order of Melchizedek." David wrote it down and stared at it. He knew about Melchizedek, but what did Messiah have to do with Melchizedek? What did a son of David of the tribe of Judah have to do with priesthood? Priesthood was invested in a different tribe, another family. True, however, to the imperative prompting of that still, small voice within, David wrote down the thoughts that God had revealed to him.

A. The Divine Oath

"The LORD hath sworn, and will not repent . . ." The word *sworn* corresponds to the word *said* in verse 1. David's Son was to be a Priest. In one sweeping statement, that abolished the entire fabric and function of the priestly order of Aaron. No wonder it was confirmed by an oath. Of course, God's naked word is enough. God's Word is His bond. God *cannot* lie.

Why then the divine oath? Because the installation of Messiah as a *priest* meant an end to a priestly order which, by the time of Christ, had been entrenched by divine decree for fifteen hundred years. Little did Caiaphas realize, when he tore his priestly robe because he believed Christ had spoken blasphemy, that this torn robe was pregnant with significance. The priesthood had indeed been torn apart.

The day Christ died, God reached down and rent the temple veil to match the rent vestment of the priest. Judaism, as it had been known, ceased to be; the Levitical priesthood was over. There was a new priest, one of David's royal line. How much of that, we wonder, was David able to grasp?

B. The Durable Office

"The LORD hath sworn and will not repent, Thou art a priest for ever . . ." Forever. The priests of Aaron's house were inducted into office when they were 30 years of age and retired when they were 50. They served for a scant 20 years, and then their office was taken by another. Sometimes death removed them from office sooner than that. David, in his lifetime, must have known of many priests whose brief ministry saw them permanently retired when they were still comparatively young. The service of God was demanding, and God wanted nothing but the best—the best years of life to be poured out in the service of sacrifice and the sanctuary. That is still what God wants.

"Thou art a priest for ever." One who would be a priest forever must live an endless life. He must count time not by years but by ages. David must have rubbed his eyes. His Son was to be a priest. That was astonishing enough, but a priest forever? If the inspiring Spirit of God had not "God-breathed" the line, he would have rubbed it out.

Thank God, we don't have to take our sins to a human priest. We come to One who knows us better than we know ourselves. He knows the worst about us and loves us just the same. He is touched with the feelings of our infirmities because He has been like us—tempted in all points as we are, yet never sinning. He is never too busy to receive us, never preoccupied, never compromising, always compassionate. Best of all, He will never die: He has already died and now He lives in resurrection power. He is a priest *forever.* Thank God for a priest like that.

C. The Distinctive Order

"Thou art a priest for ever after the order of Melchizedek."

The priestly order of Aaron was temporary; the order of priesthood that preceded it would also supersede it.

David's mind would flash back to Abraham's mysterious encounter with Melchizedek after his victory over the invading kings of the East. Who was this Melchizedek? Some think he was really Shem, founder of the godly line after the flood. Shem was about a hundred years old when the flood took place and he died when he was 600 years of age. He was still alive when Abraham set out from Ur of the Chaldees, when he went backsliding in Egypt, and when he rescued Lot from the clutches of sin-ridden Sodom and Gomorrah. It is, at least, an interesting possibility that the King of Salem, the King of Righteousness, the King of Peace, Melchizedek, was indeed the aged patriarch Shem.

Melchizedek, however, is set before us in the Bible in an astonishing way. He was a king-priest. In him church and state met and merged, as it was never allowed under the Mosaic Law. He was king of Jerusalem, a mysterious figure, mentioned only once in the Bible until David drops his name into this psalm, and mentioned only three times in all of Scripture. In Genesis he is mentioned *historically;* in Psalm 110 he is mentioned *prophetically;* in Hebrews he is mentioned *doctrinally.*

All David had was the Genesis record until, suddenly, the name *Melchizedek* came into his mind as he composed this extraordinary psalm.

A thoughtful man, David would surely meditate on the Spirit's introduction of the name *Melchizedek* in this hymn. We can imagine David calling a servant to bring his personal, handwritten copy of the Book of the Law. We can see David's forehead puckered in perplexity as he read again and again the brief Genesis account of Melchizedek.

He would conclude that his coming Son, this coming Messiah, if he were to be a priest after the order of Melchizedek, would introduce a totally new order of the priesthood.

1. A Stable Priesthood

As David knew, Genesis was a book of genealogies, yet Melchizedek was introduced into the Genesis text with no genealogy. One moment he was there, the next moment Abraham had moved on, but Melchizedek remained. No family tree. No ancestry. No heirs. Of course! The Spirit of God had written it thus on purpose. Melchizedek was, genealogically speaking, and as far as his priesthood was concerned, "without father or mother, without beginning or ending of days." He was introduced into the sacred text in such a way as to suggest an eternal priest, priest forever. A stable priesthood—one that would never know the fluctuations introduced by retirement and death into the Aaronic priesthood.

2. A Sovereign Priesthood

One of the points about Melchizedek was his position as both king and priest. He was something Aaron's sons could never be, a king. He was something David's sons could never be, a priest. "All power" then was concentrated in the same hands: all royal power, all religious power.

Thank God we know that is true of Christ today. He holds all the reins of power in His hands. Nothing can happen without His permission. Moreover, He has the ability, authority, and power to make "all things work together for good to them that love God, to them who are the called according to His purpose" (Romans 8:28).

3. A Superior Priesthood

All the priests whom David knew were sons of Aaron. Aaron was a son of Levi, who was a son of Jacob, who was a son of Isaac, who was a son of Abraham—and Abraham acknowledged Melchizedek as his spiritual superior. He paid tithes to Melchizedek.

Since Levi and Aaron and all the priests were descendants of Abraham, they too, so to speak, paid tithes to Melchizedek, in Abraham, when Abraham paid his. It followed, therefore, that any priest after the order of Melchizedek would be superior to any priest after the order of Aaron.

Indeed, the Melchizedek priesthood had absolute primacy in the Bible. It was in effect centuries before Aaron was even born, and, since David's coming Son was to have an everlasting priesthood, it would be in effect eternally, long after the Aaronic line had perished from the earth as priests.

"The LORD hath sworn, and will not repent, Thou art a priest for ever after the order of Melchizedek." Evidently the Lord had changed His mind (if such can be said of God) about the Aaronic priesthood. David would think again of priests he had known. They were good men, many of them, but he had known some bad ones too.

The Aaronic priesthood was, in fact, marked by *failure*. It had hardly been instituted when God had publicly executed Nadab and Abihu, two of Aaron's immediate sons, for offering strange fire on the altar. It had been marked by repeated failure ever since.

It was marked by *frailty*. On the awesome day of atonement even the high priest had to take the most elaborate ceremonial precautions to cover his sinfulness before he dared venture inside the holy of holies. The best human priests were fragile, fumbling, faltering men.

It was marked by *frustration*. Day after day the priests of Aaron's line offered sacrifices that could never take away sins.

It would be satisfying to think that David thought these things through while the glow of inspiration still rested upon him. It is doubtful, however, that he was able to penetrate the mysteries of the Melchizedek priesthood. The Spirit of God has made matters plain for us in the epistle to the Hebrews. Jesus is this Melchizedek priest of whom David spoke so profoundly.

III. THE MILLENNIAL PROPHECY (110:5-7)

The scene shifts to the end of the age to focus on the coming battle that will dethrone all those human and demonic forces which have usurped the government of the globe. Three features of this battle are mentioned.

A. The Day of Battle (110:5)

"The Lord at Thy right hand shall strike through kings in the day of His wrath." The psalm closes with reference to a fearful crisis. It anticipates the battle of Armageddon when the coming Priest-King will cut down those who have ranged themselves against God. It anticipates the coming day of wrath, stroke after stroke. First the crushing of the confederate kings, then the filling of the battlefield with dead bodies, and finally the crushing of the leader of God's foes.

We are living today in the day of *blessing*—the Priest-King is interceding at God's right hand; tomorrow will be the day of *battle*—God will be at the right hand of the Priest-King to strike down all His foes.

B. The Din of Battle (110:6)

"He shall judge among the heathen, he shall fill the places with the dead bodies; He shall wound the heads over many countries."

David had engaged in many battles in his tumultuous life, but he had never seen a battlefield like the one now opening up before him. He saw a battlefield filled with corpses. Then he saw the head of the rebellious nations, the lawless one, whom the Lord is to destroy by the breath of His lips and with the brightness of His coming. He saw this monstrous head crushed.

C. The Dust of Battle (110:7)

"He shall drink of the brook in the way: therefore shall He lift up the head." The head of the warring nations is crushed, and Christ, the Head of the Church and of the nations, is lifted up.

But first He drinks of the brook in the way. The word for *brook* is an interesting one. Dr. Hull tells us that it is often translated "valley" (Marion McH. Hull, *Two Thousand Hours in the Psalms*, Chicago: John A. Dickson Publishing Co.). It conveys the idea of a depression. He suggests that "the brook in the way" is a little depression in the road into which water has run from a recent rain. In other words, the coming Priest-King will actually drink out of a puddle, a muddy puddle by the side of the road.

That description expresses in a marvelous way the humiliation through which our King-Priest passed on the way to the throne. He shall drink of the mud puddle, and *therefore* shall He lift up His head. As the apostle Paul says: "He humbled Himself, and became obedient unto death, even the death of the cross. Wherefore God also hath highly exalted Him" (Philippians 2:8-9).

Jesus can be such a magnificent sovereign because He is such a magnificent Saviour. He has stooped to drink out of this mud puddle we call human life and is therefore fit to be both Priest and Prince. "Hallelujah! What a Saviour."

Psalm 111

THE LORD'S WORKS

THIS PSALM and the following one are twins. We have no idea who parented them, but there they are, standing shoulder to shoulder, alike as two peas in a pod. It is generally thought they were written after the Babylonian captivity, probably early in the post-exilic period. Both psalms are complete acrostics; both contain ten verses in our translation; both are made up of eight couplets (verses 1-8) and two triplets (verses 9-10). In each case these couplets and triplets total 22 lines, each line beginning with a different letter of the Hebrew alphabet, thus making up the complete alphabet. One psalm celebrates the *person* of the Lord; the other celebrates the *people* of the Lord.

The psalm we are studying has three major themes.

I. WORSHIP (111:1-3)

The psalm begins with the word *Hallelujah,* "Praise ye the LORD." This is a liturgical call, and stands outside the overall alphabetical structure of the psalm. Worship is the ascription of *worthship* to God. It is praising God for the glory of His person and work.

A. The Resolve To Worship (111:1)

The psalmist has made up his mind that he is going to worship the Lord. It is the rational, sensible response of a creature to the Creator, of the redeemed to the Redeemer. It is the chief end of man. We should be tuning up our souls now for the endless anthems of thunderous praise with which we shall one day make the courts of heaven ring.

1. The psalmist resolves to worship God *personally:* "I will praise the LORD with my whole heart," he says. He is resolved to put all he has into it, to summon the resources of his intellect, to engage the passions of his heart, to enlist the dynamic of his will, to harness every ounce of strength—to pull out all the stops, so to speak.

All too often our private worship is slipshod, even though God deserves our best. We should pay as much attention to singing God's praise as we would pay to any other enterprise we consider important. Take Michelangelo, for instance. His passion was sculpture. He once fell heir to a massive block of marble that had been badly handled at the quarry, and on which an inferior artist had already practiced his errors. From that block of marble Michelangelo created "David," a statue of beauty and strength. Irving Stone, in *The Agony and the Ecstasy,* tells how Michelangelo devoted himself to his task. Food, sleep, recreation, fresh clothing—all were ignored in his artistic passion. He hurled himself at the marble. When his right hand was limp with weariness, he changed hands and drove on into the marble with his chisel without missing a stroke. Not even a cold winter night could stop him, he so burned with fever to set free the David he could see held captive in that stone.

Surely we should bring a similar commitment to our work. Then, having disciplined ourselves to work with all our heart, mind, soul, and strength, we should worship with the same earnest zeal. That is what the psalmist resolved to do: "I will praise the LORD with my whole heart."

2. He resolved, moreover, to worship God *publicly:* "I will

praise the LORD . . . in the assembly of the upright, and in the congregation." To sit sleepily through a sermon, with thoughts wandering afar and attention straying to every rag or tatter of idle thought, is not worship. Worship demands active participation. It means that the "loins of the mind" are girt up, with every thought brought into captivity to Christ.

Hymns are sung that exalt the person, passion, and position of the Lord Jesus. Scriptures are read which parade before us, in the stately cadences of Holy Writ, the thoughts of God rendered into human language. Prayer is focused on Him. Words are spoken in exposition and exhortation to exalt Him. That is worship.

Private worship lifts public worship to new heights. In public worship the Holy Spirit blends together the music of many different human instruments, orchestrating the whole into a euphonious blending of joy. This person brings a heart overflowing with precious thoughts of God that have blessed his or her soul in private devotions. Another, whose heart is made glad by a glorious answer to prayer, is bursting with thanks. Another has a heart made tender by deep sorrow and by the comfort of the Holy Spirit. The Spirit of God brings together all these colors of the spectrum of private worship and blends them into the pure white light of public worship. "I will praise the LORD in the assembly," sang the psalmist as he anticipated the moment when he could contribute this new psalm to the worship of God in the congregation.

B. The Reasons for Worship (111:2-3)

1. God's Might Displayed (111:2)

"The works of the LORD are great, sought out of all them that have pleasure therein." There is, of course, God's might as displayed in His work as *Creator of the universe.* Everywhere we see the fingerprints of an omniscient, omnipotent Creator. We explore the mysteries of the atom. We reach out to the stellar empires and see evidence of that inconceivable might which can orbit a galaxy, explode a star, or lock up within an atom the power to obliterate a city. There is the power to harness an earthquake, to summon an eclipse, to erupt a volcano.

There is, too, God's might displayed as *Controller of the universe.* The Jewish repatriates from Babylon could not help but be awed by the ease with which God could control the heart of a king. The mighty Persian conqueror Cyrus had the world at his feet. His empire stretched from the gates of Greece to the waters of the Indus. Yet God so worked on his heart that he emancipated his Jewish captives, gave them his blessing, and sent them back to rebuild the promised land.

It is the essence of worship to give God our thanks, adoration, and praise for being the kind of God He is.

2. God's Majesty Displayed (111:3)

"His work is honorable and glorious: and His righteousness endureth for ever." The word *glorious* here literally means "majestic." Everything God does reveals the majestic splendor with which He robes Himself. There is nothing mean or petty about God.

Human kings surround themselves with the trappings of pomp and power. They are approached on red carpets and sit arrayed in splendid vestments adorned with the insignia of royalty. They wear diadems ablaze with precious stones and hold scepters tipped with glittering gems. They surround themselves with courtiers in impressive robes, are guarded by soldiers with splendid accoutrements, and must be approached with proper protocol. Those who come near must bend the knee.

All this is borrowed splendor, a shadow of the magnificence surrounding the presence of the living God. The ministers of His court are a flame of fire, bright spirits, sinless sons of light. His throne is high and lifted up, and His train fills the temple. The full circle of the rainbow shimmers around His throne in brightest emerald hues. A sea of glass, clear as crystal, is the glittering carpet on which He is approached. When He stooped to pitch His tent with Israel in the wilderness, He sat enthroned on a seat of purest gold, between the overshadowing cherubim. The walls of His pavilion were the richest scarlet, blue, and purple. The entire inner sanctum was ablaze with the glory of another world.

We must try to remember all this when we come to worship. We are coming to the heavenly sanctuary of our God.

II. WONDER (111:4-6)

Worship leads naturally to wonder. Thoughtful consideration of God in the sanctuary will fill the reverent soul with awe. The psalmist strikes three notes of wonder for us.

A. Apprehending What He Has Done (111:4)

"He hath made His wonderful works to be remembered: the LORD is gracious and full of compassion." Probably the psalmist is referring to God's wonders as remembered in the Passover. The Passover was to be a permanent memorial to Israel of God's majesty and splendor displayed in their redemption from Egyptian bondage. The mighty miracles by which God demonstrated His power on that occasion are celebrated throughout the psalms. They are the theme, too, of many Old Testament passages. But supremely, the exodus was to be remembered annually in the Passover.

God wants us never to forget what we owe Him. Israel remembered their redemption in the Passover. Today we remember *our* redemption in the celebration of the Lord's supper, instituted by the Lord "lest we forget." The Lord has made His wonderful works to be remembered. And of all His wonderful works, none is greater, grander, more glorious, or more gracious than the work of the cross.

We must *apprehend* what God has done. We must set our minds to that great task. We must scale the heights opened to us by the cross and plumb the depths that yawn so fearfully at Calvary—the depths the Lord has plumbed for us. We must confess that our own sounding lines are far too short to plumb those depths. Our ladders are too short to reach those heights.

B. Appreciating What He Has Done (111:5)

We must appreciate our God's faithfulness. He is dependable, utterly trustworthy.

1. God's Faithfulness to His Creatures (111:5a)

"He hath given meat unto them that fear Him." The word for *meat* is *tereph,* which literally means "the prey of a lion." The same God who feeds the forest lion faithfully provided for Israel every step of the wilderness way. He faithfully brings in seedtime and harvest, year after year, so that His creatures might be fed.

2. God's Faithfulness to His Covenant (111:5b)

"He will ever be mindful of His covenant." Those words are probably a reference to the great covenant that God drew up with Abraham, which guaranteed Israel's emancipation from Egyptian bondage and their ultimate settlement in the promised land. It might, however, allude to the earlier covenant God made with Noah. In that covenant He pledged that henceforth the seasons would faithfully continue so that man might plow in confidence and reap in gratitude. For over four thousand years He has kept that pledge in spite of human sin, ignorance, and rebellion.

C. Appropriating What He Has Done (111:6)

"He hath showed His people the power of His works, that He may give them the heritage of the heathen." This seems to be a reference to the conquest of Canaan. The Canaanites had forfeited all right to their land. Their religious system was an insult to the character of God, corrupting society, a glorification of the worst lusts of the unregenerate human heart. So God foreclosed on their land, and He handed it to Israel.

The conquest of Canaan was a further demonstration of "the power of His works." Already news of what had happened to Egypt had run ahead of Israel, demoralizing the people of Canaan. Then came Joshua, and Jericho fell. And then Ai and Gibea. Two mighty coalitions of Canaanite nations were organized to halt the Hebrew conquest, one in the south, the other in the north, but both were swept aside. In a series of brilliant campaigns, in which God made bare His arm, the promised land was conquered.

But Israel failed to appropriate what God had done. If there is one sin that is worse than forgetfulness, it is ingratitude. In Israel it made possible all the national sins and apostasies that followed. These sins climaxed in the deportation of Judah to Babylon, the destruction of the temple, and the demolition of Jerusalem. The promised land had been prostrate before them, but the Hebrews had failed to appropriate it. Instead of dispossessing the defeated Canaanites, they had compromised and settled among them. Thus, they sowed the seeds of the dreadful harvest that came to fruition in the captivities.

Similarly, God has defeated all *our* foes at Calvary. Worship will lead us to appropriate the blessings that are ours in Christ.

May we never lose the sense of *wonder* at what God has done for us at Calvary. Israel's downward path will be ours if we fail to do that. If, for instance, we lose our sense of wonder at the great truths of Ephesians, we shall soon settle for something less than God has for us, and backsliding will begin.

III. WISDOM (111:7-10)

Wisdom calls for a deliberate and active response to all that God is in Himself.

A. Fresh Regard for the Lord (111:7-9)

Knowing his need of the Lord, the psalmist again focuses attention on Him.

1. He tells us that God's work is *guaranteed by His nature:* "The works of His hands are verity and judgment; all His commandments are sure. They stand fast for ever and ever, and are done in truth and uprightness" (111:7-8). The reality that God is always true to His character is revealed in both His commandments and His covenants. Truth, justice, and uprightness are the essence of His ways in the world. In other words, God does what He does because He is what He is.

That was illustrated in His giving Canaan to the Hebrews. He was being true to His character. He had pledged the land to the patriarchs, to Abraham, Isaac, Jacob, and to their seed forever. The promise was as sure as God's integrity could make it.

God was also true to His character in dealing with the people of the land. "The iniquity of the Amorites is not yet full": that was God's explanation to Abraham for the delay in fulfilling that promise. The ultimate expulsion of the Canaanites would be a just recompense for their sins.

2. God's works are also *guaranteed by His name:* "He sent redemption unto His people: He hath commanded His covenant for ever: holy and reverend is His Name" (111:9). This is the only time the word *reverend* occurs in the King James Version, and it is exclusively a name for God. Elsewhere it is rendered "terrible" (Psalm 99:3) or "fearful" (Deuteronomy 28:58). God's name, holy and terrible, stands behind His pledges. He will never dishonor His name.

The most priceless possession a person has is a good name. God would never compromise *His* Name. Thus the name of *Jesus* becomes to us the guarantee of all our blessings in this life and the life to come.

B. Fresh Response to the Lord (111:10)

1. The psalmist tells us *where wisdom starts:* "The fear of the LORD is the beginning of wisdom." That was the basic premise in the wisdom literature of the Hebrew people. To abandon the fear of the Lord is to open the door to every wicked philosophy which the mind of man is capable of devising.

2. The psalmist tells us *why wisdom stands:* "A good understanding have all they that do His commandments." The expression "a good understanding" can be rendered "good success." "Excellent insight have all they that do those things" is Rotherham's rendering.

3. The psalmist tells us *when wisdom sings:* "His praise endureth forever."

> O worship the King all-glorious above,
> O gratefully sing His power and His love.
> Our Shield and Defender, the Ancient of
>   days,
> Pavilioned in splendor, and girded with
>   praise.

Psalm 112

THE BLESSED MAN

I. THE SECRET OF THE BLESSED MAN (112:1)
A. He Loves the Lord
B. He Loves the Word
II. THE SONS OF THE BLESSED MAN (112:2)
A. They Are Mighty Men
B. They Are Moral Men
III. THE SUBSTANCE OF THE BLESSED MAN (112:3)
He has:
A. A House Full of Riches
B. A Heart Full of Righteousness
IV. THE SERENITY OF THE BLESSED MAN (112:4)
He enjoys:
A. Guidance
B. Grace
C. Goodness
D. Godliness
V. THE SENSE OF THE BLESSED MAN (112:5)
A. He Is Compassionate
B. He Is Careful
VI. THE SECURITY OF THE BLESSED MAN (112:6-8)
A. His Is an Everlasting Security (112:6)
B. His Is an Everyday Security (112:7-8)
1. Bad News Does Not Shake Him (112:7)
2. Good News Does Not Shun Him (112:8)
VII. THE STATUS OF THE BLESSED MAN (112:9)
A. His Pity Is Acknowledged
B. His Piety Is Acknowledged
C. His Power Is Acknowledged
VIII. THE SUPREMACY OF THE BLESSED MAN (112:10)
He sees:
A. The Frustration of the Wicked
B. The Fury of the Wicked
C. The Folly of the Wicked

THIS PSALM is twin to Psalm 111. In structure (both are acrostics), content, and language these psalms are similar, without being identical.

The Jews carried much of their history and national, cultural, and spiritual heritage in their minds. Some of them performed astonishing feats of memory. For centuries, for instance, the Talmud was not written down. The rabbis memorized the whole thing, and some child prodigies already had memorized it in their teens. It was not until persecution alarmed the rabbis with the thought that if these human encyclopedias were to be killed then the Talmud itself might perish that they agreed to write it down.

During much of their history, the Jews also memorized their Scriptures and other sacred literature. That is why poetry is so popular in the Bible. Jewish poetry often had an acrostic form, with meter and a specialized structure, both a distinct aid to memory.

Most of what we get from the Bible comes from plain hard work; mental slothfulness never leads to illumination. When we pay the price of intensive reading and meditation in the Scriptures, do our homework, study the writings and teachings of others whom the Holy Spirit has illuminated and gifted, then the Holy Spirit will illumine us as well.

Here we have an acrostic psalm, a reminder that it was to be memorized as well as read. Psalm 111 puts the emphasis on the *Saviour,* this psalm puts the emphasis on the *saint.* In Psalm 110 we were occupied with *the prowess* of God. In Psalm 111 we are occupied with *the people* of God. In Psalm 110 it was *the Lord's person,* here it is *the Lord's people.* In Psalm 110 *His* works were underlined; here *our* works are underlined.

Psalm 111 tells us eight things about the blessed man who is the subject of its song.

I. THE SECRET OF THE BLESSED MAN (112:1)

He has a twofold secret.

A. He Loves the Lord (112:2)

"Praise ye the LORD [Hallelujah]. Blessed is the man that feareth the LORD." The last verse of Psalm 111 says: "The fear of the LORD is the beginning of wisdom." This psalm picks up and expands that thought.

Although human beings look everywhere for happiness, the secret of happiness is simple: blessed, or happy, is the person who fears the Lord. We remember the sad conclusion to the book of Ecclesiastes. In a wail of despair over his wasted life, Solomon (traditionally considered the author) recounts his search for happiness. He thought he could find it in *thought,* so he gave himself to wisdom and accumulated knowledge. He sought understanding from God and became a man whose wisdom was proverbial even in his own day. But *that* did not make Solomon happy.

He next thought he could find happiness in *thrills,* so he dedicated himself to pleasure. He tried everything that money could buy, or that mind could conceive. His revelry was unrestrained, yet none of it made him happy.

He thought he could find it in *things,* so he went in for making money. He became a merchant prince, with agents trading on the markets of the world for new and exotic things. Solomon was so successful that even the pots and pans in the palace kitchen were made of gold. And *that* did not make him happy either.

At the end of the book he says: "Let us hear the conclusion of the whole matter: Fear God, and keep His commandments: for this is the whole duty of man" (Ecclesiastes 12:12). That was the way he had originally started life, when he was a young man himself, but somehow he had "gone off the gold standard." He had traded the pure metal of spiritual truth for the useless alloy of the world. It cost him a kingdom, a throne, and a crown.

Here, then, is the secret of the blessed man. He loves the Lord. When the term is applied to the people of God, "the fear of the LORD" is never slavish fear. It is reverent awe that draws out the heart in wonder, love, and praise. People look for happiness, the pot of gold at the end of the rainbow, but they never find it. They must follow the bend of the rainbow until they reach its highest arch, and then look up. "Happy is the man that feareth the LORD"—it is a great aphorism for our godless, materialistic age.

B. He Loves the Word (112:2)

"Blessed is the man . . . that delighteth greatly in His commandments." We read the world's philosophers in vain for the secret of happiness. Socrates did not have it, Plato did not have it. Neither did Kant, Marx, or Engels. Some of these men had the secret of *hate,* but not the secret of *happiness.* Happiness can be found only within the pages of God's blessed book. Our society has tried to discredit this book and as a result it is unhappy, unsatisfied, and unsettled. This book makes people *good* and makes nations *great.* Happy are those who delight in God's Word. They have found the secret.

II. THE SONS OF THE BLESSED MAN (112:2)

The psalmist looks at the godly man's family and sees that his sons are:

A. Mighty Men

"His seed shall be mighty upon the earth." Are power, wealth, and position the natural inheritance of those brought up in a home where the Lord and His Word are honored? We must remember the Old Testament setting of the psalm. In Old Testament times domestic blessings were promised to those who were obedient to the covenant. Material prosperity is not part of God's promise to His people in this age, as the Sermon on the Mount makes clear. Still, the Lord delights to reach out to bless and embrace the children of those who love Him. If we are faithful, if we carefully sow the gospel seed, if we water it with our prayers, if we avail ourselves of the spiritual means of grace He has put in our hands, His promises will surely hold true.

In the Old Testament, definite material blessings were part of the Abrahamic and Mosaic covenants. The psalmist had seen examples of God's faithfulness to His pledged Word: "His seed shall be mighty in the earth." He knew a number of examples of the sons of a godly man becoming mighty men.

B. Moral Men

"The generation of the upright shall be blessed." Literally this can be rendered "a generation of upright men shall be blessed." The verse refers to the descendants of the man who fears the Lord. They become the pillars of society, a stabilizing influence, the backbone of the nation, giving moral fiber to its life. They insure that the moral tone of the nation is in keeping with the Word of God. A country with no such men at its helm is one that has lost its moorings; it is a country adrift on treacherous tides. It will make certain shipwreck apart from the grace of God in revival.

III. THE SUBSTANCE OF THE BLESSED MAN (112:3)

Next the psalmist sees two things. He sees a man who has:

A. A House Full of Riches

"Wealth and riches shall be in his house." Again we must remember the Old Testament setting of this psalm. Wealth and prosperity were guaranteed fringe-benefits under the old covenant for those who loved the Lord. That is why Job's calamities were such a puzzle to his friends. They concluded, from the disasters that had overtaken him, that he must have been guilty of some secret but horrible sin. Arguing from the premise that wealth and health are the heritage of the godly, they accused Job of sin and hypocrisy and urged him to confess.

Of course wicked men sometimes prospered, then as now, but that kind of prosperity is a house built on sand. The blessed man also has:

B. A Heart Full of Righteousness

"And his righteousness endureth forever." Words used of God in Psalm 111:8 are now applied to the godly man of Psalm 112. The character of the godly man, in other words, reflects the character of God.

The supreme example is the Lord Jesus. Every aspect of the Lord's character was a reflection of God's character. He was "God in focus" so to speak. If we take the personality characteristics and behavior of the Lord Jesus and project them into infinity we have a perfect concept of the personality and behavior of God. The Lord Jesus was literally "God manifest in flesh." The God who had been manifest for countless ages—in burning suns and shining stars, in wind, thunder and rain, in changing seasons and changeless laws—was now manifest in flesh.

IV. THE SERENITY OF THE BLESSED MAN (112:4)

The blessed man is marked by:

A. Guidance

"Unto the upright there ariseth light in the darkness." He does not have to stumble along in the dark like the ungodly man. He has light in the darkness.

A friend of mine was once overtaken in thick, African bush by the sudden darkness of the tropics. His parents were missionaries and the family was making their way by car along a forest path. He himself was still a youth. Born and raised in the jungle, he had slipped out of camp with a rifle to see if he could bag something for the pot. Hot on the trail of an antelope, he forgot the lateness of the hour. The family vehicle was far behind when the darkness fell. He tried to retrace his steps. He could hear the shouts of those who were calling for him—as well as the roar of a hunting lion. *"Put on the lights! Put on the car lights!"* he called, hoping his parents would hear him. They did, and the lights, stabbing into the darkness, enabled him to find his way back to camp. The light also frightened away the lion.

We are living in a dark world. To have light in darkness is the special blessing of those who are saved. We *know* where we are and where we are going. Jesus said: "He that followeth Me shall not walk in darkness, but have the light of life" (John 8:12).

B. Grace

The upright man "is gracious," the psalmist says. He looks at others with a benevolent smile. He is not harsh, unforgiving, malicious, spiteful, mean, unlovely. Graciousness is another God-like attribute. It, too, is what we think of when we think of the Lord Jesus Christ. Here was One who drew strong men to Himself, to whom the widow, the diseased, the broken, instinctively turned. He was One who welcomed being with children. It was said that people "marveled at the gracious words that came out of His mouth" (Luke 4:22).

C. Goodness

"He is gracious, and full of compassion." The Lord Jesus described human beings as "sheep without a shepherd." He longed to gather them to Himself. After years in the company of Jesus, Peter tells us that "He went about doing good." His heart overflowed with love for all. He had come into a world that was one vast graveyard, a world where sorrow and sickness preyed on all, a world where oppression was enthroned in the seats of power, where poverty and want were common. His heart ached for people. He tramped endless miles in tireless service of humankind. He was, above all else, a good man.

He was gracious and full of compassion, marked by the characteristics seen in the blessed man of Psalm 112, marked by qualities that ought to be seen in us. Paul could say: "I bear in my body the *marks* of the Lord Jesus." Do we?

D. Godliness

"He is gracious, and full of compassion, and righteous." Righteousness, the quality of always doing what is right, is another God-like attribute. It is of sterner stuff than goodness, though goodness is much more appealing. Paul says, "Scarcely for a righteous man will one die: yet peradventure for a good man some would dare even to die" (Romans 5:7). The man the psalmist is describing is both good and righteous. Goodness has its roots in *love;* righteousness has its roots in *law.* Thus we read, "The law was given by Moses, but grace and truth came by Jesus Christ" (John 1:17).

Here, then, we see the serenity of the blessed man. He enjoys guidance, grace, goodness, and godliness. No wonder He is a happy man.

V. THE SENSE OF THE BLESSED MAN (112:5)

"A good man showeth favor, and lendeth: he will guide his affairs with discretion." Lending is a form of gracious dealing.

When someone in need asks for a loan, the good and gracious man will be sympathetic to his needs. But that doesn't mean he is foolish. He manages his affairs with discretion. He does not foolishly expose himself to the fraudulent man. Few things can be more disquieting than to realize that you have loaned money to a person who has little or no intention of paying you back. If one knows right from the start that he is never again going to see the money he is loaning, that is one thing. In a sense it is being given. But to loan money unsuspectingly to an unscrupulous person is something else. The blessed man of this psalm is compassionate, but also careful.

Being a believer, being willing to help others, does not mean we should not take proper care of our concerns and secure our interests as well as we can. Because some people have no conscience, it is no part of Christian charity to aid and encourage their wrongdoing.

VI. THE SECURITY OF THE BLESSED MAN (112:6-8)

The blessed man enjoys:

A. Everlasting Security (112:6)

Such a person is immovable: "Surely he shall not be moved for ever." The foundation rocks of our planet will someday be removed. They will melt with fervent heat. The stars that burn and blaze in the vastness of the heavens will be folded up like a garment. On the other hand, the security of the blessed man is *forever.* That is the kind of security purchased for us at Calvary.

The memory of such a person endures: "The righteous shall be in everlasting remembrance." We all like to be remembered, and we have enough of eternity in our makeup that we would like to be remembered forever. What was it Solomon said? "The memory of the just is blessed: but the name of the wicked shall rot" (Proverbs 10:7). The Lord Jesus, in His remarkable revelation of the life beyond, mentions Lazarus by name; he was the poor man who went to the abode of the blessed. But the name of the rich man who went out into a lost eternity is not recorded. Blotted out of the book of life, he has entered eternity a nonentity, a nobody, a nameless and eternally lost soul.

The blessed man, however, has an everlasting security. He may not be remembered down here, but he is one of the nobility of heaven. Up there, he has a great name.

B. Every-Day Security (112:7-8)

Next, two things are recorded about the upright man.

1. Bad News Does Not Shake Him (112:7)

"He shall not be afraid of evil tidings: his heart is fixed, trusting in the LORD." Even the best of persons at times is overtaken by ill tidings. A loved one dies, the bank fails, lightning strikes, fire or flood cause damage, war is declared. God does not take us out of the world nor does He exempt us from life's ordinary disasters. What He does is allow us to rest our hearts on Him. We may not be able to praise Him *for* what happens, but we can praise Him *in* what happens. Bad news need not shake us; God is still on the throne.

2. Good News Does Not Shun Him (112:8)

There may be bad news, but not *all* news is bad. "His heart is established, he shall not be afraid, until he sees his desire upon his enemies." Persons of faith know that no matter how trying their circumstances, all is well. Good news is on the way. Believers are the only people in the world who have any right to be optimistic. The man who is an optimist and still in his sins is a fool. The believer need never be a pessimist because, in the end, everything is going to be all right.

VII. THE STATUS OF THE BLESSED MAN (112:9)

The psalmist acknowledges:

A. His Pity

"He hath dispersed, he hath given to the poor." Here we see the essence of practical godliness. To realize that a person is in need and not to give some practical help to that person is a denial of the faith. We are living in a needy world. Millions are starving to death; half the world goes to bed hungry. Countless Christian agencies specialize in providing relief to the hungry, to victims of disasters, to those in chronic need. Christianity teaches us to love our neighbor in the same way we love ourselves. Every believer ought to have some kind of personal program for giving to the poor.

B. His Piety

"His righteousness endureth for ever." In his great masterpiece on Christian giving, the apostle Paul quotes this verse (2 Corinthians 9:9). Giving is a grace in which all Christians should participate as a proof of righteousness. Piety without pity is lifeless—which is why the early pioneer missionaries set up clinics, hospitals, orphanages, and other institutions of mercy.

C. His Power

"His horn shall be exalted with honor." A horn epitomizes the strength of the wild beast. Throughout the Bible it is a symbol for power.

VIII. THE SUPREMACY OF THE BLESSED MAN (112:10)

The last verse sets the blessed man in contrast with the wicked man, in much the same way as the first psalm does.

We are given a glimpse of:

A. The Wicked Man's Frustration

"The wicked shall see it, and be grieved." The wicked man does not like to see the good man prospering. Time, however, is on the side of the good man. God has designed the dispensations so that, in the end, good will triumph on this planet. Wickedness can never win in the end. Divisive and self-defeating, it carries the seeds of its own destruction. The millennial reign of Christ is to be the great manifestation to the world of the principle that God is on the side of goodness.

B. The Wicked Man's Fury

"He shall gnash with his teeth, and melt away." Gnashing with the teeth is a Bible metaphor for fury and rage. The wicked are on their way to a place of gnashing of teeth. All their schemes have come to nothing and they will be forever incarcerated where their violence and vileness can no longer affect the course of the ages. They will see the blessed in heaven, Christ enthroned, and all the angels of God worshiping Him. They will see the blessed reigning on high and going from glory to glory, and will gnash their teeth in fury.

C. The Wicked Man's Folly

"The desire of the wicked shall perish." All he has lived for has come to nothing. The dreadful passions he has kindled in life consume him now with no means of quenching them. He could have been one of the blessed, he could have desired holiness and found the way to true happiness, he could have loved the Lord and loved His Word—but he didn't. He desired other things, and now, in death, he is betrayed and burned by the evil desires he cultivated in life.

And so ends this instructive psalm, a magnificent commentary on Psalm 1. May the Lord fill our hearts with right desires.

Psalm 113

HALLELUJAH!

I. THE LORD DEMANDS PRAISE (113:1-3)
   A. His Rightful Claim (113:1a, b)
   B. His Royal Name (113:1c-2)
   C. His Resounding Fame (113:3)
II. THE LORD DESIRES PRAISE (113:4-6)
   A. His Glory (113:4)
   B. His Greatness (113:5)
   C. His Grace (113:6)
III. THE LORD DESERVES PRAISE (113:7-9)
   A. His Kindness to the Downtrodden (113:7-8)
   He brings them:
      1. Up from the Pit (113:7)
      2. Into the Palace (113:8)
   B. His Kindness to the Distressed (113:9)

PSALMS 113-118 ARE KNOWN as The Great Hallel. They comprise Israel's "Hallelujah Chorus," so to speak. They were sung repeatedly throughout the year and in their entirety at the annual feasts of Passover, Pentecost, and Tabernacles. They were sung at the time of the new moon, except when the moon heralded a new year.

They teach us that God would have His people be preeminently a praising people. The word *praise* and its synonyms occur in the psalms no less than 186 times. So, no matter how sad and sorrowful some of our life situations along the way, we should learn to praise the Lord.

The thing that grips us about this particular group of psalms is the fact that they were sung at the Passover. It is impossible to read them or meditate on them without thinking of the Lord Jesus there in the upper room. The shadow of Calvary lay across His path. Gethsemane, Gabbatha, and Golgotha were only hours ahead. There He sat with Peter, James and John, Thomas and Matthew, Philip and Nathanael, and all the rest.

We can imagine that He may have led His disciples out of themselves and into the eternal truths of the will and Word of God as they sang these psalms together. Perhaps we shall sing them with Him in the glory. He, after all, is the Chief Musician and He it surely is who will lead the anthems of praise that will reverberate around the throne of God in the ages to come.

So let us look at this psalm. On the Passover night, it was sung before the meal began. We could think of it as a kind of table grace, sung to dispel the shadows of evening and to give thanks and praise to God for His love and care. As we study it, let us remember when shadows lengthen, when circumstances frown for us, that never were shadows so dark or so long as those which wrapped around that upper room. Nor were shadows ever so gloriously dispelled.

I. THE LORD DEMANDS PRAISE (113:1-3)

Praise is the first note sounded in this psalm. The Lord demands praise. The psalmist spells that out. He draws our attention to:

A. His Rightful Claim (113:1a,b)

"Praise ye THE LORD. Praise, O ye servants of the LORD." The phrase "Praise ye the LORD" is simply the Hebrew word "Hallelujah."

We note that it is the Lord's *servants* who are called on to praise Him. We serve a good Master. There is none like Him in the earth below or in the heavens above. He deserves our best, even when the tasks assigned are hard, seemingly unrewarding, sometimes tedious, often bitterly opposed by wicked men, and sometimes misunderstood and misinterpreted by other brethren. Our Lord deserves smiling service, not surly service.

We are privileged to be called into *His* service; what we *do* to serve Him is less important. Our calling may be to preach to millions or to pass on a word of testimony in a concentration camp. An angel, on commission from the King of Glory, would be as happy sweeping a chimney as ruling an empire. "Yet serve the Lord Christ" was Paul's way of phrasing it for the Colossian Christians. That concept ennobles all service.

So then, we have the Lord's rightful claim to be served. Since we are His servants, honored to be called to wait on Him and do His will, to be part of what He is accomplishing in the world, He has every right to expect we will do it with praise.

B. His Royal Name (113:1c-2)

"Praise the name of the LORD. Blessed be the name of the LORD from this time forth and for evermore." Three times in three verses mention is made of the name of the Lord. Throughout the entire Old Testament age God revealed Himself through His names: Elohim, Adonai, Jehovah Shalom, Jehovah Shammah, Jehovah Tsidkenu, Jehovah Nissi, El Elyon, El Shaddai. Name after name, revelation after revelation, until, at last we cross the great divide from the Old Testament to the New and learn the name "Our *Father*."

So, when the psalmist tells us to praise the name of the Lord from this time forth and for evermore, it is because His name is the manifold expression of who He is. We can understand that, because in a lesser sense the same is true of us. Few things are more precious in life than a good name, one we can carry with dignity and respect.

The first thing slave owners did in the American south, when they bought a new slave, was cancel out his former African name and arbitrarily give him some white man's name. Alex Haley describes the naming of Kunta Kinte, the hero of his novel *Roots*. The young man had been captured, had survived the horrors of the slave ship, had been put up and auctioned like a piece of furniture, and had been thrashed for trying to run away. Then, as the supreme indignity, the black overseer of the white master's slaves said: "You—you Toby." Kunta Kinte's rage flooded his soul with bitterness and gall. This was the final indignity: to be given a detested white man's name. Worse still, his surname for ever afterward would be that of his latest owner. His African identity was to be blotted out.

How different it is with our Master. He has bought us to set us free. He has given us the honor of bearing His name. He would keep the dignity of that royal name ever before us. We serve Him, not with a rebellious spirit because He has degraded us, dehumanized us, despoiled us. We serve Him, because He has given us back our lost dignity and has given us a high calling in Christ. He wants us to keep His name before us. Then we will properly praise Him and spread the honor of His name.

The psalmist likewise keeps before us the appropriateness of praising the Lord. Nor is that all. He emphasizes:

C. His Resounding Fame (113:3)

"From the rising sun unto the going down of the same the LORD's name is to be praised." His praises encircle the wide belt of the earth. From the distant east, around the circumference of the globe to the farthest west, the psalmist wanted the Lord's praise to be sung. And so it is.

I often think of that on a Lord's Day. By the time we arrive at the meeting place of His people to join our voices in lifting up His name, His name has already been praised in China and

Japan, in India, in the Middle East, in Europe, in the islands of the sea, in churches along our eastern shores. Nor will the praise end when we read our last Scripture verse, sing our last hymn, and offer our closing benediction. The praise will follow the sun across midwest prairies, over the Rocky Mountains, up and down the western seaboard, and on out to sea.

II. THE LORD DESIRES PRAISE (113:4-6)

The psalmist then draws our attention to three themes in order to awaken in us a desire to gratify our Lord's desire to be praised.

A. His Glory (113:4)

"The LORD is high above all nations, and His glory above the heavens." Some nations on earth today have dedicated themselves to the spread of atheism. They cannot win. "The LORD is high above all nations." They are a mere drop in the bucket to Him, and He can upset that bucket anytime He wants.

The psalmist would lift our eyes above those who think in their pride and ignorance that they can overthrow God. He says, "His glory is above the heavens. Look up!"

And now we see it: a land of fadeless day; a land where they pave their streets with gold, build their walls of jasper, and make their gates of pearl. We see a land where time is not counted in years. We see a throne, encircled round and round with a rainbow of gleaming emerald, a rainbow such as never arched the skies of earth. We see, flowing from that throne, a crystal stream. We see the lightnings play like liquid fire to form the dazzling draperies against which that throne is set.

We see the One who sits on that throne: "Thou art worthy! Thou art worthy!" we sing.

B. His Greatness (113:5)

"Who is like unto the LORD our God, who dwelleth on high." We parade before us the great ones of earth. We summon the world's thinkers—Plato, Aristotle, Archimedes, Solomon, Newton, Einstein. We summon the world's religious leaders—Buddha, Confucius, Muhammad. We summon the world's conquerors—Alexander, Genghis Khan, Napoleon, Caesar. A miserable crowd.

"Who is like unto the LORD our God, who dwelleth on high?" Nobody. All the world's great ones are dwarfed, discomfited, dismayed, before Him. Their wisdom is seen to be nothing. They are like men picking up pebbles on the seashore of knowledge and when they have gathered all they can carry, they have gleaned nothing of all that remains to be known. Their reli-

gions are seen to be false. Their conquests built them empires of
sand swept away by the rising of a later tide. They shrink away
in confusion and shame.

C. His Grace (113:6)

The grace of our Lord is the best theme of all: "Who hum-
bleth Himself to behold the things that are in heaven, and in the
earth." Although He is so high, He is willing to stoop down and
see how things are here on planet earth. He sits in heaven; He
sees on earth.

As we creep into that upper room in Jerusalem on the night
our Lord was there, we realize that our Lord clothed Himself in
humanity, humbled Himself, became obedient unto death, even
the death of the cross. "For God so loved the world, that He
gave His only begotten Son, that whosoever believeth in Him
should not perish, but have everlasting life." *That* is the supreme
manifestation of His grace. *That* should stimulate in us a desire
to praise Him as we ought.

III. The Lord Deserves Praise (113:7-9)

We are living in a world that has been ruined by sin, "a vale of
tears."

The psalmist reminds us that the Lord deserves praise because of:

A. His Kindness to the Downtrodden (113:7-8)

Our Lord does two wonderful things for the downtrodden.
He brings them:

1. Up From the Pit (113:7)

"He raiseth up the poor out of the dust, and lifteth the needy
out of the dunghill." Here we have two Old Testament meta-
phors for poverty and degradation. The refuse of a middle-
eastern town was collected and dumped in a heap outside the
walls. Beggars, lepers, those afflicted with loathsome diseases,
and other outcasts congregated there at night. They would lie
down near the ashes of the refuse fires trying to keep warm.

Although the world's great have little concern for such persons, the Lord does. He looks out over earth's cities—with their
noisome slums, the millions of people who make the streets
their home, who at best have a flimsy shanty or a spot under a
bridge for a home, and who usually go hungry to bed—and He
has an offer for them.

He offers them life everlasting—the bread of life. He offers
them a place in His kingdom—rank and royalty in the world to
come. He offers to bring them up from the pit, up from the

miry clay, up from the dust and the dunghill.

Not only does He bring them up from the pit, He also brings them:

2. Into the Palace (113:8)

"That He may set [them] with princes, even with the princes of His People." He offers to make them the aristocracy of Heaven. So we have God's kindness to the downtrodden declared.

The gospel appeal has always been to the poor. Jesus said it was easier for a camel to pass through the eye of a needle than for a rich man to enter Heaven. Paul said, "Not many mighty, not many noble are called." He didn't say "Not any" but "Not many." History has proven him right. The rank and file of the kingdom of God have come from the downtrodden of earth.

B. His Kindness to the Distressed (113:9)

"He maketh the barren woman to keep house, and to be a joyful mother of children." Verses 6 and 7 of Psalm 113 seem to be a reference to the song of Hannah (1 Samuel 2:8). Hannah wept and prayed before the Lord to be delivered from the burden of barrenness. God heard her cry and gave her a child she called Samuel ("Asked of God"). We remember how she brought him back and presented him to the Lord to be raised by the priests, to be a lifelong Nazarite, to grow up to be one of God's nobility. When she brought her little boy to Eli she thanked God for lifting her out of the dust.

Perhaps verse 7 also looks ahead to the future. When Mary learned from Gabriel that she was to become the mother of the Messiah she sang, "He hath . . . exalted them of low degree. He hath filled the hungry with good things . . ." (Luke 1:52-53).

In this psalm we see that God crowns womanhood with motherhood. Rotherham suggests that this psalm was written by a king while awaiting the birth of his firstborn. It ends on the same note with which it began, "Praise ye the LORD." Surely we can sing our own reverent Hallel.

> Man of Sorrows, what a Name
> For the Son of God who came,
> Ruined sinners to reclaim,
> Hallelujah! What a Saviour.
>
> Guilty, vile and helpless we,
> Spotless Lamb of God was He,
> Full atonement can it be?
> Hallelujah! What a Saviour.
>
> When He comes our glorious King,
> All His ransomed hosts to bring,
> Then anew this song we'll sing,
> Hallelujah! What a Saviour.

Psalm 114

HOW GOD GIVES POWER

I. The Roots of Spiritual Power (114:1-2)
   A. Separation (114:1)
   B. Sanctification (114:2a)
   C. Surrender (114:2b)
II. The Results of Spiritual Power (114:3-8)
   A. Things Begin to Happen (114:3-6)
      1. We Are Invincible (114:3-4)
         a. Obstacles Will Be Removed (114:3)
         b. Opportunities Will Be Revealed (114:4)
      2. We Are Invulnerable (114:5-6)
   B. Throngs Begin to Hearken (114:7-8)
      1. Conviction (114:7)
      2. Conversion (114:8)

A LTHOUGH THIS PSALM HAS no actual "Hallelujah," it is linked with the psalms making up the Great Hallel. Like Psalm 113, it was sung at the Passover before the meal began. For the full spiritual significance of this psalm we must imagine ourselves back in that upper room on the night in which the Lord Jesus was betrayed. We see Him there with His disciples, singing the rousing verses of this psalm.

We do not know who wrote it (Rotherham thinks it was the prophet Isaiah). Nor do we know when it was written (Rotherham thinks it was written for the Great Passover convened by godly King Hezekiah). Its position in the Hebrew hymnbook could have been assigned to it at a later date for the service of the second temple.

The Passover and the exodus marked Israel's birthday as a nation; Psalm 114 is a song of the exodus. The Passover precipitated the exodus. It was the shedding of the blood of the Passover lamb that protected Israel when the avenging angel spread his wings of death over Egypt.

From the sixth century onward the established church has

used this psalm in ministering to the dying and at the burial of
the dead. In church liturgy it was appointed also as a psalm for
Easter Day, because Israel's deliverance from bondage was seen
as a type of our deliverance from the bondage of sin.

This song is a history lesson; God does not want us to forget
the lessons of history. The Jews always regarded their deliverance from Egypt as the greatest fact in history, and God would
have us recall Calvary in that way.

We can look at this short psalm in several ways. First, we can
go back and expound the history of which it speaks: we have
the miracle recalled (114:1-2), the method recounted (114:3-6),
and the moral recorded (114:7-8). Second, we can go back and
see nature quailing and nature questioned. Third, we can study
the psalm in the light of the miracles it recalls: the water miracles at the Red Sea, at Jordan, at Horeb (Ex. 17:6), and at
Kadesh (Num. 20:11). Since we have gone over all that ground
already several times in the psalms we shall simply note those
ways to expound this psalm.

Fourth, we could carry the psalm forward to the future and
dwell on its prophetic elements, on its obvious suitability as a
song for the millennial age to come.

Or, fifth, setting aside such a temptation, we can see what
lessons the psalm has for us today. That is how we are going to
explore it, as a song of spiritual power. It tells how God gives us
victory over all the power of the enemy.

It sets before us, first:

I. The Roots of Spiritual Power (114:1-2)

The first two verses tell us that spiritual power has three
prerequisites. God does not invest His power promiscuously in
everyone who comes demanding it. A first principle for obtaining power from God is:

A. Separation (114:1)

"When Israel went out of Egypt, the house of Jacob from a
people of strange language . . ." The first secret of spiritual
power is separation. Long before Israel learned that lesson at
the Red Sea, God had begun the separating process by making a
difference between His people and the people of Egypt. For
instance, when a three-day darkness covered Egypt, we read
that "the children of Israel had light in their dwellings" (Exodus
10:23). They were children of light, not children of darkness
like the others.

The psalmist refers to the exodus from *Egypt*, not the exodus
from *Babylon*. The two experiences were dissimilar. The exodus
from Egypt was total, the exodus from Babylon was partial.

The exodus from Egypt was from slavery, the exodus from Babylon was from prosperity. The exodus from Egypt was an act of power, the exodus from Babylon was an answer to prayer. In the one case the king acted grudgingly and tried to hinder; in the other case the king acted graciously and tried to help. Both of these movements in Israel's history illustrate God's ways of power in the world.

In the case of the Babylonian exodus only a minority of God's people responded. It is easier to have a mighty movement of God among those living in poverty than among those living in prosperity. A people who know themselves to be slaves are more likely to respond to the call of God than a people who think themselves a success. In Egypt, God's people were in bondage; in Babylon, they were in business. So, when God wishes to draw attention to His sovereign power He invariably points us to the exodus from Egypt.

"When Israel went out of Egypt, the house of Jacob from a people of strange language . . ." The expression "strange language" means "stammering tongue." When the Hebrews first went down to Egypt they could not understand the Egyptian language (Genesis 42:23). When God had something to say to them He didn't say it in Egyptian, He said it in Hebrew. Turning away from those who spoke a foreign language meant they were now receptive to what God had to say.

It is an important point. This world speaks a strange language, a stammering tongue. It has no natural means of communicating the thoughts, words, and mind of God. This world may exhibit all the marks of human genius, all the evidences of intellectual power, but it cannot speak the language of Heaven. *That* language is found only in the Bible, the one book this world does not want. It has ruled it out of its public schools, colleges, and universities. Young people can read Voltaire and Marx in school, but not the Bible. They can read books that dishonor God and blaspheme His Son, books that glorify adultery and sodomy, evolution and violence. But not the Bible.

So the first way to spiritual power is separation—turning away from the world's language, the world's way of thinking, to listen to what God has to say. That kind of separation brings our intellects to rest on the language of Heaven spoken by the Holy Spirit through the pages of His book.

A second principle for obtaining power from God is:

B. Sanctification (114:2a)

"Judah," we read, "was His sanctuary." A sanctuary is a sacred enclosure where God dwells. God said of Esau that he was "a profane" person—that is, he had no enclosure in his heart where God could dwell. "Judah was His sanctuary." It was on the high hills of Judah that God at last came home to dwell when the temple was built and the Shekinah glory cloud came in and took up its seat on the ark between the cherubim.

Sanctification is the other side of separation. Separation sets us apart from the world; sanctification sets us apart for God. God will not give His power to a worldly, carnal person. That would be like putting a loaded rifle in the hands of a three-year-old. God gives His power only to those He can trust.

A third principle for obtaining power from God is:

C. Surrender (114:2b)

"And Israel was His dominion." Israel was the sphere of God's rule, the place where His sovereignty was owned. God will not give His power to those who want to use it independently of Himself. Surrender is the key to a life of victory.

A verse of Scripture we often misquote is this: "Resist the devil and he will flee from you." That, however, is not true. The devil is not going to flee from us. He is not the least bit afraid of us. What that verse actually says is: "Submit yourselves therefore to God. Resist the devil, and he will flee from you" (James 4:7). Here we see the secret of power over the enemy—personal submission to God.

Such submission would have kept Adam and Eve in the garden of Eden. That is what the serpent came to test: to see if he could persuade them to act in defiance of God. That is what He tried to persuade the Lord Jesus to do in the wilderness. That is where he tests us too. God will not give His power to those who are not in submission to Him.

These, then, are the roots of spiritual power. Now let us examine:

II. The Results of Spiritual Power (114:3-8)

Broadly speaking, we see two results of spiritual power.

A. Things Begin to Happen (114:3-6)

A glance at these four verses shows that seas flee away, rivers part wide, mountains and hills begin to shake. Surely that is what we want—for things to begin to happen. We want it to be very evident that God is at work. We also note two other ideas in these verses.

1. We Are Invincible (114:3-4)

"The sea saw it, and fled: Jordan was driven back. The mountains skipped like rams, and the little hills like lambs."
a. Let us break that down a little further. We notice first that

obstacles will be removed: "The sea . . . Jordan" (114:3). It is not difficult to perceive what those obstacles represent.

The *sea* kept them in the world. Israel marched right up to the Red Sea and there they stopped. They could go no further. They were still in Egypt's domain. They had been saved, put under the shelter of the blood, but now the enemy was coming after them. He wanted to drag them back to slavery, back to the brick kilns, the taskmaster's lash, and the ghetto on the Nile. He wanted to bring them back to the old way of life, to maintain his rule and dominion over them.

Between them and freedom was the sea, an obstacle to their further progress. It kept them there in the world, in Egypt. Then the sea fled. Why? Because Joshua was there with a few hundred brave men? Because Jethro, Moses' father-in-law, had arrived? Because Aaron prayed, or Miriam prophesied?

No, it fled because Moses, at God's command, took the rod in his hand and did what he was told. Then, over they went, over the riverbed, over onto dry land. Then, too, at the summons of that same rod, back the waters went to sweep away the foe.

Thus Israel put the waters of separation between them and the old way of life. What had been an obstacle became their protection to make it difficult for them ever to go back to Egypt and their past.

We read next that "Jordan was driven back." When that happened, the Hebrews had been saved from Egypt for a considerable time. A new, younger generation had arisen, who now stood beside the *Jordan.* That is what kept them in the wilderness. They had been in the wilderness for 40 years and had known little but defeat, discouragement, and disobedience. The life that beckoned in Canaan eluded them, because they had never crossed Jordan. Jordan kept them in the wilderness, in their grumbling, mumbling, carnal life.

Now Jordan, too, was driven back and the obstacle removed. They had symbolically passed through death, burial, and resurrection, and now they stood on the victory side of Jordan. The land was before them and, although both battles and blessings lay ahead, they were in the promised land at last.

Things begin to happen when God gets us out of the world and then out of the wilderness. Obstacles are removed.

b. We notice also that *opportunities will be revealed:* "The mountains skipped like rams, and the little hills like lambs" (114:4). Now we are in Canaan, the place where all the promises of God are "yea and amen." Look at the opportunities.

The mountains speak of the place of *fellowship.* Not everyone climbs the mountain peaks. The mountain peak is where, symbolically, we get closer to Heaven. The mountain speaks of higher ground, of nearness to God. The enemy would like to keep us in the valley, on lower ground.

But look! Those mountains skip like rams. They shake at the mighty tramp of those who are determined to scale their heights and occupy higher ground for God. Every stronghold and device of Satan to keep us down will be shaken to the ground. The way is clear now, right up to the top.

But there is more: "And the little hills [skipped] like lambs." The little hills suggest *fruitfulness*. The rolling, undulating, fertile hills were where the best crops were grown, where the cattle stood knee-deep in clover, where the vines and olives flourished.

God wants us to be fruitful. He gives us the land and has put the means of victory in our hands, but we have to go in and possess our possessions. We have to get out of the world and out of the wilderness, out of Egypt into Canaan. We have to take our stand on the ground of separation, sanctification, and surrender, and scale the heights of fellowship. We have to plough and sow the seed, and take the steps to fruitfulness. And when we do, we are invincible.

2. We Are Invulnerable: (114:5-6)

In these two verses the psalmist goes over the same ground. Only now instead of all nature *quailing*, all nature is *questioned:* "What ailed thee, O thou sea, that thou fleddest? Thou Jordan that thou wast driven back? Ye mountains, that ye skipped like rams, and ye little hills, like lambs?" What a healthy attitude for the believer to adopt.

There was no natural explanation for what happened. Only God could have produced such results. The singer does not lose his sense of awe and wonder. It was not Israel who did it, it was God.

We are invulnerable as long as we maintain an attitude of "Not I, but Christ." I was just the instrument. It is all of God. The moment we become proud, imagining that it is our zeal, prayers, intellect, eloquence, that did it, God lays us sadly aside.

B. Throngs Begin to Hearken (114:7-8)

The final verses of the psalm add a second result of spiritual power.

1. Conviction (114:7)

"Tremble, thou earth, at the presence of the Lord, at the presence of the God of Jacob." When God is moving in power, people will tremble. The Spirit of God convicts of sin, of righteousness, of judgment to come. People begin to tremble, not at the preacher, but at the presence of the God of Jacob. The name the psalmist uses is *Adon Eloah,* the Mighty Lord and Living God of Jacob. The name *Jacob* speaks to us of human frailty, of natural weakness. Adon Eloah as the God of Jacob reminds us that God's strength is made perfect in weakness. It is when *He* moves into a church service, into a soul-winning situation, into a gospel campaign, into a revival, that people begin to tremble. There is conviction.

2. Conversion (114:8)

The Mighty Lord and the Living God "turned the rock into a standing water, the flint into a fountain of waters." Two miracles are mentioned here, one from the beginning of the wilderness journey, the other at the end. In the one case the word for "rock" implies a low-lying rock; in the second case the word here rendered "flint" is *sela,* a high cliff. One speaks of Christ in His humiliation; the other of Christ in His glory.

In the first place the rock was to be *smitten;* in the second it was to be *spoken to.* In each case there were results. Water flowed; people came and stooped and drank and went away filled. Christ on the cross, smitten. Christ in glory, addressed. And the water of life flows out to thirsty, needy souls. Millions upon millions of people have been convicted and converted.

Psalm 115

IDOLATRY EXPOSED

THIS PSALM, like its immediate companions in the Hebrew hymnbook, traditionally was sung at the annual Passover feast in Israel. We do not know when it was written. We can see at a glance that it contrasts idolatry with the worship of the true God. Rotherham thinks it was written in the days of King Jehoshaphat (2 Chronicles 20) when the surrounding nations mobilized against that godly Judean king.

The surrounding peoples were all idolators. Judah itself had been infected with the same folly but Jehoshaphat had brought the nation back to God. He was assured that in the forthcoming confrontation with his foes he would not even have to fight. He was to put bands of singing Levites in the forefront of the battle. They were to march ahead of the troops, spearheading the march toward the foe. The armed men were to march behind.

What a sight it must have been—the choir out front. What an

act of faith. What folly, humanly speaking. We read that when "Judah came toward the watch tower in the wilderness, they looked unto the multitude, and, behold, they were dead bodies fallen to the earth, and none escaped" (2 Chronicles 20:24).

One can imagine the lead soloist, just at that point, ringing out the words of Psalm 115:12, "The LORD hath been mindful of us!" Rotherham is sure that the psalm was adopted later by Hezekiah for the celebration of the great Passover and that it naturally found its way into the great Hallel after the captivity.

Others think the psalm was written after the captivity. The returned remnant soon found things more discouraging than they had dreamed. The first flush of enthusiasm died away. Response to the restoration had been meager. Their great expectations came to almost nothing. The surrounding pagan nations were hostile. We can picture them sneering at the weak and ineffective Jewish remnant saying, "Where is your God now?" Some think that this psalm is an answer to that taunt.

The psalm divides into five parts.

I. APPRECIATION (115:1-3)

We begin by looking at its threefold statement about God.

A. The Sanctity of God's Name (115:1)

"Not unto us, O LORD, not unto us, but unto Thy name give glory." The name of Jehovah is forever associated with the Passover and the exodus. God had revealed Himself to Moses as the great I AM. When Moses first confronted Pharaoh with God's demand that He let the people go, Pharaoh's reply was a disdainful, "Who is the LORD [Jehovah], that I should obey His voice to let Israel go? I know not the LORD, neither will I let Israel go" (Exodus 5:2). By the time God was through with Pharaoh he knew who He was. Then he said, "Rise up, and get you forth from among my people, both ye and the children of Israel; and go, serve the Lord [Jehovah], as ye have said. Also take your flocks and your herds, as ye have said, and be gone; and bless me also" (Exodus 12:31).

Israel's redemption was therefore forever associated with the name of the Lord. And so is ours. "Not unto us, O LORD, not unto us, but unto Thy name give glory."

B. The Scoffers of God's Fame (115:2)

"Wherefore should the heathen say, Where is now their God?" There have always been plenty of people prepared to mock at divine things. We live in an age of atheism when terrible things are being said about our God by people who are influencing the thinking of millions.

One wonders why God does not smite His detractors where they stand. But He has His reasons for not doing so: immaturity in the offender, extenuating circumstances, the innocence of others who would suffer if judgment were imposed, His grace in giving time for repentance and, above all, the fact that this is not the age of judgment. In 1926 novelist Sinclair Lewis was speaking in a church in Kansas. He took out his watch and gave God ten minutes to strike him dead. When Robert G. Ingersoll made a similar challenge to God in his day, Dr. Joseph Parker, a renowned preacher, remarked: "Did the gentleman think he could exhaust the patience of the eternal God in ten minutes?"

The psalmist was up against similar scoffers of God's name.

C. The Straightness of God's Aim (115:3)

"But our God is in the heavens: He hath done whatsoever He hath pleased." God goes straight to the mark of His own sovereign will. He is under no obligation to explain to anyone why or what He does. He is above the taunts and tirades of men. How foolish their prideful expostulations must seem to God, who sublimely pursues His own unwavering purposes in spite of the noisy unbelief of His foes, and without the slightest obligation to respond.

This psalm, then, begins with appreciation for the person and purposes of God. It moves on to:

II. APPRAISAL (115:4-8)

Here we have God's estimate of idolatry, of the folly of paying homage to graven images. The psalmist begins by describing:

A. The Form of the Idol (115:4-7)

"Their idols are silver and gold, the work of men's hands. They have mouths, but they speak not: eyes have they, but they see not: they have ears, but they hear not: noses have they, but they smell not: they have hands, but they handle not: feet have they, but they walk not: neither speak they through their throat." People show as much sense talking to their garden gate as addressing a piece of metal or wood which happens to be shaped something like a human being. Especially when they know that some craftsman made it. Mouths, eyes, ears, noses, hands, feet, throats. Blind, deaf, senseless, helpless, immobile, and silent. Such is an idol. The worship of idols is a form of insanity.

One can sympathize with a pagan who worships the sun. The sun rules the daylight sky. It chases away the darkness, fills the earth with light and warmth, makes grass grow and grain ripen. But for a man to take a piece of wood and shape it to look like a cow or crocodile and then to worship it is insane. For a man to pour metal into a mold, cast it into the shape of a cat, and then worship it is folly. He might just as well kneel down and pray to an iron bedstead. For a man like Michelangelo to chip away at a huge slab of marble until he has made it into the likeness of a woman holding a dead man across her lap—and then come back and pray to it, as he did, is folly. The piece of wood is still a piece of wood, the metal is still metal, the stone, however gracefully sculpted and shapely, is still stone. To bow to it, reverence it, talk to it, is idolatry.

Nor is that folly a passing phase of human history, confined to Stone Age peoples. One can go to Korea today and see people worshiping images of Buddha or to India and see them worshiping the effigies of hundreds of so-called gods. One can cross the street to the nearest Catholic church and see people praying to a stone virgin or to the image of a man nailed to a cross-shaped piece of wood. The figure, whatever it is, has a mouth and throat that cannot speak, eyes that cannot see, ears that cannot hear, a nose that cannot smell, hands that cannot handle, feet that cannot walk. It is only a piece of metal, wood, stone, or plastic.

The psalmist also mentions:

B. The Folly of the Idolator (115:8)

"They that make them are like unto them; so is every one that trusteth in them." Idolatry has a fearful hold over the minds and hearts of millions of people in all parts of the world. It has had for countless centuries. Human beings seem continuingly to surrender their reasoning powers and become wrapped in gross superstition. Some of the world's fiercest wars have been fought in defense of idols. The Jews had just been liberated from Babylon, the land where idolatry reigned supreme over the lives and destinies of vast empires. They themselves had been infected with the same folly until it had been driven from their hearts there in Babylon, the very heartland of idolatry.

III. Appeal (115:9-11)

The heathen appraise Israel's God as helpless. The psalmist responds with a scathing exposure of the stupidity of idolatry. Then he turns his attention to those who know and love the living God of Israel. He appeals to:

A. The Covenant People (115:9)

"O Israel, trust thou in the Lord: He is their help and their shield." The sudden change to the imperative is usually explained by commentators as marking a change of voices as the psalm is being sung. The psalm, it seems, was composed for liturgical use, various parts being sung by the Levitical choir, by the choir master, and by the people. Thus the words, "O Israel, trust thou in the LORD," might have been sung by the choir leader. "He is their help and their shield" might have been the answering echo of the Levitical choir. Both parts focus attention on the faithfulness of God and His ability to hear and answer. Then the psalmist appeals to:

B. The Consecrated Priest (115:10)

Again we recognize the call and the response as the choir master and the choir take up their parts. "O house of Aaron, trust in the LORD: He is their help and their shield." If the *people* must trust in the Lord, how much more must the priests. We have every right to expect that those who have devoted their lives to the Lord's service should be able to set an example for the rest of the family of faith in trusting the Lord.

Then the psalmist appeals to:

C. The Converted Pagan (115:11)

"Ye that fear the LORD, trust in the LORD: He is their help and their shield." For the third time the choir master and choir take up their respective parts. Thus the whole family of faith—even the newest converts, the God-fearers among the Gentiles—are put on the same footing before God. There is no difference between the person brought up in a believing home, the full-time minister or missionary, and the untaught convert. One and all are to trust in the Lord and prove Him for themselves to be a help and shield.

IV. APPLICATION (115:12-15)

A. Assurance of Blessing (115:12-13)

"The LORD hath been mindful of us: He will bless us; He will bless the house of Israel; He will bless the house of Aaron. He will bless them that fear the LORD, both small and great." The blessing of the Lord does not depend on how much we know, or on whether or not we have had a spiritual education. It does not depend on our coming from a privileged family or on our being in full-time Christian ministry.

It depends on His faithfulness to those who trust Him. God finds such trust irresistible, no matter what its source.

B. Assessment of the Blessing (115:14-15)

"The LORD shall increase you more and more, you and your children. Ye are blessed of the LORD which made heaven and

earth." Is someone brokenhearted because one of their children
is far from God, dead in trespasses and sins, wandering in the
far country with a heart set against the Lord? Take courage,
and hold onto this verse. Note its context. Trust in the Lord.
Remember *who* it is who makes the pledge—the Lord who
made heaven and earth. Is any situation too hard for Him? Of
course not. If He can fling billions of stars billions of light-years
into space, and control the destinies of each one, surely He can
increase you more and more—you and your children.

V. APPLAUSE (115:16-18)

The psalm has been rising from one crescendo to another. It
ends with a ringing, reverent round of uninhibited applause.
The psalmist looks at:

A. The Globe (115:16)

"The heaven, even the heavens, are the LORD's: but the earth
hath He given to the children of men." Heaven belongs to the
Lord. It is His home. It is to be our home, but right now it is
His home, where He dwells. It is where Jesus is, where He has
been now these nearly two thousand years. Its wonders are
beyond our comprehension. Any time Scripture attempts a description of Heaven it resorts to symbolic language. It is as
though human language does not have the vocabulary to describe it. Paul came back from there and said that he saw things
"not lawful to be uttered" (indescribable).

But the earth He has given to human beings, and what a mess
we have made of it. Still, help is on the way. This tiny little
planet is the focus of great interest in heavenly places. Angels
and archangels, cherubim and seraphim, thrones and dominions, principalities and powers, the vast empires of God in regions beyond our knowledge, the dark domains of Satan—all
are intensely interested in this globe of ours. And no wonder. It
was here God was made flesh. Here He dwelt. Here is the spot
where redemption was wrought, where Jesus' blood was shed,
the spot to which He is to return. This place will be the center
of everything for all eternity.

B. The Grave (115:17)

"The dead praise not THE LORD, neither any that go down
into silence." This gloomy view of the grave is characteristic of
the Old Testament. Jesus had not yet brought life and immor-
tality to light through the gospel. Still, the Holy Spirit used even
that limited understanding to urge his hearers to praise God
while they could.

We know now that the grave is not silent. We need only read

the last book of our Bible and note the singing and shouting in praise of God to recognize that.

Last of all the psalmist looks at:

C. The Godly (115:18)

"But we will bless THE LORD from this time forth and for evermore. Praise THE LORD." Even with his limited perspective the psalmist catches fire: "We will bless the LORD for evermore," he sings. Our applause will never end. It will grow louder and louder until it awakens the echoes of the everlasting hills and fills earth below and heaven above with its joyful thunder.

"And they sung an hymn and went out into the Mount of Olives." There they go, the Lord and His disciples. The Lord is on His way now to the grave, the silence of which He is to shatter forever. "Praise the LORD."

Psalm 116

THANK YOU, LORD!

WE ARE NOT SURE when this psalm was written. Some would include it among the post-exilic collection, written after the Jews returned from Babylon. The strong Aramaic flavoring of the psalm has led some to believe that it was possibly written at rather a late date after the end of the exile. Rotherham, on the other hand, thinks it was written by Hezekiah when childless, facing death, and with the Davidic line therefore in peril of extinction. He was facing a dark and lonely hour.

It is a very personal psalm; the writer refers to himself 37 times in 16 verses. Indeed, only three verses have no direct personal reference. Yet it is not a sinful preoccupation with self; he mentions the Lord (Jehovah) 15 times.

I. THE PSALMIST'S GRATITUDE (116:1-9)

The psalmist begins with recounting:

A. The Danger He Had Experienced (116:1-4)

Evidently some alarming experience calls for his opening exclamation. In it he expresses:

I. His Present Assurance (116:1-2)

The opening statement has puzzled some commentators because of its abruptness. "I love the LORD." Surely that is a good way to begin a psalm, a day, a new business venture, a new school, a new anything. A bold confession of love for the Lord will set the sails aright and determine a great deal of what happens next.

When I was in the British army it was always my practice, when being posted to a new unit and entering the barracks, to open my duffle bag and take out a big Bible first. That Bible sat in a prominent place on my bed while I put the other things away. It proclaimed to the others in that room, "I love the Lord!" After that I was never asked to participate in their more questionable activities. The message of the Bible was loud and clear. It spoke for me when, perhaps, I might have been too nervous to speak for myself.

"I love the LORD, because He hath heard my voice and my supplications. Because He hath inclined His ear unto me, therefore will I call upon Him as long as I live." I love the LORD *because . . .* Our love is always like that, a *consequent* love. John says—and John ought to know because he was "the disciple whom Jesus loved"—"We love Him, because . . . He first loved us" (1 John 4:19).

God's love is quite the opposite from ours. His love is not a consequent love but a *causeless* love. God said to Israel, "I loved you because . . . I loved you . . ." (cf. Deuteronomy 7:8). He loves us "just because." God loves us because love is what He is. It is not what we are but what He is that makes Him love us. With us it is "I love the Lord because He hath heard."

We have, then, the psalmist's present assurance, his overflowing gratitude for the faithfulness of God. We have also:

2. His Previous Anguish (116:3)

"The sorrows of death compassed me, and the pains of hell got hold upon me: I found trouble and sorrow."

Here again we quickly realize the messianic overtones of that description. Did our Saviour recall the psalmist's words that night in the upper room, knowing that the "sorrows of death," the "pains of hell," were imminent? Reverently we assume that He did.

> His path, uncheered by earth smiles,
> Led only to the cross.

3. His Prayerful Appeal (116:4)

"Then called I upon the name of the LORD; O LORD, I beseech Thee, deliver my soul." It is practically a formula of the faith. "Whosoever shall call upon the name of the LORD shall be saved."

Let us pity those who are shouting to a deaf heaven the names of so-called saints. It is not the name of Mary, Buddha, Muhammad, or Confucius that God honors. The names of bankrupt sinners, no matter how great their reputation among men, cannot move the heart and hand of God.

Only one name opens to us all the treasures of sovereign grace, the name of the Lord. Let us never forget it. No name but *His* unlocks the storehouses of the sky.

After telling of the danger he had experienced, the psalmist next tells of:

B. The Deliverance He Had Experienced (116:5-9)

He has a twofold word here.

1. A Word about His Saviour (116:5-6)

"Gracious is the LORD, and righteous; yea, our God is merciful, The LORD preserveth the simple: I was brought low, and He helped me." How different the Lord is from the gods of the heathen. For the most part their gods are represented by cold, impassive idols. They are either distant or demanding gods. Not so the Lord. He is a gracious God.

We go back to the days of Moses. The children of Israel had made the golden calf and had been dealt with in judgment. Moses the intercessor had stood between the living and the dead. He had asked God to let the stroke of wrath fall on him in order that the people might be spared. In response, God first revealed to Moses His glory and then told him to hew out two more tables of stone to replace those he had broken. Then He told Moses to come back up the mountain once more, for the seventh and last time.

Moses made his way up alone. The mountain was deserted, even the flocks and herds having been removed. The people stood far off, afraid now to go anywhere near that place. Then, as he stood there alone, "The LORD descended in the cloud, and stood with him there, and proclaimed the name of the LORD."

What a name it was! In those circumstances! Picture the scene—the golden calf but scarcely beaten to a heap of dust, the law broken and shattered, Moses standing alone with two new tablets in his hands. We read, "And the LORD passed by before him, and proclaimed, 'The LORD, the LORD GOD, merciful and gracious, longsuffering, and abundant in goodness and truth, keeping mercy for thousands, forgiving iniquity and transgression and sin . . .' " (Exodus 34:5-7). That was how the Lord wished to be known, and thus the psalmist cries, "How gracious you are!" It was a word to His Saviour.

2. A Word to His Soul (116:7-9)

In a threefold reminder to himself, the psalmist tells his soul, first, to *rest in the Lord:* "Return unto thy rest, O my soul; for the LORD hath dealt bountifully with thee" (116:7). Then the psalmist tells his soul to *rejoice in the Lord:* "For Thou hast delivered my soul from death, mine eyes from tears, and my feet from falling" (116:8). God had brought this singer of Israel through a terrible experience. Finally he tells his soul to *resolve in the Lord:* "I will walk before the LORD in the land of the living" (116:9). The land of the living—a land of fadeless day, where eternal ages roll. It is a land where they have no graves, no cemeteries, no funeral homes, no death. Through danger to deliverance indeed!

II. THE PSALMIST'S GRIEF (116:10-11)

Touching on his grief in passing, the psalmist mentions:

A. What He Had Suffered (116:10)

"I believed, therefore have I spoken: I was greatly afflicted." We are left in the dark as to what had so overwhelmed the psalmist. If the writer of this song was Hezekiah, then we have a clue. We can picture Hezekiah after his friend and counselor Isaiah had left him with the sad news that he must prepare for death. The king turned his face to the wall and sobbed. To die, with his work scarcely begun; with no son and heir to carry on his name and the royal Davidic line, with the Assyrian threat on the horizon, to leave his people as sheep without a shepherd. And then came a glorious reprieve: the prophet returned with a 15-year extension of his life.

B. What He Had Said (116:11)

"I said in my haste, 'All men are liars.' " Most of us have spoken in haste like that. We have been disappointed—deceived, perhaps. Some great calamity comes and we say things we shouldn't say, things we wish we could recall. The psalmist has the honesty to admit that he had spoken too hastily. Now it grieved him to think about it, and he was sorry.

III. THE PSALMIST'S GOALS (116:12-15)

The psalmist now states his thinking about his life in days to come.

A. His Assessment of His Duty (116:12-14)

First he gives us *the reason* for such an assessment: "What shall I render unto the LORD for all His benefits toward me?"

How can any of us repay the Lord for His benefits? Think, for instance, of just one benefit—the Bible. What if we had no Bible, no Word from God in this sinful world, no light on our path, no assurance of sins forgiven and a home in Heaven.

The psalmist is realizing how much he owes to God. Then he gives us *the result* of his assessment: "I will take the cup of salvation, and call upon the name of the LORD. I will pay my vows unto the LORD now in the presence of all His people."

Saved. Surrendered. That is how *we* should assess our duty to the Lord in the light of all his benefits. Take the cup of salvation. Call on the name of the Lord. Pay your vows.

B. His Assurance about His Death (116:15)

"Precious in the sight of the LORD is the death of His saints." What a volume of truth is locked up in that one brief verse. He who attends the funeral of a sparrow knows what a terror death can be to us. Never mind, He says, your death is precious to me. God finds nothing precious in the death of the lost. But in the death of each of His own He finds something worth treasuring. Their death is precious. It is of great value to Him because of the death of His Son.

Again, we might reverently wonder what went through the mind of Christ in the upper room: "Precious in the sight of the LORD is the death of His saints." Did He transpose that in His mind to: "Precious in the sight of the Lord is the death of His Son"?

Rotherham changes the word from "precious" to "costly." "Costly in the sight of the Lord is the death of His saints." How much more costly was the death of His Son. God looks at the blood that was shed there at Calvary and He calls it "precious blood." The death of Jesus was costly beyond words to describe: It purchased salvation full and free for all who will come to God by Him.

So we have the psalmist's goals. Even death has lost its terrors.

IV. The Psalmist's Gladness (116:16-19)

In closing his song, the psalmist recalls:

A. His Position (116:16)

"O LORD, truly I am Thy servant; I am Thy servant; and the son of Thy handmaid: Thou hast loosed my bonds." He was a man set free. He had learned the liberating secret that true freedom comes only when a person is sold out to the Lord, to be His bondslave, to be absolutely and always at His disposal. "I am His servant"; that was his position.

B. His Promise (116:17-19)

In view of that liberation, the psalmist promises to live:

1. A Sacrificial Life (116:17)

"I will offer to Thee the sacrifice of thanksgiving, and will call upon the name of the LORD." I will say, "Thank you, Lord," come what may." The sacrifice of thanksgiving.

That is what Jesus offered in the upper room when He instituted the remembrance feast. He took bread in His hands, declared that it represented His body, *gave thanks,* and broke it. The cup, He said, represented His blood, about to be shed, and again He *gave thanks.* The sacrifice of thanksgiving.

2. A Sanctified Life (116:18-19)

"I will pay my vows unto the LORD. Now in the presence of all His People, in the courts of the LORD's house, in the midst of thee, O Jerusalem. Praise ye THE LORD."

We must think again of Jesus in the upper room. When He came into the world it was with a vow: "Not My will but Thine be done." He chose to pay that vow hanging on a Roman cross in order to bear the sin of the world, my sin and yours.

Psalm 117

INTERNATIONAL PRAISE

I. THE CALL TO PRAISE (117:1)
   A. The World in Its Totality Is Lovingly Invited to Adulate Him
   B. The World by Its Tribes Is Loudly Invited to Adore Him
II. THE CAUSE FOR PRAISE (117:2a,b)
   A. The Loving Triumph of the Lord
   B. The Lasting Truth of the Lord
III. THE COMMAND TO PRAISE (117:2c)

PSALM 117 IS MEMORABLE as the shortest psalm in the Hebrew hymnbook, the shortest chapter in the Bible, and (someone has calculated) as the center chapter of the Bible. All of that, I suspect, is intended to draw it to our attention. God does nothing without a purpose. There must be a purpose for including a psalm of just two verses and only 17 Hebrew words.

It is a *messianic* psalm. It is quoted by Paul in the New Testament in connection with the work of Christ. It includes a Passover invitation from Israel to the Gentiles, to come and join them in their Passover. As Rotherham says, "We heartily thank them for this their Passover invitation." And we hasten to join them—only we will join them on the ground not of a *foretelling* Passover but of a *fulfilled* Passover.

Then, too, this is a *millennial* psalm. It looks forward to the day when Jesus will reign, when Israel—regathered to the promised land and dwelling in peace and security as head of the nations—will invite all peoples to come to Jerusalem and join in their annual feasts of thanksgiving.

Israel belongs to the nations. It was never God's plan that the Hebrew people should exclusively and selfishly hug their blessings to themselves, snapping and snarling at other nations with a dog-in-the-manger attitude. Even in their punishment and dispersal among the nations, they are a universal reminder to all that God is sovereign in human affairs: That Jewish dispersal gave wings to the gospel.

The Jews had already spread the concept of the one true God to all nations by the time of Christ. In their law and through their prophets, the world saw evidence of their access to higher truth. When the gospel evangelists went from city to city they always made straight for the synagogue. It was the God-fearers among the Gentiles, orbiting around the outer fringes of Judaism, attracted by what they heard, repelled by what they saw, who first embraced the gospel among the nations.

Finally, this is *a missionary* psalm. Paul appealed to it in Romans 15 to show that God always had loved the Gentiles. The Jews indeed were given *light* from God which the Gentiles never had, but they were never given *love* from God which the Gentiles did not have. God loves Gentiles just as much as He loves Jews. *That* is the missionary message of this psalm.

It was because "God so loved *the world,* that He gave His only begotten Son." It is not just the world of the *elect* as the extreme Calvinist would say, or just the world of the *Jew* as the rabbis of old would have said. It is the world in its totality.

Short as it is, the psalm divides into three parts.

I. The Call to Praise (117:1)

"O praise the Lord, all ye nations: Praise Him, all ye people."

A. The World in Its Totality Is Lovingly Invited to Adulate Him

"O praise the Lord, all ye nations." The word for "praise" is *hallel* from which comes our transliterated "Hallelujah!" It means "to shine" or "to glorify" or, more commonly, simply "to praise." The invitation is given to the millions of mankind, red and yellow, black and white, oriental and occidental, from pole to pole, from sea to sea, to come and praise the Lord. "The Lord" is literally Jehovah Himself. Nobody else. Jehovah Himself—Jesus Himself.

How the heart of our God yearns over lost men and women. He sees the Russians, Chinese, Cubans, Vietnamese, and His heart longs over them. They are seeking to build secular paradises on earth, motivated by the vision of Karl Marx, the vision of man without God: brainwashed to believe that God does not exist, that all things result from the blind working of evolutionary force, that man is simply a social insect caught in the web of time. The psalmist calls to them too: "O praise the Lord, all you atheist nations."

God sees Europeans and Americans seeking a solution to their problems in humanism and materialism, in pleasure-seeking and money making, in permissiveness, in drugs and drink. He sees lands once ablaze with gospel truth now wrapped in darkness. "O praise the Lord, all you Western lands."

God sees the millions of India and Japan bowing down to wood and stone. He sees the clever Japanese make pilgrimages to shrines to worship the spirit of their ancestors. He sees Hindus chained to idols, revering cows, crocodiles, insects, vermin, and rats.

What abysmal folly to worship a *rat*, the most destructive creature on earth, which devours the grain the starving millions of India need.

Some years ago *National Geographic* carried a series of photographs, one of which showed a Hindu shrine dedicated to rats. It pictured a distinguished, grey-haired man in an attitude of worship. Other people, including a young boy, were in postures of adoration before the objects of their worship: a dozen wild rats were crowded around a dish thoughtfully provided to feed their ravenous appetites, given to them as an act of worship, an offering to the gods. God's heart weeps. "O praise the Lord, all you idolatrous lands."

B. The World by Its Tribes Is Loudly Invited to Adore Him

"Praise Him, all ye people." The psalmist now uses a different word for praise, a comparatively rare word, one that occurs only four times in the Psalms. It is translated "Laud Him!" by some scholars. It means to "sing aloud." It conveys the idea that God should be praised with a voice loud enough for everyone to hear.

It is amazing how reserved we are in most of our services. This is one reason why the charismatics are so appealing: they get excited about their religion and put enthusiasm into it. They may go to excess and sometimes border on the blasphemous. They may get carried away with tongues. They may let themselves go, foolishly handing mind and body over to the control of they know not what. But at least they enjoy their religion.

Most of us are scared to shout a loud *Amen* even when we heartily agree with what is being said. We all have either been to a ball game or seen one on television, when the bases were loaded and a home run was needed to win the game. We have felt tension mount as the last batter comes out on the field. The pitcher throws a fast ball. Strike one! He pitches a curved ball. Strike two! The batsman spits on his hand and looks anxiously at the bases, at the pitcher, at the crowd. The pitcher winds up for the kill. The ball comes flashing in. The batsman strikes.

There is a solid resounding *smack* as a good connection is made between bat and ball. The ball soars up, up, straight and true, and flies clean out of the park. And the crowd goes wild! They yell and shout, they hug each other, they rush out onto the field. All for a game that will be forgotten in a week. Yet we can't even say a loud *Amen* when someone says something about the Lord that stirs our hearts.

So we have *the call to praise.* The Holy Spirit calls on the Gentile nations to praise the Lord. When this verse was quoted by the apostle Paul (Romans 15:11), his missionary outreach was to the Roman Christians. He had been writing about accommodating the weaker brother, telling us that there are some matters about which we should be willing to give and take. We are not to do things that might cause someone else to stumble. We are to bear the burden of the weak. Love compromises.

But then he comes to a bedrock issue, a point of belief on which there can be no concession. In this case, love goes on loving but stands its ground and refuses to compromise. The issue at stake in Paul's argument was the bringing of Gentiles into the church of God on the same basis as Jews. To support his point, Paul quoted from Psalm 18:49, Deuteronomy 32:43, and Isaiah 11:10. Note that he quoted from all sections of the Hebrew Bible, from the law, the prophets, and the book of Psalms. Then, amid an avalanche of quotations he quoted from Psalm 117:1. "And again, 'Praise the LORD, all ye Gentiles; and laud Him, all ye people." (Romans 15:11). He nailed down his point with a quotation from this mini-psalm. Let us remember *that,* if we are tempted to pay it scant heed.

There is always the temptation to overlook the little fellow. This little fellow, however, has a mighty voice; he packs a powerful punch; he is not about to be ignored. Nor is he about to be overshadowed by Psalm 119. We have a pygmy and a giant among the psalms—almost next-door neighbors. Let us Gentiles remember that this little fellow puts in a powerful voice for *us.* Without him we might have found ourselves second-class citizens in the kingdom of God, poor brothers and sisters in the family of faith.

This little psalm refuses to let us be overlooked. It brings us in as joint-heirs with Christ to join our voices with those who praise His Name.

II. The Cause for Praise (117:2a, b)

"For His merciful kindness is great toward us: and the truth of the LORD endureth forever." The focus is now on Israel. The psalmist recounts:

A. The Loving Triumph of the Lord

"For His merciful kindness is great toward us." And so it is. The expression "merciful kindness" is the usual and often-used expression in the psalms, "loving-kindness." It has the Old Testament equivalent of the New Testament word *grace.* "His grace is great toward us."

This psalm is generally thought to be a song of the Jews who had returned from the Babylonian exile. God's mercy to them had just been written large on the page of history. For centuries the Jews had defied Him, turned their backs on Him, plunged into the grossest idolatry in which prostitution and child murder were common religious practices. They had filled the land with their abominations, injustice, pornography, and perversion. They had persecuted and killed the prophets.

At last God has uprooted them, allowed their temple to be burned to the ground, and ploughed Jerusalem like a farmer's field. Now He had forgiven them, regathered them, given them a second chance. No wonder they sang, "His merciful kindness is great toward us."

The repatriated remnant of the Jewish people will sing these words in a coming day when they are delivered from extermination in the fires of the great tribulation, when they look on Him whom they pierced, when they recognize at last in Jesus their Messiah. "Ransomed, healed, restored, forgiven," given a place of royalty in the millennial kingdom, they will sing "His merciful kindness is great toward us." We, too, heirs to the spiritual promises to Abraham, we should sing this song.

A section in the Museum of Science and Industry in Chicago is devoted to discoveries that have revolutionized modern medical science. Among those honored by a greater-than-life portrait is Sir James Simpson, the man who discovered chloroform. Before the discovery of chloroform even the simplest operation was a nightmare. Simpson not only let people sleep through the worst horrors of an operation, but he opened the door to medical operations before impossible.

Sir James Simpson was a Christian. Once he was interviewed by a newspaper man who asked, "Sir, what do you consider your greatest discovery?" Sir James replied, "My greatest discovery was when I discovered I was a sinner in the sight of God." The newspaper man tried again: "Thank you, Sir James. And now would you please tell me your *second* greatest discovery." "By all means," replied that great Christian. "My second greatest discovery was when I discovered that Jesus died for a sinner like me."

B. The Lasting Truth of the Lord (117:2b)

"And the truth of the LORD endureth for ever." Salvation does not rest on sentiment. It rests on truth, the truth that God cannot deny His own character. It is not *truth at the expense of mercy.* If that were so, there could be *no hope;* it would mean that God would have to deny His own holy character. It would be as though a judge opened all the prisons and set free murderers and rapists, thieves and swindlers, just because He felt sorry for them pining in prison.

Mercy at the expense of truth would turn Heaven into hell and drive God from His throne. David tried it with Absalom and, before long, he had a rebellion on his hands which drove him out of Jerusalem and into the jaws of death. God had to devise a means by which He could reconcile both His merciful kindness and His everlasting truth. The problem was solved at Calvary.

Jesus went to Calvary to die for us, the Just for us the unjust, to bring us to God. He took our guilt that we might take His goodness, took our sinfulness that we might take His sinlessness, took our ruin that we might take His righteousness. *That* was God's way of bringing mercy and truth together in an everlasting embrace. *That* is our cause for praise.

Last of all, the psalm sets before us:

III. THE COMMAND TO PRAISE (117:2c)

"Praise ye the LORD." Astronomers are now discovering that many stars are binary stars, or twins. They are tied together and act and react the one on the other. God has a binary star, the bright and morning star. That binary star is *Jesus.* When Jesus came to Bethlehem, something unique happened in the universe. God took deity and humanity and so fused the one into the other that something new was brought into being—the person of Jesus. The child of Bethlehem was the Ancient of Days; the Son of God became the Son of Man; the eternal, uncreated, self-existing One was now also a man born to die. That wondrous binary star has now made salvation possible for us.

We would be clods if we did not want to sing and shout His praise. We would advertise to the universe that we have no comprehension of Him at all, no real understanding of the greatness and the cost of our salvation.

That is the note that rings down through this Great Hallel: *"Praise the Lord!"*

Psalm 118

THE JOURNEY HOME

HERE IS A PSALM freighted down to the waterline both with history and prophecy. Its human author is unknown. Suggestions have included David, Hezekiah, Isaiah, Nehemiah, Zechariah, and Haggai. The consensus seems to be that the psalm is post-exilic; it belongs to the time when the remnant came back from Babylon to reconstitute Hebrew national life in the promised land.

We can connect it with the celebration of the feast of the Tabernacles (that annual feast of rejoicing prefiguring the millennium) recorded in Nehemiah 8. The walls of Jerusalem had been completed in spite of fierce opposition from Samaritans and others. The work was completed in the 21st year of Artaxerxes (444 B.C.) and a month later the joyful feast of Tabernacles was kept with exceptional national rejoicing. The psalm may well have been composed for that occasion.

It was Martin Luther's favorite psalm. He wrote, "This psalm has been of special service to me. It has helped me out of many great troubles, when neither emperor nor kings nor wise men nor saints could help."

It is the last of the Hallel psalms (113–118) and it was sung at the close of the Paschal Feast. In all probability this 118th Psalm was sung by the Lord Jesus Himself. We can picture Him, His voice ringing out in perfect time and tune, filling the upper room as He poured out His heart in its words. The thought should make this psalm infinitely precious to us.

It is a messianic psalm. Certain verses are forever associated in our minds with the Lord Jesus Himself and with His earthly life and ministry.

It is what I call "an envelope psalm," the first verse and last verse being the same. It is therefore possible to come to the last verse of the psalm, count it as the first verse, and begin all over again. It could be sung over and over again in that way (there is no evidence that it was, but it could have been). The psalm begins and ends with thanksgiving to God for His goodness and deathless grace.

The psalm is clearly liturgical, arranged to be sung in answering parts, choir answering choir. It was sung antiphonally at the feast of Tabernacles as the worshipers drew near to the gates of the temple proclaiming the miracle of God's magnificent deliverance of His people.

It is also prophetic, looking beyond the Lord's first coming to His coming again, to the time when He will deliver Israel from its foes at Armageddon and lead the world into the millennial age.

Then, too, the psalm sets before us a journey—a journey home, and we are going to consider it from that perspective. It is not just our journey home, or Israel's journey home, but our Lord's journey home. It takes us by way of Calvary to the land beyond the skies.

I. COMMENCEMENT OF THE JOURNEY (118:1-4)

The journey commences with praise to God for His amazing goodness and grace. We note:

A. The Worshiper's Theme (118:1)

"O give thanks unto the LORD; for He is good: because His mercy endureth for ever." What a blessing to find something that endures forever. We are living in an age of built-in obsolescence. Auto makers don't want to build a car that will last forever. No manufacturer, in fact, wants to build such a product. It would not be good for business. More and more things today are built to be disposable: soft drinks in disposable bottles, flashlights, cameras, all kinds of things.

Nothing down here lasts forever. "O give thanks unto the LORD; for He is good: because His *mercy* endureth forever." That is the theme. Imagine the Lord Jesus singing that as He faced the terrible torment of Calvary. He was about to face the undiluted *wrath* of a thrice-holy sin-hating God.

We note next:

B. The Worshiping Throng (118:2-4)

"Let Israel now say, that His mercy endureth for ever. Let the house of Aaron now say, that His mercy endureth for ever. Let them now that fear the LORD say, that His mercy endureth for ever." Here we see *public* praise—Israel; *priestly* praise—the house of Aaron; *personal* praise—they that fear the Lord.

Praising the Lord is not always the spontaneous expression of a redeemed heart. But God *is* going to be praised for all eternity by every living creature—that is a predetermined fact of the future. Not all will own Him as Saviour, but all will own Him as Sovereign and will give Him the honor and glory that belong to Him by sovereign right.

The best kind of praise is not that of "Israel," which derives from its national position. Nor is it that of the house of Aaron, the chanted responses of religious professionals. The best praise wells up from the heart of an individual who has come to appreciate the Lord. "They that worship Him must worship Him in spirit and in truth," Jesus told the woman at the well, "for the Father seeketh such to worship Him" (John 4:23-24).

II. CHARACTER OF THE JOURNEY (118:5-18)

The way home for the Lord Jesus was a long way, beset with difficulty and danger. It was no flower or palm-strewn path.

There were four major stopping places on that dreadful road our Lord was called to tread. They all seem to be mirrored here—in Gethsemane, Gabbatha, Golgotha, and glory. First we find ourselves:

A. At Gethsemane (118:5-7)

Look at:

1. The Prayer that Was Answered (118:5)

"I called upon THE LORD in distress: THE LORD answered me, and set me in a large place." Five times in this psalm the name *Jah* is used for God. In some ways it is the greatest of all the names for God. It expresses in concentrated form the eternal existence of the great I AM, the ever-present One. The title occurs 49 times in the Bible.

There is no way we can measure the distress that overtook the Lord in Gethsemane. Certainly the agony He experienced would have killed an ordinary man. In the intensity of His agony the great drops of perspiration pouring off Him looked like blood.

Yet Satan did not succeed in turning the Lord Jesus aside from His ultimate goal. He was *delivered*—for that is the force of the expression. "He set me in a large place." How large that place is we shall never know until we stand at last with Him on the vast shores of eternity and look out over the unborn ages, over the breathtaking wonders of God's new creation. Look also at:

2. The Peace that Was Assured (118:6)

"The LORD is on my side; I will not fear: What can man do unto me?" Men thought they could arrest Him, try Him, and crucify Him. Led by Judas, the mob came into the garden. Jesus met them possessed of a peace that passes all understanding. He stood there calmly, His soul filled with quiet confidence. He had won the victory. He could say, "No man taketh [My life] from Me, but I lay it down of Myself. I have power to lay it down, and I have power to take it up again. This commandment have I received of My Father" (John 10:18). When Pilate threatened Him with the cross, He replied, "Thou couldest have no power at all against Me, except it were given thee from above" (John 19:11). He had no fear of what man could do to Him.

Look, too, at:

3. The Person that Was Alongside (118:7)

"The LORD taketh my part with them that help me: therefore shall I see my desire upon them that hate me." Scholars admit that this is an awkward rendering. Rotherham puts it, "Jehovah is my Helper; so shall I gaze on them that hate me." Jesus had Someone alongside.

Let us stand with Him a little longer in Gethsemane. "Whom seek ye?" we hear Him say to that mob. "Jesus of Nazareth," they reply. "I AM" was His simple reply. They fell flat on their backs. It happened three times. At any time He could simply have walked away from them and gone anywhere He wished. But he chose to go to Calvary. The way of the cross led home. That was the path marked out in eternity before the worlds began, before He stooped down to fashion Adam's clay, before the serpent raised his head in Eden, before by one man sin entered into the world and death by sin.

So then, Gethsemane was the first stopping place on the journey home. We come now to the next stopping place. We find ourselves:

B. At Gabbatha (118:8-9)

"It is better to trust in the LORD than to put confidence in man. It is better to trust in the LORD than to put confidence in princes."

Take Simon Peter, for instance. Suppose the Lord had put confidence in him. He was a smoking flax, a broken reed. The Lord would not quench the smoking flax, nor break the bruised reed, but neither would He put confidence in it. He knew Peter better than Peter knew himself. "Though all men forsake Thee, yet will not I," Peter said. Jesus knew he would.

Look at Herod and Pilate. Suppose the Lord had put confidence in them. Nobody could trust Herod Antipas, the treacherous son of Herod the Great who had massacred the male children of Bethlehem. Herod Antipas had stolen his own brother's wife. He had murdered John the Baptist to pacify the same wicked woman. The Lord was certainly not going to put confidence in him. Nor in Pilate. Pilate undoubtedly wished Him well and no doubt would have released Him had it been expedient. He was, however, more concerned in being Caesar's friend than in doing what he knew to be right. The Lord was not going to put His trust in man.

Next comes the most dreadful stopping place of all. We find ourselves:

C. At Golgotha (118:10-13)

There we see foes massed against Him. There are:

1. The Human Foes (118:10-12)

The Lord is unimpressed by their nationalities, by their numbers, or by their nature. "All nations compassed me about: but in the name of the LORD will I destroy them [cut them off]. They compassed me about; yea, they compassed me about: but in the name of the LORD I will destroy them. They compassed me about like bees; they are quenched as the fire of thorns: for in the name of the LORD I will destroy them."

Stand for a moment on that hill of shame. But take your stand there a thousand years before the cross was reared. The armies of Israel are terrified by a giant from Gath, armed to the teeth and fierce as a jungle lion. Into the cowering camp comes David with his slingshot and staff. Down into the valley he goes to fight the foe. The Philistine sees him coming and curses him by his pagan gods. David calmly eyes him up and down. "Thou comest to me," he said, "with a sword, and with a spear, and with a shield; but I come to thee in the name of the LORD of hosts . . ." (1 Samuel 17:45). David destroyed him, cut him off, in the name of the Lord.

Now come back to Calvary where great David's greater Son hangs encompassed by His foes. The armed might of the Roman world is massed against Him. But the weapons of our warfare are spiritual and mighty through God to the pulling down of strongholds. He fights back in the name of the Lord.

His foes are compared to bees and to a fire of thorns. The bees suggest the *furious* nature of His foes. An angry swarm of bees can be formidable, almost impossible to fight. They come from all directions and inject their venom like a thousand red-hot needles. That is how the Lord's foes appeared to Him. But a bee can sting only once, and once it has made its attack it dies. Its power is forever gone. Thus our Lord intended to destroy Satan.

The fire of thorns suggests the *fierce* nature of His foe. But a fire of thorns, although it blazes up and burns fiercely, soon dies out. It has no lasting substance from which to produce new heat. One swift blaze and it is all over. That is how the Lord's foes appeared to Him. Calvary was fierce and furious, but it was soon to be over and then Jesus' foes would be powerless ever to harm Him again. He would overcome them in the name of the Lord. The name of the Lord was stronger than their swords and spears.

So much for human foes. But there is another one. There is:

2. The Hidden Foe (118:13)

"Thou has thrust sore at me that I might fall: but the LORD helped me." Commentators do not know what to make of this verse. Who is the "thou" of whom it speaks? He is not only unnamed, he is invisible. That unseen, hidden invisible foe must surely be Satan.

We know that Satan and his hosts were at the cross because the Lord Jesus triumphed over them there. Paul says the Christ triumphed over "principalities and powers making a show of them openly in His cross."

Satan was there having his final moment of seeming triumph. "Thou hast thrust me sore." The Hebrew of the passage is more graphic. It says, "Thrusting thou hast thrust me through." That final parting thrust was as vicious as the hosts of hell could make it.

We have been to Gethsemane, to Gabbatha, and to Golgotha. There is only one more stopping place now. We find ourselves:

D. In Glory (118:14-18)

The suffering phase of the journey is over. The Lord can now rejoice. We see Him rejoicing:

1. In His Redeemed People (118:14-16)

"THE LORD is my strength and song, and is become my salvation. The voice of rejoicing and salvation is in the tabernacles of the righteous." The primary reference seems to be to the tents of the pilgrims pitched outside Jerusalem at the joyous feast of Tabernacles. The ultimate reference is to a coming day when Jesus will return and set up His kingdom in Israel. The intermediate reference is to the Lord now, in Heaven, rejoicing with His redeemed people over the great salvation He has wrought.

The theme of the rejoicing is given: "The right hand of the LORD doeth valiantly. The right hand of the LORD is exalted: the right hand of the LORD doeth valiantly."

Look at that right hand of His. It is a pierced hand, engaged now in a priestly work, raised at God's right hand in answer to all the accusations of the evil one against the people of God. Satan cannot get anywhere near the throne with his venomous charges because that hand is upraised to silence every word he utters.

We see Him rejoicing also in:

2. In His Resurrection Power (118:17-18)

"I shall not die, but live, and declare the works of THE LORD. THE LORD hath chastened me sore: but He hath not given me over unto death." Calvary, with its sorrows and sufferings, is behind:

> Ne'er again shall God Jehovah
> Smite the Shepherd with the sword;
> Ne'er again shall cruel sinners
> Set at nought our glorious Lord.

He lives forever in the power of an endless life. The tree and the tomb are behind Him. He inhabits eternity, there to proclaim the merits of a finished work.

But although the Lord is now in heaven, seated at God's right hand in the rest and enjoyment of a finished work, there remains one step more.

We must consider:

III. THE CLIMAX OF THE JOURNEY (118:19-29)

The world is still in the grip of the evil one. The nation of Israel is still in its sins, living in unbelief. The closing verses of the psalm anticipate the coming climax of the age when those things, too, will be set right. The scene moves on to the close of Armageddon and to the commencement of the millennial reign.

We see the Lord in two positions.

A. The Lord Jesus at the Portals of the Temple (118:19-26)

First we have set before us:

1. The Simple Prayer (118:19-21)

The Lord will bring the rescued earthly people of Israel to the temple gates. He will demand entrance knowing that *access is rightfully His*. "Open to me the gates of righteousness: I will go into them, and I will praise THE LORD" (118:19). When Jesus lived on earth the first time He could enter the court of the Gentiles, the court of the Women, and the Court of Israel, but not one step further could He go. He was born of the royal tribe of Judah, not the priestly tribe of Aaron. He could not go where the priests could go. Now He has gone all the way in, into the holy place where only the priests could minister. Into the holy of holies (barred in olden times, hidden by the veil) where only the high priest could go—and then only once a year after elaborate preparations.

Our Lord is the priest of a new order, a priest forever after the order of Melchizedek. The old Aaronic scheme of things has passed away. Access is His by sovereign right. The temple is His.

We notice too, that *acceptance is rightfully His*: "This gate of the LORD, into which the righteous shall enter" (118:20). Reference is now made to a special gate. The Revised Version rephrases this verse to read, "This is the gate that belongs to Jehovah; the righteous may enter into it." We do not know what gate this is. Perhaps it is a gate that led directly into the temple itself.

Notice also that *acclaim is rightfully His*: "I will praise Thee:

for Thou hast heard me, and art become my salvation"
(118:21). This is His ultimate triumph—to enter the holy of
holies. The returning Christ is not only allowed in there, but
shouts of praise attend Him on His way. When King Uzziah
tried to minister there he instantly became a leper and was
thrust out with horror by the priests. But Jesus has access,
acceptance, acclaim, because of the salvation He wrought at
Calvary. Simple prayer gives way in the psalm to something else.
We have:

2. The Sudden Pause (118:22-23)

"The stone which the builders refused is become the head
stone of the corner. This is the LORD's doing; it is marvelous in
our eyes." The "stone" contemptuously despised by the Jewish
leaders when they rejected Jesus is now the stone conspicuously
displayed. There are six references to this statement in the New
Testament, three of them (parallel references in the Gospels)
made by the Lord Jesus Himself. Peter quoted this Scripture
when he and John were arrested by the Sanhedrin for healing
the lame man and for preaching Christ to the crowds.

The cornerstone or headstone was the most important stone
in the building. It was a strong stone made to cap the building
and to bond the walls together. One suggestion has been made
that the cornerstone can be likened to the capstone of a pyramid which, itself a perfect pyramid, brings to an apex all the
lines and planes of the pyramid.

The Lord Jesus is the chief cornerstone. He who was cast
aside by the builders of rabbinic Judaism, and whom they have
consistently rejected ever since, is yet to be given His rightful
place by Israel.

Then comes:

3. The Sounding Praise (118:24-26)

"This is the day which the LORD hath made; we will rejoice
and be glad in it. Save now, I beseech Thee, O LORD: O LORD, I
beseech Thee, send now prosperity [success]. Blessed be he that
cometh in the name of the LORD." A wonderful statement,
which Rotherham renders: "Ah pray, Jehovah! do save, pray! Ah
pray, Jehovah! do send success, pray!" The three English words
do, save, and *pray* in this quotation are an exact rendering, he
says, of the Hebrew compound word *hoshiah-na* which we trans-
literate into "Hosanna" (Save now!). It was the Hebrew equivalent of Britain's *God save the king!* "Hosanna!" is what the multitudes cried as Jesus rode in triumph into Jerusalem a week
before His crucifixion—making the Jewish leaders furious.

We see the Lord Jesus at the portals of the temple in a coming day. Then all the people will cry "*Hosanna!* Blessed is He that cometh in the name of the L<small>ORD</small>."

B. The Lord Jesus in the Precincts of the Temple (118:27-29)

The scene before us is clearly millennial. It had its initial fulfillment at Calvary, but now the whole journey via Golgotha is brought to a climax.

1. The Coming Sacrifice (118:27)

"GOD is the L<small>ORD</small>, which hath showed us light: bind the sacrifice [the festal sacrifice] with cords, even unto the horns of the altar." At the feast of Tabernacles, a solemn procession of the people compassed the great altar of burnt offering in the outer court. Once each day for six days they marched around it crying out, "Hosanna! Hosanna!" On the seventh day they marched around the altar seven times, still shouting Hosannas.

The practice looked forward, as did the entire feast of Tabernacles. Everything is prophetic of the coming millennial reign of Christ. The Lord will rescue Israel from her foes at Megiddo. He will cleanse the earth of all that offends, and He will restore Jerusalem, making Israel the head of the nations, the headstone of His kingdom, He will rebuild the temple according to Ezekiel's plan and then will lead the redeemed peoples of the world in a great celebration of the feast of Tabernacles. Festal sacrifices will be offered, not for their *mediatorial* value but their *memorial* value. They will be a solemn reminder of Calvary.

2. The Coming Song (118:28-29)

"Thou art my GOD, and I will praise Thee. Thou art my God, I will exalt Thee. O give thanks unto the L<small>ORD</small>; for He is good: for His mercy endureth for ever." What a day it will be when Israel sounds out this song of worship and of witness— *hosannas* for the Lord Jesus Christ. Once they said, "We have no king but Caesar." Once they said, "We will not have this man to reign over us." One day the redeemed nation will look to Jesus singing, "*God save the king!*"

Psalm 119:1-8

SING A SONG OF SCRIPTURE

The Bible Will Make:
  I. A HAPPY MAN (119:1-3)
     A. In His Way (119:1a)
     B. In His Walk (119:1b)
     C. In His Will (119:2-3)
        1. Gives Purpose to Life (119:2)
        2. Guarantees Purity in Life (119:3)
 II. A HOLY MAN (119:4-6)
     A. His Duty (119:4)
     B. His Desire (119:5)
     C. His Decision (119:6)
III. A HUMBLE MAN (119:7-8)
     A. Still Learning (119:7)
     B. Still Longing (119:8)

WE DO NOT KNOW who wrote this psalm. Suggestions have included David, Hezekiah, Jeremiah, Ezra, Nehemiah, Malachi, and Daniel. The internal evidence makes it evident that the author was a suffering saint who had to endure contempt if not downright ill treatment. His enemies included Jews who were in a position of power and able to do him harm. He was in physical danger, he was faced with laxity and even apostasy in the ranks of his people, and he had successfully resisted temptation. Some have thought he was a young man, others that he was old. Rotherham presents a strong case for Hezekiah, others an equally strong case for someone living after the exile. The fact that the singer makes no mention of the temple and of ritual law, but rather emphasizes the inward, spiritual aspects of faith, points to Daniel rather than either Hezekiah or one of the post-exilic writers. In their days the Hebrew religion was centered on the sanctuary and the sacrifices.

260

The psalm is a mosaic arranged around the central theme of God's law. The psalmist did not see God's law as harsh edict but as a source of joy and rejoicing. We do not have here any cold legalism of Mosaic precept but the warmth of one in love with the Lord. We have the passion of a poet—precept rhapsodized by poetry, law transfigured by love, demand elevated to desire, edict replaced by emotion, fact matched by fervor, enforcement made easy by enjoyment.

The Word of God is the foundation on which this poet builds; he builds on it because he loves it. He is bound to the Word of God, not by the chains of *law* but by the magnetic attraction of *love*.

The psalm, as most Bibles show, is an *acrostic*. It consists of 22 stanzas, each consisting of eight verses, and each emphasizing, in order, a letter of the Hebrew alphabet. Each verse in each stanza begins with the letter of the alphabet to which the stanza is related.

This form of writing may seem somewhat artificial and stilted to us, but probably the psalm was written that way as an aid to memory. The theme of the psalm is the law, which is referred to in 173 of its 176 verses. God is mentioned in every verse. The psalm contains 70 prayer requests. The psalmist refers to himself 325 times and mentions his suffering in 66 verses. He is resolved to know, keep, and love God's law.

The psalmist uses eight synonyms for the Word of God. (Some expositors expand the list to nine, others to ten. All are agreed on the eight.) He uses the word *Torah* ("law" or "instruction") 24 times; *Edoth* ("testimonies") 19 times; *Piqud* ("precepts") 20 times; *Chaq* ("statutes") 19 times; *Mitsoth* ("commandments") 22 times; *Mishpat* ("judgments," "decisions," or "appointments") 22 times; *Debar* ("Word") 22 times; and *Imrath* ("word," "promise," or "saying") 20 times.

Maclaren says of this psalm that "there is music in its monotony," and that although "there are but few pieces in the psalmist's kaleidoscope they fall into many shapes of beauty." Spurgeon says, "It is weighty as well as bulky." Simons says, "It is a star of the first and greatest magnitude in the firmament of the Psalms." Rotherham says, "It is a study set to the murmuring of the sea" and "The monotone . . . is that of a lullaby by which a troubled soul may be softly and sweetly hushed to rest." Someone has said, "It is the Alphabet of Divine Love."

The psalm's eulogy of the Word points us directly to *the Word made flesh*. Many a verse can best be illuminated by relating it directly to Him who truly hid God's Word in His heart. Again and again in our study of this psalm we find our best illustration of its heights and depths in the person of the Lord Jesus. In this psalm we have the Word made flesh—the Word clothed with warmth and enthusiasm such as Israel in its recurring apostasies never knew. We turn repeatedly from this psalm to Him in whom the Word was made flesh.

This first stanza shows us what will happen in the life of those who make the Word of God the center of their life. It sets before us a picture of:

I. A HAPPY MAN (119:1-3)

He is happy because the Word of God rules in three areas of his life.

A. In His Way (119:1a)

"Blessed are the undefiled in the way." The word rendered *way* occurs 13 times in the psalm, and some authorities include it as one of the synonyms for God's Word. The word suggests a course of conduct marked out by God's Word, a road trodden as a way of life, a course of action mapped out by God's law.

We can make our journey through life along one of two ways. There is the broad way of disobedience, a way that seems right to a man but ends in death; and there is the narrow way of obedience, a way that leads onward and upward to life everlasting. That is the way the psalmist has chosen.

Most people would consider that way undesirable. The picture most unsaved or backslidden people have of the Christian life is one of gloom—no gambling, no drinking, no smoking, no fun. Just prayer meetings and Bible conferences and church— boring sermons, bad music, dull people. On the other hand, how much fun is it to contract AIDS or herpes, to be hooked on drugs, to be a slave to tobacco or alcohol? The psalmist says, "Blessed is the man who chooses the way of the undefiled." We think of Daniel who refused to "defile himself with the king's meat" and of Jesus who was "holy and harmless and undefiled and separate from sinners."

The word *blessed* in the Old Testament is invariably in the plural. It means "Happy," literally "Happy! Happy!" or "Oh, the happinesses . . ." Happiness is the overflow of joy. Joy is the source; happiness is the stream. God always weds happiness to holiness. That is why an unsaved person can never know real happiness. The devil has his counterfeits, mostly based on pleasure, but they are shallow; they have no deep well from which to spring. The devil's brand of happiness depends on what happens; he weds happiness to happenings.

We tend to equate happiness with pleasure ("I want to have fun"), with prosperity ("If only I were rich . . ."), with power

("I'd show him . . ."), with popularity ("I wish everybody liked me . . ."), or with position ("I'm the boss"). God equates happiness with none of those. The failure of human sources of happiness was expressed like this by Robert Burns:

> Pleasures are like poppies spread,
>   You seize the flower, the bloom is fled,
> Or like a snowflake on the river,
>   A moment white, then gone for ever.

So the opening words of Psalm 119 strike an important note. We would all like to be happy. And not just happy, but "happy, happy." But we cannot have overflowing joy without holiness, and we cannot have holiness without the Holy Spirit—and we cannot have the Holy Spirit without salvation. So the first verse takes us back to spiritual basics.

I like to think that the supreme example of the happy, happy man was Jesus. I cannot imagine Him being miserable, sulky, out of sorts, gloomy, or pessimistic. He faced even Calvary looking beyond to "the joy that was set before Him."

"Blessed are the undefiled in the way, who walk in the law of the LORD." The ultimate secret of happiness is to live according to the principles found in God's Word. The happy man is happy because the Word of God rules his way. He is also happy because the Word of God rules:

B. In His Walk (119:1b)

"Who walk in the law of the LORD." We all once learned to walk. Watch that baby. He knows from the start that lying flat on his back, or face down on his stomach, is no position for a human being. He's supposed to stand upright and walk. So he begins to wave his arms and legs, he struggles to push himself up, and finally he gets to the point where he can. Then he crawls and soon learns to stand on two wobbly legs. Next he learns to balance himself, holding out his arms, to take a few tentative steps. At first he has many a fall, but soon he is walking around hanging onto things. And then he is off on his own, running here, there, and everywhere.

That is how it is with us and God's Word. When we first begin to read it, study it, try to obey it, down we go. We stumble and fall; we pick ourselves up and try again. Soon we are walking in the law of the Lord, making progress, moving forward, growing in grace, and increasing in the knowledge of God. There is no happiness like that which floods the soul when the Word of God has guided us past a snare or led us into a right decision.

He is a happy man because the Word of God rules:

C. In His Will (119:2-3)

The psalmist sees two things that happen when we bring our wills into captivity to the Word of God. Our wills are such that they must be brought into captivity to something. Happy is the one who has his will enslaved by the Word of God.

1. Such captivity *gives purpose to life:* "Blessed are they that keep His testimonies, and that seek Him with the whole heart" (119:2). The idea behind the word *testimonies* is that of attestation. It carries the thought that God has solemnly declared His will on matters of faith and morals. In the singular it is used to describe the Ten Commandments.

Everybody is seeking something in life. People seek to get married, be promoted at work, to be approved by a boss or a friend. Persons whose will is subject to the Word of God are seeking God with all their heart. There can be no greater purpose in life.

2. Captivity to God's Word also *guarantees purity in life:* "They also do no iniquity: they walk in His ways" (119:3). Sin will keep us from the Bible, or the Bible will keep us from sin—one or the other. Think of the Lord Jesus. He walked through life seeking God wholeheartedly and doing no iniquity. The ultimate secret of His marvelous life was the Word of God. It ruled His every thought.

He stepped off the throne on high, walked down the streets of gold, out through the pearly gates, down the star-spangled splendor of the sky to be born as a human being. His triumphant shout rings out as a challenge to all the hosts of hell and as a cheer to all the hosts of Heaven: "Lo, I come (in the volume of the book it is written of Me) to do Thy will, O God" (Hebrews 10:7). He could not sin because His life was ruled by God's Word. When Satan tempted Him, He simply referred him to God's Word.

The Bible will also make him:

II. A HOLY MAN (119:4-6)

A. His Duty (119:4)

"Thou hast commanded us to keep Thy precepts diligently." The word *precepts* occurs only in the psalms. It has the idea of "taking charge." It refers to God's mandates enjoined on the human race, His injunctions.

The psalmist calls attention to the fact that it is *God* who is the author of the law. The word *Thou* is emphatic. We could read it, "*Thou Thyself* has commanded us." That relates the commandments to duty. There really is no choice in the matter. The God who commanded light to shine out of darkness has commanded us to live by His laws. The sun, moon, and stars obey Him and so should we. There is an aspect to God's law which obliterates all choice in the matter.

B. His Desire (119:5)

"O that my ways were directed to keep Thy statutes!" Welling up from the soul of this singer is a deep desire to keep God's Word. Being mortal, he knows how easily he can wander away. But his deepest desire is to obey.

This cry was wrung from the heart of the apostle Paul at the end of Romans 7. He had been studying the secret of living a holy life. He longed to live a holy life but he found he was incapacitated in doing so by the active power of the flesh. "Who shall deliver me from this dead body?" he cried. Many an earnest believer has echoed that cry, "O that my ways were directed to keep Thy statutes."

The anguished cry summons up the picture of a storm-tossed mariner in the grip of a storm. The captain has been swept overboard, the first mate is dead, the helmsman is dead, and the ship is at the mercy of wind and wave. What it needs is a firm hand on the helm, it needs to be brought before the wind, it needs someone with a skillful hand to take over and direct it back on course. Without such a hand on the helm of our life, shipwreck on the rocks and shoals is inevitable. The psalmist's words were the passionate cry of one who knew and felt his need.

C. His Decision (119:6)

"Then shall I not be ashamed, when I have respect unto all Thy commandments." A decision is necessary here: a choice to obey God's commandments. Then and not until then, the psalmist says, will he escape being ashamed.

Note also, he chose to obey not just some of the commandments—those that were not irksome—but all the commandments. It was his commitment to keep the whole law that caused Daniel to dare to stand out against the entire Babylon establishment. The command not to eat improperly prepared meat might easily have been dismissed as a trifle, given the fact he was a captive in a foreign land and under the will of a despotic and dangerous king. He could have compromised, arguing that the kosher laws were secondary ritual laws, not moral laws. Daniel knew no such fine points, no such twisting of truth. "Has God said it? I obey it." That was his rule. There were 613 commandments in the Mosaic Law. The psalmist determined to keep them all.

III. A HUMBLE MAN (119:7-8)

He is not proud or arrogant in his determination to live a holy life. He does not look down on other people. Here is no prudish self-righteousness, no proud Pharisee praying with himself and saying, "Lord, I thank Thee that I am not as other men are . . . even as this publican . . ."

The psalmist is:

A. Still Learning (119:7)

"I will praise Thee with uprightness of heart, when I shall have learned Thy righteous judgments." The word *judgments* contains the thought of a legal decision, a ruling from the bench. It is a judicial decision which makes an authoritative ruling, a precedent for similar cases in the future. Sometimes the word is used to describe God's judicial acts in executing His judgment on the wicked.

The psalmist realized that he did not know all the cases in which God had acted thus judicially. He did not know all the precedents nor how God would act in every instance. But, he knew that when he *was* in possession of all the facts, he would praise Him with uprightness of heart.

A classic example of this is found in the Apocalypse. There we meet the four and twenty elders. They are mentioned seven times in the book of Revelation and on six of those occasions they get up from their thrones, fall on their faces before God, and cast their crowns at His feet. The only time they do not do that is the last time they are mentioned—when they are so entranced at the triumphant entry of the 144,000 witnesses into Heaven that they sit as if riveted to their thrones. All through the book of Revelation those mysterious beings act as a kind of celestial jury. They watch God's acts in judgment, they see Him setting His magnificent precedents, and time and time again they are so blessed at what they see that they fall down in worship. They praise Him with uprightness of heart because they are seeing His righteous judgments.

We too will thank God one of these days that He has always done the right thing. Vexing questions like: "Are the heathen lost? What about my lost loved ones? What about all the injustices done on earth?" will all be answered. We shall see "the Judge of all the earth" doing right and we will make Heaven ring with our hallelujahs. Right now, like the psalmist, we are still learning. We see only the shadows of His judgmental ways today because we are living in an age of grace. More often than not in this age, God stays His hand. He defers judgment until the time of the judgment seat of Christ and the great white throne. Everything will be dealt with then. Right now we are still learning.

The psalmist pictures himself as a humble man, still learning, and also as:

B. Still Longing (119:8)

"I will keep Thy statutes: O forsake me not utterly." The word for *statutes* comes from a word meaning "to hew, cut, engrave, inscribe." It stands for anything prescribed or enacted. God's law, we remember, was engraved on two tablets of stone (symbolizing its immutability).

The psalmist, conscious of failure, promised the Lord to keep His laws. He pleaded with the Lord to be patient—not to cast him off utterly, not to forsake him.

Thus David must have prayed in those dreadful weeks and months after his seduction of Bathsheba and murder of Uriah. He had committed two capital offenses, adultery and murder. Worse still, because he had sinned presumptuously he knew of no sacrifice that would cover his sin. He was haunted by the memory of King Saul and of God's refusal to speak any more to that man who had sinned once too often. David might well have prayed, "I will keep Thy statutes: O forsake me not utterly." The psalmist leaves his first stanza there, with his heart still longing for the ability to keep God's law.

Psalm 119:9-16

GOD'S WORD HID IN THE HEART

I. THE VIRTUE OF THE WORD (119:9-16)
   A. Its Cleansing Effect (119:9)
   B. Its Controlling Effect (119:10)
   C. Its Correcting Effect (119:11-12)
II. THE VALUE OF THE WORD (119:13-16)
   A. We Must Proclaim It (119:13)
      1. The Need For Diligence (119:13a)
      2. The Need For Daring (119:13b)
   B. We Must Prize It (119:14-15)
      1. Its Priceless Worth (119:14)
      2. Its Practical Worth (119:15)
   C. We Must Prove It (119:16)

THE PSALMIST BEGINS this section of the psalm knowing that sin defiles and destroys and that everybody needs some kind of protection against its deadly virus. His test case is the young man. We can think of the young man of this psalm as David in his youth, or as Daniel in Babylon, or as the Lord Jesus pursuing His immaculate journey through scenes of time.

The section divides into two main parts. It sets before us:

I. THE VIRTUE OF THE WORD (119:9-16)

The Word of God has three inherent virtues as it is applied to the life of a young person. It has:

A. A Cleansing Effect (119:9)

"Wherewithal shall a young man cleanse his way? By taking heed thereto according to Thy word." Think what a school playground was like in your day. Think of the passionate hatreds that could generate in a flash, of the fist-fights that broke out. Think of the cursing and swearing, the common language of the crowd. Think of the dirty jokes that were the password to popularity. Think how deeply some of those smutty

268

stories have become embedded in your memory, still unerasable. Think of the obsession with sex, the vile things said and done with a snicker or sneer. Think of the lying and cheating, the smoking and drinking. Think of the peer pressure to conform, the pettiness and jealousy.

As I recall such things, it seems as if our school playground was a suburb of hell for youthful wickedness. Yet in those days strict discipline was maintained on campus. We could be expelled for cheating or smoking, forfeiting the right to further education in that school. Schools are much worse now, with far more permissiveness and lack of discipline—to say nothing of the problems of drug use and alcoholism. How can a young person stay clean in such an environment? The psalmist has the answer.

The Word of God kept me from many a sin when I was young, even though I did not take an aggressive stand for Christ. Whenever I reflect on the sins of my youth in the presence of God, I blush for some of the things I said and did, and to think what a poor testimony I was. Yet at the same time I was kept from many harmful things by the Word of God. It had a cleansing effect on my life. I shall praise the Lord one of these days, in His presence, when He shows me the full story of God's Word keeping me in a clean path when I might have wallowed in filth. Young people who want to honor Christ at school should begin every day with a verse or two of Scripture and prayer:

> Keep me true, Lord Jesus, keep me true.
> There's a race that I must run,
> There are victories to be won,
> Give me power, every hour, to be true.

God's Word also has:

B. A Controlling Effect (119:10)

"With my whole heart have I sought Thee: O let me not wander from Thy commandments." Here is one of the great secrets of a holy life: "With my whole heart."

Halfhearted commitment, in my opinion, was the problem with American involvement in Vietnam. The United States had no commitment to win, only a halfhearted response to a treaty obligation. American failure there led to subsequent massacres by the communists throughout Southeast Asia. America did not have total commitment; the nation was divided. Troops were sent to Vietnam to fight a war while millions demonstrated, protested, and some even burned the American flag. It was a sure recipe for ruin.

Anyone who tries to keep God's Word halfheartedly will fail. God calls for total commitment. Yet it is the wholehearted among us who disturb us most. The apostle Pauls, the D. L. Moodys, the Patrick Henrys.

A documentary film which is the prelude to a tour of Williamsburg, Virginia, gives us exceptional insight into Patrick Henry. This revolutionary hero began by demanding that colonists have the same rights as Englishmen. Patrick Henry was a born lawyer. In six weeks with only a stack of books he taught himself enough Virginia law to force the examiners to sign his application for the bar. In three years he tried over a thousand cases, most of which he won. When the British imposed the Stamp Act of 1765 on the colonies, to make them help pay for the soldiers who guarded their Indian frontiers, Patrick Henry exploded. He saw it as a violation of the Magna Charta. When things finally came to a head he lifted his voice in Richmond: "Gentlemen may cry 'Peace, peace,' " he said, "but there is no peace. Is life so dear, or peace so sweet as to be purchased at the price of chains . . . ? As for me, give me liberty or give me death." Patrick Henry seemed a dangerous man to many. But he was a real driving force behind the American Revolution.

The Word of God also has:

C. A Correcting Effect (119:11-12)

"Thy word have I hid in mine heart, that I might not sin against Thee. Blessed art Thou, O LORD: teach me Thy statutes." After God gave the law to Moses, He commanded that it be placed in the sacred ark. That ark was made of acacia wood overlaid with gold and was covered with a lid of gold called the mercy seat. It had its place in the holy of holies beyond the veil. It was there upon that mercy seat God sat enthroned in solitary splendor.

The sacred ark, the depository for God's unbroken law, symbolized the Lord Jesus. The acacia wood of the wilderness spoke of His humanity; the pure gold symbolized His deity. Within His heart there reposed the unbroken law of God. His whole life was lived on earth with that law at the center of His being. He did always those things that pleased His Father; He was perfect, sinless, and unblemished. In Old Testament times, when the ark was carried from place to place, it was borne on the shoulders of the priests and was overlaid with a cloth of blue. It was thus that the Lord Jesus journeyed through this life, high and lifted up, enthroned above all others. The life that others saw, as they looked at Him, was a life that reflected the beauty of Heaven. Within, in His heart, where only the eye of God could see, was that unbroken law.

When Satan tempted Him in the wilderness, He answered, "It is written . . ." He defeated Satan with the one weapon God had placed in the hands of Adam and Eve. Eve had only to say, "Thus saith the Lord," and Satan would have been defeated. But Eve tossed that weapon aside and relied on her own reasoning. Adam tossed it away too and relied on his emotions. Not so the Lord Jesus.

The more we know the Word of God, the more we will love God. The more we love God, the more we will love the Word of God. It is a spiral stairway to glory.

We need to enthrone God's Word in our hearts. Then we shall be like Joseph. When Potiphar's wife made her improper suggestion to him, he said, "How then can I do this great wickedness, and sin against God?" (Genesis 39:9). The usual arguments—"It's natural. Everybody does it. Nobody's going to know. It can't be wrong if we love one another"—cut no ice with Joseph. Fornication was wickedness because it was against the known will of God. That settled it. God's Word had a correcting effect—keeping his feet on the straight and narrow way.

This psalm also sets before us:

II. THE VALUE OF THE WORD (119:13-16)

Again the psalmist has three things to say. Such a treasure as God's Word is not to be kept to ourselves.

A. We Must Proclaim It (119:13)

"With my lips have I declared all the judgments of Thy mouth." The apostle Paul would later call that "the whole counsel of God." To proclaim the judgments of God in their totality demanded:

1. Diligence (119:13a)

Obviously before we can declare all His judgments we have to study them, and that calls for time, application, and self-denial. Long hours will be spent poring over the pages of the Book, hours that might have been spent in making money, in pursuing pleasure, or in wasteful idleness. How many who say they don't have time to meditate on God's Word, daily find hours to read the newspaper, watch television, and talk on the telephone (not that those things in themselves are wrong). When we say we have no time to study the Bible, however, yet have time for everything else, we are simply exposing how wrong our sense of values is.

Nobody ever mastered the Bible by occasionally opening it

and reading a random verse or two. Nobody ever mastered it by listening to someone else preach, no matter how gifted that person might be. The only way to master this Book is to study it as diligently as a doctor studies medicine or as an astronomer studies the stars. What makes us think there is some magic formula for mastering the Bible, a special unction that makes up for mental laziness? If we studied our subjects at school or the specifics of our profession as carelessly as we so often study the Bible we would be tossed out of school or fired. First, we need diligence. The next thing is:

2. Daring (119:13b)

The psalmist said, "With my lips have I declared all the judgments of Thy mouth." That calls for daring. This Book is the most unpopular book in the world. Try getting up in a biology class to oppose Darwin with Moses. Try getting up in a philosophy class to oppose Karl Marx with Christ. Try getting up in a sociology class to oppose the common idea that human nature is basically good with Paul's statement that "there is none that doeth good, no, not one." Try getting up in a geology class to oppose its eons of time with Genesis. Try getting up in a psychology class to oppose Freud with the doctrine of original sin. We soon find out that it calls for *daring* to declare all the judgments of God.

If we want to become instantly unpopular with a great many people try publishing an article on the errors of the Roman Catholic Church, or an article claiming that sign-miracles are not for today. Or try getting up in the local PTA to make a motion that we restore the Bible to the classroom. Try taking a public stand against pornography and perversion.

What came out of the mouth of the psalmist was what came out of the mouth of God. That took courage and daring. If the writer of this psalm was Daniel, then we know with what holy boldness he confronted Nebuchadnezzar, Belshazzar, and Darius the Persian with the Word of God.

The value of the Word is such, however, that we must proclaim it. In the Bible we have all the treasures of wisdom. It contains the wisdom the politician needs in the halls of Congress for enacting wise and right legislation, the wisdom the teacher needs in the classroom for molding the lives and characters of boys and girls, the wisdom a parent needs for dealing with a difficult child.

In the bankrupt society in which we live we need to return to the gold standard of the Word of God. We need to tell people the true value of this Book.

B. We Must Prize It (119:14-15) because of:

1. Its Priceless Worth (119:14)

"I have rejoiced in the way of Thy testimonies, as much as in all riches." Suppose tomorrow you were to receive a letter from a reputable firm of attorneys telling you that you had inherited a million dollars. There would be rejoicing in your home. Yet you have something far better than that in God's Word.

On the popular television program, *The Price Is Right*, each contestant is shown a package of prizes and must guess their value, coming closer to the right price than the other contestants. The wild delight of those who win is astonishing.

We have been given a prize worth far more, yet how nonchalantly we take it. Our possession of the Word of God should send us into ecstasies of joy. The psalmist said, "I have rejoiced in the way of Thy testimonies as much as in all riches." Imagine dying without ever having heard John 3:16, without ever having heard the saving name of Jesus, without any assurance of sins forgiven and of peace with God. These things are more precious than gold.

We must prize the Word of God too for:

2. Its Practical Worth (119:15)

"I will meditate in Thy precepts, and have respect unto Thy ways." The word *ways* should be rendered "paths." Meditation in God's Word will lead our feet into right paths. The path we pursue determines our ultimate destination. A person cannot pursue a road leading southward from Chicago and expect to end up in Alaska. The Bible says, "There is a way which seemeth right unto a man, but the end thereof are the ways of death" (Proverbs 14:12). That is why it is so important to get our feet on the right path. The practical worth of this Book lies in the fact that it leads us to respect God's paths.

There are so many slippery places in life. I remember a frightening experience I had once when driving on an icy road. The road did not look slippery. It was not until I touched the brakes and the car went into a violent spin that I realized I was in serious trouble. It was my first and most hair-raising experience driving on ice. The car slid forward at about 25 miles per hour, turned slowly around until it was facing the wrong way, and continued to skid onto the wrong side of the street. The car finally came to a stop in a used car parking lot just a foot or two away from another car. Life is like that. There are slippery places.

The Bible will keep our feet away from life's slippery places.

It will keep us out of danger. It will direct our feet away from the places where Satan has hidden his snares.

The Bible is our chart and compass on life's stormy sea. A woman on board a ship that was threading its way through rocks and shoals asked the captain if he knew where all the rocks were to be found. "No, Madam," he said, "but I know where the deep water is." That's it. We cannot tell where the rocks and shoals are but we can know where the deep water is. The Bible tells us. That is its practical worth. Our task is to study this Book until we know where the deep water is. We shall then avoid shipwreck and drop anchor at last in Heaven's harbor.

C. We Must Prove It (119:16)

"I will delight myself in Thy statutes: I will not forget Thy word." It is not much use reading this Book if we immediately forget what it says. The best way to keep God's Word alive in our life's experience is to prove it, to put it to the test in our everyday affairs.

That is what David did. After years of fleeing from Saul, the day came when his enemy was delivered into his hand. David and Abishai came into the camp of Saul, crossing the barricade and finding everyone asleep. There lay Saul with his spear stuck in the ground by his pillow. Abishai knew what to do. "Now's your chance, David," he said, "God hath delivered thine enemy into thine hand . . . let me smite him . . . I will not smite him the second time." It sounded very plausible. Then David remembered a verse of Scripture, a principle of Scripture: "Touch not Mine anointed . . ." (1 Chronicles 16:22). At once he drew back his hand. It was not for him to kill Saul, however terrible and persistent a foe he was. That was God's prerogative.

That kind of practical application of God's Word, this putting it to the test, kept David from sin. It showed him to be a man after God's own heart. David could interpret even favorable-looking circumstances in the light of God's Word. What looked like an open door (circumstantially) was really a closed door (scripturally). To kill Saul would have been to violate a divine principle that we must not attack a man whom God has anointed.

The Bible abounds with such principles. We must prove them in the rush-and-bustle of our lives—at home, at work, at school, at play. As we do that, we will prove for ourselves the value of God's Word as a practical counselor in life.

Psalm 119:17-24

WONDROUS THINGS OUT OF THY LAW

I. FINDING GREAT OPPORTUNITIES IN THE WORD OF GOD (119:17-20)
   A. It Bestows Life on the Soul (119:17)
   B. It Brings Light into the Soul (119:18)
   C. It Banishes Loneliness from the Soul (119:19)
   D. It Bares Longings in the Soul (119:20)
II. FINDING GREAT OPPOSITION TO THE WORD OF GOD (119:21-24)
   A. The Antipathy (119:21-23)
      1. The Domineering Man, Cursed of God (119:21)
      2. The Disdainful Man, Contemptuous of God (119:22)
      3. The Dangerous Man, Controlled by God (119:23)
   B. The Antidote (119:24)

THIS SECTION OF THE PSALM divides in two parts. In the first part, the psalmist is taken up with the *great opportunities* he finds in God's Word. In the second part, he is taken up with the *great opposition* he finds to God's Word. The Word of God divides the whole human race like that. Some find God's Word a treasure chest of wisdom, counsel, and help. Others despise it and try to undermine its influence and power.

> Within this awesome volume lies
> Mystery of mysteries.
> Happiest they of human race
> Who from their God have gotten grace
> To read, to wonder and to pray,
> To lift the latch and face the way;
> But better had he ne'er been born
> Who reads to laugh, who reads to scorn.

I. GREAT OPPORTUNITIES IN THE WORD (119:17-20)

The psalmist found four essential things for his soul in the Word of God.

275

A. It Bestows Life on the Soul (119:17)

"Deal bountifully with Thy servant, that I may live, and keep Thy word." Here the psalmist seems to anticipate the great change in dispensations which took place at Pentecost. Some of these Old Testament saints did that, even though they had no real understanding of what that change would mean. David, for instance, was able to anticipate New Testament justification even though he had sinned presumptuously and with a high hand. "Blessed is the man unto whom the LORD imputeth not iniquity," he wrote (Psalm 32:1-2; Romans 4:7-8). David thus entered into the truth that we are not justified by the works of the law but by the righteousness of Christ. Similarly, he anticipated, by a whole millenium, the "Melchizedek priesthood" of Christ.

Here the psalmist enters into the new emphasis regarding *law* and *life* which would mark the difference between the old dispensation and the new.

In the Old Testament emphasis, *law* came before *life*. The Old Testament dictum was, "This do, and thou shalt live." Doing aright would bring *life* (Luke 10:28; Romans 10:5). In the New Testament emphasis, *life* comes before *law*. The New Testament dictum is, "If you live you will do this." "For the law of the Spirit of life in Christ Jesus hath made me free from the law of sin and death . . . that the righteousness of the law might be fulfilled in us, who walk not after the flesh, but after the Spirit (Romans 8:2,4).

The psalmist entered into the good of that: living, he would obey God's Word. The life must come first, and that life can come only from God's bountiful dealings. That life is inherent in God's Word. It is imparted to the soul in the new birth—"being born again, not of corruptible seed, but of incorruptible, by the word of God, which liveth and abideth for ever" (1 Peter 1:23).

B. It Brings Light into the Soul (119:18)

"Open Thou mine eyes that I may behold wondrous things out of Thy law." The soul is a very dark place until God's Word shines in. It is a great thing to get one's eyes opened to the Word of God, and once they are opened by the Holy Spirit we need to keep them open. In our daily quiet time we need to pray the psalmist's prayer and then start to look diligently for gems of truth.

Take, for instance, 2 Timothy 3:16: "All Scripture is given by inspiration of God . . ." It takes five English words, "given-by-inspiration-of-God," to render one Greek word which literally means "God-breathed." As the breath of a man is in each word he utters, so that words become the vehicles of his thought, so the breath of God is in the words of Scripture. Some 2,600 times the Old Testament writers claim that their words are the words of God; over 500 times the New Testament writers do the same. The Bible is God-breathed.

Equally remarkable is the economy of words used by the Holy Ghost in imparting God's thoughts in human language. In classical Greek there are 97,921 words; in New Testament Greek there are only 5,857 words. Of all the words available to Him the Holy Spirit deliberately left unused 92,064 Greek words as unnecessary for His purpose. He ignored 94 percent of the Greek vocabulary. Yet with that small percentage of words He wrote down for us the sublimest stories, the grandest truths, the greatest concepts ever penned. Surely that is a wondrous thing about the Book of God.

Those words He has uttered bring light into the soul. Think how inadequate are the best of human philosophies, how benighted the stateliest of manmade religions, when compared with the light shed into our native darkness by the Word of God.

C. It Banishes Loneliness from the Soul (119:19)

"I am a stranger in the earth: hide not Thy commandments from me." There is no loneliness like it—to be a stranger in a foreign land, to wander the streets of a bustling city, to be surrounded by millions of people, unable to read the signs in the shop windows, unable to understand a word that is being said on every hand—to be friendless and alone, to be a stranger.

That is how it was with the Lord Jesus. In the parable of the sheep and the goats He confessed Himself to be a stranger on earth. He was homeless in the world His hands had made. He longed for someone to talk to. Nobody spoke the language of Heaven so He found companionship and comfort in the Word of God. He listened to what His Father had to say to Him in His Word; He talked to His Father in prayer. The Scripture banished loneliness from His soul; it spoke the language of the land from which He had come.

It will do the same for us. We all have times when we feel lonely, when we feel that nobody understands or cares. We all have deep needs. Every man is an island. We reach across the seas of our isolation to relatives, neighbors and friends, to acquaintances and people with whom we rub shoulders every day. But at times we are spiritual Robinson Crusoes, isolated. We have all kinds of gadgets to help us banish our solitude, but lonely moments still come. *Then* it is that this Book can banish loneliness from our soul; it introduces us to the "friend that sticketh closer than a brother."

D. It Bares Longing in the Soul (119:20)

"My soul breaketh for the longing that it hath unto Thy judgments at all times." The word *longing* means "fervent desire." The person who has discovered the worth of God's Word yearns fervently to read it. It is attractive to one's soul.

A needle free to move will turn toward a nearby magnet. The nature of the magnet has affinity with the nature of the needle. As a result, put a needle on the table near a magnet and it will rush instantly to the magnet the moment it is set free to move.

When we are saved, the Lord does something to our soul. He does something to our nature. He puts His own nature in us, and that new nature responds to the drawing power of the Word of God.

There is something else, too. Let a needle keep company with a magnet for any length of time, and it will take on the same nature. A magnet gets its strength from many tiny magnetic dipoles, all laid down in an orderly way, lying together in the same direction. In an ordinary needle or piece of steel, the magnetic dipoles lie in a thousand directions. There is no order, just chaos. When a needle comes under the influence of a magnet for any length of time, a miracle takes place. The disoriented dipoles are rearranged, order is brought out of chaos, and the needle takes on the nature of the magnet. It becomes magnetized. It has a measure of the power we associate with the magnet. It has a drawing power of its own derived from the magnet.

That is what God's Word will do for us. It brings our chaotic, disorderly lives into line. We take on the characteristics of the Word of God, and the mysterious power residing in this Book is imparted to our own lives. Then we have the power to attract other people.

Nor is that all. Float a magnetized needle on water, or balance it on a pivot where it is free to move, and it will align itself so that it points toward the north, to that place where the earth's own magnetic lines of force come together. God's dwelling place, in Scripture, is said to be "in the sides [recesses] of the north" (Isaiah 14:13). That is the point to which the magnetized needle points, toward God's home. That is where the redeemed heart points, the heart that has bared its longings to the Word of God. It points toward *home*.

The psalmist had discovered longings in his soul which only God's Word could satisfy. As the needle turns toward the magnet and the magnetized needle toward the north, so his soul yearned toward God's Word and toward Heaven.

II. GREAT OPPOSITION TO THE WORD (119:21-24)

It is obvious that not all people love the sacred Scriptures. Many despise them, deride them, detest them.

A. The Antipathy (119:21-23)

Real opposition to God's Word is evident on every hand. Earlier I mentioned that when I was in the British army, I made it a point to have a Bible on my bed, out in the open where everyone could see it. Right across from me was a man from the north of Ireland, a rabid Roman Catholic. The sight of that Bible infuriated him. In those days the Roman Church actively discouraged its people from reading the Bible for themselves. "I don't believe a word of that cursed book," he sneered. "Then what do you believe?" I asked. "I believe the Church," he said.

The psalmist sensed opposition to the Word from three kinds of people.

1. The Domineering Man, Cursed of God (119:21)

"Thou hast rebuked the proud that are cursed, which do err from Thy commandments." Here we see a threefold development of sin. Pride is the root, error is the flower, the curse of God is the fruit.

It is pride that makes people think they know better than God, think that their ideas are superior to what is taught in God's Word. The principle of pride-error-curse is seen everywhere in Scripture.

It is seen, for instance, in the history of *Lucifer,* who once held the highest place in heaven, a place next to the throne of God. He was a magnificent creature, brilliant in mind and beautiful in body. His supreme task was to lead the anthems of heaven and direct the angelic choirs in their hymns of praise to God. Then pride entered. He thought *he* should have the worship he directed to God. Pride was followed by error. He deceived himself into thinking that he, a creature, could dethrone the Creator. Deception was followed by rebellion and the curse of God which in his case was a curse without remedy. He fell from glory and has wandered the spaces of the universe—a demented, hell-bound, twisted being ever since.

That principle is seen in the history of King Uzziah. He reigned for a long time in Judah and was able to restore the fortunes of his troubled land. He put all his foes beneath his feet. Then pride entered, and on the heels of pride came error. He set aside God's Word, which taught that only a son of Aaron might enter the holy place of the temple and engage in the service of the sanctuary. Why should he share power with anyone, even with God's appointed priests? One tragic day he seized a censor, pushed his way into the forbidden place, and at once came under the curse. He was smitten with leprosy and lived a leper until the day of his death.

The psalmist knew such people. We, too, know such persons, those whose intellectual pride drives them to force their godless notions on all around them. Our schools and colleges are full of them.

The psalmist also sensed antipathy toward the Word of God from:

2. The Disdainful Man, Contemptuous of God (119:22)

"Remove from me reproach and contempt; for I have kept Thy testimonies." The psalmist was up against people who scorned him for his adherence to the Word of God. Reproach and contempt from those who disdain God's Word are directed against the godly, against those who adhere to the Word of God. In many a college classroom young people from godly homes are held up to scorn and ridicule because they prefer God's account of creation to the atheist's evolutionary concepts. Let them take courage. People poured scorn on Jesus too. We remember, for instance, the day Jesus raised the daughter of Jairus from the dead. When He came into the room where the little girl lay, He commented, "She is not dead, but sleepeth." They laughed Him to scorn. We remember, too, how they gathered like vultures around the cross to wag their heads and to mock Him as He died. "Remove from me reproach and contempt for I have kept Thy testimonies" might well have been His prayer.

Few things are harder to take than scorn. Few things cause young persons at school or in college to hide their faith more than the fear of scorn. Let us remember, people may laugh us into hell but they will never laugh us out.

Then opposition came from:

3. The Dangerous Man, Controlled by God (119:23)

"Princes also did sit and speak against me; but Thy servant did meditate in Thy statutes." The psalmist is now contemplating a man in a position of power, able to use that power to put down the humble believer. This man could harness the resources of the state to banish the Bible and to persecute believers. History tells countless tales of such, but God has His sovereign way of dealing with them and confounding their boasts and plans.

The Emperor Diocletian was one such man, he and his co-emperor and son-in-law Galerius. The pair of them set out to put an end to the faith, committing countless atrocities against Christians. One of their chief goals was to eradicate the Bible from the face of the earth. The fact that we have no extant manuscripts of the New Testament older than the middle of the fourth century is proof of the widespread destruction of Christian writings during the reign of Diocletian. All the pains that iron and steel, fire and sword, rack and cross, and wild beasts could inflict were employed to ban the Bible and interdict Christianity.

It was all in vain. Galerius died eaten up of a loathsome disease so vile that he was deserted by all his friends. Diocletian abandoned his empire, retired to private life, and became more interested in cabbages than Christians. His death is shrouded in obscurity. Gibbon, ever willing to cast the enemies of Christ in favorable light, says that he died a suicide but adds a reluctant footnote to the effect that Diocletian probably died a raving madman.

God controlled this dangerous man and forced him off the throne he had abused. Then, when all was done, He summoned him on high to answer to Heaven for his crimes on earth. As for the Bible he banned and burned, it has long since witnessed the burial of the Roman empire just as it will see the doom of all its foes.

The psalmist entered into the sense and spirit of this. In his own day he sensed antipathy toward God's Word from all kinds of people, but he was unmoved. His response was to open his Bible afresh and to meditate in the truths of God's Word.

B. The Antidote (119:24)

"Thy testimonies also are my delight and my counselors." The more the scornful sought to discredit the Bible, the more the psalmist found his delight in it. In the pages of God's Book he found a multitude of counselors able to lead him and guide him even though his path was beset with peril.

It is better to seek the counsel of Solomon than of Dr. Spock and his kind when it comes to raising our children. All these people can give us is the wisdom of this world but Solomon can give us wisdom from on high. It is better to seek the counsel of Moses than Darwin when it comes to the origin of life. All Darwin can give us is supposition, theory, and ever-changing guesses. Moses can tell us what really happened. It is better to seek the counsel of the Bible than *The Wall Street Journal* on the kinds of investments to make with your money. All *Barron's* can give us is advice on how to get a 15 percent increase on invest-

ments; the Bible tells us how to get 10,000 percent (a hundred-
fold). It is better to go to the Scriptures than to a psychiatrist
with our guilt, depressions, frustrations, anxieties, and inhibitions. A psychiatrist can identify, perhaps, the source of the
problem; yet if he is ignoring "the law of sin" he is often wrong
even then. The Scriptures not only diagnose our problems, they
can transform our personality.

The psalmist learned to seek the counsel of God's Word rather than the counsel of worldly people. Abraham, Isaac, Jacob
and Joseph, David and Daniel, Moses and Joshua have far more
meaningful things to say to us than all the celebrated sages of
the world.

Come what may, the psalmist chose to find *his* answers in the
Bible. He was a wise man indeed.

GLEAMS AMID THE GLOOM

I. WHAT THE PSALMIST REALIZED (119:25-29)
God's Word:
  A. In Conviction (119:25)
  B. In Confession (119:26)
  C. In Consecration (119:27)
  D. In Contrition (119:28)
  E. In Contrast (119:29)
II. WHAT THE PSALMIST RESOLVED (119:30-32)
  A. His Decision to Live for God (119:30)
  B. His Determination to Live for God (119:31)
  C. His Desire to Live for God (119:32)

SOME GREAT SORROW has overtaken the singer. He is over-whelmed with grief. In his extremity he prays. This is the first of nine prayers in this psalm for God's "quickening" in his life. The psalmist finds a gleam amid the gloom in the fact that God is still on the throne, still mighty to save, still sovereign over all the situations and circumstances of life.

The psalm divides into two main parts. We have, first:

I. WHAT THE PSALMIST REALIZED (119:25-29)

The psalmist realized that God's Word has the answer to every need. We see him applying God's Word to his life in five fundamental ways.

A. God's Word in Conviction (119:25)

"My soul cleaveth unto the dust; quicken Thou me according to Thy word." We don't know what it was that so prostrated the psalmist before God. It may have been an overwhelming sense of his own guilt (guilt will do that). And that, after all, is the first function of God's Word—to expose guilt. The Holy Spirit's first work in the soul is to convict of sin, righteousness, and judgment to come.

283

There can be little doubt that the psalmist was in the grip of deep depression. He was flat on his face in the dust. He had come to the end of himself and his own resources.

At this point our society would advise us to see a psychiatrist, seek professional help. There may be times when a Christian psychologist can help, but that was not the solution the psalmist discovered.

Sometimes when people go to a psychiatrist, they are put into group therapy and encouraged to let it all "hang out." They are to talk openly about their problems to others, who have problems too. Everybody comments on the problems, criticizing hangups, attitudes, personality traits, weaknesses, and shortcomings. All that is supposed to help.

The psalmist makes a different suggestion. He says to the Lord, "Quicken *Thou* me." He was going to air his problems all right, but he was going to take them to the Lord. He was going to seek a counselor—the counsel of the Word of God. There are very few problems in this life that cannot be solved by a thorough-going, honest exposure of one's life to the Scriptures. To do that is the greatest therapy in the world.

The psalmist asked God to "quicken him," that is, to put *new life* into him. What he needed was a stiff dose of Scripture, taken with a mixture of faith, every day. Try it. Read your Bible consistently. Say with Samuel, "Speak, Lord, Thy servant heareth." The Bible is a book of people and principles. Sooner or later, God will confront us in the pages of His Book with the basic cause of our problem and with His inspired, infallible solution to that problem. The psalmist had discovered the best way of all to handle depression.

But we must be prepared. The Bible will not hedge or redefine sin. It will put its finger unerringly on the sin question, frequently at the root of other problems of life.

Next we have:

B. God's Word in Confession (119:26)

Confession is also marvelous therapy. "I have declared my ways, and Thou heardest me." The psalmist confessed his wrongdoing to the Lord.

Usually when we confess to somebody else, we succeed only in transferring the load from us to them. A young man came up to me once and said, "I have a confession to make to you." I said, "Oh, what is it?" He said, "I have never liked you." That came as rather a shock to me since I hardly knew him. To the best of my knowledge I had never done him any harm. I suppose telling me that did *him* some good, but it didn't do me any good at all. I found I had the greatest difficulty liking *him* after that! Fortunately, the acquaintance was only a very casual one and I soon forgot all about it as the events of life came crowding in and our paths diverged forever. Now I cannot even remember his name, and when I do occasionally think about him it is with an inward smile at how foolish we can be.

The psalmist took his problems to the Lord. He lay down, so to speak, on the Great Physician's couch and poured out his soul to *Him*. He took his confession to the Lord and, first and foremost, that is the place to take it.

Right from the beginning, the Bible teaches us that. When God came into the garden of Eden to confront Adam with his sin His first question was, "What hast thou done?" He said: "Now tell *Me* all about it. What has happened?" No permanent solution could be found to the shame and guilt of Adam's soul until he had confessed to God. No permanent solution can be found to a personality problem that leaves out confession to God. That is one reason why so much modern counseling falls short of the mark.

Jesus is far more interested in us than any psychiatrist could ever be. And He is far more knowledgeable too.

C. God's Word in Consecration (119:27)

"Make me to understand the way of Thy precepts: so shall I talk of Thy wondrous works." God does not let us off lightly. When God has finished listening to our confession and has exposed us to His Word, His counsel will be that henceforth we are to adjust our ways to His Word. It is not blind obedience that God commands. He wants to show us how His precepts *work*. The psalmist made an intelligent request. He said, "Make me to understand *the way* of Thy precepts."

We find an example in Leviticus 11 where God spelled out for Israel His dietary laws—what animals they could and could not eat. We understand, of course, that we are not under law any more in such matters. What we are interested in here is the way those precepts worked for godly Israelites who regulated their lives by God's commands. If they were observed in the right spirit, those dietary laws would lead the Israelite:

1. In the Way of a Healthy Life

God forbade, for instance, the eating of pork, rabbits, scavenger fish, crabs, lobsters, carrion fowl, and beasts of prey. We now know that, unless the greatest care is taken, pork can lead to intestinal parasitic invasion. Crab meat can cause serious allergies. God simply forbade the Israelites to eat such foods. Obeying God's law led to a healthy life. The same is true of most of God's laws. Breaking God's moral laws leads to guilt and worry which in turn, lead to ulcers and to all kinds of other physical ailments. So the way of God's law is the way of a healthy life.

Observing God's dietary laws would also lead the Israelite:

2. In the Way of a Holy Life

The body of the believer is the temple of the Holy Spirit. Leviticus 11, with its long list of dietary restrictions, contains the explanatory command, "Be ye holy for I am holy." The underlying principle of that chapter, as it bears on Christian life today, is that we are not to put into our body things that would grieve the indwelling Holy Spirit and hinder Him from having undisputed sway over us. Such enslaving things as alcohol, drugs, and tobacco should be avoided on principle by believers. The Holy Spirit says, "To make a difference between the clean and the unclean [holiness and unholiness] and between the beast that may be eaten and the beast that may not be eaten [between health and ill health]."

In addition, those dietary laws would lead the Israelites:

3. In the Way of a Happy Life

A holy life—a life free from guilt, from the gnawings of conscience, from psychologically-based illnesses—is far more likely to be happy than a guilt-ridden, pain-wracked life.

No psychologist can adequately deal with guilt apart from the Word of God. Guilt can be washed away only in the blood of Christ.

The psalmist, then, asks God to make him understand the *way* of His precepts, how they work. He promises that he will then talk of God's wondrous works. He will spread the word.

Next we have God's Word:

D. In Contrition (119:28)

"My soul melteth for heaviness: strengthen Thou me according unto Thy word." The word *melteth* is a poetic way of expressing weeping. Thus it was that Jesus wept, not for His own sins, but for ours. One lesson of the prophet Hosea is that sin breaks not only God's laws, it breaks His heart.

Jesus wept at *Bethany* over what sin had done to an *individual*. His friend Lazarus was dead and in his grave. Sin had slain him as it slays everybody who enters this world. Our progress is steadily from the womb to the tomb. Jesus wept over that.

He wept over *Jerusalem*, over what sin had done to a *nation*. It had caused the nation of Israel to reject Him, and eventually to crucify Him. That sin would be visited in horror on that nation.

Within a generation those hills would be black with crosses.
Jesus wept over that.

He wept in *Gethsemane* over what sin had done to the *world*.
Sin had turned this fair paradise into a graveyard. The penalty
of sin, which soon He must bear, was so terrible, so full of
horror, so appalling in its issues that He wept.

So we well might weep over our sin. "My soul melteth for
heaviness" cried the psalmist as the Word of God bit into his
innermost being.

Finally we have God's Word:

E. In Contrast (119:29)

The psalmist now prays, "Remove from me *the way* of lying:
and grant me Thy law graciously."

He doesn't simply pray, "Remove *me from* the way of lying," as
though his feet were ensnared in a net. He prays, "Remove *from
me* the way of lying." He was conscious of the deep things of
Satan in his own soul, that it was bent, warped, and twisted by
indwelling sin. His heart was deceitful above all things and
desperately wicked. He needed to have the way of lying taken
from his soul.

We are all prone to tell lies; nobody has to teach a child to lie.
Some people lie occasionally, when they find themselves in a
tight corner. Others will look you in the face and, with every
outward evidence of sincerity, string together a whole pack of
lies and swear on the Bible that they are telling the truth. They
will do it so convincingly that, although you know better, you
still believe them. They lie seemingly without a qualm of conscience, as though lying were their natural language—which it
probably is. Today lying is a way of life, accepted almost without
question. Nothing so betrays our fallen human nature.

School textbooks lie to us, politicians lie to us, businessmen lie
to us, advertisers lie to us, newspapers lie to us, our children lie
to us. Worst of all, when we get sick of it all and look for a way
out, we find we are hedged around with religious lies. Buddhism is a lie. Islam is a lie. Much that passes for Christianity is a
lie.

When Jesus stood before Pontius Pilate, He told the truth
because He *is* the truth. Pilate, who had been lied to under oath
many times, who had so often witnessed in court the perfidy
and falsehood of the majority of men, who now scarcely expected the truth out of anybody, cynically demanded of Jesus, "*What
is truth?*" And then, just as cynically, he walked away without
waiting to be told.

The Word of God stands in contrast to the way of lying. The

Bible tells the truth, the whole truth, and nothing but the truth. "Thy word is truth." The psalmist wanted God to straighten him out inside.

He saw, in God's Word, the answer to his need. He did not see God's law as something imposed on him *governmentally,* but as something imparted to him *graciously.* God's law to him was a blessing, not a burden.

Now the emphasis changes. We are told:

II. WHAT THE PSALMIST RESOLVED (119:30-32)

The psalmist made three resolutions.

A. His Decision to Live for God (119:30)

"I have chosen the way of truth: Thy judgments have I laid before me." He has just asked God to remove from him the way of lying; now he deliberately chooses the way of truth. He records his decision to live for God.

A classic example of such an attitude is Daniel, who purposed in his heart not to defile himself with the king's meat. We can picture him alone in his room, that first night there in Babylon. He is overwhelmed with impressions. The grandeur and splendor of that capital city, paganism on every hand. He and his friends had been chosen by the king. Their obvious intelligence, high rank, and attractive persons had secured for them impressive prospects. They were to be groomed for high office. The world lay at their feet. Daniel was to go to school in Babylon, to be trained for an important position in the administration. He was to mix with the intelligentsia, the nobility, the social elite of Babylon—at a price. The price was the compromise of his convictions. Tomorrow he would be assigned his place at the table of his peers, along with scores of others. He would be offered the best food in Babylon, with rare dainties from the royal kitchens and viands from the king's own table. The king no doubt wanted these selected courtiers of his to be the picture of good health.

Daniel took out his Bible and began to read. Passages in the Mosaic Law spoke of what kind of meat could or could not be eaten and how that meat must be killed. It must contain no blood. Well he knew that the meat which would be placed before him the next day would not meet these rigid standards of the law. He saw before him two paths. He could dare the king's wrath or he could set aside the law of God. The one path led to *promotion,* the other to *peril;* one was the path of *delight,* the other the path of *danger;* one path entailed *compromise,* the other *conviction;* the one path demanded saying "yes" to the *world;* the other path demanded saying "yes" to the *Word.* He read the Scriptures, he prayed. He said, "I have chosen." He chose to live for God.

Sooner or later that choice faces every child of God, the choice between compromising some biblical principle and complete obedience to the Word of God—even if it means offending friends, family, or employer.

Further, the psalmist records:

B. His Determination to Live for God (119:31)

A decision to live for God is the crisis; a determination to live for God is the process. The psalmist uses an interesting expression to describe his determination. He says, "I have stuck unto Thy testimonies: O LORD, put me not to shame." That word *stuck* means exactly what it says. It means "attached" or "adhered." It conjures up a picture of a man who has adhered himself to the Word of God. He is not stuck *with* it (as though it were some kind of a burden), he is stuck *to* it. He cannot be separated from it. Note also that he has stuck himself to it.

Every now and then we see an advertisement on television for super glue. We see someone put a spot of this glue on a two-thousand pound car, and a little dab on the end of a piece of wood suspended from a crane. Then the tip of the wood is brought in contact with the glue on the car and a fast bond is made. Then, wonder of wonders, the car is hauled thirty feet into the air, dangling from a piece of wood, stuck with super glue. That is how the psalmist was stuck to God's Word. Nothing could pry him loose.

"O Lord, don't let me down," he says. As though God ever could. Once adhere yourself to God's Word and He will see you through, no matter what happens. The bonding is perfect.

That is the kind of bonding we need nowadays. We send a young person off to college and the first thing one of his professors says to him is, "Now you can forget all your parents told you . . ." This psalmist says: "Not me! I've been glued to the Book!" That is the kind of young person to send to college. In fact, if that kind of bonding has not taken place it is probably best he or she stay out of a secular college. It is better for a person to spend life pumping gas or waiting tables than to lose one's soul in a college classroom. That is what Jesus meant when He said that it is possible to lose one's life for His sake and yet to find it.

Last, the psalmist records:

C. His Desire to Live for God (119:32)

"I will run the way of Thy commandments, when Thou shalt enlarge my heart." Sin narrows us. By nature we are chronically addicted to our own ways. God's wants and wishes do not appeal to us at all. Sin has narrowed our hearts so that our circle of desire is circumscribed by self. As for God's vast and eternal interests, we scarcely have a thought for them at all.

The psalmist realizes that if ever he is to have an enlarged *horizon,* he must first have an enlarged *heart. God* must enlarge his heart. Such things as the prayer meeting, the communion service, the demands of the mission field, the daily quiet time, the meeting place of the people of God, must all be interests *God* implants in the soul. The psalmist's desire is to live for God. He asks God to enlarge and increase that desire so that he will end up *running* eagerly in God's ways.

Psalm 119:33-40

FOUR PICTURES OF A MAN OF GOD

    I. SOJOURNER (119:33-34)
    He promises to follow God's direction:
    A. Faithfully (119:33)
    B. Fully (119:34)
   II. SOLDIER (119:35-36)
    He underlines:
    A. The Discipline Needed (119:35)
    B. The Desire Needed (119:36)
 III. SERVANT (119:37-38)
    A. A Discerning Servant (119:37)
    B. A Devoted Servant (119:38)
 IV. SAINT (119:39-40)
    He wanted to be:
    A. A Good Man (119:39)
    B. A Godly Man (119:40)

I N THIS SEGMENT OF THE PSALM we have four pictures of a man of God. We see him as:

I. SOJOURNER (119:33-34)

Life is a journey. A man of God is a wanderer in this world. Here he has no continuing city but he seeks one to come. Like Abraham he is a stranger and sojourner on the earth. This world is not his home, he is only passing through. And, as one who is passing through an alien scene, he needs directions. Here he is seen asking God to guide him on his way.

He promises to follow God's directions:

A. Faithfully (119:33)

"Teach me, O LORD, the way of Thy statutes; and I shall keep it unto the end." He sees God's Word as a path to be followed, a sure way through the wilderness.

It is not much use asking directions if we don't remember them when they are given or if we don't follow them when we

291

get them. I dislike stopping to ask directions when driving. This is what usually happens. My wife will say, "Why don't you stop and ask how to get there?" I keep on driving, hoping something will turn up. She soon has another suggestion, "Here's a gas station. Stop and ask." I have a full tank of gas, and I hate to pull into a gas station to ask for directions without buying gas, so I pretend I don't hear. Eventually, after driving around aimlessly for half an hour, I pull in and ask directions. They usually go like this: "Go down here to the second intersection, turn right, go about one mile, turn left, go about five miles. At the top of the hill, turn left. There's a barn there. You'll see it."

The inevitable happens. After driving a mile down the road I can't remember if the man said to turn left or turn right. After making a guess and driving for some time I can't remember if it was five miles or ten miles to the hill or if I was supposed to turn left or right there. Sometimes, even when I remember what was said and come to the right turn it seems the man must have made a mistake, because a right turn will put me on a dirt road leading nowhere whereas a left turn is a well-paved highway.

We need guidance. We need to pay heed to the Lord's leading and follow it carefully, even though sometimes the Lord's leading seems contrary to what our own thoughts on the matter might be.

We have an example of that in the case of Israel. As soon as the waters of the Red Sea closed behind them they faced the wilderness journey. There were no maps, no paths, no signposts—just the cloudy pillar, which in those days represented God's leading for His people. And, instead of heading eastward across the Sinai in a direct line for Canaan, the cloudy pillar turned south. The path became indescribably difficult. South of Elim the landscape changed and the going became harder than ever. Even before Elim the people had struggled over pebbly ground, through weary wadis and along bare limestone hills. South of Elim they found themselves marching through a dreary flat desolate waste, a land inhospitable and forbidding. After Sinai it was worse. The ground beneath their feet was hard, strewn for endless miles with small sharp pieces of polished flint in which lurked serpents and scorpions. It is justly called "that great and terrible wilderness" (Deuteronomy 8:15). Added to that were enemies. The watchful Amorites and Edomites were waiting for an opportunity to attack. Yet that was the way God led—every difficult, dangerous step of it.

God does not promise us an easy path to Heaven. He does promise us a safe one. So the psalmist prays, "Teach me *the way* of Thy statutes." Not just His statutes, but the *way* of His statutes. He is determined to follow that way faithfully no matter how difficult the road. He is a sojourner in a hostile world and needs God's leading home.

He also promises to follow God's directions:

B. Fully (119:34)

"Give me understanding, and I shall keep Thy law." Understanding is better than knowledge. A man can fill his head full of knowledge and still have no real understanding of what he is doing. Here is knowledge: "The square on the hypotenuse is equal to the sum of the squares on the two sides containing the right angle." That is knowledge about geometry. A person may learn that and even learn how to prove it correct on paper without really understanding it. When a carpenter lays out a floor plan, however, he wants to get perfect 90° angles at the corners. All he does is apply Pythagorean theorem by drawing a 3-4-5 triangle on the floor. He may not be able to give a mathematical proof that the theorem concerning a right-angle triangle works. To prove the theorem on paper is not that simple. He may not have that knowledge, but he has understanding. Knowing that a triangle whose sides are 3-4-5 is a right-angle triangle, he understands that drawing such a triangle on the floor where he wants it will guarantee that his corners will be square.

We have knowledge of God available to us by reading the Bible. That does not mean we understand biblical principles. And it is *understanding* them that enables us to see the sense in them. There are times, of course, when God calls for blind obedience, a simple willingness to say, "Yes, Lord," even when we can't understand why. More often than not, however, meditation on God's Word will give us understanding. Behind all God's commands are two goals God has in mind. One has to do with *our good*—God never has anything else in mind for us than that. The other is *His glory*. God always acts in ways that reflect His glory.

So, first of all, the man of God is seen as *a sojourner* determined to be guided through the wilderness of this world by the Word of God. He is also seen as:

II. SOLDIER (119:35-36)

Life is a battle. The psalmist realized that if he was to keep his life in line with God's Word there would be a struggle. He mentions first:

A. The Discipline Needed (119:35)

"Make me to go in the path of Thy commandments, for therein do I delight." That is a paradox. Imagine having to ask God to *make* us do something we love doing. We do not have to make a little boy eat ice cream! We might have to make him eat spinach or parsnips but we have trouble keeping him away from the cookie jar. We might have to make him practice his piano lessons but we won't have to force him to run and fetch one's wallet when he is going to get some pocket money.

The only explanation of the psalmist's paradox is that we are not one person but two. There is "the old man" and there is "the new man." That was the problem with which Paul wrestled in Romans 7. He said, "For I delight in the law of God after the inward man: But I see another law in my members, warring against the law of my mind, and bringing me into captivity to the law of sin which is in my members" (7:22-23). The new man loves the path of God's commandments; the old man loathes that path. So the fight is on. As a result we tend to swing back and forth like a pendulum.

The psalmist says, "Lord, I need a discipline higher than anything I possess. I need You to make me to go in the path of Your commandments." That is the mark of a true believer. That is the difference between the prodigal's going-away petition and his coming-home petition: "Father, *give* me," and "Father, *make* me."

The psalmist wanted God to make him obedient. He wanted God to make his decisions correspond with his desires.

B. The Desire Needed (119:36)

The psalmist has just told us that he delights in God's law. But he needs that to be reinforced and strengthened. "Incline my heart unto Thy testimonies, and not to covetousness." We all know the problem of vacillation—the see-saw effect in our spiritual life of inclining first this way and then that. The psalmist wanted the scales permanently depressed on the side of God.

One problem in his life, however, was covetousness, as it was also in Paul's life (as he tells us in Romans 7). With that tenth commandment—"Thou shalt not covet," or "thou shalt have no evil desire"—we come under conviction. We have been challenged at a meeting or the Lord has met us in our quiet time. We rise determined to do God's will. The impression fades and soon we are lusting after something else. We need what Paul needed, what the psalmist needed—deliverance.

III. SERVANT (119:37-38)

The psalmist wanted to be:

A. A Discerning Servant (119:37)

"Turn away mine eyes from beholding vanity; and quicken Thou me in Thy way."

One law of spiritual victory we need to learn is to look the other way. A great deal of temptation comes to us through our eyes. Satan used Eve's eyes to lead her into sin. "When she saw," we read, "when she *saw* . . . the tree . . . " she saw in it a chance to become like God. Instead of becoming like God she became like Satan. And no sooner was she a sinner than she became a temptress.

Sinful things have great attraction for us. How often we find ourselves gazing with ever-growing desire at something suggestive, something sensual, something sinful—we are almost unable to turn our eyes away. That is why the psalmist prayed, "Quicken me in Thy way." We need all the new life we have in Christ to turn our eyes from beholding the vanities Satan would put before them. Never was that more so than today when moral standards are lax, when tempting literature is paraded before us everywhere, when our television screens bombard us with sights we would do well to decline to watch.

Reading John 8, I was struck by what Jesus did when the scribes and Pharisees brought the woman taken in adultery to Him. He deliberately averted His eyes. He suddenly became very taken up with the ground. He acted as though He could not hear them and certainly He refused to stare at the poor woman. When they insisted He stared at them. And looked right through them. It was not until they were gone that He looked at her, and then it was with a look of compassion and forgiveness.

Thus the psalmist wanted *his* eyes to be controlled. This is one of the psalmist's nine prayers for "quickening," for being made alive. He wanted inner strength to keep his eye on the Master.

B. A Devoted Servant (119:38)

"Stablish Thy word unto Thy servant, who is devoted to Thy fear." This is not slavish fear but reverential awe. This is a healthy master-servant relationship. The servant must stand in awe of his master, must hold him in respect, must measure the distance between them. There are at least three ways we can read the Bible.

There are those who read it and *forsake* it. They deliberately turn their backs on it, putting it out of their minds. They want no part of it. Its demands cut across the path they have chosen in life so they forsake it.

There are those who read it and *forget* it. They are not deliberate rebels or sworn enemies of the truth of God. They simply allow it to be crowded out of their lives. They have so many other interests. The cares of this world, the deceitfulness of riches, and preoccupation with other things push it out of the conscious, active part of their minds.

There are those who read it and *fear* it. It gets a hold on them. They realize that it deals with eternal issues. There is a Heaven to be gained, a hell to be shunned.

The psalmist takes his stand with those who fear God's Word, with those who have healthy respect for it, who know it is the final arbitrator of life. God's Word is already established in Heaven; the psalmist wanted that Word to be established in his life. God has billions of servants in the unseen world who exist solely to please and obey Him. The psalmist wanted to become that kind of devoted servant. Such service is never one-sided. God establishes His Word to such servants. They can depend on His promises.

IV. SAINT (119:39-40)

The psalmist wanted to live the kind of life that God demands of people, a holy life. The essence of the Mosaic law was that God demanded, "Be ye holy for I am holy." Such a command would be impossible were it not for the fact that God's commands are always God's enablings. There is power in His Word—power to create galaxies, power to bring forth life in myriad forms, power to raise the dead from their graves, power to enable us to do what God demands.

The psalmist, as a saint, wants God's Word to:

A. Make Him Good (119:39)

"Turn away my reproach which I fear: for Thy judgments are good." The word *reproach* means "scorn" or "contempt." The psalmist felt the sting of those who scorned him for his efforts to live a life ruled by God's Word. He wanted that life to be justified by having the inherent goodness that is part of God's Word become part of his life. Not much criticism can be leveled against sheer goodness. But a person who professes to live life by God's Word, but whose behavior is inconsistent, earns the ridicule rather that the respect of those who despise God's Word.

The word *reproach* is found frequently in the Bible. One example was during the wilderness wanderings when Israel neglected the important covenant seal of circumcision. Failure to administer that seal cut the Hebrew off from the Abrahamic covenant (Genesis 17:14).

Such neglect had begun in Egypt, so it is called "the reproach of Egypt." The Israelites had the worldliness of Egypt about them; their disobedience was a reproach, as much a reproach as the disobedience of Pharaoh or the vileness of the Canaanites.

Israel had to be brought into line with God's Word before dealing with God's foes. There could be no victorious living in Canaan until everything that savored of Egyptian disobedience was put away.

Thus the psalmist prayed. He felt that some areas in his life brought discredit on him as a believer. He felt the scorn of the ungodly. He wanted to be good; he wanted the goodness of the Word of God to become evident in his life.

God never asks us to do anything wrong, anything bad, anything not good. God's commandments are good because *He is good*. His commandments are *for our good*, and further, they are designed to *make us good*.

The psalmist wants God's Word also to:

B. Make Him Godly (119:40)

"Behold I have longed after Thy precepts: quicken me in Thy righteousness." The psalmist did not want merely to be good, he wanted to be like God Himself. Again we find echoes of this section of the psalm in Paul's experience in Romans 7 and 8.

Romans 7 records Paul's *longing for victory*. He longed to be able to live a victorious life, longed to be holy. He says: "How to perform that which is good, I find not. For the good that I would I do not: but the evil which I would not, that I do" (Romans 7:18-19). As Paul's longing after a holy life came to a head, he agonized, "O wretched man that I am! Who shall deliver me from the body of this death?" (Romans 7:24). His old nature was like a rotting corpse to which he was tightly bound. He longed to be free of it.

In Romans 8 we see Paul *living in victory*. The psalmist knew that only life can deliver from death, and Paul too found the liberating secret: "The law of the Spirit of life in Christ Jesus hath made me free from the law of sin and death" (Romans 8:2).

The psalmist longed after God's precepts, longed to live the kind of life set forth in God's Word. "Give me the life! Your life! Give me Your righteousness." He had anticipated by centuries the liberating secret of the great epistle to the Romans.

Psalm 119:41-48

FLASHES OF LIGHT FROM GOD'S WORD

The psalmist wants to:

THE SINGER OF THIS PSALM knew that not everyone shared his trust in the Word of God. In this segment of the psalm we see him striking the flint of God's Word with his hammer of conviction; we see the sparks of his testimony fly. In Hebrew each verse begins with the word *And*. We can picture the psalmist hitting out in all directions as though saying, "Take that *and* that *and* that." Yet at the same time he is talking to God and to himself.

He wants to:

I. EXPERIENCE THE PROTECTION OF GOD'S WORD (119:41)

"Let Thy mercies come also unto me, O LORD, even Thy salvation, according to Thy word." The psalmist knows he needs to be garrisoned about with the mercies of God: the Scriptures abound with examples of God's mercy coming to others.

We recall, for instance, the way God's mercies came to *Abraham* when he was a man in Ur of the Chaldees. Those mercies rescued him from darkness. The light of God's Word burst in on his soul; he heard God's voice speaking to him. He recognized that Word for what it was, the revelation of the true and living God, speaking with authority and majesty, and he responded at once. He was rescued forever from the darkness of Babylonian religion to become the father of all those who believe.

We recall the way God's mercies came to *Jonah* when he was inside the whale. Jonah called it "the belly of hell." There he experienced the horrors and pangs of a lost eternity—to which he had been only too willing to consign the people of Nineveh. As that mighty fish sounded the deeps of the sea, Jonah's heart sank with it. Then God's Word came to him, rescuing him from despair. He tells how he prayed using quote after quote from the psalms. God's Word brought light into that dreadful prison, set his soul free, brought him to the place where he pledged himself to obey God's Word and thus to a change in his hopeless circumstances.

God's Word offers us protection on the journey home, protection from doubt and despair, from sin and from the sorrow it brings. God's Word is one of the three strands in that threefold cord of confidence which holds fast when strong tides lift and cables strain. Our assurance of salvation rests on *the Word of God, the work of Christ,* and *the witness of the Spirit.* The psalmist is thankful for the Word of God which tells him about the mercies of God and the salvation He provides.

II. EXERCISE THE POWER OF GOD'S WORD (119:42)

"So shall I have wherewith to answer him that reproacheth me: for I trust in Thy word." Behind that word *reproacheth* is the idea of contempt and mockery. The wisdom of this world is opposed to the wisdom of God's Word. As has been said, young people entering college soon have to make a choice between God and man. Brilliant minds confront them, subtle philosophies entangle them, clever arguments will seduce them unless they take a stand immediately on the Word of God. Like Martin Luther, facing the massed power of the enemy, each must say, "Here I stand; I can do no else; so help me, God."

There is power in the Word of God, power our adversaries cannot withstand. Satan's first goal in the garden of Eden was to persuade Eve to set aside God's Word. The moment she did that he could tell her anything.

If the attack does not come from man, it will come from those unseen enemies which haunt the spirit world, ever watchful to insert a doubt, denial, or delusion into the mind of the believer. The story is told of a young boy who had been saved reading John 3:16. In bed that night, however, doubts assailed him. Was it true? Had anything really happened? He didn't feel any different. Perhaps he really wasn't saved after all. His child's mind then concluded that this was Satan tormenting him. He had been told that Satan loved darkness and, since the darkest place in the room was under the bed, perhaps Satan was lurking there. So he opened his Bible to John 3:16, put his finger on the verse, thrust the Bible under the bed, and said, "Here! Read it for yourself."

The psalmist decided likewise to exercise the power of God's Word. "Here, read it for yourself" is the best answer to scoffers. There is power, mighty power, in God's Word. We don't have to defend the Bible; it is able to defend itself.

III. Express the Proof of God's Word (119:43)

"And take not the word of truth utterly out of my mouth; for I have hoped in Thy judgments." The psalmist wanted nothing in his life or circumstances that would give his enemies a handle against him.

Often we find ourselves in situations where it seems as if God's Word has failed. The foe is quick to pounce on such things. The skeptic picks out some grave injustice done to a believer and says, "There! Explain that." Many things in life seem to nullify the truth of the Bible—to the satisfaction of the unbeliever.

God, however, is not working to the puny time scale of microscopic man. He is working for eternity, and His Word is made of the stuff of which eternity is made. The ultimate truth of God's Word may sometimes be seen at once, sometimes not for centuries.

When God promised Japheth that he would know enlargement, that his descendants would be the masters of the world and that his people would inherit the spiritual blessings deposited with his brother Shem, *that* promise was for the distant ages, not the immediate future (Genesis 9:27). Scoffers of old must have really made fun of that Scripture as centuries came and went. First the Hamitic peoples rose to empire, then the Semitic peoples. The Japhetic peoples came to nothing. With the coming of Cyrus the Persian, however, world power passed, as promised, into Japhetic hands and it has been there ever since. It will remain there, too, until it is taken away from the beast and his confederate kings at the battle of Armageddon by the returning Christ of God.

Likewise the promise that Japheth would dwell in the tents of Shem took a very long time to be fulfilled. It had to await Pentecost and the subsequent conversion of Cornelius before it began to stir into life. Believers, however, should not be troubled by seeming delays. They know that God's Word is true no matter what immediate circumstances say. Like us, though, the psalmist longed that circumstances would vindicate the truth of God's Word.

One can imagine Abraham praying such words. He left Ur of the Chaldees secure in the promise of God's Word that God would give him both a *possession* and a *posterity.* He never did live to see his people established in the promised land. As for the promised posterity, it looked as though he might live without even seeing a son born to perpetuate his name. It was not until he was an old man, and his wife long past the age of bearing children, that God fulfilled His Word and Isaac was born.

We can picture Abraham looking enviously at Lot's children. He had just rescued Lot and his family from the kings of the East. Now Lot is packing his bags and preparing to go back to Sodom once more. "Well, Uncle Abraham, it's like this—the King of Sodom has offered me a position in the government of Sodom. It's an opportunity I can't afford to turn down. My wife is keen on it too. She likes Sodom. The people aren't that bad, you know. You've got a phobia against them. I have the word of Sodom's king that my future is made. As for those promises you talk about—where are they? Just how many acres do you actually own in Canaan? How many children do you and Sarah have? How long is it now since you first got this idea that God is going to give you a son? There seems to be nothing to it. I'm going to settle for certainties. I'm going back to Sodom."

All Abraham would be able to say to that kind of talk would be, "Let God be true, and every man a liar, but I believe God." Abraham, taking the long view, was right, and Lot, taking the short view, was wrong. So we must not be downhearted because God's promise about some matter seems to be taking a long time to materialize. It will come to pass. And, when it does, it will silence the critic. We have to learn to wait. There is a *time* element as well as a *trust* element in God's promises.

IV. EXPLAIN THE PERMANENCE OF GOD'S WORD (119:44)

"So shall I keep Thy law continually, for ever and ever." Temporary delays and seeming setbacks were not going to undermine the psalmist's faith. He would bring his life into line with eternal verities, not just temporal advantages. He would link himself to the permanence of God's Word.

That is what D. L. Moody did. It explains why he was so successful an evangelist and why, unlettered man that he was, the agnostics, intellectuals, and skeptics of his day could not defeat him.

During his 1883 campaign in Britain, D. L. Moody challenged the freethinkers and atheists of the country to come to a

meeting and he would speak just to them. At the time Charles
Bradlaugh was the reigning champion of atheism. As soon as he
heard of the challenge he ordered all the clubs he had formed
to go and take possession of the hall and deal with this American upstart. When the meeting was well under way, Mr. Moody
turned to his text: "Their rock is not as our Rock, even our
enemies themselves being judges" (Deuteronomy 32:31). He
began to pour out broadside after broadside of incidents from
his own experience at the deathbeds of Christians and infidels.
He challenged his listeners. Who had the best foundation on
which faith and hope could rest?

Before long, tears began to flow from some eyes, but the
great mass of men, with a dark and determined defiance of God
on their faces, sat seemingly unmoved. Moody continued to
speak to them in their most vulnerable points—their hearts and
their homes. At the end of the meeting Moody said, "We will
rise and sing 'Only Trust Him' and while we do so the ushers
will open the doors so that anyone who wants to may leave.
After that I will have the usual meetings for those who want to
be led to the Saviour." Instead of stampeding for the door the
great mass of five thousand men rose, sang the hymn, and sat
down again.

Mr. Moody then explained in simple terms the steps to take
to become a Christian. After a few minutes one man said, "I
can't." Moody acknowledged him and told him to keep listening. He continued to explain the plan of salvation. He asked,
"Who will say, 'I will believe Him'? One man shouted, "I won't."
D. L. Moody, his heart overcome with tenderness and compassion, burst into broken tearful words, half sobs. "It is *I will* or *I
won't* for every man in this hall tonight," he cried. Then he told
the story of the prodigal son. "The battle is on the *will*," he
cried, "and only there. When the prodigal son said, '*I will arise*,'
the battle was won."

"Men," he said, "you have your champion there in the middle
of the hall, the man who said 'I won't.' " There was silence.
And, as no man arose, Moody burst out, "Thank God, no man
says '*I won't*.' Now who'll say '*I will*?' " In an instant the Holy
Spirit seemed to break loose on the crowd of Christ's enemies.
The men sprang to their feet, their faces wet with tears, shouting, "I will, I will," until the whole atmosphere was changed and
the battle was won.

Moody knew how to stand on eternal verities. He knew *his
Rock* was better than their rock. "So shall I keep Thy law continually, for ever and ever," sang the psalmist. He had cast his
anchor into the stormy sea and it had taken hold on a rock that

could never be moved. He knew he was safe. He had taken hold of the permanence of God's Word.

V. EXPLORE THE PATH OF GOD'S WORD (119:45)

"And I will walk at liberty: for I seek Thy precepts." Most people would not describe walking according to God's laws the way the psalmist did. They would describe the life of faith as bondage rather than liberty. "You can't do this, can't do that, can't go here, can't go there." To the unsaved man, it seems like a life hedged about with restrictions. The psalmist saw God's law as the perfect law of liberty. It did not mean he could do whatever he wanted; it meant he could do whatever God willed. And that, he says, is true freedom.

Those who refuse to walk in God's ways bring themselves into frightful bondage. They are soon bound by the shackles of sin. Jesus said, "He that committeth sin is the slave of sin." How many millions of people are slaves to drugs and drink, to tobacco, to bad temper, to pride, to evil passions.

Libertarians, today, would like to abolish all restraints on human behavior, especially the restraints God has imposed on society. In the name of freedom and liberty we must have abortion on demand, perversion raised to respectability, criminals coddled and their rights respected above those of their victims. As a result, we have a drug culture destroying millions, divorce making a shamble of homes, a sexual revolution that has lured millions into lifestyles that mock at God's law. That is not liberty but lust. People who live like that soon find their bodies enslaved and ruined by disease. Ask the woman hooked on heroin if she is enjoying liberty or the man dying of AIDS if he likes the fruit of his freedom. Ask the children of divorce how they like the new freedoms of our age.

The first lie propagated on this planet promised liberty from having to do what God required. Eve swallowed Satan's lie and her husband was the first victim of the freedom she had discovered. The human race plunged into bondage.

VI. EXPOUND THE PRINCIPLES OF GOD'S WORD (119:46)

"I will speak of Thy testimonies before kings, and will not be ashamed." Paul did that, Jesus did that, Joseph did that, Daniel did that. We have nothing to be ashamed of in God's Word. It has stood the test of time. It has commanded the allegiance of some of the world's finest thinkers. We stand alongside some of the greatest human beings who ever lived. We need not be ashamed of this Book. It has the answers to all the questions of mankind.

VII. EXTRACT THE PLEASURES OF GOD'S WORD (119:47)

"And I will delight myself in Thy commandments, which I have loved." Not many people do that. Not too many get their pleasure out of studying God's Word.

Paul says of the Old Testament Law that it was our "schoolmaster, to bring us to Christ." And a stern schoolmaster it is. It will stand for no nonsense; it will enforce its lessons with a ready use of the rod. Yet it is a kindly old schoolmaster just the same.

In the movie version of the sad-sweet story, *Goodbye Mr. Chips,* we find a helpful illustration. Mr. Chips taught in an English boarding school in the old days when schools were run on strict lines and when schoolmasters believed that their job was to cultivate a boy's morals as well as his mind. The story opens with Mr. Chips being thoroughly detested by the boys because of his stern discipline. But the story ends with Mr. Chips being cheered to the rafters by the boys who had come to love him for being the fine noble character he was.

In the psalmist's day, the "schoolmaster" was still ruling the classroom with his firm hand. Old Dr. Law was there to cultivate the mind and morals of the people of God. The psalmist was one of those students in the school who had come to appreciate his teacher to the full.

VIII. EXAMINE THE POTENTIAL OF GOD'S WORD (119:48)

"My hands also will I lift up unto Thy commandments, which I have loved; and I will meditate in Thy statutes." The psalmist's hands are upraised, reaching up to grasp God's law. That is what the law was intended to do—make us reach up. It was given on a mountain peak. Because it expresses God's holiness, its standards are those of perfection. God does not lower His standards, He does not compromise with sin, He does not accommodate Himself to our low level of behavior. He makes us reach up. He makes us lift up our hands to His commandments. That means we have to lift up our hearts as well.

But with all the will in the world, with all our reaching up, we still cannot reach high enough. That is why *He has reached down.*

Psalm 119:49-56

HOPE

I. WHAT THE PSALMIST REQUESTED (119:49)
II. WHAT THE PSALMIST RECOGNIZED (119:50-51)
   God's Word was:
   A. Life to Him When Injured (119:50)
   B. Law to Him When Insulted (119:51)
III. WHAT THE PSALMIST REMEMBERED (119:52-56)
   A. The Lord's nature (119:52-54)
      1. It Comforted Him (119:52)
      2. It Consoled Him (119:53-54)
   B. The Lord's name (119:55-56)
      It had:
      1. Become Precious to Him (119:55)
      2. Become Part of Him (119:56)

REPEATEDLY IN PSALM 119 we see the psalmist wrestling with the problem of adverse circumstances. His unhappy situation was caused by wicked men who hated him because he was godly. In this section he grapples again with this problem. We note:

I. WHAT HE REQUESTED (119:49)

"Remember the word unto Thy servant, upon which Thou hast caused me to hope." Hope has to do with the future; it looks forward to something. Hope allies itself with our emotions. But hope is only as good as the promise to which it is related. It is often dashed because of the unreliable nature of the objects to which it looks. As a result, we tend to see hope as a rather anemic quality. If we ask someone, "Are you saved?" and he says, "I hope so," we feel that to be an unsatisfactory answer.

Hope, however, does have its stronger side. When we hope in God's Word, we can be sure that our hope is well placed. The future is bright.

305

In this psalm we see that the psalmist's hopes have been raised. The promises, principles, and precepts in God's Word meet a definite need in his life. They are not promises guaranteed only to certain individuals under certain circumstances. They are open, general promises. They are "blank checks" for the people of God to present any time they like at the "bank of Heaven." The psalmist is presenting one of those checks now. He wants his hopes to be confirmed.

II. What He Recognized (119:50-51)

The psalmist recognized that God's Word was:

A. Life to Him When He Was Injured (119:50)

"This is my comfort in my affliction: for Thy word hath quickened me [kept me alive]." We don't know what had afflicted the psalmist. Perhaps he was sick, even desperately ill. Perhaps he had suffered a severe financial reverse, or was out of work and unable to find a job. Perhaps people were telling lies about him. Perhaps his wife had died. Whatever it was, something had gone wrong in his life. The kinds of things that upset us would also upset him.

Facing affliction, the psalmist turned to the Scriptures. Affliction should drive us to our Bible. With many people, that is about the last place they think to go in their troubles. They rush off to a specialist—to a doctor if they are ill, to a lawyer if they are being attacked, to job placement people if they are out of work. Which, of course, makes some sense. The Bible never militates against common sense. But the first place to go is to the *Book*, as did this sensible psalmist. He rushed to his Bible. As a result, his gloom lifted; God was still on the throne.

There was a time when our young son was rebellious. We were in despair to know what to do. The Bible was a great solace to us in those days. There came a time when my wife determined she would avoid the usual distractions—the telephone, the TV set, getting out of the house, going places. She would shut herself up with the Lord until she received some assurance that all would be well, that the boy would be saved and our other children made to walk in God's ways. She turned to Isaiah and found many verses that brought fresh hope and new life. One in particular was, "And all thy children shall be taught of the Lord; and great shall be the peace of thy children" (Isaiah 54:13). She underlined it in her Bible. She shared it with everybody. And sure enough, in time, God saved our son. He even worked it out so that he went to a Christian university for his education, the last place on earth he would have considered going in his wayward days. And one by one the

Lord brought our other children to Himself, graciously fulfilling His promise.

God's word comforts us; it keeps us going on when times are hard. Thus it was with the psalmist. Thus it was with our family. Thus it can be for any of us. God's Word brings *life* when we are injured.

The psalmist recognized also that God's Word was:

B. Law to Him When Insulted (119:51)

"The proud have had me greatly in derision: yet have I not declined from Thy law."

Into the grand and gilded court of Pharaoh there once came a shepherd from the desert. He knew those courts well. He had been reared there years ago, though it is doubtful the present Pharaoh knew who he was. All he saw was a shepherd, and Pharaoh on his throne had not the slightest interest in this shepherd. He eyed him with disfavor. Then came the fellow's unbelievable, impudent demand, a message from some tribal deity—the deity of Pharaoh's Hebrew slaves, no less. (Some kind of God they had, one that allowed His devotees to live in slavery and squalor!) "*Let my people go!*" What was that? How ridiculous! We can imagine the whole court rocking with laughter, a laughter suddenly silenced as Pharaoh, his beard bristling with wrath, proudly mocked that divine imperative: "I know not the Lord. Neither will I let this people go."

But he did. "The proud have had me greatly in derision: yet have I not declined from Thy law," Moses might have said.

Here is another example. Into the camp of Israel one day there came another shepherd, this one a boy. He arrived in time to hear the Philistine giant Goliath roar out his challenge and blaspheme the God of Israel. "Why doesn't somebody fight him?" the boy wanted to know. "Go on home," his brothers snapped. But he insisted. *He* would fight this giant, he was not afraid of *him*. Down into the valley he went, to be met by the scoffing laughter of Goliath. That laughter was soon cut off by a stone from David's sling.

A classic example is our Great Shepherd, Jesus, when He arrived at the house of Jairus, whose daughter was dead. "She is not dead, but sleepeth," He said. "And they laughed Him to scorn." They did the same later when He hung crucified on the tree. "The proud have had me greatly in derision, yet I have not turned from Thy law," He might have said. Our Lord held steadfastly to God's law all through His life and on through the valley of death to the triumph on the other side.

God's law was the rule of the psalmist's life, no matter who might deride. Let people insult him if they would. That is a lesson our young people need to learn before they face the sneers and ridicule of the ungodly.

III. What He Remembered (119:52-56)

The psalmist remembered:

A. The Lord's Nature (119:52-54)

God is a God of integrity and righteousness, a God who always does what is right. Nothing can change that. The Lord's nature:

1. Comforted the Psalmist (119:52)

"I remembered Thy judgments of old, O LORD; and have comforted myself." Our circumstances change; God's Word is permanent. His testimonies are "of old." They have stood the test of time.

Laws today are often made under pressure, they are often tentative, they often reflect compromise or social, economic, or political bias. Lobbyists and interest groups significantly influence legislation. We have hundreds of thousands of laws seeking to accomplish what God effected in ten commandments. The psalmist, however, was not brought up in a land where legislation was at the mercy of lobbyists. He was brought up in a land where the law was mandated from heaven—handed down by God on two tables of stone, fixed and firm. The law was therefore perfect. The psalmist could comfort himself in the fact that God, who legislated such personal righteousness, public responsibility, and pure religion, was a God of wisdom, love, and power. The law reflected God's nature, just as our laws reflect our national character. God's laws reflect *His* character. That was a comfort to the psalmist. God's laws reflect a holy and righteous God, a God of compassion and love.

The Lord's nature, as revealed in His law:

2. Consoled the Psalmist (119:53-54)

"Horror hath taken hold upon me because of the wicked that forsake Thy law" (119:53).

The psalmist first speaks negatively of his horror. The margin of some Bibles suggests the alternative reading, "indignation," but we can let the reading stand as it is. Our souls should be filled with horror at the deeds and certain doom of the wicked. One wonders how they can sleep at night. It is not that they never knew God's Word. Many were brought up in Sunday school, exposed to the truth of God, taught from the Scriptures what God is like and what He thinks about sinful human behavior. That makes no difference. They lie, steal, commit adultery,

and think they can get away with it. The psalmist was horrified
at such people. Surely we should be horrified too. We should be
horrified at the harvest they will reap from such sowing, horrified at what awaits them at the great white throne. The horror
should drive sleep from our eyes and drive us to our knees.
General William Booth used to say he wished every one of the
soldiers in the Salvation Army could be held over hell for half
an hour. It was their driving horror of sin and its consequences
that drove the Salvationists into the streets and slums of the
world's cities, to work miracles of grace. If such horror would
seize hold of *us,* maybe similar horror would seize hold of *them,*
our loved ones and friends outside of Christ. That would put
them in a hurry to be saved.

Then the psalmist speaks positively of his happiness: "Thy
statutes have been my songs in the house of my pilgrimage"
(119:54). Some render the word *pilgrimage* as "sojournings" or,
as we would say today, "journeys." A sojourner is someone away
from home, perhaps in a far country. The psalmist was not in
the far country as a prodigal. He had not rushed off somewhere
to get away from God and from the influence of a godly home.
He may have been in the far country as a prisoner, as one of the
exiles. He was away from his beloved land, whatever the reason,
but his longings were all toward home.

To sing in a land of exile would be a glorious *triumph.* Singing
hymns, psalms, and spiritual songs is a mark of the Spirit-filled
life. This psalmist has risen above his circumstances. Like Paul
and Silas in the Philippian jail, he sang. To sing the *Scriptures* in
a foreign land, in the land of exile, would be a glorious *testimony.*
It was the Bible that consoled him, that tuned up his harp, that
put a song in his soul, that came irrepressibly from his mouth.
We can picture him in Babylon, the land of exile. Foreigners
rule over him. His beloved homeland is in ruins, its temples
burned, its altars forsaken. He serves a foreign master, yet as he
goes about his duties he sings. We can almost hear him:

> The Lord's my shepherd, I'll not want
> He makes me down to lie;
> In pastures green, He leadeth me
> The quiet waters by.
>
> Yea, though I walk in death's dark vale,
> Yet will I fear no ill,
> For Thou art with me, and Thy rod
> And staff me comfort still.

His master comes along, a big, burly Babylonian, a pagan
idolater, a man with no knowledge of God at all beyond the
crass superstitions and dark infamies of his pagan worship.

"Hey, there, what's that you're singing?"

"It's one of the songs I learned as a lad, my lord."

"How does it go in Babylonian?"

The singer translates a few lines.

"Those are beautiful words. Who wrote them?"

"These words, my lord, were written half a century ago by a shepherd boy who became a king. His name was David. He founded the ruling dynasty in Israel. He became the hero of my people as a youth, when alone and unaided he fought and killed a giant in the Valley of Elah."

"Is the Valley of Elah the same as the valley of the shadow?"

"No, my lord. The 'valley of the shadow' is a poetic expression for the valley of death. This song tells how we can have peace in that valley, how our true and living God will be with us there to conduct us safely to the other side."

"You speak as though your God were a living God."

"And so He is, my lord."

"I take it, then, that you don't think much of Bel and Marduk and the other gods of Babylon?"

"My lord, I know the true and living God. The One who gives peace in the valley."

"You have to be born a Hebrew, I suppose, to know this God of yours?"

"No, my lord. He is the God of creation, the Lord of the universe. He rules in all lands. My lord could come to know Him, too . . ."

B. The Lord's Name (119:55-56)

The psalmist tells us two things about the Lord's name. It had:

1. Become Precious to Him (119:55)

"I have remembered Thy name, O LORD, in the night, and have kept Thy law." The Bible has a lot to say about the night. It is a time of *terror.* Picture, for instance, the terror of the rich fool in the Lord's parable. He was congratulating himself one night on having made his fortune. He was laying his plans for a life of prosperity and pleasure. Then the voice of God rang in his soul: "This night shall thy soul be required of thee . . ." Psalm 91:5 speaks of "the terror by night." Many a person has awakened in the night, their soul gripped with stark horror at the thought of death.

Night is a time of *trouble.* Isaiah warned his godless age, "The morning cometh, and also the night" (Isaiah 21:12). The prophet's words sum up what is ahead for the world: a glorious morning for the church when it will be ushered by way of rapture into a land of fadeless day. The morning cometh. And also the night: the dark night of despair when the devil's messiah will seize the planet and inaugurate a reign of terror the like of which has never been known on earth in all its long and tragic history.

The night is a time of *tears* (Psalm 22:2), a time of *temptation* (1 Thessalonians 5:7), a time of *tragedy*—Judas went out and it was night (John 13:30), a time of *truth* (Daniel 2:19). How often God speaks to us during the night, bringing a verse of Scripture to mind or a word of testimony. And so night is even a time of *triumph.* Job spoke of His Maker giving him songs in the night (Job 35:10).

It was so with this psalmist. The Lord's *name* gripped his soul in the night watches, that glorious, manifold name by which God had progressively revealed Himself to His people in Old Testament times. If we honor it, that name will keep us true to His law.

Finally, the psalmist says that the Lord's name had:

2. Become Part of Him (119:56)

"This I had, because I kept Thy precepts." We must supply the ellipsis, the subject to which the *this* refers. Some suggest, "This (comfort) I have had (all this comfort and steadfastness and joy in the midst of trials) because I have kept Thy precepts." Perhaps, however, the ellipsis should go back further. "This I had (Thy Name, O Lord) because I kept Thy precepts." In other words, the singer is identified with the Lord because of his adherence to the Lord. Today we take the name of Christ, we who are *Christians.* His name becomes our name. We are identified with Him. What we do and say reflects on His Name. What a difference *that* should make to the way we live.

Psalm 119:57-64

RUINED BUT STILL REJOICING

IT SEEMS LIKELY from this segment of the psalm that the singer has suffered material loss—but not loss of his joy. Like the noble Hebrew Christians, the psalmist accepted joyfully what may have been the ruin of his goods (Hebrews 10:34). That calls for more than the usual amount of grace. It is not everyone who could shout a loud Hallelujah over such a loss.

We are to examine:

I. THE PSALMIST'S FIND (119:57-58)

The psalmist found that what he had left to him was far more than what he had lost. (Robbers lose far more than those they rob. Their victims lose their purse; thieves lose their integrity.)

A. What He Realized (119:57a)

"Thou art my portion, O LORD." Nobody could rob the psalmist of that. His treasure was laid up in heaven where neither moth nor rust can corrupt and where thieves do not break in and steal. "*Thou* art my portion . . . I will keep Thy words

312

. . ." That is the genius of the Bible. The *person* comes before the *precept*. In the New Testament the Lord Jesus expressed it like this: "If ye love *Me*, keep My commandments." Fall in love with Jesus and it will be easy enough to do what He says.

Abraham, too, discovered that the Lord was his portion. He had that sad experience with Lot over the matter of money. The land was not big enough to support all of Abraham's cattle as well as all of Lot's, so Abraham gave way. He let Lot choose first. With a greedy eye to gain, Lot chose by sight and not by faith. He took the well-watered plains of Jordan regardless of the character of the Sodomites who lived down there.

Abraham watched him go. Then the Lord appeared to him, as He did so often in the crises of Abraham's life. Abraham still had the Lord and, having Him, he had everything. He really hadn't lost anything. He was going to get it all back (Genesis 13:14-18).

He learned the same lesson in the next chapter of his life— still over Lot's selfishness. He had rescued Lot from the kings of the East. Instead of being grateful, Lot had gone back to Sodom. He had staked his claim to those well-watered plains and to the prosperous cities that dotted them, and he was not about to give them up. Abraham sadly watched him go. Again God appeared. "Fear not, Abram," He said, "I am thy shield, and thy exceeding great reward" (Genesis 15:1).

In the Lord we have a very large portion. We remember how Joseph dealt with his brothers in Egypt. As yet they did not know the man at the right hand of the Pharaoh. They had no idea who he was, although he knew them. He sat them down to feast in his presence, and gave them all a portion. He was related to all of them, so he gave them all a portion. But he gave Benjamin a special portion—five times as much as any of the others, for Benjamin was more closely related to him than all the others. It looked forward, typically, to the day when the glorious One at God's right hand will manifest to His own all the splendor He has out there beyond the skies. All Israel will feast in His presence. All Israel will receive their portion. But there is a Benjamin, the church. The church is to get a special portion, a worthy portion, since the church is related to Him in a special and unique way.

When the land was divided between the twelve tribes by lot, Levi was not included. Ephraim and Manasseh represented Joseph, so in them Joseph received a double portion. But Levi received no territorial grant, just a number of towns scattered here and there throughout the tribes. Still Levi did not lose out by getting the Lord as his portion—not even financially. Levi received the tithe from the other eleven tribes. By law, those tribes had to tithe their income. Each tribe had nine-tenths left after the tithe and eleven one-tenth portions went to Levi. Each tribe received nine-tenths, Levi received eleven-tenths, so even in terms of cold cash, Levi had more. But that was not the point. The point was that Levi had the Lord.

And we have the Lord. "*Thou* art my portion, O Lord." We can sing with Charles Wesley:

> Thou, O Lord, are all I want
> More than all in Thee I find . . .

B. What He Resolved (119:57b)

"I have said that I would keep Thy words." The sneering skeptic might say, "So, you have been robbed! Now where's your God?" The psalmist would say, "Just where He always is, close by my side. Nothing has changed. I am still going to keep His words. I can think of no better rule for life and certainly not the rule of life exemplified by those who just ran off with my purse. If you think I am going to change my philosophy of life, rooted and grounded as it is in the Word of God, just because some-body else has no respect for God's Word, you are mistaken."

The psalmist resolved that he would keep God's Word no matter what might happen.

C. What He Requested (119:58)

"I intreated Thy favor with my whole heart: Be merciful unto me according to Thy word." The psalmist knew that he too was a sinful, erring man, just as much in need of mercy as anyone else.

It is one of God's characteristics that He loves to show mercy. Shakespeare says:

> The quality of mercy is not strained;
> It droppeth as the gentle rain from heaven
> Upon the place beneath. It is twice blest:
> It blesseth him that gives and him that takes.
> 'Tis mightiest in the mightiest; it becomes
> The throned monarch better than his crown . . .

When a person throws himself on the mercy of a human court, he relies on the temper and whim of the judge. An appeal to God's mercy is on surer ground. That mercy, as the psalmist reminds God, is "according to Thy word." God has *promised* mercy. He would rather show mercy than wrath. He is a God of tender mercy. His mercy, however, is to be implored in accordance with the terms revealed in His Word.

Jesus once told a story that shows how the mercy of God

works. He told of two men who went up to the temple to pray. One of the men was a smug, complacent, self-righteous Pharisee who came to tell God how good he was. Jesus says with fine sarcasm that he "prayed with himself." God did not even hear him. The other man was a wretched publican, burdened down with a sense of sin and shame. He would not so much as lift up his eyes but beat his breast in an agony of despair. "God, be merciful to me a sinner," was his cry. He went away forgiven, freely and forever. *That* is the condition of God's mercy: We must seek it conscious of our deep need.

We do not plead our innocence but our guilt. We do not appeal our case. We plead *guilty* and sue for *mercy*. That is what the psalmist requested. The word translated "favor" is *face* in the orginial text. "I intreated Thy face." There is nothing like face-to-face contact when seeking a favor.

II. The Psalmist's Feet (119:59-60)

The psalmist has something to tell us about the path he has chosen as he journeys through life. He has chosen the way of:

A. Perfect Obedience (119:59)

"I thought on my ways, and turned my feet unto Thy testimonies." Here we see four aspects of his obedience. First was *deliberation*. He says, "I thought." It is a good sign when we stop and think. That is one thing the devil does not want us to do. He has a thousand diversions to dangle before us to prevent us from thinking. It comes out, for instance, in our word *amusement*. "Muse" means "to think." The idea of musing, however, is turned into a negative by the addition of the letter *a*. "Amuse" means "don't think." It is the first sign of hope in a sinner when he says with the psalmist "I thought . . ."

Second, his thoughts had a *destination*: "I thought on my ways . . ." He sat down to think about the way he was living. "Where is all of this getting me?" he asked himself. The first sign of spiritual sanity in the prodigal son was when he began to talk to himself about his ways. He thought about his destination. He had already arrived at one stopping place on the broad road to destruction and discovered it no pleasant place to be. He found himself arrayed in rags, clutching a pig-pail, sitting on a garbage dump, and eating slops intended for the hogs. "I will arise and go to my father," he said.

Which brings us to the next point the psalmist made: there was *determination*. "I thought on my ways, and turned my feet." This was the turning point in his life. Just as Moses came to the turning point in his when he said, "I will now turn aside, and see this great sight, why the bush is not burnt" (Exodus 3:3). There has to be a decision. A person has to decide for Christ. God does not push people into the kingdom. He will persuade and plead but He will not push. He woos but never ravishes.

Finally, there was *discrimination*: " . . . unto Thy testimonies." The psalmist did not turn to some manmade philosophy or to some religious system. He turned to God and to God's Word. That was discrimination. That is the story of every conversion:

> I've wandered far away from God
> Now I'm coming home;
> The paths of sin too long I've trod,
> Now I'm coming home.

Take a good look at the psalmist's feet. For all the glowing sentiments expressed in his long and eloquent ode to the Word of God, the psalmist did not *always* love God's Word, did not always walk in obedience to it. There came a turning point in his life when he made up his mind that henceforward he would walk in God's ways.

B. Prompt Obedience (119:60)

"I made haste, and delayed not to keep Thy commandments." A proverb says, "Procrastination is the thief of time." We have an inbred tendency to delay, to put off until tomorrow something that often would far better be done today. We resolve that we are going to walk in God's ways—tomorrow.

Robert Laidlaw, in his booklet *The Reason Why*, concludes his presentation of the gospel by confronting Satan's final tactic in the soul of one who is "almost persuaded"—the tactic of delay. He puts it like this:

> "Tomorrow," he promised his conscience,
> "Tomorrow I mean to believe,
> Tomorrow I'll think as I ought to,
> Tomorrow the Saviour receive.
> Tomorrow I'll conquer those habits
> Which hold me from heaven away."
> But ever God's Spirit insisted
> One word, and one only—TODAY.
>
> Tomorrow, tomorrow, tomorrow,
> Thus day after day it went on.
> Tomorrow, tomorrow, tomorrow,
> Till youth, like a vision, had gone;
> And age, with its passions had written
> The message of fate on his brow;
> And out of the shadows came Death
> With his pitiless syllable—NOW.

We squander away days and weeks, months and years, which might have been invested for eternity; we delay and stall and postpone obedience to God. We think that obeying God is going to be a *burden* whereas all the time God wants to make it a *blessing*. How foolish we are. The psalmist went in for *prompt* obedience.

III. The Psalmist's Foes (119:61)

"The bands of the wicked have robbed me: but I have not forgotten Thy law." That verse might have been the text of Adoniram Judson, the man who took the gospel to Burma. In the annals of foreign missions, few people have been as abused as he was. On one occasion he was driven in chains across a desert, beaten and bruised, his feet bleeding, and falling at last utterly exhausted, beneath the lashes of his captors and praying for God to put an end to his sufferings. Another time he was imprisoned for two years in unspeakable conditions, and baited and persecuted without mercy. Meanwhile, the mission house in which he lived was plundered of all he possessed; his wife, driven almost to distraction, was left without even a chair to sit on. One of the most pathetic pages in the story of this man's suffering tells of his return home. Judson himself was maimed and forever scarred, a living skeleton, but he scarcely recognized his wife. She was dressed in rags, her hair shorn from her head, and in the depths of privation.

Nonetheless, the two determined to carry on. Their enemies could not rob them of their faith in God. That burned as brightly as ever. By the time their witness here on earth was over, people were turning to Christ by the thousands.

How like our Lord. On the cross He could have said, "The bands of the wicked have robbed Me." There, at the foot of the cross, the soldiers gambled for His clothes. "But I have not forgotten Thy law," He might have added. He died with the Word of God on His lips, robbed of everything except what mattered most.

IV. The Psalmist's Fervor (119:62)

"At midnight I will rise to give thanks unto Thee because of Thy righteous judgments." People in the psalmist's day went to bed early. To rise at midnight was to rise in the middle of the night. To get up at midnight in order to pray and give thanks to God indicated an extraordinary measure of devotion and love for the Lord. It wasn't that he couldn't sleep, that he tossed and turned on his bed with sleep driven from his eyes by the haunting horror of his sin. It was nothing like that.

It was just that he was so grateful to God for "His righteous judgments." He loved the Lord and was grateful that He was the kind of God He was. He wanted a time when he could be

free from the disturbances and distractions of the day, when all
would be peaceful and still—and the best time for that was in
the middle of the night. So he saw to it that he got up in the
midnight hours to be alone with God.

Jesus did that also. We are told that He rose up "a great while
before it was yet day" to talk to His Father in Heaven, to tell
Him how much He loved Him, how He appreciated Him, how
He was grateful for His love and for His leading in His life. To
talk over with Him the events of the day just passed; to speak to
Him about Zacchaeus, perhaps, or blind Bartimaeus, or the
woman He had met at the well; to share with Him something
Peter had said, or something Matthew had done; to tell Him
about the deepening shadows—to go over with Him again what
the Scriptures said about the cross, and to unburden His heart
about the approach of Calvary.

V. The Psalmist's Friends (119:63)

"I am a companion of all them that fear Thee, and of them
that keep Thy precepts." The second act of God in creation was
to separate the waters from the waters, to divide the waters
above from the waters below. Between the two God put a firmament, an atmosphere. That is always God's second act. His first
act is to bring light into the darkened soul; His second act is to
make a difference between those who know Christ personally
and those who don't. He separates the believer from the unbeliever by putting an atmosphere between them. The unbeliever
likes the atmosphere of the bar, the dance hall, the smoke-filled
pool room, the suggestive and impure atmosphere of Broadway
or Hollywood. The believer prefers the atmosphere of the
prayer meeting, the communion service, the place where God's
people meet to read and study God's word.

People are known by the company they keep. "Birds of a
feather flock together" is a simple fact of nature. "Being let go,
they went to their own company" says the Holy Spirit of the
apostles after they had been threatened by the Sanhedrin (Acts
4:23). "Hereby we know that we have passed from death unto
life," says John, "because we love the brethren." The psalmist
was known by his choice of friends, and so are we.

VI. The Psalmist's Facts (119:64)

Two great facts filled the soul of this singer as he contemplat-
ed the glorious goodness of God. He tells us:

A. What He Discovered (119:64a)

"The earth, O Lord, is full of Thy mercy." Everywhere he
could see something only redeemed eyes can see—the earth full

of God's mercy. *That* is something we do not see in *nature*. Those who worship God in nature miss the message of His mercy. They see nature "red in tooth and claw." Nature does not teach forgiveness. If a man falls off a fifty-foot cliff, it does him no good to say to nature, "I'm sorry! I slipped." The law of gravity works on relentlessly heedless of his apology.

Redeemed eyes see God's mercy everywhere. It was mercy that provided a coat of skins for Adam and Eve so that the shame of their nakedness might be covered in the presence of God. It was mercy that branded Cain instead of burying him, thus giving him a span of time in which to repent and seek the salvation of the God he had despised. It was mercy that waited some fifteen hundred years before sending the flood on the vile and godless antediluvian world. It was mercy that built the ark and offered man a way of escape from the wrath to come. It was mercy that hung the rainbow in the sky and gave those emerging from the ark a new pledge of God's patience with the children of men.

It was mercy that marched to meet Abraham after his disastrous backsliding in Egypt, and mercy that met him again when he was flushed with his victory over the kings of the East. It was mercy that pulled Lot out of Sodom before he was engulfed in its flames. It was mercy that saved Jacob at Bethel and sanctified him at the Jabbok. It was mercy that lifted Israel out of the house of bondage. It was mercy that washed away the stain of David's sin. It was mercy that turned the tide of history and brought the Jews back from Babylon to the promised land.

It was mercy—"wide, wide as the ocean, high as the heavens above"—that held back God's wrath from the human race when men hammered His Son to the tree. It was mercy that transformed the cross from a symbol of infamy into a symbol of salvation.

It is mercy that has lengthened out the day of grace for two millennia. It is God's mercy that has met us a thousand, thousand times already in our own brief journey through life. "It is of the Lord's mercies that we are not consumed." Think of the times we have sinned. Think of the number, the nature, the nastiness of our sins. If God visited us in judgment for even the least of them, we would be cut off forever in the lake of fire, but He has met us with mercy. "The earth, O Lord, is full of Thy mercy." *That* is what the psalmist discovered.

Then, note:

B. What He Desired (119:64b)

"Teach me Thy statutes." Grace *unstinted* must be followed by growth *unstunted*. God's mercy must be the foundation on which to build a new kind of life. Mercy and truth must kiss each other. Life under the mercy of God must be a life shaped by the truth of God. Do we, like the psalmist, desire to be taught God's statutes?

Psalm 119:65-72

IT IS WELL WITH MY SOUL

I. The Psalmist's Word of Testimony (119:65)
II. The Psalmist's Wish for Teaching (119:66-68)
   A. What He Expressed (119:66)
   B. What He Experienced (119:67)
   C. What He Expected (119:68)
III. The Psalmist's Way in Testing (119:69-71)
   A. His Reaction to Those Who Affronted Him (119:69-70)
      1. To Their Sneers (119:69)
      2. To Their Smugness (119:70)
   B. His Reaction to That Which Afflicted Him (119:71)
IV. The Psalmist's Wealth of Treasure (119:72)

THROUGHOUT THIS PSALM we are reminded that the psalmist's situation was anything but pleasant. Enemies surrounded him and tried to make his life a misery.

The constant gnawing of adverse circumstances can wear down even the most committed believer. Yet, as the constant washing of the waters smooths the pebbles and the constant wearing of the sand rounds the ragged edges of even the roughest rocks, so the unremitting adversities of the psalmist were doing their work of polishing and refining his soul.

This segment of the psalm divides into four. We have:

I. The Psalmist's Word of Testimony (119:65)

"Thou hast dealt well with Thy servant, O Lord, according unto thy word." Even when things go wrong, all is well. That surely sums up, for instance, the life of Joseph. Nothing could have seemed worse for Joseph than the events that overtook him and promised to overwhelm him in the early years of his life.

There was the bad temper of his older brothers and their

321

undisguised dislike. There was their callous betrayal of him for cold cash, into the hands of foreigners. There was the knowledge that they would have killed him had not the cash motive inserted itself.

Then, too, there was the ignominy of slavery after having once been the favorite of his father, with every prospect of inheriting the patriarchal rights and privileges. Now his father thought him dead. There was the constant dread of his master's wife as she pursued him with her hot passions and unwanted favors. One can well imagine the terror this must have inspired in Joseph. His master was an influential man in Egypt. For him to be caught in a compromising situation with the man's wife, he, a slave, with no rights, augured certain death. There was the added sting that anyone else would have accepted the situation philosophically and helped himself to what was offered.

There was also the horrible realization that his refusal had been in vain. He had been accused of the sin anyway; his denials had been useless. His integrity was in shreds, his honor gone, his testimony ruined. He had been falsely accused. The lying evidence had been convincing. He was finished.

There was his bitter incarceration in prison, twelve long years without hope. His father was sure he was dead—his brothers' lies had guaranteed that. His master thought he was an ungrateful libertine—his wife's lies guaranteed that. All he could see ahead was prison until he died. What a waste to a promising life.

But when at last the sun broke through the clouds, when he saw that those years were not wasted years, but years in God's rigorous school, and that in an instant change of circumstance he was taken from prison to the palace—why then he could sing with the psalmist, "Thou hast dealt well with Thy servant, O LORD, according to Thy word."

Joseph's dreams had come true. God's Word had been tested and tried and was *true*. How often he must have been tempted to abandon his faith, to decide there was nothing to it after all, that God's Word was a mirage on the sands of time, a lovely dream that taunted and mocked while it offered comfort and hope.

No matter what the *situation* says, the *Scripture* is sure. God's Word is utterly dependable.

II. THE PSALMIST'S WISH FOR TEACHING (119:66-68)

The psalmist had barely touched the fringe of the garment of God. He was like a child on the seashore paddling in the rippling shallows. There was so much more.

A. What He Expressed (119:66)

"Teach me good judgment and knowledge: for I have believed Thy commandments." When we *believe* a person we willingly listen to what they have to say. The character of a teacher adds strength to the instruction he or she imparts. The psalmist believed God, believed His Word, believed His commandments. He was ready for more instruction. Knowing God's Word to be reliable, he wanted that conviction translated into action in his life: "Teach *me* good judgment and knowledge," he prayed.

A believer has a decision to make. It may concern his business, perhaps, or some situation at home. He is not sure what is the right thing to do. Should he take that promotion even though it means moving to a distant city? Should he allow his daughter to date that young man? If not, how should he put a stop to it? He prays, "Teach me good judgment and knowledge." Then he quietly reads the Scriptures. He is not in a hurry. He reads them quietly and consecutively, waiting for God to speak to his situation. Any decision he makes, of course, will be in keeping with God's Word; he has already established *that* as the basic principle of life. He finds that God meets him in His Word, shows him a specific verse, a divine principle, a life-example. Or, just by a general reading of God's Word, he discovers that the Holy Spirit quietly but assuredly sways the balance of his judgment and leads him to the right decision. That is what the psalmist wanted. He wanted to be sure that God's Word would be translated from abstract dogma into practical decision in his daily life.

B. What He Experienced (119:67)

"Before I was afflicted I went astray: but now have I kept Thy word." First there was *confession:* "I went astray." That is true of every child of Adam's race. "All we like sheep have gone astray, we have turned everyone to his own way . . ." To stray is as natural to a sinner as it is to a sheep.

Then there is *conversion:* "Before I was afflicted I went astray." As long as he was left to himself he did as he pleased. But affliction came and he was brought to his senses like the prodigal son in the far country. He went astray *before* he was afflicted. He no longer goes astray.

Then there is *consecration:* "But now have I kept Thy word." That is the value of affliction: it brings us swiftly to an end of ourselves. So David discovered. Under the chastening rod of God he saw his sin as God saw it. God's chastenings of His children are *parental* not *punitive:* "Whom the Lord *loveth* He chasteneth" (Hebrews 12:6). It is a sorry parent who never chastens his child.

C. What He Expected (119:68)

"Thou art good, and doest good; teach me Thy statutes."

God is holy, so all His ways are holy. God is love, so love characterizes all He does. God is good, so goodness character-izes all His purposes. God is kind, so kindness marks all His dealings with us. To blame God, even indirectly, for the suffer-ing, sickness, sadness, and sorrow in this world is to slander Him. He is good. It is impossible for Him to be cruel, unkind, or vengeful.

"O God, I should like to be like You," the psalmist prayed. What higher ambition is there in all the world than that?

III. THE PSALMIST'S WAY IN TESTING (119:69-71)

The psalmist records a twofold reaction.

A. His Reaction to Those Who Affronted Him (119:69-70)

1. He tells us of his reaction to *their sneers.* "The proud have forged a lie against me: but I will keep Thy precepts with my whole heart" (119:69). Nothing is harder to accept than to have one's character smeared by a deliberate lie invented and propa-gated with malice and success. When mud is thrown it sticks. It is only after time has done its work that the worst of it can be brushed off; and even then it often leaves a stain.

That is one of Satan's favorite tactics. He is "the proud one" of whom the psalmist speaks. He is also the father of lies. He has plenty of people willing to do his dirty work for him in this world. The sad thing is that all too often Christians are far more ready to believe something bad about a believer than they are to believe something good.

Someone had forged a lie against this singer of psalms, yet the lie caused him only to cling closer to God's truth: "I will keep Thy precepts with my whole heart."

2. Then he tells of his reaction to *their smugness.* "Their heart is as fat as grease; but I delight in Thy law" (119:70). With a few words he pictures the individuals who were lying about him. He was too honest to pretend to like them or to forgive them.

Fatness, in the Bible, was not something necessarily culturally negative as it is among us. It was a sign of prosperity and wellbeing. In Jotham's parable, when the trees of the forest invited the olive tree to come and reign over them, it refused: "Should I leave my fatness, wherewith by me they honor God and man . . . ?" replied the olive (Judges 9:9). The fat of an animal was always reserved for God as the most desirable part of the offering.

But "fat as grease" is something else. It suggests something repulsive even if flourishing. This is not the fatness of spiritual blessing but the fatness of sensual bloating. This is the Eglon-type fatness, suggesting gross development of the carnal man (Judges 3:17,22), something revolting. It is the flesh run wild.

The psalmist describes his enemies as having fat hearts. The heart, of course, represents a person's inner life. A heart "fat as grease" suggests a life larded over with the flesh in its more repulsive forms.

"But I delight in Thy law," he said. His enemies had indulged their lusts and lies and had become vile. He had been indulging himself in God's truth. They had been getting on in the world; he had been getting on in the Word. They had become gross; he had become godly. The psalmist's refused to become like them. He found his Bible the best protection against their kind of life.

B. His Reaction to That Which Afflicted Him (119:71)

"It is good for me that I have been afflicted; that I might learn Thy statutes." That, surely, is the last thing we think about, that our afflictions are *good*. Of all the insufferable meddlers we meet in Scripture, the worst, surely, are Job's comforters. With endless variations on the same theme, they tell the poor man that his afflictions are good for him; that he is under the chastening hand of God, that he should consider himself happy that God has decided to take him in hand. But the revelation of that goodness should come from the Holy Spirit, not from the well-meant but often exacerbating comments of other people.

The child of God finds goodness in affliction if he does not rebel against it. Any affliction that drives him to his Bible and to his knees is surely worthwhile.

Think of the Lord Jesus. What did He do when He was tempted or taunted, troubled or tried? He went at once to the Word of God. When Satan came with his subtle temptations, Jesus met him with Scripture. The temptations were real enough. Take, for instance, the first of them, that He command stones to turn into bread. Jesus had been without food for forty days. "He afterward hungered," the Scripture says.

A fast cannot last much longer than forty days without terminating in death. For a considerable period, after the first three days, the hunger pangs die away, but at the end they come back with renewed force. Jesus was hungry, and He had the power to change stones into bread. He could change water into wine. He could multiply loaves and fishes. He had the power. The very thought of something to eat must have awakened all the power of appetite in His starving body. However, He recognized the temptation for what it was and answered the devil with an appropriate verse of Scripture.

Jesus did that all His life. He quoted the Bible when challenged by His foes. He appealed to it when dying on the cross. He knew its value in every crisis.

IV. THE PSALMIST'S WEALTH OF TREASURE (119:72)

"The law of Thy mouth is better unto me than thousands of gold and silver." It is, after all, a matter of priorities. In which world am I investing? Where do I most want to succeed? In the world of business, or in the world of Bible? Very few people succeed in both, because both are totally demanding if success is to be more than nominal.

Jesus said, "Ye cannot serve God and mammon." The psalmist said, "The law of Thy mouth is better unto me than thousands of silver and gold." He had a better treasure in his Bible than in all the gold in the world. He had made his decision; he knew for which world he was living. His treasure was in heaven.

Psalm 119:73-80

IN GOOD COMPANY

I. THE LORD'S HAND (119:73-75)
   A. In Making Him (119:73)
      He was sure the Lord had:
      1. A Part in Making Him
      2. A Purpose In Making Him
   B. In Motivating Him (119:74)
   C. In Molding Him (119:75)
II. THE LORD'S HEART (119:76-77)
   He wanted the Lord to:
   A. Show His Love to Him (119:76)
   B. Share His Love with Him (119:77)
III. THE LORD'S HELP (119:78-80)
   He wanted to be:
   A. Successful in the Fight (119:78)
   B. Secure in the Fellowship (119:79)
   C. Sound in the Faith (119:80)

IN THE HEBREW each verse in this section begins with the letter *Jod*, the small letter referred to by the Lord Jesus when He said, "Verily I say unto you, Till heaven and earth pass, one jot or one tittle shall in no wise pass from the law, till all be fulfilled" (Matthew 5:18). Such is the integrity of God's Word in the original autographs. Not only is every book, every chapter, every verse, every word, every letter inspired, but even the smallest letter is put in its place by God and kept there—by the same omniscient genius that keeps the stars in the sky.

This little letter of the alphabet, which begins every verse in this stanza, introduces some very big subjects. The psalmist is going to sing now about God's *hand,* God's *heart,* and God's *help.*

I. THE LORD'S HAND (119:73-75)

The psalmist looks at God's hand from three points of view. He sees:

327

A. The Lord's Hand in Making Him (119:73)

1. He knew he was not the end product of blind forces of chance. He was sure that the Lord had *a real part in creating him.* He says, "Thy hands have made me and fashioned me" (119:73a). The best work, the work that displays the most tender, loving care, is work done by hand. A machine may turn out work faster and in a more uniform way, but anything made by hand has a value all its own. Sometimes when we are shopping we see an article displaying a sign, *Handcrafted* or *Handmade.* We know that such an object has special workmanship.

In olden times, of course, all work was done by hand. Cathedrals in Europe, which took hundreds of years to build, display the most exquisite craftsmanship. Carvings embellishing the rafters and cornices show the artisan's meticulous care. Even high up on the roof can be seen figures of cherubim, whose back sides are carved as painstakingly as the front—because, the workers reasoned, God could see the back as well as the front.

In creation God simply *spoke* worlds into space. Billions of worlds sprang into being in infinite space, burned and blazed, expanded and exploded, shone and shimmered in a prodigious output of exuberant energy. To create, God had only to speak. Genesis 1 records God's first ten commandments.

> And God said: Light be, and light was.
> And God said: Let there be an atmosphere.
> And God said: Let the waters be gathered to one place.
> And God said: Let the earth bring forth grass.
> And God said: Let there be two great lights.
> And God said: Let the waters bring forth abundantly.
> And God said: Let the earth bring forth the living creature.
> And God said: Let Us make man in Our image.
> And God said: Be fruitful and fill the earth.
> And God said: Behold, I have given you fruit for food.

When it came to the making of man, however, God did more than speak. He rolled up His sleeves, so to speak, put His mighty hands into the red clay of Eden, and fashioned man's body by hand. Man was something special, set apart from the rest of creation. The making of man called for craftsmanship. God, it might be said, mass-produced the universe; He made man with His own hands.

When Jesus came, He demonstrated again and again that to perform a miracle He needed only to speak. He spoke, and the wild, tempestuous sea hushed to immediate rest. He had only to speak and Lazarus came forth from the dead. One word from Him and demons hurled themselves into the bodies of swine, leaving their human victim possessed of his senses and at peace.

Some of His work Jesus deliberately did by hand. Thus it was He touched a leper. Thus it was He took the daughter of Jairus by the hand and gently lifted her back from death to life. Thus it was He made clay and anointed a blind man's eyes. Thus, too, He accomplished the work of redemption. The hands of Jesus, deeply scarred, bear evidence of that.

"Thy *hands* have fashioned *me*," said the psalmist. God attends the birth of a baby. His hands are involved in the creation of each and every human life. Every child of Adam's race comes into the world with God's touch on him. Each one is a person, infinitely precious, *handmade*, special. There is not a single human being for whom God does not care, about whom He does not feel deep compassion, concern, and absorbing interest. The psalmist realized that.

To say that we are the result of chance is to insult God. We are not just a mass of atoms. We are not a product of the slime of the sea, nor are we descended from anthropoid apes. We come from the hand of God. The evolutionary propaganda of our day, cleverly orchestrated, hotly espoused by thousands of scientists, philosophers, and educators, is a satanic myth designed to debase and dehumanize man and make him kindred to the beast when God says he is kindred to Himself.

2. Then, too, the psalmist was sure that the Lord had *a real purpose in creating him*. "Thy hands have made me and fashioned me: give me understanding, that I may learn Thy commandments" (119:73b). Underline the word *me* in this verse. "Thy hands have made *me* and fashioned *me:* give *me* understanding that I may learn Thy commandments."

Our most important task in life should be to discover *why* God has made us. Each human being is a unique individual. Never before, never again will there be another just the same. Nobody else has the same parents; the same mix of genes and chromosomes; the same nature, disposition, and character; the same background of circumstances; the same blend of thoughts and emotions; the same fusion of decisions and ambitions. If no two blades of grass are alike and no two snowflakes identical, it is certain no two human beings are alike. God has a sovereign will for my life. Paul could say that he was separated in his mother's womb for the work God eventually called him to do. God told Ananias that Paul was "a chosen vessel." And so are we all. Our prayer should be, "Give me understanding that I may learn the things, O God, You have especially to say to me to direct me in my life."

B. The Lord's Hand in Motivating Him (119:74)

"They that fear Thee will be glad when they see me; because I have hoped in Thy word." This singer's hope in God's Word was basic in his motivation. The horizons of his life were contained within the covers of God's Book. It was not just that His *love* was for God's Word or that his *faith* was in God's Word, but his *hope* was in God's Word. Hope has its stake in the future, and that is one area in which the Bible is unique. It addresses itself to the future. It sets before the people of God the certain hope of glorious things to come. It tells us that we have laid up for us "joy unspeakable and full of glory."

Unsaved persons have a hopeless future. They may indulge in wishful thinking, clinging to one of the devil's delusions, but they are fantasizing. They have no future.

One of nature's cruelest tricks is played on travelers in the desert. They often tell stories of being deceived by a mirage. Lost and thirsty, they suddenly see an oasis. It looks near, perhaps three or four miles away, with glittering water and waving palms. They struggle forward, convinced that relief is just ahead, only to find when they crest a sandy hillock that the expected oasis was a mirage. The delusion is caused by the refraction of light. The physical explanation is simple enough but the subsequent disappointment is beyond words. How tragic to stumble forward over the sand, frantic with thirst, only to find nothing. The unsaved are like that. They are deceived.

Not so the children of God. Our hope is in the infallible Word of God. But we, too, need to be careful that we are not deceived, careful that we are handling the Word aright. Some popular preachers proclaim false hope. They come on the air with the promise that "something good is going to happen to you today," meaning something good materially or physically. People want to think that they are going to get well, going to get more money, going to see their problems miraculously melt away. The mirage lies in the fact that the statement has enough truth to make it seem real. God *has* promised that "all things work together for good to them that love God, to them who are the called according to His purpose." But *that* good might involve sickness, the death of a loved one, financial loss. That, however, is not what these popular preachers mean. They are popular because they spread optimism—but optimism, apart from the Word of God, is a mirage.

> God has not promised
> Skies always blue
> Sunny green pastures
> All the way through.

Persons whose hope is in the Word of God, however, can be cheerful. Something good is indeed going to happen to them. The worst that can happen to children of God is death. To be instantly absent from the body, eternally present with the Lord, what could be better than that? No circumstance of life, however threatening, can prevent God from bringing good things into our lives. They may not be the things we would have chosen, they may even be things we ourselves would not call "good," but in the end we shall see how good they really were.

"They that fear Thee will be glad when they see me," the psalmist says, "because I have hoped in Thy word." People cheered up when he came around. They felt good just to see him coming in through the door. He shed good cheer about him everywhere he went. What a challenge. Do I spread gloom or glory as I journey through life? It depends on what motivates me.

C. The Lord's Hand in Molding Him (119:75)

"I know, O LORD, that Thy judgments are right, and that Thou in faithfulness hast afflicted me." In other words, God makes no mistakes, even when things seem to go wrong from our limited point of view. Many of God's dealings with us are designed to change our character, to make us more like His Son. They also further the sublime ends toward which He is guiding human affairs.

God would not be faithful to us if He saw we needed some kind of affliction and withheld it from us. Nor would He be true to His character. If God simply let us alone we would go on our own careless ways. God is too loving to be unkind, and too faithful to His own character to neglect our training.

Moreover, the psalmist says, His judgments are always right. God suits the correction to the occasion. It would be an unnatural father who thrashed a three-year-old for dropping a glass of milk. It would be an unfaithful father who simply said, "Naughty, naughty," to a son arrested for stealing a camera. God matches the discipline to the deed.

II. THE LORD'S HEART (119:76-77)

"Let, I pray Thee, Thy merciful kindness be for my comfort, according to Thy word unto Thy servant." He wanted the Lord to:

A. Show His Love to Him (119:76)

Glance at the remaining verses in this stanza. In each of them the psalmist asks the Lord to let something take place, to let certain things happen.

Here he is in need of comfort. But where can comfort be found? Certainly not in the pagan religions of the world. The religions of the psalmist's day were fierce and cruel. Who would think of going to the child-killing Moloch or to the fish-god Dagon for comfort? Cold is the comfort, too, offered by Islam, Buddhism, or Hinduism. Who wants to be told that if they fail to live up to certain religious standards they will be sent back to earth as a fruit fly or a toad?

Not that false Christendom does much better. What merciful kindness can be found in a theology that sends people to purgatory to atone for the residue of their sins? Here is a priest standing by the bed of a dying man. All his life this person has faithfully followed the dogmas of his church. He has impoverished himself with sacrificial giving. He has gone to confession and done penance. He has received the sacraments and absolution. Now the priest is there to administer the last rites to this devout and faithful church member. And what does Rome tell him to expect when he dies? Fire and flame. Purgatory. For how long? Nobody can say. Prayers must be made for him after he's dead. Masses must be said for his soul. Money must be paid. What comfort is there in *that*?

The psalmist flees directly into the arms of God. He flies to a God who is merciful. Alan Redpath says that *mercy* is God's "weak point." He holds a nation guilty for its sins to the third and fourth generation of those that hate him, but He shows mercy to those who love Him and keep His commandments. We can always storm the heart of God if we lay siege along the line of His mercy. Mercy is an attribute of God, certified and verified in the Word, made good to the soul of this singer, so that he tunes up his harp and cries, "Let, I pray Thee, Thy merciful kindness be for my comfort, according to Thy word unto Thy servant."

But he isn't through yet. He also wants God to:

B. Share His Love with Him (119:77)

"Let Thy tender mercies come unto me, that I may live: for Thy law is my delight." The psalmist now speaks of God's tender mercies. Not just kindness, but *merciful kindness.* Not just *mercy,* or even *mercies,* but *tender mercies.*

Suppose for a moment that God were not like that. Suppose He stood revealed as the opposite, as a God of *unrelenting cruelty.* Suppose the Bible had been written in some fierce and savage strain. Suppose God were like the gods of the Aztecs, with an insatiable appetite for cruelty and blood. Suppose He were revealed in Scripture as completely indifferent to the fate of humankind. Suppose He had said: "I made you perfect, I gave you a flawless environment. I restricted you along only one line. I warned you of the consequences of disobedience. Now then, live with those consequences. I wash my hands of you. You made your bed, now lie on it." Suppose God were like that.

What hope would there be of salvation? None. There would be no hope, no Heaven, no help, no home. There would be no salvation, no song. Unspeakable horror would haunt us all the days of our life and we would dwell in the house of the damned forever. But, blessed be His name, He stands revealed as a God of merciful kindness, a God of tender mercies. Thank God it is possible for us to pray as the psalmist did.

Finally, the psalmist tells us of:

III. THE LORD'S HELP (119:78-80)

The singer now turns to specific petitions. He wanted:

A. To Be Successful in the Fight (119:78)

"Let the proud be ashamed; for they deal perversely with me without cause. But I will meditate in Thy precepts." Here we have two men. One is ruled by his *pride*, the other by God's *precepts;* one has an *inflated idea* of his own *importance*, the other has an *informed idea* of *God's importance;* the man who is ruled by pride *deals perversely*, the man who is ruled by God's precepts *waits patiently.*

God's Word says, "Pride goeth before destruction, and a haughty spirit before a fall." Those who are ruled by God's Spirit know that time is on their side. Those who are ruled by pride are heading for disaster.

The fall of the proud will lead to one of two consequences. It will lead to their *ruin*, as it did in the case of Haman, or it will lead to their *redemption* as it did in the case of Nebuchadnezzar. The psalmist prays that he might be successful in the fight—by leaving it all with God.

He also wanted:

B. To Be Secure in the Fellowship (119:79)

"Let those that fear Thee turn unto me, and those that have known Thy testimonies." The psalmist was a marked man, as we learn from the previous verse and from many other verses in this psalm. He was being persecuted by those in power. It was not safe to be associated with him. He felt keenly his loneliness.

Particularly he felt he was being avoided by the Lord's people, and that was—as Mark Antony said when Julius Caesar was stabbed by his closest friend, Brutus—"the most unkindest cut of all." It is understandable that the unsaved should stand aloof. But the Lord's people?

We think of Paul in prison. It was not really safe to visit Paul, indeed no longer safe to know him. Paul now was not only chained but was treated as a malefactor. Most people abandoned him. A few noble souls dared the dangers of being known as his friend: Onesiphorus had diligently sought him out. Linus, Pudens, and Claudia stood by him. So did his beloved physician Luke. But when it came to his trial, *nobody* stood by him (2 Timothy 4:16). He was forsaken by all, left friendless except for that Friend that "sticketh closer than a brother." With the certainty of death awaiting him, Paul experienced profound loneliness.

At this moment, in Iron Curtain countries, there are those who face a similar loneliness. The heart craves the face of a brother or sister in Christ, someone in love with the Lord. And not only those in prison. Many an aged or suffering saint in the hospital, many a widow could cry the same: "Let those that fear Thee turn unto me . . ." The psalmist wanted to be secure in the fellowship of believers.

He also wanted:

C. To Be Sound in the Faith (119:80)

"Let my heart be sound in Thy statutes; that I be not ashamed." To be sound in the Scriptures means, of course, that we must apply sound principles of Bible interpretation to its truths.

We must proceed first of all on the principle that God says what He means and that He means what He says:

—that when He uses symbols or poetic language He does so according to the usual usage of language, not to make things mysterious or to give reign to the human imagination, and that He explains His own symbols;
—that we must always make a difference where God makes a difference, not mixing up dispensations and covenants, resurrections, and judgments indiscriminately;
—that the context is always crucial in determining the meaning of a verse of Scripture;
—that we must see the whole before concentrating on the part;
—that there is an underlying structure to any book or passage that needs to be discerned;
—and that our hermeneutics must be consistent. (For a thorough treatment of hermeneutics, see *Bible Explorer's Guide,* by this author, published by Loizeaux Brothers.)

The psalmist, however, goes beyond all that. He says that it is possible to be sound in God's statutes—and yet to miss the mark. One's theology might be correct, but if all one has is intellectual knowledge of divine truth, then the real purpose of Scripture has been missed altogether. The psalmist prays, "Let *my heart* be sound in Thy statutes; that I be not ashamed." We must get sound doctrine into our hearts.

The psalmist was anxious to get his heart right. That was the most important thing.

Psalm 119:81-88

A BOTTLE IN THE SMOKE

I. A TROUBLED SOUL (119:81-83)
   A. He Needed Revival (119:81-82)
      1. His Soul Was Fainting—Longing for a Work of God (119:81)
      2. His Sight Was Failing—Looking for a Word from God (119:82)
   B. He Needed Restoration (119:83)
II. A TRYING SITUATION (119:84-87)
   He is faced with:
   A. Seeming Delay (119:84)
   B. Systematic Deceit (119:85)
   C. Serious Danger (119:86-87)
      1. What He Sought (119:86)
      2. What He Survived (119:87)
III. A TRUSTING SAINT (119:88)

THROUGHOUT THIS PSALM we are made aware that the singer is in trouble. We would like to know who he was—David, perhaps, or Daniel, or Hezekiah. But since he has remained anonymous (making this psalm one of the "orphan psalms" of the Hebrew hymn book) the Holy Spirit intends his sufferings to be of universal significance. Any beleaguered saint of God can put his or her name at the head of this psalm and sing it themselves.

First we have:

I. A TROUBLED SOUL (119:81-83)

The psalmist needed two things, needed them badly.

A. He Needed Revival (119:81-82)

The circumstances in which he found himself were trying. He was despairing. He tells us that:

336

1. His Soul Was Fainting—He Was Longing for a Work of God (119:81)

"My soul fainteth for Thy salvation: but I hope in Thy word." Salvation is a concept of various textures and tones. The biblical context must always determine what kind of salvation the writer has in mind. There is, of course, salvation from sin—its penalty, power, and presence. There is salvation from sorrow as well as salvation from situations. This last aspect of salvation is in view here, although we do not know what the singer's situation was. We do know, as the Scripture puts it elsewhere, "Hope deferred maketh the heart sick."

I remember one time taking off in a plane straight into a bank of heavy clouds. The day had been completely overcast, a leaden sky scowling down on a gloomy landscape. The plane taxied down the runway, took off, and instantly a gray world enveloped us. Looking out of the window, I could see nothing except a blanket of foggy vapor so thick it even streamed down the windows. Then suddenly the plane broke through and we were above the clouds. The sky was a blazing sapphire, the sun was shining. Looking down at the clouds, now far below, I saw them transformed into things of beauty, billowing fleece of whitest wool. The blue skies were there all the time and, seen from above, the dark clouds were already being hurried away by the wind.

The Word of God is like the sun, shining always in the sky, our frowning circumstances are the clouds. When we stare up at them from down below, they appear threatening. But when we allow God's Word to change our viewpoint we see them as temporary troubles, soon to vanish, and, in any case, glorious from Heaven's point of view. The psalmist goes on.

2. His Sight Was Failing—Looking for a Word from God (119:82)

"Mine eyes fail for Thy word, saying, When wilt Thou comfort me?". So prolonged was the dry spell in this singer's soul, he might as well not have had the Scriptures, for all the comfort they seemed to offer him. That is a common enough experience for those who have waited beside a bed of suffering, for those who have found themselves in prison for conscience' sake, for those who have yearned over the waywardness of a beloved child. So often, for all our pleading and praying, nothing seems to change.

John the Baptist had a similar experience. He had preached repentance to the nation, had seen thousands baptized (even

many of the hardest cases had been reached through his ministry). He had seen revival. A great awakening had taken place
under his preaching about the imminent coming of Christ.

Then he had introduced Christ to the nation, had sent his
best disciples to Jesus, had gladly seen his own ministry decrease so that the ministry of Christ might increase. He had
confidently stepped back to watch the coming of the kingdom.
He had burned the ears of Herod by denouncing him for his
immoral life.

Then he had ended up in jail but had confidently expected
that the new Prophet of Nazareth would come and set him free.
But nothing happened. Days became weeks, weeks became
months. He became discouraged, disillusioned.

We can have no doubt that John had searched the Scriptures
earnestly to see what would be the signs of Christ's coming.
There in prison he must have turned it over and over in his
mind. The *Stone*, cut without hands, was to smite the Gentile
world power. Israel was to rule the world. Jerusalem was to
become the world's center. The Christ was to reign as Lord of
all lands. The desert was to blossom as the rose. *And none of it
was happening.* Either that, or he had made a colossal blunder
and Jesus was not the Messiah after all. There, in Herod's dark
dungeon, awaiting the executioner's ax, he must often have
wept.

So he sent messengers to Jesus. "Are you *He?* Have I made a
mistake?" Jesus simply pointed to His works. The blind were
being made to see, the lame were being made to walk, lepers
were being cleansed, demons were being cast out. Jesus also
pointed John to another Scripture, Isaiah 35:5-6; 6:1. John had
made no mistake. In other words, Jesus said, "Dry your eyes,
John. Everything is proceeding according to plan. Right now
I've come to show God's *grace;* I'm coming back later to show
His *government.*"

So often, when the Bible seems to be silent, or seems to be
saying wrong things, it is not the Bible that is wrong but our
viewpoint or our interpretation. For instance, many, when sick,
do what it says in James. They call for the elders of the church,
have themselves anointed with oil, and expect to be healed.
When healing doesn't take place they become confused. They
doubt the Scriptures, or think something is wrong with their
faith.

God has not failed. They have invested a passage of Scripture
with a meaning it does not have. Nowhere does God unconditionally guarantee healing to sick believers every time they are
ill. Even the great apostle Paul was a chronically sick man, in

need of the care of an attendant physician. Obviously God is not going to heal everyone every time. Otherwise, believers would never die. The passage in James, as the context shows, has to do with the healing of a person who has become sick as a result of sin and consequent church discipline.

So the psalmist needed revival in his discouragement. God's Word seemed to be letting him down.

B. He Needed Restoration (119:83)

"I am become like a bottle in the smoke; yet do I not forget Thy statutes." A bottle (a wineskin) in the smoke. Ancient peoples made containers for wine and water out of the skins of animals. It doesn't take much imagination to see what smoke would do to such vessels. Exposed to the smoke they would soon be useless; the contents would take on an unpleasant odor and taste of the smoke. The smell of smoke is tenacious, too. Once get it into a fabric and it is difficult to get out.

The *psalmist* was that wineskin. The smoke was the penetrating, pervasive, polluting influence of the world. He felt contaminated by its atmosphere. Worse, he felt that God could no longer use him. The wine of salvation, the water of the Word—how could it be poured out from him? The bad odor of the world spoiled everything. He needed restoration.

"Yet do I not forget Thy statutes," he said. There was one way to get rid of that smoke. The Word of God was able to cleanse deep within. The contaminating power of the world is more than counteracted by the cleansing power of the Word.

That is a good thing to know. We cannot escape the world. We have to live in it—rub shoulders every day with people who curse and blaspheme, tell dirty jokes, live godless lives, espouse filthy causes—but we have God's Word to restore us when we feel we have taken on the bad odor of the world.

So, we see first *a troubled soul.* We see next:

II. A TRYING SITUATION (119:84-87)

The psalmist is face to face with:

A. Seeming Delay (119:84)

"How many are the days of Thy servant? When wilt Thou execute judgment on them that persecute me?" The psalmist thinks: "Why is God delaying? Why is He waiting so long? Time is running out. My days are slipping fast away and my prayers remain unanswered." Apart from God's Word, there is no answer to the seeming indifference of God to the sufferings of His saints. There is no answer to His mysterious silences. His people pour out their hearts in impassioned, importunate pleas, but God remains silent.

Numerous people in the Bible help us understand the reason for these strange delays in God's handling of situations which, we would think, call for instant redress. The stories of Job and Jonah, Jeremiah and Jesus help us see that God is working out a wise, vast plan. The sufferings of His own are being woven into a cosmic tapestry in which grays and blacks and somber browns are as essential as reds and yellows and greens.

Our problem is we do not have a large enough perspective; our views are too limited. We know only the surface facts. Tom is sick and is going to die. Dick has run away from home and wants no part of the gospel. Harry has lost his job. Jerry has failed to get an important promotion at work. *Why?* We will never get the right answer if the surface facts are all we know. A *real* story lies behind all that, a story related to the eternal counsels of God.

The psalmist finds himself face to face also with:

B. Systematic Deceit (119:85)

"The proud have digged pits for me, which are not after Thy law." God's law does not employ evil means to attain its end. With God the end never justifies the means, nor does He set traps for people. Satan does; God never does. He has the resources of His own omniscience, omnipresence, and omnipotence at His disposal. He does not need to dig pits. That is a device of the evil one.

Potiphar's wife dug such a pit for Joseph with her looks, lusts, and lies. The rulers of Babylon dug such a pit for Daniel with Darius's decree. The scribes, Pharisees, and Herodians dug such a pit for Jesus when they baited Him, trying to get Him to say an incautious word.

God does not do that kind of thing. Such things are "not after Thy law," as the psalmist says. Nowadays we call such efforts to snare people "entrapment." God does not resort to such devices.

We must remember, however, that there is a difference between entrapment and detection. God is a great detective. He says, "Be sure your sin will find you out." We leave our fingerprints on everything we do, our voiceprints on everything we say. God has His own methods of facing us with the evidence of our sins.

The psalmist, however, complained that men, men who evidently knew the law, were using snares and traps against him. It was a trying situation. He was faced with systematic deceit.

He also was faced with:

C. Serious Danger (119:86-87)

Knowing that, he tells us:

1. What He Sought (119:86)

"All Thy commandments are faithful: they persecute me wrongfully; help Thou me." The psalmist was still painfully aware of what Shakespeare called "the slings and arrows of outrageous fortune" but now he meets those arrows with the shield of faith. He prays, "Help Thou me."

His prayer was *very simple*. When a person is desperate, he does not make a speech. He simply calls out, "Help!" If a man who can't swim falls into a river and sees a man on the bank, the drowning man has no use for flowery language. He doesn't say: "I say there, my friend, I wonder if I could persuade you to divest yourself of your garments and plunge into this swiftly flowing river and save me from a watery grave. I shall be forever obliged to you for your kindness and consideration. I am about to be inundated by these waters. Please come to my aid." No, he simply shouts, "HELP!" That is what the psalmist did.

God does not need long speeches. We are not heard for our much speaking.

His prayer is *very specific*. He wants help and he wants God to help. But he does not presume to tell God how the help should come. That is God's side of it. He has all the resources of deity. When He does deliver the psalmist it will be in a way consistent with His character and eternal purposes.

2. What He Survived (119:87)

"They had almost consumed me upon earth; but I forsook not Thy precepts." Two words stand out, *almost* and *but*. They had almost consumed him. God, however, had drawn a line in the sand beyond which they could not go. It was like that when Laban pursued Jacob. He had his sons and servants with him, and a rough crowd they were. He was infuriated with Jacob, and no doubt determined to send him on his way a beggared wayfarer. We can imagine how all along the Fertile Crescent he spurred his horses and camels, breathing out threats and slaughter, nursing his rage and resentment, fanning the coals of his fury to white hot heat. Then, having come some four hundred miles, he saw Jacob's camp on the horizon. Perhaps he rubbed his hands with glee; he would make short work of Jacob. But then God stepped in and drew the line: "Take heed that thou speak not to Jacob either good or bad," He said (Genesis 31:24).

When the psalmist wrote this he was looking back at some experience through which he had come, able to see how close he had come to the brink of disaster.

"But I forsook not Thy precepts." That was the ultimate triumph. That is what the psalmist's enemies had wanted, that denial of the faith, that pinch of salt on the altar of Caesar's godhead. Hallelujah for that "*but.*" The more they attacked him, the more the psalmist clung to God's Word. Their persecution had the opposite effect from what they hoped. That is what persecution often does.

Last of all we see:

III. A TRUSTING SAINT (119:88)

"Quicken me after Thy lovingkindness; so shall I keep the testimony of Thy mouth." God's Word has come straight from God's mouth. As Paul tells us, it is "God-breathed." Further, the God who inspired this Book is the creator of the universe. The Bible can never get out of date, never be wrong. When God talked with Abraham in Ur of the Chaldees He knew all about the structure of the atom. He did not tell Abraham anything about it—that was not His purpose—but He knew more about the atom than our most brilliant nuclear physicists will ever know. When God talked with Moses at the burning bush He knew all about space technology. He had been orbiting galaxies for billions of years. This is the God who has spoken to us in this Book.

But knowing that, even acknowledging that, does not guarantee our obedience. Such is the strength of human self-will, and the power of satanic and self-deception, that even when there is a deep, heartfelt desire to keep God's Word, we often do not have the strength to do so. That is why the psalmist prays, "Quicken me after Thy lovingkindness; *so* shall I keep the testimonies of Thy mouth." He had the law; what he needed was *life.* He needed to be quickened. Then, when he had the *life* he needed the *love:* "Quicken me after Thy lovingkindness."

So this troubled soul, in this trying situation, becomes a trusting saint. He says, "Lord, even though I know that everything You have to say is right and good and perfect, and even though I say *yes* to it all, and even though I really do want to be obedient to You—I don't have the strength. I need You to quicken me. I need You to breathe into me the life-giving, life-transforming power I need."

> Breathe on me, Breath of God,
>   Fill me with life anew,
> Until I love what Thou dost love,
>   And do what Thou wouldst do.

Psalm 119:89-96

SETTLED IN HEAVEN

I. THE PERMANENCE OF GOD'S WORD (119:89-91)
   A. Why (119:89a)
   B. Where (119:89b-90)
      1. In the Glory (119:89b)
      2. On this Globe (119:90)
   C. When (119:91)
II. THE PROTECTION OF GOD'S WORD (119:92)
III. THE POWER OF GOD'S WORD (119:93-95)
   A. To Save Him (119:93-94)
     How It:
      1. Quickened His Faith (119:93)
      2. Quelled His Foes (119:94)
   B. To Safeguard Him (119:95)
IV. THE PERFECTION OF GOD'S WORD (119:96)

THE PSALMIST BEGINS THIS SEGMENT of his song with a grand word—*forever.* By it, God's Word is lifted above all the changes wrought by time, above all the vicissitudes of life, above the temporality and transience of earth.

The psalmist begins with:

I. THE PERMANENCE OF GOD'S WORD (119:89-91)

He tells us:

A. Why (119:89a)

"For ever, O Lord, Thy word is settled . . ." The Word is permanent because it is the Lord's word. That is why God does not have to change His mind. In His omniscient wisdom, God knows everything—everything possible and everything that is. He is acquainted with every fact, every detail, about everything and everyone in Heaven, earth, and hell. He may be invisible to us, but we are not invisible to Him. He saw Adam and Eve hiding in the garden, saw Cain murder his brother, heard Sarah

343

laugh in the privacy of her tent. One of the first revelations of God occurs on the Bible's opening page: seven times the Holy Spirit says, "And God saw."

God knows every detail about everything that has happened in the past. He knows everything going on right at this moment throughout all the vast reaches of space. He knows every event, from the smallest to the greatest, that will ever happen in the ages and eternities to be. If it were possible for something to happen that God did not know about, He would cease to be omniscient; He would cease to be God. "Known unto God are all His works from the beginning of the world" (Acts 15:18).

Then the psalmist tells us:

B. Where (119:89b-90)

God's Word is settled, first of all:

1. In the Glory (119:89b)

"For ever, O LORD, Thy word is settled in heaven." It is beyond the reach of man. No person, however clever, confident, or confused, will permanently change God's Word. Foolish is anyone who tampers with God's Word. Foolish is the one who tries to get rid of God's Word. As has been said, Diocletian harnessed the resources of the Roman empire to stamp out the Bible; he might as well have tried to stop the blowing of the wind. Voltaire held up a copy of the Bible and said, "In fifty years I'll have this book in the morgue." In fifty years he was in the morgue and the Geneva Bible Society owned his house and used it as a place to store Bibles.

God's Word is settled in heaven. The galaxies will pass away, but God's Word will remain, far beyond the reach of all its foes, forever settled in Heaven.

The psalmist tells us that God's Word is settled also:

2. On this Globe (119:90)

He says, "Thy faithfulness is unto all generations: Thou hast established the earth, and it abideth." The psalmist turns back to Scripture's first page. "There," he says, "read it for yourself." God's Word established the earth.

On the *first* day of creation God established the *laws of light*. He ordained that light should travel at 186,000 miles per second, that it should dispel darkness, that its speed should be one of the constants of our universe—so that thousands of years later a Jewish scientist, reading in nature's vast book, could introduce the atomic age with an equation containing the speed of light. "$E = MC^2$" he concluded. "Energy equals mass multiplied by the speed of light squared."

On the *second* day of creation God established the *form of the firmament,* separating the waters from the waters and setting in motion all those vast forces of evaporation and condensation which renew and replenish the earth.

On the *third* day of creation God established the *lay of the land,* separating the oceans from the continents and ordaining the depths and bounds of the sea.

On the *fourth* day of creation, God established the *service of the sun,* ordaining the sun to rule the day and the moon to rule the night, ensuring the regular round of the seasons and giving humankind a celestial timepiece to measure the passing of days and months and years.

On the *fifth* day of creation God established the *fish and the fowl* in the sea and the sky and set in order the laws of their being.

On the *sixth* day of creation God established *life and lordship* on this planet, making all forms of animal life and crowning man monarch of all he surveyed.

Thus it has been, from that day to this, sunshine and shadow, seedtime and harvest, summer and winter. And everywhere, to earth's remotest bounds, to the outer edges of the universe, God has established His Word. Everywhere there is evidence of law. All modern science is predicated on the fact that the laws of nature do not change. "Thou hast established the earth and it abideth." The laws of light and electricity, of heat and sound, of magnetism and gravity, of chemistry and physics, of biology and mathematics—all are established by the Word of God. And such is the power of that word that the entire established order of nature sprang into being in response to *ten commandments.* Ten times we read in Genesis, "And God said."

God's Word, settled in heaven, settled on earth, is settling to my soul. Its permanence gives us something solid on which to rest our faith.

Then the psalmist mentions:

C. When (119:91)

"They continue *this day* according to Thine ordinance, for all are Thy servants." People speak of the "laws of nature" and of "providence." The Bible speaks of God. Such expressions as "nature" and "providence" are depersonalized synonyms for God, used to avoid having to acknowledge God as the author and sustainer of the universe. Behind the vast fabric of nature and its laws is God.

The psalmist observed that the laws established by God in

creation still stood unchanged. The same is true today. When we put a kettle on the stove to heat water we don't expect a few minutes later to get a block of ice. If we drop a lead weight we don't expect it to fly off into the sky.

Kettles and weights are His servants. Even the exceptions prove the rule. When Jonah ran away from God, God simply summoned His servants, the wind and the whale, and sent them to arrest the disobedient prophet. When Pharaoh dug in his heels and defied the living God, He directed Moses to summon frogs and flies, locusts and lice, blood and boils, and thus lay Egypt in the dust.

When the Lord Jesus stilled the storm the disciples said, "What manner of Man is This, that even the wind and the sea obey Him?" (Mark 4:41). Of course they did. They had been obeying Him ever since they were made.

So then, the psalmist sings about the *permanence* of God's Word. It is a source of comfort to him to know that he has invested his faith in a "bank that can never fail." God's faithfulness is to all generations, as changeless as His Word. Everything was settled in heaven before God ever put it into writing.

Next the psalmist speaks of:

II. THE PROTECTION OF GOD'S WORD (119:92)

"Unless Thy law had been my delights, I should then have perished in mine affliction." The Word of God helped the psalmist keep his sanity; it gave him something to hang onto when his world was falling apart. It was a rock, an anchor. He was able to get his feet on the solid rock when surrounded by the quicksand of menacing circumstances. He was able to throw out his anchor and feel the cable hold his drifting boat against rising wind and perilous reef.

John Bunyan must have had such thoughts when sitting in Bedford jail, imprisoned for preaching the Word, knowing he was unable to support his wife, thinking too of his little blind daughter. But John Bunyan had his Bible. Nobody could take that away from him. If they took away his tattered Testament, he had it graven in his mind. They put Bunyan in that jail but out of it came Christian and Pliable, Mr. Great-heart and Madam Bubble, Atheist and Mr. Worldly Wiseman, Giant Despair and Mr. Valiant-for-truth, and all the other charcters that came alive in the pages of *Pilgrim's Progress*. Bunyan kept his sanity with his Bible, finding company in the characters he created from his knowledge of God's Word.

God's Word protected him from despair, boredom, and decay. Others, locked up in prison, have told of their desperation—counting the nails in the floorboards, counting the stones in the wall, counting the stars in the sky. John Bunyan had something better to do. He allowed God's Word to leap to life in his soul to become his first line of defense against Satan's attempts to drive him into the Slough of Despond.

III. THE POWER OF GOD'S WORD (119:93-95)

The psalmist saw the power of God's Word operating in various ways in his life. It had power to:

A. Save Him (119:93-94)

God's Word was at work in a saving way in his heart. That Word had:

1. Quickened His Faith (119:93)

"I will never forget Thy precepts: for with them Thou hast quickened me." God's Word had breathed new life into him.

God's words are not merely legislative, they are executive. God said, "Light be," and light *was.* He said, "Let the seas bring forth abundantly," and so they did. When the Word was made flesh and dwelt among us, it was the same. The incarnate Word had instant, executive power. When a leper came saying, "Lord, if Thou wilt Thou canst make me clean," He said, "I will; be thou clean." When howling wind and heaving wave threatened to sink the ship in which He slept He simply said, "Be still!" There was instant calm. When He stood at the tomb of Lazarus who had been dead for four days and whose body was in the process of decomposition, He said, "Lazarus, come forth." And "he that was dead came forth."

As God's Word is stored in our memory so can it be used by the Holy Spirit to quicken us in a moment of temptation, trial, decision, doubt. "Thou shalt not steal." "Forsake not the assembling of yourselves together." "Let no corrupt communication proceed out of thy mouth." There it is, God's Word, commanding us, able to quicken us.

The Word of God also:

2. Quelled His Foes (119:94)

"I am Thine, save me; for I have sought Thy precepts." The psalmist was not yet out of the woods; his foes were still in a position to do him harm. But a new note of confidence has crept in. He stakes everything now on a threefold proposition, a threefold cord of Scripture not easily broken.

He says, "*I belong* to You, Lord." That took care of one of his deepest psychological needs, the need to be accepted, to be a part of someone's circle of care. When I first came to North

America, I was a stranger in a strange land, thousands of miles from home. I felt a deep sense of isolation and vulnerability. If I were to fall sick, who would really care? If I were to die, to whom would it make the slightest difference beyond some temporary inconvenience? After I married, I belonged. The psalmist said: "I belong! I am Yours. I know You care. You understand me. You love me. For anyone to interfere with me means that they are tampering with one of Yours."

He says, "Save me." That reduces things to basics, to two words. That is all it takes, a two-word prayer. True prayer does not consist in making speeches to God. Prayer is the soul's urgent cry, the kind Peter prayed when he felt himself sinking beneath the waves. "Lord, save me!" This is prayer stripped of verbiage, pious phrases, and empty oratory. It is the most persuasive prayer of all—"Save me!" It links my urgent need to His glorious wisdom, love, and power.

He says, "I have sought Thy precepts." He may have stumbled, his efforts may have been feeble, he may have made mistakes, his falls may have been frequent—but his motive was right, his heart was right. That is always a powerful argument with God. The psalmist did not want to be delivered so he could live a selfish life. He wanted to be delivered in order to have greater freedom to walk in God's ways. This is what Jabez prayed when he asked the Lord to bless him and added, "And keep me from evil." Such prayer delights the heart of God.

The Word of God also had power to:

B. Safeguard Him (119:95)

"The wicked have waited for me to destroy me: but I will consider Thy testimonies." David could have said that—or Daniel, or Jeremiah, or Hezekiah, or any other of a long line of God's suffering saints. Two things that stand out here are the *persistence* of the wicked and the *patience* of the psalmist.

One would have thought that the wicked would give up. They don't; they persist. Nothing is more galling to the wicked than the righteousness of a genuine saint. The supreme example, of course, is the Lord Jesus Himself, whose unblemished goodness lashed the guilty conscience of His foes. Because He was good, He told them the truth, unpalatable as it was to them. So they waited for Him in order to destroy Him—and they persisted until they saw Him crucified and slain.

"But I will consider Thy testimonies," says the psalmist. One can picture the Lord Jesus repeating those words to Himself when faced with the persistence of His foes. One can picture Him repeating those words to Himself in moments when He retired from His disciples to be alone with His Father in Heaven.

What would He consider as He sat on the well or lay on the grass of some isolated woodland glen? He would think of Abraham and Isaac and Mount Moriah, perhaps, or the story of Jonah. He would think, perhaps, of the story of Moses, the riven rock, the water that immediately flowed. He might recall Scriptures that foretold His birth, spoke of His anointing and ministry to the poor, Scriptures that told of His death. On such occasions He might recall other words of the psalmist: "Thou wilt not leave my soul in hell nor suffer Thy holy one to see corruption." He considered God's testimonies. That was what enabled Him to manifest patience in the face of bitter hatred, malicious lies, growing opposition, and certain death by crucifixion.

The Word of God safeguarded Him—and it will safeguard us. It will give us a broader view, a wider horizon, and a sense of divine purpose which no immediate circumstance can change.

IV. THE PERFECTION OF GOD'S WORD (119:96)

"I have seen an end of all perfection: but Thy commandment is exceeding broad." Or, "I have seen an end, a limit, to all things, but exceedingly spacious are Your commandments." In the view of the average person, the Bible is a very narrow book. Not so. The Bible takes the broadest view of life and death, of time and eternity, that it is possible to take. All human philosophies are finite, limited, inadequate, bent, and harmful because they all are clouded and tinctured by sin. Sin fogs issues, clouds the intellect, narrows the vision, inflates the ego, and biases opinions. It is not the Bible that is narrow, but rather our human understanding—even when we loudly proclaim our openness, broad-mindedness, and catholicity of viewpoint.

Take, for instance, the popular theory of evolution, which leaves out God. That is its primary mistake. It then tries to explain the universe in material and mechanistic terms. It speaks of giant forces at work, impersonally and impartially following inevitable laws over enormous eons of time. It enlists the support of the academic community and the unthinking acquiescence of masses. When logically applied to the human race, it produces such philosophical stepchildren as Nazism, communism, and humanism. It can give no hope beyond the grave; it offers no comfort to the weak, the sick, the handicapped, the maimed, the dying, the lost. The theory is narrow because it refuses to accept a vast, revealed dimension of truth—the reality of the unseen, the spiritual, the supernatural.

All human philosophies, religions, and theories share that problem. They are narrow. They leave out the Word of God, and, in the end, they are discarded because they are inadequate.

The Bible, however, gives us a total and adequate view of all issues because it reveals the heart and mind of an omniscient God. "Spacious exceedingly are Thy commandments." The Bible gives us a true account of the origin of the universe. It alone tells us the truth about God. Nowhere else can a comprehensive and completely reliable plan of salvation be found. The Bible offers life evermore and warns against the horrors of a lost eternity.

Above all, it tells us about Jesus, God manifest in flesh. It records His teaching, morality, truth, and love. It sets before us a wholly satisfying and all-embracing view of life. It gives solace to the suffering and dying, salvation to the lost. It tells of life everlasting in a dimension beyond our imagining and of a duration that knows no end. There is nothing else to say.

Psalm 119:97-104

A SCHOLAR AND A SAINT

I. THE SOURCE OF TRUE SCHOLARSHIP (119:97-100)
   A. The Glorious Occupation of the Psalmist (119:97)
   B. The Glorious Outcome for the Psalmist (119:98-100)
   A mind sharpened by the Word of God is better than wits sharpened by:
   1. Enmity (119:98)
   2. Education (119:99)
   3. Experience (119:100)
II. THE SOURCE OF TRUE SANCTITY (119:101-104)
   A. A Separated Life (119:101)
   B. A Steadfast Life (119:102)
   C. A Satisfied Life (119:103)
   D. A Sterling Life (119:104)

GREAT PREMIUM IS PLACED on scholarship. Young persons hoping to get anywhere in our society must first demonstrate their academic ability by graduating from college. If individuals cannot produce a college diploma these days, no matter how vast their experience in the field, they are generally considered unable to fulfill the requirements for a particular job. There is little or no respect for the Word of God in today's educational institutions.

Yet the Bible is the source of all true scholarship. The English language contains about 400,000 words; the King James Bible has a vocabulary of about 6,000 words. But the impact of those words, as they are put together in the English Bible, can never be measured. The Bible has left a lasting impact on the English-speaking world. Its influence will never be eradicated from English law, social justice, art, music, and literature.

Addressing a body of students years ago, newspaper editor Charles A. Dana declared: "Of all books, the most indispensable and the most useful, the one whose knowledge is the most effective, is the Bible . . . There is perhaps no book whose style

351

is more suggestive and instructive, from which you can learn more directly that sublime simplicity which never exaggerates, which recounts the greatest events with solemnity, of course, but without sentimentality or affections . . . which you open with such confidence and lay down with such reverence."

Again and again our great literary figures have gone back to the Bible for their words, phrases, and ideas. Dr. Odell Shepherd, professor of English at Trinity College in Hartford, Connecticut, said: "America rests upon four cornerstones—the English Bible, the English language, the common law, and the tradition of liberty—but liberty, language and law might have been drawn from the Bible alone. Had we brought nothing with us across the sea beside this supreme book, we might still have been great. Without this book, America could not have become what she is, and when she loses its guidance, the wisdom of America will be no more. The breath of the prophets was in the sails that drove the Mayflower. . . . From those beginnings until now the Bible has been a teacher to our best men, a rebuke to our worst, and a noble companion to us all."

The first half of this psalm tells us that the Bible is:

I. THE SOURCE OF TRUE SCHOLARSHIP (119:97-100)

We have first:

A. The Glorious Occupation of the Psalmist (119:97)

"O how love I Thy law! It is my meditation all the day." Wise man that he was, the psalmist occupied himself daily with God's Word. There is so much to love about the Bible. There is, for instance, its sound common *sense*. It is filled with the distilled wisdom of the ages. Through the pages of the Bible omniscient wisdom speaks to all the issues of life and death. It tells us how to make a marriage work, how to raise our children, how to be truly successful in life, how to face tragedy, how to live forever.

There is its *structure*. The Bible is a magnificent mosaic of truth, a never-ending poem of literary styles. Verse balances verse; truth is weighted against truth. The way the Bible uses numbers, symbols, and words is a never-ending kaleidoscope of wonders.

Then there is its *simplicity*. The Bible deals with the sublimest truths ever conceived. Wise men and sages have delighted in its unfathomable depths. Scholars have spent lifetimes exploring the archaeology, vocabulary, and theological immensities of the Bible. Its chief charm, however, lies in its simplicity. A child can grasp its truths. Harriet Beecher Stowe caught this aspect of the Bible in *Uncle Tom's Cabin*. She pictures poor, old, ignorant, unlettered Uncle Tom picking out words from his Bible: "For-

God-so-loved-the-world-He-gave-His-only-be-gotten-Son. . . ."
"Fortunately," she said, "he was reading from a book which loses
nothing by being read with such slow, painstaking care." A key
text of Luke's Gospel reads: "The Son of man is come to seek
and to save that which is lost." There is not a single two-syllable
word in that sentence. Such is the simplicity of the Scripture.

We can pick up this book day after day, year after year, and
come back to old, familiar passages, or we can venture into
unexplored territory, but we will always find something to delight our hearts and minds. The psalmist was saturating his soul
in the Scriptures, earning for himself a valuable degree in the
school of God.

B. The Glorious Outcome for the Psalmist (119:98-100)

The psalmist shows that his mind, sharpened by the Word of
God, is keener than the wits of those sharpened by the philosophical grindstones of the world. He describes three kinds of
persons and compares himself with each one of them in order to
show that he has more wisdom than any of them—for instance,
those whose wits are sharpened by:

1. Enmity (119:98)

"Thou through Thy commandments hast made me wiser
than mine enemies: for they are ever with me." A classical
biblical example is David, especially in the early fugitive years
of his life. We remember, for instance, what happened after the
overthrow of Goliath. Jonathan came to David and David was
given command over Saul's men of war and thereafter sent on
this, that, and the other commission. We read, "And David went
out whithersoever Saul sent him, and *behaved himself wisely*"
(1 Samuel 18:5).

Then the spirit of jealousy seized Saul. On two occasions he
threw a javelin at David and twice David escaped. Saul became
afraid of David. He appointed David captain over a thousand
men but removed him from court. Again we read, "And David
behaved himself wisely in all his ways, and the LORD was with him"
(1 Samuel 18:14).

Then Saul offered his daughter to David to be his wife, hoping to snare him into some incautious word and also trap him
into a fight against hopeless odds with the Philistines. Later still,
another of Saul's daughters, Michal, fell in love with David,
married him, and took his side. Then Saul "became David's
enemy continually." Soon afterward the lords of the Philistines
initiated hostilities again against Israel and we read, "David
behaved himself more wisely than all the servants of Saul" (1 Samuel
18:30).

This wisdom of David was "the wisdom that is from above" which "is first pure, then peaceable, gentle, and easy to be intreated, full of mercy and good fruits, without partiality, and without hypocrisy" (James 3:17). David was always ready to forgive Saul and be his friend. Twice he refused to kill him when he had opportunity.

Geoffrey Bull, recounting his experience in a Chinese communist prison camp, tells of three years he had to live without a Bible. The communists hoped to cut him off from his source of spiritual solace and strength. It was a vain hope. He had for years been storing up that Word in his heart. Then they began brainwashing him. He describes the nagging and noise, the scrutiny and spying, the tension. He tells how they would threaten him with execution—threats always baited with a promise of pardon if he would reform and acknowledge his crime against the people. The tension was aggravated by ceaseless provocation and baiting, by attacks on his integrity and self-respect, and by endless prying into his thoughts. From morning to night, day after day, month after month it went on—argument, haranguing, criticism, and struggle. Every movement he made was under intense scrutiny. Officials, wardens, fellow prisoners kept at it. For fear of their own future they dared not relent. There was no love, no peace, nothing but indoctrination and examination. The whole thing was aimed at a single end: to bring his mind into captivity to Marx.

In the end they gave him back his Bible. Geoffrey Bull describes the ecstasy with which he once again held it in his hands: "Ringing in my ears were forty months of man's words, man's wisdom, man's arguments, man's hurt. Now on the page before me ran the quiet yet pungent words of Holy Scripture: 'Where is the wise . . . where is the disputer of this world?' " Long after his release he wrote, "Even today, I feel like running up and down the corridors of learning shouting out: 'Yes, where is he?' After the mad haranguings and fanatical ragings of the Marxists, let me ask. . . . 'Where is the wise? Hath not God made foolish the wisdom of this world?' "

Geoffrey Bull's tormentors had their wits sharpened by enmity. His mind was sharpened by God's Word. He was wiser than they.

There are those whose wits are sharpened by:

2. Education (119:99)

"I have more understanding than all my teachers: for Thy testimonies are my meditation." The psalmist does not say he will have more *knowledge* than his teachers. The young people who sit in college classrooms today cannot hope to match wits with their professors in the matter of knowledge. When it comes to chemistry, psychology, anthropology, or biology they can quickly squelch young believers who try to do battle with them on the grounds of mere cleverness. The Bible does not say we shall have more knowledge; it does say we shall have more wisdom. The Bible does not aim at making us clever; it aims at making us right.

The classic example of this, of course, is the Lord Jesus Himself. He entered human life at Bethlehem and went through all the normal stages of growing up. We see Him, for instance, as a boy of twelve, sitting before the learned teachers in Jerusalem "both hearing them, and asking them questions." What questions they must have been. So thoroughly had He mastered the Scriptures that Luke says, "All that heard Him were astonished at His understanding and answers" (Luke 2:46-47).

The rabbis had spent their lives learning the Midrash and Mishna—the Midrash with its allegories, homilies, and unsophisticated commentaries, and the Mishna which sought to wed rabbinical learning to Greek reasoning—a type of departure from the simple truth of God's Word brought to its full flower by Hillel shortly before the birth of Christ. They had spent years mastering the Midrash and the Mishna; Jesus had spent His short life mastering Moses and Malachi. He had more understanding than all his teachers.

But that was only the beginning. Jesus "increased in wisdom and stature, and in favor with God and man" (Luke 2:52). He was twelve when He met with the teachers; He was thirty when He began to preach. There were another eighteen years of carpentry and intensive study. By the time He was through He had total understanding of the spiritual significance of the Scriptures; He knew all that the prophets had written. No wonder He spoke "with authority and not as the scribes." The Jews marveled at Him saying, "How knoweth this Man letters, having never learned?" (John 7:15). He had been educated in the finest university in the world. He had been taught by the Holy Ghost.

When Jesus came, the world had been given five hundred years to find out what philosophy and religion could do. Buddha and the Greek philosophers had come and gone. Yet their learning and wisdom does not compare with His in its significance for this life and for the life to come.

And what about us? The Bible will give us an understanding of human behavior that surpasses psychology and psychiatry. It will enable us to face life and also death with assurance and courage. Those whose minds are sharpened by the Word of God will have understanding that worldly wisdom can never give. Then there are others whose wits are sharpened by:

3. Experience (119:100)

"I understand more than the ancients, because I keep Thy precepts." The psalmist here underlines two principles. First, *old* is not necessarily better and, second, light cannot be divorced from life. It often happens that truth is replaced by tradition. Not that traditions are always bad, but the person whose thinking is controlled by the Bible will be able to distinguish good traditions from bad ones. The Lord Jesus confronted the elders of His day on this very issue. Their traditions concerning the Sabbath had turned the Sabbath from a day of rest into a day of burdens.

The Catholic Church, for instance, has many dogmas that are venerated because they are old. The ancient church fathers promulgated them. When Martin Luther challenged those dogmas, he proved that his insights into the Word of God gave him more understanding than the ancients. It was not long before the reformers were challenging other aspects also of Catholic teachings, many of them made venerable by centuries of practice, yet scripturally invalid.

The Bible, however, does not command our veneration because it is old, but because it is right. Something is not true just because it is old.

The word translated "ancients" in this verse is rendered "elders" by some. It refers to those who, by their age and experience, deserve and demand the respect of others. But to be old does not necessarily mean that one is wise. A person who has grown old in error is no safe guide.

The Bible is also:

II. THE SOURCE OF TRUE SANCTITY (119:101-104)

The psalmist says that God's Word will direct him into:

A. A Separated Life (119:101)

"I have refrained my feet from every evil way, that I might keep Thy word." Our feet carry us to many places where eye, hand, mind, and will are exposed to temptation. One way to look at the closing four verses of this stanza is to relate them to the experience of Daniel in Babylon. It did not take Daniel long, teenager that he was, to make up his mind on certain matters. The first of these was separation. He determined that he would not do certain things forbidden by the Word of God even though others might think them harmless and that he was a fool. He purposed in his heart, for instance, that he would not defile himself with the king's meat. And that was that.

Then, too, God's Word directed the psalmist into:

B. A Steadfast Life (119:102)

"I have not departed from Thy judgments; for Thou hast taught me." There came a time in Daniel's life when he was called on to interpret one of Nebuchadnezzar's dreams. But what a dream. When Daniel was told the dream and understood what it meant he was almost afraid to tell the truth to the king. Nebuchadnezzar, after all, was an absolute monarch, hot and hasty of temper. How do you tell such a king that he is going to become insane? Nothing but Daniel's determination never to depart from God's judgments kept him true in that trying hour. He had learned the secret of a steadfast life.

God's Word also directed the psalmist into:

C. A Satisfied Life (119:103)

"How sweet are Thy words unto my taste! Yea, sweeter than honey to my mouth." We come again to Daniel's determination not to defile himself. How succulent that meat must have been—the choicest cuts, the thickest steak, the tastiest hams, the finest legs of lamb—but all killed with the blood undrained and all offered to idols. How flat and insipid must have been the bean soup he chose to eat instead. Yet the conscious knowledge that he was pleasing God brought Daniel its own compensation. Obedience to God's Word brings into life a special dimension of joy.

Last, the psalmist says that God's Word assures:

D. A Sterling Life (119:104)

The term *sterling* has been associated with silver since the thirteenth century. At that time England's coins were so debased through lack of silver content as to be practically worthless. The only coins containing large amounts of silver were minted in Germany. These coins were called "easterlings" to distinguish them from the low-grade English coins. The word *sterling*, derived from that term, became synonymous first with silver of high quality and then, by metaphor, with a life of high quality.

"Through Thy precepts I get understanding: therefore I hate every false way." Thus we see Daniel, after the Persians had swept away the Babylonian empire, becoming an intercessor for the nation of Israel. God's Word had given him understanding. He knew the time had come for prophecy to be fulfilled. Because he hated every false way, the sins of Israel loomed large in his thinking. The enormous sin that had made the exile a necessity had never been confessed. Daniel therefore gave himself to earnest prayer. Behind those marching pioneers that shortly afterward left for the promised land we can see an old man by the name of Daniel praying in Babylon.

God's Word points out a twofold path, to true *scholarship* and to true *sanctity.* May all of us ever walk thereon.

Psalm 119:105-112

THE LAMP

I. GOD'S WORD GUIDES US (119:105-108)
   A. In Our Walk (119:105-106)
      1. The Way Found (119:105)
      2. The Way Followed (119:106)
   B. In Our Weakness (119:107)
   C. In Our Worship (119:108)
II. GOD'S WORD GUARDS US (119:109-110)
   A. Hushes Our Fears (119:109)
   B. Hinders Our Foes (119:110)
III. GOD'S WORD GLADDENS US (119:111-112)
   It will remind us of:
   A. Our Happy Heritage (119:111)
   B. Our Heavenly Home (119:112)

BELIEVERS HAVE AN IMMENSE ADVANTAGE over the unsaved. Believers know where they are going as they journey through life, and they know how to get there. They have God to help them, and the Bible to show them the way.

I remember once being lost in a forest in northern British Columbia. At the time I was working as an accountant for a lumber company. One day an urgent message came into the office and someone had to go to the logging camp to deliver it. I drove out to where the camp was, but all the men were in the bush. The cook gave me vague directions and pointed out a path. Some time afterward I realized I was lost. I stood there alone and afraid. All the paths looked the same. An eerie stillness was in the air, a slight hint of menace, and all around me, on every hand, hundreds of square miles of trees. I learned a lesson about being lost that day. If you don't know where you are going, you are lost.

That is the condition of every unsaved man and woman on earth. The Bible does not use the word *unsaved* to describe the condition of those without Christ; it uses the word *lost*.

Christians have found the way. They are going home. The psalmist here points out three essential things about the Bible. It has been given to us to *guide us* (105-108), to *guard us* (109-110), and to *gladden us* (111-112). No wonder Christians regard the Bible as their greatest treasure on earth. It is our road map to glory. It has been given to us to say, "This is the way, walk ye in it" (Isaiah 30:21).

I. GOD'S WORD GUIDES US (119:105-108)

The psalmist underlines three areas in which God's Word guides us.

A. In Our Walk (119:105-106)

The psalmist tells of:

1. The Way Found (119:105)

"Thy word is a lamp unto my feet, and a light unto my path." A light on the path shows us the direction in which we are heading; a lamp shows us the next step. A light, no matter how bright, will not show us all the twists and turns ahead on the road, but it will give us a general sense of direction. That is what the Bible does. It lights the sinner's path to Christ; it lights the believer's path to glory. "The path of the just is as the shining light that shineth more and more unto the perfect day" (Proverbs 4:18).

The Bible does not unroll the whole map of life before us. If it did, we would be too terrified at some of the steeper crags or darker valleys along the way. God did not begin with Abraham by asking him to give up his son; He began by asking him to give up his father. Only years later was that demand made of Abraham, that he offer up Isaac. The Bible, for the most part, especially in the New Testament, sheds its light on our way by giving us broad, general principles. In the days of the spiritual infancy of the race, God gave Israel 613 specific and detailed commandments. In the New Testament all this is reduced to several principles.

In His Word, God does not say explicitly, "Tom, marry Susie" or "Jane, do not marry Wally." It simply says we are not to be unequally yoked together with unbelievers and that Christian marriage must be "in the Lord."

Of course there are occasional exceptions to every rule. I know of two instances where people thought they saw their names in the Bible, where an individual sensed God's guidance in an unusually explicit way.

Some years ago, in England, there lived a man named Goodman, a well-known servant of the Lord. He told of an incident in his life, when he was seeking guidance from the Lord as to whether or not he should undertake a certain journey. He opened his Bible and his eyes fell on the words, "The steps of a *good man* are ordered of the Lord." He read his own name (Goodman) into the text, assured that he was to go ahead with his trip.

My father knew of a woman who was much troubled about the lost state of her soul, but somehow, no matter how many preachers she went to hear, she couldn't believe that the message of salvation was for her. Her name was Edith. One day she was taken to hear a preacher who had a slight speech impediment. He recited the text, "This man receiveth sinners and eateth with them." The way he pronounced it, it sounded as though the text read, "This man receiveth sinners and *Edith* with them." The woman heard her name, and her doubts dissolved.

Such incidents are exceptional. The Bible, for instance, does not say: "Thou shalt not smoke or dance or drink or take drugs." It says that our body is the temple of the Holy Spirit and that we are not to defile it—that takes care of all the specifics. The Bible is a *light* unto our path.

It is also a *lamp* unto our feet, for there *are* times when we need something more specific than a general principle. We need to know exactly what the next step should be. At such times the Holy Spirit sometimes suddenly illumines a specific text or passage of Scripture and makes it speak directly to the need of the moment. Saintly George Mueller used to say that often the *stops* as well as the *steps* of a good man are ordered of the Lord. It is a matter of vital importance that, once God has indicated the way we are to take, we obey His leading.

2. The Way Followed (119:106)

"I have sworn, and I will perform it, that I will keep Thy righteous judgments."

A promise is one thing; performance is something else. Although many people make promises to the Lord in life's desperate hours, not many keep their word. Israel in the wilderness promised, "All that the Lord hath spoken we will do," but before the month was out, the nation was dancing around the golden calf.

The only One who has ever really said, "I have sworn, and will perform it, that I will keep Thy righteous judgments," is the Lord Jesus. He kept God's word to the letter, every chapter, every verse, every line. As He stepped out of eternity into time He said, "Lo I come, in the volume of the book it is written of me, to do Thy will, O my God." He kept God's righteous judgments. And not just those righteous judgments as they were recorded in the Mosaic Law and in the prophets—but those judgments as they were interpreted by Himself in the Sermon on the Mount. He took those grand edicts of old, lifted them far beyond our reach, and then kept them—not just in letter but in Spirit, not just in their content but in their intent. He paid His vows. He is the only One who ever really has.

Then God's Word guides us:

B. In Our Weakness (119:107)

"I am afflicted very much: quicken me, O LORD, according unto Thy word." The psalmist was suffering from affliction and consequent depression, not an unusual combination. Where could he go for help? Only one solution occurred to him. He would go to God's Word—where else?

His *affliction* came from the *outside.* We gather from numerous statements in this psalm that the psalmist was the object of the active dislike of a number of powerful and influential enemies. God's Word lifted his thoughts above them all, right up to the throne, right up to the Lord, to One who was mightier than all his foes. That is the *objective* perspective we get from God's Word when we are aware of our weakness and vulnerability. The Bible gives us a frame of reference outside ourselves. It points us to someone bigger than our circumstances. A God who can create a hundred million galaxies is not to be thwarted by a mere man no matter what power he wields.

The psalmist's *depression* came from the *inside.* He needed to be "revived" or "quickened." He had allowed his circumstances to get him down. The Bible ministers to our inner person, to our spirit. That is the *subjective* perspective we get from God's Word. It fortifies our heart and soul and revives us. It deals with anxiety, guilt, and depression; with inhibitions and fear; with all those other negative feelings that torture us within. It assures us we are known, loved, and wanted by the most important person in the universe. It links our weakness to His strength.

Then, too, God's Word guides us:

C. In Our Worship (119:108)

"Accept, I beseech Thee, the freewill offerings of my mouth, O LORD, and teach me Thy judgments." The psalmist was familiar enough with the freewill offerings demanded under the law. The greatest of the freewill offerings was the burnt offering. He knew the instruction for the burnt offering in Leviticus 1 and he sensed that the detailed ritual had to mean something. But what? Why, for instance, did the priest get the skin of the burnt offering? And why, if a person was so poor that he could afford to bring only two turtle doves, did the priest help him with his burnt offering, whereas if a man brought an ox he received no help at all? All this makes sense to us who are living on the other side of Calvary, but it made little or no sense to Old Testament believers like this psalmist. No wonder he asks God to "teach him" His ordinances.

But then he takes a giant leap. He asks God to accept quite a different kind of freewill offering, the praise of his mouth. That shows what a spiritual giant this unknown singer was. He rose above the majority. He had insight into God's Word not given to most. He saw that there was much more to worship than bringing a bull or a goat and shedding its blood. The mere form of ritual religion profited little. God is a spirit and those who would worship Him must worship Him in spirit and in truth— in spirit because of who He is and in truth because of what we are. He wanted to worship in spirit: "Accept, I beseech Thee, the freewill offerings of my mouth"; he wanted to worship in truth: "and teach me Thy ordinances."

II. God's Word Guards Us (119:109-110)

The psalmist now takes up a different aspect of his subject. God's Word is not only a guide, it is a guard that:

A. Hushes Our Fears (119:109)

"My soul is continually in my hand: yet do I not forget Thy law." That initial clause is an idiom. Where we would say, "My heart was in my mouth," the Hebrew would say, "My soul was in my hand." "My life was in my hand" would be another way he might express the same thought. Thus Jephthah, at great personal risk, delivered Israel from danger. He immediately ran into criticism from the tribe of Ephraim who were ashamed of themselves for standing idly by while Jephthah won his great victory. They threatened to burn his house down. Jephthah told them he had called them and they did not respond. So he *put his life in his hands*, and Israel was delivered (Judges 12:3).

The same expression is used in connection with David. David had saved Israel from Goliath, and King Saul, insanely jealous, issued orders that David was to be killed. Jonathan, indignant, stood up for David: "He did *put his life in his hand*, and slew the Philistine," he said (1 Samuel 19:5).

An identical expression was used to King Saul on another

occasion. In his early zeal, Saul had rooted out witchcraft from Israel and had put to death those who practiced it. Later, when he found that God would not speak to him, he resorted to one of the few surviving witches in the land. He commanded her to summon up Samuel from the dead. The witch, naturally enough, thought it was a trap but, her fears finally allayed, she did what Saul demanded. She went through her incantations to establish contact with her familiar spirit so that it might impersonate Samuel. Instead, Samuel himself came with a message of doom for the guilty king. Saul was beside himself with terror and the witch tried to comfort him. "Behold," she said, "thine handmaid hath obeyed thy voice, and *I have put my life in my hand,* and have hearkened unto thy words" (1 Samuel 28:21).

Thus it was with the psalmist. His dangers were real, he was afraid, his heart was in his mouth, but God's word hushed his fears.

God's Word also:

B. Hinders Our Foes (119:110)

"The wicked have laid a snare for me: yet I erred not from Thy precepts."

The psalmist's heart was in his mouth because of his danger of being snared. Traps were being set for him. Again David comes immediately to mind.

King Saul set his first trap for David by offering him Merab, his eldest daughter, to be his wife. David had slain Goliath and thus met Saul's condition (1 Samuel 17:25). The snare Saul set for David was obvious to David: Saul wanted to see if David had political ambition, a secret desire to usurp the throne, to climb to the throne by way of Merab. David was careful. He told Saul that he was a nobody, unfit to aspire to so high an honor as to be son-in-law to the king (1 Samuel 18:18).

Then Saul deliberately married Merab to someone else. It was another snare. He wanted to see if David would make an incautious comment. David said nothing (1 Samuel 18:19).

It was then that Michal, a younger daughter of Saul, fell in love with David and wanted to marry him. When Saul heard of it, he was pleased. "I will give him her," he said, *"that she may be a snare to him"* (1 Samuel 18:21). Then he laid a trap for David to see what his reaction would be to the news that he was to be the king's son-in-law after all (1 Samuel 18:22).

David knew God's Word enough not to respond in kind. The Lord steered him safely around such snares because he honored God's precepts. Thus God's Word can guard us also from wrong-doing.

III. God's Word Gladdens Us (119:111-112)

The Scripture never lets us lose sight of:

A. Our Happy Heritage (119:111)

"Thy testimonies have I taken as an heritage for ever: for they are the rejoicing of my heart." A heritage is something we inherit. The most priceless heritage we have is the Bible. Nothing can compare to it down here. The Bible, however, is like some other inheritances people receive—it yields its treasures only under certain conditions.

A man owned a vineyard and his sons believed their father to be very wealthy. Since he was secretive about it they could not be sure, but they hoped to inherit a fortune when he died. On his deathbed he told his sons that the secret of his wealth was to be found in the vineyard. The boys immediately began to dig, hoping to find the treasure they believed to be hidden under the vines. They toiled for months, being careful not to damage the vines. In the course of time they dug over every inch of the vineyard and discovered nothing. But that fall their vineyard produced the finest crop of grapes on record. Then they realized what their wise old father had done. He had forced them to stop loafing around and instead to cultivate the vineyard. The secret of his wealth was the vines which, properly cared for, would keep them rich.

Our heritage, too, is priceless but it will not yield its wealth to us without work. When we work at it, the Bible never fails to yield its riches to our souls.

Finally, the Bible never lets us lose sight of:

B. Our Heavenly Home (119:112)

"I have inclined mine heart to perform Thy statutes alway, even unto the end." A tired horse will move faster and pull harder when it is heading for home, when the end is in sight. Most people find keeping God's Word to be uphill, tiring work. Not the psalmist. He was heading home. He had inclined his heart in that direction.

As a boy I used to ride a bicycle along some of the country roads of Wales. Those backroads were hilly and steep. It was hard work pedaling up them and sometimes quite impossible. Then it was necessary to get off the bicycle and push it up the hill. As often as not, however, once the brow of the hill was reached there would be a steep slope down the other side. That made up for it. My companions and I would jump on our bicycles and off we would go, soaring down the hill, the wind rushing past our ears, whooping for joy. Then, as the bottom of the hill came in sight and another rise loomed up ahead we would pedal as fast as we could, while the going was still easy, to get up as much momentum as possible to carry us at least halfway up the approaching rise.

No doubt the psalmist found that keeping God's Word gave him momentum, so that when steep places came they were already more than half conquered. He never lost sight of the end of the journey.

Psalm 119:113-120

TRUSTING AND TREMBLING

I. WHOM THE PSALMIST TRUSTED (119:113-117)
 A. His Vacillation Is Assessed (119:113)
 B. His Victory Is Assured (119:114)
 C. His Virtue Is Assailed (119:115-117)
 He expresses his need for:
 1. Separation (119:115)
 2. Scripture (119:116)
 3. Support (119:117)
II. WHY THE PSALMIST TREMBLED (119:118-120)
 A. At the Justice of God (119:118-119)
 1. In His Dealings with the Wayward (119:118)
 2. In His Dealings with the Wicked (119:119)
 B. At the Judgment of God (119:120)

IN THIS SEGMENT OF HIS SONG, the psalmist is preoccupied with the evildoers of his day. He talks to them about God and he talks to God about them. Throughout he declares, as always, his adherence to the Word of God.

We are told:

I. WHOM THE PSALMIST TRUSTED (119:113-117)

We notice first that:

A. His Vacillation Is Assessed (119:113)

"I hate vain thoughts: but Thy law do I love." The word for "vain thoughts" could be rendered "divided thoughts." The idea is to be doubled-minded. With constant pressure on him from his foes, the psalmist assesses his tendency to vacillate. There is the battle between his own see-saw thoughts and his basic fidelity to the Word of God. We all experience moments when doubts assail and when compromise looks attractive.

The root of the word for *vain* or *divided* thoughts is used on a significant occasion elsewhere in the Old Testament. Picture

367

Elijah as he summons the people to Mount Carmel to confront them, once and for all, with the folly of their idolatry and with conclusive evidence that the Lord God Jehovah was indeed a true and living God. The people had been awed and dazzled by Jezebel with her forceful personality, her exotic ways, her false gods. Ahab, her husband, was useless as a shepherd of the people. Elijah looked at the assembled multitudes tossed this way and that between the old paths and the heathen practices introduced by Jezebel. Then he formulated his memorable challenge. "How long halt ye between two opinions?" he demanded. "If the LORD be God, follow Him: but if Baal, then follow him" (1 Kings 18:21). The word Elijah used for *halt* literally means "to leap." That is what a double-minded, vacillating person does—leaps first this way and then that way. The psalmist hated it, especially when he saw it in himself.

He made up his mind to take one final leap and land with both feet squarely on the Word of God. The Scriptures would be the law of his life, the arbitrator of his conscience, the ruler of his will, the love of his heart, and food for his thoughts.

"I *hate* . . . I *love*." The law of opposites. Every negative has its positive. Night is offset by day. Centripetal force is balanced by centrifugal force. Extremes, thus balanced out in nature, need to be balanced out in life. It is no good to hate vacillating thoughts unless they are offset by love for God's Word. Once God's Word is given a balancing role in our lives, instead of leaping this way and that, we become stable, steadfast, unmovable. John Bunyan illustrated this in *Pilgrim's Progress* by introducing Mr. Pliable into the story, a poor wisp of a man with no mind of his own.

B. His Victory Is Assured (119:114)

"Thou art my hiding place and my shield: I hope in Thy word." We need a hiding place when danger threatens: we need a shield when danger makes its thrust. A hiding place suggests that the danger, though real enough, is not yet at hand. It can still be averted perhaps. A shield is needed when the hiding place no longer affords protection. The danger has become immediate, a present-tense peril.

The psalmist's first line of defense against his foes is God, and his final line of defense against his foes is God. He has no other defense, nor does he need any. His hope is not in his friends or family, in his own resources or resolution, in his skill with sword or spear. His hope is in God and in God's Word. Since that cannot fail, his victory is assured.

God cannot deny Himself. He must honor His Word, must be true to His character. So much is at stake in God's honoring His

Word that the psalmist does not consider for a moment the possibility of anything else.

Our thoughts go back to Abraham, when he had just won a tremendous victory. With a few hundred of his retainers and a motley force of ragtag and bobtail allies, he had taken on an invading army from the East which, flushed with victory, was returning on its triumphant way back toward the Euphrates. Then had come the reunion with Lot. We can imagine excited talk and chatter, with Abraham delighting in it all. He would talk of old times with Lot, and earnestly counsel him to remain committed to the Lord. There would be reminiscences of Lot's wife, about life in Sodom. There would be laughter and games with Lot's children. Then it was all over. To Abraham's dismay, Lot headed back to Sodom, arm in arm with Sodom's king. In the silence that descended on the patriarch's camp, the aging pilgrim looked at his beloved wife, now growing old. The silence that reigned in his camp seemed only to emphasize the fact that they had no children. Brooding over it all was the possibility that the eastern army, robbed of its spoils, might return to take summary vengeance on this petty chieftain who had caught them by surprise.

Then came the I AM of God, one of the first of the mighty I AMs of Scripture: "Fear not, Abram: I am thy shield . . ." (Genesis 15:1). And behind that shield Abraham rested. No weapon forged by hell could penetrate it. He was safe from the kings of the East. He could rest in God's promise of a son. The psalmist rested in the living God: "Thou art my hiding place and my shield," he says. "I hope in Thy word."

C. His Virtue Is Assailed (119:115-117)

In view of the unrelenting pressure from his enemies, the psalmist relied on three things. First he realized:

1. His Need for Separation (119:115)

"Depart from me, ye evildoers: for I will keep the commandments of my God." It is a good thing to put distance between ourselves and those who would persuade or push us into doing something wrong. History would have been very different if Eve had said to Satan, "Depart from me, ye evil doer," or if Adam had chosen to go along with God's one prohibition.

"Be off with you!" That is the essence of what Jesus said to Satan when the evil one made the last of his loaded offers to the Lord in the wilderness. He offered Jesus an empire—in exchange for His soul. Jesus said, "Get thee hence, Satan." "Depart from me," says the psalmist to those who in his day wished to lure him from the path of virtue.

Another classic example of a man putting distance between himself and temptation is Joseph. From what we know of Egyptian social life, Egyptian women did not deprive themselves of sensual pleasures. Numerous popular tales tell of the wives of Egyptian lords nonetheless doing as they pleased—casting their eyes on younger men. It is not surprising, therefore, that Potiphar's wife cast lustful eyes on Joseph, who seems to have inherited his mother's good looks. When her open propositions were refused, she began to lie in wait for him. The more Joseph drew back, the more she came on to him. At last, she physically accosted him. Joseph fled. He put distance between himself and the temptation.

The psalmist saw separation as a means of maintaining a holy life: "It is no use you people trying to entice me into some kind of wickedness. I am committed to keeping God's Word."

2. His Need for Scripture (119:116)

"Uphold me according unto Thy word, that I may live: and let me not be ashamed of my hope." God's Word is what undergirded the psalmist's faith and stiffened his resolve. He knew the value of Scripture as a bulwark against evil. He staked everything on it, leaned heavily on its counsel. He said that if God's Word failed him, if *that* let him down, he might just as well die. But he had made no mistake. The Bible was well able to uphold him, come what may.

A dear Christian friend once told me how he staked his all on the Word of God. He was a pioneer missionary in the Yukon. In those days we lived in northern British Columbia, and in his comings and goings he often visited us. In his early days as a pioneer in the remote wilds of the Canadian north, he carried a gun with him. The journeys he undertook often called for long tramps through desolate country. It was not unusual to meet wild animals, some of them fierce. He felt he needed the protection of a gun.

It was his policy to call on lonely homes along the Alaska highway as he journeyed, leaving people with a word of greeting, some gospel literature, and a word of testimony. One day he came to a house and walked up the drive carrying his gun slung as usual over his shoulder. The woman challenged him about it. "You tell me," she said, "that you trust God and that God is all powerful. Then why do you carry a gun?" My friend was confounded. He didn't know what to say. He mumbled a few words and went on his way, embarrassed and ashamed. Then God began to speak to him. Verses like "Lo, I am with you always" came to his mind. At last he came under such conviction that he tossed his gun into a ditch and resolved never to carry a weapon again. He would trust God, the God who promised to supply all his need, including the need for protection, the Lord who promised to be with him always.

Not long afterward he was put to the test. Coming up over the brow of a hill he came face to face with a grizzly bear. Both stopped dead in their tracks. Then, claiming God's promise and acting on a maxim from his army days that surprise often wins the day, he yelled, waved his arms, flourished his Bible—and charged straight at the bear. It turned tail and fled.

3. His Need for Support (119:117)

"Hold Thou me up, and I shall be safe: and I will have respect unto Thy statutes continually." Here we have the threefold law of "life in the vine."

The first thing a vine learns is to *cling.* It must have outside support. It cannot hold itself erect and throw out its branches like an ordinary tree. "Hold Thou me up," says the psalmist. I must have Someone to cling to.

That was a lesson Jacob had to learn, and it took him some twenty years to learn it. All his life he had schemed and planned, even in the things of God. He had schemed to get the birthright, then to get the blessing, then to get a bride, then to get a business, then to get back a brother. All the time he needed to be broken. He needed to learn to cling. Thus God met him at the Jabbok and thus we see Jacob clinging to his mysterious Visitor, saying, "I will not let Thee go, except Thou bless me" (Genesis 32:26).

The second law of life in the vine is to *climb:* "Hold Thou me up, and I shall be safe." Jacob learned that lesson next. He discovered that his little camp was surrounded by an armed angelic guard. He did not need to be afraid of Laban and his furious sons, nor of Esau with his four hundred armed clansmen. Thus Jacob began to grow. He went on growing in grace, increasing in the knowledge of God all the rest of his eventful life. He had learned the second law of life in the vine: how to climb.

The third law of life in the vine is to *cluster:* "Hold me up . . . and I will have respect unto Thy statutes continually."

When a grapevine has learned to cling and to climb, it can then fulfil the law of its Creator and begin to bear fruit. A vine simply stays where it is placed; it leaves the problems of pruning, planning, and protecting to the husbandman, and eventually it delights the world with its grapes. It was not until Jacob had learned those lessons that he became spiritually fruitful. The Jacob we see in the closing chapters of his life, blessing his sons, foretelling the future, demanding that his bones be buried in Canaan since he had no part or lot with Egypt, is a Jacob bearing magnificent clusters of fruit.

II. Why the Psalmist Trembled (119:118-120)

A. At the Justice of God (119:118-119)

1. In His Dealings with the Wayward (119:118)

"Thou hast trodden all them that err from Thy statutes: for their deceit is falsehood." The word translated "trodden down" can be rendered "set at naught." That is how God dealt with the wayward, with those who set at naught the Word of God. God set *them* at naught. What they taught was deceit and falsehood.

Any teaching is false, no matter how many millions of adherents it can muster, no matter what backing it might have in the halls of the learned or in the corridors of power, if it sets aside God's Word.

The psalmist uses the past tense to tell the fate of moral, religious, political, and cultural cheats. In actual fact he was still in the thick of it, his enemies were still flourishing, but they are through! They had no future, God had set them at naught. They will all come to nothing in the end—collectively at the return of Christ and individually at death. The psalmist trembled, too, at the justice of God:

2. In His Dealings with the Wicked (119:119)

"Thou puttest away all the wicked of the earth like dross." Sometimes it happens in great, sweeping holocausts of judgment as at the flood and the overthrow of Sodom, as in times of war, famine, and pestilence. God allows wickedness in society to be heated until it is brought to a boil, until it rises to the surface, until it is a horrible scum on the face of society. Then He skims it off.

But even when He is not dealing with human wickedness in such dramatic ways, He is still dealing with it. Every man, woman, boy, and girl born, eventually dies. One by one God skims off like dross men like Nero and Caligula, Voltaire and Marx, Hitler and Stalin. Ordinary men and women, whose lives and sins are mediocre but none the less damning, are also skimmed off. No one lives a day longer than God permits for their repentance. The thought of it awed the psalmist. He trembled at the righteous justice of God. He trembled, too:

B. At the Judgment of God (119:120)

"My flesh trembleth for fear of Thee; and I am afraid of Thy judgments," he said. If we were to render that idiom in modern terms, we might say, "My flesh creeps for fear of Thee . . ." Contemplating the judgment of God on the wicked instilled fear into the psalmist's soul.

The kind of God envisioned by liberal religionists has no basis in fact. They depict God as too kind and merciful to send people to hell. Their God is a kind of cosmic Santa Claus. Their God is certainly not the God of the Bible who, while He is a God of infinite love, is also a God of awesome and terrifying holiness. God would never have us become so familiar with holy things that familiarity breeds contempt. He loves us, and He wants us to love Him; the supreme revelation of God in the Bible is the revelation of God as a Father. He yearns over us as a father yearns over a little one. But He will never let us forget His holiness.

We see this illustrated in the ark, the most sacred object in the tabernacle. It contained God's unbroken law, a symbol of God's *goodness,* a goodness as inflexible and as adamant as the stone upon which the law was engraved. It contained a pot of manna, a symbol of God's *grace,* grace that remembered that His people were but flesh and blood, grace that ministered to their daily physical needs. It contained Aaron's rod that budded, a symbol of God's *government,* His swift and certain wrath poured out on rebels and apostates. The ark was covered with the mercy seat, a symbol of God's love—splashed with blood, an awesome reminder of His holiness—and surmounted by figures of the cherubim, symbolic guardians of His creatorial and redemptive rights on earth.

When that ark was moved, it was first covered with a blue cloth, not only to hide it from the gaze of the curious but also to turn their thoughts toward Heaven where God really sat enthroned. It was carried high on the shoulders of the priests, with a measured distance between them and the rest of the people. Even God's redeemed people were to keep their distance. When the men of Bethshemesh dared to look inside the ark they were smitten with instant death. When Uzzah put out his hand to touch it, he died where he stood. All this brought home to the Hebrew people a sense of the holiness and awesomeness of God. That is why the psalmist trembled. He trembled at the justice of God and at the judgment of God. And so should we.

Psalm 119:121-128

LORD, IT IS TIME

I. HIS SERIOUS CONCERN (119:121-124)
   He wanted God to act:
   A. In Government (119:121)
   B. As Guarantor (119:122)
   C. With Grace (119:123-124)
      1. Saving Him (119:123)
      2. Strengthening Him (119:124)
II. HIS SWEET CAPTIVITY (119:125)
III. HIS SOLE COMPLAINT (119:126)
   A. How Daring He Was (119:126a)
   B. How Discerning He Was (119:126b)
IV. HIS SIGNIFICANT CLAIM (119:127-128)
   A. The Treasure He Loved (119:127)
   B. The Truth He Lived (119:128)

A S THIS SEGMENT OF THE PSALM SHOWS, the singer is still surrounded by watchful and vengeful foes. Now, however, a hint of impatience creeps into his songs and supplications. He tells the Lord it is time for Him to be up and doing. We may smile at that, because we have often told the Lord, with astonishing arrogance, much the same thing.

I. HIS SERIOUS CONCERN (119:121-124)

The psalmist was concerned that God should act in a threefold way. First:

A. In Government (119:121)

"I have done judgment and justice [righteousness]: leave me not to mine oppressors." Thus Jesus might have prayed in the garden of Gethsemane.

Here we have the seemingly endless problem of *right* forever on the scaffold, *wrong* forever on the throne. It is the age-old problem of the suffering of the godly, the theme of the book of

374

Job. In a short-term view, the problem has no answer; in the long run, all will be well. God is not dead, He is not asleep, His silence is not the silence of indifference but the silence of infinite patience.

The psalmist tells the Lord *he* has done the right thing. So why doesn't God likewise do the right thing?

Job is a case in point. After his three friends had done all they could to prove that he must have been a wicked sinner and a surpassing hypocrite, Job gave his final answer. In three chapters particularly (29–30–31) he proclaimed his own righteousness. In the space of those three short chapters he used personal pronouns no less than 195 times: *I, me,* and *my.* Then, having nothing else to say, Job rested his case, as it were. Even though his remarkable statement might seem to have a flavor of self-righteousness, it is nevertheless a noteworthy claim—especially for a man who did not have a single word of written Scripture in his hand.

"I have done justice and righteousness," he says in effect. "I have been a good neighbor, I have paid my debts, I have a clean conscience."

The psalmist believed that trusting in God would make a difference in how things go. "Leave me not to my oppressors," he says. He had fallen on hard times. Evil men had him in their power and had not hesitated to use their position and influence against him. Although many might lose their faith altogether under such circumstances, or else blame God, the psalmist retained a sense of proportion. Losing faith in God leads only to greater despair. The psalmist simply dug in. The triumph of the wicked *had* to be temporary. He wanted God to act in government. Anyone who has been at the mercy of an unscrupulous person knows exactly how he felt.

He also wanted God to act:

B. As Guarantor (119:122)

"Be surety for Thy servant for good: let not the proud oppress me." This is the only verse in this psalm which does not employ one of the ten synonyms for God's Word. There is a reason. Throughout this psalm the psalmist is like a man who has a written guarantee to secure him in case of need. That guarantee was God's written Word. Again and again he has taken out this guarantee, finding encouragement in its sweeping and, for the most part, unconditional clauses. He has underlined those precious promises that form the warp and woof of his Bible. More than once he has put his finger on a pledge or promise and said, "I believe that."

But his enemies were still there and his circumstances seem to have remained unchanged. The guarantee reads well enough, the divine signature is legible enough, but nothing seems to have happened. So in this verse he puts down the written Word and goes directly to the Living Word, to the Guarantor Himself. "Be surety for Thy servant for good," he says. "Let not the proud oppress me." We can be sure he did not appeal to God in vain.

The whole idea behind God's plan of salvation is in focus here. *He* is our sole hope of heaven, our unfailing resource in life. Nothing delights God more than when we take Him at His Word—unless it is when we come directly to Him and tell Him face to face how dependent we are on Him.

There is something else. The psalmist wanted God to act:

C. With Grace (119:123-124)

1. By Saving Him (119:123)

"Mine eyes fail for Thy salvation, and for the word of Thy righteousness." The picture is that of a shipwrecked mariner. Like a hapless Robinson Crusoe he has climbed to some vantage point on his lonely island to scan the far horizons in search of a sail.

Or the picture is that of a beleagured garrison. The enemy has the fortress surrounded, food supplies are running low, and water is in short supply. A trusted soldier has been secreted through the enemy lines to see if aid can be summoned. The commander climbs to the tower to scan the distant hills in hope that help will arrive.

Both sailor and soldier continue to look, with failing hope.

The psalmist has staked everything on his Lord's assurances. God simply cannot let him down. After all, he is not a sailor scanning uncharted seas for sight of a sail he has no reasonable right to expect. He is not a soldier who has no real assurance his messenger has cleared the enemy lines. The psalmist has the promise of God. There can be no question about his prayers getting through. Help has been promised. What he calls "the word of Thy righteousness," what we might call "Thy righteous word," cannot fail. It would be simpler for the stars to cease to shine.

Thus it was with Abraham who "against hope believed in hope." What hope had he of a son? His expedient of bringing a son to birth through Hagar had been a disaster. True, he had a child, Ishmael, and the familial complications that ensued—as well as thirteen years of the silence of God. As for Sarah, she was now too old for childbearing.

And yet, didn't he have God's word for it that he *would* have a son and that his seed would be countless as the stars in the sky?

Surely *that* would suffice. So, Abraham settled for God's Word, wise man that he was, father of all them that believe as he was, friend of God as he was. His eyes might fail, his strength might fail, his days might fail, but *God* could not fail. This psalmist, in his pressing and perilous circumstances, took his stand with Abraham against all odds. He wants God to act in grace in saving him, and he really has no doubt that He will.

Then, too, he wants God to act in grace:

2. By Strengthening Him (119:124)

"Deal with Thy servant according unto Thy mercy, and teach me Thy statutes." The psalmist needed to be strengthened by the Holy Spirit in the inner man. If God was going to make him go on waiting for the redemption of His promise, then he needed to be fortified within by the Word of God.

Note how the psalmist instinctively links his need of God's mercy with his need to grasp God's laws. After all, mercy and morality go together. A classic example of mercy being extended at the expense of morality is that of Absalom. David forgave Absalom for the crime of murdering his brother, since there was considerable provocation and some possible justification. Absalom, however, had taken the law into his own hands, and David, as head of state, could not ignore that. So, although he forgave Absalom, he banished him from Jerusalem. In the end he gave in altogether and welcomed Absalom home. But Absalom was unrepentant. He felt his crime was justified, he had done no worse than his father had done, he was an avenger of blood, he had sentenced and executed a man who deserved to die—a man the king was too weak to execute. So, far from being reconciled, Absalom was resentful, and the mercy extended to him was worse than wasted. It bred rebellion.

"Deal with Thy servant according to Thy mercy," said the psalmist, appealing to a mercy wider than the ocean and higher than the heavens. Wisely he added, "And teach me Thy statutes." Mercy and morality hold hands.

The psalmist speaks next of:

II. His Sweet Captivity (119:125)

"I am Thy servant; give me understanding, that I may know Thy testimonies." The psalmist, like Paul, described himself as a bondslave. This singer of old delighted in a sweet captivity to the will and Word of God. Like the Hebrew servant he said, "I love my master... I will not go out free." By law such a devoted servant was taken to a nearby post and his ear was bored. Henceforth he carried on his body the slavebrand of his master. That pierced ear proclaimed to the world what a wonderful master he served and that his whole life was being poured out in sweet captivity.

God has the right to demand our unquestioning obedience, and sometimes He *does* demand that kind of obedience. But God is no tyrant. Often He does give us insights into His mind and will—but only if we study His Word.

So the psalmist prays for understanding. He wanted to know what principles lay behind the bare commandments so that he might intelligently serve his beloved Master.

Now that the Holy Spirit has come to lead us into all truth we can have even deeper insights into God's ways than could this devout singer of old.

Then the psalmist speaks of:

III. His Sole Complaint (119:126)

A. How Daring He Was (119:126a)

"It is time for Thee, LORD, to work: for they have made void Thy law." As though we can tell God when He ought to go to work! Like Job, we think we have all the answers. Like Job too, we find that we really know nothing at all about the great issues, of the working of those "wheels within wheels" of His will.

The only person who can pray like that, with any authority or assurance, is a person who lives close enough to the Lord to know God's Word very well. Such a person can appeal to God on the basis of intimate knowledge of His will. Daniel could do that. He had so thoroughly mastered the Word of God as given to Jeremiah, he had so marked the passing of the years, he was so conversant with the signs of the times that he could pray, "It is time, O Lord, for Thee to work."

George Mueller also could do that at times. He was so sensitive to the leading of the Lord in his life that he could say, in effect: "It is time, O Lord, for Thee to work." On one occasion George Mueller was sailing down the Saint Lawrence into Montreal to keep an appointment he knew to be in the will of God. A heavy fog came down and the ship reduced speed to a crawl. The captain of the ship was a believer so Mr. Mueller approached him and asked him if they would make Montreal on time. The captain said, "Not unless this fog lifts at once." Said George Mueller, "Very well, we shall ask the Lord to take the fog away." He knelt down and in a simple prayer made his request. When the captain was about to pray, Mr. Mueller gently put his hand on his arm. "Don't you pray," he said. "Why not?" the captain asked. "You don't really believe the fog will lift. Besides, it has already gone!" said Mr. Mueller.

B. How Discerning He Was (119:126b)

"It is time for Thee, LORD, to work: for they have made void Thy law." Here is another occasion when God *must* act—when moral apathy and spiritual apostasy are such that God's Word has been completely set aside by the wicked, and when His control over human affairs appears to be totally undercut by sin.

We are rapidly arriving at that state of affairs in the world today. And so the Lord will work—in rapture, ruin, or revival.

The psalmist's sole complaint was that he even had to *ask* God to work. He couldn't understand why he needed to mention the matter at all.

Finally, we have:

IV. HIS SIGNIFICANT CLAIM (119:127-128)

A. The Treasure He Loved (119:127)

"Therefore I love Thy commandments above gold; yea, above fine gold." That is a magnificent claim. The psalmist staked his claim in God. He now appears as a prospector who has struck a rich mine. He stakes his claim in God. Note *his first love;* it is not gold, but God. What he coveted most was not the wealth of the world, but the wealth of the Word. What human beings won't do for gold! Men will sell their souls for money, women will sell their bodies. People will traffic in soul-destroying drugs for gain.

Note also *his fine logic:* "Therefore," he says, "I love Thy commandments above gold." The word *therefore* links us to what has gone on before. He loves God's Word so much because of the claim it gives him on God. He has just been exercising his claim by telling the Lord it is time for Him to work. Surely to have a claim on God like that is worth more than all the wealth of the world.

B. The Truth He Lived (119:128)

"Therefore I esteem all Thy precepts concerning all things to be right; and I hate every false way." That is a great statement, a great place to take one's stand in life. The previous verse put a *monetary* value on the Bible—it is worth more than gold; this one puts a *moral* value on the Bible—it is always right.

When the Bible says something about *creation,* that settles it. The Bible is right. Let the world bring on its paleoanthropologists and its origins researchers. If what they have to say contradicts what the Bible has to say, they are wrong and the Bible is right.

When the Bible says something about *crime,* that settles it.

The Bible endorses capital punishment, for instance. Let the world's psychologists and sociologists take the stand the Bible takes or else be wrong.

When the Bible says something about human *conduct,* the Bible is right. The Bible teaches that the basic law of human behavior is "the law of sin." Humankind is bent; we are sinners by birth, choice, and practice. No amount of contradictory arguments by psychiatrists and humanists will make the Bible wrong. If their theories contradict the Bible, it makes no difference. The Bible is right.

When the Bible speaks about *conversion,* that's it. Let the world bring on its religions and its cults, its gurus and disputers. If what they have to say contradicts the truth of the Bible, that people need to be born again, born from above, born of the Spirit of God—then let God be true and every one of them a liar.

Every issue to which the Bible speaks is right. Let us side with the psalmist: "Therefore I esteem all Thy precepts concerning all things to be right; and I hate every false way." Others may say that such a conviction makes us bigots; we say, it makes us believers.

Psalm 119:129-136

GOD'S WONDERFUL WORD

I. THE PSALMIST AS TRIUMPHANT (119:129-131)
   A. Living by God's Word (119:129)
   B. Lighted by God's Word (119:130)
   C. Longing for God's Word (119:131)
II. THE PSALMIST AS TREMBLING (119:132-136)
   A. Distance Is Sensed (119:132)
   B. Direction Is Sought (119:133)
   C. Deliverance Is Supplicated (119:134)
   D. Darkness Is Scattered (119:135)
   E. Disaster Is Seen (119:136)

IN THIS SEGMENT OF HIS SONG, the psalmist is seen both triumphing and trembling. His circumstances have not altered; he still fluctuates between contemplation of his situation and contemplation of the Scriptures. He still has difficulty with the fact that God has not stepped in sovereignly and delivered him. But he is singing.

I. THE PSALMIST AS TRIUMPHANT (119:129-131)

The singer expresses his triumph on three levels. First, he tells us that he is:

A. Living by God's Word (119:129)

"Thy testimonies are wonderful: therefore doth my soul keep them." God's Word *is* wonderful, in all kinds of ways. It is wonderful in its *sufficiency.* The Mosaic Law was stated in 613 commandments. That was sufficient. What other nation could conclude all its legal business within such narrow compass? In the United States we keep thousands at work in Congress, the Senate, and state legislatures just to keep adding new laws to the statute books. God stripped the entire government processes in Israel down to manageable proportions. He Himself passed the laws and did so with a remarkable economy of re-

381

quirements. Yet they were sufficient. The entire personal, political, financial, moral, religious, and social life of the Hebrew people was covered by those laws.

God's Word is wonderful in its *simplicity*. The laws that made up the Mosaic legal code were divided into two major categories. There were *moral* laws and *ceremonial* laws. Failure to keep God's law was punished. Failure to keep God's law incurred a debt to society which had to be paid; it also incurred guilt before God which needed to be atoned. Provision was made in the ceremonial laws for that guilt to be covered.

None of the laws was complicated. They contained none of the verbiage so dear to the legal mind today. They were stated in straightforward language. A child could memorize the whole legal code in a matter of weeks. What could be simpler than "Thou shalt not kill—thou shalt not steal—thou shalt not commit adultery—thou shalt not bear false witness—thou shalt not covet . . ."? Only a few words each. Words that immediately ally themselves to the conscience so that nothing more needs to be said.

God's Word is wonderful in its *sagacity*. No wiser laws have ever been framed. They were marked by *sternness* ("an eye for an eye and a tooth for a tooth") but also by *sympathy* ("Thou shalt not seethe a kid in his mother's milk"). They were *punitive*, carrying the death penalty for things like murder, adultery, kidnapping, witchcraft, sodomy, and bestiality; they were *protective*, containing wise provisions for health and hygiene. They were *menacing* ("Beware, beware"), but they were *merciful* (as, for instance, the provision of cities of refuge for the man guilty of accidental manslaughter).

No wonder the psalmist could say, "Thy testimonies are wonderful: therefore doth my soul keep them." With a complete Bible before us we can surely say a resounding "Amen!" to that.

The psalmist was also:

B. Lighted by God's Word (119:130)

"The entrance of Thy words giveth light; it giveth understanding unto the simple." The psalmist here underlines:

1. The Chief Blessing of God's Word

God's Word gives light. People can shut light out of their life, of course, and remain forever in the dark, or they can open the windows of their soul and let that light flood in.

Light reveals dirt. There was a time when I lived in a cold climate, where every year storm windows had to be put in place to help keep out the cold. That annual chore always necessitated washing windows. The storm windows, stored all summer, had to be cleansed of the dust and dirt that had accumulated on them. The regular windows had to be cleansed, too—by strict order of the lady of the house. Finally, after an exhausting day, the last storm window would be fitted into place and with a sigh of relief I would sit back, thankful that the job was done for another year. The next day the sun would come out and the slanting rays would shine on the windows and reveal the streaks, the spots, the places that were missed. The light revealed the dirt. The windows had looked quite acceptable in yesterday's shadows, but in today's sunshine all the grime was conspicuously revealed.

Light reveals disorder. Things may be badly out of place in a room and, as long as it is dark, it makes no difference. But when light is turned on, the mess and muddle can be clearly seen. Just so, God's Word reveals the disorder of our lives.

Light reveals direction. A man stumbling through the darkness may have no idea where he is or what immediate perils lie at his feet. Light changes all that. It gives us a sense of direction, enabling us to see signposts and landmarks. This is one of the chief blessings of God's Word. It gives *light.*

The psalmist also underlines:

2. The Chief Beneficiary of God's Word

"The entrance of Thy words giveth light; it giveth understanding unto the simple." Not to the sophisticated, but to the simple. Many are too clever to believe the Bible. They have listened to what Paul calls "philosophy and vain deceit" or, as J. B. Phillips renders that, "intellectualism and high-sounding nonsense." The Bible speaks to the teachable. It has little or nothing to say to those who wish to argue and contradict. God's Word is not given as the starting point for debate, but as the starting point for obedience. It gives understanding to the simple. The little girl, for instance, who worked for Naaman's wife, had a deeper understanding of God and His ways than did the king of Israel in all his pomp and majesty. That country boy from Canaan, sold by his jealous brothers to the Midianites and resold as a slave to Potiphar, had more wisdom and insight than all the magicians of Egypt.

The psalmist was also:

C. Longing for God's Word (119:131)

"I opened my mouth, and panted: for I longed for Thy commandments." The psalmist may have had in mind a dog lying panting in the sun. Or a mountain deer with its mouth open, its flanks heaving as it gasps for air or for a drink from a distant stream. He had often seen such a sight—expressive of the whole being longing and yearning with a craving that will not be denied and which is a torture to the body. In just such a way his soul panted after God's Word. He needed it. He could not live without it. It was the breath of life to his soul, the water of life to his inner being.

Such a desire for God's Word is certainly not the normal human experience. Most people, even Christian people, ignore their Bibles—just as they ordinarily ignore the stars. Stars are a spectacular phenomenon but we are so used to them that we scarcely give them a passing glance. Someone has commented that if the stars came out only once every five hundred years people would certainly wait up all night to see them. They would never stop talking about the marvelous sight. But as it is, the stars are such a common sight that people generally ignore them.

They do that with the Bible. It is in our mother tongue. We have a score of versions from which to choose. It is available in any bookstore for a few dollars. There are societies organized to give it away free. Most Christians have several, if not dozens of, copies in their home. We take it for granted.

Martyrs gave their blood to make it available to us, scholars gave their lives to translate it, yet we so often yawn over it or let our thoughts wander when it is read.

But let it be taken away from us! Let the communists come in and ban this Book from bookstores and libraries, arrest those who preach it, make it an offense against the state to read it. Then its value will be known. Then, like the psalmist, we will long for it. Why wait until it is taken away to appreciate it?

So we see the psalmist as a triumphant man, his whole life revolving around the Bible as the earth revolves around the sun. Next we see:

II. THE PSALMIST AS TREMBLING (119:132-136)

In the next five verses the psalmist depicts five states of soul. He senses danger without and within. His see-saw experiences are not foreign to us; we experience them too. Moments of exultation, as we revel in some delightful truth from God's Word that has gripped our soul, are followed by a swing of the pendulum, and we give way to depression and defeat.

A. Distance Is Sensed (119:132)

"Look Thou upon me, and be merciful unto me, as Thou usest to do unto those that love Thy name." The psalmist feels that there is a barrier somewhere, a reason why God does not act for him as He has acted so often for others in the past. But at the same time he does not lose his confidence in God's Word.

In this situation he has three things to say about God. He says first that *God is able to see:* "Look Thou upon me." God sees. Our attention is focused on that fact on the very first page of Holy Writ. Seven times we read in Genesis 1 that "God saw." What was true of creation was true of redemption. When God called Moses to go down to Egypt to be the kinsman-redeemer of Israel, He said, "I have surely seen the affliction of My People" (Exodus 3:7). Nothing happens that God does not see. Hagar's cry was, "Thou, God, seest me." That, of course, can be a frightening thought if He sees us doing something wrong, but it can be a comforting thought when we are in peril.

The psalmist says that *God is anxious to save:* "Look Thou upon me, and be merciful unto me." Such is the nature of God. He is merciful to nations, much more willing to bless them with revival than to blast them with ruin. Thus He sows His messengers into the world, a William Carey here, a John Wesley there. He is merciful to individuals. Calvary is God's long-standing advertisement of that fact. But we need to make it personal. "Be Thou merciful unto *me.*"

The psalmist says that *God is always the same:* "Look Thou upon me, and be merciful unto me, as Thou usest to be merciful unto those that love Thy name." God is no respecter of persons. He is always the same. The God of Abraham and the God of Isaac can become the God even of Jacob. The Lord who met with Moses, who delivered David, who sought out Solomon, has not changed. In effect, the psalmist says: "Lord, You must treat me the same way You have treated others. You were merciful to Jacob, merciful to Job, merciful to Jonah. You must be merciful to me."

B. Direction Is Sought (119:133)

"Order my steps in Thy word: and let not any iniquity have dominion over me." The two always go together: the *overcoming* life and the *obedient* life. The psalmist wanted his steps to be ordered by God. God gives the orders; we supply the obedience. God will not order our steps if we have no intention of doing what He says. If we have run into a period in our lives marked by silence from God, then it is likely that somewhere along the line we have stopped being obedient to God or have trusted in some human expedient instead of in Him.

We see an example of that in the case of King Saul, who was so persistent in his rebellion against God's Word that Samuel had to rebuke him: "Behold, to obey is better than sacrifice" (1 Samuel 15:22). The time came when God so completely stopped speaking to Saul that, without chart or compass, he soon made shipwreck of his life on the quicksands of witchcraft. No wonder Samuel said to Saul, "Rebellion is as the sin of witchcraft" (1 Samuel 15:23). It was about the last thing Samuel ever said to him.

An obedient life, on the other hand, is always an overcoming life. The psalmist says, "And let not iniquity have dominion over me." A person whose steps are ordered of the Lord will be led in the paths of victory.

The New Testament tells the same story. God says, "Let not sin therefore reign in your mortal body" (Romans 6:12). We take our stand by faith on that command and then God says, "Sin shall not have dominion over you" (Romans 6:14). We take our stand with God against sin and its power is broken in our lives.

James states the same principle: "Submit yourselves therefore to God [that comes first]. Resist the devil, and he will flee from you." That is the natural consequence.

"Order my steps in Thy word, and let not sin have dominion over me." That is the kind of prayer God is always going to answer. He will make it His business to stop the growth of iniquity in our lives. So Abraham discovered. His prior meeting with the king of Salem fortified him against his coming meeting with the king of Sodom. Abraham was able to take his stand on a fresh revelation from God and treat with indifference the offer of the king of Sodom—"Give me the souls, and you can take the spoils." Lot, who evidently had no such prior ordering of his steps in God's Word, fell an easy prey to the suggestion of vile Sodom's king.

C. Deliverance Is Supplicated (119:134)

"Deliver me from the oppression of man: so will I keep Thy precepts." It would seem that, when he prayed this, the psalmist was in a situation that made it difficult for him to keep God's precepts. Since we do not know who this psalmist was, we cannot say what his circumstances were. Perhaps he was in prison. He was certainly being oppressed. His enemies had the upper hand and had him under surveillance or under lock and key. Many duties enjoined by the law were impossible for him to keep, but he wanted to keep them and he would have if he were free.

D. Darkness Is Scattered (119:135)

"Make Thy face to shine upon Thy Servant; and teach me Thy statutes." The sun always shines. It shines even on the dullest day. Even when it is pouring rain, the sun is still shining. A breath from heaven can blow away the clouds.

Just so, God's face never ceases to shine on us. His smile is warm and bright even when circumstances arise that seem to obscure Him from us. Satan can trap us in some error, the flesh can cause us to fall, the world can oppress us, just as it did the psalmist, as he says in the previous verse. Or as the earth, rotating on its axis, takes us away from the sun and plunges us into darkness, so we ourselves can turn away from God, following the natural laws of our wayward hearts. But God does not change.

"Make Thy face to shine upon Thy servant." The psalmist felt that some dark, obscuring cloud had come between him and his God. He wanted that cloud removed.

So might David have prayed after his sin with Bathsheba, when the darkness rolled in, when he sat on his throne terribly conscious that God was no longer shining on him, acutely aware of what had happened to King Saul. After his repentance he was willing once more to be taught of the Lord.

> Sun of my soul, Thou Saviour dear,
> It is not night if Thou art near;
> Oh, may no earth-born cloud arise
> To hide me from my Saviour's eyes.

E. Disaster Is Seen (119:136)

"Rivers of waters run down mine eyes, because they keep not Thy law." Suddenly the psalmist's heart goes out to his oppressors, to those who are persecuting him. He feels sorry for them, since they are men like himself. But they are lost; they need God. The psalmist is transported right out of his own dispensation into ours. He prays as Jesus prayed when men hammered His hands to the tree, as Stephen prayed when men took up rocks to stone him.

The psalmist did more than pray for his foes. He wept for them. This is the spirit that brings revival. It seems that nothing gets done for God in this world apart from tears. Sin, as Hosea tells us, not only breaks God's law, it breaks His heart. Thus Jesus was "a man of sorrows and acquainted with grief." Tears were never far from His eyes. He looked into hearts and homes, and what He saw there broke His heart.

Sin has ploughed this planet with sorrow. It has planted every graveyard, it has made necessary every hospital, it has built every prison, every psychiatric institution, every slum. Were it not for sin we could disband our armies, dissolve our police forces, open our prisons, dismiss our legislators, unlock our doors. As Jesus looked at the ravages of sin He wept.

So, far from hating his enemies, the psalmist pitied them and wept for them. It is the secret of revival:

> Weep o'er the erring one,
> Lift up the fallen;
> Tell them of Jesus, the mighty to save.

Psalm 119:137-144

GOD'S WORD IS RIGHT

I. The Psalmist's Discernment (119:137-138)
   The righteousness of:
   A. The Lord's Character (119:137)
   B. The Lord's Commandments (119:138)
II. The Psalmist's Devotion (119:139)
III. The Psalmist's Delight (119:140)
IV. The Psalmist's Distress (119:141-143)
   A. His Correct View of Self (119:141)
   B. His Correct View of Scripture (119:142)
   C. His Correct View of Suffering (119:143)
V. The Psalmist's Desire (119:144)

THE PSALMIST CONTINUES with his inexhaustible theme, occupied with the most wonderful Book ever written, a Book without parallel in the world's libraries. He is occupied with the Word of God.

In this section we begin with:

I. The Psalmist's Discernment (119:137-138)

Now the psalmist turns to the general theme of divine righteousness. He begins with:

A. The Lord's Character (119:137)

"Righteous art Thou, O Lord, and upright are Thy judgments." God is always right. He is right in His character and He is right in His commands. That is one of the most basic lessons to be learned in life, a lesson some people never learn.

If God speaks *to instruct us*—as He does, for instance, in the matter of the origin of the universe, the species, and the human race—then what God says is right. In the end, all other teachings will be proven wrong. It may take a long time. It may seem that error has a firm grip on humanity and is all-triumphant. It may rule supreme for now in the halls of science, but, in the end, what God says will be seen to have been right all along.

For instance, the Bible has always said that the world was a sphere and hung upon nothing. For centuries people believed it was flat. The Bible was right; they were wrong. Today the popular theory is that man and the anthropoid apes have a common ancestor. The Bible says that God created man in His own image and after His own likeness. It flatly contradicts the theory of evolution. And God is right.

If God speaks *to inhibit us*—as He does, in hundreds of commandments that cut across our sinful wants and wishes—then what He says is right. Today, for instance, society permits sexual perversion as an alternate lifestyle. God says that it is wrong and that those who indulge in homosexual practice will come under His severest displeasure. Society may say what it will, but society is wrong and God is right.

If God speaks *to inspire us*—as He does, for instance, when He sets before us the plight of a lost world, the preciousness of a single soul, the infinite cost of Calvary, the eternal destinies that await all of us beyond the grave, the priceless privilege of being a child of God and joint-heir with Jesus Christ, and the appalling disaster of a lost eternity—then God is right. All lesser views of life are wrong. Our highest, holiest, happiest destiny lies in being conformed to that "good and acceptable and perfect will of God." That will of His may put us in a slum or send us to the Senate. It may put us to preach in a pulpit or put us to preach in a prison. But God's will is always right. It is impossible for God to be wrong, for Him to make any mistakes, for Him to do or say anything but what is right. The psalmist's discernment had taught him that.

Then he speaks about the righteousness of:

B. The Lord's Commandments (119:138)

"Thy testimonies that Thou hast commanded are righteous and very faithful." It is impossible for God ever to lead us astray, for Him ever to ask us to do something wrong.

In the halls of the American Congress one finds two kinds of people, the legislators and the lobbyists. The politician is there to make the laws. The pressure groups are there to influence those laws, to see that the only laws passed are the ones their particular group wants. The gun lobby wants no laws that will interfere with the right of people to own weapons. The pro-abortionist wants no laws that will restrict a woman's right to end unwanted pregnancies. The sexual deviant wants laws that will protect his lifestyle. Thus it is with our laws. All too often, instead of being righteous and faithful, they simply reflect the interest of whichever side can bring the most pressure to bear on politicians.

God's laws are not like that. He is not swayed by public opinion. He is not running for office. Nor is He running this planet along democratic lines. His laws are not influenced by polls or pressure groups. God's laws are righteous and faithful. They are impartial, imperial, impeccable.

They are magnificent in scope and substance. In His law, God has spoken to moral issues, political issues, social issues. He has spoken His mind about sex, sanitation, stealing. He has spoken about diet and dress, family and financial matters, warfare and welfare. He has addressed Himself impartially to sovereigns and to slaves.

Moses led about three and one-half million people out of Egypt, many of them comprising what the Holy Spirit calls "a mixed multitude," people who were not Hebrews by birth, but a conglomeration of people who participated in the emancipation and were accepted by God's grace.

The entire mass of people, Hebrews and fellow-travelers alike, were newly liberated slaves. They had no central government, no social conscience, no systematic religion. Yet within three months thay had the most comprehensive and compassionate legal code the world has ever known. The Mosaic Law was not the product of human reasoning. It was not modeled by Moses on Egyptian law learned during his days as prince in Pharaoh's court. It was a law handed down to him intact by God, given by direct divine revelation, and intended to be a model of legislation for all mankind.

Next we note:

II. THE PSALMIST'S DEVOTION (119:139)

"My zeal hath consumed me, because mine enemies have forgotten Thy words." The psalmist sets his devotion to the Scriptures in contrast with his enemies' forgetfulness of God. As Joseph's goodness shines all the more brightly in Genesis because it is set against the background of Judah's sin and the spite of his other brothers, so the psalmist's devotion to God's Word is brighter because it is set like a diamond against the background of general disinterest in the Scriptures by those around.

"My zeal hath consumed me," he says. We are reminded at once of the Lord Jesus. The scene is Jerusalem, the courts of the temple are in view, especially that portion of the temple courtyard assigned to the Gentiles. There, with contempt for God and Gentiles alike, the merchants and money changers had set up shop. The time was Passover as Jesus came into the Holy City, His first visit since beginning His public ministry. One sweeping glance around that courtyard and His holy soul took fire. The place had been converted into a market. Behind the somewhat dubious transactions taking place was the power of the Sadducees who had vested interests in the temple and who farmed out the concessions—for a price.

The Lord Jesus took it all in, and then He deliberately drove them all out—one glorious Man against the system and the syndicate. The disciples watched Him and Scripture came instantly to their minds: "The zeal of Thine house hath eaten me up" (John 2:17). It was a quotation from Psalm 69:9. It could equally have been a quotation from this one.

Jesus had to do it all over again later, at the end of His ministry. This time He showed that they had indeed forgotten God's words: "It is written," He said, "My house shall be called of all nations the house of prayer, but ye have made it a den of thieves" (Mark 11:17; Isaiah 56:7). The first time his zeal consumed him it led to a conversion—Nicodemus came for that famous midnight talk with Jesus. The second time it led to a conspiracy—the scribes and Pharisees consulted together to get rid of Him.

This Old Testament singer, too, much as he might pity and pray for his enemies, nevertheless felt his soul stirred at what they were doing. It was not so much what they were doing to him; it was what they were doing to the Lord—that was what incensed him. That was what caused him to catch fire and what made his soul blaze out: "*Mine* enemies have forgotten *Thy* word," he says.

It is evident from this that his enemies were people who had once known God's Word. It made them all the more culpable. It is better never to have known God's Word than, having known it, to set it aside as of no account—which, of course, is the capital sin of multitudes of people today, brought up in Christian homes, taught God's Word since childhood, who now are living in total disregard of God's laws.

III. THE PSALMIST'S DELIGHT (119:140)

"Thy word is very pure: therefore Thy servant loveth it." God's Word is not pure because it has been refined. It is pure because God is its author, and that is the way He is.

Anyone who has done any writing knows how severe is the refining process through which a manuscript has to go before it is ready to appear in print. First comes the rough draft, usually typed, double-spaced with plenty of margin space top and bottom and on the sides. The resulting pages of copy must be read with a critical eye. Usually it is repetitious—too wordy, sentences are clumsy, there are spelling errors and grammatical mistakes. Sometimes whole paragraphs need to be deleted, put in as footnotes, or rewritten. The author decides that this illustration is redundant or that thought is ambiguous. He gets busy with his pencil and, by the time he has finished, it all needs to be retyped.

The second draft is better, but again changes have to be made before it can be submitted to a publisher. Then the editors take over, revising and refining things still more. Even when the work has gone to the typesetter, and the galleys appear, the author can still see changes he wishes to make.

At last the work appears in print and, horror of horrors, in reading it through, the author finds he has made a mistake. He has put in a wrong date or he has misquoted a source. And even when the book has gone through a first half dozen printings the author sees areas that need to be altered, so he suggests a complete or partial revision in the light of changes that have taken place in the field or because his own thinking has matured. Not so God's Word.

The psalmist loved God's Word because it was so pure. He could drink in God's Word without fear of contamination. Such, certainly, cannot be said about the writings of the world's false religions, many of which are polluted at their source. God's Word can make the reader pure as well.

IV. THE PSALMIST'S DISTRESS (119:141-143)

Again the fact that the psalmist is in trouble comes to the fore. Yet in spite of his distress an element of assurance and hope is evident, based on the Word of God.

We note:

A. His Correct View of Self (119:141)

"I am small and despised: yet do not I forget Thy precepts." In this brief statement the psalmist makes three observations. First he says, *I am small.* Being small in size tends to make a person feel inferior. In our society we have come to admire bigness, as though quantity could ever be a substitute for quality.

King Saul was physically big. The trouble was he was not big enough. He stood head and shoulders above others and that is what attracted the people to him. The problem with being merely big is that sooner or later we meet somebody bigger than ourselves, as Saul discovered when he ran into Goliath. Then his own bigness was no use. A stripling by the name of David was ten times the man Saul was when it came to fighting giants. So the psalmist tells the Lord that he was small. That cast him upon the bigness of God.

Then he says, *I am scorned.* The small man very often is. David was. When he presented himself to Saul with his offer to fight the Philistine giant he ran into three sets of critics. There were the *family* critics, his brothers who told him to go on home where he belonged. There was the *official* critic, King Saul, who told him he was a mere youth, no material for a duel with a giant. Finally there was the *enemy* critic, Goliath himself who ridiculed him for thinking he could fight *him,* the mighty champion of Gath.

Then the psalmist says, *I am smart:* "Yet do I not forget Thy precepts." David could see the shortsightedness of measuring a man by his height. Nor should a man be measured by the number of degrees he has after his name. That is the world's yardstick, not God's. God measures a man by His Word—and for that reason this small man was a very large man indeed (and he wrote the longest psalm!). He was very much bigger than the enemies he mentioned in the previous verse.

B. His Correct View of Scripture (119:142)

"Thy righteousness is an everlasting righteousness, and Thy law is the truth." Righteousness is that quality in God which causes Him always to say and do what is right. Does God decide to create a hundred million galaxies? He does it because it is the right thing to do. We may not understand why He has done it. We may not see much sense in billions of tons of red-hot matter floating in space. But then, we don't know very much. They are there because it is right that they should be there.

Does God create angels and archangels, cherubim and seraphim? He does so because it is the right thing to do.

When Lucifer falls and drags a multitude of the heavenly host with him, does God hold His hand from judgment—even though He knows that Satan will involve the human race in ruin and spread sin like a plague across the planet? He does so because it is right. We may not think it right, but God knows it is right.

This quality of the everlasting righteousness of God underlies the Bible. If we want to be right about anything we need only to see what the Bible says about it. If the Bible speaks to any subject, the Bible will always be right. The psalmist had a correct view of the Scriptures.

C. His Correct View of Suffering (119:143)

"Trouble and anguish have taken hold on me: yet Thy commandments are my delights." Trouble and anguish are two of the devil's jailors. He uses them to imprison our souls. The best way to get free from their clutch is to reach out for the golden key the psalmist here puts into our hand: "Yet Thy commandments are my delights." It is this that has given the martyrs triumph in the face of death.

It has often been observed that sometimes criminals can face death with calmness and courage. The political prisoners in the Bastille could face the guillotine with a haughty indifference, fierce pride of class making them scorn to show fear. But Christian martyrs have met death with jubilation, facing the fangs of wild beasts in the arena with hymns of praise to God, singing in the fire when burned at the stake, pouring out praises to God and praying for their tormentors.

Trouble and anguish, Satan's grim jailors, could not silence the song of the psalmist.

V. The Psalmist's Desire (119:144)

"The righteousness of Thy testimonies is everlasting: give me understanding, and I shall live." The Bible is made out of the same stuff as eternity. Jesus said, "Heaven and earth shall pass away: but My words shall not pass away" (Mark 13:31). "Forever, O God, Thy word is established in heaven." That is the Holy Spirit's witness.

Some books become classics and outlive their authors. They become national treasures and survive from age to age. But even the classics can fall out of vogue. The Bible, however, is not just a classic, dependent on the whims of an age for its popularity. The Bible will outlast the universe. It transcends time. It was hammered out of the eternal ages. It is the very breath of God.

No wonder the psalmist sings, "Give me understanding, and I shall live." The everlasting life inherent in the Scriptures can be transmitted to the human soul. "Being born again," says Peter, "not of corruptible seed, but of incorruptible, by the word of God, which liveth and abideth for ever" (1 Peter 1:23). The God who breathed into Adam's clay so that Adam became a living soul breathes now by His Holy Spirit through His Word into human hearts so that we can become quickened spirits. "Give me understanding and I shall live"—live for evermore. That was the psalmist's desire.

Psalm 119:145-152

CRYING WITH THE WHOLE HEART

IN THIS SEGMENT OF THE PSALM the singer's adverse circumstances continue unchanged. He is still raising his voice in cries of desperate appeal to God. Indeed, the first half of the segment is a sustained cry. We hear the psalmist crying, calling, and finally confessing.

I. THE PSALMIST CRYING (119:145-148)

We notice three things about the psalmist's cries as they rise heavenward and then echo down the ages of time.

A. How Fervent He Was (119:145)

"I cried with my whole heart; here me, O LORD: I will keep Thy statutes." There are many kinds of cries, as anyone who has been around a baby for any length of time knows. There is the bad temper cry, when the baby is just plain mad and when it wishes to advertise to the world that it is a true child of Adam and has inherited, tiny as it is, a fallen human nature. That kind of cry can be amusing to watch if one is not deafened by the din. The little fellow screws up his face, waves his little arms, goes fiery red, opens his mouth, and yells. It is best ignored. The sooner he learns that *that* kind of behavior is unacceptable,

396

and gets him nowhere, the better.

There is the peevish cry, the whining, nagging cry of a child who is bored or miserable or sulking because he cannot get what he wants. The child often doesn't know what he wants or wouldn't be satisfied with it even if it was given to him.

Then there is the cry of a child in pain, of a child who has been hurt or frightened. *That* kind of cry calls for immediate attention. *That* is the kind of cry the psalmist raises here. "I cried with my whole heart," he says. He was frightened, he was in need, he needed help. Our loving heavenly Father recognizes that kind of cry and always responds to it—not always in the way we would expect perhaps, nor on our limited time scale. But He never ignores a cry like that.

Alexander Whyte, in commenting on Elijah's prayers, says that although Elijah was a man subject to like passions as we are, Elijah put his *passions* into *prayers*. In other words he knew how to cry with his whole heart. That was why he was able to see such mighty miracles wrought for God. Like him, the psalmist here puts his passions into his prayers. But he does something more.

He puts his promises into his prayers as well: "Hear me, O Lord: I will keep Thy statutes." Those are two very good ingredients in the recipe for prayer—the emotional and the volitional. The one says, "I am desperate"; the other says, "I am determined." The one says, "Rescue me!" The other says, "Rule me!" The answer to such prayer is never far away.

B. How Frustrated He Was (119:146)

"I cried unto Thee; save me, and I shall keep Thy testimonies." Here the psalmist repeats himself. He says the same things, in different words perhaps, but the same thing. Again he promises that he will keep God's Word, out of sheer gratitude if for no other reason. This repetition of the prayer and the promise is a kind of twofold witness. The psalmist, of course, was familiar with the legal demand in Israel that there be two or three witnesses if every word was to be established. Since he had no other witness to corroborate his testimony he repeats himself to make his own pledge and promise its own second witness. This was not *vain* repetition. This was *validating* repetition, the psalmist's way of taking his oath before God.

Often, when in desperate straights, people will promise the Lord to live better lives (or whatever), if only He will act on their behalf. In itself that may not be bad. Sometimes it is the very reason why God turns on the heat. He did that, for example, with Jonah. It was not until Jonah found himself in what he calls "the belly of hell" that he broke down. "I will pay my vows," he said and within moments he was a free man and his promise put to the test. The word of the Lord came to him a second time telling him to get going to Nineveh. Jonah had seen enough of one of God's prisons never to want to get into another. But frequently people do go back on their promise to God. God, however, is not to be mocked like that. To the man He healed at the pool of Bethesda, Jesus said, "Sin no more, lest a worse thing come unto thee" (John 5:14).

Here, the psalmist wanted to make his promise doubly sure, so he repeated it.

We think of Lot. We cannot help but wonder what went on in the mind of that misguided individual when he and his family were in chains, being forced-marched toward the distant east, destined for the slave markets of the orient. His fortune was gone, his family was in ruins. Did he pray? Did he make great promises to God for the future if only he were delivered from his plight? Probably he did. Surely Lot prayed, "Save me, and I shall keep Thy testimonies." If so, it didn't take him long to go back on his word. All it took was the whispered promise of Sodom's king that he could "sit in the gate of Sodom." He could be elected to high office in the government. And Lot was gone—to face a far worse disaster later on.

We notice not only how fervent this psalmist was, and how frustrated. He had prayed. His prayer had not been answered. He had promised. He promises again.

C. How Forward He Was (119:147-148)

His was persistent, importunate prayer. He not only knocked, he kept on knocking. He not only prayed, he pestered God's throne.

He tells us how forward he was in:

1. Praying before Rising in the Morning (119:147)

"I prevented [anticipated, forestalled] the dawning of the morning, and cried: I hoped in Thy word." How true that is to life. We have been in the same place ourselves, worrying, fearful, desperate. Sleep is driven from our eyes; we anticipate the morning. Bed becomes an instrument of torture and we get up because we can no longer toss and turn. This is the third time the psalmist has mentioned his crying, the third time in three verses. There can be no doubt he is in trouble.

"I hoped in Thy word," he said. That is the worst part of it. Even God's Word seemed to have failed. Verses like this, which sound so much like our own experience, drive us back to Job. There were times when Job lost hope. But even then, in his darkest hours, when the heavens seemed as brass and his pain and anguish more than he could bear, even then God was watching over him. Job did not know *why* these disasters had overtaken him. He knew nothing about the secret counsels of the most high, of that insolent challenge flung in God's face by the father of lies. He did not even know if his sorrows would ever end. His own wife had already actually suggested suicide as an answer. "I hoped in Thy word," Job might have said. The silence of God was the greatest trial of all. But if God was silent, He certainly was not absent. Not a single stroke fell on Job that God had not measured first.

> The soul that on Jesus hath leaned for repose
> I will not, I will not desert to his foes;
> That soul, though all hell should endeavor to shake,
> I'll never, no never, no never forsake.

2. Praying before Retiring in the Evening (119:148)

Long before his bed became a wrack, he would pray. Lying in bed waiting for sleep to come, he would pray. "Mine eyes prevent [anticipate, forestall] the night watches, that I might meditate in Thy word." He turned those moments before sleep came into good use. He composed himself for sleep by prayerfully turning over the Word of God in his mind. In other words, he had what today we would call a quiet time.

Surely most of us waste far too much time. Someone has calculated that the average believer, if he lives to be 75 years of age, spends 25 years asleep, 17 years at work, 6 years in traveling, 7½ years in dressing, 9 years in watching television, 6 years being sick, and only 4 years in prayer and Bible study. Imagine 4 years out of 75 preparing for eternity, less than half the time spent watching television. Suppose we converted half the travel time, mostly idle time, into praying or memorizing Scripture instead of daydreaming. Suppose we invested most of the time spent dressing engaging our minds in prayer. Suppose we took an hour less sleep a night and devoted the time to concentrated Bible study. Suppose we cut two-thirds of the time spent watching television and devoted that time to reading the Bible, studying the Word, and praying for family, friends, missionaries, and all those hundreds of other things we say we are too busy to pray about. Why, we could increase the time we spend in prayer and Bible study by 19 years. Instead of a paltry 4 years, we would spend 23 years in getting ready for the judgment seat of Christ.

F. W. Boreham used to tell the story of a gypsy he knew in his youth. She would come to the village green near where he lived and open her chest of treasures. From that chest she would take all kinds of things, fingering and fondling the items one by one and offering them for sale. She would announce the price, permit no haggling, offer the item, and unless it was purchased at once, back it went into the chest. On no account would she take it out again and give the people standing around a second chance to purchase it. The bargain had to be taken at once or the chance was gone.

"Redeeming the time," says Paul. God offers each of us a fleeting moment of time. We can seize it and freight it down with something for eternity, or it passes back unredeemed into God's keeping to be a witness against us at the judgment seat. Life's golden moments never return. This wise old singer made it his plan to buy up the time.

II. THE PSALMIST CALLING (119:149-151)

A. His Simple Plea Is Described (119:149)

"Hear my voice according unto Thy lovingkindness: O LORD, quicken me according to Thy judgment." The word *hear* is emphatic. It could be rendered, "O do hear." The psalmist wanted the Lord to respond *with love*. He based his plea on the lovingkindness of God.

He asked God to "hear *my* voice." Only God could do that. At this very moment there are over five billion people in the world, all talking at once, many of them addressing themselves to God. Who but God could single out one solitary, individual voice out of such a babel?

All of us have stood in the lobby of a church or public building as a service or performance ends. People pour out and linger for a few minutes to talk before going on their way. The resulting noise is bedlam, a total confusion of sound. Occasionally one voice, more strident than the rest, will rise for a moment above the general din. The listener might catch a phrase or two, but it is soon lost again in the general clatter of conversation. By straining one's ear it is possible occasionally to pick up a stray strand of conversation from someone nearby, but after a snatch or two it is lost again. Certainly it is not possible to follow a conversation between two people several feet away. God can, and does, because He is omniscient. Omniscience is an attribute of deity alone—that is why it is such folly to pray to the virgin Mary or to one of the "saints." When the psalmist asks God to hear *him*, he has no doubt that God can.

As we have seen, he based his plea on God's love. Occasionally when preaching I have seen a woman quietly rise from her seat and slip out. More often than not I am right in my guess, especially if the nursery happens to be close to the auditorium. Between that woman and her baby is a wall. In that nursery is the clamor of a dozen children. But that mother is first and foremost a mother. Love quickens her ears. She hears her baby's cry. *That* is how the psalmist wanted the Lord to respond—with love.

He also wanted God to respond *with life*. He says, "Quicken me according to Thy judgments." He wanted God to make him alive to what He had to say to him in the circumstances of life. He wanted to be as swift and sensitive to recognize the voice of God as he wanted God to be to recognize his. That is a lesson worth learning.

B. His Sudden Plight Is Described (119:150)

"They draw nigh that follow after mischief: they are far from Thy law." Some render that, "They draw nigh that follow after me maliciously." *Near* and *far*. That describes them perfectly.

They were far from God. They were in the far country of the prodigal. They had long since departed from God's law. The distance between them and God was not to be measured in miles, however, but in malice. The quickest measure of how far a person has departed down the road that leads to destruction can be seen in the question, "How much is this person like Christ?" Who could imagine Jesus being spiteful or malicious, moody or mean, jealous or hostile, bitter or deceitful, or any such thing? Such a thought is impossible. *That,* however, is the real measure by which we mark out the miles we or any one else has drifted from God—especially now that the Word has been made flesh.

They were far from God but they were near to the psalmist. "They draw nigh" he said. They were after him. Their tongues were sharp, two-edged swords. Their words were poisoned arrows. They were intent on mischief and motivated by malice. Against such persons there was no defense apart from God.

C. His Safe Place Is Described (119:151)

No one could protect him except God. "Thou art near, O LORD; and all Thy commandments are truth." In the previous verse the psalmist had said that his enemies were near. Now he says that God is near. That was enough.

An illustration of this comes from the exodus. Pharaoh, frightened out of his wits by the death of his firstborn and the loud lamentations all over the land of Egypt, finally consented to let his Hebrew captives go. Some three million or more left after having first despoiled the Egyptians of enormous stores of wealth. Then came second thoughts. Pharaoh thought of the land of Egypt lying desolate and ruined by the plagues. Cattle were dead in countless herds, crops were destroyed, his people were dead by the thousand, vast amounts of treasure had been carried off by the Hebrews. It was as though Egypt had been ravaged by Assyria or Babylon. And millions of able-bodied slaves, the backbone of the Egyptian labor force, had gone.

As the shock of the Passover visitation subsided, Pharaoh's wrath arose. Enraged and humiliated, he made up his mind. He would bring them back. He would make them pay. Oh, how he would make them pay! The army was mobilized and its swift war chariots raced out onto the plains. Hard behind came the eager, shouting cavalry. Soon the rearguard of Israel saw the coming storm. Word was passed to Moses, who appealed to God. And God acted. The Shekinah glory cloud moved as a rearguard between Egypt and Israel. To get at *them* Pharaoh had to get past *Him*. Israel was safe.

So was the psalmist. His enemies were near, but so was God. That was all the protection he needed, the safe place he describes.

III. The Psalmist Confessing (119:152)

"Concerning Thy testimonies, I have known of old that Thou hast founded them for ever." It would be easier for everything else to fail than for God's Word to fail.

Forever takes us back a very long way. It takes us back before the Spirit of God inspired Moses to write the first page of Genesis, back before the fall of man, before the creation of man. It takes us back before the creation of the planet, before the creation of the galaxy, before the creation of all the galaxies in one fiery big bang. We go back for ever. And when we reach back as far as eternity in that direction, *that* was when this Word was founded. It has been around for a very long time—much longer than its critics.

Forever takes us on ahead a very long way. It takes us on past the sum of our life's short span, on past the soon-coming rapture of the church, on past the dark days of the great tribulation and the battle of Armageddon, on past the millennial age, on past the coming holocaust of the heavens, and on into the deathless ages of the new creation. On, forever on, as long as there is a God in Heaven! Forever. That is how long God's Word will endure. It will see the burial of all its foes. God's Word, founded before time was, will be firm and changeless when time shall be no more.

Such is God's Word. The psalmist confesses his faith in that.

A life insurance company has as its logo the rock of Gibraltar, a symbol of stability. It offers its policy holders "a piece of the rock." That is what God offers us—*a piece of the Rock forever.*

Psalm 119:153-160

WHEN AFFLICTION COMES

I. THE PSALMIST'S ASSESSMENT (119:153-156)
   A. His Situation (119:153-155)
      It made Him:
      1. More Thoughtful in Prayer (119:153-154)
         He Opens His Life to:
         a. God's Inspection (119:153)
         b. God's Intervention (119:154)
      2. More Thankful in Prayer (119:155)
   B. His Saviour (119:156)
II. THE PSALMIST'S ASSAILANTS (119:157-158)
   He was:
   A. Troubled by Their Attacks (119:157)
   B. Troubled by Their Attitude (119:158)
III. THE PSALMIST'S ASSURANCE (119:159-160)
   A. His Devotion to God's Word (119:159)
   B. His Discernment of God's Word (119:160)

A S SO OFTEN IN THIS PSALM, we find the singer once more tuning his harp to a minor key. The persecution he is facing is again preying on his mind. For the moment he is back in the valley, but he will not stay there for long. He takes himself in hand and looks again to the Lord, the source of his strength.

I. THE PSALMIST'S ASSESSMENT (119:153-156)

A. His Situation (119:153-155)

There is no doubt that what Cowper calls "a frowning Providence" can nag like a toothache. It is hard to forget or ignore. The one good thing that comes out of it is a new sense of our dependence on God.

The psalmist confesses here that his situation made him:

403

1. More Thoughtful in Prayer (119:153-154)

He opens his life, first, to:

a. God's Inspection (119:153)

"Consider mine affliction, and deliver me: for I do not forget Thy law." He draws attention here to a most important truth: Not all suffering and affliction are punitive. A growing segment of the Christian community thinks otherwise; if a person is sick, for instance, there must be sin in his life. Sickness is considered to be incompatible with spirituality. If one were "right with God," one would not be ill. If one had sufficient faith, there would be instant and miraculous healing.

That kind of teaching is a distortion of Scripture and is contrary to experience. The New Testament does not equate health and wealth with spirituality. The Sermon on the Mount begins with a series of beatitudes which ring strangely in the ears of "positive thinkers." Something *good* from God's point of view might be a desperate illness which suddenly puts eternity's values into perspective, or a crippling financial reverse which shows the deceptive transience of material things. The saints of the Old Testament era had far more right than we to claim physical and material wellbeing as their heritage; those things were part of the Old Covenant. They are not necessarily part of *our* inheritance in this world. The Gospels and the epistles warn us to watch out for stormy weather no matter how spiritual we might be.

"Consider mine affliction, and deliver me: for I do not forget Thy law," says the psalmist. That was sound foursquare gospel in his day. In the Old Testament the blessing promised was "the blessing of the LORD [that] maketh rich, and He addeth no sorrow with it" (Proverbs 10:22). There were however, exceptions even then, as the book of Job makes clear. Men like Jeremiah and Ezekiel were bluntly told by God that they were going to suffer. It is certain that affliction can be part of God's wise plan for His people today, a means of grace, an instrument in His hand to develop character and conviction.

The psalmist also opens up his life to:

b. God's Intervention (119:154)

"Plead my cause, and deliver me: quicken me according to Thy word." We have God's Word for it (though the psalmist did not have nearly such a clear statement on it in his day) that we do have an advocate with the Father: Jesus Christ the righteous. We have One of the highest authority, greatest skill, most compassionate nature, tenderest sympathy, and of the closest kin to plead our cause.

In fact, we have *two* advocates. We have the Lord Jesus and we have the Holy Spirit. "The Spirit Itself maketh intercession for us with groanings which cannot be uttered, and He That searcheth the hearts knoweth what is the mind of the Spirit, because He maketh intercession for the saints according to the will of God" (Romans 8:26-27).

The Spirit knows my heart, He knows His own mind, and He knows God's will. He is therefore able to bring all three into line. He is therefore eminently able to plead our cause—that every word of God for us might be established. We have that One of whom Job dreamed and for whom he groaned. Job, of course had Him too, had Him all the time, although he did not know it. All through his long and severe sufferings there was One ever standing in the shadows, drawing the line beyond which Satan in his malice might not go.

We have that One whom Joshua the high priest saw in the days of Zechariah. There Joshua stood in his filthy garments, in the presence of God, with Satan standing at his right hand to resist him (Zechariah 3:1). But he too had an advocate. He had Jehovah Himself to represent him, to redeem him, and to robe him.

We have the One whom Balaam met when hurrying headlong to curse the people of God, the One whom Laban met when he was furiously following Jacob. We have One, sitting there on the throne, in the supreme court of the universe, to plead our cause and to deliver us and to revive us according to God's Word.

The psalmist's situation, then, made him more thoughtful in prayer. It also made him:

2. More Thankful in Prayer (119:155)

"Salvation is far from the wicked: for they seek not Thy statutes." This is a solemn word to the unsaved. There are times when salvation is near, times when the Holy Spirit is at work, times when the conscience is on the wrack and the heart tender. The Holy Spirit warns us not to miss such moments. "Call ye upon Him while He is near," says the Old Testament prophet. "Jesus of Nazareth passeth by," says the Gospel text.

We often think of the wicked as being far from salvation and very often so they are. They are like the prodigal son in that far country. It was a long way home for the penitent prodigal. He had no idea he had gone so far until he started back. But there came a moment when the distance was dramatically shortened. "When he was yet a great way off" the father saw him, had compassion, and ran to meet him. Not, however, before many weary, woebegone miles lay behind.

"For they seek not Thy statutes" is the psalmist's explanation as to why human beings continue on in sin. There are none so blind as those who will not see. Equally, there are none so lost as those who will not seek. No condition is worse than being lost and not knowing it—to go on and on down a wrong path. What a terrible plight is that of the lost: to be lost, to be blind and deaf and past feeling, and not to realize it. It is bad enough for the wicked to be far from salvation. But when salvation is far from the wicked that is ten thousand times worse. "They seek not Thy statutes." That is the *root*. "Salvation is far from the wicked." That is the *fruit*.

All this made the psalmist thankful that he was not numbered among them any more. His eyes had been opened. Having assessed his situation, he found it very much better than that of the man who afflicted him. He speaks next of:

B. His Saviour (119:156)

"Great are Thy tender mercies, O LORD: quicken me according to Thy judgments." "Thy mercies." "Thy judgments." The psalmist strikes first a white note, then a black note. Both played together make a harmonious chord. Thus it is that God orders our lives—now sunshine, now shadow, and never too much of either, just enough so that like our Lord we might "grow up before Him as a tender plant." How wise our Saviour is.

It is not all mercy. It is not a blanket pardon absolving us not only from all guilt but also from all consequences of sin. If it were, we would never learn, never grow, never become responsible citizens of the kingdom. Often He lets the scars, inconveniences, memories, remain to remind us of the serious consequences of sin. He did that with David. "God hath taken away thy sin," Nathan assured the broken king. Nevertheless the sword was not to depart from his house so that he might never sin thus again. It is not all mercy.

It is not all judgment. It is not all stern application of the letter of the law. If it were, we would be prostrate in hopelessness and despair. The sword, indeed, might not depart from David's house but it would smite only four times in accordance with the judgment he himself had deemed right. And even those sorrows were tempered, since he was allowed to keep Bathsheba as his wife and she was later permitted to bear him Solomon for a son. No wonder David was such a singer of psalms of praise.

II. THE PSALMIST'S ASSAILANTS (119:157-158)

The psalmist was:

A. Troubled by Their Attacks (119:157)

"Many are my persecutors and mine enemies; yet do I not decline from Thy testimonies." It is easy to go downhill. Anyone who rides a bike knows that. It is easy to go zipping along on a flat road; that calls for very little effort. But going uphill is another matter. Even a slight incline calls for more determination, and taking on a steep grade calls for all the strength and resolution a person has. But going downhill? Anyone can do that. Many a cyclist, faced with a really stiff hill, will simply turn around and coast back the way he came. The reason, of course, is that he was not really going anywhere in the first place. After all, he was just out for a joyride.

Being a believer, however, is no joyride. The psalmist was facing a stiff grade: "Many are my persecutors and mine enemies," he said. Everywhere he looked he saw unfriendly faces. The temptation was to give up. "Yet do I not decline from Thy testimonies," he added.

As a boy I was brought up in a town that was avidly devoted to soccer. It was the big game. On Saturday afternoons thousands of people would flock to the stadium to see the weekly match. In those days most people walked, took the occasional bus, or rode a bicycle. Very few people had cars. When the match was over and the crowds poured out of the stadium the sidewalks would be jammed with people walking back toward town. Anyone could have gone *with* that crowd. A small person could have picked up his legs and been carried along by the crowd, the people were so tightly packed. But try going *against* it—that was different. To go against the crowd called for determination. It was a struggle every single step.

It is no coincidence, surely, that the epistle to the Ephesians has two major themes. The one has to do with our *blessings* in the heavenlies. We climb the Alpine heights of the faith. We catch a panoramic view of all the marvelous blessings we have in Christ. But then we are told that not only are all our blessings up there on the heights but all our *battles* are in those same heavenlies. Our wealth is there, but so is our warfare. We cannot have the one without the other.

So, although the psalmist was troubled by the attacks of his foes, he had no intention of giving up. He did not take the easy path, go with the crowd, shrink from the battles.

He was also:

B. Troubled by Their Attitude (119:158)

"I beheld the transgressors and was grieved; because they kept not Thy word." We note *what he saw:* "I beheld the transgressors . . ." The word he uses literally means "traitors" or "treacherous men." He was surrounded by men of no principle, men devoid of honor, men he could not trust. He saw men who would sell him if they thought it worth their while. They were men without conscience or scruple, the hardest kind to deal with.

We note also *what he suffered:* "I was grieved," he said. *Grieve* is a love word. We do not grieve over those we do not love. We are grieved when someone we love turns against us, betrays us, lets us down. The treacherous men with whom he was surrounded were men he loved. But they did not love him.

The psalmist was evidently a man filled with the Spirit; the Spirit of God grieves over men. Three New Testament words describe the Holy Spirit and His relationship to humankind. He can be resisted, quenched, and grieved. He is resisted by the ungodly; He can be quenched by the church; He is grieved by the individual believer. The Holy Spirit loves us and we are those who can grieve Him. The psalmist suffered because he was being betrayed by those he loved.

We note also *what he said:* "Because they kept not Thy word." That is really what grieved him. It was not so much what they were plotting against him, but the fact that those he loved had no regard for God's Word. In the end such an attitude could spell only judgment, and that grieved him more than what they were doing to him.

III. THE PSALMIST'S ASSURANCE (119:159-160)

The psalmist turns away from his assailants to look once more at the Lord, deriving comfort from the Word his enemies despised. His assurance is based on two factors:

A. His Devotion to God's Word (119:159)

"Consider how I love Thy precepts: quicken me, O LORD, according to Thy lovingkindness." The word *quicken,* used so often in this psalm (nine times—vv. 25, 37, 40, 88, 107, 149, 154, 156, 159), literally means "give me life" or "keep me alive." From this we learn that it is impossible to be attached to the Word of God without knowing its quickening, reviving power.

Mere Bible study, however diligent, does not make a person spiritual. Knowledge of Bible truth, hours spent in memorizing Scripture, synthesizing Bible truths, analyzing Bible books, extracting truth by the application of hermeneutical principles, and all the rest of it might add to one's knowledge of the Bible, one's expertise in exploring its truths. But that in itself is no guarantee of spirituality. "The letter killeth," the Bible warns.

"Consider how I love Thy precepts," the singer says. There was nothing wrong with his devotion to the Word of God. He could pass inspection in that. He could invite God to make a full investigation of his attachment to the Scriptures. He not only knew his Bible, he loved his Bible. But he was feeling as dry as a brick kiln, as barren as the wilderness of Sinai.

Devotion to the *Word* is not the same as devotion to the *Lord*. The Bible—great, inspired, important as it is—does not save us or sanctify us. Its function is to point us to Christ. The Bible is like a sign on a highway. A man might come to that sign and note its direction carefully to make sure he knows which way to go. He might even thoroughly investigate the signpost itself—measure it, photograph it, walk around it—and make no progress at all. It is only a sign. A man who became so infatuated with a signpost that he pitched a tent beneath it so as to be close to it instead of following the directions it gave would be a fool.

The inspired Word of God points us to the incarnate Word of God. It is when we get to *Him* that revival begins. The Bible is indispensible in pointing the way, but it is not itself the way. Jesus is the way. The psalmist felt his need of revival despite his love for the Word.

Yet his devotion to the Word of God gave him assurance just the same. It marked him out in contrast to the transgressors who had no love for God's Word at all.

B. His Discernment of God's Word (119:160)

"Thy word is true from the beginning: and every one of Thy righteous judgments endureth for ever." Even if the Word of God cannot save us, it gives us assurance of salvation. God speaks to us through His Word. We must not deprecate God's Word nor its role in our lives, but, rather, make sure we don't give it a role it doesn't have.

And if we are to get assurance from God's Word we must say with the psalmist, "Thy word is true from the beginning." From the beginning. Let us take the words at their most literal and go back to the beginning and see.

"In the beginning *God*. . . ." That is true. God is eternal, timeless, dateless. He did not begin before eternity began. He did not begin at all. He always existed in an unimaginable form of being that transcends time. The skeptic's argument, "If God made everything, who made God?" is spurious. That would make of the first cause, the second cause, which is a mathematical impossibility. Nobody made God. He always was.

"In the beginning God *created*. . . ." That is true. Matter is not eternal, nor did matter make itself. The idea is ludicrous. Out of nothing, nothing. When I was a boy in school we had a math teacher who delighted in setting us problems in mental arithmetic. He would call out a number of steps in a problem. We would have to work them out in our heads and be ready with the answer. For instance, he might say: "Multiply 25 by 9. Now add 51. Multiply the answer by 3. Now subtract 178." The process could go on and on. Then he would demand the answer. But sometimes he would play a trick on us. After we had sweated through a particularly long sum he would say, "Multiply the answer by zero." Of course, the answer was always zero. It made no difference whether the previous answer was 78, 964, or something in the millions. Any amount of nothings is nothing. I can toss around a billion nothings for countless billions of years and all I get is nothing. God created. That's true. Only God can make something out of nothing.

"In the beginning God created the *heavens*. . . ." That is true. Every sun, every star, every satellite in space, carries the fingerprints of God. The clear-cut evidence of law and order in the universe is proof that there has to be a lawgiver. Chaos does not resolve itself into order. The size, age, complexity, and power of the universe all point, too, to a lawgiver who is ageless, omnipotent, and omniscient.

"In the beginning God created the heaven *and the earth*. . . ." That is true. Every atom, every molecule, every chemical, every stick and stone, every rock and rill, every shoreline and sea, every fish and fowl, every plant and tree, every animal and every human being come from God. It makes as much sense to say that an atom evolved as it does to say that an automobile evolved. Every natural law discovered and documented by science only adds to the evidence that we are living in a planned and orderly universe which did not come about by the blind laws of chance and random change.

It is true. It is all true. The very first word that begins the Bible is true and everything else it says is true. No manmade theories are going to change *that*.

So the psalmist, experiencing affliction grieved at the unbelief of those about him and did the sensible thing: he retreated to the one source of certainty in the universe, the Word of God. It is the one great constant. Meditating on that Word garrisoned his heart against whatever deviltries man might devise against him.

He cast his anchor into the deep and took firm hold of the Word of God. Now let the storms come if they will.

Psalm 119:161-168

PEACE IN SPITE OF PERSECUTION

I. THE PERSECUTED MAN (119:161)
II. THE PRAISING MAN (119:162-164)
   A. What He Discovered (119:162)
   B. What He Detested (119:163)
   C. What He Did (119:164)
III. THE PEACEFUL MAN (119:165)
IV. THE PATIENT MAN (119:166)
V. THE PASSIONATE MAN (119:167)
VI. THE PERFECT MAN (119:168)

FOR THE LAST TIME THE PSALMIST mentions the persecution with which he is threatened. Just one more time. Then he will rise permanently above it. It will cease to haunt him, he will have victory, God's Word will have done its work in his heart. In this segment of the psalm he picks up his old lament, then drops it at once and turns his face resolutely away from it.

I. THE PERSECUTED MAN (119:161)

"Princes have persecuted me without a cause: but my heart standeth in awe of Thy word." Given the choice of standing in awe of a sovereign or standing in awe of the Scriptures, most people's hearts would stand in awe of the prince of the realm— especially if he were all powerful and contemptuous of God. It is a choice many a person has had to make in this dark world of which Satan is the ultimate prince.

We must always stand more in awe of God's Word than of those who would persecute us or who have it in their power to do us harm. After all, the most powerful and despotic of them is only another human being. And God is God. Long after the petty tyrant is dead and all accounts like that are settled at the great white throne, or the judgment seat of Christ, the consequences of our decisions will remain. Let "no man take thy

411

crown" (Revelation 3:11) is the apt warning of the Holy Spirit.

So we see the psalmist, first, as the persecuted man but one whose heart stood in awe of God's Word. He feared God far more than he feared man. Harriet Beecher Stowe tells us how poor Uncle Tom fell into the hands of the cruel Simon Legree, a brutal slave owner who hated Tom. He had Tom beaten to within an inch of his death by two other slaves. As Uncle Tom lay groaning, broken, and bleeding in an abandoned room of the gin house, among pieces of broken machinery, piles of damaged cotton, and other rubbish, Simon Legree came in.

He was determined to break Tom's will. Giving his slave a cutting blow with his riding whip, he said: "How would you like to be tied to a tree, and have a slow fire lit up around ye: wouldn't that be pleasant, eh, Tom!" "Mas'r," said Tom, "I know ye can do dreadful things; but"—he stretched himself upward and clasped his hands, "but, after ye've killed the body, there an't no more ye can do. And oh, there's all *eternity* to come after that." That was it. The downtrodden slave had fallen in love with Jesus and stood in awe of His Word far more than he stood in awe of his brutal master. He saw accounts settled in full in eternity. They always are.

II. The Praising Man (119:162-164)

The psalmist now resolutely turns his back on the problem that has haunted him throughout. From now on he will climb the heights and leave the lowlands.

A. What He Discovered (119:162)

"I will rejoice at Thy word, as one that findeth great spoil." Popular on television these days are programs that offer valuable prizes in exchange for guessing correctly the price of something, or for spinning a fortune wheel to the right combination of numbers, and so on. The programs are rigged to elicit the maximum amount of expectation and excitement from both the participants and the audience.

Let us imagine a contest modeled after one of these giveaway shows. The contestant is chosen and given a glimpse of the prize. It includes a trip to some exotic playground of the world such as Tokyo or Paris, a grand piano, a complete set of silverware, a late model Jaguar sports car. The contestant has to guess the value of the prize. He must not go over the total value and he must come within $100 of its value. The audience shouts suggestions and gives encouragement. The contestant ponders, panics perhaps, but then makes a wild guess or a shrewd calculation. He wins!

But now a new feature is added. The program host takes the

contestant to a curtain. He says: "Behind that curtain there is an alternative prize. To get that prize you must forfeit what you have just won. All I can tell you about the mystery prize is that people have died to own it. There are people in the world today who would give all they have to possess it. There are those who do have one who would rather die than be without it. You have a choice. You either can take what you've won or you can take what's behind that curtain instead."

The contestant hesitates, then takes the plunge. He decides he'll have what lies behind the curtain. The curtain slowly rises. On a table is a small box. The host gives it to the contestant who, with trembling hand, opens it. It contains a plain, unadorned Bible. What kind of reaction do you think would ensue?

We know the psalmist's. He says, "I rejoice at Thy word, as one that findeth great spoil." If it came to a choice between the wealth of the world and the Word of the living God, it would be the Bible for him. Do I rejoice at God's Word as one that findeth great spoil? Do I count myself blessed by God because I have it in my own language and in my own hand?

B. What He Detested (119:163)

"I hate and abhor lying: but Thy law do I love." We see two sets of contrasts in this verse. On the one hand we have the words, "I love" and "I hate." On the other hand we have the words, "Thy law" and "lying." The word used for *lying* suggests the falsehoods of false religion.

Somehow we shrink back from using the word *lying* to describe false religion, but that is what it is. The tendency today is to try to emphasize the good points in a false religion, to see where we can accommodate it. God's *Word* is *truth,* not relatively but absolutely, not partially but wholly. Anything that is contrary to God's Word is false—*lying* is the word the Holy Spirit uses.

No doubt those who propagate religious lies believe them to be the truth, but that does not make them the truth. In the days of Columbus many believed that the world was flat and that if one sailed too far he would fall over its edge. Their arguments seemed to make sense. People could not imagine other people living and working on the upside-down side of a globe. That did not make it flat.

Some time ago I was trying to find a street in a strange town. I stopped and asked a man for directions. He thought for a moment, hesitated, and then gave me some. I was to go back two miles and I would see a gas station. I was to turn left and go for about a mile until I came to a traffic light. I was to turn right and I would see the place I was looking for. He was telling me lies. He really had no idea where the place was, but he was not going to admit it. Instead he sent me off on a wild goose chase. When I did finally find the place it was in a completely different direction from the way he said.

That is what false religions do. The people who propagate them have not the slightest idea of how to get to Heaven, yet they talk convincingly and persuade people to follow their directions. Jesus called them "blind leaders of the blind." To be charitable, perhaps the man who gave me those false directions was mistaken himself. Perhaps he did think that was the way to go. That did not alter the fact for one moment that he led me astray, that his directions were worthless. Intentionally or not, what he told me was a lie.

Taking a stand for the truth is not calculated to make a person popular with false religious teachers. But then, God's Word has never been popular; it has simply been right. It is not a question, of course, of hating people, even people who give false information. It is a question of hating falsehood, especially religious falsehood, because religious falsehoods are the most dangerous falsehoods of all. They not only deceive, they damn.

C. What He Did (119:164)

"Seven times a day do I praise Thee because of Thy righteous judgments." Not just morning, noon, and night. The psalmist would greet his *waking* moment with a word of praise: "Thank You, Lord, for this new day and for all I shall learn today of Thy wondrous love and care." He would come down for breakfast and here was another opportunity to praise the Lord. If he had been living in our day, come mid-morning he would have a coffee break and again he would lift his heart in praise. Then would come lunch, and later afternoon tea, and still later his evening meal, and each would be the occasion for another round of praise. Finally he would go off to bed and, before closing his eyes, he would say: "Thank you, Lord, for this day. Thank you for all your kindness to me today. Before it passes from me forever into eternity let me load it down with a parting benediction of praise." Seven times a day—if we want to take the expression in its most literal way.

It would be a good example for us all to follow. Not just pausing seven times a day to pray, to ask God for gifts or for guidance or for grace—but simply to praise Him. To thank Him for being the kind of God He is, loving and kind and omniscient and omnipotent and omnipresent and faithful and true. To thank Him, as the psalmist says, "for all His righteous judgments," for overruling the way He does in the everyday affairs of our lives. Such a pattern of praise would transform us.

III. THE PEACEFUL MAN (119:165)

"Great peace have they which love Thy law: and nothing shall offend them." The word for *offend* is literally "make them stumble." Those who love God's Word are armored against the fiery darts of Satan; their feet are guided so they do not fall into his snares.

Situations cannot make them stumble. On the contrary they can say with the apostle Paul, "The things which happened unto me have fallen out rather for the furtherance of the gospel" (Philippians 1:12). Thank God for that!

Scholars cannot make them stumble. They are in touch with *truth* itself, truth imparted by the omniscient wisdom of the Holy Spirit. The theories and philosophies of men are like surging seas which break themselves at last against the massive headlands and coastlines of the Word of God.

Sovereigns cannot make them stumble. "The king's heart is in the hand of the LORD, as the rivers of water" (Proverbs 21:1), said Solomon, one of the most imperious of kings. "He turneth it whithersoever He will." A human government can do nothing that God does not permit. God has His ways of hanging this world's Hamans on the gallows they prepare for His Mordecais.

Sinners cannot make them stumble. The temptations they put before them do not entice them; the terrors they threaten do not intimidate. "Great peace have they that love Thy law and *nothing* shall make them stumble."

Such is the peace of the psalmist. It is a peace the world cannot give, a peace it can not take away. It is a peace that does not depend on what happens.

IV. THE PATIENT MAN (119:166)

"LORD, I have hoped for Thy salvation, and done Thy commandments." It is a great thing to have a good conscience toward God and man, to be able to look God in the face and say, "I have done Thy commandments."

The thing that stung David after his fall was the tormenting knowledge that he had *not* done God's commandments but had broken them. As a result he lost all sense of assurance of his salvation. He paid a terrible price for his sin. And by no means the least part of that price was the torment of soul which overwhelmed him when he thought he had severed forever his communion with God. In Psalm 51 he moans, "Take not Thy Holy

Spirit from me." No doubt he was tormented by the vision of King Saul, abandoned by the Spirit of God and a prey to evil spirits from the pit.

The singer of this psalm, however, had a conscience void of offense. Such a person can hope (in the strong way that word is used in the Bible) for God's salvation. The "hope" side of salvation is always that side that has to do with the future. It is brought most sharply into focus in the phrase, "the blessed hope," the bright prospect of Christ's return. Persons who have a good conscience toward God can make that blessed hope the bright and shining star in any darkened sky. They need have no fear of being ashamed at the second coming of Christ. Not even the prospect of the judgment seat is alarming. They can look forward to it as the time when they will be *crowned*, not *condemned*.

V. THE PASSIONATE MAN (119:167)

"My soul hath kept Thy testimonies; and I love them exceedingly." We note that superlative—*exceedingly*. For us to say of God's Word, "I love it, I love God's Word," would be a strong statement—much stronger, for instance, than the comparatively weak, "I like the Word of God." The psalmist says of God's words, "I love them exceedingly."

We note the use of the superlative elsewhere in the Bible. For instance, God did not say to the surging seas, "Let the waters bring forth." He said, "Let the waters bring forth *abundantly*" (Genesis 1:20), and instantly myriad forms of life swarmed through those seas with a variety and prodigality that astonishes us still.

When Moses described the overthrow of Pharaoh's hosts in the waters of the Red Sea, he did not say, "The Lord hath triumphed." He said, "The LORD . . . hath triumphed *gloriously*" (Exodus 15:1). The whole world would resound with the tidings of *that* victory and the Canaanite tribes would look with doubt and dismay at their manmade idols of wood and iron and stone.

When Israel found fault with the manna in the wilderness the Holy Spirit does not say, "The anger of the Lord was kindled." He says, "The anger of the LORD was kindled *greatly*" (Numbers 11:10). Their offense in despising what the Holy Ghost calls "angels' food" (Psalm 78:25) greatly incensed God who thus had spread a table for them in the wilderness.

When God gave His people a once-for-all opportunity to contribute toward the building of the tabernacle He did not simply say that the offering was to be taken "of every man that giveth." He said it was to be taken "of every man that giveth it *willingly*" (Exodus 25:1). God does not want high-pressure methods to be used in raising money for His work. Those who give grudgingly or under pressure might as well not give at all.

"My soul hath kept Thy testimonies." It is not difficult to do something you love to do anyway. In the Old Testament, God's will was largely a matter of *law*; in the New Testament it is largely a matter of *love*. Jesus said, "If ye love Me, keep My commandments" (John 14:15). The loving and the keeping are thus wedded together by Him. This Old Testament singer had entered somewhat into the truth of that. He was not ruled by *law* but by *love*.

VI. The Perfect Man (119:168)

"I have kept Thy precepts and Thy testimonies: for all my ways are before Thee." The psalmist knows that all his ways are seen by God. His first motive for keeping God's Word was from the heart, his second motive was from the head. If love moved him to keep it, so did logic. It simply made good sense to him to keep God's Word because he knew God's eye was always on him.

"All my ways are before Thee." All of them. God knows when I get up in the morning and when I go to bed. He knows when I go out and when I come in. He pulls up His seat at my table at mealtime. He is the unseen guest at every meal, the silent listener to every conversation. He sits with me in my office and rides beside me in my car. He reads my thoughts and knows the intent of my heart. It makes good sense to keep His precepts.

"Thou, God, seest me." That text hung on my bedroom wall as a boy—and a very disconcerting text I found it at times. Yet it is also a comforting text—to know that God sees *me*. Whether that text scolds me or soothes me depends on whether or not I can say, "I have kept Thy precepts."

Psalm 119:169-176

A FINAL PLEA

I. LORD, HEAR ME (119:169-172)
    A. The Prayer (119:169-170)
        1. For Enlightenment (119:169)
        2. For Enablement (119:170)
    B. The Promise (119:171-172)
        1. He Would Praise the Lord (119:171)
        2. He Would Proclaim the Word (119:172)
II. LORD, HELP ME (119:173-176)
    A. Lord, Save Me (119:173)
        1. The Ground of the Appeal
        2. The Greatness of the Appeal
    B. Lord, Satisfy Me (119:174)
    C. Lord, Strengthen Me (119:175)
    He wanted something:
        1. Wrought in Him
        2. Brought from Him
        3. Taught to Him
    D. Lord, Seek Me (119:176)
    We see him:
        1. Straying
        2. Praying

THE SINGER HAS NOW COME to his last stanza. Letter by letter he has alternately sung and sobbed his way through the letters of the Hebrew alphabet. Again and again he found that his tears turned into rainbows when he looked through them at the Word of God; his triumphs turned into hymns. Now he is about to conclude his rhapsody on the wonders of the Word, a Word that has met him in every need of his life.

His closing prayer is in two parts. He says, "Lord, hear me," and, "Lord, help me." As he begins the last lap of this journey through the alphabet of God's Word he can still see some bumpy spots in the road ahead. The devil's hue and cry after the saved soul continues right to the gates of death itself. Indeed, many a harassed child of God has gone plunging headlong into the Jordan with the devil's bloodhounds baying furiously in pursuit. Pharaoh's chariots and horsemen pursued redeemed Israel right to the banks of the Red Sea, yes, and even into the mysterious corridor the living God had ploughed for His people through the rushing sea. But that was the end. Once across the sea, Israel could sing a new song. The power of the enemy was broken at last and forever.

I. LORD, HEAR ME (119:169-172)

A. The Prayer (119:169-170)

1. For Enlightenment (119:169)

"Let my cry come near before Thee, O LORD; give me understanding according to Thy word." As has been said, understanding is better than knowledge. Anyone can acquire knowledge. All one needs for that is a good encyclopedia. Knowledge is merely the accumulation of facts. Understanding is the ability to comprehend those facts and to relate them to other situations.

I might have a lot of knowledge, for instance, about a friend's illness. He has appendicitis and he is to go into the hospital for an operation. "It is usually a routine operation," I tell him (from my fund of facts), "but it cannot safely be delayed—because, if your appendix ruptures, peritonitis will set in and your whole system will be poisoned. So, a sensible fellow like you will have the operation. You will be up and about again in a day or so and, apart from having to avoid lifting things, you'll be fine." That's knowledge. Anyone can acquire that kind of knowledge. He can even acquire the knowledge and skill to take the knife and make the cut and remove the offending organ.

Understanding is different. If I have ever had an operation, I have understanding. I can sympathize with the pain and suffering involved. I know how much it can hurt, how long it takes to feel better.

The psalmist knew God's Word. He could recite by heart many of the great promises it contains. He had knowledge. He could quote a dozen texts that suited his situation. But he did not have understanding. His circumstances remained as stringent as ever, despite his pleadings and prayers. He had knowledge; he wanted understanding. He wanted to be able to enter more deeply into the principles of God's dealings with him, to understand not just the *what* but the *why.*

That desire represents a great spiritual advance. It is not so much a prayer for immediate alleviation of his situation, much as he wanted that. It was a prayer of acceptance, based on God's ways as revealed in God's Word. This singer knew that any understanding must come from God's Word. There and there alone would he find answers to life's most difficult questions. The world does not have those answers. This world's learning does not help us much when the ultimate issues of suffering and death are in view. Its philosophies are so much "high sounding nonsense" when it comes to the deeper issues of the soul.

In the life of Moses we see an interesting illustration of the difference between knowledge and understanding. We read of God that "He made known His *ways* unto Moses, His *acts* unto the children of Israel" (Psalm 103:7). There's a big difference. Grumbling Israel could know only God's acts. They saw the plagues in Egypt, the parting of the Red Sea, the move south instead of east, the leading of the fiery-cloudy pillar, the manna, the quails, the bitter water made sweet, the water from the riven rock, and all the rest of it. They saw the acts. Moses saw God's ways. They had knowledge of the facts, but Moses had an understanding of what God was doing in bringing those experiences into their lives.

2. For Enablement (119:170)

"Let my supplication come before Thee: deliver me according to Thy word." The word *deliver* comes from a root meaning "to rescue" or to pluck out of the hands of an enemy. Such were the psalmist's continuing circumstances. He had prayed and prayed. Nothing had happened. He wanted God's enabling in his life to be able to understand why nothing had happened. He not only wanted to be delivered from his difficulties, he wanted to be delivered from his doubts.

Only three conclusions were possible. There was the impossible conclusion that something was wrong with *the promises.* He could put his finger on hundreds of promises that he could claim as an Old Testament believer. Those promises pledged God's blessing and help for the righteous. The Abrahamic, Mosaic, and Davidic covenants all assured him of God's continuing, unfailing goodness to His people and, in the Old Testament, this goodness included the guarantee of physical well-being and material prosperity as the reward for godly living. He searched through those promises again, certified by the living God. He decided there was nothing wrong with them. They are the gold coin of the kingdom, minted in Heaven, the recognized currency of the bank of Heaven.

If there was nothing wrong with the promise, maybe something was wrong with *his performance.* Perhaps his life was out of line with the conditional clauses in some of the promises. Maybe he was out of the will of God. Perhaps there was unconfessed, uncleansed sin in his life. But, as far as he knew, he was conscientiously seeking to walk in obedience with God's will. His many expressions of love for God's Word show that his heart was right.

So then, something had to be wrong with *the petition.* It was not that he was asking for the wrong thing. Under the Old Testament covenant he had a right to expect, as Job's friends expected and as he himself expected, that if he behaved himself then the blessing of the Lord was "the blessing of the Lord that maketh rich and addeth no sorrow thereto." So, it was not that he was asking for the wrong thing. What else, then, could be wrong with the petition? It was being hindered. It was not getting through: "Let my supplication come before Thee," he says.

Something was breaking the circuit, hindering the flow of power. As Daniel learned, satanic forces are sometimes at work to hinder answers to prayer. The New Testament teaches that principalities and powers, the rulers of this world's darkness, and wicked spirits in high places are all ranged against the child of God to hamper the prayers of God's people (Daniel 10:1-2, 12-21; Ephesians 6). The psalmist wanted the obstructions removed and the power to flow. He wanted enablement to reach him and rescue him.

B. The Promise (119:171-172)

The psalmist makes two promises to God.

1. He Would Praise the Lord (119:171)

"My lips shall utter praise, when Thou hast taught me Thy statutes." He had learned God's statutes from others. That is where most of us begin. We start, in many cases, when we are children learning the Bible stories, the Ten Commandments, some of the great psalms, the Sermon on the Mount, favorite Bible texts. We move on and begin to study the Bible for ourselves. We make our first feeble ventures into exploring the Bible on our own account. We try our hand at exegeting a passage of Scripture, a verse, a chapter, a Bible character, a doctrine, an aspect of prophecy, a principle of holy living. We still rely heavily on others, turning diligently to our commentaries and concordances. But we are on the way.

We learn the great principles of Bible interpretation, the golden rule, the law of context, the survey principle, and so on. We learn that we must have a consistent hermeneutic, that we cannot switch back and forth between the literal and the allegorical, that what we say about this Scripture must harmonize with what we say about that Scripture. We learn the importance of language and grammar; of culture, geography, and history; of putting things into their proper perspective. We begin to see the organic structure of the whole Word of God.

But happy is he who is taught of the Lord. The Holy Spirit is the ultimate interpreter of the Bible just as He was the original inspirer of the Bible. It is a great day when we begin to see things for ourselves in Scripture, fresh gleams of light, new glimpses of truth. "God is His own interpreter" is the great principle to discover.

The psalmist said, "My lips shall utter praise, when *Thou* hast taught me Thy statutes." The word for *utter* literally means "to pour forth" or "to bubble over." Truly there are few joys to be compared with being taught by God and learning from Him the depths of His Word.

2. He Would Proclaim the Word (119:172)

"My tongue shall speak of Thy word: for all Thy commandments are righteous." Our tongues usually speak our own words, and what words they are. So often deceptive, defiant, defiling, derisive, disrespectful, damaging. James says that if a man can control his tongue he is perfect. He can control his whole body. The tongue is an unruly member. Men can bridle wild horses more easily than they can tame their tongues. They can steer great ships with little rudders more easily than they can guide their conversation. The psalmist said, "My tongue shall speak of *Thy* Word." If only we could harness our tongue like that.

Of course, if our tongue is to speak God's Word, then that Word must first get down into our heart. It is "out of the abundance of the heart that the mouth speaketh," Jesus said.

In recent years men have invented a new language, one never used on earth until the twentieth century. No barbarian tribe invented the language. It was invented by brilliant men of science. It is a strange language. It has only two words in it, the mathematical equivalents of *yes* and *no*. It is "binary" computer language. With that language men can solve problems in arithmetic at almost the speed of light. They can use that language to guide spaceships to the stars.

Programmers, who write the instructions for their computers in that new language, have an expressive word to describe the way things work out when that language is spoken to the machines they have made. It is the word *GIGO*. The word GIGO means: "Garbage in, garbage out." In other words, if they put misinformation *into* the computer's electronic brain they will get misinformation out when the machine responds.

If my tongue is to speak God's Word, if that is what I am to get out, that is what I have to put in. I shall never be able to *proclaim the Word* if I do not meditate on that Word day and night, saturating my soul with its treasures of wisdom.

II. Lord, Help Me (119:173-176)

In concluding his psalm, the psalmist has a fourfold petition.

A. Lord, Save Me (119:173)

"Let Thine hand help me; for I have chosen Thy precepts." There is no mistaking:

1. The Ground of the Appeal

"For I have chosen Thy precepts," he says. On that ground the psalmist has every expectation of help from on high. He is a citizen of the kingdom, an heir of grace, a chosen one of God. And he has made a choice himself. He has chosen God's Word as the law of his life. He therefore has every right to expect that Heaven will act on his behalf. He needs no other argument, employs no other plea. He is on solid ground.

2. The Greatness of the Appeal

"Let *Thine* hand help me." No lesser hand would do. He did not want help from some man, no matter how great and influential that man might be. He did not want help from an angel, not even Michael, the archangel, field marshall of the armies of heaven. That would not do. For even Michael did not dare to rail on Satan when disputing with him over the body of Moses but referred that fallen prince to God (Jude 9). If the writer of this psalm was Daniel, he knew well, by divine revelation, that the angels—great and mighty as they are—have their limitations.

No, he appealed directly to the throne. What a sensible man. What folly to pray to the virgin Mary, to some dubious saint, or to an angel when we are bidden to "come boldly unto the throne of grace, that we may obtain . . . grace to help in the time of need" (Hebrews 4:16). So, still preoccupied with his troubles, the psalmist takes his case to the supreme court of the universe.

B. Lord, Satisfy Me (119:174)

"I have longed for Thy salvation, O Lord, and Thy law is my delight." The desire for deliverance had not dimmed his delight in the Scriptures. Many persons, faced with a protracted period of difficulty, distress, and doubt would have taken out their frustrations on God. It is a foolish thing to do, but a common one. Many have abandoned the Bible altogether. Not this singer.

The disciples of the Lord Jesus had a spirit like his. Others were becoming discouraged and drifting away, especially after the Lord's hard teaching about the bread of life. When Jesus said to them, "Will ye also go away?" Simon Peter answered, "To whom shall we go? Thou hast the words of eternal life" (John 6:68).

That's it. There is nowhere else to go. If we allow Satan to trap us into abandoning the Bible (the oldest trap ever laid for the human race by the evil one) to whom are we going to turn? To Buddha? Shall we go to one whose religious teaching offers countless ages of endless reincarnations, a relentless law of retribution in thousands of lives, and an eightfold path of good works leading to nirvana, the ultimate goal of it all—to *nothingness?* Are we going to turn to Marx, to dialectic materialism with its endless law of thesis, antithesis, synthesis? Can Marx, who has unloosed untold misery upon mankind, help us? Are we going to turn to the humanist? To the libertine? Can those who advocate freedom from all restraint and a path of lust and wickedness and inevitable guilt help us?

No. There is nowhere else to go. If we abandon the Bible we abandon hope. There is no salvation in the scientific theories of men, in the social philosophies of our age, in the religious ideologies of the world. God has shut us up to His Word, and that's an end of it.

This ancient singer was a happy man. He was longing for deliverance from his threatening circumstances but he had God's Word and in that Word he trusted and rejoiced. It was his delight—he did not doubt it for a moment. And it rewarded him with a joy in his soul which the world could not understand, duplicate, nor erase.

C. Lord, Strengthen Me (119:175)

"Let my soul live, and it shall praise Thee; and let Thy judgments help me." This was really a threefold prayer—and a perceptive and provocative little prayer it is.

First the psalmist wanted something:

1. Wrought in Him

He prays, "Let my soul live." He was aware of a deadness, a dryness within. Over and over he has expressed his delight in God's Word and his dependence on it. Yet his soul was as dry as

Aaron's rod before it spent a night in the presence of God. Thereafter that rod budded, blossomed, and bore fruit—evidence of a new life, evidence that a miracle of renewal had been wrought in that dry old stick Aaron had carried around in his hand for years. That is what the psalmist wanted.

Because life is a divine monopoly, any change from dryness and deadness of soul must come from God. How true and sad a fact it is that we can spend months and even years in God's Word and still be unchanged in our lives. There has to be a touch from God.

He also wanted something:

2. Brought from Him

"Let my soul live, and it shall praise Thee." Life flowing in, love flowing out, a living soul expressing itself in lilting song. The first evidence of life in a newborn babe is a cry. Charles Dickens, in describing the birth of poor little Oliver Twist, put it like this: "After a few struggles, Oliver breathed, sneezed, and proceeded to advertise to the inmates of the workhouse the fact of a new burden having been imposed upon the parish by setting up as loud a cry as could reasonably be expected from a male infant . . ."

New spiritual life also advertises itself, not in sad wails but in joyful song. Praise is the evidence of a new heartbeat in the breast. So the psalmist wanted something brought from him: praise.

Further, he wanted something:

3. Taught to Him

"And let Thy judgments help me." He wanted God's own spoken Word to aid him in expressing the new life within. The highest form of praise is that which employs God's own Word as a vehicle for praising Him. For example, few people in modern times have prayed like George Mueller of Bristol. This seasoned suppliant used to say that he considered it the first and most important business of the day to get his own soul happy in the Lord. To do that he meditated on the Scriptures, letting the Holy Spirit teach him divine truth. Then he took the words that had been an enlightenment to his own soul and converted them into the language of prayer. When he used words, "the Holy Ghost supplieth," God's Word lent wings to his prayers. He would use the words of Scripture in praying for his wife, his family, his friends, his orphans, his own soul.

The singer has one last prayer request before he finishes this monumental psalm. He says:

D. Lord, Seek Me (119:176)

"I have gone astray like a lost sheep; seek Thy servant; for I do not forget Thy commandments." This last verse takes us some-what by surprise. One would have thought that, after 175 verses devoted to the Word of God, this singer would have become a super-saint. Far from it. The older we grow, the further along we get in the life of faith, the more we realize the entrenched wickedness and treachery of our hearts.

In this last verse we have a final glimpse of this unknown singer before he vanishes into the anonymity from which he emerged. We see him:

1. Straying

We hear first an honest confession from a transparent soul: "I have gone astray like a lost sheep." It is the nature of a sheep to stray. It does not do it to be wicked or wanton. It does it because that is what a sheep is like. Likewise, it is human nature to go astray. Nobody has to take a course in theology to know that. Our sin nature is bent that way. It is not necessarily that we deliberately make up our minds to neglect our daily quiet time, the place of prayer, the gathering of God's people. We just allow the crowding concerns of everyday life to loom too large. We do what comes naturally. We stray.

Then we see him:

2. Praying

"Seek Thy servant," he says. He feels his lostness keenly. He is lonely, vulnerable, afraid. He doesn't know how to get back where he belongs. He adds something which perhaps he means as an inducement: "For I do not forget Thy commandments." It is more in the nature of an indictment. There is far more excuse for a sinner to stray than there is for a saint. To have God's Word stored up in our hearts, to be able to write a Psalm 119, to know the secret of victory and praise, to know the reality of a new life and still to stray, that is a serious matter— much more serious than to be lost out of ignorance of God's Word.

There the singer ends the psalm, on a somewhat doleful note. But at least he is still praying. And the Holy Spirit does not end it all there. He goes on to add new psalms, new books, a New Testament. He goes on to tell of One who came "to seek and to save that which was lost."

We may lose sight of Him and stray like a foolish sheep, but He does not lose sight of us.

Psalm 120

THE WAR LORDS

PSALM 120 INTRODUCES a series of fifteen psalms, all with the inscription, "A song of degrees." Scholars, divided over what that expression means, have made various suggestions:

—It may mean "A song of the higher choir" or "In a higher key."

—It may have to do with stages on the journey back to the promised land after the Babylonian captivity.

—It may be of a prophetic nature, referring to the final ingathering in a coming day of the Jewish exiles from their worldwide dispersion.

—Some have suggested that these songs are related in some way to the restoration of the ark to Jerusalem.

—Others think they refer to fifteen stages in the annual ascent to Jerusalem by the tribes in their periodic pilgrimages to the holy city.

—Perhaps these songs were sung on the steps of the temple. We know there will be fifteen steps in Ezekiel's future temple, seven in the outer court and eight in the inner court (Ezekiel 40:22, 31). However, we do not know that Solomon's temple had fifteen steps.

Obviously all of the above views cannot be correct.

The Hebrew text uses the definite article in this expression; it is not just "*A* Song of degrees" but "*The* Song of degrees." Naturally, that leads us to the question, "*What* degrees?" Only one set of degrees is mentioned in the Bible: those related to the sundial of Ahaz. When King Hezekiah was deathly ill, his importunate prayer was answered and he was given a fifteen-year extension to his life. He was also given a sign by the prophet Isaiah as proof that he was going to recover. The shadow on the sundial of Ahaz went back by ten degrees. The Holy Spirit evidently wants to draw our attention to the degrees on the sundial because they are mentioned six times in 2 Kings 20:8-11 and five times in Isaiah 38:8 (in the original text). On recovering from his sickness, the king said: "The LORD was ready to save me: therefore we will sing *my songs* to the stringed instruments all the days of our life in the house of the LORD" (Isaiah 38:20).

These fifteen "Songs of Degrees" correspond to the number of years added to Hezekiah's life. He himself wrote ten of them (corresponding to the number of degrees the shadow went back on the sundial); the other five were selected from extant hymns of David and Solomon and added to the collection. Of these five, David wrote four and Solomon one. The psalm by Solomon (Psalm 127) is set in the center of the fifteen psalms, with two of David's psalms coming in the group of seven before and two coming in the group after (122, 124, 131, 133). The ten psalms by Hezekiah are not given any title; there would be no need for Hezekiah to append his name to them because he has already called them "my songs."

The life of this remarkable king is of great interest. The story of his sickness and of the Assyrian invasion (the two great events of his life) is recorded in three books of the Bible: 2 Kings, 2 Chronicles, and Isaiah. A study of the incidents recorded by the Holy Spirit reveals many points of comparison (*The Companion Bible* lists fifteen) between Hezekiah's experiences and the theme of these songs.

The psalms in this series can be arranged in five groups, each containing three psalms. The first psalm in each triad records *trouble,* the second in each records *trust,* and the third records *triumph.* These psalms may have been sung by the pilgrims going up to Jerusalem; they may have been sung by the returning captives, especially when the hills of Judah burst upon their sight; they may record the experiences of the dispersed of Israel in the coming great deliverance from the power of the beast. But first and foremost they are linked with Hezekiah.

The psalmist strikes four notes in Psalm 120, which begins the series. We begin with:

I. THE PSALMIST'S DISTRESS (120:1)

"In my distress I cried unto the LORD, and He heard me." The psalmist has just experienced the reality of God's hearing and answering prayer. If this was Hezekiah speaking, and if the scene and setting of this psalm are the Assyrian invasion, then the psalmist had just had a very recent and very remarkable experience of God's answering prayer.

Let us put the events of Hezekiah's life in sequence. He came to the throne of Judah in a desperate hour. The Assyrians were expanding their empire and pressing down from the north. In the line of their advance lay little Judah. With news coming in constantly of the warlike preparations of this great imperial expansionist northern power, Hezekiah did what he could to put his little nation in a posture of defense.

Then he was taken violently ill and it seemed as if he was going to die. In answer to Hezekiah's prayer, Isaiah was sent to tell him he would get better, would live for another fifteen years, and the sign of all this would be seen on the sundial of Ahaz. Hezekiah recovered.

About this time he received ambassadors from Merodachbaladan, the king of Babylonia who was himself facing war with Assyria. This great king of the east sent to Hezekiah ostensibly to congratulate him on his recovery, but undoubtedly to try to arrange a military alliance between Judah and Babylon against Assyria. Hezekiah was flattered and, no doubt, tempted. But the Lord wanted no such dependence on man. Isaiah was sent to rebuke Hezekiah, who had so foolishly shown all his treasures to the Babylonians.

Far from being a source of help, the Babylonians would be a source of sorrow. It was not the Assyrians whom Judah had to fear, but the Babylonians. The future world empire would not belong to Assyria, but to the currently hard-pressed Babylonians. Judah's judgment would come, not from the present and greatly dreaded Assyrians, but from the Babylonians, with whom Hezekiah was now considering alliance. Shortly after this the Assyrian invasion against Judah was launched. Many cities were taken and Hezekiah was shut up in Jerusalem like a bird in a cage.

It can be seen, then, that if this psalm was written during the time of the Assyrian invasion Hezekiah could well state, "In my distress I cried unto the LORD, and He heard me." He had cried during his sickness. He had been delivered from death, the king of terrors. Now he wanted to be delivered from the king of Assyria.

II. THE PSALMIST'S DECEIVERS (120:2-4)

He mentions first:

A. What He Wanted (120:2)

"Deliver my soul, O LORD, from lying lips, and from a deceitful tongue." There can be little doubt that this is a reference to Rabshakeh, a golden-tongued orator in the pay of the Assyrian king. He was history's first propagandist. Rabshakeh assured the Hebrews that Egypt, to which country some in Judah were looking for aid, was a broken reed. He told the Jews that God had forsaken them because Hezekiah's religious reforms had insulted the gods. As for Jehovah, He was just a tribal deity; the Assyrians made short work of the gods of other nations, and Judah's God would be no exception.

Like all successful propaganda it was a clever mixture of truth and lies, promises and threats. When Hezekiah asked Rabshakeh to speak in the Syrian tongue, that only encouraged the propagandist to speak even more loudly in Hebrew—so that the rank and file defenders on the walls could hear. The psalmist wanted to be delivered from this lying tongue, this tongue that was anxious to subvert the defense of Jerusalem. False and slanderous utterance is always very difficult to endure and even harder to counter.

We are told also:

B. What He Wondered (120:3)

"What shall be given unto thee? or what shall be done unto thee, thou false tongue?" The real problem was how to extinguish not only the fires set ablaze by the falsehoods and insinuations of the enemy, but the lying tongue itself. Hezekiah commanded the citizens of Jerusalem to make no reply to Rabshakeh. Silence was the only answer he could conceive. To deny or argue would only strengthen the force of the enemy's claims.

Similarly for us, when we are attacked verbally, silence is often the only answer, but so often that seems too passive a solution. Retribution, however, must lie with God; it is He who must pay back the deceitful person. The psalmist wondered how He would do it, but he had no doubt He would.

The justice of God ensures that all wrongs be either forgiven or settled. With propaganda, people become the victims of their own lies. They come to believe the untruths they tell and so victimize themselves. Then we note:

C. What He Wished (120:4)

"Sharp arrows of the mighty, with coals of juniper." The psalmist wanted to see the enemy repaid in kind and in full—it was not, of course, a Christian prayer, but one appropriate to his day and age.

The word translated "juniper" is the Hebrew word for broom, a plant from which even today the Arabs make charcoal of the finest quality (charcoal that makes the hottest fire and retains its heat for the longest time). That was what the psalmist wished: He wished he could take those poisoned arrows of the enemy, affix them to red hot charcoal, and shoot them back at him. Next, we note:

III. THE PSALMIST'S DWELLING (120:5)

"Woe is me, that I sojourn in Mesech, that I dwell in the tents of Kedar!" *Mesech* is mentioned in Genesis 10:2 as a son of Japheth. In the psalmist's time the people of Mesech lived between the Black Sea and the Caspian Sea, and *Mesech* probably refers to the Moschi of whom the Greek historian Herodotus speaks. *Kedar* is mentioned in Genesis 25:13 as the second son of Ishmael. The name stands for one of the wild Arab tribes that roamed the Arabian desert (Kedar is the general rabbinic name for Arabia). The names Mesech and Kedar cannot be taken literally here; the psalmist could not possibly have been living at the same time in places so far apart. Rather, the names are used symbolically for a merciless people.

The psalmist felt that his enemies were ruthless, like the people of Mesech, and untamed, like the people of Kedar. The Greeks would have called them "barbarians"; we might call them "vandals." Perhaps members of these remote tribes were mustered in the Assyrian army now encamped around Jerusalem.

Whatever the reality was, the psalmist felt he was dwelling among such people. Perhaps he was referring not only to the enemy outside the nation but also to the enemy inside. Again we need to pause and recall the situation. Hezekiah had instituted widespread reforms and had cleansed the nation of its abounding idolatries. His father, a weak man and a dedicated pagan, had given royal support to the apostasies, but Hezekiah, tutored and helped by his friend Isaiah, had put an end to all

that. Holiness, however, cannot be legislated, even though idolatrous practices can be made illegal, and it is evident that Hezekiah's religious reforms had not converted everybody. Many
only feigned obedience to the new laws and in enforcing them
Hezekiah had many enemies, not a few of them people of
considerable power. How greatly Hezekiah's efforts to bring
about a revival failed is seen in the swift way court and country
reverted back to idolatry after his death.

Then, too, many were resentful of Hezekiah's political policies. Some influential opinion makers wanted an alliance with
Egypt; others thought Judah should come at once to terms with
Assyria. After all, how could tiny Judah fight such a superpower as Assyria?

Hezekiah knew there were traitors in his country. He felt
surrounded by them; he felt as though he was living right in the
tents of Kedar or in Meshech itself. His whole posture of defense was being undermined and eroded by subversion from
within. He groaned in despair.

But we must not miss the prophetic overtones in this psalm.
Mention of Meshech directs our thoughts to Ezekiel 38 and 39
and to the possibility of a coming lineup of nations headed by
Russia. Mention of the tents of Kedar, too, might remind us of
Arab hatred of Israel, a hatred never more vocal and virile than
it is today, and one that has given Russia an opportunity to
move into the Middle East. Russia's plans will be treated with
the same decisive intervention by God as were those of Assyria
in the psalmist's day. Finally we have:

IV. The Psalmist's Desire (120:6-7)

He mentions:

A. The Warlike Attitude by which He Was Surrounded (120:6)

"My soul hath long dwelt with him that hateth peace." More
than anything the psalmist wanted peace. But there was no
peace. How could there be peace in the world as long as Assyria
brooded up there in the north, determined to expand its empire, determined to rule the world? There could be appeasement, but there could be no peace. Plenty of people were willing to march for peace in Jerusalem; let them try it in Nineveh!
How up-to-date it all sounds—people mistaking peace for appeasement.

Hezekiah had tried appeasement, his father Ahaz had tried
appeasement, but appeasement never works. Hezekiah had beggared the kingdom, hoping to buy off Assyria. But he soon

discovered that appeasement only encourages the enemy to ask for more and more, and in the end to demand unconditional surrender.

The psalmist wanted peace; the enemy wanted the world. "My soul hath long dwelt with him that hateth peace," he complains. No terms were possible, except abject surrender and then the prospect of becoming a pawn in the enemy's plans for further expansion.

Substitute the word *Russia* for the word *Assyria* and we can put this psalm into the context of today's world. There is a convenient ambiguity in the Russian language of which the Russians take full advantage every time they say they want peace. When the Russians say "We demand peace," the same words mean "We demand the world." That is the kind of peace they are interested in. "My soul hath long dwelt with them that hated peace" might well be the language of many a western statesman today.

Finally the psalmist mentions:

B. The Wonderful Attitude in which He Was Sustained (120:7)

"I am for peace: but when I speak, they are for war." According to Hebrew scholars, two words in this statement are emphatic: the words *I* and *they*. "I [emphatic] am for peace: but when I speak they [emphatic] are for war." War was the ultimate instrument of their policy; peace was the ultimate objective of his. Despite all the discouragements, despite the seemingly impossible international situation, he was still for peace. The fact that the enemy was for war did not alter his own fundamental desire for peace—not peace at any price (he was ready to fight the Assyrians to the last man) but true peace. That is why this psalm is really a prayer. How can you have peace with a power that makes war the basic instrument of its policy? All you can do in a case like that is prepare to defend yourself the best way you can and trust in God to do the rest.

History has shown how God dealt with the Assyrians; prophecy shows how God will deal with the Russians. This psalm simply assumes that God is still on the throne, that there is a higher power in the world than a superpower, and that ultimately God does vindicate the right. God was not intimidated by the size of the Assyrian army nor impressed by the weight of heavy metal it could put in the field. Neither is He intimidated by the Russian war machine.

Napoleon once said that God was on the side of the big batallions. In other words, that He was on the side of *might*. That is not true; God is on the side of *right*.

Psalm 121

SAFE IN THE ARMS OF JESUS

I. THE LORD IS MY KING (121:1-2)
   A. The Awe-Inspiring Hills (121:1a)
   B. The All-Sufficient Helper (121:2)
II. THE LORD IS MY KEEPER (121:3-8)
   He takes care of:
   A. The Problem of Weariness (121:3-4)
   He knows how easy it is for me:
    1. To Slip (121:3a)
    2. To Sleep (121:3b-4)
   B. The Problem of Weakness (121:5-6)
   I am vulnerable:
    1. On All Sides (121:5)
    2. At All Seasons (121:6)
   C. The Problem of Wickedness (121:7)
   D. The Problem of Waywardness (121:8)

A S WE HAVE SEEN, this series of psalms was probably written in the days of Hezekiah, when the Assyrian army was threatening Judea and Jerusalem. They could have been adapted later for use by the returning exiles from Babylon. They could have been used by the pilgrims in their annual journeys to Jerusalem to participate in the feasts of the Lord. One can picture the Lord Jesus as a boy of twelve singing out these songs as He and His parents made their way to the holy city. We can picture Him, too, singing them with His disciples on the occasions when they went up to Jerusalem. The psalms are versatile in their applicability. They can be adopted by God's praying and praising people and reflected on or sung whenever the occasion arises.

In this study we are going to picture Hezekiah, shut up in Jerusalem, awaiting the onslaught of the invader. Humanly speaking, the situation was desperate, and a psalm such as this

434

might well have been composed to match it. There are at least two speakers in the psalm. The first two verses are in the first person singular; the singer is looking for help and is encouraging himself in the Lord. The remainder of the psalm is in the third person singular; the speaker is being answered by another, one who points him with unwavering finger to an omnipotent God. Perhaps the first singer was Hezekiah, and the second one the prophet Isaiah. It seems that when this hymn was finished and added to the Hebrew hymnbook it was intended to be sung by several groups, one group chiming in to answer another. Possibly a soloist sang the first two verses to be answered by the choir with thunderous volumes of sound.

In any case, here is a psalm to turn to when shadows deepen and the future looks bleak.

I. THE LORD IS MY KING (121:1-2)

News has come that the Assyrian is on the march. Or perhaps news has come that the dreaded army has completed its mopping-up operations in the surrounding areas and is now headed directly for Jerusalem. Terrible stories of what might be expected would be whispered by husbands and wives. Many people in Jerusalem had relatives who had come through the dreadful siege of Samaria. They had loved ones who had been tortured to death, flayed alive, even impaled on spikes to shriek away their last hours on earth. Many had loved ones long since deported and lost forever.

There was plenty of cause for fear. The choices were unthinkable. Surrender—and face deportation, with forced marches over vast distances under harsh conditions. Not many would survive, certainly not the little children, the enfeebled old folk, the sick, the maimed. Surrender—or siege. Battle and bloodshed, unceasing war, famine, pestilence. And, if surrender came at last, sacking by an infuriated army would follow. Wholesale slaughter, rape, torture, harsh slavery.

The worried king seems to waver. Perhaps it would be best to give in. He looks first at:

A. The Awe-Inspiring Hills (121:1)

"I will lift up mine eyes unto the hills, from whence cometh my help." Most commentators are agreed that this rendering should be changed. It is not that the psalmist thought his help would come from the hills, perhaps already occupied by the Assyrians. Those hills, up until very recently when Hezekiah had instituted his religious reforms, had been scenes of idolatrous worship. The high places of Baal had crowned them; licentious rites had been enacted there. Israel was now paying for polluting the hills. There was no help in the hills.

They were impressive enough, those hills. Jerusalem was enthroned on them, surrounded by them. Jerusalem was not situated on or near a broad river as were other national capitals—Babylon, Memphis, Rome. It did not have a great harbor fronting the sea like Tyre, Sidon, or (later) Carthage and Corinth. It was not on the main highways between Egypt and the east. It was off the beaten track. All Jerusalem had was hills. The Tyropoeon valley, the Kidron valley, and the valley of Hinnom gouged through the environs of the city, leaving it cresting or commanding some half dozen hills. The city stood on a rocky plateau 2,550 feet above the level of the Mediterranean and 3,800 feet above the level of the Dead Sea. But there was no help in those hills.

The singer lifts up his eyes to the hills to drink in their scenery and to fill his mind with a thousand memories of sacred history hammered out on them. "I will lift up mine eyes to the hills," he says. "Whence cometh my help?" He lifts his eyes higher than the hills.

It was not the awe-inspiring hills that strengthened his resolve to resist the demands of Sennacherib. He looks higher than the hills to:

B. The All-Sufficient Helper (121:2)

"My help cometh from the Lord, which made heaven and earth," he says. There was a Helper, the God who made those hills. Had Isaiah the prophet already shared with Hezekiah those words that later found their way into his book? "O Jerusalem . . . be not afraid; say unto the cities of Judah, Behold your God! Behold, the Lord God will come with strong hand. . . . Who hath measured the waters in the hollow of His hand, and meted out heaven with the span, and comprehended the dust of the earth in a measure, and weighed the mountains in scales, and the hills in a balance?" (Isaiah 40:9-12).

The king, standing there on the high walls that surrounded his city, would see those hills. He would think to himself that God, his God, had made them. His God had a mighty hand, a hand that could pick up mountains and swing them to and fro in His scales. So why be afraid of Sennacherib?

The Lord was his King, the Lord who made heaven and earth, the Lord who could take all the vast reaches of space, the enormous distances between the stars, billions upon billions of light years—the Lord could take all those inconceivable distances and, anthropomorphically speaking, hold them between His little finger and His thumb. What a God! What a King! Why should he fear a human king, even one as great and terrible as Sennacherib? Sennacherib had taken on the living God of Israel, the God in whom Hezekiah trusted. That was Hezekiah's defense.

So ends the first segment of the psalm. Now comes the response.

II. THE LORD IS MY KEEPER (121:3-8)

The Lord is able to take care of every problem. That idea is repeated six times in this segment (verses 3, 4, 5, 7, 8). The psalm mentions:

A. The Problem of Weariness (121:3-4)

The response to the new confidence of the king is intended to strengthen and support his faith.

1. The Lord knows *how easy it is for us to slip.* "He will not suffer thy foot to be moved" (121:3a). The word for *not* here is a qualified negative; it expresses a wish that it might be so. It is subjective desire, a cautious statement. It can be rendered: "May He not suffer thy foot to slip."

The king has taken a bold stand. No other nation that defied the Assyrian lasted long, and the vengeance meted out by the conqueror was swift, marked by chilling savagery. The singer hopes that God will not allow the king to slip, now that he has taken such a stand. He takes courage in the fact that the Lord knows how easy it is for us to slip. We all know how often we have second thoughts after making some bold commitment to God.

Second thoughts are not always the best. It is the more cautious, the more calculating side of ourselves which appears in our second thoughts. The highest medal for bravery in the British Army is the Victoria Cross, awarded sparingly and always for some act of outstanding daring and bravery. It is said that most of the men who have won this medal have done so by responding to the impulse of the moment. Others had the same urge, but they hesitated. Hezekiah has won his "Victoria Cross" and the second singer hopes he will not tarnish it now.

2. Then, too, the Lord knows *how easy it is for us to sleep.* "He that keepeth thee will not slumber" (121:3b). Here again we have the qualified negative which could be rendered: "May

He that keepeth thee not slumber." It is so easy, having made some commitment to God, to settle down and get nothing done after all. The king would need to stay awake now, and so, the subjective desire is voiced that God might keep a watchful eye on him.

At this point the psalmist recovers himself and takes his stand on higher ground: "Behold, He that keepeth Israel shall neither slumber nor sleep" (121:4). God is not like a human sentinel likely to fall asleep at his post. There is really no need for such a prayer—as though God could get tired. Hebraists tell us that this is a positive negative. This is not subjective desire; this is objective certainty.

Every star, every galaxy, every burning orb in space, is an object lesson in sheer physical energy. Take our sun, for instance, a ball of fire that astronomers classify as a moderate star, neither small nor large on the stellar scale. It has a diameter of 864,000 miles, but it is all gas. Two billion billion billion tons of gas. Over every square inch of the core there presses down a crushing weight of a million million pounds of matter. The only thing that keeps the sun's core from collapsing is energy, inconceivable floods of energy that raise the sun's internal temperature to twenty-five million degrees Fahrenheit. Consuming 657 million tons of hydrogen each second, the sun can still go on burning for another fifty billion years. And that's just one moderate star. The amount of energy being put out by all the suns and stars of space is beyond human computation.

A God who has that kind of energy is not likely to need an afternoon nap, so we can forget the problem of weariness. We humans get tired, but God never does. His watchful eye is on His people.

B. The Problem of Weakness (121:5-6)

The singer realizes that we are very vulnerable.

1. We are *vulnerable on all sides.* "The LORD is thy keeper: the LORD is thy shade upon thy right hand" (121:5). The right hand is the sword hand. The singer sees God taking up His stand on the king's right hand so that His right hand, His sword hand, might be unencumbered and free to defend the king on all sides. Hezekiah was going to need a defense like that once the Assyrian army was drawn up around the city's walls.

Our weakness is offset by God's strength. He deliberately takes up a position from which He can defend us, no matter from which quarter the attack comes.

And we never know where the attack will come from—sometimes from our families, sometimes from a friend. Sometimes the enemy attacks along the line of our weakness, which he knows only too well; sometimes he attacks at the point of strength. Elijah's strong point was his courage, yet he fled in abject fear from Jezebel. Moses' strong point was his meekness, yet he lost his temper and smote the rock. Abraham's strong point was his faith, yet down he went to Egypt in unbelief.

Because we all are vulnerable, we all need the Lord to stand on our right hand with His right hand outstretched to defend us no matter from which quarter the offensive comes.

2. We are also *vulnerable at all seasons.* "The sun shall not smite thee by day, nor the moon by night" (121:6). Sunstroke is both common and dangerous in the east. Moonstroke also was thought to be injurious. The name given to disordered people for centuries was the word *lunatic,* from the Latin *luna,* moon. (I remember as a boy its being said that people in asylums behaved more irrationally during a full moon.)

The point of the above observation by the psalmist, of course, is that we are vulnerable at all seasons but God is able to keep us by day or by night. It makes no difference to Him.

That takes care of the problem of our weakness. Then there is:

C. The Problem of Wickedness (121:7)

"The Lord shall preserve thee from all evil: He shall preserve thy soul." Technically the word *evil* here literally means something wicked or injurious. It comes from a root signifying the breaking up of all that is good and it is used especially of moral depravity. Its Greek equivalent is *ponēros,* from which we derive the English word *pornography.*

The ancient Assyrians were the embodiment of this. Their monuments and inscriptions glory in their cruelty and wickedness, gloating over the terrible things they did to other people. No instrument of policy was too vile if it furthered their goals. Hezekiah was faced by an absolutely unscrupulous power which was restrained by no moral principle. There was no Geneva Convention to constrain it. It would use anything that came to hand, if it furthered its ambitions.

The verse speaks to our hearts. We carry around within us a slumbering volcano; we are capable of any sin. The flesh is utterly depraved. Paul says, "In me (that is, in my flesh,) dwelleth no good thing" (Romans 7:18). How can we hope to overcome? The answer lies with the Holy Spirit. In the New Testament, whenever the flesh is mentioned, so is the Spirit:

"That which is born of the flesh is flesh; and that which is born of the Spirit is spirit" (John 3:6). "The flesh lusteth against the Spirit, and the Spirit against the flesh . . ." (Galatians 5:17). "The works of the flesh are . . . the fruit of the Spirit is . . ." (Galatians 5:20). "My spirit shall not always strive with man, for that he also is flesh" (Genesis 6:3).

When the flesh rises to overthrow us, the Holy Spirit raises up a standard against it in our hearts. Thus we can borrow the language of this singer of old and say, "The LORD will preserve me from all evil: He will preserve my soul." That is part of our salvation—not only deliverance from the penalty of sin, but deliverance from the power of sin.

Last, the Lord takes care of:

D. The Problem of Waywardness (121:8)

"The LORD shall preserve thy going out and thy coming in from this time forth, and even for evermore." In the historical setting Hezekiah was shut up in Jerusalem. There could be no going out and coming in. But that was only a temporary imprisonment. Soon, very soon, God would smite the Assyrian army and the gates of Jerusalem would again be opened wide so that the king could come and go as he pleased.

The verse, however, goes far beyond that. Under the Mosaic law it was incumbent on a devout Jew to inscribe verses from the Mosaic law on his gates. Thus each time he went out he took with him a word from God. That word was to keep him alert in all his journeys, business dealings, and contacts with others. He was a member of the family of God and he must conduct himself as such. Upon his return home, as he passed his gate again, he would once more be reminded of his relationship to the law. He could review his activities since last he passed his gate to see if he had been true to God's Word. And on his way back into his home, he would be reminded again that he must conduct himself as a believing man to all those who lived under his roof.

Devout Jews to this day keep a small metal cylinder fixed to the right-hand door post of their homes. The cylinder contains a parchment inscribed with the words of Deuteronomy 6:4-9 and 11:13-21. As they pass in and out of the house they touch this cylinder and recite the last verse of Psalm 121. We might well emulate the spirit of that, if not the actual letter.

Such a spiritual exercise will take care of waywardness. It will keep our feet away from places where God's name is dishonored, from places where His holy standards are debased and disregarded. It will keep us honest in business and pure in social contact. It will keep us mindful of the One to whom we belong and whom we serve. It will garrison us around so that we might be preserved from many a wrong step in life.

Psalm 122

JERUSALEM! JERUSALEM!

I. A SURGE OF HAPPINESS AT THE SIGHT OF JERUSALEM
   122:1-3)
   A. A Word of Delight (122:1)
   B. A Word of Determination (122:2)
   C. A Word of Description (122:3)
II. A SOURCE OF HOLINESS IN THE STREETS OF JERUSALEM
   (122:4-5)
   A. Holiness Is Encouraged
      Spiritual Power Was Evident (122:4)
   B. Holiness Is Enforced
      Secular Power Was Evident (122:5)
III. A SENSE OF HEAVINESS AT THE STRESS OF JERUSALEM
   (122:6-9)
   A. Request for Prayer for Jerusalem (122:6a)
   B. Reasons for Praying for Jerusalem (122:6b-9)
      Praying for Jerusalem will prove to be:
      1. A Blessing (122:6b)
      2. A Bulwark (122:7-9)

THIS IS AN envelope psalm—it begins and ends with a reference to the *house of the Lord,* and it is a song about Jerusalem and the temple.

It bears the superscription, "A Song of degrees of David," which suggests that David was its composer. This has been questioned by some, chiefly on the ground that the temple, the psalm's opening and closing theme, was not built in David's day. That, however, does not invalidate the overall Davidic authorship. The psalm may have been edited and adapted by Hezekiah under the guidance of the Holy Spirit. The first and last verses, which have special reference to the temple, may have been added by Hezekiah.

There are fifteen psalms in this collection, of which ten are

442

anonymous, four are attributed to David, and one, the central one, to Solomon. The fifteen psalms are arranged in five groups of three psalms each. The Davidic psalms occur in a discernible pattern:

Group 1: 120, 121 *(122 David)*
        Group 2: 123 *(124 David)* 125
                Group 3: 126 *(127 Solomon)* 128
Group 4: 129, 130 *(131 David)*
        Group 5: 132 *(133 David)* 134

In the first and fourth groups David's psalms come last, and in the second and fifth groups David's psalms are in the middle. To deny the Davidic authorship of Psalm 122 destroys the structure. The psalm might have been written by David soon after the removal of the ark to Jerusalem, when he himself planned to build a house for God. David no doubt intended the song to encourage the tribes of Israel to regard Jerusalem as the rallying center of the nation.

In Hezekiah's day the psalm, in its final form, was used for the same purpose. The first thing Hezekiah did, when he came to the throne, was clean up the temple and get rid of the idolatrous imports which cluttered its courts. He then invited the remnant of the ten tribes—the scattered, isolated, and lonely survivors of the Assyrian holocaust—to come to Jerusalem, as yet unscathed and untouched by the invader, to worship. As an added incentive, he reinstated the long-neglected Passover as an annual feast. This psalm was probably used by the northerners on their renewed pilgrimage to Jerusalem, a pilgrimage neglected for many long, sad centuries.

The psalm divides into three parts. We have:

I. A SURGE OF HAPPINESS AT THE SIGHT OF JERUSALEM (122:1-3)

A. A Word of Delight (122:1)

"I was glad when they said unto me, Let us go into the house of the LORD." The temple of Jerusalem was the place where God promised to meet His people. When the temple was finished, in accordance with the instructions given to David, Solomon dedicated it, making repeated references to it as the place where God was to be found. The Shekinah glory cloud, resting on the temple in former times, confirmed that this was so.

Ever since the division of the kingdom, in the days of Jeroboam and Rehoboam, the northern tribes had kept away from

Jerusalem. Jeroboam made the cleavage with Jerusalem as permanent as possible because he did not want his tribes to feel nostalgia for Jerusalem. He deliberately set up competing shrines at Bethel and at Dan to offset the pull of Jerusalem. For centuries the rift had remained. The northern tribes had paid for their apostasy by being carried into captivity by the Assyrians. "Come on back to Jerusalem to worship," King Hezekiah of Judah said to the remnant. "Come and celebrate the Passover with us." It was mandatory under the law of Moses that the tribes make a pilgrimage to Jerusalem three times a year (Exodus 23:17; 34:23; Deuteronomy 16:16).

This psalm might well record the feelings of some of the northerners when they received the invitation. All too often the Lord's people find it more of a duty than a delight to go to the place where God's people gather in the name and around the person of the Lord Jesus. Not so with this psalmist. "I was glad," he said.

B. A Word of Determination (122:2)

"Our feet shall stand within thy gates, O Jerusalem." Some translators render that: "Our feet are standing within thy gates, O Jerusalem." One suggests, "Our feet have stood (and shall still stand) within thy gates, O Jerusalem." There seems to be a determination voiced here that this great Passover will not be the last.

The first person singular is changed to the first person plural. The implication is that when the pilgrims finally reached the city of David they halted for awhile just inside the gates, spellbound by the magnificence of the city and overwhelmed by racial and religious memories. This would be especially true of those from the northern kingdom, not swept away by the Assyrian storm. Here, at long last, was home.

We need to recall the importance of Jerusalem in the counsels of God. There was never a city like it. Even today, draw a circle with a radius of about nine hundred miles, and you will take in nearly all the Middle East. The circle will embrace Athens, Istanbul, Antioch, Beirut, Damascus, Baghdad, Jerusalem, Alexandria, Cairo, and Mecca. Much of western civilization is the offshoot of what transpired in those ten cities. Some idea of the importance of Jerusalem to God can be gathered from the number of times He mentions it in the Bible. About 465 verses in the Old Testament and about 24 verses in the New Testament (489 verses in all) speak of Jerusalem and its future. Many of the predictions have been fulfilled but many more await fulfillment. The city itself is named more than eight hundred times in the Bible.

The siege of Jerusalem by Sennacherib, which casts its shadow on all these "songs of degrees," is in itself the subject of more long parallel accounts in the Bible than any other single event in Israel's history. The invasion and siege were prophesied by Isaiah at least two years before the event took place. The subsequent deliverance of the city was also spoken of by the prophet at the same time, the promise being repeated a year later when the armies of Sennacherib surrounded the city (Isaiah 30:19; 31:4-5; 2 Kings 19:32-34; etc.).

God has things to say about Jerusalem that He never says about any other city in the world. He calls it "the city of the great King" (Psalm 48:1-2), "the city of God" (Psalm 46:4), "the holy city" (Isaiah 48:2).

The pilgrim, standing within the gates of Jerusalem, was standing where history was made. He was standing in a city with a continuous recorded history dating back to the days of Abraham and Melchizedek. The Jews, even in Hezekiah's day, could trace its story back for some thirteen hundred years. Memories, associated with those centuries, made up the heart of the race-memory of this people. No wonder the pilgrim would pause inside the gates of Jerusalem just to soak up the atmosphere. Modern visitors do the same. Now that Hezekiah had restored the temple, the atmosphere of Jerusalem would link the Hebrew visitor to the living God of Abraham, Moses, and David. With a surge of emotion the pilgrims would make up their minds: "This won't be the last time!"

C. A Word of Description (122:3)

"Jerusalem is builded as a city that is compact together." Many of the pilgrims would have been used to village life which, as often as not, revolved around a street or two, a well, and a few farms situated up the hillside. Here was a walled city with busy thoroughfares, marketplaces, an awe-inspiring temple, great iron gates, palaces and towers, and all the other amenities of an urban center. The pilgrims were impressed. There was a sense of solidity and permanence about Jerusalem.

II. A SOURCE OF HOLINESS IN THE STREETS OF JERUSALEM (122:4-5)

The singer was further impressed by two things to be sensed in a city over which brooded the Shekinah glory cloud.

A. Holiness Is Encouraged

Spiritual power was evident. "Whither the tribes go up, the tribes of the LORD, unto the testimony of Israel, to give thanks unto the name of the LORD" (122:4). This was a tactful reminder to the remnant of Israel that here was a duty long neglected. The singer was tactful because, after all, the tribes had not come to Jerusalem to be reprimanded for their long absence. They had come at long last to the house of God to worship. The singer does not say, "Whither at long last the tribes have come up, which they should have been doing for centuries." He happily acknowledges that they have come. The people of God were united again in the holiest of bonds. They were together again in the meeting place, to worship.

"Not forsaking the assembling of ourselves together, as the manner of some is" is the Holy Spirit's New Testament counterpart to this—with the added word, "And so much the more, as ye see the day approaching" (Hebrews 10:25). The place of corporate worship, neglected by many, is an essential part of Christian life. There we derive strength, encouragement, and help. There we forge links of love with others of "like precious faith" which God uses to strengthen our spiritual resolves. There Jesus has promised to be and to meet with His assembled saints. There the Word of God is expounded, there we pray as a body, there we sing the grand hymns of the faith. When those who neglect the meeting place do come, it is no time to scold but to encourage.

Note, too, how this singer describes the tribes. True, they are the tribes of Israel, but that is not how he describes them. They are "the tribes of the LORD." The word he uses is *Jah*, frequently used of God to depict the concentration of His power. There they were, the feeble, frightened remnant who somehow had escaped the vengeance of the Assyrian. Here they were at last, all that was left of the ten tribes after centuries of apostasy, and the Holy Spirit calls them "the tribes of the LORD." Such is His way. That is what God thinks of His people, even the ones who are barely able to make it spiritually.

Even more than that, they represent "the testimony of Israel," not just the testimony of Judah but of all Israel. This gathering was a testimony to the pagans round about, the kind of testimony God always intended His people to have in their annual feasts. "What mean ye by this service?" was to be the question the strangers would ask.

That is another reason for not neglecting the meetings convened by the Holy Spirit for His people. It was recorded of the apostles that "being let go, they went to their own company"

(Acts 4:23). Of course they did. We always do. It was a testimony to the leaders of the Sanhedrin. The Lord Jesus said, "By this shall all men know they ye are My disciples, if ye have love one to another" (John 13:35).

But there was something else about Jerusalem. The pilgrim sensed that here:

B. Holiness Is Enforced

Secular power was evident. "For there are set thrones of judgment, the thrones of the house of David" (122:5). J. B. Rotherham thinks that when the northern pilgrims came to Jerusalem they saw empty thrones placed in a public area as a sort of a forum, the idea being to bring home to the wanderers that it was at Jerusalem that justice was to be administered. Now that Samaria was no more, now that the northern tribes were scattered, there was no need for further schism in the nation. A people who are united in worship should also be united in government.

Others suggest that the use of the plural for thrones here means that the king's sons were associated with him in administering justice. More likely the plural here is the "plural of majesty" as when, for instance, the Queen of England refers to herself publicly as "we." It is not the plural of multiplicity but the plural of majesty: the great throne was there, in Jerusalem. God's throne was there. Hezekiah, as God's regent, had his throne there. Again, it is a suggestion to the remnant of the northern tribes that Jerusalem was not only their *gathering* center but also their *governing* center.

This is another function of the corporate gathering. It is a place for and a means of administering discipline among the people of God. The One who enthrones Himself among us is the Lord. His regent is the Holy Spirit. Discipline of God's people by scripturally recognized leaders is a New Testament truth.

Finally, there is:

III. A Sense of Heaviness at the Stress in Jerusalem (122:6-9)

Although this was a high-water mark in many centuries both for Israel and Judah, there was still a great deal of stress. Not everyone in Jerusalem liked the reforms and the revival. Not everyone was pleased that at last a great and uncompromisingly godly king sat again on the throne of David. Not everyone was thrilled with the evangelistic preaching of the prophet Isaiah.

Not everyone liked to see the entrenched cults swept out of places of privilege, influence, and power. Everybody went along with the revival because of the powerful backing it had in the king, but not everyone was pleased.

Then, too, the undercurrents of tension at home were matched by rising tension abroad. The Assyrians were by no means through. Hezekiah was still a prime target for attack. It was no small matter to throw off the Assyrian yoke that Ahaz, Hezekiah's father, had forged and fastened on Jerusalem. It was no small matter to stop paying tribute to Nineveh, no small matter to refuse proffered alliances from Egypt and Babylon. It was no small matter, indeed, for the king, encouraged by his court preacher Isaiah, to refuse to rely on worldly expedients for the defense of Jerusalem.

Tension was in the air. The sad visitors from the north knew what resistance to Assyria cost. The smouldering ruins of Samaria, the heaps of the dead, the cries of the deported captives were still vivid in their minds. No one would need to be an astute student of domestic politics and international affairs to sense the heaviness in the streets of Jerusalem. Coming to the feast was serious business. Taking a stand for God in a hostile world is always serious business. This testimony would soon reach the ears of the king of the north. Hence the stress. This heaviness and stress resulted in a statement about prayer; the singer has not lost sight of God.

A. Request for Prayer for Jerusalem (122:6a)

"Pray for the peace of Jerusalem." It is doubtful if any city in all the world has so belied its name in the course of its history as Jerusalem. The name means "city of peace" but it has known little or nothing of peace in its long history. History records nearly three dozen sieges of Jerusalem. It has been besieged by Shishak, king of Egypt; by Rezin, king of Syria; by Pekah, king of Israel; by Sennacherib, king of Assyria; by Pharaoh-Necho, king of Egypt; by Nebuchadnezzar, king of Babylon (on three separate occasions—once in the days of Jehoiakim, once in the days of Jehoiachin, once in the days of Zedekiah); by Ptolemy Sotes, king of Egypt; by Antiochus the Great; by Antiochus Epiphanes; by Pompey, the Roman general; by Vespasian and Titus; by Rome again in the days of Bar Kochba; by Muslims and by Crusaders. It has been fought over repeatedly in modern times. Britain wrested it from the Turks, and the Israelis wrested it from the Jordanians. The Russians will surge down toward this city, the antichrist will take it and ravish it, the armies of the world will dedicate themselves to its destruction at

Megiddo. It will become the object of attack again at the end of the millennium.

Well might the singer say, "Pray for the peace of Jerusalem: They shall prosper that love thee." Jerusalem is yet to rise from the rubble of the ages and become the city of the great King, the city of peace, the center of a world government ruled by Jesus and administered by the twelve apostles.

Finally we have:

B. Reasons for Praying for Jerusalem (122:6b-9)

There are two main reasons to pray for Jerusalem, one personal and the other providential. Such prayer will prove to be:

1. A Blessing (122:6b)

"They shall prosper that love thee." Ultimately, of course, this promise is millennial in scope and character. It looks forward to the day when Jerusalem will be the world's gathering center, when love for Jerusalem will reflect love for Jesus.

But even today, with Jerusalem the center of international controversy, the peace of the world largely depends on what happens in Jerusalem. The hatred and strife that swirl around Jerusalem, engendered by the bitter hostility between Arab and Jew, have more than once brought America and Russia to the verge of war.

Also, praying for Jerusalem will prove to be:

2. A Bulwark (122:7-9)

"Peace be within thy walls, and prosperity within thy palaces. For my brethren and companions' sakes, I will now say, 'Peace be within thee.' Because of the house of the LORD our God I will seek thy good." In those days the temple still stood in Jerusalem and was still the house of the Lord. The King was still in residence.

In Britain you can always tell whether the Queen is in residence at Buckingham Palace, at Windsor Castle, at Sandringham in Norfolk, or at Balmoral in the Scottish Highlands— because when the Queen is in residence the royal standard flies over the palace. *The King was in residence in Jerusalem.* The Shekinah glory cloud, the royal standard of heaven, hung over the temple.

That was Jerusalem's ultimate bulwark. Prayer invoked the aid of heaven against the invader. That was the ultimate reason for praying for Jerusalem. It cast everything back on God. Prayer always does.

Psalm 123

SCORNED

I. THE SIMPLE CONCERN OF THE FEW (123:1-2)
   A. The Far Look (123:1)
   B. The Fixed Look (123:2)
II. THE SCORNFUL CONTEMPT OF THE FOE (123:3-4)
   A. The Full Measure of That Contempt (123:3)
   B. The Foolish Motivation of That Contempt (123:4)

THIS IS ANOTHER of the songs of degrees which have no named authorship and which, we suggest, were written by King Hezekiah. As has been noted, the setting was probably that of the Assyrian invasion of Judah and the encirclement of Jerusalem by the armies of Sennacherib. The immediate occasion was probably the blasphemous, contemptuous speech of Rabshakeh in which he tried to subvert the loyalty of the besieged defenders of the city.

When this psalm was sung, it is possible that Hezekiah himself sang the first verse, leading the congregation in worship. Then the choir picked up the psalm and sang out the remaining verses.

The psalm divides into two main parts.

I. THE SIMPLE CONCERN OF THE FEW (123:1-2)

The simple concern of the defenders of Jerusalem was that they might be in an attitude of dependence and obedience before God so that He would hasten to their aid. The song begins with the upraised voice of the king expressing his personal faith. Note:

A. The Far Look (123:1)

"Unto Thee lift I up mine eyes, O Thou that dwellest in the heavens." The force of the verb is that the speaker has already

450

lifted up his eyes, that he is still doing so, and will continue to do so. The upward look is sometimes the only one left.

If Hezekiah looked within he saw the natural fear and terror of his own heart; he was a man of like passions as we are. If he looked without he saw the Assyrian army so strong, so victorious, with its dreadful reputation for military thoroughness and savage revenge. Humanly speaking, it seemed ridiculous for the Jews to think they could be victorious in a contest with Assyria. So Hezekiah might well have feared.

If Hezekiah looked at the people, he saw horror and hopelessness on their faces. They did not have the faith he had (many were but lately weaned from paganism and many were reluctant converts). If he looked again, beyond the walls, he saw the endless ranks of Assyrian soldiery, the siege engines, the sappers and engineers, the pavilions and banners of the officers, the disciplined march of infantry, the arrogant ranks of cavalry, waiting to pursue any who sought refuge in flight. There was no place to look but up.

He lifted his eyes higher now than the hills, he looked to the heavens. He stood on the roof of his palace to pray, raised his eyes, saw the countless stars. He may have recalled that brief comment in the first book of Moses: "He made the stars also." These five words dismiss with a wave of the hand, as it were, whole volumes in the story of God's omnipotence.

The stars. He would see several thousand of them, just the brightest ones, those visible on a clear night to a viewer on earth looking heavenward with the naked eye. He could see some of the stars that make up the Milky Way, that grouping of some one hundred billion stars that carpet our corner of space. Perhaps he thought of God's words to Job: "Canst thou bind the sweet influences of Pleiades, or loose the bands of Orion? Canst thou bring forth Massaroth [the twelve signs of the zodiac marking the path of the sun in the heavens] . . . or canst thou guide Arcturus with his sons? Knowest thou the ordinances of heaven? canst thou set the dominion thereof in the earth?" (Job 38:31-33).

That would give the worried king something upon which to meditate. Like Job, he stood in ignorance of these things. He would gaze at mighty Orion, the great hunter of the sky with his battle club upraised, with his brilliant sword in his blazing belt, with the skin of the slain lion in his hand, and with his right foot upraised as though to trample the foe.

Turning to the neighboring constellation of Taurus, the bull, he would see that famous cluster of stars called Pleiades, the seven sisters. The brightest star of the group bore the name Alcyone, "the center." Perhaps, like so many others, the king thought he was gazing at the center of the universe.

Did Hezekiah know that Pleiades and Orion are true star clusters? There are other groupings of stars in the heavens. There is that group of stars, for instance, we call the Big Dipper. The two stars at the opposite ends of the Big Dipper are moving in one direction; the other stars in the cluster are moving in more or less the opposite direction. In other words, the Great Dipper is in the process of disintegrating. In the course of time there will be no Big Dipper in the sky, but Pleiades and Orion are different. They are true star clusters with all the stars in their groups moving together in the same direction in space. They are bound together by God's omnipotent power. No man could bind the sweet influences of Pleiades nor loose the bands of Orion. It must have been a comforting thought to Hezekiah: to think of the power of the Assyrian and then of the power of God.

And there were Arcturus and his sons. Arcturus is the brightest star in the constellation of the Bear Driver (Bootes). Next to the sun it is the fourth brightest star seen from the earth. Actually, it is eighty times brighter than the sun. The king had no way to guide Arcturus, that blazing point of light, on his journey through the sky. Apart from God's word to Job he could not even know that Arcturus needed guiding, even that it was moving at all. In actual fact it is moving at a speed of seventy miles a second, four times the speed of Earth as it rushes around the sun. The movement of Arcturus was one of the first clues modern astronomers had that the stars are not fixed but are hurrying on endless journeys through space. The God who could guide Arcturus and its sons could certainly guide Hezekiah in his trouble, doubt, and perplexity in this great crisis of his life.

This, then, was *the far look*—beyond the towering ramparts of the city, beyond the highest stars, to the dwelling place of God: "Unto Thee lift I up mine eyes, O Thou that dwellest in the heavens." Or, as some render that, "O Thou that sittest enthroned in the heavens." All those mighty stars are the splendid carpet that surrounds the throne of God.

The reference, too, seems to point to Hezekiah's prayer when he received the insulting letter from Rabshakeh. We read that "Hezekiah went up into the house of the LORD, and spread it before the LORD. And Hezekiah prayed before the LORD, and said, 'O LORD God of Israel, *which dwellest between the cherubims*, Thou art the God, even Thou alone, of all the kingdoms of the earth; *Thou hast made heaven and earth*" (2 Kings 19:14, 15).

So the far look paid off. It encouraged Hezekiah to go into the temple, to lay matters before a God who, having created stars, was not likely to be intimidated by Assyrian soldiers. When Hezekiah set Sennacherib in balance against the creator of the stars, he regained his sense of proportion.

B. The Fixed Look (123:2)

The choir now picks up the theme: "Behold, as the eyes of servants look unto the hand of their masters, and as the eyes of a maiden unto the hand of her mistress; so our eyes wait upon the LORD our God, until that He have mercy upon us."

The picture is that of an oriental slave. In an oriental home, the master was supreme and even the mistress ruled her slaves with an iron hand. A well-trained slave did not need to be told what to do. It was not necessary to issue loud commands. All that was needed was a gesture: a beckoning finger, a palm held outward in a cautioning gesture, a thumb significantly cocked. That was all. The slave would know that he must approach or that he must stay where he was or that he must watch his step or that he must attend to the needs of a guest. He would keep his eye on the master's hand.

The defenders of Jerusalem knew that their destiny was in the hand of God. Their duty was to obey His wishes. The Master would not fail to supply the needs of His obedient servants. There was mutual responsibility: the responsibility of the slave to *heed* the slightest wish of the Lord and the responsibility of the Lord to *help* when the servant needed divine resources to fulfill the Master's wishes.

The singers take their places as dutiful servants. They expect that God's hand, the hand that created the stars, will work on their behalf. These besieged servants of God had their eyes glued on heaven, waiting for the move of God's hand.

This, then, was the simple concern of the few. They were concerned that God should make the needed move. They would then know what *He* intended to do and they would know, too, what *they* were intended to do. Looking at the heavens reminded them what a mighty hand it was which, as they eagerly expected, would soon move on their behalf.

The second part of the psalm deals with:

II. THE SCORNFUL CONTEMPT OF THE FOE (123:3-4)

The psalmist speaks of:

A. The Full Measure of That Contempt (123:3)

"Have mercy upon us, O LORD, have mercy upon us: for we are exceedingly filled with contempt." The defenders of Jerusalem were enduring not only the privation, hardship, and uncertainty of a siege, but also the jeering mockery of the foe.

Hezekiah had received a letter putting in writing the contempt the Assyrians felt for the God of the Hebrews: "Let not thy God in whom thou trustest deceive thee, saying, 'Jerusalem shall not be delivered into the hand of the king of Assyria.' Behold, thou hast heard what the kings of Assyria have done to all lands, by destroying them utterly: and shalt thou be delivered? Have the gods of the nations delivered them which my fathers have destroyed; as Gozan, and Haran, and Rezeph . . ." (2 Kings 19:10-13)?

This letter equated the Lord with the idols of the heathen nations round about. The Assyrian argued that *their* gods had not saved *them,* so Jehovah could not save the Jews. They considered the Lord as useless as the gods of the pagans, and they did not hesitate to say so. The Assyrians were waging a propaganda war on God, pointing to their successes to prove they were right.

We do not have to look far to find their counterpart in the world today. Russian communism, being exported around the world, is at its heart an out-and-out attack on God. The communist vision is that of man without God; the communist goal is that of a world without God. No person can be a member of the communist party without declaring himself an atheist. Lenin described religion as "a kind of spiritual gin in which the slaves of capitalism drown their human shape." When Lenin seized power in Russia in 1917 he declared war on the church. Anyone in Russia today, who openly and regularly attends church, forfeits all chance of personal advancement. He gets no promotions at work, his name goes to the bottom of the waiting list for housing or anything else, his children have the greatest difficulty getting into college, and he lives with the certain knowledge that at any moment he might be arrested and sent to Siberia. To export their attack on God it is not unusual for the communists to spend over $2 billion in propaganda every year.

In our age atheism, as financed and backed by militant communism, is likewise contemptuous of God and of the Christian ethic. In Hezekiah's day anti-God propaganda was the specialty of the Assyrian. Like Russia today, Assyria believed that the tide of history was on its side. It could point to numerous successful conquests in the world. It could afford to be belligerent. Its policies were backed by armed forces that had no equal. All this bellicose, blasphemous contempt of God was centered on the land of Israel. The God of the Bible was the ultimate target. Behind this Assyrian menace was Satan, seeking as always to further his goal of bringing the whole world into open contempt of God. Hezekiah had had enough. He had a full measure of the contempt of the foe, and he told God so.

But the psalmist is not quite through. Now he speaks of:

B. The Foolish Motivation of That Contempt (123:4)

"Our soul is exceedingly filled with the scorning of those that are at ease, and with the contempt of the proud." Behind the Assyrian's boastful attitude was his evident success. Lesser nations trembled before him. The tide of history seemed to be running his way, and that tide had been running for nearly two centuries.

First had come Ashurnasirpal II (883-859), who had lifted Assyria out of its long decline and who had converted his country into a military state. Cruelty was his key to statecraft and terror the instrument of his policy.

Then had come Shalmaneser III (858-824). He took the war machine built up by his father and began to export terror abroad. He called himself "the mighty king, king of the universe, the king without a rival, the autocrat, the powerful one of the four regions of the world, who shatters the might of the princes of the whole world."

In due time came Tiglath-pileser III (745-726), a warrior and statesman. He set about making Assyria a world power. He conquered Babylon, overran Israel, deported whole conquered populations to distant parts of his empire.

Then came Shalmaneser V (726-722), who began the fateful siege of Samaria which lasted three long, dreadful years.

He was followed by Sargon II (721-705), best known of the Assyrian emperors. In his reign Samaria fell and the ten tribes vanished into captivity.

And now had come Sennacherib (704-681). One of his first acts was to thrash Babylon for trying to throw off the Assyrian yoke, taking seventy-five cities and four hundred smaller towns and villages. His conquests were carried out with a heartless cruelty that characterized Assyrian conquests. He executed campaigns of intimidation against the Medes. Then he appeared suddenly in the west and a number of city-states, like Sidon, fell before him. Many petty princes hastened to make their peace with him. The Assyrian army then descended on Judah and, according to Assyrian records, some forty-six Judean towns were overrun and 200,150 captives deported. Now it was Jerusalem's turn.

The psalmist speaks of the seeming prosperity and the swelling pride of the conqueror. He has no place to go but to God, so he lays it all out before Him. He tells the Lord that he is heartily sick of hearing of Assyrian victories, of listening to Assyrian insolence.

With that, he ends. What more is there to say? Surely God was heartily sick of listening to it too.

It happens from time to time that those who live for God in this Christ-rejecting world have to face the sneering contempt of other people. How we handle it makes all the difference. Take the case of William Carey. He began life as the village cobbler. Every two weeks or so he would tramp the country roads to the government contractor taking with him shoes he had repaired and tramping back again with another consignment.

But Carey had an eager mind. While cutting leather and hammering nails he learned languages: Latin, Greek, Hebrew, French, and Dutch. By the time he was in his teens he could read the Bible in six languages. On the wall of his workshop he had a map made of scraps of leather, a map of the world. On a shelf was a copy of the *Voyages* of Captain Cook. This young man was about to open a new era for the Christian church, the era of modern missions.

He went to India and threw himself into the work of opening up the Hindu subcontinent to the gospel. He became professor of oriental languages in Fort William College in Calcutta. He helped found a printing press. He assisted in the translation of the Bible, or portions of it, into thirty-six languages and dialects. He translated Indian classics into English. He prepared grammars and dictionaries in various languages, opened mission stations in India, Burma, and the East Indies, helped advance horticulture and agriculture in India, and helped make the Bible accessible to more than three hundred million people. He helped put an end to the burning of child widows in India. He ran into opposition from the powerful East India Company, but he carried on.

One day he was on board a ship going back to India. He sat at the captain's table along with officers from the Indian army, aristocratic young men, graduates from Sandringham, Eton, Harrow, and Oxford. He sat with officials of the East India Company, with members of the British administration and members of the diplomatic corps. One of them, who resented sitting at table with a man like Carey, in a cultured accent and with icy contempt said, "I understand, Carey, that before going to India you were a village shoemaker." With all the snobbery of the English upper class he was going to put the missionary in his place. "No, sir," William Carey said politely, "I was not a village shoemaker. I was a village cobbler. I did not make shoes, I mended them." Thus he put to silence the insolent pride of a foolish man.

ESCAPED

THIS IS THE second of the "songs of the steps" with an author's name attached to it. In this case the author is given as David. There are a number of occasions in David's hectic life when he could have written this psalm. He could have written it when he went alone into the valley to face Goliath, or when Saul eyed him with sullen hate at court, or when time and again he and his men escaped by a seeming hairbreadth from Saul's executioners, or when Absalom rebelled and the fate of the nation hung poised in the balance, or during some of his wars with Syria and Edom. There is no reason why David could not have been the author of this psalm.

However, granted its Davidic authorship in the original, Hezekiah seems to have adopted it. The situation in his day was so perilous, so analogous to some of David's experiences, that he seems to have picked up this psalm and incorporated it in this series of songs that revolve around the Assyrian invasion. Hezekiah could find no better words to express the way he and his people felt as they saw the last of that dreaded foe.

One of the supreme values of the Word of God is that it puts into words for us those deep feelings of our hearts we would have trouble expressing any other way. This is an ideal psalm to sing after some personal or national deliverance. It is a psalm of deep emotion. Notice its repetitions: *if, if, then, then, then, against us, against us, our soul, our soul, our soul*. Let us begin with:

I. RECOGNITION OF THE LORD'S PRESENCE (124:1-2)

A. The Double Declaration (124:1-2a)

" 'If *it had not been* the LORD who was on our side,' now may Israel say, 'If *it had not been* the LORD who was on our side.' " This fact is so real that the psalmist is almost incoherent. He falters in his speech. Here we note the italics which indicate that missing words in the original have been supplied by the translator.

There is a kind of rugged grandeur about this kind of writing. It is emotion-packed writing, writing from the heart, writing too hot, too fervent, to be bothered about ideal syntax.

The most important word here is the little word *if*—"*if* it had not been the LORD who was on our side." There were those who would have settled for something much less than that.

There were those who would have been content to have Egypt on their side. There had been many warrior pharaohs in the past, pharaohs well able to mobilize great armies, pharaohs who had carried victorious Egyptian arms to the cataracts of the Nile and to the banks of the Euphrates. But the days of the Thutmoses and the Ramessides had long since departed from Egypt. The great Egyptologist, James Breasted, in covering the years of Assyrian ascendency in the world, calls this period of Egyptian history "the decadence." He tells us how weak and divided Egypt had become. Ethiopians had seized the kingdom, and their main concern was to conceal the weakness of Egypt from the Assyrians. By inciting the Syro-Palestinian states to rebel against Assyria, they hoped to provide Egypt with some kind of buffer against the common foe.

The prophet Isaiah warned Judah not to rely on Egypt, which he likened to a drunken man staggering in his own filth (Isaiah 19:14). No wonder Rabshakeh, Sennacherib's propaganda chief, told the Jewish defenders of Jerusalem that Egypt was a broken reed, and that if anyone tried to lean on it, it would simply break and pierce his hand (2 Kings 18:21). It was no use having Egypt on their side.

There were those who thought it would be good to have Babylon on their side. But Babylon was to be an even more terrible enemy for Judah than Assyria—and far more successful. Isaiah roundly rebuked Hezekiah for thinking that some kind of Babylonian alliance might be helpful against Assyria; it was no use looking to Babylon. The only place to look was to the Lord.

After all, what hope did Assyria have of conquering Jerusalem when the Lord was on their side? None. When Peter pulled out his sword to defend the Lord, Jesus told him not to rely on worldly weapons. Why, He simply had to say the word and twelve legions of angels would descend from heaven and deal with His foes.

When things go wrong, it is always a temptation to see if we can work things out ourselves—not that human help is always wrong. But there are times when God chooses to shut us up to Himself, so that when deliverance comes all the glory will be His.

B. The Deadly Danger (124:2b)

"Men rose up against us," the psalmist says. The word he uses is *adam*, and it is in the singular. It refers to Sennacherib, the dreadful Assyrian warlord, a *man* in the most fearsome expression of pride, ferocity, and power. Nonetheless, the Lord, the God who keeps faith with His own, was the key to all that had happened.

We can picture the morning when the news came. We can picture the worried king talking to the prophet Isaiah. We can visualize Isaiah seeking to strengthen the king's hand in God: "The Lord is on our side."

The king would paint a gloomy picture. The situation was desperate. What were walls however high, moats however deep, to the Assyrians? Ahead loomed months of siege, battle, flame and smoke, attacks and counterattacks. Sappers would seek to tunnel beneath the walls; siege ladders would be brought up against them; battering rams would hammer at the gates; mobile towers, erected by the enemy, would command the city walls and drive away the defenders. Hunger, famine, desperation, would stalk the streets. People would die in battle, as well as of starvation and disease. And then the inevitable would come. The walls would be breached. The terrible Assyrian storm troops would be in the city raping, torturing, slaying.

Then came the messenger, breathless, wild-eyed. "My lord, king! There is a strange stillness in the enemy camp. There have been no morning parades, the trumpeters are silent, there are no campfires. All is silent and still." The Lord was on Jerusalem's side. That made the difference. There was a recognition of the Lord's presence.

How much better to trust in the Lord than in some nonentity of a conqueror whose name none can recall today.

II. Recognition of the Lord's Protection (124:3-5)

This assault on Jerusalem, after all, was part of Satan's plan. He hated and feared the Hebrew people. He knew that from this people would come the Christ of God. He would spare no pains to get rid of them. His strategy throughout the entire Old Testament age was to prevent the birth of the promised Messiah. This was just another of his efforts. He would mobilize armies, motivate kings. What did he care for human life? He has no love for people. He hates them.

The psalmist tells how the Lord protected His people:

A. From Being Devoured (124:3)

"Then they had swallowed us up quick, when their wrath was kindled against us." Judah's enemies were like wild beasts, fierce as hungry lions. Judah's enemies were like the grave, opening up to swallow its victims.

We can well believe that the enemies' wrath was kindled. Every day that Sennacherib had to deploy the bulk of his army outside the walls of Jerusalem was another day during which he could not march them against Egypt, where the real spoils of war were to be found. In Egypt the tombs of a hundred kings waited to be plundered; temples, rich with the offerings of a thousand years, waited to be despoiled. And he had to remain here, in these barren Judean hills, tethered to this detestable city with its massive walls and iron-girt gates. He had tried intimidation, propaganda, threats, promises. It had taken his predecessors three costly years to take Samaria. Who could tell how long it would take to subdue Jerusalem, far more formidable than Samaria? We can well believe "their wrath was kindled against us." But if so, the wrath of God was kindled against *them*. The Assyrians did not know it, but they had touched the apple of His eye. Before they were through, they would pay for it fearfully, and to the full.

Nonetheless, the fear of being devoured alive was very real in Jerusalem in those days. The wrath of the enemy was so great that it would not wait to kill its victim; it would devour it alive. There could be no hope of mercy. Assyrian vengeance was truly something to be feared.

But God protected them from being devoured. He also protected them:

B. From Being Drowned (124:4-5)

The psalmist changes the figure of speech. He now describes the Assyrian invasion as a flood. "Then the waters had overwhelmed us, the stream had gone over our soul: then the proud waters had gone over our soul." The flood is seen steadily rising. First water, then the raging torrent as it burst its banks carrying devastation with it, then the wild waters of the sea, the mighty ocean waves.

That is what the Assyrian invasion was like. The enemy had come in like a flood, inundating city after city throughout the land. All that was left for the proud waves to conquer was Jerusalem, and the triumph would be complete. Between Jerusalem and disaster had been nothing but the thickness of a stone wall—and God.

I remember Britain's desperate hours during the second world war. Hitler's panzer divisions were drawn up at Dunkirk and just twenty miles of water stood between Britain and the foe. The government organized what it called the Home Guard: old-age pensioners and men unable to pass the physical to get into the regular armed forces, anybody who could hold a gun and patrol the coastline. Except they had no guns. They paraded with broomsticks.

Hitler had his immense Luftwaffe, his U-boats prowling the seas, and his all-conquering armies, flushed with victory. Britain had some thousands of troops demoralized by defeat and practically devoid of equipment, her Home Guard, a navy stretched to its limits—and God. For Britain had a godly king, a man who knew the Lord personally, knew how to pray, believed in prayer, and who called Britain as a nation to prayer. Many in those desperate hours agreed that only God stood between Britain and defeat, the concentration camps and slavery worse than death.

There was a recognition, then, of the Lord's protection. Without God, all was lost. Without the Lord there was no hope.

III. RECOGNITION OF THE LORD'S PREEMINENCE (124:6-8)

The psalmist is now seen:

A. Blessing the Name of the Lord (124:6-7)

He blesses Him first for:

1. Hindering (124:6)

"Blessed be the LORD, who hath not given us as a prey to their teeth." Anyone who has lived through a desperate war knows the sudden relief when it is all over and the danger is past. I remember when they first blacked out our streets and when car headlights and traffic lights were marked so that only a sliver of light showed. I remember the air raids and how the Germans rigged their bombs with whistles so that we could hear them screaming all the way down.

Then it was over! Lights went on again. People went wild with delight. Buildings were decked with flags and bunting. Huge crowds chanted and cheered, singing and dancing in the streets.

When Hezekiah sang this psalm, his acknowledgment of God was sincere. As far as he was concerned, it was all the Lord. The swift visitation of death which had come upon the Assyrian camp was proof enough. As his scouts came back, it became increasingly clear. All that remained was to send out armies of men to bury the dead.

We are reminded of the poem by Lord Byron, "The Destruction of Sennacherib."

> The Assyrian came down like the wolf on the fold,
> And his cohorts were gleaming in purple and gold;
> And the sheen of their spears was like stars on the sea,
> When the blue wave rolls nightly on deep Galilee.
>
> Like the leaves of the forest when Summer is green,
> That host with their banners at sunset were seen:
> Like the leaves of the forest when Autumn hath blown,
> That host on the morrow lay withered and strown.
>
> For the Angel of Death spread his wings on the blast,
> And breathed in the face of the foe as he pass'd;
> And the eyes of the sleepers wax'd deadly and chill,
> And their hearts but once heaved, and for ever grew still!
>
> And there lay the steed with his nostril all wide,
> But through it there roll'd not the breath of his pride:
> And the foam of his gasping lay white on the turf,
> And cold as the spray of the rock-beating surf.
>
> And there lay the rider distorted and pale,
> With the dew on his brow, and the rust on his mail;
> And the tents were all silent, the banners alone,
> The lances unlifted, the trumpet unblown.
>
> And the widows of Ashur are loud in their wail,
> And the idols are broke in the temple of Baal;
> And the might of the Gentile, unsmote by the sword,
> Hath melted like snow in the glance of the Lord!
>
> —*George Gordon Byron*

So Hezekiah blessed the Lord for hindering. He blessed Him also for:

2. Helping (124:7)

"Our soul is escaped as a bird out of the snare of the fowlers: the snare is broken, and we are escaped." Thus the Lord turned Sennacherib's boastful words against him.

In the British Museum is a cylinder which records eight expeditions of Sennacherib. One of these is the record of his siege of Jerusalem. The hexagonal cylinder contains 487 lines of closely written and perfectly legible cuneiform text. Here are lines 11-24:

> . . . And of Hezekiah [king of the] Jews, who had not submitted to my yoke, forty-six of his fenced cities, and the strongholds, and the smaller cities which were round about them and which were without number . . . I besieged. I captured 200,150 people, small and great, male and female, horses and mules, and asses, and camels, and men, and sheep innumerable from their midst I brought out, and I reckoned [them] as spoil. [Hezekiah] himself, like a caged bird, within Jerusalem, his royal city, I shut in . . .

The connection between Sennacherib's boast and Hezekiah's song is evident. The cylinder goes on to record Sennacherib's boasts. He says of Hezekiah that "he was overwhelmed by the fear of the brightness of my lordship" (line 30). He does not record what happened next, or Hezekiah's escape from his cage. It was no part of that ancient Assyrian's character to record such a humiliating defeat.

But God records it, in the boastful words of the proud Assyrian himself. Sennacherib may have securely locked the cage but the living God of Israel came after him and unlocked it. "We are escaped!" cries the exultant king. The "we" is emphatic— "*We* are escaped!" It seemed too good to be true. "Blessed be the LORD!" There was a recognition of the Lord's preeminence, blessing for the wonderful name of the Lord, the name that guaranteed that God would be the great I AM to all the needs of His people.

Finally the psalmist is seen:

B. Broadcasting the Fame of the Lord (124:8)

"Our help is in the name of the LORD, who made heaven and earth." What chance did the Assyrian generals have against a God who had all of nature at His command?

Let us make an application. We find ourselves in a difficult situation. We may have an unsaved loved one, or we may face an illness, the loss of employment, or some other heartache. There seems to be no way out. We are caged in. God has a thousand ways to effect a solution. It is never a question with

Him, "How can I do this?" It is always a question of, "Which way shall I do this?" The resources at His disposal are infinite.

"Our help is in the name of the LORD, who made heaven and earth." A God who can do that can do anything.

Psalm 125

SAFE

THIS LITTLE SONG has to do with the security of the believer. It is a security that cannot be threatened by outward circumstance. As Paul puts it in Romans 8,

> Can anything separate us from the love of Christ? Can trouble, pain or persecution? Can lack of clothes and food, danger to life and limb, the threat of force of arms? Indeed, some of us know the truth of the ancient text: For Thy sake we are killed all the day long; we are accounted as sheep for slaughter. No, in all these things we win an overwhelming victory through Him who has proved His love for us. I have become absolutely convinced that neither death nor life, neither messenger from heaven nor monarch of earth, neither what happens today nor what may happen tomorrow, neither a power from on high nor a power from below, nor anything else in God's whole wide world has any power to separate us from the love of God in Jesus Christ our Lord (Romans 8:35-39 JBP).

The Old Testament singer couldn't go as far as that, but he went as far as he could. He knew very little of the eternal security of the believer, but he knew about the security of the nation of Israel. So, with the object lesson of the Assyrian overthrow before him, while the great deliverance was still fresh in his mind, the singer wrote this song of the security of the saint.

I. THE VICTORIOUS SAINT (125:1-4)

A believer is safe in two ways.

A. Safe as to His Person (125:1-2)

The psalmist speaks first of:

1. The Essential Security of the Believer (125:1)

"They that trust in the LORD shall be as mount Zion, which cannot be removed, but abideth for ever." The name Mount Zion rings out again and again in the psalms. It is used in at least three different ways in Scripture.

It is used *prosaically* as the name of the old Jebusite stronghold in Jerusalem (1 Chronicles 11:4-9; 2 Samuel 5:6-10). The Jebusites considered it invincible and boasted they could defend it against David with their blind and their lame. It was wrested from them in an act of high and resourceful courage by Joab, for which he was appointed David's commander-in-chief. Called Zion, the fort, the castle, or the city of David, it was situated on the southwest eminence of Jerusalem. It was where David made his home when in the city and was the political heart of his empire. The actual name *Zion* means "castle."

Zion is used *prophetically* to depict the administrative center of the millennial kingdom (Psalm 2:6; Isaiah 2:3). Isaiah says, "Out of Zion shall go forth the law" (Isaiah 2:3). He goes on to describe the consequent abolition of war and tells of swords being converted into plowshares and spears into pruning hooks.

Zion is used *poetically* to describe heaven and the hope of the New Testament believer (Hebrews 12:22). It is set in contrast with Mount Sinai. These two mountains, Zion and Sinai, are contrasted to emphasize the difference between the hope of the Old Testament believer and the hope of the New Testament believer. The security of God's Old Testament people hinged on the *law;* the security of His New Testament people hinges on the *Lord.*

In Psalm 125, as most frequently in the psalms, Zion is used prosaically to depict Jerusalem. "They that trust in the LORD shall be as mount Zion, which cannot be removed, but abideth for ever." From the beginning Zion was intended to be God's ultimate seat of sovereign power on earth. It was designed to stand the test of time. "Those who trust in the Lord shall be like that," says the Hebrew singer.

Hezekiah had not trusted in his armed might. He had done all he could to protect himself from the Assyrian, but it was little enough. He had safeguarded the city's water supply, had made sure that adequate food was laid in to withstand a siege, had seen to the walls and the gates. When it came to the bottom line, however, his trust was in God alone.

The opening words of this psalm illustrate the essential security of the believer. Armies can come and go, empires rise and fall, kingdoms wax and wane, but those ordered hills will outlive them all. As God chose Zion, so God has chosen us.

2. The Eternal Security of the Believer (125:2)

"As the mountains are round about Jerusalem, so the Lord is round about His People from henceforth even for ever." Now that the Assyrian threat was removed, the way was open again for pilgrims to come to Jerusalem to keep the annual feasts. The first thing they would see as they approached the holy city would be the hills.

No matter where you are in Jerusalem you see hills. The Mount of Olives is on the east side of the city. On the southwest side of the city is the Mount of Offense (so called, it is believed, from the idolatries that Solomon once practiced there). On the south is the Hill of Evil Council (as it is now called, and so named because there it was that Caiaphas had his house in which the evil decision was made to have the Lord Jesus put to death). To the north the terrain is not quite as rugged, so it was from the north that attacks usually developed.

These mountains, of course, were not Jerusalem's real defense. Any determined army could surmount the obstacles they represented. But they were illustrations, symbols of stability and security. Their encircling ramparts depicted God's embracing arms. To get at Jerusalem an enemy had to get past the mountains. To get at God's people, an enemy must first get past God. And that is more than any enemy can do, human or satanic.

"For ever." The psalmist writes it down twice. The circle God drew around His people, not just in mountains and hills, but in love and power, made them invulnerable to the foe as long as they rested in His arms, as Zion rested among the hills.

This is illustrated in the book of Job. When God drew Satan's attention to Job, Satan sneered: "Doth Job fear God for nought? Hast not Thou made an hedge about him, and about his house, and about all that he hath on every side?" (Job 1:9-10). So God took away the first circle of protection He had about Job. Immediately Job fell prey to Satan's malice. His property was stripped away from him in a series of disasters. He was left bankrupt and bereaved.

Again God challenged Satan about Job and again Satan jibed: "Skin for skin, yea, all that a man hath will he give for his life. But put forth Thine hand now and touch his bone and his flesh, and he will curse Thee to Thy face" (Job 2:4-5). God took away the second circle of protection, and Job's flesh was tormented with a painful and incurable disease. There was yet a third circle about Job: "Save his life," God said to Satan. Satan was not allowed to cross that line.

God draws circles around all His saints. There is the circle God draws around the redeemed so that we shall never perish. There is the circle of His perfect will and the circle of His permissive will. So Job, the psalmist, and we, too, are safe as to our person.

The psalmist was also:

B. Safe as to His Possessions (125:3-4)

1. The Problem (125:3)

"The rod [cudgel] of the wicked shall not rest upon the lot [the heritage—that which God has allotted] of the righteous." Note the *sad truth* (125:3a) that the rod of the wicked does come down on the heritage of the righteous. We live in a wicked world where Satan holds sway. But that word *rest* literally means "continue forever." God has drawn a line beyond which Satan cannot go.

We have, too, the *subtle temptation:* "Lest the righteous put forth their hands unto iniquity." The word for *iniquity* suggests falling into a course of deceitful behavior. When being ill-treated it is so easy to react in kind. That is only natural, but God's people are not to react naturally, but spiritually.

There is a remarkable illustration of this in the history of Israel. When Syrians had invaded Israel, a little girl had been taken captive and carried away to Damascus. There she was acquired by Naaman, captain of the Syrian army, and she became a slave to Naaman's wife. It was not long before that little girl discovered that her master was a leper. What did she do? Did she shrink from him in horror? Did she say to herself: "It serves him right. I'm glad. He stole me from my family. He invaded my homeland. He killed my friends. He has made me a slave. I'm glad he's a leper." No. She pointed him to the one who could save him. What a wonderful little girl.

It was like that also with Joseph. When his brothers were delivered into his power he said, "Ye thought evil against me; but God meant it unto good" (Genesis 50:20).

So, even when the rod of the wicked does come down on the lot of the righteous, it will not remain there. It cannot remain there, but, since God has permitted it to happen, the thing to do is not to react in a natural way but in a spiritual way.

2. The Prayer (125:4)

"Do good, O LORD, unto those that be good, and to them that are upright in heart." Often in life it seems as though those who do good are the victims of those who do evil. The trouble is that our focus is too short and the image is blurred. We cannot see end results, so we judge by immediate circumstances. God will always do good to those who are good.

When my wife was a little girl her mother contracted tuberculosis and had to be placed in a sanitorium, for her own good and for the good of her two children. The two little ones were deprived of their mother for their own good, even though at the time the separation must have seemed to them to have been heartless and cruel. My wife, Jean, was given a home by an aunt. This dear lady was poor, but she was a woman who loved the Lord and who was committed to good works. During the years of the great depression, when there was so much unemployment, she still had a job—even if it wasn't much of a job. She kept the facilities clean on a ferry. It did not pay much, but at least it was something. Come payday, this good woman would put aside the bare minimum she needed for the week. The rest she used to buy groceries for those in greater need than herself. And, beside that, she took in motherless Jean and gave her a comfortable home.

The years came and went. When the aunt grew old and could no longer work, the Lord raised up others to take care of her. Her declining years were spent in the company of Christian people; she had congenial fellowship with all her needs met. Then the time came when she could no longer care for herself. Old age robbed her of her faculties. Then a niece came along and became a daughter to her, lavishing goodness on her so that her last years were filled with the goodness she had once shown to others.

The Lord does good to those who are good. Nor does it all end at the grave. Beyond the gloom of the valley of the shadow lies the light and splendor of the glory. Jean's aunt has long since crossed over Jordan and, at the feet of Jesus, she now receives in full measure, pressed down and running over, abundant reward for all those cups of cold water (and bags of groceries) given so long ago.

The psalm now picks up a second theme:

II. The Vanquished Sinner (125:5)

A. The Evil Man's Crooked Dealings (125:5a)

"As for such as turn aside unto their crooked ways . . ." Do you remember a nursery rhyme you may have learned as a child?

> There was a crooked man
>   And he walked a crooked mile,
> And he found a crooked sixpence
>   Upon a crooked stile;
> He bought a crooked cat
>   And it caught a crooked mouse,
> And they all lived together
>   In a little crooked house.

That little nursery rhyme has an outer jacket of nonsense but an inner waistcoat lined with truth. A crooked man walks down many a crooked mile. His business dealings are crooked. The money he puts in the bank is crooked money. He likes crooked things and likes to see others as crooked as himself. Even his homelife is crooked. He doesn't know what it means to be honest. Devious ways suit him best. He will pull a fast one in business. He will buy deceitful pleasures for himself. He will cheat on his wife. We rightfully call such a man a crook. God says that He knows all about the crooked man. He is not nearly as clever as he thinks he is.

B. The Evil Man's Coming Downfall (125:5b)

"The LORD shall lead them forth with the workers of iniquity." The word for *iniquity* is one generally connected with idolatry. God says that the crooked man and the idolater are a pair well met. (Idolatry is religious crookedness, a twisting and distorting of the truth of God into a lie.) God says that He will lead the pair of them forth—to judgment. They will follow their crooked paths down the bends and twists in the road, the incline becoming ever steeper and more difficult until, at last, turning the final bend, they slide into a lost eternity.

"The LORD shall lead them forth." That is what God says also about the great northern power that is one day to invade Israel. "I will bring thee forth," He says, "and all thine army" (Ezekiel 38:4). Later in the chapter we hear Russia saying, "I will go up to the land . . . I will go to them that are at rest" (Ezekiel 38:11). But Russian foreign policy is not being decided in the Kremlin; it has already been decided in heaven. Inflated with pride, armed to the teeth, filled with a deadly hatred of God, determined to seize control, Russia says: "*I* will . . . *I* will. . . ." God says: "*I* will. *I* will bring thee forth." It is a bringing forth for judgment. The same is true here in Psalm 125.

In Hezekiah's day, the army of Sennacherib had set forth on its mission with banners flying and drums beating, determined to extend Assyrian imperial ambitions in the Middle East. It had been encouraged by many seeming victories along the way. It was oblivious of the fact that the God it insulted, derided, and denied was bringing it forth. He had already drawn the line. Brazenly, carelessly, chanting its war songs, reciting its victories, the juggernaut rolled on toward the south, crossing that unseen line the moment it crossed into the land of Israel. But God had His hooks in the jaws of this leviathan of the north. He was playing it as a fisherman plays a trout. All the time He was drawing it forth to the place where His judgment angel stood, silently watching its approach, with his sword drawn ready in his hand.

There is one final note in this psalm, an appendage.

III. THE VIRTUOUS SIGH (125:5c)

"But peace shall be upon Israel." It is an audible sigh of relief. Peace means that the war is over. The Assyrian is no more. The land has rest at last. God has vindicated Himself among the nations.

For us, peace is the legacy of Calvary, the peace of God that passes knowledge, a peace that the world cannot give and cannot take away.

Psalm 126

FREE AT LAST

F REE AT LAST! The horrors of siege and sack are removed. The numbing terror of fear is gone. The world superpower has been flung back by the miraculous intervention of God. Such is the background of Psalm 126.

It contains only six verses, but they throb with relief—as though a person wracked with cancer should suddenly be healed.

Look at this leper, an outcast of society living in poverty, associating only with other lepers. A foul disease is slowly eating his life away. He hears of Jesus. He dares to come, ignoring the warnings of his friends that he will be stoned. He braves the crowds, crying, "Unclean! Unclean!" and resolutely holds to his way. When the crowds melt before him, he feels a certain grim satisfaction—though he never knows when a well-aimed stone will fell him. At last he stands before the Master. "Unclean! Unclean!" he weeps. He feels a touch. Jesus has taken him by the hand (nobody has done that for years). His hand is little more than a stump of putrefaction. He looks. He stares. His hand is healed, whole. He is clean! He might well have gone on his way singing this psalm.

We picture Bunyan's Pilgrim, bowed beneath the load of sin

473

on his back, fleeing from the City of Destruction and urged on
by the words he reads in the little black book in his hand. He is
under deep conviction of sin. But where can he go? How can he
escape? How can he get rid of the burden on his back? Evangelist shows him the way to the cross. He sets out but soon falls into
the Slough of Despond. He is in despair but, though mired and
fouled by the swamp, he struggles out, but on the side farthest
from the city of doom. At last he comes to Calvary. He passes an
open sepulchre, climbs the hill, and sees the dying form of One
who suffered there for him. And, wonder of wonders, the burden is gone. His sin has gone. It has rolled into the mouth of
that tomb. He goes on his way rejoicing.

> Blest cross! Blest Sepulchre!
>   Blest rather be,
> The One who there was put to shame for me.

So Christian sang in the joy of sins forgiven, in the joy of peace
with God. And so we sing. And we could just as well employ the
language of this little Hebrew hymn, Psalm 126.

I. THE REALITY (126:1-2a)

At first the reality of the Lord's deliverance seemed like a
dream.

A. Deliverance (126:1)

"When the LORD turned again the captivity of Zion, we were
like them that dream." Most dreams are like the mirage seen by
a thirsty traveler as he plods across the sands. The oasis looks so
real, so near, just over yonder. But when one gets there, it's
gone. It was never there at all. It was just a mocking trick played
by the light. The reality of burning sands and raging thirst is all
the worse for the traveler's disappointment.

Dreams are like that. We awake from them to find the realities of life unchanged. A dream may have been pleasant enough
while it lasted, but, like a bubble seized in the hands, it bursts
within seconds after we awake. And there it is, the reality of
life, the stab of familiar pain, of disgrace. Soon the dream is
forgotten; its images fade and even the impression it made melts
away. "We were like them that dream," said the psalmist. The
reality was so good as to be unbelievable. Surely they would
wake up and find it was all a dream—that the enemy was still at
the gate, that resources were still running low, that help was as
distant as the moon.

But it was no dream. Sennacherib's hordes were dead. The drums of war were stilled. Never again would that army or any army from Assyria ravish Israel and Judah. In a day or two the whole Assyrian encampment would be a valley of dry bones bleaching in the sun, with no one to recall them to life.

The Lord "turned the captivity of Job" (Job 42:10). He restored his fortunes, gave him back wealth and health, home and happiness. Ezekiel makes it clear that "to turn again the captivity" has to do with a return to a former happy state. It was an idiomatic expression used to emphasize a return to a former good condition (Ezekiel 16:53, 55). Such was Hezekiah's deliverance from the Assyrians.

Such, too, will be Israel's coming deliverance from its present oppressors and still later deliverance from the beast. Such has been the deliverance of numerous ones of the Lord's people. Such was Peter's deliverance from Herod's prison, and that, too, seemed like a dream (Acts 12:9).

So Geoffrey Bull must have felt when at last the gates of his communist prison opened and he was allowed to walk out of China. So General Edmund Allenby must have felt in the first world war when a superstitious dread of his name, as rendered in Arabic (Allah Bey), seized the Turks and caused them to fling down their arms and flee so that Jerusalem could be taken without a shot being fired. Humbly he dismounted from his horse, bared his head, and walked like a pilgrim into the city— as one that dreamed. God does not always perform these kinds of miracles, of course—just frequently enough to confirm our faith, never so many as to allow us to presume.

B. Delight (126:2a)

"Then was our mouth filled with laughter, and our tongue with singing." Who wouldn't sing after so great a deliverance? One would need to be a clod not to sing as the sealed gates of the city rolled open at last and the cooped-up people were set free to roam the surrounding hills if they wished.

In Paul and Silas, however, we see a different response of faith. In prison, with their backs still bleeding and their feet in stocks, they sang nonetheless. Those dismal prison walls had never heard the like. And what singing! About Jesus and His love. About Christ and the cross. Singing until the prison foundations moved, the walls shook, the gates burst open wide! Not a prisoner moved. They sat there spellbound by two men who could sing in circumstances like that.

II. The Reaction (126:2b-3)

A. The Astonished Reaction of the Heathen (126:2b)

"Then said they among the heathen, the Lord hath done great things for them." Is that our testimony among the unsaved? The world is waiting to see something extraordinary take place among the people of God.

In those days the heathen knew that something extraordinary had happened. They saw the vultures coming in great flocks and swooping down toward Jerusalem. They must have thought at first that another ominous victory had been added to the long tale of Assyrian triumphs. But then the news leaked out. Sennacherib's vaunted army was no more. The pall of gloom that had descended on every nation in the Middle East vanished like morning mist. Explanations and speculations would quickly circulate. It was an earthquake. It was the plague. It was this; it was that. One thing was certain: it wasn't the Jews. But Israel's testimony, backed by laughter and song, convinced them: "The Lord hath done great things for them," they said.

Of all people on earth we have something to sing about. We have been saved! What happy, joyful people we should be.

Charles Dickens had the right idea. You see that sour old miser, Ebenezer Scrooge, hopping and skipping around his bedroom on Christmas morning and you know that something has happened to him. You see him flinging open his window and whooping like a schoolboy to a passing youngster, ordering the biggest turkey in town to be sent to poor Bob Cratchet. He went to bed miserable; he woke up with joybells ringing in his soul. That is the evidence of conversion. That is what the world is waiting to see.

B. The Affirming Reaction of the Hebrews (126:3)

"The Lord hath done great things for us; whereof we are glad." The Jewish people now pick up that theme. What heathen people could ever show that their idols had miraculously overthrown a determined superpower that had surrounded their city, determined to take it and destroy it? What heathen king, dying of an incurable disease, had been raised to health and strength by his idols and had his recovery certified by the backward-moving shadow on a sundial?

"What advantage then hath the Jew?" Paul could say in a later age. "Much every way," he could reply, "chiefly, because that unto them were committed the oracles of God. For what if some did not believe? shall their unbelief make the faith of God without effect?" (Romans 3:1-3).

Expanding on the theme later in his letter, he could say of the Hebrew people: "Who are Israelites; to whom pertaineth the adoption, and the glory, and the covenants, and the giving of the law, and the service of God, and the promises, whose are the fathers, and of whom as concerning the flesh Christ came, who is over all, God blessed forever" (Romans 9:4-5). The heathen knew little or nothing about all that. The biblical dimensions of salvation eluded them altogether.

Now let us move from the Old Testament into the New Testament. Consider the regenerating, baptizing, indwelling, securing, filling, and anointing ministries of the Holy Spirit. Consider the five-times-repeated "much more" of Romans 5. Consider the new and better sacrifice, the new and better sanctuary, and the new and better security which form the backbone of our faith as expounded in the epistle to the Hebrews. Consider also the better priest, the better promises, the better prospects which run through that book. Consider what it means for us to be children of God, joint-heirs with Jesus Christ, seated with Him above all principalities and powers and every name that is named not only in this world, but also in the world to come. Consider our *position*—seated with Christ in the heavenlies; consider our *perfection*—declared to be righteous, to be partakers of the divine nature; consider our *power*—God says to us, "Submit yourselves unto God, resist the devil and he will flee—flee—flee from you." To all of which we can add Paul's resounding benediction at the end of the second major section of his Roman epistle: "O the depth of the riches both of the wisdom and knowledge of God! how unsearchable are His judgments, and His ways past finding out!" (Romans 11:33).

III. THE REQUEST (126:4)

"Turn again our captivity, O LORD, as the streams in the south." The word *streams* is literally "torrents." On the surface, Hezekiah wanted God to restore the ravished country to its former beauty and bounty. The south is the Negev, the area that the Jews today have made to "blossom as the rose" (Isaiah 35:1).

But the prayer is much deeper than a prayer for physical prosperity. Hezekiah was too godly a man to be content with that. This is a prayer for spiritual revival. To be saved was one thing. To be filled with the mighty flowing river of the Spirit of God was something else.

True, in Hezekiah's day, there had been some measure of

revival under the evangelistic preaching of the prophet Isaiah and the godly example of the king. The great passover had been celebrated with enthusiasm. But that was just a passing shower of blessing. What was needed was a torrent. It needed for God so to open the floodgates of heaven that torrential revival rains might descend and His people be caught up in the flood of a tremendous spiritual tidal wave that would sweep all before it and leave the national life of Israel purified and deepened and beautified forever. Such a revival never came.

Nor are there signs of such a revival on the dismal spiritual horizons of our day. This needs to be our prayer: "Turn again our captivity, O Lord, as the streams in the south—a spiritual awakening that will revive the church, reach our rebellious wayward children, convert thousands of unsaved people to Christ, and thoroughly cleanse our land of its pollutions and sins."

IV. The Reply (126:5-6)

The reply is simple. There is a price to be paid for revival. Revival doesn't just happen. Spiritual laws bring it about. The cost of revival is high, far higher than most of us ever want to consider.

There is:

A. A Time for Weeping (126:5-6a)

"They that sow in tears shall reap in joy. He that goeth forth and weepeth . . . shall doubtless come again with rejoicing." Is that a price we are prepared to pay? Are we prepared to weep over lost souls, lost sons, lost neighbors and friends?

In our society, weeping is considered too emotional (and certainly we need to beware of shallow emotionalism). But someone needs to care if people are to be saved. Jesus shed His blood; surely we can shed some tears. Paul could say to the Ephesians that he had warned them night and day with tears.

Years ago a young minister visited Dundee, Scotland, deeply concerned that his ministry was producing such meager results. He decided to visit the scene where years before the saintly Robert Murray McCheyne had ministered in such evident power of the Spirit of God. McCheyne died at the age of thirty, but not before he had moved Scotland to its depths. The visitor asked the old sexton at St. Peter's if he could tell him the secret of the amazing influence of Robert McCheyne. The old man led the young minister into the vestry. "Sit down there," he said. "Now put your elbows on the table." He did so. "Yes, that was the way McCheyne used to do it," said the old man. "Now put your face in your hands." The visitor obeyed. "Now let the tears flow! That was the way McCheyne used to do!" said the sexton.

"He that goeth forth weeping . . ." The trouble is, our ministry is not watered by tears. That is why so little fruit is seen, even when we get professions of faith.

Jesus wept. Three times in the Gospels we are told that He wept. "Strong crying and tears" is the Holy Spirit's description.

Jesus wept once for *a man,* a dead man, His friend. Standing before his tomb, sensing the heartbreak around Him, Jesus wept. Knowing that in a moment He would perform the greatest of all His miracles and bring back to life a man rotting in the tomb, He wept at the sorrow and anguish that sin and death brought in its train.

Jesus wept once for *a nation.* He stood on the heights outside the city and wept because Jerusalem and the nation had rejected Him. He could see into the future. He could see the appalling things that would happen within the generation. He wept because a nation that had received so many blessings could be so obdurate, so stubborn and foolish in its rejection of Himself.

He wept once for *the world,* for the whole world of lost and ruined human beings. In Gethsemane the tears rolled down, mingled with blood—so great was His agony—as He thought of a lost, lost world.

B. A Time for Reaping (126:6)

"He that goeth forth and weepeth, bearing precious seed, shall doubtless come again with rejoicing, bringing his sheaves with him." First comes the sowing, "bearing precious seed." There is power in a seed. There is life in a seed. There is life in a seed that can crack concrete. There is power in the Word of God, power to overcome all opposition. We must go out and plant it. We must spread the Word. We must broadcast the gospel.

But what if people do not receive it? That is not our concern. That is God's concern. He is able to take care of that.

Recently I was staying in the home of a farmer. He told me how he was saved. He had been a bitter, hard-drinking, foul-mouthed sinner. He couldn't understand what people saw in church. It made no sense to him to sit and listen to a preacher when he could be out fishing. His wife kept on urging him and one Sunday he went with her to church. He forced himself into collar and tie and Sunday suit and sat awkward and unhappy through the sermon. But something that was said convicted him. He went home knowing he was a lost sinner. The next morning he had his breakfast and prepared to go out. He had his foot poised over the threshold of his house when a voice said to him, "If you go out in your sins and have an accident, you'll be in hell." He moved his foot back, went into the living room, lit a cigarette, and thought it over. He decided he was imagining things. He finished his smoke and headed for the door. As soon as he reached the threshold the same voice said, "If you go out in your sins and have an accident, you'll be in hell." He went back into the house, went upstairs, knelt by his bed, and said: "God, I don't want to go to hell. Please save me for Jesus' sake. Amen." Then and there he was saved and his life transformed. His foul mouth was cleansed. His cigarettes went into the fire. He began to lead others to Christ.

We sow the seed. God takes care of the results.

". . . Shall *doubtless* come again with rejoicing, bringing his sheaves with him." God doesn't promise that everyone will be saved. He doesn't promise that everyone we speak to will be saved. He does promise that sooner or later we shall get a harvest, that we shall come with rejoicing with shouts of joy as at harvest time.

Barry Goldwater once said, "The political battles of this generation will be won on the doorstep." That is where the harvest is. The Mormons realize that, the Jehovah's Witnesses realize that. They are harvesting on the doorsteps of America, Britain, Japan, India, the world.

"He that goeth forth and weepeth . . ." That is the challenge. There is a time for reaping. If we will plant and water the seed, God will guarantee the harvest.

Psalm 127

BUILDING HOUSE AND HOME

I. A PROPER SENSE OF VANITY (127:1-2)
   A. Working in Vain (127:1a)
   B. Watching in Vain (127:1b)
   C. Worrying in Vain (127:2)
II. A PROPER SENSE OF VALUES (127:3-5)
   Children are:
   A. Our Heritage (127:3)
   B. Our Helpers (127:4)
   C. Our Happiness (127:5)

PSALM 127 IS central in the series of fifteen songs that make up the "songs of degrees." According to the title it is a psalm "for" (or "by") Solomon. Much in this little song clearly relates to Solomon; much, too, applies to Hezekiah's day. It is likely that Solomon composed this psalm and that when Hezekiah added it to the Hebrew hymnbook, he did so because it ministered to him in such a wonderful way, thereby proving its divine origin.

The circumstances described in this psalm, both the external and internal threats to the line of David, suited Hezekiah's situation. With Sennacherib and his hosts threatening the demise of the *promised land* and the king's *princely line*, Hezekiah needed some word from God. He found it in this word out of the past. This poem spoke to his need, as the voice of God to his soul.

When he came to make up his collection for the "songs of degrees" this psalm naturally found its way into the anthology and thence into the Book. As we can see for ourselves when we read it, it speaks with the voice of divine authority. The wonder is that it should have taken so long to be adopted into the Hebrew hymnbook. It is another illustration of how cautious

481

the Hebrews were before adding anything to the recognized
Word of God.

The psalm divides into two parts.

I. A PROPER SENSE OF VANITY (127:1-2)

Echoing Solomon, the psalmist underlines three things that
are vain. As an old man Solomon wrote a whole book on the
subject of "vanity," the book of Ecclesiastes. He had become
increasingly convinced that a life that left God out of account
was a life lived in vain.

A. Working in Vain (127:1a)

"Except the LORD build the house, they labor in vain that
build it." Some such thought might well have been in the mind
of Solomon as he hired Hiram's craftsmen, drafted his enormous levies, opened up the vast and incalculable treasures of
David, set about quarrying the massive stones for the foundations, and launched his ambitious seven-year plan to build the
temple of David's dreams in Jerusalem. Over and over again, as
he followed the blueprints David had received from heaven, as
he saw the vast building rise on its awesome foundations, Solomon must have said: "I wish my father were here to see this.
Wouldn't David have been thrilled to see that?"

The Holy Spirit gives us some idea of the enormous amount
of treasure David had accumulated in his forty-year reign and
dedicated for the building of this house for the Lord. When
Solomon received his charge from David, David first showed
him the plans: "All this," said David, "the Lord made me understand in writing by His hand upon me, even all the works of this
pattern" (1 Chronicles 28:19). Like the tabernacle before it, the
temple was to be built to divine specifications.

Then David said to the entire assembled congregation: "Solomon my son . . . is yet young and tender, and the work is great:
for the palace is not for man, but for the LORD God. Now I have
prepared with all my might for the house of my God the gold
for things to be made of gold, and the silver for things to be
made of silver, and the brass for things of brass, the iron for
things of iron, and wood for things of wood: onyx stones, and
stones to be set, glistering stones, and of divers colors, and all
manner of precious stones, and marble stones in abundance"
(1 Chronicles 29:1-2). Then David went on to list the extras he
had accumulated for this work: "Even three thousand talents of
gold of the gold of Ophir, and seven thousand talents of refined

silver, to overlay the walls of the houses" (1 Chronicles 29:4).

David then challenged the leaders of the nation to follow his example and give. And give they did—in abundance. Again the Holy Spirit writes it down: "Of gold five thousand talents and ten thousand drams, and of silver ten thousand talents and of brass eighteen thousand talents, and one hundred thousand talents of iron. And they with whom precious stones were found gave them to the treasure of the house of the LORD" (1 Chronicles 29:7-8).

So when Solomon began to build the house he had no lack of materials; David had seen to that. David could not build the temple, but he could certainly give. Then Solomon set to work (2 Chronicles 3:1-4; 22; 1 Kings 5-7). He drafted thirty thousand Hebrews and sent them to Lebanon, ten thousand at a time, to cut wood. Massive stones were quarried, shaped, and transported to Jerusalem for the foundation. All that wealth could command, all that skill and craftsmanship could devise (within the framework of the blueprint), all that zeal and enthusiasm could do, went into the building of that house. It was the supreme work of Solomon's life. Much else that Solomon did was tainted and spoiled, but not the temple. Never was there a richer temple; fragrant and beautiful wood of cedar, gold, silver, precious stones, rich and royal fabrics—all went into that temple. Yet Solomon, young, full of zeal, devoted to the task, was able to say: "If the Lord build not the house, they labor in vain that build it."

Little did he know what its history was to be. He could not have foreseen the neglect, the outright pollution, that would disgrace that lovely building. Little did he think, in those golden days of his youth, of the vile things he himself, in his old age, would import into Jerusalem; how those things would take root and flourish until, in the end, God Himself would walk out of that temple and hand it over to the Babylonians to be sent up in flames.

As Hezekiah pondered this psalm, he had an inkling of it. He had seen what his father Ahaz had done to that temple, how much rubbish his own men had to cart away before it could be once again dedicated to sacred use.

"If the Lord build not the house, they labor in vain that build it." The truth applies to us as much as to Solomon. It applies to every local church and assembly, to every effort made down here to build God's house, that great "habitation of God through the Spirit." It is not going to be built by super-programs, by slick advertising, by TV commercials; it is not going to be built by oratory in the pulpit or by excellence in the choir;

it is not going to be built by high-pressure evangelism, by vast sums of money, by well-organized missions. It is going to be built by the Holy Spirit, by Christ living in and through believers.

B. Watching in Vain (127:1b)

"Except the LORD keep the city, the watchman waketh but in vain." The people of Jerusalem believed their city, sheltered by mountains and hills, to be virtually invincible. Certainly none of the petty princelings of Canaan would be able to take Jerusalem. The enemy's supply lines would be long and vulnerable, his need for water a constant problem. The enemy's troops would become dispirited and discouraged long before they reached the city. Then its towering walls would face him with a new set of problems calculated to give pause to even the most determined foe. But even those battlements were not Jerusalem's best defenses. Jerusalem's real defense was in God.

When the armies of Assyria deployed before Jerusalem's walls, the city was up against a new kind of foe, a world superpower well-versed in storming the highest battlements and breaching the strongest walls. When Sennacherib's battle-hardened veterans flung their cordons around the city and put in place their proven siege artillery, the watchman might well have stayed awake in vain.

The only other superpower the Hebrews had known was Egypt, but the Egyptians were children compared with the Assyrians. The Assyrians were experts at sacking cities. The thorough way they went about preparing to take Jerusalem must have caused the bravest hearts to tremble. War was hazardous business at best. Nobody knew better than Hezekiah that it was really the Lord who kept the city. If He abandoned it, of what use would watchmen be? When he resurrected this old song of Solomon, Hezekiah no doubt first read it with sober agreement. Perhaps he had it sung and sung and sung by the temple choir in the hope that some of its sublime statements would sink in. Perhaps the citizens of Jerusalem would realize at last how important that great passover had been.

The principle remains unchanged. This psalm might well be read in every legislature, parliament, strategy-planning meeting in the western world. The very clauses in the Constitution intended to keep church and state in balance and accord are now being used against the church. The Bible is banned from classrooms and the soul-destroying humanism and evolutionary philosophy are so entrenched that God as creator is denied a hearing in the schools. The higher halls of learning are frequently in the hands of humanists. The vile sins of Sodom are allowed to parade themselves unblushing and unashamed. Drunkenness and dishonesty haunt the corridors of power. The will to resist aggression is being sapped. Drugs are destroying the nation all the way from grammar school to the most esteemed professions. "Except the LORD keep the city, the watchman waketh but in vain."

The principle holds good also for individual believers. We do not fight the good fight of faith in our own strength. The devil is not the least bit afraid of us. The world and the flesh will sap the resistance of the most committed person—once the main line of defense is down, the place of prayer neglected, the Bible's authority set aside, the daily quiet time allowed to decay. So Samson fell, so David fell, so Peter fell. So may you and I fall.

C. Worrying in Vain (127:2)

Many of us are "anxious about many things." We worry a lot. Solomon points out three things about worrying. It is an *exacting thing:* "It is vain for you to rise up early, to sit up late." That does not help matters. If a developing situation is beyond our control, it is beyond our control. Yet somehow worry comes in and compounds the problem by harrying us. A tyrannical master, once it gets in, it nags us so that we can think of little else.

It is an *excruciating thing:* "It is vain . . . to eat the bread of sorrows." A person in the grip of anxiety and worry is a person in torment. Worry has a way of preying on the mind and driving the victim to distraction.

It is an *exhausting thing:* "For so He giveth His beloved sleep." The solution is in the Lord. All worry does is wear us out until our nerves are frayed, our tempers short, and our health gives way. Our worry is in vain. When we have worried ourselves sick, we have not changed the situation at all; it is still there. All we have done is decrease our ability to cope with it. Incidentally, the name *Beloved* was one of Solomon's names (Jedidiah) given to him by Jehovah Himself (2 Samuel 12:25).

Coming back to the situation in Hezekiah's day, we can well imagine the worry that gnawed at the good king's heart when he realized that diplomacy and defiance alike had failed. The enemy was at the gates. One can well imagine the sleepless nights in Jerusalem.

First, the tidings had come that Sennacherib's invincible troops were on the march. Destination: Jerusalem. The northward walls of Jerusalem would be thronged with anxious watchers. News would filter in as refugees came straggling down the northern highway, dreadful news of taken cities, ravaged populations, rapine and torture and mass deportation. People would rise up early in the morning to scan the horizons anxiously, to exchange whispers with the watchmen. They would sit up late at night, reluctant to go to bed, eager to hear the final newscast of the day, dreading to go to bed lest the enemy should come in the night. They would eat the bread of sorrows, thinking, as they ate, of tales of atrocity. Their sleep would be haunted by nightmares. Mothers and fathers would slip into children's rooms when they were asleep, look with yearning and longing at their little faces, and a thousand fresh fears would arise.

Then the day came when the watchmen on the walls sounded the alarm. The flags and banners of Assyria were visible on the distant hills. The enemy was in sight. Fear would be redoubled. In horror and dismay, people would watch the greatness of the approaching army, observing the efficient way they set up camp and sealed off the highways of escape. Then would come the great engines designed to batter walls and burst gates open and breach defenses.

Sleep? Sleep was impossible. Next came Rabshakeh's insolent propaganda. One can imagine the rumors, alarms, the undercurrent of whispered talk, the mounting fears, despair, the efforts of the king to counteract the demoralization of his defenses by the psychological warfare of the foe.

And what about God's beloved in all of this? What of Hezekiah? Well, one suspects that Hezekiah put his finger resolutely on the last part of verse 2 of this psalm: "For so He giveth His beloved sleep." As a father picks up a fretful child, holds him in his arms, close to his heart, hums a lullaby to the little one so that presently he settles down, safe and secure, and goes to sleep—so the Father gives His beloved sleep. It is one of God's great gifts. Thus Jesus could sleep amid the storm. Thus Peter could sleep in Herod's prison, knowing that the warrant of his execution had been signed and that he was destined to meet the headsman the next day.

The text, however, goes far beyond the passive, to the positive. It is not merely that "He giveth His beloved sleep." Rather it is "He giveth to His beloved *in* sleep." And not just the restoration of our physical fiber, worn and torn with the daily business of life, not just the soothing of our jangling nerves—it is more than that. Often in sleep the answer comes to our problem. We go to sleep committing the whole matter to Him; we wake up knowing just what we have to do and perhaps with some intimation of what God intends to do. So it was with Daniel, when knowing that next morning he must tell Nebuchadnezzar his dream, or perish. He simply went to bed and went to sleep, and God gave to His beloved while he slept. So too He gave to Solomon (1 Kings 3:5-15), to Adam (Genesis 2:21-22), to Abraham (Genesis 15:12-13).

So too he gave to John Bunyan. When his enemies forbade him to preach the gospel and then locked him up in Bedford jail for defying them, little did they know what a pen they were going to set loose on the world. Says Bunyan, in the opening paragraph of his masterpiece:

> As I walked through the wilderness of this world, I lighted on a certain place, where was a den; and I laid me down to sleep: and as I slept, I dreamed a dream. I dreamed and behold I saw a man clothed with rags standing in a certain place, with his face from his own house, a book in his hand, and a great burden upon his back.

Thus begins the immortal *Pilgrim's Progress* and the delightful allegory of man's pilgrimage via Calvary to the Celestial City. God gave to His beloved in sleep.

The psalm continues with:

II. A PROPER SENSE OF VALUES (127:3-5)

The second half of the psalm was equally relevant to Hezekiah's needs. It turns from contemplating battles to considering babies. Hezekiah wanted less of the first and more of the second. How heavily he must have underlined these last three verses before handing the manuscript to the temple choir.

He contemplates the fact that children are:

A. Our Heritage (127:3)

"Lo, children are an heritage of the LORD: and the fruit of the womb is His reward." Today there is a trend, even among Christians, to refrain from having children. They are not looked on as a blessing but as a burden. Nowadays so many people have heart-rending problems with rebellious children that some are suggesting it might be just as well to refrain from having children at all. After all, why spend one's life—one's strength, money, and emotions—bringing up children only to have them repay it all with defiance? To have them disobey, trample on one's ideals, spurn the living God, involve themselves in drugs and sex and open sin? The chances against seeing one's children avoid all the terrible pitfalls set for them by society today are so slim that increasing numbers of people are concluding they would be better off without them.

Then, too, the world is becoming increasingly dangerous. The superpowers are glaring at each other across the width of the world, armed with ICBMs tipped with multiple nuclear warheads. Terrorism is on the rise. Vice and violence are barely checked by society. Foul sins are accepted as permissible, even smiled upon. The church has lost its authority and most of its power. Why have children? Wouldn't it be best to avoid bringing little ones into such a dangerous world? It is an appealing philosophy and it is occurring to many.

But that is not what the Bible says. The Bible says that children are a heritage of the Lord. Suppose the parents of Elijah had reasoned that it was sinful to bring children into such a world as theirs. Suppose they had said, "Omri is king, and he's such a wicked man—he walks in the sins of Jeroboam the son of Nebat who made Israel to sin. In fact, he is worse than all the kings before him. It would be best for us to have no children." Suppose the parents of Moses had reasoned like that. Suppose they had said, "Pharaoh has commanded all boy babies to be thrown into the Nile. We are living in a ghetto. It's not safe to have children."

"Children are an *heritage* of the LORD: and the fruit of the womb is His *reward.*" God is the only one who can make a baby. He is the one who decides which babies should be born black and which should be born white. He decides which ones should be born of rich parents and which should be born of poor. He decides which babies should be gifted and which ones should be retarded. He decides which ones should be born in this generation and which in some other. When He sends a baby into a family it is because He has some wise and wonderful purpose in creating that particular child. As F. W. Boreham once said, "When God sees that in this poor old world a wrong needs righting or a truth needs preaching, or a benefit needs inventing—He sends a baby into the world to do it." Which is why, nearly two thousand years ago, He sent a Child to be born at Bethlehem.

Children are also:

B. Our Helpers (127:4)

"As arrows are in the hand of a mighty man; so are children of the youth." Arrows in the hand of a mighty man are arrows he intends to use, and use effectively. Those arrows are going to go where he wants them to go and do what he wants them to do.

Not everyone can make arrows do what they want. The ability to direct an arrow, so that it accomplishes what the mighty man has in mind, assumes quite a number of things, not least of which is discipline on the part of the mighty man. Before he can discipline his arrows he must discipline himself. He must learn how to direct arrows. He must master the art of archery, learn how to bend a bow, how to take aim, how to judge distance, direction, the strength and quarter of the wind. He must learn how to draw back the string, how to keep his eye on the target. Then, too, he must know how to fashion arrows. They must be made straight. He is not going to hit the target with bent and crooked arrows.

Children who turn out well are not the product of a haphazard home life. Bringing up our children is the single most important task we have in life—far more important than excelling as a biochemist, a pathologist, or a professor of economics. We need to study child raising. We need to study our children. We need to know the various stages through which they pass as they grow from babyhood to adulthood. Above all we need to study the Bible so that we will know and apply what God has to say about this matter. Then our children will grow up to be our helpers. They will help us accomplish our goals in life, and we will help them discover their own place in God's plan. They will be extensions of our own commitment, able to help us in our prime and willing to support us when old age overtakes us, when our own mightiness has passed away.

Finally, children are:

C. Our Happiness (127:5)

"Happy is the man that hath his quiver full of them: they shall not be ashamed, but they shall speak with the enemies in the gate." The word *happy* here is the word "blessed." Literally, the expression is, "Happy, happy is the man . . ." The parents who have many children have many happinesses.

Jesse was such a man; imagine having a son like David. Happy, happy was Jesse, down there on the farm, when the prophet Samuel appeared with the news that Israel's next king was to be chosen from among Jesse's sons. "Well," Jesse might have said, "you will have plenty to choose from." And what a handsome, strapping, impressive group of sons he was able to parade before the prophet. As each one, big, burly, and commanding, stood before the prophet he said: "Surely this is the one." As far as Samuel was concerned, any one of Jesse's sons, humanly speaking, was suited to be a prince of Judah.

Or imagine being the father or mother of Joseph, Daniel, Moses, or Noah! Just imagine being an Amram or a Jochabed and having a Moses, an Aaron, and a Miriam come out of your bow. What happiness.

Hezekiah had no children. I can imagine him reading this psalm over again one more time with great longing in his soul.

Psalm 128

THE WELLBEING OF HOME AND NATION

I. THE SANCTITY OF OUR HOME LIFE (128:1-4)
    A. The Secret of the Lord's Blessing (128:1a)
        1. A Proper Center: The Lord
        2. A Proper Circumference: The Law (128:1b)
    B. The Scope of the Lord's Blessing (128:2-3)
    He will take care of:
        1. Our Finances (128:2a)
        2. Our Feelings (128:2b)
        3. Our Future (128:2c)
        4. Our Family (128:3)
    C. The Surety of the Lord's Blessing (128:4)
II. THE SECURITY OF OUR HOME LAND (128:5-6)
    A. Security at the Center (128:5a)
    B. Security in the City (128:5b)
    C. Security for the Country (128:6)

THIS PSALM IS a companion to the previous one. Its theme is simple yet sublime. The welfare of the state depends on the welfare of the home, and the welfare of the home depends on the spiritual condition of the head of that home. An unspiritual father will often produce unsaved children and unsaved children will build an unstable state. That is the general principle underlying this psalm. The safety of the state depends on the sanctity of the home, and the sanctity of the home depends on the spirituality of the parents. No psalm in the Hebrew hymnbook needs to be preached more insistently than this one.

I. THE SANCTITY OF OUR HOME LIFE (128:1-4)

The psalm begins with a threefold thought:

490

A. The Secret of the Lord's Blessing (128:1)

"Blessed is every one that feareth the LORD; that walketh in His ways." The word *blessed* is the usual word found throughout the Old Testament. It is in the plural. It is the word for "happy." It can be rendered: "Happy, Happy." "Happy, happy is everyone that feareth the Lord."

The Lord lays down two conditions for such happiness. To be happy one's life must have a proper *center* and a proper *circumference*.

1. A Proper Center (128:1a)

"Happy is everyone that feareth the LORD." If we are to be happy, our life must be centered in *the Lord*. The fear referred to is not slavish fear, but spiritual fear (combining the elements of reverence and trust). If we fear God we shall fear nobody else. With most people, that is about the last thing they would think of when thinking of happiness. People think that money will make them happy or that marriage will make them happy. The last thing they think of is that fearing God will make them happy.

Such was the experience of Barbara Hutton whose death on May 21, 1979, made the obituary column of *Time* magazine. She died at the age of 66, a celebrity. She was the granddaughter of F. W. Woolworth, and at the age of twelve she inherited $25 million, a fabulous fortune in those days. But her money did not make her happy, nor did her marriages. She married seven husbands, among them a Laotian prince, a Lithuanian prince, a Russian prince, a Prussian count, and a Hollywood film star. She was plagued with sickness. Her illnesses ranged from kidney disease to cataracts. She died of a heart attack. The last years of her life found her a recluse, often bedridden, weighing only eighty pounds. The newspapers used to call her a "poor little rich girl." Happiness is not to be found in marriage or in money. Something else is needed: True happiness cannot be divorced from God. Peace, harmony, and order have their center in God.

In the world of nature, God, the author of creation, shows us the importance of order and a proper center. If we take our telescopes and explore the world of the infinitely large, everywhere we find order. We find that we belong to a solar system which revolves around the sun. The solar system is populated by a single star, the sun, and by nine planets, thirty-two moons, some 100,000 asteroids, and about 100 billion comets. The word planet comes from the Greek word *planetai,* which means "wanderers," so called by the Greeks because the planets seemed to drift among the fixed stars. The Greeks were wrong. The planets do not wander; they obey fixed laws. On the outer fringes of the solar system is Pluto, which orbits around the sun on an eccentric path which takes it to within 2.7 billion miles of the sun to as far away as 4.6 billion miles. Roaming the icy fringes of the system are the comets. The sun, however, has the power to exert its gravitational sway far far beyond the comets, to a distance of some thousand times beyond the distance of Pluto. The solar system exists solely because it has a center. Without that center it would disappear. But the sun itself is not the center of everything. It, too, has a center.

The sun is one of billions of stars that make up the Milky Way. With the unaided eye we can see about 7,000 of the stars which make up this, our home galaxy, but 100 billion stars are said to be in the Milky Way. Of these, the sun is a mere infant, a fifth-magnitude star up to 100,000 times fainter than its closest neighbors in the galaxy and so faint that it adds nothing to the blue glory of the galaxy's spiraling arms. It shines with a pale yellow light, some 30,000 light years from the hub around which it hurries on its ordained orbit—completing the journey once every 200 million years. The Milky Way would not exist if it did not have a center.

If we explore the world of the infinitely small, we discover that the atom is a miniature solar system with electrons revolving around a nucleus made up of protons and neutrons. These electrons move at inconceivable speeds. They complete billions of trips around their nucleus in a millionth of a second. Atoms themselves consist mostly of empty space. They are so small that a million hydrogen atoms lined up side by side would measure less than the thickness of a sheet of paper. As in the world of the infinitely large, so in this world of the infinitely small, the Creator has written the same lesson. There must be order. There must be a center.

When all is said and done, the fact remains that God is the ultimate center of everything. He must also be the center of our lives. There can be no happiness for those who forget this.

But there also has to be:

2. A Proper Circumference (128:1b)

"Happy is everyone that feareth the LORD; that walketh in His ways." Our life must have proper boundaries. As its center is the Lord, so its circumference is *the law*, the limits set by God Himself. Some things are out of bounds. There are some places we should not go, some books we should not read, some people we should not admire. We must draw the line where God draws the line.

We will find happiness only inside the circumference of God's Word. Outside it we will find guilt, fear, sorrow, and death. "Blessed is everyone that . . . walketh in His ways." Not our ways, not the ways of a particular crowd, not the ways permitted by a godless, humanistic, sinful society—but the ways spelled out by God. That is the secret of the Lord's blessing: a proper center and a proper circumference to life.

B. The Scope of the Lord's Blessing (128:2-3)

The Lord promises four things to those who get the center and circumference right. He will take care of:

1. Our Finances (128:2a)

"For thou shalt eat the labor of thine hands." In other words, to borrow the expressive language of the Old Testament prophet Haggai, we will not put our money in a bag with holes (Haggai 1:6). God will take care of our incomes and our expenditures. He will safeguard our savings. He will see that when we plough and plant we shall also reap the harvest. It will not go to the locust, to the vagaries of nature, to be the spoil of the invader. A bad year will be followed by a good year. He will see to it that we are not left destitute. David could say, "I have not seen the righteous forsaken, nor his seed begging bread" (Psalm 37:25). The Lord may not give us all we want; He will certainly see that we have all we need. Paul puts it this way: "My God shall supply all your need according to His riches in glory by Christ Jesus" (Philippians 4:19).

That is not to say He will never try us, but God guarantees that if we get the center and circumference right, He will take care of everything in between. "For thou *shalt* eat of the labor of thine hands." The guarantee, of course, does not underwrite laziness. God does not promise to prosper indolence. Indolence means that we have the center and circumference out of adjustment in our lives.

2. Our Feelings (128:2b)

"Happy shalt thou be. . . ." There will be no guilt, no grudges, no guile, to bring consequent unhappiness into our lives. Happiness is the most elusive commodity in this world. People spend their lives pursuing it. The slightest breath of adversity and it withers and dies. It is a plant that blooms best in paradise. On earth, it is an exotic transplant and, ever since the fall, blooms only where the soil of the soul is right.

None of the pleasure-providers in this world can issue an unconditional warranty that their particular recipe will please. God can and God does. He says: Get the center and the circumference right and I will unconditionally guarantee happiness.

A camera illustrates the need for getting center and circumference right if happiness is to result. My camera has a system for enabling me to get things in focus and in proportion so that I am assured of a pleasing picture. First, there is an arrangement for getting the picture properly in focus. When I look through the viewfinder of the camera I see in the very center a split-image rangefinder and microprism rangefinder. There is a small circle there, right in the center of the camera. It is made up of tiny fragments which cause a shimmering effect when the picture is out of focus. And in the very center of the camera is an even smaller area which breaks the image in two horizontally. The lens is in focus when the top and bottom halves come together and when the shimmering effect is cleared up. The point is that I have to concentrate on the center. When I have taken care of the center I know that I am going to get a clear, sharp picture. If I ignore the center it doesn't matter how expensive my camera may be, what accessories I have, how carefully I adjust for the light—I am not going to be happy with the result.

When I look through the viewfinder of my camera I can see something else. There is a red rectangle there. I have to make sure that, when I sight through the viewfinder, everything I want included in the picture is inside that red rectangle and everything I don't want included in the picture is outside that rectangle. If I don't take care of the circumference, as represented by that red rectangle, I am going to be unhappy with the results. When the picture is developed I am going to discover that I have cut off Aunt Mary's head or I have chopped off Uncle Harry's legs. Or I will find I have included too much in the picture. I have somehow included the garbage can or that unpleasant neighborhood dog.

I do not know a great deal about cameras. I know even less about how they work. I cannot make sense of much of the manual which talks about such things as depth of field and stopped-down metering and backlight control, but I do know that—and this is basic—I must take care of the center and the circumference. And if I do, I will be happy when the results come in. The people who make the camera promise me that. Just about everything else on my camera is automatic. All I have to do is take care of the center and the circumference and press the button.

God says the same. He says, "Everything else is automatic. You take care of the center and the circumference, and all the rest is automatic. Get Me in the center. Clear up that fuzzy area on the viewfinder. Look at things through Me. If, when you look at a proposal or a prospect through Me, it doesn't look so good, leave it alone. It cannot make you happy in the end." Take care of the center.

"Blessed is everyone that feareth the LORD . . . happy shall he be." There is no way you can be happy if things are blurred when you look at them through Christ. Let me illustrate what I mean.

When I was in high school I was greatly tempted to start smoking. It was considered the smart thing to do, though it had to be done secretly because in those days a boy could be expelled from school for smoking. By the grace of God, however, I was able to see the thing through the proper center, through Christ. Try as I would, I could not get that picture in focus. I could not see the Lord Jesus walking around the temple courts puffing on a low-tar, filter-tipped cigarette. I could not see Him taking a final drag, blowing out a cloud of smoke and butting out the fag end on the temple wall. I could never get the thing in focus when I looked at it through Christ.

And now I am glad. Some years ago my brother, who is one of the leading pathologists in North America, took me into his laboratory in one of the great hospitals where he worked. He showed me half a human lung on a dish. The thing was black, literally black. The person from whose chest it came was a smoker.

I'm quite sure I have been happier as a nonsmoker than I would have been as a smoker. I have never awakened craving a cigarette, never lost the taste of food, never assailed my lips and throat and lungs with cancer-causing tars. In that, at least, to name just one example, I was able to see things in the light of the center. I have been happy ever since that I never had to go through the struggle of trying to stop smoking.

Then God says: "Now take care of the circumference. Make sure you get into the picture just those things I want you to have in the picture. Don't be getting any garbage cans in the picture."

When I was a young man in the army I found myself in a country where certain kinds of immorality were accepted by society. Downtown there were brothels where men could go and foul up their lives with government approval. You can imagine what a temptation those places were to men, living in a barrack room, starved for affection, burning with lust, separated from all the restraints of home. I didn't have to think twice about that one. I knew that God had drawn a red rectangle, clear and well-defined in His Word, that prohibited that kind of behavior. There was no way such conduct could be included in a Christian's life, no way that kind of thing could be included in the picture.

I remember one fellow who thought it could be. I remember, too, his horror when he discovered he had picked up a venereal disease as a result. Nobody had to be told that he wasn't happy. I am not saying that I have never gotten some things out of focus or that I have never included some things which God forbids. I am saying that such things have made me unhappy.

God helping us, let us get the center right and the circumference right from now on. If we do, God guarantees to make us happy.

I do not know how He makes it work any more than I know how my camera works. I only know that our God controls all the factors of time and space. He sovereignly overrules all the thousands of things that crowd into our daily lives. He controls the changing mosaic of life's kaleidoscope. That side of it is His concern. He is the one who makes "all things work together for good to them that love God, to those who are the called according to His purpose" (Romans 8:28). I have God's unconditional guarantee that He will take care of my happiness. If I will take care of the center and the circumference, He does the rest.

He says: "Blessed [happy, happy] is every one that feareth the LORD; that walketh in His ways. For thou shalt eat the labor of thine hands: happy shalt thou be." Notice the change of pronouns from the general to the specific.

3. Our Future (128:2c)

"And it shall be well with thee." Who else can guarantee that? Not only am I going to be happy, but I am going to go on being happy. "It *shall* be well with thee." Only an omniscient, omnipotent, omnipresent God could guarantee that. And, praise His name, so He does.

Adam and Eve were happy in the garden of Eden. God had blessed them. He had given them a glorious place to live; He had given them Himself and each other to love; He had given them a congenial sphere in which to labor. They had all things richly to enjoy. He was the center of their life; His will was the circumference of their life. In the cool of the day He came down to visit with them. The whole world was before them;

they were monarchs of all they surveyed within the compass of
His will. The red rectangle was very small, just drawn around
one tree, that was all. There was no sin, no sorrow, no sickness,
no suffering, no shame, no strife, not even the shadow of sadness. Adam and Eve were delightfully, deliriously happy. Theirs
was "joy unspeakable and full of glory"—until they lost their
center and violated their circumference.

Into that scene of pristine happiness came Satan, the great
spoiler of happiness. He offered to make them happier. He
offered them a life without limits, offered to broaden their
views, to emancipate them from the restrictions imposed on
them by God. He assured them they could do their own thing
and find fulfillment and achievement in godlike independence.

It was all lies. Satan is the great spoiler. Desperately unhappy
himself, he takes a sardonic satisfaction in making others unhappy.

Adam and Eve listened to that old liar and from this stemmed
all the unhappiness of the human race. The human race today
is adrift from its center; it has crashed through every circumference God has drawn around life. And, apart from the intervening grace of God, men and women are heading to a lost eternity, to everlasting, desperate unhappiness beyond the grave.

God, however, offers a guarantee for the future. "It *shall* be
well with thee," He says. There will be bliss beyond anything
that can be imagined in a sin-spoiled world. Who else can make
an offer like that?

4. Our Family (128:3)

But God isn't through yet. He promises that "Thy wife shall
be as a fruitful vine by the sides of thy house: thy children like
olive plants round about thy table."

I see three things about the vine that illustrate the contented
wife of a happy man. The first thing a vine does is *to cling*. It
puts out its tendrils, it takes firm hold of the supporting wall or
trellis, and it clings. By denying the mutual interdependence of
married partners, our age has defied the circumference drawn
by God around things sacred. God knows what is best for a
marriage relationship. Both husband and wife are to cleave to
each other, the wife clinging to her husband, the husband providing support.

A second thing a vine does is *to climb*. Once it has found the
support it requires, it begins its development to maturity. Its
roots go down, its branches grow out until it embraces all the
space provided for its growth. Given proper protection, given
support, given room for growth, soon that vine will cover the

wall. It will turn that wall into a thing of beauty, covered with wide green leaves and rich purple grapes. That is God's idea of an ideal wife.

A third thing a vine does is *to cluster.* It brings forth fruit in abundance. It richly repays the care and cultivation lavished on it by producing an abundant yield. Children, blessings from God, are a result of the union of marriage.

The godly wife is her husband's greatest pride and joy. He has given her the support, as she *clings* to him, that she needs to be secure; he has given her the room she needs to grow, *climbing* like a healthy vine—growing in grace and increasing in the knowledge of God; they share the joy of producing a *cluster* of children, to raise up for the Lord.

No wonder this man is a happy man. And see how infectious his happiness is in the circle of his own home. See how his loving wife has flourished and grown under his care. Look, too, at what God says about his little ones: "Thy children like olive plants around thy table." The olive grows best in hard, rocky soil; it is in austere ground, so to speak, that it is best rooted. Its roots go down, finding their way into the clefts and crevices from whence they draw the olive's richest stores of oil.

The olive is slow to grow, and the planter must be patient while it is growing. Normally, it will bear no berries until the seventh year, nor will the crop be worth much until the new tree is from ten to fifteen years of age. But then it will continue to yield its fruit to extreme age. The discipline and patience of those developing years will pay off for the rest of the lifetime of the tree. The Roman Catholic Church used to have a motto. It said: "Give us a child until he is seven. You can do what you like with him after that." How important those first seven years are. As the twig is bent, so the tree will grow. By the teens the future of the child is pretty well set, apart from some direct intervening act of God.

As has been said, a properly rooted olive tree will grow to a great age. And, as long as a fragment remains, even though externally the tree looks as dry as a post, it will continue to yield olives. For twenty generations owners can gather fruit from an old patriarch. That is why the commandment concerning children is the first commandment with promise—and the promise has to do with living a long life (Exodus 20:12).

Once the olive is well established it needs little supervision. It will take care of itself. Even if long neglected it will revive again when the ground is dug or plowed. Vineyards neglected soon die out, but not olive groves. "Train up a child in the way he should go: and when he is old, he will not depart from it," says the Holy Spirit (Proverbs 22:6).

The olive is an evergreen. If properly set in the soil it will display its beauty no matter what season it is. God's goal with our children is to turn them into evergreens, to give them eternal life, so that they might live forever.

The olive tree casts off its flowers by the millions, as if they were of no more value than the snowflakes they resemble. Children, well trained, will be like the olive. They will cast off the empty glories of this world as of little worth. The empty flowers signify nothing to the olive. All its strength goes to producing fruit. Well-trained children will be able to discriminate between what is of value and what is of little worth in this life, no matter how attractive and eye-catching those things might be. They will concentrate on the things of real value, not only for this life but for the life to come.

There are wild olive trees as well as good olive trees. In its natural state, the wild olive bears no berries, or only a few, and these small and destitute of oil. You cannot graft a wild olive branch onto a good olive tree and expect the good to overcome the bad. The opposite will happen. The wild will conquer the good. It is important that children learn that. They must learn the importance of the friendships they form, of the partnerships they propose, of the marriages they make. It is asking for trouble to take a wild olive graft in marriage, to marry an unbeliever in defiance of the plainly stated Word of God.

Finally, the psalmist speaks of children being like olive plants around the table. Thompson describes for us an aged olive tree, decayed and almost through, surrounded by young and vigorous shoots that have sprung from the roots of the venerable parent tree. They surround it as though to protect it and continue for it its long and useful life. Thus do good and affectionate children gather around the table of godly parents, becoming the joy and rejoicing of their hearts, the stay and comfort of their old age.

Having set before us the secret and scope of a happy life, the Holy Spirit adds a word about:

C. The Surety of the Lord's Blessing (128:4)

"Behold, that thus shall the man be blessed that feareth the LORD." I like Rotherham's rendering of that: "Lo! surely thus shall be blessed the man who revereth Jehovah." The blessing is sure. God will take care of the fortune, feelings, future, and family of the man who puts the *Lord* as the center of his life and the *law* as the circumference of his life. The blessing is as sure as God's guarantee can make it.

The psalmist then turns his attention to:

II. THE SECURITY OF OUR HOME LAND (128:5-6)

The closing two verses contain three circles of security.

A. Security at the Center (128:5a)

"The LORD shall bless thee out of Zion." We have discovered time and time again in the psalms that Zion stands for the political heart of Jerusalem, the citadel of David, Israel's "tower of London." During the millennial age Zion is to be the center of all political power throughout the length and breadth of the Lord's worldwide empire. He who held Zion, held the city and the nation. Let a nation's family life be right and everything else will be right. God will take care of the center of national life. If there is corruption and decay at the center, than all is lost.

It might not be amiss to compare Zion to our political advisory board, the Cabinet, the place where decisions are made, where policy is determined, where a nation's internal and international affairs are decided. If that is rotted away, there is no hope for the nation. If those who make the decisions are atheistic, humanistic, godless, the rot has reached the heart.

The Lord promises security at the center if we take care of our center. "The LORD shall bless thee out of Zion." The nation's deciding issues will be made under the smile and approval of God. What a word for our land in this dark and dangerous hour.

B. Security in the City (128:5b)

"The LORD shall bless thee out of Zion: and thou shalt see the good of Jerusalem all the days of thy life." Jerusalem was the nation's capital. Hezekiah and the Jews had seen this principle work in a very practical way during the Assyrian invasion. Hezekiah had taken care of the center and the circumference by endeavoring to bring the nation back to God. God had hurled back their foes. What a message for the nations of the world in this crisis hour! The best defense we have against hostile military power is in God, the God whose name we have stamped on our coins, and whose Word as a nation we have so greatly neglected, ignored, and banished from our schools.

C. Security for the Country (128:6)

"Yea, thou shalt see thy children's children, and peace upon Israel." Instead of young men being marched away to war, instead of the nation's youth being slaughtered on the battlefields, they would grow up to have families of their own and live their days in peace. God would defend the land from all its foes.

There is something almost pathetic about Hezekiah's references to children in this and the previous psalm. The thing that troubled him most, when his sickness overtook him, was the fact that he had no children, no son to be his heir and carry on his name and the royal Davidic line. He was still childless when the Assyrians were laying siege to Jerusalem. The promise of God to David seemed about to fail (2 Samuel 7:12). Not until three of the fifteen years added to Hezekiah's life had passed did the king finally have a son.

Hezekiah triumphed over all his testings and troubles. He lived to see Jerusalem safe and secure all the days of his life, as God said. He lived to see a son born and grow to the threshold of manhood. And if he was disappointed in Manasseh's disinterest in spiritual things, he now had no doubt that God could take care of the royal line. Hezekiah's great grandson was Josiah, one of the godliest of all the kings.

Thus ends this psalm. It underlines the truths that one cannot divorce the *security* of the homeland from the *sanctity* of the home; and one cannot divorce the sanctity of the home from the *spirituality* of the parents. That is its message to us today.

Psalm 129

ISRAEL AND HER FOES

I. ISRAEL VICTIMIZED (129:1-3)
  A. Frequent Persecution (129:1)
  B. Fruitless Persecution (129:2)
  C. Frightful Persecution (129:3)
II. ISRAEL VINDICATED (129:4-8)
  A. The Lord's Righteousness Declared (129:4)
  B. The Lord's Retribution Desired (129:5-8)
    1. Their Unsuccessful Schemes (129:5)
    2. Their Unproductive Show (129:6-7)
    3. Their Unblessed Souls (129:8)

THIS IS THE LAST in the second group of five psalms in the songs of degrees (or "songs of the steps," as J.B. Rotherham describes them). It is another of those psalms which seem to revolve around the circumstances of Hezekiah and the Assyrian invasion. In this short hymn we see Israel and her foes. Israel has always been surrounded by hostile neighbors, yet no nation that has persecuted her has ever done so with impunity. The blessing of the Lord is with this nation as with no other nation on earth. This psalm, which divides into two parts, brings that into clear focus.

I. ISRAEL VICTIMIZED (129:1-3)

The psalmist points out that Israel has been victimized by:

A. Frequent Persecution (129:1)

" 'Many a time have they afflicted me from my youth,' may Israel now say." In 701 B.C. the Assyrian invasion of Israel carried the tide of conquest to the gates of Jerusalem. Hezekiah could look back over more than eight centuries of Hebrew

502

national history, from the time of the pharaohs until the time of the Assyrians. He could have compiled an impressive list of afflictions and persecutions, starting with the oppression in Egypt.

Israel spent its youth in Egypt; it was there that the nation grew to manhood. Jacob went down there with his family (about seventy people in all). Four hundred years later the nation marched out of Egypt some 3 million strong. It was in Egypt that Israel grew up. It was in Egypt that anti-Semitism, hatred of the Jew, first raised its head. Since then it has been endemic in all Gentile societies having contact with the Jews and periodically it has become epidemic.

Anti-Semitism first assumed epidemic proportions in Egypt when the reigning pharaoh viewed with growing dislike and apprehension the multiplying millions of Hebrews in the land of Goshen. He decided upon what Adolph Hitler later called "the final solution" to the Jewish problem: genocide, the murder of a race. Goshen became the pharaoh's "gas chamber." Hebrew boy babies were the victims. Pharaoh hoped that within a generation he would have solved his problem by wiping out this dreaded and detested people. Within a generation, however, Egypt suffered the most humiliating and horrifying series of disasters and defeats ever recorded of any nation in all of history.

God sent Moses back to the courts of Pharaoh, armed with miracles that beggared Egypt. Then, when Pharaoh still persisted in defying God's orders, God met him and his armies in floodtides of wrath at the Red Sea. There He inflicted on him a defeat that is still recounted and remembered today, nearly 3,500 years later. God wanted the world to learn a basic lesson: "Don't tangle with Israel." That was history's first major affliction of Israel, and God made a summary example of it.

Soon after Israel left Egypt there was war with Amalek, then war with the remnants of the giants, then war with Moab and with the kings of Canaan. No nation prospered that lifted the sword against Israel; no nation ever will. Then came the days of the judges and constant harassment from the surrounding nations—afflictions God permitted as chastisement of Israel's national sins, but afflictions He never failed to avenge. We can trace the same story through the long history of the Israeli and Judean kings. Nations warred against Israel and in the end paid for it in full.

Syria to the north and Egypt to the south, both became major offenders. Then at last came a world superpower, Assyria, whose tyrannies and atrocities dwarfed those who had gone before. Assyria carried ten of the tribes into captivity. The land was desolated and its peoples marched away into oblivion. The

overwhelming defeat of the Assyrian army outside the walls of
Jerusalem was the first herald of the coming storm for Assyria,
the first intimation that God had suffered long enough this
nation's invasions and insults. Next time there would be no
Jonah to preach repentance to Nineveh—just a Nahum to
preach retribution.

So the singer mentions the frequent persecution of Israel. He
goes on to show that it was:

B. Fruitless Persecution (129:2)

"Many a time have they afflicted me from my youth: yet they
have not prevailed against me." There is a reason for the persistent phenomenon of anti-Semitism in the world. It has its roots
in the fact that Satan is the god of this world, this world's
prince. Behind the nations of the world he works, using his
fallen angels and demons to effect his will. He has divided the
heavenly hierarchy into nations to correspond with the nations
of earth; over each nation of mankind he sets his own secret
government in the unseen world. Over each nation he sets a
prince. These princes make up the "principalities and powers"
spoken of by Paul in Ephesians 6:12.

The truth of this is seen in the book of Daniel, where the
prophet was told by Gabriel that an answer to his prayer was
held up for three weeks by an angelic being he called "the
prince of Persia"—obviously not a human prince. Having delivered the message, the angel told Daniel he was returning to
fight with the prince of Persia and that the prince of Greece was
also involved. "There is none that holdeth with me in these
things, but Michael your prince," he added (Daniel 9:12-21).

To understand this we need to go back even farther. It would
seem that when God called Abraham and promised to make of
him a great nation (Genesis 12:1-3) He not only laid the foundations of the Hebrew nation, but He did something else. He
created a nation over which Satan had no prince. Instead, God
put Michael, the archangel, the head of the armies of heaven, as
prince over Israel.

This explains the mystery of anti-Semitism. Satan loathes and
detests the nation of Israel because it is one nation over which
he has no direct authority. All the other nations he received as a
grant from Adam when Adam, in whom God had vested dominion of the earth, fell. But Israel is an exception. Israel was
created by direct fiat of God. Down through history Satan has
tried to get rid of this nation. He has tried assimilation and he
has tried extermination and he has failed. There is not a leader

in any one of the twenty leading countries of the western world today who does not have to take the influence of its Jewish population into account when determining internal and international affairs.

So, throughout history, Satan has tried to rid himself of this thorn in his side—the nation of Israel. In 586 B.C., after two previous invasions, the Babylonians sacked Jersusalem and burned the temple. In 473 B.C. Haman instigated a decree aimed at the extermination of the Jews in the Persian empire. In 169 B.C. Antiochus Epiphanes polluted the temple and began a bloodbath of persecution. In A.D. 70 the Romans besieged Jerusalem, killed a million Jews, deported 97,000 captives, and glutted the slave markets and arenas of the world with Jewish slaves. In A.D. 135 the Romans crushed the Bar Kochba rebellion and banished all Jews from the country which Hadrian renamed Palestine (after the Philistines, a hereditary enemy of the Jews for centuries). In 399 Constantine issued edicts against the Jews. In 439 Theodosius II issued further edicts against them. In 630 the Byzantine emperor Heraclius allowed priests and monks to massacre the Jews of Palestine. In 722 Leo II ordered all Jews to become Christians or face the consequences. In 1066 the Moslem rulers of Grenada in Spain killed 4,000 Jews in a single day. In 1096 Pope Urban II proclaimed the First Crusade, which was preached throughout Europe by Peter the Hermit. Christian knights made it a side show of the Crusades to massacre Jews whom they called "Christ-killers." As crusade followed crusade many Jewish communities adopted what they called *Kiddush ha-Shem* ("the tradition of sacrifice"—i.e., mass suicide to escape the horror they knew awaited them when the brave knights rode by). And so it continued. In 1290 Edward I ordered all Jews out of England. In 1306 Philip IV ordered them out of France. In 1475 all Jews in Trent, Italy, were massacred. In 1371 all Jews in Seville were murdered. In 1483 the infamous Torquemada took charge of the so-called Holy Office in Spain and taught the Jews a new lesson in horror as he turned the Inquisition against them. In 1492 all Jews were driven out of Spain. In 1506 Spanish Jews who had sought refuge in nearby Portugal were massacred. And so it went— until in the middle twentieth century Germany cheered Adolph Hitler to power and gave itself over to history's most infamous attempt to exterminate the Jews. And now the mantle of Jew-hate has fallen on the Russians and the Arabs.

"Many a time, many a time," says the psalmist. "Many a time have they afflicted me from my youth, yet they have not prevailed against me." The reason is found in the Abrahamic covenant. When God first presented that covenant to Abraham He promised to bless those that blessed him and to curse those that cursed him. History is one long record of the outworking of that principle. Nations that have harbored and protected the Jews have prospered. Nations that have persecuted them or turned against them have eventually paid for it in full.

The psalmist points out, further, that Israel has been victimized by:

C.   Frightful Persecution (129:3)

"The plowers plowed upon my back: they made long their furrows." When they think of that statement our thoughts go at once to Gabbatha. Is not this what Pilate did to Jesus? "I will scourge Him," he said, "and let Him go." And so he did; he scourged Him. But he did not let Him go. That was beyond his power.

The Roman scourge was made of cords or thongs made more terrible by pieces of lead or brass or small, sharp bones attached to the lashes. People condemned to crucifixion were usually scourged before being led away to execution. The victim was stripped to the waist and bound in a stooping position, hands behind his back, tied to a post. The suffering was excruciating, the body lacerated. Sometimes under a scourging the veins would be laid bare and even the inner muscles, sinews, and internal organs exposed. "The plowers plowed upon my back," says the psalmist, perhaps one of those prophetic foreviews of the suffering Messiah seen so often in the Old Testament.

In its historical context, however, the statement refers to the nation of Israel and its sufferings at the hands of its foes. In Hezekiah's day the land was being thus scourged by the Assyrians whose armies had already thoroughly plowed up the northern part of the country and left it desolate. The statement may look forward, too, to the future sufferings of the nation. After the capture of Jerusalem by Titus the plow was drawn through the city by Terentius Rufus. The same thing was done again by Hadrian's troops after the suppression of the Bar Kochba revolt.

The picture of plowing on a person's back is a graphic way of depicting frightful sufferings. Who can read the history of the Jews in the Middle Ages without being deeply moved at the sufferings of this people? The barbarities of the Nazis demonstrated that anti-Semitism is still very much alive. Atrocities against the Jews will come to a head in the great tribulation yet to be launched by the antichrist.

II. ISRAEL VINDICATED (129:4-8)

Israel's enemies never have the last word. God does, and God is on Israel's side.

A. The Lord's Righteousness Declared (129:4)

"The LORD is righteous: He hath cut asunder the cords of the wicked." The reference seems to be to the cords which bound the victim of the lash. The Lord steps in and cuts free the victim, throwing back in confusion those ill-treating him. The reason why "the cords of the wicked" cannot ultimately prevail is because the Lord is righteous. If wickedness were allowed to triumph finally on the earth, then either the Lord would not be impeccable or else He would not be omnipotent. Since He is both good and great, the cords of the wicked can never prevail in the end. He may allow wicked men to flourish for a little while—He even uses them to discipline others—but in the end He cuts their cords and vindicates His righteousness.

The context here is clearly national. History affords us countless examples of God cutting the cords of the wicked when they transgressed once too often against His people. A classic example is that of the British empire, which in its heyday embraced a quarter of the globe. It was held together by the most tenuous cords. In many ways the empire was thrust upon Britain. Here, one of Britain's sons, a Wolfe or a Clive, would add another subcontinent, a Canada or an India; there, an adventurer would bequeath another vast segment as did Cecil Rhodes when he handed over North and South Rhodesia, a tract of territory in Africa as large as Germany, France, and Spain together. Here, traders, missionaries, or explorers would add some more; there, the exigencies of a growing world trade would necessitate the annexation of these vital straits or that strategic island or those key countries. And it was all bound together with cords that led to London.

Two Jews did as much to make the empire possible as did anyone. One was Benjamin Disraeli, Britain's imperialist prime minister, the man who purchased the Suez Canal and secured for Britain continuing access to vast dominions in the east. The other was Chaim Weizmann, who rescued Britain from certain defeat during World War I by discovering how to manufacture a synthetic cordite out of horse chestnuts. A grateful British government issued the famous Balfour Declaration in which it pledged itself to help establish a national home for Jews in

Palestine after the war. But Britain soon forgot her indebtedness.

The League of Nations mandated Palestine to Britain to administer with a view to establishing a national home for Jews in the area. The Balfour Declaration of 1917 envisioned Palestine as comprising both banks of the Jordan. In 1921 the British colonial secretary Winston Churchill decided to divide Palestine along the Jordon river and award the eastern portion to Britain's ally, King Emir Abdullahibn-Husein, thus creating the state of Jordan, a national home for the Arabs. Presumably he assumed that the Arabs would be content and that Britain could then fulfill its pledge and establish a national home for the Jews in the western half of the country.

It did not work out that way. With increasing troubles looming on the horizon, with vast, oil-rich lands at stake, with the Germans intriguing with the Arabs against the Jews and against Britain, the British began a series of betrayals against the Jews which were to have awesome consequences. First they issued a so-called White Paper to restrict further Jewish immigration into the country. This was done just when the holocaust was beginning and when the Jews desperately needed a place to go. That was the moment Britain chose to slam the door of the promised land. God remembered that. Then, after World War II, Britain elected a leftist government which had no particular love for the Jews and began a policy which led, in the end, to Britain's ignominious withdrawal from Palestine. The Mandate came to an end in bitterness and recrimination and a disgruntled British administration saw to it that the key military installations in the land were left in anti-Semitic hands. For that final spiteful act she paid in full. God cut the cords of empire and Britain lost everything.

History tells us that the Lord's righteousness is upheld. He holds to His original pledge to Abraham to bless those who bless him and his seed, and to curse those who curse him.

B. The Lord's Retribution Desired (129:5-8)

The psalmist mentions three things about those who trouble Israel—and here the psalm takes on the character of an imprecatory psalm, and also a prophetic dimension which embraces the coming day of divine retribution. The psalmist underlines:

1. Their Unsuccessful Schemes (129:5)

"Let them all be confounded and turned back that hate Zion" (129:5). The Lord had done just that, of course, to the Assyrians. The psalmist prays that He might do it always to those who persecute His people. He is invoking one of the basic clauses of the Abrahamic covenant in which God had promised so to do.

Again we could fill books illustrating the fulfillment of this psalmist's prayer. One example will suffice. When Hadrian came to the throne, the Roman empire he inherited from Trajan was vast. It was more than two thousand miles in breadth, more than three thousand miles in length. It stretched from the great wall built across the north of Britain to the Tropic of Cancer and from the Atlantic seaboard to the Euphrates river. It comprised more than sixteen hundred thousand square miles, for the most part fertile and well cultivated. Peace and prosperity under law were the hallmarks of that vast domain.

Then came Bar Kochba, a passionate Jew who proclaimed himself messiah and took possession of the ruins of Jerusalem. The emperor Hadrian, flattered that all was well in the east, was infuriated. He summoned his best generals and sent them against the upstart. So great and severe was the struggle that Hadrian, in announcing to the Roman senate the conclusion of the war, refrained from using the usual congratulatory phrase. To revenge himself against the Jews, Hadrian set about obliterating Jersusalem. Its very name was changed to *Aelia Capitolina*. A temple was erected in Jerusalem to the pagan god Jupiter. A statue erected to the divine majesty of the Caesar was set on the site of the holy of holies. Jews were banned from the city and for hundreds of years Jerusalem passed out of history, no Jew daring to approach it.

So Hadrian won his petty triumph. And he signed the death warrant of his empire. With him the empire reached its high-tide mark. For a few more years the eddies of the flood rippled on the outer frontiers, but the Roman empire was through. It took centuries for it to be evident, but God had drawn the line in the sand. Hadrian had strode across that line in fury, and the end was only a matter of time. H. G. Wells, who certainly could not be suspected of any undue bias toward God, Christianity, or the Jews, commenting on Hadrian, said, "The full tide of Roman expansion was past." He stated that already, in the reign of Hadrian's successor, the frontier in northern Europe was actively on the defensive. The Teutonic and Slavic tribes had had enough.

Next, the psalmist underlines:

2. Their Unproductive Show (129:6-7)

"Let them be as the grass upon the housetops, which withereth afore it groweth up; wherewith the mower filleth not his hand; nor he that bindeth sheaves his bosom." The roofs of eastern houses were flat. Sometimes seed carried by the wind fell on these roofs and found a lodging place in the dirt accumulated there. This seed would germinate but because it had no depth of soil it would soon come to nothing. The psalmist prays that the schemes of Israel's enemies might be like that, that they might come to nothing before they could come to flower and fruit.

The schemes of those who hate the Jewish people may flourish at first, but they are counterproductive. In the end they come to nothing. God dries them up and blows them away. Their success is futile and profitless. God has only to blow on it and it is gone. OPEC is a prime example. When the oil-producing Arab states suddenly realized what a potent weapon oil could be in their hands, they set about blackmailing the world. They realized fabulous fortunes from the wealth that lay buried beneath the sand of their desert lands as the price of oil soared. Inflation gripped the world. Nations borrowed money feverishly just to stay afloat. Undeveloped nations particularly suffered.

The new wealth was invested in world banks, in assets in foreign countries, in fabulous spending sprees at home, in bankrolling terrorism, in buying sophisticated pro-Arab anti-Israel propaganda around the world. God has shown how easily He can blow upon this newfound wealth. Nations tightened their belts, found unsuspected oil resources, researched possibilities for alternate energy. The Arab stranglehold on oil flourished for awhile, but then economic depression hit the industrial, oil-consuming nations and oil prices fell. OPEC members began squabbling about quotes and prices and suddenly the cartel did not seem nearly so omnipotent as it had been. The Arabs have found themselves saddled with vast socialistic enterprises at home and falling revenues. They are particularly vulnerable to upheavals within, to invasion from without, and to the seizure of their invested wealth in foreign lands. Their power in the world is like the grass on the housetops—of swift and spectacular growth, but of shallow and unsubstantial roots.

Finally the psalmist underlines:

3. Their Unblessed Souls (129:8)

Those who curse and afflict the Jew reveal a state of soul completely out of touch with the living God of Abraham, Isaac, and Jacob. "Neither do they which go by say, 'The blessing of the LORD be upon you: we bless you in the name of the LORD.' " Such was the cheery greeting of those passing by the harvest fields in Israel. The enemies of the Jew know nothing of the blessing of God on their lives.

The psalm teaches us a great truth—God has a covenant tie with Israel that He has with no other nation on earth. Nations which attack Israel will have God to contend with. All history proves that to be true. Let the nations of the earth beware.

Psalm 130

A PENITENTIAL PSALM

I. PERSONAL EXPERIENCE (130:1-6)
   A. The Psalmist Is Depressed (130:1-2)
      1. Desperate Condition (130:1)
      2. Desperate Cry (130:2)
   B. The Psalmist Is Defiled (130:3-4)
      1. A Sad Fact (130:3)
      2. A Sure Forgiveness (130:4)
   C. The Psalmist Is Determined (130:5-6)
      1. Spiritual Exercise (130:5)
      2. Splendid Expectation (130:6)
II. PUBLIC EXHORTATION (130:7-8)
   A. There Is Hope in the Lord (130:7)
   B. There Is Help in the Lord (130:8)

THIS IS THE SIXTH of seven penitential psalms. In this psalm Hezekiah pours out his heart to God. His confession of sin is both personal and public, that is, he assumes the role of a true mediator, taking on himself the sins of his people and pouring them out before the Lord as though they too were his own.

The world does not know many such individuals. It is a serious thing for the world when no one is concerned enough at national sins to cry to God for the poor lost lands of earth. The world will never know what it owes to the presence in its midst of a few godly intercessors who pour out their souls before God for the land in which they live.

This penitential psalm divides into two parts. In the first part we have:

I. PERSONAL EXPERIENCE (130:1-6)

We see the psalmist in three states of soul. First:

A. The Psalmist Is Depressed (130:1-2)

1. Desperate Condition (130:1)

"Out of the depths have I cried unto Thee, O LORD." The psalmist was in the depths of despair. Like Jonah in the belly of the whale, he had touched bottom. Billows of despair surged over his soul like the billows of the sea.

If the psalmist was Hezekiah, as seems likely, we do not have to look far for the source of his sorrows. We see a close correspondence between the words in this psalm and the "writing of Hezekiah king of Judah, when he had been sick, and was recovered of his sickness" (Isaiah 38:9). Even though he had recovered, he was still haunted by his circumstances.

There was, for instance, the problem of *barrenness*, either of himself or his wife. He had no son to carry on his name. Worse, he had no son to carry on the royal Davidic line. Even after the prophet had given him the sign of the sundial, the sign that doubtless inspired the writing and collecting of these "songs of degrees," no son was born. There were three long years of that "hope deferred" which "maketh the heart sick" before a son was born.

There was the problem of *battlefields;* he was surrounded by the din and noise of battle. Assyria was on the march, and that was enough to plunge anyone into despair. Nineveh had been a potential world threat for centuries, but now, armed to the teeth, aggressive, untameable, it was on the march. It had one supreme ambition: to rule the world. Out of the north it had come, an Old Testament Soviet Union, bent on conquering the Middle East. It saw the little Hebrew nation as an obstinate and annoying hindrance to its plans. Samaria had been besieged and by this time, perhaps, had been taken. Hezekiah wavered, his foreign policy uncertain. He had tried appeasement but it did not work. Babylon beckoned with vague promises of an alliance and Egypt encouraged him to take a firm stand, but Isaiah told him to trust neither. There was no help either in the far east or in the west. Hezekiah was surrounded by battlefields. And they were coming closer.

All the horrors of conflict and carnage, siege and slaughter, loomed ahead—either that, or surrender on unthinkable terms of deportation and the seeming dissolution of the Old Testament kingdom of God.

There was another problem too; the problem of *behavior*. Apostasy had ruled the land for years. Apostasy had brought the northern kingdom of Israel to a terrible end in blood, fire, and ruthless deportation. Judah was just as bad. Hezekiah's own father, a weak and wicked king, had brought Judah to an all-time low of idolatry and apostasy. Hezekiah's religious reforms, great and zealous as they were, had produced only a surface reformation. The nation's heart remained untouched. The worst vices had been curbed, the law had been enforced, national religion had been revived, but the hearts of people and prince alike remained untouched. It was politic to conciliate the king in these things, but, within a few years of Hezekiah's death, the vile sins he sternly repressed would flourish again. The son he longed for would reign longer than any other Judean king but would be the worst king ever to disgrace the throne of David. The nation would never recover from Manasseh's disastrous rule. In the end the Assyrian threat would be replaced by the Babylonian. "Out of the depths have I cried unto Thee, O LORD," sobs the psalmist.

Such is the setting of the song. The sad realities faced by the singer are reflected in the verses that follow.

2. Despairing Cry (130:2)

"LORD, hear my voice: Let Thine ears be attentive to the voice of my supplications." In his despair the psalmist turned to God. "Lord," he says, "Hear *my* voice." He did what here and there a noble soul does in every generation; he became a mediator, a daysman. He stepped into the gap. The Lord would not hear the majority who were wedded to their sins but perhaps He would hear him.

Israel could not have found a better intercessor. In later years the rabbis made much of Hezekiah. The famous rabbi Hillel, who flourished just before the coming of Christ, was so enraptured with Hezekiah that he said, "Israel shall have no more messiahs; for they had him in the days of Hezekiah." An erroneous statement, but one that shows the reverence with which later Jews regarded this godly king. Of course, Hezekiah was no messiah, but he certainly was a mediator. He pleaded with God as Moses had done.

In the very first year of his reign he had repaired and reopened the doors of the temple. He had assembled the priests and Levites, charging them to clean up the temple and get rid of the filth that disgraced it. So much rubbish had accumulated in the temple it took the entire priestly clan two whole weeks just to cart the stuff out. Then Hezekiah had restored the temple worship, reinstating the long-neglected sacrifices and reorganizing the choir. It had all been done "suddenly" the Scripture says (2 Chronicles 29:36), doubtless to face the opposition with an accomplished fact (idolatry had long been entrenched in the city). Hezekiah had then convened a great Passover celebration, the first to be kept for many years. He had sent invitations to all Judah and to the remnant of Israel in the north, urging all to join in a great national celebration of worship. He urged his people not to repeat the sins of their fathers which had brought the nation so low. Many in Ephraim, Manasseh, and Zebulun mocked Hezekiah's messengers, but some from the scattered tribes had responded, and so did all the tribe of Judah. In preparation, Hezekiah destroyed all altars to false gods throughout the country.

The Passover was kept with great rejoicing and with such outward enthusiasm that the celebrations were allowed to run on for a full week. Hezekiah then extended his reforms, rooting out idols wherever they were discovered and extending his activities to the former tribal territory of Israel in the north. Finally, he reorganized the priesthood and revived the law for setting aside tithes and offerings for the Lord's servants.

The revival of religion in Judah was largely the work of two men, Hezekiah and Isaiah the prophet. No wonder Hezekiah could say, "Lord, hear my voice." Hezekiah, however, was not content with a single prayer; he kept on praying.

Looking at his second state of soul we see that:

B. The Psalmist Is Defiled (130:3-4)

Although the king was a godly man, one of the best of men, he was still terribly conscious of his own shortcomings and sins. The burden of his prayer was sin, Israel's sin, his own sin.

1. A Sad Fact (130:3)

"If Thou, LORD, shouldest mark iniquities, O LORD, who shall stand?" How many sins make one a sinner? Just one. James says that if we keep the whole law yet offend in one point we are guilty of all. What hope do we have if God were to mark every single sin, call us to account for every piece of misbehavior? Our condition would be beyond hope.

The problem, even with confessing sin, is that we do not remember all our sins. Our hearts are corrupted, our minds confused. We are indulgent of our sins. We do not understand at times what constitutes sin. Still less can we properly confess all our sins. But God can mark them. Hezekiah prayed that God would not do that. Who could stand if He did?

2. A Sure Forgiveness (130:4)

"But there is forgiveness with Thee, that Thou mayest be feared." The "fear of the Lord," in the Old Testament, was not slavish fear, but reverential awe and trust; it included the hatred of evil. Praise God, He does forgive sin. Sin has to be forgiven at the point of guilt. If a man sins against his wife, he must put it right with his wife; if he sins against his neighbor, he must put it right with his neighbor. It is no use a man asking his wife to forgive him for something if he did wrong to someone at work. Above all, sin has to be confessed to God since all sin is also against Him.

This was the essence of the removal of guilt under the sacrificial system of the Old Testament. Sin had to be dealt with at its point of guilt. The *sin offering* dealt with the *principle* of sin—I am not a sinner because I sin; I sin because I am a sinner. I do what I do because I am what I am. The *trespass offering* dealt with the *practice* of sin. It entailed first putting things right with the one who had been injured, then coming and putting things right with God.

"There is forgiveness with Thee that Thou mayest be feared," the psalmist said. When the Holy Spirit does His gracious work of conviction in our hearts and when He ministers forgiveness to us, He plants in our hearts a reverential awe. It has cost God so much to forgive. Calvary is the price. So God plants, in the penitent's heart, a deep disgust at sin itself—something no human priest can do.

When Dr. G. Campbell Morgan went to Wales to see for himself the Welsh revival, he heard a Welshman praying in English. He was praying in English but thinking in his native tongue, translating as he went along. He started to quote these words, "There is forgiveness with Thee, that Thou mayest be feared. . . ." He stumbled at the second line. After one or two attempts to express the idea, he put it like this: "O Lord, we thank Thee that there is forgiveness with Thee enough to frighten us." That's it. Sin should frighten us. The sinner is afraid God will punish him; the saint is afraid he might sin again.

We come to the psalmist's third state of soul. We see that:

C. The Psalmist Is Determined (130:5-6)

He is determined to watch and pray, to do the two things Jesus asked Peter, James, and John to do in Gethsemane. We have seen him praying; now we see him watching.

1. Spiritual Exercise (130:5)

"I wait for the LORD, my soul doth wait, and in His word do I hope." There is nothing else to do but wait. God is never in a hurry. The work He wants to do in our hearts takes time. We want things hurried up; God is working for eternity and takes whatever time He needs to bring our souls into line with His will.

The Moody Bible Institute has a film entitled *Time and Eternity.* To make this film, the Moody Institute of Science staff used cameras with which they could play visual tricks with time. They sped time up on the screen so that things that normally take hours, days, weeks, even months, to develop can be seen all at once, in a matter of moments: the opening of a flower, the rising and setting of the sun. They slowed time down so that something that happens in a flash can be stretched out and can be seen happening in a slow, drawn-out way: the fall of a steel ball into a glass of milk, the flight of an arrow through the heart of an egg. The resulting effects are fascinating to watch.

One of the sequences in this film takes the viewer through the Panama Canal at the speed of sound, another takes him on a weekend vacation—the entire event in five or ten minutes. The activities of days are telescoped into a few seconds. The viewer sees traffic in a busy intersection arriving, stopping, starting again, flashing off into the distance, all at high speed. He watches a football game being played at the same pace.

The stadium fills in a moment; the game is a series of darts and dodges—here, there, everywhere; the stadium empties and it's all over and done with. The overpowering impression one receives is one of exhaustion and a sense of relief. What if life were lived at a pace like that? What a blessing that God has slowed it down to a day at a time. We want to speed it up; God makes us wait.

God keeps telling us He has not forgotten us; He hears us. If we are watching out for Him, He is watching out for us.

2. Splendid Expectation (130:6)

"My soul waiteth for the LORD more than they that watch for the morning. I say, more than they that watch for the morning."

Here is a Hebrew priest, one of thousands; the company of priests was so vast it had to be divided into twenty-four courses. Only for one month every two years does his division have the privilege of service in the sanctuary. In his course there are hundreds of priests, so his turn might come only once in his lifetime. But now it has come. He is going to offer the morning sacrifice. He has been up all night (he could not trust himself to sleep lest he oversleep). All his colleagues will be watching, priests and Levites alike; the king will be watching; thousands in Jerusalem will be watching. Nothing must go wrong. The responsibility is his. He has rehearsed this moment in his mind a hundred times. He has thought how he must hold the knife, where he must make the cut, how he must catch the blood, how to flay the sacrifice, how to place it on the altar, how to arrange the wood, how to apply the fire. God will be watching as he leads the people redemptively by way of the morning sacrifice.

Like that priest, like a lover awaiting the arrival of the beloved, so the psalmist waited for the Lord. Deliverance? Yes, he wanted that, but much more than that he wanted the Lord.

Certainly, we want the Lord to act in our situations. We would be less than human if we didn't. But do we want Him most of all? Can we sing with Fanny Crosby:

> Oh the dear ones in glory, how they beckon me to come,
> And our parting at the river I recall;
> To the sweet vales of Eden they will sing my welcome home,
> But I long to meet my Saviour first of all.

So then, we have the psalmist's *personal experience.* Next comes his:

II. PUBLIC EXHORTATION (130:7-8)

The psalmist concludes by pressing home to the conscience of his nation the need for a personal and national relation with God. There is such a thing as national religion as well as personal religion. He points out:

A. There Is Hope in the Lord (130:7)

"For with the LORD there is mercy, and with Him is plenteous redemption." The nation of Israel was founded on the principle of redemption. God redeemed Israel from bondage in Egypt. The Passover was intended to commemorate that fact and keep it annually before the conscience of the nation. With the Assyrians threatening disaster from the north it was imperative that Israel keep her eye on the Lord. The northern kingdom had perished for trusting in idols.

How true for us today. However rich their spiritual heritage, nations cannot survive apart from spiritual renewal.

The expression "plenteous redemption" reminds God's people that He has a thousand ways to effect salvation for those who put their trust in Him. His patience and mercy had not been exhausted by the nation's long and persistent rebellion. Confession and contrition would soon open the floodgates of His lovingkindness.

B. There Is Help in the Lord (130:8)

"And He shall redeem Israel from all his iniquities." Again the psalmist puts his finger unerringly on the sore spot, the source of all the nation's woes. Its iniquities were the reason for its perils.

The psalmist here lifts the psalm out of its historical setting and puts it down in the tribulation age. Its prophetic overtones are too obvious to be overlooked. The psalm anticipates Israel's perils during the great tribulation and the earnest waiting of the instructed Jews for the coming of the Messiah. Indeed, beginning with the setting up of the beast's idol in the temple and the consequent persecution, the godly will be able to begin a countdown. They will know that the coming of Christ to reign will take place in exactly 1,260 days. They will be able to mark off the days on their calendars. What a comfort that will be in those terrible times!

The sudden appearing of the Lord in the sky will be the turning point for Israel. "He shall redeem Israel from all its iniquities." They will "look on Him whom they pierced." The nation will be "born in a day," born from above, redeemed at last. May God speed the day.

Psalm 131

A HUMBLE BELIEVER

I. TRUE HUMILITY (131:1-2)
  A. Crucified Pride (131:1)
  B. Cautious Prudence (131:2)
    Beware of:
    1. Undue Independence
    2. Undue Insecurity
II. TRIUMPHANT HOPE (131:3)

THE TITLE TELLS US that this is "a song of degrees of David." It breathes the spirit of David in his years as a shepherd boy, as a courtier in the palace of King Saul, and as a fugitive on the hills patiently awaiting the day when God would make good to him His promise of the throne. Above all, the psalm sounds like David, the youngest son of an insignificant farmer, suddenly projected by circumstances into the society of the nation's ruling elite—with courtiers for his companions and rivals, with the king's son for his friend, with palace plots and politics all about him (dangerous pitfalls), and with gossip enough in his ears to scandalize scores of the great names in the nation.

The psalm is short. It is just a little step in these "songs of the steps," as some call them. Its theme is humility.

That may seem like a step down to us, but it is really a giant step up in the counsels of the Most High. Nor is the step that small. It is a tricky one indeed to negotiate. Many a person has refused to attempt it at all. And some who have made the attempt have ended up slipping and sliding all the way to the bottom.

I. TRUE HUMILITY (131:1-2)

David begins with mention of:

A. Crucified Pride (131:1)

Only a truly humble man could write, "LORD, my heart is not haughty." Imagine broadcasting one's own humility. That is either gloriously true or an astonishing exhibition of self-deception. Humility is an exceedingly difficult plant to grow in the soul's garden of grace.

Often, humility is misunderstood. We think of it as a kind of self-abnegation, a wretched groveling, a pretending not to have abilities that we know we have. In *Screwtape Letters*, C. S. Lewis, with his usual incisiveness, tells us that true humility does not consist in pretending we do not have gifts and abilities we know we have and everyone else knows we have. He says that true humility is, for instance, to have the ability to design and build the most magnificent cathedral in the world—but to be just as happy if someone else were to have that ability.

"LORD," says David, "my heart is not haughty, nor mine eyes lofty: neither do I exercise myself in great matters, or in things too high for me." It is, of course, an incidental proof of David's genuine humility that those words were not intended by him for publication. Those words were breathed by him in prayer. He wrote them down for his own edification and guidance in the conduct of his affairs. This is not a psalm he sent, signed and sealed, to the chief Musician to be incorporated in the temple repertoire. Nobody in David's day suspected, I feel sure, that such a psalm existed. Nobody announced that today the choir was going to sing about David's humility. Probably David never suspected that this psalm would ever see the light of day. We have no idea how it came to be in Hezekiah's hands. But when it was finally added to the sacred songs of Israel, its author had been dead for over three hundred years.

We can picture David, fresh from the farm, plunged into the exciting world of high politics in the court of the king. The Old Testament history book says that "David behaved himself wisely." The Old Testament hymnbook tells us what went on in David's heart. He kept himself in his place; he refused to meddle in the politics of the palace; he kept clear of matters that were beyond him and that were none of his concern. In so doing, he not only saved his own life, but he showed himself fit for those important matters of government he so studiously set himself to avoid.

The spirit of the world tells people to "get ahead." This world's educational systems are designed to help the young advance. Parents want to see their children make their mark, which is all well and good, as far as it goes. God, however, is running His own school in this world, especially for His own.

Moses learned that. He spent forty years in man's school, learning to be *somebody*. He ended up by murdering an Egyptian. He
spent forty years in the wilderness, in God's school, learning to
be *nobody*—and then God could use him in a marvelous way.

David avoided all that. He brought with him into Saul's court
a humble spirit which kept him clear of meddling in affairs he
rightly judged were too great for him as a shepherd lad.

This is a practical principle. When a young fellow leaves
school and finds himself suddenly thrown into the business
world he would do well to lie low; adopt a teachable spirit; be
willing and cheerful, conscientious and obedient, stay away
from the gossip of the place and from criticisms of his supervi-
sors; sedulously avoid the politics of the job. Those things are
too high for him.

I remember my first job. I was fifteen years of age, a recent
graduate from high school. I thought I owned the world. I
obtained a job with Barclay's Bank in South Wales, one of the
world's largest banking institutions. I thought I had the most
important job in Britain. In fact, I was just a junior clerk, the
lowest of the low, at everyone's beck and call, responsible for
changing the blotting paper for the manager and making sure
his inkwell was full.

I remember the new feeling of freedom and importance that
was mine my first morning out of school and on the job. I was
sent on an errand from the bank and I can still remember
swaggering down High Street, astonished at myself for no longer being in school, half expecting to be apprehended by the
authorities for truancy. What a big man I thought I was when I
first went into Newport Station and bought a season ticket for
the train to Cardiff. I remember how important I felt, looking
over the counter at customers. I was sure they had all come in
to look at me and to admire me. So many times as a little boy I
had gone into the bank with my mother to stand and watch with
awe as the tellers took her money, flipped their way profes-
sionally through a stack of banknotes, and counted the change
with a dash and splash that left me envious. Now I was the one
on the other side of that counter. No matter that I had not yet
attained to the dizzy height of teller, able to take people's money
and stamp their deposit slips with those impressive-looking rub-
ber stamps. I was a banker!

Yet with it all there was an underlying grain of common sense
painstakingly drilled into me by my sensible father. I knew
really I was nobody. I was only the "junior" at everyone's nod
and summons. On the wall near where I stood was a phone. It
had connections to various officials in the bank: to the head of
the securities division; to the chief clerk's office; to the remote,

plush, and awesome quarters where the manager presided in terrible isolation and dignity. That phone was equipped with a small red warning light. When that phone rang and that light came on—that was it! Upstairs in this bank building was the Local Head Office which presided over the affairs of hundreds of branches of Barclay's Bank all over South Wales. When the light went on, that meant that the BIG MAN himself, the regional director, was on the line. Then, no matter what one was doing—adding up in one's head a long column of figures in pounds, shillings, and pence, or trying to meet a daily deadline with the mail under the harassment of half a dozen other people—when that light went on, somebody ran. To that phone, up those stairs, into the "presence," there to wait, awed and insignificant, for whatever directions the Big Man might have to give. And woe betide the bank employee—junior or chief clerk—who kept that Big Man waiting.

It was a wholesome reminder of the true scale of things. I was a nobody and a novice. What a fool I should have been if I had tried to meddle in matters of high finance. What an idiot to have entered into the conversation of my betters and passed an opinion to the manager on his decision concerning a loan to the giant dockyard down the street. I would have had my ears pinned back in a hurry.

David knew better than to meddle in matters that were over his head and that were no concern of his. Think of all the harm done by gossip among the people of God. How much of it would die an instant death if David's principle were applied to it, the simple principle of minding one's own business and letting other people get on with theirs.

B. His Cautious Prudence (131:2)

"Surely I have behaved and quieted myself, like a child that is weaned of his mother: My soul is even as a weaned child." The weaning of a child marks a stage in its growth. It marks its first venture into *independence*. The child can now eat many kinds of food and venture farther afield. It is growing up, but it is still a child and in no position to make any more than the simplest decisions and those only under parental permission and guidance. And, at times, it has a nostalgic longing for the old closeness.

Think, for instance, in adult context, of a person who first learns to fly a plane. To begin with, he is very fearful. He is venturing into a strange new world, the world of aerodynamics, where different rules apply than those to which he has been accustomed all his life. The laws of this new world are adamant.

One false move, one mistake, and he is lost. It is an unforgiving, relentless world of unbending law. So he heeds well his instructor. He learns how to taxi a plane down the runway, in touch with the control tower, noting the direction of the wind, keeping the plane trim. He learns how to climb, dive, bank, and, hardest of all, how to land. And for the first few weeks he is very glad to have an instructor sitting by his side with experienced hands hovering over a duplicate set of controls.

However, the student pilot goes on learning. He learns to navigate, to adjust to the weather, to use his instruments. His confidence grows with every hour of flying time and he begins to become irritated at his instructor's hands tensed to seize control should he make a mistake—because he isn't going to make a mistake. He knows how to fly now. He learns how to handle stalls and spins, how to extricate himself from trouble.

Then he is weaned. He flies solo. The first flight fills him with nervousness, but the feeling of independence is pleasant too. With each successive flight his confidence grows. He can fly an airplane; he can fly it as well as his instructor; he can fly better than the Red Baron. And therein lies the danger. He grows too confident. He imagines his skills to be greater than theirs are. He takes chances with the weather. He takes off despite warnings from the tower. He flies over terrain for which he has little training and for which his skills are inadequate. The mountains below cause strange currents, unexpected turbulence. Lulled by his previous successes, he suddenly finds himself in serious trouble. Bad weather blows in, he is lost, his fuel is running low.

That is the danger with being weaned, but we have to be weaned. We cannot remain babies forever. But there is danger when we think we know more than we do. We must beware of:

1. Undue Independence

After David had been in court long enough to know the ropes came the dangerous phase, the equivalent of being weaned. The time came when the novelty of being among important people wore off. The newness of being Saul's son-in-law passed, and his new familiarity with the court and with the king could have blunted the knife-edge of his dangers. His successes as a soldier might easily have prompted David to assert too much independence. But David was saved from those quicksands. He knew the danger of independence, the first danger of being weaned. We know from 1 Samuel 18 how wisely David behaved himself during those initial, perilous years in Saul's court.

2. Undue Insecurity

The weaning of a child, however, marks not only the first venture into independence, with its attending perils; it marks also the first real taste of insecurity. The weaned child toddles off quite happily at first. But then, all of a sudden, comes that surge of fright, loneliness, and insecurity. It wants to run back to its mother. And wanting to go back to a former stage of growth is as bad as anticipating a future stage of growth.

David wanted to cultivate a state of soul in which he knew just as much of independence as God wanted him to know and just as much of insecurity as God wanted him to have so that he would not wander away from Him. He was wise enough to know the dangers as well as the delights of being a weaned soul.

God does want to wean us, and therein lies both our potential and our peril. Nobody has illustrated this better than C. S. Lewis in the second volume of his science-fiction trilogy. In *Perelandra*, Lewis re-enacts the temptation of the race, setting the scene on Venus, a strange world of surging seas, floating islands, and fixed land. To that world comes Ransom, the hero of the tale. On that world lives a woman, dwelling in innocence and perfection on one of the floating islands. Ransom meets this woman and learns the law of life on Perelandra. She has every floating island on the planet on which to live, each one a paradise. The Fixed Land she can visit. But Eleldil, the Creator, has told her that on no account must she spend a night on the Fixed Land. That is reserved for him. Then comes the tempter. He tries to persuade the woman that she *should* spend a night on the Fixed Land; that is her right as an intelligent being; that is part of growing up. Eleldil really *wants* her to spend a night on Fixed Land. The prohibition is a test—to see whether she will accept her maturity and responsibility as a being with a will of her own and dare to be all that she has the potential to be. Eleldil does not want her to remain a child forever. He wants her to grow up. He wants her to act independently of him. And how else could she show him that she had grown up but by daring to do what he had prohibited? The woman grows older with every passing moment. And, almost she is persuaded to act on her own, in independence; and ever she is held back by a sense of insecurity, by a haunting sense that something is wrong in the flattering platitudes of the tempter.

So David—ruled by his deliberate acceptance of the fact that he was a shepherd boy wandering in high places, ruled by a humble, teachable spirit—away from home and aware of the pitfalls of life, behaved himself like a weaned child. He had learned the secret of keeping things in balance. He had the rare gift of objectively seeing himself as he was, not as pride would have him see himself.

So we see David's crucified pride wedded to cautious prudence. We have set before us his true humility.

II. TRUIMPHANT HOPE (131:3)

David turns now from himself to his nation, the nation over which one day he was to be king. "Let Israel hope in the LORD from henceforth and for ever." The holy anointing oil had already been poured on David's head by Samuel, out there on the family farm. All the while that he was walking so carefully before Saul he knew that he was to be king. David also had enough sense to keep that to himself. It was not up to him to get rid of Saul. That was up to God. His job was to hope in the Lord.

In the same way, Israel was to hope in the Lord. The Lord had destined Israel for great things among the nations, but Israel could never attain her destiny by independence of God nor by a groveling feeling of insecurity when faced by the world superpowers. It needed the same sense of balance that David had achieved: crucified pride and cautious prudence.

All this, of course, was especially relevant in Hezekiah's day. The overthrow of Sennacherib's host was a major step in Israel's spiritual development. The danger now was that the nation would become cocky and independent, forgetting that God had given the victory. Or else, horrified and appalled at the devastation wrought in the land by the invader and fearful that the Assyrians might come back, the nation might feel a debilitating sense of insecurity. "Let Israel hope in the LORD from henceforth and forever." Words could not be more appropriate to Hezekiah's need at this crisis hour in trying to bring before his people the spirit that should motivate the nation.

One can picture him handing this short psalm over to the choirmaster. "Note this last verse," he might say. "When the choir comes to this verse, make them sing it out with all they have. Pull out all the stops."

Psalm 132

GOD'S COVENANT WITH DAVID

I. DAVID'S OATH RECORDED BY THE LORD (132:1-10)
  A. A Reminder of David's Sincerity (132:1-6)
    1. David's Afflictions (132:1)
    2. David's Affirmations (132:2-6)
      a. Wording of the Pledge (132:2-5)
      David promised he would be:
        (1) Truthful in His Promise (132:2)
        (2) Tireless in His Purpose (132:3-4)
        (3) Triumphant in His Performance (132:5)
      b. Witnesses to the Pledge (132:6-7)
  B. A Request for David's Sake (132:8-10)
  The matter of:
    1. A Finished Work (132:8)
    2. A Faltering Worship (132:9)
    3. A Fervent Wish (132:10)
II. DAVID'S OATH RECIPROCATED BY THE LORD (132:11-18)
  A. The Promise Regarding the Scepter (132:11-12)
    1. The Lord's Integrity (132:11a)
    2. The Lord's Intention (132:11b-12)
  B. The Promise Regarding the Sanctuary (132:13-15)
    1. A Selected Place (132:13)
    2. A Sacred Place (132:14)
    3. A Satisfying Place (132:15)
  C. The Promise Regarding the Saints (132:16)
  D. The Promise Regarding the Site (132:17-18)
  A central point for:
    1. Vitality (132:17)
    2. Victory (132:18)

THIS PSALM IS symmetrical in structure. The first ten verses deal with David's promise to God to build Him a house in Jerusalem; the remaining verses deal with

God's promise to David to build a house (dynasty) for him. Because of his longing for a son and heir, Hezekiah was haunted by these two houses. Several of the psalms in this series are haunted in the same way. The specter of childlessness, of the possibility of the royal Davidic line becoming extinct after him, horrified Hezekiah.

It would have been a good thing if it had. It became extinct anyway in Jeconiah, as far as the line through Solomon was concerned and as far as the throne was concerned. It would have been a good thing if the dynastic line to David, the throne line, that is, had finished on a high note with godly King Hezekiah. Instead it finished on a low note after the disastrous reign of Manasseh (the son and heir Hezekiah eventually had) and after the equally disastrous reigns of some of his successors. Anyway, this psalm is Hezekiah's plea to God to give him a son—a plea solidly based on God's promise to David and mistakenly embracing the idea that the Messiah was to come through Solomon.

I. DAVID'S OATH RECORDED BY THE LORD (132:1-10)

A. A Reminder of David's Sincerity (132:1-6)

1. David's Afflictions (132:1)

"LORD, remember David, and all his afflictions." David's afflictions were many; all kinds of things conspired to keep him off the throne and to drive him back off it once he was seated there. But there is a deeper significance to this opening plea. The word *afflictions* is really "anxious care." Despite all the other ups and downs of his colorful life, David had one "anxious care" and that was to build a temple for God in Jerusalem. His wars, work, and wealth were all dedicated to this goal. Hezekiah's "anxious care" was also for the temple. Like his illustrious forebear, no sooner was he securely seated on the throne than he made God's house the supreme concern of his life.

2. David's Affirmations (132:2-6)

The psalmist now paraphrases and poeticizes David's oath to make the building of God's house the special concern of his life.

a. We note *the wording of the pledge* (132:2-5). He made a threefold pledge to the Lord. He promised God to be *truthful in his promise:* "How he sware unto the LORD, and vowed unto the mighty God of Jacob" (132:2). That is, he pledged himself to the mighty One to whom Jacob in his day made his vow. That vow was made at Bethel when Jacob was running away from home, and on the night when he learned that the God of Isaac his father, the God of Abraham his grandfather, could become the God of even Jacob. He "vowed a vow" (Genesis 28:20), or, as we would say today, he made a solemn vow. Thus David, about to become the founder of the Hebrew temple, appeals in a vow to the God to whom Jacob appealed when he was about to become the founder of the Hebrew tribes. He pledged that he would be truthful in his promise.

He pledged that he would be *tireless in his purpose:* "Surely I will not come into the tabernacle of my house, nor go up into my bed; and I will not give sleep to mine eyes, or slumber to mine eyelids, until . . ." (132:3-4). He would allow himself no rest until he had secured a place where God could rest among His people. It was a noble thought. How God loves to have those who will take spiritual things so seriously that all thought of personal convenience is driven from their lives. They will have no rest, they say, until God comes into His.

D. L. Moody was led to Christ by a man with such a one-track mind, by a man who had a single, unswervable determination to win boys and girls to Christ. This was a man who, having had young Moody in his class for some time, walked into the back of the shoestore one day, where Moody was at work, and said to him, "Now then, Dwight, you've heard it long enough; it's time you accepted Christ." Moody became a Christian, probably the noisiest and most rambunctious and objectionable Christian the staid church he attended had ever known. He flung himself into the Lord's work right from the start. He heard someone say, "The world has yet to see what God can do through a man wholly yielded to Him." He said, "By the grace of God, I'll be that man."

That is what David had: a sense of purpose, an urgent passion, a resolution never to rest until he had done something about the house of God on earth. He promised to be tireless in that purpose.

He promised he would be *triumphant in his performance:* "Until I find out a place for the LORD, an habitation for the mighty God of Jacob" (132:5). It was going to take years before he found that place. There were to be wars and rumors of war, there was to be upheaval and pestilence. In the end he found it—a mighty rock on Mount Moriah where, centuries before, Abraham had gone all the way with God (Genesis 22). Through all those changing vicissitudes of his life David never lost sight of his goal, to find the right place.

b. We note also *the witnesses to the pledge* (132:6-7). "Lo, we heard of it at Ephratah: we found it in the fields of the wood."

News of David's vow ran through the kingdom. Down there at Ephratah the tidings were told. This fresh evidence of their illustrious brother's consecration to the things of God, of his devotion to the Lord that not even success could spoil, infused new life into his relatives: "We will go into His tabernacles: we will worship at His footstool."

Such is the impact of the consecration of a man like David. A man's relatives are often the most difficult people in the world for him to reach. David's inspiring commitment to the house of God had its impact on his parents and his brothers. A consecrated life is bound to make an impression. In David's case, the immediate impact of his commitment resulted in his own family rediscovering the place where the sacred ark resided "in the fields of the wood." They sought out the place where God had put His name. The ark was in Kirjath-jearim (1 Chronicles 13:5), long neglected, under a tent beneath some trees in a forest. It should have been in the center of Israel's national life. David's kinfolk, the people of Ephratah, decided they had neglected the ark too long. It must have been a happy day for David to know that his consecration had this impact on his family, friends, and neighbors in his hometown. All too often, a prophet is not without honor except in his own country and among his own people.

B. A Request for David's Sake (132:8-10)

The psalmist brings before the Lord the matter of:

1. A Finished Work (132:8)

"Arise, O LORD, into Thy rest; Thou, and the ark of Thy strength." Solomon had used these words, "Arise O LORD God, into Thy resting place, Thou and the ark of Thy strength" (2 Chronicles 6:41), when dedicating the magnificent temple he had built. Hezekiah, when rededicating the temple, might have used the same words, though in his day the Shekinah glory cloud had not yet departed from the temple.

What God must have endured in longsuffering silence all the years of Ahaz and his predecessors! These godless men had not been content with neglecting the temple; they had insulted the living God with false altars and they had filled the chambers attached to the temple with all kinds of rubbish. We do not know how God visibly manifested His anger with these things. Maybe that mysterious Shekinah pillar (fire by night, cloud by day) grew dark, or fiery red, as an expression of God's wrath; maybe it dimmed until it could scarcely be seen at all. We are not told. But that God should have sat there, on the mercy seat, through those dark apostasy-ridden years and not have destroyed the temple, Jerusalem, and the nation in one fiery holocaust is a tribute to His patience and grace.

Well might Hezekiah, borrowing the language of Solomon, have assured the Lord that now He could rest. The temple had been cleansed; the work of purifying and rededicating the temple was finished.

2. A Faltering Worship (132:9)

"Let Thy priests be clothed with righteousness; and let Thy saints shout for joy." Hezekiah had done his best to restore the priesthood and Levitical service but he could not clothe them in righteousness. That was God's work. He had urged on them the need for being right with God but he could do no more. He asked God to make His saints "shout for joy." There had been so much fear, war, hardship, death, and desolation. Now let joy fill the hearts of God's people.

It had been thus in David's day, when in anticipation of building the temple, he had brought the sacred ark up to Jerusalem. We read: "Thus all Israel brought up the ark of the covenant of the LORD with shouting, and with sound of the cornet, and with trumpets, and with cymbals, making a noise with psalteries and harps" (1 Chronicles 15:28).

3. A Fervent Wish (132:10)

"For Thy servant David's sake turn not away the face of Thine anointed." Hezekiah thus comes to the point of his prayer: he needed a son. When he had been so sick that his friend Isaiah had told him to prepare for death, Hezekiah had turned away his face. He had turned to stare in stunned silence at the wall. It could not. It must not be. For David's sake it should not be. Hezekiah did not plead in his own name. He did not parade before the Lord his own good deeds and his own devotion to the temple. He pleaded the name of another greater than himself. He breathed before God the name of David, "the man after God's own heart." It was the greatest name he knew. Similarly, when we come to the Lord, distressed at our lack of fruit, at the seeming failure of our lives at vital and critical points, we too plead the name of another, a greater name than David's, a name guaranteed to command attention at the throne above—the name of the Lord Jesus Christ.

The second half of the psalm shows:

II. David's Oath Reciprocated by the Lord (132:11-18)

Four promises are recorded in these verses.

A. The Promise Regarding the Scepter (132:11-12)

In this section the speaker is the Lord Himself, ratifying and guaranteeing His promise to David and to David's heirs.

1. The Lord's Integrity (132:11a)

"The LORD hath sworn in truth unto David; He will not turn from it." Hezekiah had taken care of God's house (the temple); now God must take care of the house (dynasty) He had promised to David. That God would make good His promise could not be questioned. God's word was enough to guarantee that. But He had gone further; He had sworn to David. It was impossible that God's integrity could fail. It was bold of Hezekiah to write afresh into his psalm the solemn pledge and promise of God. Bold, for he was still childless, and also reassuring.

2. The Lord's Intention (132:11b-12)

"Of the fruit of thy body [David's] will I set upon thy throne. If thy children will keep My covenant and My testimony that I shall teach them, their children shall also sit upon thy throne for evermore." The promise to David concerning the establishment and maintenance of the Davidic dynasty on the throne of Israel was unconditional (2 Samuel 7:16). However, when that promise was renewed to Solomon, a condition was appended to the original contract: Solomon and his descendants must walk in obedience to God (1 Kings 3:14). This conditional aspect of the covenant, reflected in Psalm 132:12, must have haunted Hezekiah. He did not know what kind of a son he was going to have, but he knew what kind of a father he had had: a weak and wicked man.

One of Hezekiah's descendants was a man named Jehoiachin (also called Jeconiah and sometimes merely Coniah—2 Kings 24:6; 2 Chronicles 36:9; 1 Chronicles 3:16; Jeremiah 22:24-28; 24:1). This man pulled down God's curse on the Solomonic line. He was a youth of eighteen when he came to the throne and he reigned a scant three months, long enough for the world to see what kind of a king he would be. He was carried off to Babylon by Nebuchadnezzar. He was so thoroughly bad that Jeremiah contemptuously cut down his name from Jeconiah to

Coniah. Because the name Jeconiah meant "let Jehovah establish," Jeremiah lopped off the divine prefix to signify that God had cut Himself off from Jeconiah. Jeremiah called "this man Coniah" a "despised broken idol." Then he apostrophized the earth: "O earth, earth, earth, hear the word of the LORD. Thus saith the LORD, Write ye this man childless, a man that shall not prosper in his days: for no man of his seed shall prosper, sitting upon the throne of David, and ruling any more in Judah" (Jeremiah 22:28-30). In actual fact, Coniah was not childless; he had eleven sons (1 Chronicles 3:17-18). But he was childless as to the throne, since none of his sons sat on the throne of David. In him the royal line to Christ through Solomon came to an end.

Thus the threat, inherent in the conditional clause when the Davidic covenant was renewed with Solomon, came into effect. The Lord Jesus, by birth, was not a son of David through Solomon. He was not born of that branch of the Davidic family. Joseph was, but Joseph was not the father of Christ. Jesus claimed the throne through a collateral line. David had two surviving sons through Bathsheba: Solomon (through whom the *regal* line is traced to Joseph in Matthew) and Nathan (through whom the *legal* line is traced to Mary in Luke). Jesus was to be "the seed of the woman." It was through Mary He inherited His right to be Israel's king, although when Mary married Joseph the two lines, the regal and the legal, were joined as well. Thus God kept faith with David and remained true to His warning to Solomon.

Hezekiah did not know all this. He did know that the Davidic line through Solomon had already been badly tarnished but he did not live to see how dreadfully it would be tarnished by his own (as yet unbegotten) son, Manasseh.

B. The Promise Regarding the Sanctuary (132:13-51)

The Lord ratified to David three things about the temple and its site. It was:

1. A Selected Place (132:13)

"For the LORD hath chosen Zion; He hath desired it for His habitation." Zion is used here in its broadest sense, as including Moriah where the temple actually was built. It was to Zion that David brought the ark and found a place for it pending the final settlement of the ark on Moriah. God did not forget David's thoughtful act. Zion is embraced by Him as being part of the nation's heart. This is brought out clearly in Psalm 24.

2. A Sacred Place (132:14)

"This is My rest forever: here will I dwell; for I have desired it." God has put His own name there, and that name is not associated with a Muslim mosque. The temple site belongs to God and to the Hebrew people. Those who forget that will find themselves entangled with a God who has claimed it for His own.

3. A Satisfying Place (132:15)

"I will abundantly bless her provision: I will satisfy her poor with bread." Verses 13-15 which deal with Zion and the sanctuary here take on a millennial dimension. They anticipate the day when Jesus will make Jerusalem and Zion the center of a world empire. It will be obvious to all then that God's blessing rests on the place He has chosen for Himself.

C. The Promise Regarding the Saints (132:16)

"I will also clothe her priests with salvation: and her saints shall shout aloud for joy." This was a direct answer to Hezekiah's prayer that Zion's priests might be clothed with righteousness. It was a worthy prayer. Before a man can minister as a priest, he must be right both with God and with man. Before he can be righteous, however, he has to be saved. So God promises to clothe His priests with salvation. That was their first and foremost need. Righteousness apart from salvation is self-righteousness, something God hates and man despises.

An unsaved priest—an unregenerate man, the product of a religious education, consecrated by a religious system, given so-called sacramental powers, functioning in the name of God, a blind leader of the blind, pretending to have powers of sacrifice and absolution—leads all who follow him to a lost eternity.

D. The Promise Regarding the Site (132-17-18)

The chosen place in the holy city will become a central point for:

1. Vitality (132:17)

"There will I make the horn of David to bud: I have ordained a lamp for Mine anointed." Two things are inherent in this promise.

a. *Life would show there.* Assurance is given that Hezekiah will have a son, a bud, an heir to David's throne. A bud has great promise for the future but, in itself, is small and insignificant. Hezekiah's son would amount to no more than that. He would not come to anything for God.

In contrast, the Holy Spirit describes the Messiah as the Branch, one of Isaiah's favorite terms for this coming One. Hezekiah had doubtless heard his friend refer to the Messiah in this way: "In that day shall the Branch of the LORD be beautiful and glorious" (Isaiah 4:2). But not thus did God see Manasseh, the unworthy son who would be born to Hezekiah. He was to be a mere "bud."

b. *Light would shine there.* In the Old Testament, a lamp is a symbol for the continuing existence of the divine purpose. It is first used in this connection when God formally signed the Abrahamic covenant (Genesis 15:7). When David was almost killed by Ishbibenob, the son of the giant, David's men said, "Thou shalt go no more out with us to battle, that thou quench not the light [lamp] of Israel" (2 Samuel 21:17). The symbol is used again when God determined to rend ten of the tribes away from Solomon. Ahijah told Jeroboam: "I will take the kingdom out of his [Solomon's] hand and will give it unto thee, even ten tribes. And unto his son will I give one tribe, that David My servant may have a light [lamp] alway before Me in Jerusalem, the city which I have chosen Me to put My name" (1 Kings 11:35-36).

Perhaps, in their private talks together, Isaiah had shared with Hezekiah his own concept of the millennial kingdom: "For Zion's sake will I not hold My peace, and for Jerusalem's sake I will not rest, until the righteousness thereof go forth as brightness, and the salvation thereof as a lamp that burneth. And the Gentiles shall see thy righteousness, and all kings thy glory" (Isaiah 62:1-2).

Manasseh was to plunge the land into worse darkness than it had ever known before. Hezekiah did not know that, but God did. Faithful, however, to His purpose, God gave Hezekiah the assurance that the lamp would remain alight until the dawning of the new day at the coming of the Christ. Then, indeed, the holy city will become the center of all vitality for a thousand years.

Finally, the chosen place in the holy city will become a central point for:

2. Victory (132:18)

"His enemies will I clothe with shame: but upon himself shall his crown flourish." This was certainly not true of Manasseh

who, for awhile, was dragged away to Babylon in shame. It will
be true of Christ. When He comes, His enemies will be covered
with shame. The dreadful things they have said and done will
be exposed and judged. The Lord Jesus, crowned King of kings
and Lord of lords, will rule "from the river to the ends of the
earth."

Thus ends this psalm, this eulogy of the Davidic covenant,
upon which Hezekiah pinned his hopes and which, indeed, is
the only hope of our world as well.

Psalm 133

THE UNITY OF THE SPIRIT

I. THE BEAUTY OF UNITY (133:1-3a)
   A. A Declaration about Unity (133:1)
   B. A Description of Unity (133:2-3a)
     1. An Illustration from the Sacred Realm
       We are taken to the cloister and shown a ministering priest
     2. An Illustration from the Secular Realm
       We are taken to the country and shown a mountain pasture
II. THE BLESSING OF UNITY (133:3b)

AN OLD STORY tells of a father who had a family of quarrelsome sons. One day he called his sons before him and, picking out the strongest of them, handed him a stick. "Snap it," he said. The son did so with a gesture of contempt. The man handed him two sticks. "Snap them," he said. Again the son did so. The old man handed him ever increasing numbers of sticks. "Snap them," he said—a bundle of four, five, six. Soon the young man was having to strain to snap the sticks and, finally he had to admit defeat.

"Unity is strength," the old man cautioned his sons. "A house divided cannot stand. Anyone can overthrow you one by one. But stand together, in unity, and your united strength will give your enemies second thoughts."

This little psalm is about true unity, the unity of the Spirit, a unity that gives strength and on which God pours His blessing.

I. THE BEAUTY OF UNITY (133:1-3a)

A. A Declaration about Unity (133:1)

"Behold, how good and how pleasant it is for brethren to dwell together in unity!" It is a sight worth seeing. It is what

537

God covets for His people. It is what Satan dreads and what he works night and day to undo. It is that for which Jesus Himself prayed beneath the lengthening shadow of the cross. It is the one thing, God says, that will convince people that the church has something the world does not have. It is what the Holy Ghost came to achieve in His baptizing work. It is what the Jews saw so convincingly displayed in the infant Jerusalem church— a church where one and all, rich and poor, bond and free, great and small, young and old, gifted and retarded, had all things in common. The unity God wants for His people is not deadly uniformity, not an imitation ecumenism; it is not a unity brought about by doctrinal compromise, political expediency, or organizational efficiency. (The church is not an organization but an organism; it's symbol for this age is a body, not a business.) The unity of the Spirit is not a unity brought about by some extrabiblical experience indulged at the expense of sound doctrine; the early church continued steadfastly in the apostles' doctrine, as well as in fellowship.

Unity. How rare and exotic a plant it is on earth. "How good and how pleasant it is for brethren to dwell together in unity." Shadows of Cain and Abel at once start to life. Man's first sin separated man from God; his second sin separated man from man. Abel's blood, seeping into the soil, crying aloud to heaven for vengeance, put an end to the brotherhood of man.

Nobody can organize brotherhood. People can join lodges and clubs, they can found United Nations organizations and promote ecumenical movements all in vain. There can be no universal brotherhood of man apart from a universal fatherhood of God, and the Bible makes clear that God is not the father of all. He is the creator of all, but He is the father only of those who are born again, born from above, born of the Spirit of God. What the world is looking for is a practical demonstration of brotherhood and unity among the children of God.

Years ago I was part of a detachment of troops stationed on Haifa docks in Palestine. There were about twenty men in the barrack room, drawn from all strata of society and from all walks of life. On my first Sunday morning I left camp to find a place where I could fellowship with the people of God. Making my way up to Mount Carmel I saw a small building half a block down a side road. It bore a sign that read: "Gospel Hall." I knew at once what it was. It was an assembly of believers known as Brethren. I had been raised in such a group in South Wales. A few minutes' conversation with an aged man at the door convinced him that I knew and loved the Lord, that I was a baptized believer in fellowship with a likeminded group of believers back home, and as such I was made welcome. I was at home. I was with people who knew and loved the Lord. I was part of a worldwide family of God's people.

After the morning service I was invited to the home of a young Christian Arab. There I was made welcome, entertained at his table, introduced to his aged mother and his sisters, and shown Christian love and hospitality. In that home I forged links of love that lasted for many years and which proved true and real even in distant lands in later times.

I was also invited that Sunday to have supper with a Russian brother and his wife. Here, too, new links of love were forged and a friendship formed which stood the test of time. After the evening service I was invited to the home of a Palestinian Jew.

I arrived back at camp quite late at night. The first question I was asked by a curious group of men was, "Where have you been all day?" I said, "I went to church this morning. I had lunch at the home of a Palestinian Arab along with his mother and his sisters. I had supper at the home of a Russian. I have just come back from the home of a Jew." I shall never forget the comment with which this astounding piece of news was received. The men in this unit had been there for months. They knew nobody outside their own circle. Incredulously one of them asked, "What kind of a lodge do you belong to?"

It was no lodge. No lodge on earth can provide its membership with what I enjoyed that day. When I walked into that Gospel Hall I walked into a family, my family, the family of God. I enjoyed something of that unity of the Spirit which exists nowhere outside Christ but which, within the wide circle of the family of God, is known to all who love the Lord. I have experienced this family unity in more than twenty countries around the world.

This psalm is one of the "songs of degrees" that bears David's name—its words are fitting to have come from David's pen. It was David who united the tribes. He found them a dozen warring, divided entities, a prey to their enemies and suspicious of one another. He forged them into a united kingdom.

It was David who gave cohesion to the nation and centralized everything in Jerusalem. It was David who planned for its temple to be a national symbol of spiritual unity for the twelve tribes of Israel. It was David who saw that true unity for the nation had to be centered in common faith in the living God in accordance with the Word of God.

Later, that unity was shattered by Jeroboam, its foundations having been sapped by Solomon—Jeroboam, "the son of Nebat, who made Israel to sin." It was Jeroboam who led the northern tribes in open revolt. It was Jeroboam who capitalized on the stresses to national unity brought about by the selfish orientalism of Solomon. It was Jeroboam who invented an unblessed rival religion based on calf-worship in the name of Jehovah. It was Jeroboam who changed the feast days and who ordained commoners as priests. It was Jeroboam who saw that he must undo what David had done in unifying the tribes if his revolt was to last. He clearly saw that the temple in Jerusalem and the annual pilgrimage of the people to Jerusalem were ties that had to be broken if his rival kingdom was not eventually to succumb to the lure of Jerusalem.

Hezekiah in his day saw at once the value of this forgotten psalm of David. He incorporated it into his "songs of degrees." Israel had paid in full for its apostasies, so let the remnant of the various tribes come and worship in Jerusalem. Let them be reconciled with God. Let the old divisions be healed. Let the people, north and south, unite, heart and voice, in true unity around the Word of God. Some came; some stayed away, nursing old resentments. Glad for those who did come, for those who did respond to his invitation, Hezekiah resurrected this old psalm of David and gave it its place toward the end of the Hebrew hymnbook that, for all the remaining ages of time, God's people might be able to sing in heavenly harmony about the unity of the people of God.

B. A Description of Unity (133:2-3a)

David has two illustrations: one from the sacred realm and one from the secular realm, one from the cloister and one from the countryside, one having to do with the ministering priest and one with a mountain pasture.

1. An Illustration from the Sacred Realm

"It is like the precious ointment upon the head, that ran down upon the beard, even Aaron's beard: that went down to the skirts of his garments." We think of the *manifestation* of that ointment in the deliberate, purposeful anointing of Israel's high priest. We think also of the *manufacturing* of that ointment according to a formula of which God in heaven had an absolute and abiding monopoly (Exodus 30:22-23).

a. *Manifestation.* The psalmist, himself an anointed man, dwells upon the manifestation of the ointment in the anointing of Aaron, Israel's first high priest. David has five things to say about that. First that oil was poured on Aaron's head, which suggests the glory of his position. It speaks of Christ in His *majesty,* Christ the head of the church. We have an anointed head in heaven.

Nothing can change that. No failure on the part of any member of the body can ever affect or change the fact that the head is anointed. His majesty is manifest, His fragrance fills all heaven.

Then the ointment went down over Aaron's beard. That speaks of Christ in His *manliness.* He was a true man, He was every inch a man, a man's man, God's man. There was a fragrance about Him. He was holy, undefiled, and separate from sinners. Yet at the same time He was loving, gracious, kind, forgiving, and generous. He was never effeminate, never weak, never anything less than a perfect man. All that manliness of His was anointed by the Holy Spirit so that everywhere He went it was seen and sensed. Strong men like Peter, James, and John put down their nets, left their careers, and followed Him instantly, even to death. Women like Mary Magdalene and Mary of Bethany loved Him. Children were drawn to Him, climbed on His knees, looked into His face, and received His blessing.

The ointment ran down on Aaron's garments. That speaks of Christ in His *ministry.* Aaron's garments were the garments of a ministering priest. The Lord Jesus came "not to be ministered unto, but to minister, and to give His life a ransom for many" (Mark 10:45). He had a Calvary ministry, and He has a continuing ministry at God's right hand.

The ointment went down to the skirts of Aaron's garment. That speaks of Christ in His *mercy.* His grace reaches right down to the ground. He has a down-to-earth ministry—not just a remote, distant ministry in heaven, but a ministry that reaches down to where we are on earth. He is touched with the feelings of our infirmities. He was made like unto His brethren. We can come to Him and find "grace to help in time of need." His ministry is fragrant, attractive, appealing. His mercy is not cold but compassionate, understanding, sympathizing, personal, kind.

But, we observe, the ointment was poured on Aaron; it ran down Aaron's beard. That speaks of Christ in His *members.* Although Aaron was not Christ, during Christ's absence and during his own lifetime, Aaron represented Christ. He stood for Christ, he reminded people of Christ, he ministered as Christ, on Christ's behalf. His was an anointed ministry. The fragrance of that wondrous ointment clung to him. That is what people sensed when they came into his presence; they sensed something of the fragrance that belongs to Christ alone. And so it is with us today. We are Christ's representatives on earth, here to carry with us something of the loveliness that belongs to Him, the head of the body of which we through the Spirit are members.

b. *Manufacture.* Before leaving this theme let us think of the manufacture of that ointment. The formula is given, the spices are named, the quantities are specified. We know the various parts but the whole was God's alone.

The fragrance of that ointment was spread over all. In the outer court the brazen altar and the brazen laver were anointed with it. In the holy place the candlestick, the table, and the altar of incense were also anointed. Inside the veil, where the ark and the mercy seat stood, there too the oil was applied. Aaron was anointed with it. His sons were anointed with it. They could not come into God's presence with the odor of the flesh clinging to them. They had to be washed and anointed so that the fragrance of Christ would cling to them.

The ointment was made of myrrh and of sweet cinnamon, of sweet calamus and of cassia, all blended together with olive oil. The various weights of each precious spice were given and the needed amount of oil. Upon the blending of the splendid whole, God pronounced a solemn warning—it must never be imitated, for nobody can imitate Christ. Either He, by the ministry of the Holy Spirit, is poured on us to make our lives fragrant like His—or else nothing. Anybody who tried to imitate it or who poured it upon something common was cut off by God from among God's people.

Now, as the blending of the various parts produced a harmonious whole—five-hundred shekels of this, five-hundred shekels of that, two-fifty shekels of this, two-fifty shekels of that, all the ingredients, myrrh and cassia, cinnamon and calamus, mixed and mixed to merge into one, all blended together by the oil— so is the unity of the Spirit. Christ in me, Christ in you, Christ in this brother, Christ in that sister, all blended into one body by the gracious unifying work of the Holy Spirit. Such is the unity Christ looks for in His own. It cannot be imitated.

So, as those various ingredients, mixed and merged into one unifying whole, were then poured on Aaron and his sons, so that each of them carried about with him that rare fragrance that spoke of Christ—so now Christ is set forth to the world by the body of Christ, each member anointed by the Holy Spirit to be a sweet-smelling savor of Christ in a dead and decaying world.

Let the beauty of Jesus be seen in me,
All His wondrous compassion, and purity;
O, Thou Spirit Divine,
All my being refine
Until the beauty of Jesus be seen in me.

2. An Illustration from the Secular Realm

"It is . . . as the dew of Hermon, and as the dew that descended upon the mountains of Zion." In the hot Mediterranean climate, dew is vital to plant life. The dew the psalmist describes here is better understood if we leave out the italicized words ("and as the dew"). The northern tribes (Hermon) and the southern tribes (Zion) are encompassed by the life-giving embrace of that refreshing, copious, summer mist.

The dew is a fit symbol of the unity of the Spirit. It is distilled in the night season—and never after a storm. It forms only when all is still and at rest. Strife, rush and bustle, worry and ceaseless activity, will never bring about the unity God envisions for His people. The dew cannot be manufactured. It is God's gracious gift to an otherwise dying world.

In Hezekiah's day there had been a momentary display of this spiritual, heavenly dew. The tribes had been given a unique opportunity to show to a warring world the oneness and unity of the people of God in the great Passover. Though many stayed away, many from the northern tribes did come. Judah was in its heart and soul. For one brief week the nation knew such a time of spiritual refreshing as had not been known among God's people for centuries. It was brief, but it inspired Hezekiah to take this forgotten psalm of David and include it in the hymnbook so that God's people might learn something of the beauty of unity.

II. The Blessing of Unity (133:3b)

"For there the LORD commanded the blessing, even life for evermore." God's Spirit is quenched by a squabbling church. It is not where quarrels abound that souls are saved and newborn babes in Christ grow strong in the things of God. People cannot be fooled. They know when they have come into the company of a people who love God.

A friend of mine helps pastor a large and growing church in the United States. When asked the secret of the growth of this church he said: "It rests on three things: our people love God, they love each other, and they love the lost." It is there that the Lord is commanding "the blessing, even life for evermore."

That is what the world is waiting for—for this church and that church and the other church to show signs of being one in Christ; for this believer here and that brother there and that sister to become one. When God sees *that*, He will bless.

Psalm 134

WITHOUT A CLOUD BETWEEN

I. Rendering Blessing to the Lord (134:1-2)
    A. Who (134:1a)
    B. When (134:1b)
    C. Where (134:1c-2)
    D. What (134:2a)
II. Receiving Blessing from the Lord (134:3)
    A. The Lord's Ability (134:3a)
    B. The Lord's Abode (134:3b)

THIS IS THE LAST of the songs of degrees, or, as some have suggested, the songs of the steps—so called because it is assumed they were sung on the steps of the temple by pilgrims to Jerusalem. Let us allow that assumption to stand for a moment. The singer has ascended three flights of steps. He can now look back down to the bottom step, far below the fifteenth step on which he stands. He can go no higher. There is nothing now between himself and the Savior. He has planted his feet, step by step, on higher ground, and now he is at the top. Also, spiritually, he is far above the place where he was when he began with his, "Woe is me," in Psalm 120. He bursts out into an ecstatic, "Bless the LORD!"

It is worth looking at the way by which he has ascended. Pause, for a moment, with this blissful singer. See the ascending flights of stairs by which he has arrived at this high point. These "songs of degrees" can be divided into three groups of five psalms each. First the singer is seen down at the bottom, looking up. He is *beholding the Lord* (120–124). In Psalm 120 the psalmist was *groaning*. He was very low down indeed. He bewailed his distress. Everything was dark and depressing. He was a defeated man.

In Psalm 121 he began his upward way. He left that low-lying step where his feet felt like lead and his soul was in despair. The

544

psalmist was no longer groaning; he was *glancing*. He had his eyes on the hills.

When an artist paints a picture, one of his first concerns is composition. He has to have a central point of interest. Every line in his drawing must eventually carry the eye of the beholder to that focal point. The branches and trunk of a tree, the winding path, the way the peasant's arm is resting on the fence—all carry the eye by stages to the main feature of the picture. Thus it is that the psalmist's eyes, resting on the distant hills, are carried up, up, up, to the crags on the heights and on up, up, up, to the cloudy sky to contemplate the Lord, maker of heaven and earth. In Psalm 121 the psalmist was glancing upward to the skies and beyond the skies to that throne, high and lifted up, and to Him whose train fills the temple. Looking up, he inevitably steps up.

In Psalm 122 the singer was to be seen *glorying*. "I was glad," he says, "when they said unto me, 'Let us go into the house of the LORD.'" Although God's throne was on high, in His condescending grace He also had a seat on earth; there in the temple, behind the veil, between the cherubim, on the sacred ark, the Shekinah cloud sat enthroned upon the mercy seat. The thought of Jerusalem, as God's earthly dwelling, filled the singer's soul with exultation. God was not remote, far away. He was here, in Jerusalem, at the top of these very steps.

In Psalm 123, on the fourth step, the singer could be seen *gazing*. The glance can save, but it is the gaze that sanctifies. There was "life for a look" when the serpent was raised on the pole by Moses. But it is the steady gazing into the face of Jesus that brings out His image and His likeness in the soul. As Paul puts it, "We all, with open face beholding as in a glass the glory of the Lord, are changed into the same image from glory to glory, even as by the Spirit of the Lord" (2 Corinthians 3:18).

In Psalm 124 the singer was to be heard *gasping*. He had arrived at the fifth step, he had ascended the first flight and for a moment, like Peter on the surging sea, he took his eyes off the Master. He looked back. He gasped at the perils and pitfalls he had already escaped but which he could see more clearly now. "Our soul is escaped as a bird out of the snare of the fowlers," he cried out. But quickly he brought his thoughts back to the Lord, who had made heaven and earth. It is the only thing that stopped him from tumbling back down the whole flight of stairs. When we are climbing, we must keep looking up, not looking down.

He had negotiated the first flight of steps. The secret was simple: *Beholding the Lord*. By keeping his eye on the One who reigns above and who encouragingly beckons him on, the psalmist gained the first flight. He was now ready for the second flight. The secret of the second flight of steps was just as simple: *Believing the Lord.* He would take God at His Word and climb to even higher ground (125–129).

In Psalm 125 *dangers were minimized.* "As the mountains were round about Jerusalem, so the LORD is round about His people." No foe can harm us, no fear alarm us. We're on the victory side.

In Psalm 126 *dreams were realized.* "When the LORD turned again the captivity of Zion, we were like them that dream." Job must have felt the same when the Lord restored him. No more pain, poverty, persecution. No more problems. The wonder of his restoration was so great, Job might have thought he was only dreaming. The psalmist put his dangers in perspective, realizing that those who sowed in tears would reap in joy.

In Psalm 127 *desires were verbalized.* The singer had a deep desire to become a fruitful man, to have the joy of seeing sons born into his home. He realized that this could not be accomplished in the energy of the flesh: "Lo, children are an heritage of the LORD." He made it a matter of believing prayer, that God would reward him with fruit.

In Psalm 128 *delights were multiplied.* He embraced the joy of being a fruitful person. He saw children as olive plants around his table. His faith rang out: "The LORD *shall* bless thee out of Zion."

In Psalm 129 *dreads were crucified.* He arrived at the top of the second flight of steps and again, just as when he arrived at the top of the first flight, he almost slipped. He thought of the afflictions he had experienced in his pilgrimage, "many a time, many a time." But before he could slip and slide all the way back to the bottom he took a fresh grip on God. "The LORD is righteous," he said. His dreads were crucified: "He hath cut asunder the cords of the wicked."

Having successfully ascended two significant flights of steps, the psalmist was ready for the third and final ascent. Now we see him *blessing the Lord.* The last five psalms are all about *Him.*

In Psalm 130 the psalmist sang of the *pardon of the Lord.* "If Thou, Lord, shouldest mark iniquities, O LORD, who shall stand?" We shall never climb so high that we are beyond the need for pardon. The higher we get, the more we see the abysmal wickedness of our own evil hearts. Paul could describe himself in his unregenerate days as "a Hebrew of the Hebrews" (Philippians 3:5). Later on, he was one who came "not a whit behind the very chiefest apostles" (2 Corinthians 11:5). Later still he was "less than the least of all saints" (Ephesians 3:8). In the end he called himself the chief of sinners (1 Timothy 1:15) and "not meet to be called an apostle" (1 Cornithians 15:9). It was not that the apostle was backsliding; it was just that he was climbing higher and seeing in ever sharper focus how much he owed to the pardon of the Lord.

In Psalm 131 the singer told of the *patience of the Lord*. He described himself as a weaned child. He thought of that wonderful God who treated him the way a loving mother treats her child.

In Psalm 132 he sang of the *promises of the Lord*. He held God to His covenanted word to David, that David should never lack a descendant to sit on his throne. And he received the Lord's prompt answer that He had not forgotten.

In Psalm 133 he sang of the *people of the Lord* and told aloud the wondrous story of their unity and blessing. Life for evermore! he exclaimed.

And now he has arrived at the top. In Psalm 134 he sings of the *power of the Lord*. It is a note he has struck twice before in the series. "Bless ye the LORD . . . that made heaven and earth." He has come a long way from that first faltering step taken with fear and trembling but with hope in his heart.

We are now ready to *bless the Lord*, which is what this short psalm is about. This is what we shall be doing for all eternity: blessing and praising and worshiping the Lord who has done great things for us. This final psalm of the series divides into two parts. We see the psalmist:

I. RENDERING BLESSING TO THE LORD (134:1-2)

The psalm begins by underlining:

A. Who (134:1a)

"Behold, bless ye the LORD, all ye servants of the LORD." It is the Lord's servants who are best equipped to render to Him the praise and blessing that belong to His holy name. Take, for example, a man who is tone-deaf. He is at a concert. He sees everyone else obviously enjoying themselves, drinking in the sounds. But he really cannot appreciate all that other people get out of it. For the sake of appearances, perhaps, he might pretend that he too is enjoying the performance. And, no doubt, the movement and rhythm, the color of the costumes, the bright and shining instruments, the scenery and draperies, might please him. But the full beauty of the music—that eludes him. Something is lacking in his life. His ears are simply not finely attuned to music.

The souls of unsaved persons, not attuned to worship,

may substitute *religion* for reality. They may make do with stained-glass windows, orchestras and choirs, pulpit oratory, benevolent good works. But worship? That is the prerogative of those whose souls have been born anew by the regenerating work of the Holy Spirit of God. So the psalmist says *who:* "Bless ye the LORD, all ye servants of the LORD." Let us note that *all*. From the least to the greatest, from the king on his throne to the slave in the field, all God's people are to praise Him. The only qualification for worship is to be constituted one of the Lord's servants by being born again. The new birth is the key to everything: to being a child of God, to being a servant of God, to being a saint of God.

B. When (134:1b)

"Ye servants of the LORD, which by night stand in the house of the LORD." Not only servants, but sentinels. In the first year of his reign Hezekiah opened the doors of the temple, which evidently had been closed up at some time in the past. Then he brought priests and Levites into the temple courts and commanded them to sanctify themselves: "My sons," he said, "be not now negligent: for the LORD hath chosen you to stand before Him, to serve Him" (2 Chronicles 29:11). The great Passover was kept and again we read of the priests and the Levites: they "stood in their place after their manner, according to the law of Moses" (2 Chronicles 30:16).

When that Passover was over, there was a general housecleaning throughout the cities of Judah; idols were chopped down and their shrines demolished. Then Hezekiah "appointed the courses of the priests and the Levites after their courses . . . to minister, and to give thanks, in the gates" (2 Chronicles 31:2). Everything was done decently and in order. Every man had his place and function.

The porters were sentinels, appointed to guard the gates. They were Levites who might have thought themselves low down on the scale. Like the priests, they were descendants of Levi, but, unlike the priests, they had no anointing to serve in the holy place or at the altars. They were not entrusted with work around the temple nor were they members of the temple choir. Their job was simply to stand at the gates as watchmen. They might have felt that theirs was not a very significant job— and especially the porters mentioned in this psalm, the *night* watchmen. Very few people even saw what they did for the Lord.

But their service was essential. The sentinel's job was to guard the gate. He was to stand there and keep a watchful eye on everything that came in and went out of the city. Their job was to see that nothing was allowed into the holy city that might bring down the displeasure of God.

From Nehemiah's day we have a graphic illustration of the importance of this post.

> "In those days," said Nehemiah, "saw I in Judah some treading wine presses on the sabbath, and bringing in sheaves, and lading asses . . . which they brought into Jerusalem on the sabbath day. . . . There dwelt men of Tyre also therein, which brought fish, and all manner of ware, and sold on the sabbath unto the children of Judah, and in Jerusalem. Then I contended with the nobles. . . . And it came to pass, that when the gates of Jerusalem began to be dark before the sabbath, I commanded that the gates should be shut, and charged that they should not be opened till after the sabbath: and some of my servants set I at the gates. . . . So the merchants and sellers of all kind of ware lodged without Jerusalem once or twice. Then I testified against them, and said unto them, 'Why lodge ye about the wall? if ye do so again, I will lay hands on you.' . . . And I commanded the Levites that they should cleanse themselves, and that they should come and keep the gates, to sanctify the sabbath day" (Nehemiah 13:15-22).

So the watchmen had an important task. They were responsible to see that the city was kept undefiled, as befitted a place where God chose to dwell.

The spiritual application of all this is obvious. We need to keep a close watch on our eyes, ears, mouths, to make sure that nothing comes in and out of our lives that might displease the indwelling Spirit of God.

The sentinels whom Hezekiah urges to praise and bless the Lord are those who watch by night. The post might have been a lively one during the day. It was a lonely one at night. But that had its advantages. During the night watches, the sentinels while keeping a wakeful eye on the gates could pass the long hours blessing the Lord. They could commune with Him, meditate and pray, and thus pass the hours. What a privilege.

C. Where (134:1c-2)

"Behold, bless ye the LORD, all ye servants of the LORD, which by night stand in the house of the LORD . . . in the sanctuary." The singer is thinking of those who are afar off, cut off from God, born in unblessed lands, raised to worship idols and to embrace fierce ideologies. And here were the Levites, standing in the temple courts, entrusted by the Lord with a special service, with a post of danger and responsibility. Their task was to take care of things during the night, a post of rare trust. Yet so faithless and restless is the human heart that these men needed exhortation.

Here we see the ever-present danger of becoming unduly familiar with holy things. We can take spiritual privilege for granted, as a matter of course, and yawn over a place of privilege which others would covet. We can be guilty of grumbling and complaining because the Lord has not given us some more meaningful position to fill.

Imagine having to exhort any of those who stood "in His sanctuary" to bless Him. Yet how often in our own day and age do we find it necessary to be exhorted to be at our post, in the right spirit, with hearts overflowing with gratitude and praise. How many there are who infrequently attend the house of the Lord, who serve Him indifferently, carelessly, grudgingly. The word comes ringing down the centuries. "Behold! Wake up! "Bless *ye* the Lord!"

D. What (134:2a)

"Lift up your hands in the sanctuary. . . . " To lift up one's hands was a symbolic gesture that showed three things. First, it showed that the hands are *clean*. As David said in Psalm 24: "Who shall ascend into the hill of the LORD? . . . He that hath clean hands." God does not insist that our hands be clever.; He does insist that they be clean. Those that handle holy things are not required to pass an aptitude test or have a degree in theology. But our lives must be pure. Defiled and dirty people are barred from sanctuary service. The New Testament principle for worship is this: "Let a man examine himself, and so let him eat . . ." (1 Corinthians 11:28).

Second, the hands were lifted to show that the hands are *complete*. In the law book of Israel, detailed instructions were given for service in the sanctuary. The priests and the Levites were occupied with holy things, with the things of God. Those who were in any way blemished were not permitted to serve in the sanctuary. Such imperfect ones were allowed to *sit* but not to *serve* with their brethren. There were areas in which a believer could serve—but not in the sanctuary.

The New Testament principle is much the same. It is not physical disability now that bars a person from certain types of service but there are still things that prohibit. A person may be incapacitated from certain types of service by a crippling defect in his testimony—a divorce, for instance.

Third, the hands were lifted to show that they are *consecrated*. A man lifting up his hands in the sanctuary would either hold up hands that were empty—and thus available to be filled and used; or hands that were employed—holding some implement necessary for the work of God in which he was engaged. We cannot serve the Lord if our hands are already full of other things. How hard it is to get people to let go of the things they are grasping, things that profit only for this life—if they profit at all.

The remainder of the psalm shows us the other side of the coin. No one can render blessing to the Lord without:

II. RECEIVING BLESSING FROM THE LORD (134:3)

In this last verse the psalmist makes mention of:

A. The Lord's Ability (134:3a)

"The LORD that made heaven and earth . . . " Here, again, we see *from whence our assurance comes*. No wonder this is the top step of the series. We are to bless the Lord who "made heaven and earth." Every sun and star in space, every blade of grass, every stick and stone on earth—He made them. That is why the psalmist urges us to bless Him. He doesn't ask us here to serve Him, but to bless Him, to worship Him.

B. The Lord's Abode (134:3b)

"The LORD that made heaven and earth bless thee out of Zion." That tells us *from whence our answer comes:* out of Zion, out of the place where the Lord had put His name. It is impossible for us to bless God without having Him bless us. The God who has the genius to create a galaxy and who has the grace to come and live among His people is surely a God who knows how to bless us. What more could we ask than that?

Psalm 135

WORSHIP

I. INVOKED WORSHIP (135:1-2)
Worship should be inspired by:
  A. His Person (135:1a)
  B. Our Position (135:1b-2)
II. INTELLIGENT WORSHIP (135:3-14)
  A. For His Goodness (135:3-4)
    1. His Personal Charm (135:3)
    2. His Peculiar Choice (135:4)
  B. For His Greatness (135:5-13)
    1. Declared (135:5)
    2. Displayed (135:6-12)
      a. His Creation Is a Witness (135:6-7)
      b. His Conquests Are a Witness (135:8-12)
    3. Described (135:13)
  C. For His Government (135:14)
III. INSENSATE WORSHIP (135:15-18)
  A. The Foolishness of Idolatry (135:15-17)
    1. Idols Are Manufactured (135:15)
    2. Idols Are Meaningless (135:16-17)
  B. The Foolishness of Idolators (135:18)
IV. INSISTENT WORSHIP (135:19-21)
  A. Full Participation in Worship (135:20)
    1. By the People (135:19a)
    2. By the Priests (135:19b-20a)
    3. By the Proselytes (135:20b)
  B. Fervent Participation in Worship (135:21)

PSALMS 135 AND 136 ARE A PAIR of almost identical twins. Both are orphan psalms, but what orphans. Here we have two of the happiest orphans in the world. "Praise the LORD. . . . Praise the LORD. . . . Give praises to the LORD. . . . Bless the LORD. . . . Give thanks unto the LORD!" Such are the themes of both these psalms.

Probably they were written by Hezekiah in the joy and overflow of his soul after his double deliverance—first from sickness, then from siege. The text itself, however, does not say so.
The Holy Spirit prefers to let them stand "without father or
mother, without beginning or ending of days"—as Melchize-
deks, so to speak, owning no father but God (Hebrews 7:3).

The theme of Psalm 135 is worship. First we have:

I. INVOKED WORSHIP (135:1-2)

The psalmist looks first at the Lord and then at His people.
He says that our worship should be inspired by:

A. His Person (135:1a)

"Praise ye the LORD!" "Hallelujah!" or, as we should perhaps emphasize it: Hallelu-jah. The name *Jah* is a contraction,
a concentration, of the great name *Jehovah*, just as *El* is a contraction for the name *Elohim*. *Jah* is God the eternal One, inhabiting eternity and also inhabiting the praises of His people. The
name first occurs in Exodus 15:2 where, in the first song in
Scripture, Moses leads Israel in rapturous celebration of the
overthrow of Pharaoh. In that song Moses drew the attention of
the ecstatic people to the One who had really delivered them.

We have much to be thankful for. Praise should be a constant
habit of our lives. Yet how often we have to be reminded to
praise the Lord. How often when we spread like a peacock the
gorgeous plumage of our satisfaction at some singular blessing
or mercy from the hand of God do we have to be called back to
a consideration of the blackness of our fallen nature.

But we are not only to praise the Lord. The psalmist says we
are to "praise the name of the LORD." This time there is no
contraction of the name. Jehovah is the God of covenant, the
God of promise, the God who keeps His Word, the God who is
forever all that His people need. Throughout Scripture, salvation in all its aspects is closely linked with the name of the Lord:
that saving, sanctifying, sovereign name of Jehovah in the Old
Testament and of Jesus in the New. We are to praise His name.
His person should inspire worship; the mere thought of His
name should inspire songs of praise.

Our worship should also be inspired by:

B. Our Position (135:1b-2)

"Ye that stand in the house of the LORD, in the courts of the
house of our God." Those that "stand in the house of the LORD"

are the *priests;* those that stand "in the courts of the house of our God" are the *people.* Nobody has a monopoly on praise. One does not need to be an ordained minister to offer praise to God. A little child can praise, for "Out of the mouths of babes and sucklings Thou hast perfected praise. . . ." A little child singing

> Jesus loves me this I know
> For the Bible tells me so. . . .

brings as much delight to the heart of God as the ordered cadences of some mature and thoughtful saint of God. When it comes to praise, God is no respecter of persons. There are no class distinctions with God.

The psalmist points out that their position should evoke praise. The consecrated priest in the temple and the concerned Hebrew in the outer court were both in the place where God had put His name. When we stand in the house of the Lord and gather with His people, praise should be as natural as the air we breathe. One does not look for people to praise the Lord in a tavern, theater, dance hall, or casino, but one does look for praise in a place where God's people congregate.

II. INTELLIGENT WORSHIP (135:3-14)

The psalmist states three grounds for worship. We are to worship God:

A. For His Goodness (135:3-4)

1. His Personal Charm (135:3)

"Praise the LORD; for the LORD is good: sing praises unto His name; for it is pleasant." He is good! Suppose He were not good. Suppose it were all a dream, and that, after all, the gods of the heathen were the true gods. Suppose it turned out that God were like Dagon or Baal or Moloch. Suppose Baal were God, that He delighted in temples which were really brothels and in priests and servants who were really pimps and prostitutes. Suppose the Hindus were right, that God were the kind of multiform god found in their temples. Or suppose Moloch were God, that He had an insatiable thirst for blood. Thank God He isn't like that at all. And the Lord is not just passively good, but absolutely and actively good, ever looking for ways to express His goodness.

"Sing praises unto His name; for it is pleasant." The name of Moloch brought fear into the hearts of worshipers. The names of the fierce Aztec gods inspired horror. The name of the Lord inspires song. What lovelier name was there to the Hebrews than the name Jehovah, a name expressing the inexpressible and telling the Hebrew people of a God who loves and cares. What lovelier name is there in all the universe than *Jesus!*

> There is no name so sweet on earth
> No name so sweet in heaven,
> Than the name which at His lowly birth
> Was to our Savior given.

2. His Peculiar Choice (135:4)

"For the LORD [Jah] hath chosen Jacob unto Himself, and Israel for His peculiar treasure." The psalmist's mind goes back to Exodus 19, to the third month since the Hebrews left Egypt. What an eventful three months they had been, packed with proofs of God's goodness. Now they had come to Sinai. Seven times Moses would ascend and descend that mountain. The first time, answering God's call, he went up alone and God rehearsed before him His initial dealings with Israel as a nation. Then He said: "Now therefore, if ye will obey My voice indeed, and keep My covenant, then ye shall be a peculiar treasure unto Me above all people: for all the earth is Mine. And ye shall be unto Me a kingdom of priests, and an holy nation" (Exodus 19:5-6). The expression "a peculiar treasure" denotes a treasure reserved for one's self (as in Matthew 13:44 where the Jewish people are compared with a treasure hidden in a field).

This was the psalmist's illustration. As God had chosen the tribe of Levi to be a priestly tribe, so He had chosen the nation to be a priestly nation to minister to all the world. Above all, He chose the nation to be His own special treasure on earth. The goodness of God in doing this has not yet been seen on earth because of Israel's dismal failure. But it will be seen during the millennial age.

We are to worship God, moreover:

B. For His Greatness (135:5-13)

First, that greatness is:

1. Declared (135:5)

"For I know that the LORD [Jehovah] is great, and that our Lord [Adonim] is above all gods." That Jehovah was great was evident. He was so great that His very name was protected by Old Testament law. It was not to be taken in vain nor would the Lord hold him guiltless who took that name in vain. But He was not only Jehovah, the revealer; He was also Adonim, the ruler. More, He was *"Our* Adonim," our Lord. The word *Adonim* is seldom used of man. It is the plural of *Adon* (which signifies the Lord as ruler in His relationship to earth) and because it is plural it carries the thought of that rulership to a greater degree. Adonim is especially the Lord who rules His own.

No wonder Sennacherib met with disaster on the mountains of Israel. God's people were protected by the best of all pacts: they were under the special protection of God. Israel is the only nation with which God has signed a treaty. It is a vassal state of heaven and, despite its faults and failures, the concordat stands. Israel as a nation is God's peculiar treasure, He is their ultimate ruler, and any nation that attacks them attacks Him. As for the gods of the nations which do not acknowledge Israel's God, they will be brushed aside.

Then, that greatness is:

2. Displayed (135:6-12)

In this section the psalmist summons two witnesses to the greatness of God.

a. His Creation Is a Witness (135:6-7)

"Whatsoever the LORD [Jehovah] pleased, that did He in heaven, and in earth, in the seas and all deep places" (135:6). The Lord is sovereign from the farthest reaches of space to the depths of the seas (the last two frontiers man has left to explore). God pleased Himself in creation; if what He has done has pleased us too, that is incidental.

First the psalmist gazes at the heavens. The celestial galaxies whirl and dance to please the Lord. Their mass, their movements, their vastness, their velocities, their atomic fires, their awesome futures—all exist to bring Him pleasure. God lets us paddle on the shorelines of His vast creation with our telescopes and shows us how tiny we are and how little we know.

The psalmist turns his eye to earth. Highlands and lowlands, frozen poles and burning sands, pampas and prairies, forests and fields, the hidden treasures of the rocks, the open pleasures of a sunlit sky—all exist to please Him. He it is who paints the sunset, who makes grass grow, who clothes a mountain range with trees and caps it with eternal snow. Every living creature is a tribute to His inventive genius.

The psalmist looks at the sea. The seas were God's idea. He set their bounds, sloped their shores, sounded their depths, salted their waters, stirs their waves. He filled their dark depths with fish, ordained their tides, mapped their movements. In all of those creative acts He first of all pleased Himself.

The psalmist thinks next of the second day of creation: "He causeth the vapors to ascend from the ends of the earth; He maketh lightnings for the rain; He bringeth the wind out of His treasuries" (135:7). When God separated the waters from the waters He set in motion some of the mightiest forces on this planet. The process of evaporation, condensation, and precipitation was largely a mystery to the ancients. The inspired psalmist, however, links the lightning with the rain. It has remained for modern science to reveal the astonishing accuracy of that statement. Even today, however, with all our equipment, weather satellites, and computerized information, we still cannot infallibly predict tomorrow's weather. Still less can we control it. God does what He pleases to demonstrate His sovereignty.

Creation is God's witness to His greatness.

b. His Conquests Are a Witness (135:8-12)

The psalmist appeals now to the sacred history of the Hebrew people. He shows that God's greatness was evidenced:

(1) *In Bringing Israel out of Bondage.* "Who smote the firstborn of Egypt, both of man and beast. Who sent tokens and wonders into the midst of thee, O Egypt, upon Pharaoh, and upon all his servants" (135:8-9). The psalmist was impressed by the *solemnity* of God's judgment on Egypt. When the final stroke fell, it fell on the firstborn (and only the firstborn) of both man and beast.

What an evidence of God's omnipotence. Had any other creature died that night except the firstborn, God would have failed in His purpose. But He knew just which child and animal to smite; in every home in the stricken land, from the palace of the pharaoh to the poorest hovel in the country, in every barn and field, it was always and only the firstborn. Such was the solemnity of God's action in judgment on Israel's foes.

The psalmist was impressed, further, with the *significance* of God's judgment. He "sent tokens," he says. That was all, just tokens, mere illustrations of His power. Sea and water turned to blood; lice, locusts, and lightnings came and went; frogs and flies had their turn; darkness and death descended on the land—all mere tokens. Each was a warning that further stubbornness on the part of the pharaoh would be judged by a living, omnipotent God. Such was God's greatness in bringing Israel out of bondage.

God's greatness was also evidenced:

(2) *In Bringing Israel into Blessing.* "Who smote great nations, and slew mighty kings; Sihon king of the Amorites, and Og king of Bashan, and all the kingdoms of Canaan: and gave their land for an heritage unto Israel His People" (135:10-12). When God brought Abraham into the land, He told him that all would be his, but there would be a delay of four-hundred years in actual possession because the "iniquity of the Amorites is not yet full" (Genesis 15:13-16). By the time of Joshua it was.

The cities of Sihon and Og, on the wilderness side of Jordan, were Amorite cities, and Og himself was one of the giants. "And we took all his cities at that time, there was not a city that we took not from them, threescore cities," said Moses in describing the overthrow of Og (Deuteronomy 3:4). "There was not one city too strong for us" was Moses' comment on the overthrow of Sihon (Deuteronomy 2:36). Walled cities, giants, coalitions of armies, all melted away before Israel's advance because God had deeded Canaan to Israel, and no confederation of Canaanite kings could keep them out.

The psalmist appeals to all this as a basis for intelligent worship. The greatness of God, declared and displayed, in creation and in conquest, should stimulate praise. Then, too, that greatness is:

3. Described (135:13)

"Thy name, O LORD, endureth for ever; and Thy memorial O LORD, throughout all generations." This exclamation brings us to the heart of intelligent worship. We may indeed praise God for what He does, but ultimately we worship God for who He is. And who is He? He is the eternal One whose name endures for ever. Throughout the Old Testament period we find God revealing Himself to His people through His names: Jehovah Jireh (the One who provides), Jehovah Shalom (the Lord our peace), Jehovah Tsidkenu (the Lord our righteousness), Jehovah Ropheka (the Lord who heals).

Now, He has revealed Himself in the name of Jesus.

We are to worship God not only for His goodness and greatness, but also:

C. For His Government (135:14)

"For the LORD will judge His People, and He will repent Himself concerning His servants." The word *judge* can be translated "vindicate"; the phrase "repent himself" means "have compassion." We can rephrase this verse: "The Lord will vindicate Himself, and He will have compassion concerning His servants." That is the kind of God He is. His government goes hand in hand with His grace, His judgment is never divorced from His mercy. Thus, when Israel first came to the frontiers of Canaan they turned back in unbelief into the wilderness and He judged them; later He brought them back in mercy. In Hezekiah's day, He judged Judah for its national sins by allowing the armies of Sennacherib to invade the land, and then in mercy He turned them back.

We can trace the same principle in our own lives.

III. INSENSATE WORSHIP (135:15-18)

The psalmist now turns his attention to the kind of "worship" practiced by the pagans and particularly to the worship of idols. In his day, idolatry was still a prevalent snare to Israel. He speaks of:

A. The Foolishness of Idolatry (135:15-17)

The psalmist strikes at the roots of idolatrous worship by pointing out that:

1. Idols Are Manufactured (135:15)

"The idols of the heathen are silver and gold, the work of men's hands." Silver and gold (the most precious metals) and men's hands (the most practical of our bodily members) are brought together to make—an idol! To make a big fat Buddha, a fierce-faced Kari, a serene-looking virgin, idols of all kinds. What skill it takes to convert a slab of marble into a Madonna. What skill to melt and mold metal into a Moloch. And behind those clever hands is a clever mind, able to conceive the thought and direct the grand idea—all coming together to create a man-made god or goddess. But when all is said and done, they are manufactured. They bear the label, "Made by man."

2. Idols Are Meaningless (135:16-17)

"They have mouths, but they speak not; eyes have they, but they see not; they have ears, but they hear not; neither is there any breath in their mouths." How foolish to pray to them. Imagine a person talking to a gatepost. It makes as much sense. Think of the folly of anyone who addresses a piece of metal, wood, or stone, however attractively sculptured and shaped.

Idol worshipers talk to a senseless god that cannot *speak*, to a god unable to talk to its devotee, unable to reveal itself, unable to make itself heard, unable to answer a single question, quiet a single fear, encourage a single aspiration.

Image worshipers pray to a god who cannot *see,* a god blind to all that is happening in the world, unable to see the person bowing before it. They pray to a piece of painted wood.

Idol worshipers talk to a god that cannot hear the slightest *sound.* The idolater comes to it, pours out his heart to it, prays to it, pleads with it. He might as well talk to a brick wall. Idol worshipers adore a god that cannot *save,* a god that has no life, no existence. Take an axe to it and it cannot save itself.

No wonder the psalmist talks of:

B. The Foolishness of Idolators (135:18)

"They that make them are like unto them: so is every one that trusteth in them." Idols are senseless, they have no life, they cannot love. The Holy Spirit says that those who make them and trust in them are as the wood, metal, and stone before which they bow. It is foolish to make them and even more foolish to worship them. Yet countless millions do.

The psalmist closes with a word about:

IV. INSISTENT WORSHIP (135:19-21)

Now the topic comes back to true worship. The psalmist demands that those who know the Lord worship *Him.* He calls for:

A. Full Participation in Worship (135:19-20)

1. By the People (135:19a)

"Bless the LORD, O house of Israel." Bless the Lord. Bless the Lord. Bless the Lord. Three times in swift succession the psalmist insists that people worship the true God. This insistent note sounds all the louder against the immediately preceding verses. People should praise the Lord, for He can see, He can speak, He can hear, He can save. He is a living God, a loving God. If we had nothing else for which to worship Him, that would suffice. We shall spend all eternity blessing Him.

2. By the Priests (135:19b-20a)

"Bless the LORD, O house of Aaron: bless the LORD, O house of Levi." This is a call to those in fulltime work for God. The priests ministered in the sanctuary, the Levites helped with the service; both were consecrated to fulltime ministry. It was theirs to handle holy things. They of all people should bless God.

3. By the Proselytes (135:20b)

"Ye that fear the LORD, bless the LORD." This imperative refers to people who came to be known in New Testament times as "the God-fearers," men and women like Cornelius. These were people from other nations who had come to trust in the God of Israel.

B. Fervent Participation in Worship (135:21)

"Blessed be the LORD out of Zion, which dwelleth at Jerusalem. Praise ye the LORD." The psalm ends with a resounding Hallelujah. Think who He is! Think where He is! Think how near He is!

The last sentence in this psalm ("Praise ye the LORD") takes us back to the first ("Praise ye the LORD"). Such a repetition makes it an envelope psalm, closing on the same note with which it begins. It invites the singer to go all the way through the psalm again—and again and again and again. The round continues forever.

We can picture Hezekiah singing such a song after the Assyrian army had been miraculously slain as it prepared its assault on Jerusalem. No wonder he says, "The LORD . . . dwelleth in Jerusalem." There indeed—and everywhere else.

Psalm 136

THE KINDNESS OF GOD

I. THE CALL TO THANKSGIVING (136:1-3)
  A. The Goodness of God (136:1)
  B. The Greatness of God (136:2-3)
    1. His Deity (136:2)
    2. His Dominion (136:3)
II. THE CAUSES OF THANKSGIVING (136:4-25)
  A. The Lord Created All Things (136:4-9)
    1. God's Personal Uniqueness (136:4)
    2. God's Perfect Universe (136:5-9)
      a. The Original Chaos (136:5-6)
      b. The Original Cosmos (136:7-9)
  B. The Lord Controls All Things (136:10-24)
    1. How the Lord Delivered Israel (136:10-15)
      a. His First Act of Deliverance (136:10)
      b. His Further Act of Deliverance (136:11-14)
        (1) In Saving Them (136:11-12)
        (2) In Separating Them (136:13-14)
      c. His Final Act of Deliverance (136:15)
    2. How the Lord Directed Israel (136:16-22)
      a. In Their Ways (136:16)
      b. In Their Wars (136:17-22)
        (1) Their Conspicuous Triumphs (136:17-20)
        (2) Their Conquered Territory (136:21-22)
    3. How the Lord Defended Israel (136:23-24)
      a. Remembered Them (136:23)
      b. Rescued Them (136:24)
  C. The Lord Considers All Things (136:25)
III. THE CONCLUSION OF THANKSGIVING (136:26)

PSALMS 135 and 136 are twins. *The Companion Bible* shows that each psalm has an independent structure of its own but, when put side by side, they have a structure in common. Both were probably written by Hezekiah. These psalms form an appendix to the songs of degrees (Psalms 120–134). As we have seen, Psalm 135 rehearses parts of Israel's history and underlines the folly of worshiping false gods; Psalm 136 rehearses parts of Israel's history and underlines the wisdom of worshiping the true God, the God whose "mercy endureth forever." That expression occurs like a chorus in every verse.

We can divide the psalm into three uneven parts.

I. THE CALL TO THANKSGIVING (136:1-3)

The psalmist introduces his theme of thanksgiving with a twofold emphasis. First, we are to give thanks because of:

A. The Goodness of God (136:1)

"O give thanks unto the LORD; for He is good: for His mercy endureth for ever." The theme of this psalm is "mercy's vast, unfathomed sea." Twenty-six times the psalmist lowers his sounding line into the ocean of God's mercy. Twenty-six times he finds that his line is too short. "No bottom here," he says. As a chorus puts it:

> Wide, wide as the ocean,
> High as the heavens above
> Deep, deep as the deepest sea
> Is my Saviour's love.

Theologically, of course, God's love is deeper, far deeper, than that. The psalmist looks first at God's goodness manifested in His mercy. The word for *mercy* is the usual word for "grace" or "lovingkindness." That mercy endures forever. Its brightest rays blazed forth against the dark background of the cross when Jesus cried, "Father, forgive them; for they know not what they do" (Luke 23:34). The very spear that pierced His side drew forth the blood that saves. Here we have:

> Love that no thought can reach,
> Love that no tongue can teach,
> No love like His!

This love and mercy outshines the sun and outlives the stars. Thank God for that. Suppose it lasted only for a hundred billion years and then ran out. Suppose, after that, His wrath overcame His mercy. How thankful we should be for this inspired revelation of the character of our God.

The psalmist tells us to give thanks also for:

B. The Greatness of God (136:2-3)

Here we see two examples of God's greatness, both calculated to set the joybells ringing in our souls.

1. His Deity (136:2)

"O give thanks unto the God of gods: for His mercy endureth for ever." God is merciful because He is God. It is His nature as God to be merciful. When Moses in his memoirs sought to explain to Israel why God set His heart's affections on them he said, "The LORD did not set His love upon you, nor choose you, because ye were more in number than any people; for ye were the fewest of all people, but because the LORD loved you" (Deuteronomy 7:7-8). Why does He love you? Just because He loves you. That's the way He is. He needs no other reason.

Moreover, He is "a God of gods," Elohim of the elohim. Are these *elohim* other "gods" or earthly rulers? The gods of the heathen are idols and vanities. Behind them, however, lurk the fallen elohim, the fallen angels of Satan, the lords of the underworld, the princeling powers of the air. We can let the word stand as it is printed in our text: He is "the God of gods." This view is supported by the previous psalm where the folly of idolatry is exposed.

The expression, "the God of gods," is matched in the next verse by the expression, "the Lord of lords." Since earthly rulers are in view in that verse, heavenly principalities are probably in view in this verse. This "God of gods," however, is not like them. He is celebrated for His mercy, a mercy that lasts forever. Long after the mischief wrought in the universe by Lucifer and his angels has been dealt with, the God of gods will reign on in majesty and mercy.

2. His Dominion (136:3)

"O give thanks to the Lord of lords: for His mercy endureth for ever." He is not only Elohim of the elohim, He is Adonim of the adonim. All power in heaven and earth is His. The "mystery of iniquity" works its woes in this world, empires wax and wane, kingdoms rise and fall, man's cruelty to man goes on and on, nations lord it over nations. Suffering and sorrow, war and famine, oppression and injustice, misery and woe, inundate the planet from pole to pole and from sea to sea. But God in His mercy sets limits to it all. Evil men like Stalin and Hitler die. In time, oppressions are overthrown; in the end, God wins. We turn from the pages of history to the scroll of prophecy and we read of a day when the Lord Jesus will come again. He will set up His kingdom, and the prayers of centuries will be answered: "Thy kingdom come. Thy will be done in earth, as it is in heaven." In the light of this, faith sings out: "O give thanks to the LORD of lords: for His mercy endureth for ever."

II. THE CAUSES OF THANKSGIVING (136:4-25)

Our reasons to be thankful, though numerous and varied, can be summarized in three categories.

A. The Lord Created All Things (136:4-9)

Here the psalmist draws our attention to two things:

1. God's Personal Uniqueness (136:4)

"To Him who alone doeth great wonders: for His mercy endureth forever." I remember watching a tiny spider run across my desk. The little fellow was no bigger in body than the period at the end of a sentence. He was going for all he was worth, trying to get away from the enormous monster who was eyeing him. He had eight legs—just tiny wisps of hair they seemed. He had eight eyes, no doubt all staring out of his head with fright (they were too small for me to see). Think of the wonder of it, that God could pack so much creative genius into so small a space. Inside that tiny dot of a body, that minute creature had a heart, a circulatory system. He had senses and instincts, genes and chromosomes. He could see, eat, walk. And doubtless, tiny as he seemed to me, there were creatures in *his* world that looked on *him* as an awesome monster.

We have a God who "doeth wonders." The universe is full of such wonders. From the inner mystery of the atom to the outer mystery of black holes in space, all creation bears tribute to the wonder that this God is a God whose "mercy endureth for ever."

2. God's Perfect Universe (136:5-9)

a. The Original Chaos (136:5-6)

"To Him that by wisdom made the heavens: to Him that stretched out the earth above the waters: for His mercy endureth for ever."

He put the *stars* in space. He is the one who "by wisdom made the heavens." The farther back we push the frontiers of known space, the more stars we find. What a God we have. And to think that His mercy is commensurate with His might—"His mercy endureth for ever."

Then, too, He put the *seas* in their place. He is the One who "stretched out the earth above the waters." Except for Him those waters would long since have come back and claimed their ancient domain; they once covered the world in one vast shoreless sea. He it was who heaved up the continents from their watery grave. Once, as punishment for human sins, He allowed those waters to come back. Afterward He hung a rainbow in the sky to advertise the fact that He will never again allow the world to be inundated by a flood. That rainbow says, "His mercy endureth for ever."

b. The Original Cosmos (136:7-9)

He gave the sun and moon their form: "To Him that made great lights: for His mercy endureth for ever" (136:7). How great they are. One is a giant reactor generating heat and light with an efficiency beyond anything ever dreamed of by the ancients; the other is a great reflector to catch the light of the absent sun and throw its beams on the darkened earth.

Think of the greatness of the sun. Over its entire surface it radiates about seventy thousand horsepower per square yard every second. Read that last sentence again. In the time it took to do so, the sun consumed twelve million tons of gasses. If we used our planet's stores of fuel at the same rate, there would be none left in three or four days. The sun's mass, however, is so great that millions of years from now it will have scarcely diminished at all. God has ensured that the sun will shine as long as there is life on earth.

He also gave the sun and moon their function: "The sun to rule by day: for His mercy endureth for ever: the moon and stars to rule by night: for His mercy endureth for ever" (136:8-9). The division of time into night and day is ruled by the sun, the slow but steady change of the seasons is ruled by the sun, the division of time into days and years is ruled by the sun. The division of time into months is ruled by the moon, the rise and fall of the tides is ruled by the moon. Our knowledge of the movement of the sun itself is derived from the stars.

Think of the orderliness of the sun, the moon, the stars—the way they obey the laws of God as they undertake their journeys through space. Think of the mathematical precision of their movement. If there were no such order, what a chaotic universe it would be. We would never know for sure the length of a day or be assured of the coming of a season. Our lives would be at the caprice of chance and we would live in disorder and confusion. The set rule of the sun, moon, and stars is another proof that God's mercy "endureth for ever."

B. The Lord Controls All Things (136:10-24)

The psalmist shows:

1. How the Lord Delivered Israel (136:10-15)

With a threefold development in mind, the psalmist draws our attention to:

a. His First Act of Deliverance (136:10)

"To Him that smote Egypt in their firstborn: for His mercy endureth for ever." Mercy? To smite the firstborn? The baby in the crib, the boy at school, the grown man in the field, the old grandfather in his bed? To smite the firstborn of every beast, of the calf in the stall, of the old mule by the mill? Mercy? Yes. It could have been everyone. Nor did that stroke of doom come until He had manifested to Pharaoh and to Egypt both His pity and His power nine times. Not until He had been lied to and played with and resisted by the pharaoh and his court nine times did God smite. Mercy? Yes. This is indeed one of those incidents in history which prove that, in wrath, God remembers His mercy.

b. His Further Act of Deliverance (136:11-14)

(1) In Saving Them (136:11-12)

"And brought out Israel from among them: for His mercy endureth for ever; with a strong hand, and with a stretched out arm; for His mercy endureth for ever." It was the strong hand of which Jesus spoke when He drew attention to a salvation far greater than that of the Hebrews from Egypt. "My sheep hear My voice, and I know them, and they follow Me: and I give unto them eternal life; and they shall never perish, neither shall any man pluck them out of My hand. My Father, which gave them Me, is greater than all; and no man is able to pluck them out of My Father's hand" (John 10:27-29).

That too was the arm which is not shortened that it cannot save, the arm we see outstretched on the cross.

(2) In Separating Them (136:13-14)

"To Him Which divided the Red sea into parts: for His mercy endureth for ever: and made Israel to pass through the midst of it: for His mercy endureth for ever."

When Pharaoh, in a final fit of fury, hardened his heart for the last time and harnessed his chariots of war to pursue Israel, that mighty arm was outstretched to bar his way. The Shekinah glory cloud came around and stood between Israel and Egypt's cavalry. Then followed the greatest miracle of the Exodus: the waters of the Red Sea parted so that this saved people might pass over on dry land to the other side. What a sight it must have been—those towering walls of water held back by omnipotent power, and Israel's multitudes, with flocks and tents, hurrying down that long, rumbling lane to the other side of the sea. Thus they were "baptized unto Moses in the cloud and in the sea" and forever separated from the old way of life.

c. His Final Act of Deliverance (136:15)

"But overthrew Pharaoh and his host in the Red sea: for His mercy endureth for ever." The foolish Pharaoh thought that unbelievers could do what believers could do. So he spurred his horses and he and his regiments leaped forward into the bed of the sea. Halfway across, his chariots broke down. Then, back came the thundering waters of the sea. God had not saved Israel from Egypt in order to surrender them to their foes. What a mercy it is for mankind that, sooner or later, tyrants like Pharaoh meet their match in God. All history bears witness to that. If He does not strike down the tormentor in the first acts of his defiance it is because He loves the poor deluded tyrant too.

Then the psalmist shows:

2. How the Lord Directed Israel (136:16-22)

In Hebrew history we see how God directed His people:

a. In Their Ways (136:16)

"To Him which led His People through the wilderness: for His mercy endureth for ever." God's daily guidance of Israel was as great a demonstration of His mercy as was His salvation. He led them down around the rim of the Sinai Peninsula because "the longest way around was the shortest way home." He led them into experiences that would develop and discipline

them, into experiences that would delight them. He fed them
with bread from heaven, gave them water from the riven rock,
gave them victory over Amalek, led them to an oasis of rest
along the way. Above all He bore their murmurings, complaints, and chronic unbelief. He bore with their worldliness
and carnality, just as He puts up with ours.

b. In Their Wars (136:17-22)

Blessings and battles go hand in hand in this dark world. The
psalmist draws attention to:

(1) Their Conspicuous Triumphs (136:17-20)

"To Him which smote great kings: for His mercy endureth
for ever: and slew famous kings: for His mercy endureth for
ever: Sihon king of the Amorites: for His mercy endureth
for ever: and Og the king of Bashan: for His mercy endureth
for ever." We perhaps would not think of smiting great kings as
an act of mercy, but rather an act of judgment. But what dreadful kings these were. There were nephilim kings; remnants of
the giants; products of sorcery and spiritism; hybrid, demon
men such as roamed the world before the flood. To rid the
world of such wickedness was an act of mercy to all the rest of
humankind. The people of Canaan were infecting surrounding
nations with their polluted religion, and these nephilim kings
were monstrous proponents of a spreading system of wickedness. Nobody thinks a surgeon cruel because he cuts deep with
his knife into the flesh of a patient suffering from cancer. God's
surgery on the Canaanites and their kings was an act of mercy
on the body politic to remove a malignant society which threatened the moral health of the world.

(2) Their Conquered Territory (136:21-22)

"And gave their land for an heritage: for His mercy endureth
for ever: even an heritage unto Israel His servant: for His mercy
endureth for ever." When God began to populate this planet He
divided the lands among the various families. He it was who first
decided who should live where. In His eternal counsels the land
between the Euphrates and the Nile was to be Israel's. In due
time, therefore, He deeded it to Abraham, Isaac, and Jacob.
The fact that this land was seized and occupied by a dozen
Canaanite tribes; that it was sought and fought over by empire-
hungry Pharaohs, Assyrians, Babylonians, Persians, Greeks,
and Romans; that parts of it were invaded and settled by Philis-

tine warriors from the west; and that part of it was held tenaciously by Phoenician merchant princes to the north made no difference. The title deeds were Israel's; they still are. Israel, out of the promised land, signifies that there is a limb of the body that is out of joint, a source of pain and trouble. For although the "wandering Jew" is a source of blessing to nations that give them a temporary home, they are also their bane. They belong in the promised land. Today the nations that still are fighting tooth and nail to keep Israel out of the land are hurting themselves, inflaming an old wound, hindering the healing of the nations. God, who smote great kings for Israel's sake in days gone by, and who gave them their inheritance in the promised land, is able to do the same today. He has not changed His mind nor revoked Israel's title deeds. He will yet settle Israel in its heritage, and thereafter heal the hurts of all nations (as many a Bible prophecy declares).

The psalmist shows too:

3. How the Lord Defended Israel (136:23-24)

The psalmist now briefly scans Israel's history in the land, pointing out that the Lord:

a. Remembered Them (136:23)

"Who remembered us in our low estate: for His mercy endureth for ever." Our merciful God remembers us. How terrible it would be if we had a forgetful God. Suppose it were possible for God to forget His promises! But, no matter how low our estate, how far we have fallen, how frail and forgetful we are—He remembers. He remembered Israel for four hundred years in Egypt. He remembered them during the seventy years of their Babylonian captivity. He has continued to remember them for the almost two thousand years since the Romans sacked Jerusalem. We do not forget those we love, and neither does God.

b. Rescued Them (136:24)

"And hath redeemed us from our enemies: for His mercy endureth for ever." The word *redeemed* means "rescued." It comes from a root meaning "to break" and occurs only here. God knows how to rescue His people. If, as we may suppose, Hezekiah added this psalm to the Hebrew hymnbook after the destruction of Sennacherib's host, then words such as these are especially appropriate. The Lord had rescued Israel in a remarkable way, and His actions served to warn the rest of the world.

c. The Lord Considers All Things (136:25)

"Who giveth food to all flesh: for His mercy endureth for ever." The human race has no monopoly on God's goodness and mercy. He cares just as much for the wild beast of the forest or an insect on the wing. Every creature has its place in God's ecological balance of nature. He provides for them all. Jesus said His Father is aware of the death of every sparrow. God clothes the grass of the field and finds food for the fish of the sea. The Mosaic Law even forbade the wholesale depletion of the nest of a bird. Such is our God.

III. THE CONCLUSION OF THANKSGIVING (136:26)

And behold, it is no conclusion at all: "O give thanks unto the God of heaven: for His mercy endureth for ever." The psalmist directs our thoughts upward again. The round goes on and on.

The title, "God [El] of heaven," is an interesting one, first occurring in 2 Chronicles 36:23 (the last verse of the book, and the last verse of the Hebrew Old Testament). It is a title of God found on the lips of Cyrus the Persian, who ended the Babylonian captivity. It is a title peculiar to the times of the Gentiles, when God acts from heaven and not from between the cherubim as the God of Israel. Thus the psalm ends by leading us on to our own age, where likewise "His mercy endureth for ever."

Psalm 137

JERUSALEM, BABYLON, AND EDOM

THIS IS A TALE of three cities—or rather, it is the tale of two cities and the neighboring hostile country of Edom. It is a tale of Jerusalem and Babylon—with Edom thrown in because of its special, venomous hatred of Israel.

Babylon was and will be one of *Satan's* world capitals. It was there that idolatry was first invented and institutionalized by Satan as a means of enslaving mankind and diverting worship to himself. It was there, in Babylon, that the secret mysteries took form. It was from Babylon that all false religion spread over the face of the world. Babylon was its source.

Babylon was where men first conceived the idea of world empire. It was in Babylon that the first league of nations was formed. It was there that man first embarked on a one-world society, held together by common political, religious, and cultural ties. It was at Babylon that Satan first introduced the

572

concept of a superman, a great rebel. Nimrod was the lawless one, the "man of sin" of his day, the world's first antichrist in type. It will be at Babylon that these early prototypes of Satan's plans will be replaced by reality. It was to Babylon that God ultimately banished the Jews for their idolatry and persistent rebellion against His rule, so that there, in the capital of idolatry, they might be cured of idolatry.

Jerusalem was and will be *God's* world capital. It was there that He was pleased to place His name, there He had the temple built, there He took up residence on earth. It was to Jerusalem that the tribes were to come to worship at the feasts. It was from Jerusalem that they were to be ruled. It was there that, in David, He set up a dynasty from which the Messiah would come. It was from Jerusalem that men were to learn about the true and living God. It was called "the city of the great King."

It was to Jerusalem that the Lord Jesus came, riding on an ass, to fulfill an ancient prophecy and to present Himself formally as the long awaited, but now rejected, King. It was at Jerusalem that He was crucified and buried. It was at Jerusalem that He rose in triumph from the tomb. It was at Jerusalem that the church was born and it was from Jerusalem that the gospel first began to be spread to the nations of the world.

It will be to Jerusalem that the antichrist will come. It will be there he will inaugurate a new world religion, set up his image, and desecrate the rebuilt temple. It will be from Rome that he will exert his *political* power and from Babylon his *economic* power; but it will be from Jerusalem that he will enforce his *religious* power.

It will be to Jerusalem, rescued, cleansed, enlarged, and rebuilt, that Jesus will finally come to inaugurate a new kingdom on earth.

And what about Edom? Edom was Israel's hereditary foe, right from the start. Jacob and Esau were twins; Israel and Edom, their descendants, were foes. All through Israel's occupancy of the land there was desultory warfare between Edom and Israel. Throughout its tenure of the land, Israel not only had to face the hostility of world superpowers, but also faced running guerrilla warfare with her immediate and perennially hostile neighbors—Edom and Ammon and Moab—the three countries of old which comprise Jordan today. Of them, Edom was the most bitter.

So then, this is a psalm of two cities: Babylon and Jerusalem, and of a next-door neighbor, Edom, which detested everything Israel stood for.

We are uncertain as to when this psalm was written. The internal evidence suggests it was written by a Hebrew who had been carried away into captivity by the Assyrians and who, along with others, had ended up in Babylon. The position of the psalm in the Psalter suggests it was included in the collection by Hezekiah. However, in Hezekiah's day, Babylon, though a rapidly growing power in the world, had not yet assumed the status of a world power or anything like the importance it later attained. This unknown poet had been able to make his way from Babylon back to Jerusalem where, overwhelmed with a fresh realization of all that Jerusalem meant to the Hebrew people, he burst into song.

Some, however, think the psalm was written by Jews in Babylon. If so, judging by the last two verses, it must have been written before the fall of Babylon. The likelihood is that it was written before the Babylonian captivity, that it came to Hezekiah's attention, and that he added it to the Hebrew hymnbook. The psalm is in two major divisions.

I. THE WOEFUL MISERY OF THE EXILES (137:1-4)

The poet records first:

A. The Distress of the Captives (137:1-2)

The Jews had been uprooted and deported and were far from their ancestral home. The sins of the nation had overtaken them. The judgment of God had fallen. They were exiles in a foreign land. Their hearts were broken. They are filled with nostalgia for their lamented homeland.

The poet mentions:

1. The Waters of Babylon (137:1a)

"By the rivers of Babylon, there we sat down." And great rivers they were. On the east was the Tigris, a river first mentioned in connection with the garden of Eden. In Genesis 2:4 it is called Hiddekel, the Accadian name for the Tigris. Upon this river was built Nineveh, the capital of Assyria. Then there was the Euphrates, another river connected with the garden of Eden. This great river flowed through the center of Babylon. Past and future conquerors of Israel all held the rivers of Babylon in the heyday of their power. The Euphrates will be the eastern boundary of the land deeded to Abraham, Isaac, and Jacob by God. The four great prophetic world empires (Babylon, Persia, Greece, and Rome) became world empires in the prophetic sense of Scripture only when they held the Euphrates.

The river figures largely in prophecy, especially in the book of Revelation.

Such were the rivers of Babylon. There it was the exiles sat. They would have gladly exchanged these mighty waterways for the humble Jordan or the even humbler Jabbok. They sat down because this was the end. They had been marched northward and eastward, mile after endless weary mile. Now they had arrived in "the land between the rivers." Their thoughts would wander through the recorded history of their people. It was from this very land that God had drawn their father Abraham, hundreds of years before. It was back to this land that Abraham had refused to allow his servant to go to seek a bride for Isaac. Now they were back where it had all begun. How miserably they had failed.

So they sat down, conscious of a finished work, the work of deliberately undoing all that God had done. This was "the far country" for these Old Testament prodigals. They had been brought up in the father's house, but they had squandered their substance with riotous living. Now they could only stare with empty, hungry souls at the pig trough of their destitution. The rivers of Babylon might once have flowed out of Eden; nothing could make them flow back into Eden. The rivers of Babylon marked the end of their long, wasted journey. There was no place else they could go. And like the New Testament prodigal, their thoughts turned nostalgically homeward, conscious of all they had thrown away for the garbage pails of sin.

2. The Wistfulness of Babylon (137:1b)

"Yea, we wept, when we remembered Zion." Zion was the poetic and prophetic name for Jerusalem. These exiles had looked dismally at the great cities of Assyria and the Euphrates valley. What cities they were. Nineveh was one of the greatest cities of antiquity, so large that it took three days to travel around it. It was protected by towering walls and frowning ramparts which dwarfed human beings standing down below. Anyone who has visited the British Museum and seen the colossi (the giant man-headed bulls and similar sculptures which once adorned the city) can gather some idea of this city's might. Babylon, too, was an up-and-coming city, soon to rival Nineveh.

What did these exiles care about Nineveh's might or Babylon's glories? Their thoughts turned toward Zion. To think that they, the northern tribes, the people of Israel, had scorned Zion in their day. They had neglected the city of God. They had ignored all that Jerusalem stood for in the eternal counsels of

God. They had disregarded the city of the great King, the city of David, the chosen city of God. They had overlooked the temple on Mount Moriah, with its hallowed service and sacrifices and, above all, the Shekinah glory cloud. They hardly knew the temple at all. Long years ago the northern tribes had substituted Samaria for Jerusalem and the golden calves at Bethel and at Dan for the great altars of the temple.

But now what would they not give to see Zion? All around them in Babylon were the monuments of idolatry and astrology. There were the towering ziggurats with their winding stairs and lofty heights dedicated to the mysteries of the stars—reminders, too, to these exiled Hebrews, of their own idolatrous ways. A few of the exiles, perhaps, might once have been to Jerusalem. They would, perhaps, describe a pilgrimage there. Now they could only weep, "Yea, we wept, when we remembered Zion."

3. The Willows of Babylon (137:2)

"We hanged our harps upon the willows in the midst thereof." We are all familiar with willows. We call them weeping willows. They grow near water, to a considerable height, and let down long, leafy streamers. They are droopy-looking trees, with an air of sadness about them. By the Babylonian willows, beside the wide flowing waters, these exiles sat down to weep. There were the rivers running, ever running, from a long forgotten Eden, just as these exiles had spent their lives running, ever running, from a long-forgotten God. There were the willows bowing in their nameless sorrows over the whispering waters, and there were the exiles bowing in their all-too-well-remembered sins over the waters of a foreign land. It was all so appropriate somehow, and these expatriated Hebrews fell in easily with the mood. With a symbolic gesture they took their harps and hung them on the weeping willows. They were through forever, it seemed, with laughter and song, with music and mirth.

But then the poet describes:

B. The Demand of the Conquerors (137:3-4)

The pagans around them saw those harps hanging on the trees. Ignoring the tears of these peculiar Hebrews, who could not enter into the spirit of things in Babylon—Babylon with its pleasures and treasures, with its glittering opportunities and imperial future—they demanded that the captives sing. The poet remembered that.

1. What the Conquerors Required (137:3)

The Babylonian victors required two things. First they said, "Sing us one of your *happy* songs." "For there they that carried us away captive required of us . . . mirth." They said, "Come on, sing! Sing us something that has some joy in it." Sing? That was the last straw. They had expected to be enslaved; they had hardened themselves to that. The chains on their wrists, when they were marched away to the north, had prepared them for that. They were fortunate still to be alive. But sing?

How could they sing in captivity, whether in Assyria or Babylon? They were reaping the due reward for their deeds. That is why they sobbed. But sing? And to the very ones who were wasting them? Wasting them—what a significant expression. Had they not wasted their lives before their captors took them away? Had they not wasted their time, treasures, and talents on idle pleasures and pagan superstitions? We need only turn to Hosea, Amos, and Micah to see how terribly they had wasted the glorious opportunity to know and serve the true God.

Sing us a happy song? It was more than flesh and blood could stand. When that was not forthcoming, the command was: "Sing us one of your *holy* songs. If you cannot sing us something merry, sing us a hymn. If you can't sing a tavern ballad or a love song or a marching song, then sing us a song of Zion. Sing us a psalm. Come on, you Jews! Things aren't so bad as all that. You may be captives and exiles, but you are free to settle among us. You can go into business and get on in the world if you like. Sing!"

No need to tell Paul and Silas that! Made fast in the stocks in the inner prison in the jailhouse at Philippi, with backs bleeding but spirits unbroken, Paul and Silas burst into song. They so praised God in song that an earthquake unloosed their shackles and the jailor and his family came to a saving knowledge of the Lord (Acts 16).

2. What the Captives Replied (137:4)

"How shall we sing the LORD's song in a strange land?" Imagine that. But that was the very reason why God had chosen Israel, separated Israel, taught and trained Israel—so that her people might become heralds to the nations of the greatness and goodness of God. "The Lord's song!" What an opportunity for them to witness to the pagans all about them of the saving power of their God. Suppose they had taken down those harps, had tuned up the strings, and had sung:

> The Lord's my Shepherd, I'll not want;
>   He makes me down to lie
> In pastures green; He leadeth me
>   The quiet waters by.

Surely they could have sung that. And then followed it up with one of David's penitential or prophetic psalms. But no, they sat and sulked and wallowed in the miseries they had brought on themselves.

"How shall we sing the LORD's song in a strange land?" How? By taking down their harps, of course. By tuning up their hearts. They could have said: "We'll sing you the very first song in our hymnbook. It is an anonymous psalm. Here's one of the lines—we'll recite it to you while we get ready: 'Happy is the man that walketh not in the counsel of the ungodly . . . whose delight is in the law of the LORD. . . . He shall be like a tree planted by the rivers of water.' These rivers of Babylon remind us of that." So the psalmist recounts the woeful misery of the captive. He next records:

II. THE WAKENED MEMORY OF THE EXILES (137:5-9)

At this point the psalmist seems to have stopped reminiscing about the days of his exile. He is back in the promised land and alive once more to the blessing of being associated with the place where God had put His name.

He remembered:

A. How Favored Jerusalem Was (137:5-6)

This memory, he feels, should color:

1. Every Pursuit of Life (137:5-6a)

"If I forget thee, O Jerusalem, let my right hand forget her cunning. If I do not remember thee, let my tongue cleave to the roof of my mouth." Never again would he permit himself to forget Jerusalem. Henceforth everything he did, everything he said, would be governed by thoughts of Jerusalem. He would rather never be able to do a day's work again, never be able to utter a single word again, than forget Jerusalem and all that Jerusalem stood for in the spiritual life of God's people.

2. Every Pleasure of Life (137:6b)

"If I prefer not Jerusalem above my chief joy." Never again would this poet allow life's pleasures to blot out the memory of

Jerusalem. No matter what his chief joy—wife and children, fame and fortune, success in business, sports or politics, distinction in the arts and sciences—no matter what his chief joy, Jerusalem would come first. God would come first.

What a challenge for us, only the challenge for us lies in the New Jerusalem. God would have us set our affections on things above, where Christ sits at the right hand of God. He would have us subordinate our chief joy to the interests of the world to come. He would have us get the celestial city in focus and so allow it to fill our vision that our treacherous memories may never again betray us, so that we might not be ashamed at the coming of Christ.

Then the psalmist's thoughts take a sudden ominous turn. He thinks of Edom and Babylon. Those thoughts remind him that God has a long account to settle with those two nations in particular. The closing verses are terrible imprecations (such as occasionally blaze out in the psalms).

B. How Fitting Judgement Was (137:7-9)

The psalmist's thoughts went out to Edom, the nagging next-door neighbor filled with treachery and spite, and to the growing world superpower far away. His mind was filled perhaps with some of Isaiah's prophecies of Babylon as the nation that would threaten Jerusalem in a far more terrible way than Nineveh ever did.

He thinks of:

1. The Vicious Attitude of Edom (137:7)

"Remember, O LORD, the children of Edom in the day of Jerusalem; who said, 'Rase it, rase it, even to the foundation thereof.'" It would seem that the Edomites had encouraged the Assyrians, when their armies surrounded Jerusalem. They did not actively help them, as they later did when the Babylonians besieged Jerusalem, but they gave them verbal encouragement to take, sack, and demolish Jerusalem. This unknown poet now calls on God to remember Edom's spite.

The Arab nations today are Edom's heirs. They are quite willing to encourage the Soviets as long as Russia will do their work for them in ridding the Middle East of the State of Israel. As has been said, God does not forget such hatred toward His chosen people. He has pledged Himself to curse those that curse His people. The psalmist, therefore, was not mouthing venomous spites of his own, he was simply allying himself with the declared Word of God.

2. The Violent Atrocities of Babylon (137:8-9)

"O daughter of Babylon, who art to be destroyed; happy shall he be, that rewardeth thee as thou hast served us. Happy shall he be, that taketh and dasheth thy little ones against the stones." The psalmist had been in Babylon and knew what the Babylonians were like. They were as cruel in war as the Assyrians, whose place upon the world stage they were soon to take. Like many another world superpower they raged ruthless war and committed horrible atrocities against their enemies.

At this point the poet becomes a prophet. He was doubtless familiar with the whole range of Isaiah's prophecies against Babylon (Isaiah 13–14, 46–48). He knew that Isaiah had foretold this fate for the babies of Babylon: "Their children also shall be dashed to pieces before their eyes . . ." (Isaiah 13:16). Prophetic vision dissolves the distance imposed by time.

With his poetry married to his prophecy, the singer sees the future Babylonian invasion of Jerusalem. He has no hope that the Babylonians will be kinder to ravished Jerusalem than they have been in their other wars. He could imagine the bitter and stubborn resistence of Jerusalem to the coming invasion, could picture the frustration of the Babylonians at having to take Jerusalem in long and bloody siege. He could gauge the temper of the troops when at last the walls were pierced and, with their blood lust fanned to white-hot heat by their anger over the difficulty of the siege, they stormed the city streets looting, raping, killing, even hurling babies to the ground.

It is not so much the poet's hope that the Babylonians in turn might suffer a like terrible fate. It is the relish with which he utters it that troubles us: "Happy shall he be, that taketh and dasheth thy little ones against the stones." This surely has to be the most perplexing beatitude in the Bible: actually to bless those who commit such acts of ferocity against the innocent children of a foe.

The psalmist seems to have in mind, however, the poetic justice of God. The fires of his spirit have been stoked by his contemplation of the sanctity and sublimity of Jerusalem. But to picture a man, inspired by a passionate love for Jerusalem, calling down a blessing on those who murder the children of an enemy is beyond us (which, of course, goes to show how much our own thinking has been influenced by the grace of God and by the spirit of the gospel of Christ).

Perhaps if we had lived in the psalmist's day, if we had seen what he had seen, been where he had been, we might have a better understanding of his point of view. Or if we had lived through an invasion, if we had been subjected to atrocities wrought by the hand of a cruel enemy, if our children had been thus callously murdered before our eyes, we might not have so much objectivity. Let us hope that our Christianity would carry us through, but perhaps we would have more sympathy with this Old Testament poet-prophet just the same.

In actual fact, the ultimate fall of Babylon at the hands of the Medes and Persians was relatively mild. So perhaps, after all, this prophecy has an even more significant focus. Perhaps it focuses on the end times, to the final manifestation on the earth of Babylonian world power as led and inspired by the beast. If so, then such imprecations are appropriate and take on a new note and higher purpose altogether.

Psalm 138

TRUSTING WHEN THINGS GO WRONG

THIS IS A PSALM of David written when he was surrounded by enemies. We do not know when he wrote it, but since thoughts of "the temple" were in his mind it is possible it was at the time of Absalom's rebellion. Hezekiah, in the midst of his troubles, surrounded by his enemies, and with every likelihood, humanly speaking, of being forced to evacuate Jerusalem, doubtless found solace in this psalm. He recognized its inspiration and added it to the hymnbook. It revolves around five themes.

582

I. GLADNESS (138:1-2)

The gladness ringing through the opening verses is an expression of the psalmist's joy in God. Note:

A. David's Inner Compulsion to Worship (138:1)

1. Its Totality (138:1a)

"I will praise Thee with my whole heart." Isn't that just like David! In deep trouble, his life threatened, not knowing which way to turn, his life hanging by a thread, no idea where his next meal is coming from—and praising God. If there is one time most of us stop praising God it is when our little worlds cave in. We *petition* God, perhaps, we besiege His throne with prayer requests, but *praise* Him? There are those foolish people who, when things go wrong, forsake God or accuse God. Others doggedly hold on to their faith. But praise Him? David did. David knew God well enough to expect a miracle. Man's extremity is God's opportunity.

2. Its Testimony (138:1b)

"Before the gods [the *elohim*] will I sing praise unto Thee." The word *elohim* in this context means the rulers, rather than "gods." David had nearly always borne fearless testimony before rulers—before Saul, before Goliath. The only time David was ashamed to bear testimony for God was when he pretended to be mad before Ahimelech, king of Gath—but David was in a backslidden condition at that time or he would not have gone to Gath in the first place.

Then, too, gladness expressed:

B. David's Inspired Comprehension of Worship (138:2)

David's comprehension of the meaning of worship arises from:

1. The Temple that Was so Solidly Real to Him (138:2a)

"I will worship toward Thy holy temple." In David's day the temple was not yet built, though the thought of it had been in his heart for many a year. At the time of the Absalom rebellion not even the site of the temple had been selected, though David had already begun to accumulate the enormous treasure he eventually left to enable Solomon to build God's house. In David's day, the sacred ark reposed in the special tent David had pitched for it in Zion. Yet his faith soared far beyond. In his mind's eye the gorgeous temple was already built. Perhaps he already had in hand the divine blueprints, a copy of the reality in the heavens (David was seer and prophet enough to know that).

David, also, was too great a saint to imagine that any one spot on earth could have more than symbolic value in localizing God's earthly habitation. Temples and shrines and sacred spots on earth often prove to be more of a hindrance than a help in focusing our attention on spiritual realities. David, turning his heart toward God's house, is simply David preparing his soul for worship. The temple was so real to him because he was in touch with a God that "dwelleth not in temples made by hands" and because David habitually worshiped God in His heavenly temple.

Still the thought of a literal temple on earth made him glad. He might be able to make do with thoughts of it; others would need something more substantial. Not all believers had attained his spiritual maturity.

2. The Topic that Was so Sweetly Refreshing to Him (138:2b)

"And praise Thy name for Thy lovingkindness and for Thy truth." The word *lovingkindness* is the usual word in the psalms for grace. Grace and truth—that turns our thoughts at once to Jesus. "The law was given by Moses," wrote John, "but grace and truth came by Jesus Christ" (John 1:17). The law was *given*. Moses was its mediator. Sinai flamed and shook as the people stood afar off, terrified by the sights and sounds that heralded the giving of that law. No wonder it had to be delivered into the hands of a mediator. But grace and truth *came*. And in what wondrous guise it came. It came clothed in flesh and blood, as a baby wrapped in swaddling clothes and lying in a manger. It came as a holy child, as a bright, intelligent boy who excelled at everything. Grace and truth came as a youth delighting in the temple, astonishing the doctors, thrilled to be about His Father's business. It came as a man with the keenest mind in the universe, with muscles hardened at the workbench, with an attractive personality. It came as One who was holy, undefiled, separate from sinners.

And grace! Grace to "weep o'er the erring one, lift up the fallen." Grace to forgive the ones who nailed Him to the tree. And truth! Truth to tell Nicodemus that he needed to be born again. Truth to spell out the Sermon on the Mount—and then the transparent honesty to live it out every single moment of every day He lived. "I will . . . praise Thy name for Thy lovingkindness and truth," said David—although in David's day "the half had not been told."

3. The Truth that Was so Suddenly Revealed to Him (138:2c)

"I will praise Thee . . . for Thou hast magnified Thy word above all Thy name." In the Old Testament, God's Word and God's name were inextricably interwoven. God invariably revealed Himself by His name. *Elohim* was His name as creator and sustainer of the universe, the name of the omnipotent, omniscient, omnipresent God, the God of the galaxies, the maker of molecules, the One who fashioned cherubim and seraphim, angel and archangel. Elohim. God has exalted His Word above that name.

Adonai. That was His name as sovereign Lord and supreme ruler. It is the name of Him whose throne is above the stars, the One whom all created beings and things must obey. He has exalted His Word above *that* name.

Jehovah. That was His name as the eternal One, the One who reveals Himself, the One who enters into covenant relationship with us, who makes promises, whose Word is His bond. He exalts His Word above that name.

He is *Jehovah Jireh,* the One who provides, who takes care of all our wants, who provided Himself to be the Lamb for the burnt offering. He is *Jehovah Shalom,* the Lord our peace; He is *Jehovah Ropheka,* the Lord who heals; He is *Jehovah Tsidkenu,* the Lord our righteousness; He is *Jehovah Shammah,* the Lord is there; He is *Jehovah Nissi,* the Lord our banner; He is *Jehovah Mekaddishkem,* the Lord who sanctifies. Such is His name.

He jealously guards that name. He does not allow human beings to take that name in vain. He has declared that no one will be held guiltless who lightly speaks that name. Throughout the Scriptures He has exalted and extolled His name.

Jesus added a new name for God—He taught us to call Him *Father.* Surely that is the greatest name of all.

Yet God says that He exalts *His Word above His name. That* is what God thinks of His Word. How dare men and women doubt that Word? How dare they deny that Word? How dare they disregard that Word? Yet they do. They lightly set God's Word aside as though it were the product of a human pen. A day of accounting is coming for such persons.

So, then, David's soul was filled with gladness as he tuned his heart to worship. The second theme of this psalm is:

II. GRACE (138:3)

"In the day when I cried Thou answeredst me, and strengthened me with strength in my soul." That is how the Lord answered David's prayer. He did not remove the problem, though He intended to do so in time. Instead, He strengthened David in his soul. God allows things to happen to us for that very reason. He intends to do something in our souls which will make us stronger believers than we were before. Often God answers our prayers by giving us what we need in order to live with the problem.

The apostle Paul had what he called "a thorn in the flesh." He had just been given a vision of glory. He had been caught up into the third heaven and had seen indescribable things. Lest he become so heavenly minded as to be no earthly use, God balanced the thrill with a thorn. Paul called it "a messenger of Satan," the purpose of which was to "buffet" him. The phrase, "a messenger of Satan," can be rendered "an angel of Satan." As Job was attacked by Satan, so was Paul. The apostle was devastated. He could see this thing hindering his ministry. We do not know what the affliction was—some have speculated an eye affliction; others have suggested epilepsy. Whatever it was, on three separate occasions Paul asked for it to be removed. Three times God said no. "My grace is sufficient for thee," he said, "for My strength is made perfect in weakness" (2 Corinthians 12:9). God said to Paul, "Paul, I am going to enable you to live with this thing for My glory." Paul said, "Most gladly therefore will I glory in my infirmities, that the power of Christ may rest upon me" (2 Corinthians 12:7-10).

David had a similar experience. He said, "In the day when I cried Thou answeredst me, and strengthened me with strength in my soul."

The third theme of this psalm is:

III. GLORY (138:4-5)

"All the kings of the earth shall praise Thee, O LORD, when they hear the words of Thy mouth. Yea, they shall sing in the ways of the LORD: for great is the glory of the LORD." That day has not come yet, but it is on the way. Its arrival is anticipated time and time again in the prophetic Scriptures. Many of the psalms strike this note of anticipation. From pole to pole and from sea to shining sea the rulers of the world are going to praise the Lord. They will praise Him more and more as, under His control, the earth again puts on the verdant splendor of Eden. The deserts will become a paradise. Love will be the mainspring of His empire, the Sermon on the Mount the prevailing guide. Sin will be kept down with an iron rod. The boundaries of the nations will be redrawn, and war will become a thing of the past.

The kings of the earth will hear the words of His mouth, as David says. They will say, "Never man spake like this man." They will come, like the queen of Sheba, from the ends of the earth to see Him, to listen to Him. Each will return saying, "Behold, the half was never told me."

And they will sing! When the rulers of the world meet in conference now, they do not open their sessions with song. They neither sing nor pray. There is not much to sing about and most of them do not believe in prayer. The rulers and delegates of the nations meet to discuss the storm clouds that hang, now here, now there, over the world, or to discuss this crisis or that outrage or this famine or that economic woe. What with the hostilities, rivalries, and jealousies of both superpowers and lesser powers, there is not much to sing about (though there is plenty to pray about) when the nations convene in conference. They squabble now. They will sing then.

The next theme of this psalm is:

IV. GOVERNMENT (138:6-7)

David here sets before us two truths.

A. An Amazing Fact (138:6)

"Though the LORD be high, yet hath He respect unto the lowly: but the proud He knoweth afar off." How high *He* is. "I saw . . . the LORD . . . high and lifted up," said Isaiah. He is higher than the highest heaven, His throne is exalted above the stars. Between Him and the highest archangel of glory is a gulf so vast as to be infinite.

How lowly *we* are. When Isaiah saw the Lord he became aware at once of his own despicable condition. "Woe is me," he said, "I am undone." Prophet that he was, gifted man that he was, confident before kings as he was, one glimpse of the Lord and Isaiah was filled with a sense of his unworthiness and shame. Even his lips, the words he spoke, horrified him. Yet the Lord had respect for him and lifted him up.

How foolish to be proud. "The proud He knoweth afar off." So much for Lucifer's thought to be like the Most High God. God read that thought afar off, even before Lucifer suborned the loyalty of his first follower among the angel hosts. He reads our own proud thoughts from afar. How far out in space is the remotest star, wending its lowly way in deepest darkness, in frozen isolation? How far back in time is the time when there was no time? He reads our thoughts afar off, as far off as that. So much for all the schemes and plans of the proud. In His sovereign government of the universe God makes His moves and can bring those plans to nothing.

But if David is awed by this amazing fact, it does not stagger him; it stimulates him. He gives evidence of:

B. An Abundant Faith (138:7)

"Though I walk in the midst of trouble, Thou wilt revive me: Thou shalt stretch forth Thine hand against the wrath of mine enemies, and Thy right hand shall save me." God knew Absalom's thoughts afar off. He knew cunning Ahithophel's thoughts. This amazing fact fired David's abundant faith and gave him a twofold confidence in the government of God. First:

1. God Will Revive Him (138:7a)

He has nothing to worry about. His despondency and despair will be banished the moment he sees the situation in the light of God's omnipotence and omniscience. No matter that he walks in the midst of trouble—an all-powerful, all-knowing, all-loving God is with Him.

Then:

2. God Will Rescue Him (138:7b)

God will stretch out His hand against the wrath of His enemies. The stretching forth of God's hand is a well-known Old Testament synonym for judgment. No power in the universe can withstand the stretching out of God's hand.

It was stretched out in the days of Daniel, when proud Belshazzar mocked the living God by using the sacred vessels of the temple for a drunken feast. What a display of pomp and world power was manifested in the palace that night. Everyone who was anyone was there: the great of the land, lords and ladies, the chiefs of the military. What a feast! What revelry! What ribald mocking of Jehovah! What scenes of debauchery! Then suddenly, silently, out of the sleeve of the night came the outstretched hand of God. Across the palace wall that hand moved, leaving behind it a message none could read. That was all it took to reduce proud Belshazzar's pride. God is able to humble the haughtiest of persons.

The last theme of the psalm is:

V. GROWTH (138:8)

"The LORD will perfect that which concerneth me: Thy mercy, O LORD, endureth for ever: forsake not the works of Thine own hands." Here is the ultimate secret of God's seeming delays in delivering us from the apparent triumph of the enemy: He is working on us. He uses adverse circumstances to perfect us, to accomplish some wise and wonderful purpose He has in mind for us.

Years ago I met a potter who made his home in Bethlehem. His little place was on a side road off the beaten track where he had found a field of suitable clay. I went in and there he was with a piece of clay in his hands. He was working it over, holding it first in this hand, then in that, as he punched and pounded it. It was cold, hard, stiff, and he was making it warm, soft, malleable.

Next he put that piece of clay on his wheel, drew up his stool, moistened his hands, and went to work. For awhile he exerted pressure on that clay with his hands from the outside, and that outside pressure made it grow. The clay grew taller and taller as he kept the pressure on. Without that pressure it would have remained a shapeless lump, but with it the clay grew.

Then he moistened his hands again and with his thumb made a hollow in the top of that clay cylinder. As soon as the hollow was deep enough he began pressing inward and downward with his fingers until he could get his whole hand inside the cavity. He was now putting pressure on the inside. That inside pressure gave the clay shape and form and capacity. Without it, it would have remained a cylinder of clay, incapable of holding anything.

The potter then took his vessel off the wheel and put it in the furnace, a very primitive furnace, fired by pieces of wood. I didn't stay for the whole process, but for hour after hour that clay was there, in the furnace and the heat. All the time the potter was there, feeding the furnace, knowing just how hot to keep it. He never allowed it to get too hot or too cold. At last it was finished. The potter took out the finished piece and put it on display on a shelf outside his shop—a tribute to the skillfulness of his hands. All through that process the potter was perfecting his work; now it was on display. That is what David discovered: "Thou wilt perfect that which concerneth me; Thy mercy, O LORD, endures for ever. Forsake not the works of Thine hands."

Psalm 139

FROM EVERLASTING THOU ART GOD

I. WHAT THE PSALMIST REALIZED (139:1-18)
  A. The Truth of God's Omniscience (139:1-6)
    1. David's Examination of This Truth (139:1-5)
      a. The Truth Stated (139:1)
      b. The Truth Studied (139:2-5)
        (1) You See My Every Movement (139:2a)
        (2) You Sound My Every Motive (139:2b)
        (3) You Search My Every Moment (139:3-4)
          (a) My Walk—Every Single Step (139:3)
          (b) My Talk—Every Single Statement (139:4)
        (4) You Surround My Every Maneuver (139:5)
    2. David's Exclamation at This Truth (139:6)
  B. The Truth of God's Omnipresence (139:7-12)
    1. Death Does Not Hide Us from God (139:7-8)
    2. Distance Does Not Hide Us from God (139:9-10)
    3. Darkness Does Not Hide Us from God (139:11-12)
  C. The Truth of God's Omnipotence (139:13-18)
    1. He Created Me (139:13-16)
    2. He Considers Me (139:17-18)
II. WHAT THE PSALMIST REQUESTED (139:19-24)
  A. That the Lord Would Save Him (139:19-22)
    1. David's Assurance (139:19-20)
    2. David's Assertion (139:21-22)
  B. That the Lord Would Search Him (139:23-24)

ALTHOUGH THE TITLE of this psalm declares it a psalm of David, some scholars have challenged that. They say the psalm contains a number of Chaldean expressions, so David could not have written it; it must have been written at a much later date than David's day. In that case, where did the title come from?

Why should we assume that David had no contact with Chaldea? Wasn't his empire a phenomenon that would interest other great powers like Egypt, Assyria, and Babylon? Didn't his kingdom stand astride the most important trade routes of the ancient world? Wasn't Israel at one end of the Fertile Crescent and Chaldea at the other end? Hadn't Abraham himself come from Chaldea? Wouldn't the Chaldeans want to establish diplomatic relations with this new power in the west, if for no other reason, to insure the safety of their caravans? Why should David not know some Chaldean words and why should he not use them?

Other scholars point out that the words, supposedly of Chaldean origin (in 139:3, 4, 8, and 20), are found in earlier books of the Bible written before the days of David, books like Leviticus and 1 Samuel. So why not let David have the credit for this psalm?

The writer is obviously a poetic genius and a man who knew and loved God. God is referred to by name six times and by personal pronoun thirty times. The psalmist refers to himself fifty times. It is a song of profound spiritual experience. All such experience is, by its nature, personal and intimate—the engagement of a soul with God.

If David wrote it, we might well ask when. An inference from verse 17 ("How precious also are Thy thoughts unto me, O GOD! How great is the sum of them!") perhaps gives us the key.

David had united the nation, defeated its foes, put its internal affairs in order, and settled down to be a shepherd-king to Israel. Then it occurred to him that the living God of Israel, the God he had hymned in scores of psalms, the God to whom he owed everything, still lived in a tent. He determined to build God a temple—a temple fitting for such a God as Jehovah. He broached the subject to his court chaplain, Nathan the prophet, who gave immediate approval, an approval he had to modify almost at once when God Himself spoke on the matter. David's son would build that temple, but God would see to it that, since David was concerned about God's house, God would be concerned about David's house. He would establish David's house as a permanent dynasty until the coming of Christ.

That promise rang in David's soul. He told the Lord so, as we learn from 2 Samuel 7:18 and 1 Chronicles 17:16. His heart overwhelmed at the greatness of God's thoughts toward him, David might have gone to his room that night, not to sleep, but to write this hymn.

Herder has expressed what any commentator must feel when contemplating this magnificent hymn: "Language utterly fails me in the exposition of this psalm." Where does one begin? What does one include? The psalm is so full, intricate, detailed, grand in concept, and thrilling in its statements and stanzas. It seems a crime to leave any word unexplored. Yet obviously, to do it justice would call for more space than can be given here and so we restrict the commentary to its major themes.

The psalm begins by telling us:

I. WHAT THE PSALMIST REALIZED (139:1-18)

The psalmist realized he was in touch with an omniscient, omnipresent, omnipotent God. Nowhere else in Scripture does the Holy Spirit give us such a detailed exposition of these three essential attributes of God.

A. The Truth of God's Omniscience (139:1-6)

God is all-knowing. Nothing escapes His all-seeing eye, His awesome, all-knowing mind. Note:

1. David's Examination of this Truth (139:1-5)

a. David begins by *stating the truth of God's omnicience:* "O LORD, Thou hast searched me, and known me" (139:1). The word *searched* literally means "to pierce through." We sometimes speak of seeing right through a person. That of course is poetic but when it comes to God it is simple fact. Not that David shrank from this truth. The word he used for *searched* also carries with it the idea of searching for treasure. God was looking for what He could bless, could approve of and reward. When Hagar burst out, "Thou God seest me" Genesis 16:13, it was not an exclamation of terror, but a grateful acknowledgment that God, Abraham's God, took notice even of her, an unwanted slave.

b. David continues by *studing the truth of God's omniscience* (139:2-5). He makes a fourfold confession about God's ability to see him through and through, at all times, in all places, in his outward words and deeds and in his innermost thoughts. We all live under such an eye. Whether we regard that as thrilling or as threatening depends on the way we live. Studying this awesome and somewhat disconcerting truth, David realized four things.

(1) He says, *Lord, You see my every movement:* "Thou knowest my downsitting and mine uprising" (139:2a). God observes our most casual acts. He notices when I sit down and when I get up again, when I go to bed, when I can't sleep and get up in the middle of the night. He sees my every movement, and He is interested.

(2) David says, *Lord, You sound my every motive:* "Thou understand-est my thought afar off" (139:2b). The word *Thou* is emphatic; it is

God alone who possesses this kind of knowledge. No law court in the land would convict a person on the testimony of a witness who professed to be able to tell the court what the accused thought. God can. At least twice in the Gospels we read of the Lord Jesus that "He knew their thoughts." One of those occasions was critical. After seeing so many of the miracles He had performed, the Pharisees decided that Jesus cast out demons by the power of Satan. "Jesus knew their thoughts," Matthew says (12:25). From that moment He accused the Pharisees of blaspheming the Holy Ghost, and began to teach in mysteries. He knew their thoughts, and He knows ours too—whether lofty, lewd, compassionate, cruel, noble, or niggardly. He knows every single thought that has ever crossed our minds—He knows each and every one.

(3) David says, *Lord, You search my every moment*—You know my walk—every single step. You know my talk—every single statement. "Thou compassest my path and my lying down, and art acquainted with all my ways. For there is not a word in my tongue, but lo, O LORD, Thou knowest it altogether" (139:3-4). He knows when I leave the house. He knows whether I walk to work, take my car, or ride the bus. He knows when I go for a coffee break, when I leave for home, and when I walk back in the door. There is not a step, from my first efforts to toddle as a young child to my last faltering steps as an old-age pensioner, that He does not know.

He knows, too, every word I say. It has been said that every day the average articulate man speaks enough words to fill a good-sized volume and in the course of a lifetime enough words to make enough books to fill a college library. We forget by far the great majority of them, but every one of them is known to God. Jesus said, "Every idle word that men shall speak they shall give account thereof on the day of judgment." If that does not cause us to bridle our tongues, nothing will. God knows our mean and spiteful words and our kind, thoughtful, helpful, encouraging words. The Lord knows, too, every word we have uttered in worship and praise, and He has promised that if we confess Him before others, He will confess us before His Father and the holy angels in a day to come.

(4) Then David says, *Lord, You surround my every maneuver:* "Thou hast beset me behind and before, and laid Thine hands upon me" (139:5). The word *beset* literally means "to be cramped or limited"; it is the word used for besieging a town. God hems us in on every side so that there is no escape. None of life's little disguises deceive Him. We use them all the time with each other but He sees through them. None of our petty eva-

sions fool Him. He sees through all the games people play for exploiting each other and acquiring psychological benefits for themselves. David realized this.

2. David's Exclamation at This Truth (139:6)

David follows through with an exclamation: "Such knowledge is too wonderful for me: it is high, I cannot attain unto it." Instead of trying to shrink God's omniscience, David reveled in it. If he wrote this psalm just after learning that God was to establish the messianic dynasty in him he had good reason to be glad God knew him thus.

An emphasis of Greek philosophy was: "Man, know thyself." The dictum brought people face to face with the impossible. Nobody can know himself. We are bundles of contradictions. David realized that although he did not know himself, God knew him.

He also realized:

B. The Truth of God's Omnipresence (139:7-12)

Giving three illustrations, the psalmist came to the conclusion that nothing can hide us from God.

First he points out that:

1. Death Does Not Hide Us from God (139:7-8)

"Whither shall I go from Thy spirit? Or whither shall I flee from Thy presence? If I ascend up into heaven, Thou art there: if I make my bed in hell, behold Thou art there." That is the ultimate folly of suicide. Suicide does not solve problems; it simply hurls persons into eternity where they come face to face with God—with all their problems unresolved and their guilt aggravated by self-murder. God is present everywhere, on both sides of the grave.

Of course, we expect to meet Him in heaven. When John describes the celestial city he tells us of the gates of pearl and the streets of gold, the walls of jasper and the foundations agleam with precious stones, of the tree of life and the crystal stream. He tells us of the absence of night. He says there will be no sin in heaven, no suffering, no tears. There will be no need of a temple. But he keeps the best until last. The final bliss of that glorious place is this: "They shall see His face!" Jesus will be there. God the Father will be there, God the Holy Spirit will be there, Jesus the Son of the living God, our beloved Savior, will be there. As the hymnwriter puts it:

When by the gift of His infinite grace,
I am accorded in heaven a place;
Just to be there and to look on His face
Will through the ages be glory for me.

We expect God to be there. But the sinner will meet God in hell as well. People who have ruled God out of their lives will wake up in hell to discover that He is there, that His eye is on them. The dreadful sentence will have been passed: "He that is unjust, let him be unjust still: and he that is filthy, let him be filthy still . . ." (Revelation 22:11). Death does not change character. Those who are lost will plunge into eternity possessed of all the reprehensible attitudes, consumed by all the dreadful lusts, they lived with on earth. Incarcerating a man in prison does not change his nature; rather, it puts him in a place where he cannot abuse law-abiding citizens. In a lost eternity people will burn with horrible passions but will have no way to satisfy them. God will be there but only as judge. The thought should send a shudder through the sinner's soul: death does not hide us from God.

2. Distance Does Not Hide Us from God (139:9-10)

"If I take the wings of the morning, and dwell in the uttermost parts of the sea; even there shall Thy hand lead me, and Thy right hand shall hold me." That is a comforting thought for the child of God. No matter where he goes, that presence is with him. Jesus said, "Lo, I am with you always, even unto the end of the world." In the strength of that, women and men have dared untold dangers to spread the gospel to earth's remotest bounds.

Sir John Franklin, who lost his life looking for the Northwest Passage, found it so. He wanted to blaze a trail through the snow-clad polar regions to the Pacific. In 1845 he led one of the best-equipped expeditions ever to enter the Arctic. None of the team ever came back. Years later Sir Francis McClintock discovered what remained of the expedition, including a collection of books and bones. Among the books was Franklin's copy of John Todd's *Students' Manual,* turned down at a particular page as though the dead explorer's finger were pointing to the place. On that turned-down page, almost the last page in the book, is to be found this dialogue:

"Are you not afraid to die?"

"No!"

"No? Why, does the uncertainty of another state give you no concern?"

"Because God has said to me: Fear not; when thou passest through the waters, I will be with thee. . . ."

That was it. In the frozen north Sir John Franklin knew the abiding presence of God. A monument was erected to the memory of this navigator of the north. Lord Tennyson wrote its inscription:

> Not here!
> The White North has thy bones,
> And thou, Heroic Sailor Soul
> Art passing on thy happier voyage now
> Toward no earthly Pole.

Distance does not separate from God. The unsaved discover that as well. When the Russians put the first men in orbit they came back to earth to announce they had seen no sign of God. Foolish men! He was there all right, but it was not His time to make them aware of His presence, that was all.

The word David used for *hold* is of interest—"Even there Thy right hand shall hold me." It literally means "to snatch." Jonah discovered that. Away he went, fleeing toward the west, hoping he had left God behind. We can picture him sound asleep in the bottom of the boat. But now comes the wind at God's bidding and that little ship is picked up and hurled like a piece of driftwood on the angry waves. God is about to snatch Jonah from his bed and return him, by way of a fish's belly, to the coast from which he fled.

3. Darkness Does Not Hide Us from God (139:11-12)

"If I say, 'Surely the darkness shall cover me; even the night shall be light about me.' Yea, the darkness hideth not from Thee; but the night shineth as the day: the darkness and the light are both alike to Thee." The trouble is that "men love darkness rather than light because their deeds are evil." It is under the cover of darkness that most of this world's crimes are committed. The darkness effectively hides man from man but it does not hide him from God. Darkness and light are both alike to Him.

One swelteringly hot night in July 1977 New York's power supply broke down. Immediately tens of thousands of people poured from their tenements to loot and burn the city. Roving bands of men, women, and children pulled down steel shutters and grills from storefronts, shattered plate glass windows, and hauled away everything they could carry. Some of them even rented trucks to haul off the loot. Fires were started. Firemen fought over one thousand of them and received seventeen hundred false alarms to decoy them and the police away from the looting.

Thieves even robbed each other. One teenage girl complained to friends that some boys had offered to help her carry some clothes and radios she had stolen and had then made off with them. "That's not right," she said. "They shouldn't have done that." Only a fraction of the looters were arrested. Over two thousand stores were plundered or damaged at the cost of $1 billion. Most of those arrested thought society owed them this windfall and showed no regret except at having been caught. One young woman told a reporter: "It's really sort of beautiful. Everybody is out on the streets together. It's like being at a party." One boy said, "This is better than going to Macy's."

All this because it was dark—as though God could not see in the dark! But darkness does not hide from Him; God is omnipresent. He was there on the dark streets of New York that night and saw each and every act of robbery, arson, and violence. He is present on all dark streets every night, noting the behavior, good and bad, of all people everywhere.

Then the psalmist realizes:

C. The Truth of God's Omnipotence (139:13-18)

Two facts awe the singer. He says:

1. He Created Me (139:13-16)

"For Thou hast possessed my reins: Thou hast covered me in my mother's womb. I will praise Thee; for I am fearfully and wonderfully made: marvelous are Thy works; and that my soul knoweth right well. My substance was not hid from Thee, when I was made in secret, and curiously wrought [the word suggests embroidery] in the lowest part of the earth. Thine eyes did see my substance, yet being unperfect; and in Thy book all my members were written, which in continuance were fashioned, when as yet there was none of them." David knew nothing of the modern science of embryology, nothing of the mysterious process by which a baby grows in the womb. He had only the haziest of ideas about these things, but he knew enough to be awed at the process.

If David knew enough to be awed, what about us? We know that every living creature is made up of microscopic cells so small that the letter O on this page would contain between thirty to forty thousand of them. Each microscopic cell is a world in itself, containing an estimated two hundred trillion tiny molecules of atoms. Each cell, in other words, is a micro-universe of almost unbelievable complexity. All these cells put together make up a living creature.

Each cell has its own specialized function and each works to an intricate time table which tells it when to grow, when to divide, when to make hormones, when to die. Every minute of every day, some three billion cells in the body die and the same number are created to take their place. During any given moment in the life of any one of these cells, thousands of events are taking place, each one being precisely coordinated at the molecular level by countless triggers. The human body has more than a million million of them—a million in each square inch of skin, thirty billion in the brain, billions of red blood cells in the veins.

Obviously, such a complicated and unerring development of cells cannot possibly be the result of chance. "He *created* me!" David exclaimed.

2. He Considers Me (139:17-18)

"How precious also are Thy thoughts unto me, O God! How great is the sum of them! If I should count them, they are more in number than the sand: when I awake, I am still with Thee." God does not leave the making of a human being to the mechanistic forces of chance. He is directly involved in each stage of the process. Nor does His tender care cease once the individual is launched into the world; His care continues. He thinks about us all the time. We are the objects of His constant care and concern. His thoughts toward us are more than the grains of sand on all the world's seashores. How sad that so few people in this world ever come to realize that. How criminal are those godless systems of philosophy which rob us of this comfort— and which also rob God of our appreciation and love.

II. What the Psalmist Requested (139:19-24)

Contemplation of the omniscience, omnipresence, and omnipotence of God led David to pray for two things. He prayed:

A. That the Lord Would Save Him (139:19-22)

At this point David looked about him and realized that he still had plenty of foes, some of them his own countrymen. No man can advance from farmhand to absolute monarch without, intentionally or not, making enemies. David had plenty of them. Most of them were lying low, waiting for a favorable opportunity to join forces against him, but they were there and David knew it. Man's enmity, however, was a puny thing to David, now that he had a proper perspective of God.

We note two things:

1. David's Assurance (139:19-20)

"Surely Thou wilt slay the wicked, O God: depart from me therefore, ye bloody [bloodthirsty] men. For they speak against Thee wickedly, and Thine enemies take Thy name in vain."

To take the name of God in vain is to insult Him. To profane His person and His name is a horrible sin. God has not so marvelously put together a human being so that he or she might do that with impunity. God can just as easily unmake persons as make them. Let boasters and blasphemers beware.

David wanted no part with such men. After Joab's murder of Abner, although Joab was far too solidly entrenched in a position of power to be easily uprooted, David began to put distance between himself and Joab. In the end, he handed him over to Solomon for execution.

We do well to watch the company we keep. It is no light thing to be close friends with those who hate the living God.

2. David's Assertion (139:21-22)

"Do not I hate them, O LORD, that hate Thee? And am not I grieved with those that rise up against Thee? I hate them with perfect hatred." There is such a thing as holy hatred, being righteously indignant and angry, abhorring those who mount attacks on the creator and sustainer of the universe. David declared that he hated those who hate God.

Finally, he prayed:

B. That the Lord Would Search Him (139:23-24)

It is no light thing to hold such hatred in one's heart. It can easily turn sour. It can lead to a bitter spirit. David prayed for protection against this sort of thing.

"Search me, O God, and know my heart: try me, and know my thoughts: and see if there be any wicked way in me, and lead me in the way everlasting." The psalmist was no hypocrite. He knew that there were depths of wickedness lurking in his own heart. He knew its secret lusts. Like a sensible man, faced with the omniscience of God, he did not try to hide his inner thoughts. He opened them up to God's inspection. He pleaded that the Lord would lead him in the way everlasting—that not only his inward life, but his outward life might be pleasing to the God he cannot escape (and, clearly, from whom he had no desire to escape).

Psalm 140

DELIVERANCE FROM THE WICKED

I. Asking for Deliverance (140:1-11)
We note how David:
A. Places His Case before the Lord (140:1)
B. Pleads His Case before the Lord (140:2-11)
How the evil man's plans are:
1. Conceived (140:2-4)
a. Belligerent Thoughts (140:2)
b. Bitter Words (140:3)
c. Brutal Deeds (140:4)
2. Conducted (140:5)
3. Confounded (140:6-11)
By:
a. A God Who Responds (140:6-7)
b. A God Who Restrains (140:8)
c. A God Who Rules (140:9-11)
II. Assurance of Deliverance (140:12-13)
A. For Those Rejected by Men (140:12)
B. For Those Right with God (140:13)

THE SUPERSCRIPTION to this psalm says that it is a psalm of David. And, all the doubts thrown upon it notwithstanding, there seems no reason why we cannot let the title stand. Certainly occasions in David's life fit the psalm. Perhaps it was picked up and used by Hezekiah when Rabshakeh's glib tongue was seeking to subvert the Jerusalem garrison. Perhaps it was picked up and used by the restored captives. The so-called "reminiscences of earlier psalms" might be nothing of the kind. They might be quite original compositions. The books of Jude and 2 Peter are similar in content and approach when dealing with the theme of apostasy. Why should we suppose that the Holy Spirit cannot inspire different people at different times to express themselves along similar lines when facing similar circumstances? And, as for the suggestion that this and its companion psalms are given David's name because they are "imitations of psalms believed to be his," those who accept the Bible as the inspired Word of God see no sense in even discussing such a notion.

Clearly Psalms 140, 141, 142, and 143 are bound together by common composition, common circumstances, and common characteristics. For instance, several Hebrew words occur only in these psalms. They can easily relate to David and to the difficulties he experienced in Saul's court, surrounded as he was by plots and counterplots. They can just as easily relate to circumstances surrounding him in the tragic days of the Absalom rebellion. In this psalm it is evident that David was being slandered and that violence was lurking in the background, waiting to strike once slander had done its poisonous work.

This is an imprecatory psalm. It is therefore fitting to treat it as prophetic, relating it to the persecution of the Jewish people during the days of the antichrist and his poison-tongued prophet. The psalm divides into two parts.

I. ASKING FOR DELIVERANCE (140:1-11)

There was an evil man in the court of Saul whose name was Doeg. His name comes from a Hebrew root meaning "to move slowly" or "to glide." Anyone who has seen a reptile moving through the grass will recognize the significance of that name. Doeg was an Edomite. It was he who ran to Saul with the news that David had been to Ahimelech the priest, that he had accepted from him Goliath's sword and the showbread from the Lord's table for the feeding of his men, and that he had vanished toward the Philistine frontier.

Doeg was then commissioned by the furious Saul to make an end of the priests of Nob. In cold blood this wicked man massacred eighty-five of them, including Ahimelech. That atrocity must have haunted Saul the rest of his life (1 Samuel 21–22). Doeg was one of the men in Saul's court with whom the young David had to contend. Many a time David must have prayed words such as those in this psalm about Doeg and his like.

We note how David:

A. Places His Case before the Lord (140:1)

"Deliver me, O LORD, from the evil man: preserve me from the violent man." When such persons insinuate themselves into positions of influence and power they are a plague to society. We are living in a *vicious* world. The word used here for *wicked* emphasizes that. It has to do with the breaking up of all that is good and desirable. The comparable Greek word *ponēros* is the root from which we derive our word *pornography*. There are individuals with vile and filthy minds who hate good people. David wanted to be preserved from such persons.

We are living in a *violent* world. David prayed to be delivered from such men—"men of violent deeds" is J. B. Rotherham's rendering. Such men in Saul's court wanted to get rid of David. Both his bravery and his behavior irritated them. David's situation in Saul's court was perilous. He was not much more than a youth. He had been brought up to be a sheep farmer, not a soldier or courtier. He was held at Saul's court by royal decree because of his skill on the harp which had a soothing effect on Saul's nerves. Yet Saul hated and feared him.

Having thus, in general terms, placed his case before the Lord, David moves on. He now:

B. Pleads His Cause before the Lord (140:2-11)

David has three things to say to God about the evil men who would accomplish his ruin. We learn from this psalm how the evil man's plans are:

1. Conceived (140:2-4)

David draws attention to his:

a. Belligerent Thoughts (140:2)

"Which imagine mischiefs in their heart; continually are they gathered together for war." Some people stir up strife out of sheer mischief, others because they think they can personally profit from the situation they hope to create.

There were those in Saul's court who were conspiring to get rid of David. Slander and lies were their weapons. Against these could be urged the indictment later to be penned by Solomon: "These six things doth the LORD hate: yea, seven are an abomination unto Him: a proud look, a lying tongue, and hands that shed innocent blood, an heart that deviseth wicked imaginations, feet that be swift in running to mischief, a false witness that speaketh lies, and he that soweth discord among brethren" (Proverbs 6:16-19). It is very difficult to fight a carefully planned and deliberately propagated campaign of lies. David knew that his only resource was in God.

He draws attention also to the evil man's:

b. Bitter Words (140:3)

"They have sharpened their tongues like a serpent; adders' poison is under their lips." This verse is quoted by the Holy Spirit in the summation of His case against the human race in Romans 3. There He speaks of man's vile thoughts, man's venomous tongue, and man's violent temper. Here, David compares the poisonous words of his foes to the attack of a serpent.

A serpent has a sharp, forked tongue that flickers in and out of its mouth. A snake does not use its tongue to pierce and poison its victims; it uses it to detect vibrations and to "taste" odors, either in the air or on the ground. The sense of scent through the nostrils, usual in other animals, gives way in the serpent to the action of the tongue. The forked tips of the snake's tongue picks up microscopic particles from the air, earth, or water. Drawing in the tongue, the snake inserts the forked tips into two tiny pits in its mouth. These pits are lined with keen sensory cells and give the snake the precise scent and feel of its immediate environment.

In some snakes these pit organs also serve as night vision sensors. They are like infrared "eyes" enabling the snake to strike accurately in the dark, the strike being guided by infrared radiation emitted by warm-blooded prey.

"They have sharpened their tongues like a serpent," David says of his malicious enemies. They deliberately were using conversation as a means of tracking him down. Their tongues were being used as weapons to set him up for the strike.

He says: "Adders' poison is under their lips. Selah." The particular Hebrew word for *adder* is used only here in the Old Testament. In a poisonous serpent, the fangs are elongated hypodermic needles which enable the snake to inject its poison deep into the body of its prey. The whole action, from the striking of the head forward until the return to the original position with closed jaws, is lightning fast. The human eye is unable to follow it.

At the instant of biting, muscles in the snake's upper jaw contract, press against the poison gland, and inject venom down through the hollow fangs. The flash of withdrawal of the fangs is almost as quick as the strike itself and the serpent is ready for another strike. Often the bitten animal drops with scarcely a quiver. In any case, consciousness is very short and the serpent waits, assured of the result. Its prey cannot escape.

David's enemies were waiting for the chance to drive home the poison. It takes only a little snake poison to attack the system in flaming rivers of liquid fire. David's enemies injected their poison into Saul. They kept his raw nerves jangling with their insinuations that David wanted to take his throne. They did all they could to make bad blood between him and David. David knew what they were doing. He called them *snakes*.

He draws attention also to their:

c. Brutal Deeds (140:4)

"Keep me, O LORD, from the hands of the wicked; preserve me from the violent man." That, of course, is just what they wanted to do—get their hands on him. God answered David's prayer and never allowed them to do so. Instead, on two occasions He actually delivered Saul into David's hands. Both times, despite the urging of his less spiritual followers, David resolutely refused to lay his hand on his chief enemy. He trusted God to keep him safe from Saul.

The enemies of the Lord Jesus wanted to do the same to Him, and God allowed them to have their way. They put their hands on Him, their wicked hands. They pulled out His beard, they punched Him in the face, they scourged Him to the bone, they crowned Him with thorns, they hung Him on a cross.

So, David tells how the evil man's plans are conceived: thoughts pass into words, words pass into deeds.

Then he tells us how the evil man's plans are:

2. Conducted (140:5)

They wanted to use cords to trip him, nets to trap him, and gins or snares to take him. "The proud have hid a snare for me, and cords; they have spread a net by the wayside; they have set gins for me. Selah." It was all premeditated. They had considered his way of life, just as a hunter considers the way of life of an animal he wants to catch, a bird he wants to snare, a fish he wants to take. The hunter studies the ways of his intended prey and then sets his traps accordingly. He uses its own habits and instincts against it. When a hunter thoroughly knows his prey, knows its haunts and habits, then he constructs his trap or his lure.

David's enemies studied him until they knew their man. When they knew all about him, knew his habits and manner of life (probably better than he knew them himself), they set about trapping him. They planned to use his own lifestyle against him. His own way of life was to be the blueprint for their snare.

That is what Daniel's enemies did as well. They studied him. They said, "The only way we'll ever get anything on Daniel is in the matter of his God. He prays three times a day. We'll have to think of something along that line. He'll never tell a lie, take a bribe, never act against the king. We'll have to think of something that has to do with his habit of prayer." There is something particularly wicked about that.

It is also what wicked men did to Jesus. They studied Him— not because they wanted to trust Him, but because they wanted to trap Him.

But then David tells how the evil man's plans are:

3. Confounded (140:6-11)

The plans of evil men are brought to nothing by:

a. A God Who Responds (140:6-7)

"I said unto the LORD, 'Thou art my GOD': hear the voice of my supplications, O LORD. O GOD the Lord, the strength of my salvation, Thou hast covered my head in the day of battle." David appeals to God as *El*, God the omnipotent one, God as the one who puts all His power into operation, the God who knows everything (as suggested by the first use of the name in Genesis 14:18-22) and who sees everything (Genesis 16:13). *El* is God as the one in whom all the divine attributes are seen in their fullest concentration.

David appeals to God as "GOD the Lord," as Jehovah Adonai (Jehovah, the God who reveals, and Adonai, the God who rules). He is the one who not only pledges Himself to His people but who works out those promises in life down here on earth.

David was still quite a young man when he wrote this psalm, if he wrote it, as has been suggested, when a courtier in Saul's palace. Yet how well he already knew God. What could these lying tongues and scheming brains and violent hands do against a man who could invoke the aid of one who holds all power in His hands, who can read the thoughts of the wicked, and is pledged to establish His own righteous purposes on earth?

David realized that God had covered his head in the day of battle (140:7). He knew a God who responds. He did not remove him from the battle: rather, He protected him in it.

The expression used for battle means "to touch" or "to join" and, hence, "to kiss." It is what we have in Psalm 2 where the Holy Spirit warns Christ's enemies to "kiss the Son." In other words, David was so protected that his enemies would be well advised to make peace with him, to become his friends, to express submission by kissing his feet rather than face him in battle in the armor of God's providing.

b. A God Who Restrains (140:8)

"Grant not, O Lord, the desires of the wicked: further not his wicked device; lest they exalt themselves. Selah." The expression, "wicked device," is really *plots*, so it is evident that David was the object of a court intrigue. The next psalm tells us more about that. In this one we know only that deliberate plans were being made by his enemies at court to bring about his downfall. It must have been a frightening situation for him to be caught up in high society for which he was never trained— and with his every step a potential disaster.

In verse 5 David says, "They have spread a net by the wayside." The word he uses for *wayside* is unusual. It literally means "by the hand of the paths." We can picture a broad path suddenly forking into five possible ways for the traveler to take. Such was the path that David trod in Saul's court. Only one could be the right one. Any of the others could lead to sudden death, and all those paths were undoubtedly loaded with snares. David was appealing to a God who is able to restrain even the wickedest men.

c. A God Who Rules (140:9-11)

Now comes the imprecation which is at the heart of this psalm. It breathes what to us may seem like a spirit of vengeance and vindictiveness, although it is not really that. It breathes really a sense of fair play, inherent in the Mosaic Law: "An eye for an eye, a tooth for a tooth, a life for a life." It is the same spirit that lies at the root of the biblical warning, "Whatsoever a man soweth, that shall he also reap" (Galatians 6:7). David was invoking God along the lines of His character as a God who believes in fair play, in doing what is right. In other words, he wanted to see the justice and judgment of God at work in *confounding* evil men: "As for the head of those that compass me about, let the mischief of their own lips cover them" (140:9). He wanted their plots to boomerang, to recoil on their own heads. That is just what happened in later years to those men who plotted to get Daniel thrown into the den of lions. When their schemes were uncovered, into the den of lions *they* went.

David wanted to see the justice and judgment of God at work in *condemning* evil men: "Let burning coals fall upon them: let them be cast into the fire; into deep pits, that they rise not up again" (140:10). Fire falls from above, fire rages below—fire from heaven, fire in the pit in hell.

That such justice and judgment are to overtake the wicked is the uniform testimony of the Word of God. The Bible solemnly warns us against believing Satan's primeval lie, "Thou shalt not surely die." David allied himself to the judgment side of God's character, whereas we, in this age of grace, ally ourselves to the mercy side of God's character; we pray that grace rather than government might overtake our foes. In so doing we "heap coals of fire" on their heads. That is the kind of vengeance Christ wanted for His enemies: He wanted to enroll them in the ranks of the redeemed, write their names into life's eternal book, wash them in the blood He had shed, save them by His grace.

A time is coming, however, when the age of grace will end, when these Old Testament imprecations will come into their own. An age of judgment is on the way when fire will fall from heaven. Fire awaits those who ally themselves to the devil's messiah and his lying prophet. In that age God's people will rightfully take these words of David and pour them out in passionate entreaty to the God of all the earth who always does what is right.

David also wanted to see the justice and judgment of God at work in *controlling* evil men: "Let not an evil speaker be established in the earth: evil shall hunt the violent man to overthrow him." There is no way to measure the power and influence of an evil speaker. In the Hebrew the word for *evil speaker* is literally "a man of the tongue." That is what the false prophet will be, a man of the tongue. He will be a silver-tongued orator, able to convince the world that the devil's messiah is the world's only hope, its true savior. It will be a sad day for this world when this "man of the tongue" is established on the earth, especially since he will be the mouth of that violent man, the beast. At last, however, all these satanic plots and personages will come to a fiery end.

So, finally, David comes into rest. We see his:

II. Assurance of Deliverance (140:12-13)

David sees two classes of people coming into blessing. There is assurance of deliverance:

A. For Those Rejected by Men (140:12)

"I know that the LORD will maintain the cause of the afflicted, and the right of the poor." How wonderful it is to know that God has a special concern for the persecuted and the poor. Although they have never had a square deal on earth, things will change when Jesus comes back. Even now His eye is on them, His heart yearns over them. David was among their number when he prayed this prayer.

B. For Those Right with God (140:13)

"Surely the righteous shall give thanks unto Thy name: the upright shall dwell in Thy presence." There will be blissful rejoicing. They shall give thanks to His name. They will gather up all the wondrous names for God in the Bible and sing them out in hymns of praise. There will be blessed reward. They shall dwell in His presence—first in the millennial earth, basking in the sunshine of His love, and then in the eternal state, forever assured of their acceptance before Him. So David's faith soars, until he comes at last into the assurance of deliverance. His actual circumstances remained unchanged, even became worse, but he had the guarantee from God that all was well.

Psalm 141

A CUNNING PLOT

THIS PSALM IS closely linked with the preceding one. There is, however, a change in David's circumstances. In Psalm 140 danger to David arose from the lying tongues of others; in this psalm the danger lies in his own tongue. David was being tempted to say something that could implicate him. As in later years our Lord's enemies tried to entangle Him in His talk, so here with David.

Rotherham suggests that some of the courtiers in Saul's attendance were planning to get rid of Saul. There can be no doubt that Saul was anything but an ideal king. Under him the nation was going to ruin. The countryside was beset by outlaws: those in debt, those in distress, those filled with discontent. Many of these drifters later joined up with David, under whose wholesome influence they were transformed into an efficient body of fighting men. Saul himself was lashed periodically by fits of demonic, ungovernable rage. Worst of all, the nation was a constant prey to its enemies, particularly the warlike Philistines against whom King Saul had no success at all. Jonathan, twice the man his father was, vacillated between loyalty to Saul and love for David. In any case, he made no effort to conceal his conviction that he would never be king, that the throne belonged to David.

Those who desired to get rid of Saul would use David as a catspaw to further their own ambitions. They would befriend him, play on his fears and ambitions, and use him to assassinate Saul. Then they would make short work of him and place their own man on the throne. The evidence for such a scenario is not historical but circumstantial. It suits the exigencies of the psalm. Unprincipled men like Cush the Benjamite and Doeg the Edomite were quite capable of such plotting.

With that background, this psalm divides into five parts.

I. David's Devotion (141:1-2)

The psalm begins with David praying. Whether or not David realized the extent of his danger we cannot know. It would seem from some of his later statements that he could see through the crafty schemes of his foes. Certainly, if overtures were made to him by Doeg, his honest soul would instantly be filled with suspicions. So David turned to God in prayer. He was looking for:

A. Action from His Prayer (141:1)

"Lord, I cry unto Thee: make haste unto me; give ear unto my voice, when I call unto Thee." Note the *impertinence* of it, the sheer outrageous audacity of it. David, not much more than a youth, a former shepherd boy, youngest son of a large family where even his father Jesse was a nobody in Israel, speaking to God like that. "Make haste!" One wonders whether the angels in heaven did not look at each other with astonishment.

Yet at the same time, note the glorious, holy boldness of it, the *impressiveness* of it. David was coming to the Lord, to the God of promise. He was taking his stand on the promises of God, daring to believe that—his life being right with God, he being blameless and in the center of God's will—he had the right to speak so to God.

A friend of mine tells of a simple believer who used to address God like that. He would come to the Lord and say, "Hello, Jesus, this is Jim." Then he would make known his prayer request something like this: "Hello, Jesus, this is Jim. Mary's sick. Would You attend to her, please?" Or, "Hello, Jesus, this is Jim. I sure enjoyed that verse about You the preacher quoted in church today." Then came Jim's time to die. A friend who was visiting him reported Jim's last words. "Jesus just came," he said. "And do you know what He said to me? He said, *Hello, Jim, this is Jesus.*"

David was just such a soul. He reveled in having a simple, personal relationship with the Lord: "The LORD is *my* Shepherd." So he simply says, "Hello, Lord, this is David." "I call upon the LORD," he says. That is like Paul's "I appeal to Caesar!" Only it is a much higher, more certain appeal.

B. Acceptance of His Prayer (141:2)

"Let my prayer be set before Thee as incense [there was sweetness in that]; and the lifting up of my hands as the evening sacrifice [there was surrender in that]." David was no priest; not even a Levite. Certainly he could never enter into the holy place of the Most High and offer incense on the golden altar. Nor could he officiate in the court of the tabernacle at the brazen altar. It was not for him to offer up the evening sacrifice. Only a priest could take the evening sacrifice, shed its blood, flay it, and put its parts on those flames that burned on the brazen altar. Only a priest could take that holy fire from the brazen altar, carry it into the holy place, put the burning coals on the golden altar, sprinkle sweet-smelling incense on those coals, and watch the smoke ascend like prayer toward heaven. Not once in all his days would David see that, not even if he lived to be as old as Methuselah or lived to rule the world.

Yet young as he was, rare soul that he was, he had already progressed in his spiritual life from ritual to reality, from shadow to substance, from type to ultimate truth. He could be a priest—not a priest after the order of Aaron, but he could enter into that holy place "not made with hands, eternal in the heavens." He might not be able to bring a Mosaic offering, but he could bring a meaningful offering: "Let my prayer be counted as incense, and the lifting up of my hands as sacrifice."

David took his stand on "New Testament ground" a thousand years before his time. No need for him, like wretched Uzziah, to push his way into the holy place and usurp the prerogatives of the priests. He had advanced beyond that. God looked down on His young servant. He must have listened with delight to this spiritual prayer and it thrilled His heart. One can almost see

Him pointing David out to the angels and saying, "There! That's a man after My heart."

II. DAVID'S DESIRE (141:3-4)

David now prayed for three down-to-earth things in the light of his perilous circumstances. He wanted God to guard him in:

A. His Conversation (141:3)

"Set a watch, O LORD, before my mouth, keep the door of my lips." David could remember the day Saul's soldiers stood guard outside his gates waiting for him to come out so they could seize him. He wanted God to do that—to mount guard over his mouth, to stifle any incautious word he might utter. He knew he could not control his tongue. Who can? James tells us that the person who can do that is perfect.

Not only Saul, but those who surrounded Saul, were waiting for an incautious word to be uttered by David. It would have given them the excuse they needed to accuse him of high treason or, in the case of some of Saul's courtiers, to get him in their power. David knew his peril.

David was a spiritual man, but he was still human. Natural feelings of resentment against Saul's treatment of him could easily have surfaced in his soul and spilled out of his mouth. So David asked God to muzzle him, to choke off any unwise word before it reached the itching ears of Saul's spies. Graham Scroggie reminds us that when Demaratus was asked whether he held his tongue because he was a fool or for want of words, he replied, "A fool cannot hold his tongue."

B. His Conduct (141:4a)

"Incline not my heart to any evil thing, to practice wicked works. . . ." With rare common sense and with the Holy Spirit's enlightenment, David realized that it was not enough for his conversation to be guarded at the mouth or for his conduct to be overruled. The problem of behavior must be settled at a much deeper level: it must be resolved in his heart. Centuries later Jesus would say, "Out of the abundance of the heart the mouth speaketh" (Matthew 12:34). David entered into the truth of that. David wanted his heart to be kept against "wicked works." The word he used for *wicked* was one that has to do with the essential restlessness of fallen human nature. It is used in Scripture to describe the active lawlessness of impious and ungodly men (Isaiah 53:9). In this passage the word *wicked* (the same word David uses here) can be translated "criminals." David had seen his own heart.

David's supreme concern was that his heart be right. Then everything else would be right: character, conduct, conversation. So he asks God to guard his outward behavior by guarding his innermost being.

C. His Companionships (141:4b)

"Incline not my heart to any evil thing, to practice wicked works with men that work iniquity: and let me not eat of their dainties." This verse reveals the dangerous ground on which David stood. There were those at Saul's court, as we have seen, who wished to kill two birds with one stone. They wanted to get rid of both Saul and David. They wanted to get rid of Saul because he was so obviously unfit to be king, and they wanted to get rid of David because he was so obviously fit to be king. They disliked Saul because he was so bad, David because he was so good.

As has been suggested, they began to cultivate David. He suddenly found himself popular in unexpected quarters. These men hoped, it seems, to use David to do their dirty work for them. As he had rid the nation of Goliath, so perhaps he could be used to rid the nation of Saul. He was invited to be guest in their homes. He was invited to banquets, to feasts, to come and break bread with them, to enter into fellowship with them. David saw through it.

He was nobody's fool. Well he could see that if he did kill Saul (something he had no intention of doing under any circumstances since Saul was the Lord's anointed), he would be open to a charge of treason. If he did attend these social functions and keep company with these wicked men, then some charge would be trumped up against him. His words could be twisted. Perhaps he might even say something unwise which could be used against him.

In those days David "behaved himself more wisely than all the servants of Saul" (1 Samuel 18:30). One can see now that Saul's attempts on David's life, which drove him into the wilderness and away from those cunning men, were a blessing in disguise.

Perhaps there was a time when David did feel inclined to respond to the overtures of these men, even though his heart mistrusted them. After all, a man in David's perilous position needs all the friends he can get. But God overruled. Being driven into the wilderness was God's answer to David's prayer, although he may not have realized it at the time.

III. DAVID'S DISCERNMENT (141:5-6)

David now records his discernment of two factors in life.

A. The Faithful Rebuke of the Saints (141:5)

"Let the righteous smite me; it shall be a kindness: and let him reprove me; it shall be an excellent oil, which shall not break my head."

In an eastern home, hospitality included washing of the guest's feet with water and anointing of the guest's head with oil. It was an act of rudeness for Simon the Pharisee to invite the Lord Jesus to his home and to ignore these common courtesies. David now envisions himself as a guest in the home of a godly man, rather than in the home of a wicked man. He says that it would be a blessing for him to sit at such a man's table and be rebuked by him, since true friendship does not flatter; it speaks out even though the words may sting.

In later years God answered this prayer of David, that he might have faithful friends who were not afraid to rebuke him when such a reprimand was deserved. There came a day when God sent Nathan the prophet to David to smite his conscience, to reprove him for his sin with Bathsheba. That rebuke proved to be an anointing of oil in David's life. Had Nathan not spoken out, David might well have died in his sin.

It was thus that Paul rebuked Peter at Antioch. That was no easy thing for Paul to do. Peter had a wide and deserved following in the early church. Peter had been with Jesus from the beginning, had been the Holy Spirit's instrument at Pentecost to bring three thousand Jews into the fellowship of the church, had suffered for Christ when Paul was still a Pharisee and a committed foe of the church, had been the Spirit's chosen instrument to fling open the door of the faith to Paul's beloved Gentiles. Peter was a great-hearted, lovable, impulsive man. It was Peter who had put in the telling argument at the Jerusalem conference which liberated Gentiles from the insufferable yoke of the Mosaic Law. Yet when Peter came to Antioch and dissembled over the matter of breaking bread with Gentiles in their homes because of his fear of James—then Paul took matters into hand. "I rebuked him to his face," he said. The wounds he inflicted were the wounds of a friend. Thus David prayed that he might know the faithful rebuke of the saints.

Then David records his discernment of:

B. The False Reasoning of the Sinner (141:6)

"When their judges [rulers] are overthrown in stony places, they shall hear my words; for they are sweet." The word rendered "sweet" is a cognate word with the word *dainties* (141:4).

David was a man of sound common sense. He knew it was no good quoting Scripture to these people who surrounded Saul. They would simply scoff at such words of wisdom, though doubtless David could have thought of a dozen passages of Scripture he might have put before them.

David was a believer in constituted authority. He believed that "the powers that be are ordained of God" even though rulership was in the hands of a man like Saul and his sycophantic courtiers. David believed that when a ruler turned into a tyrant it was God's work to remove him, not his. Saul was still the Lord's anointed. It was his duty to pray for Saul, not to promote conspiracy against him.

So David might have found verses to quote to those who had no scruples along these lines. He might have quoted Abraham: "Shall not the Judge of all the earth do right?" (Genesis 18:25). Or Hagar: "Thou God seest me" (Genesis 16:13). He might have referred to God's convicting word to Job: "Wilt thou also disannul My judgment? . . . Hast thou an arm like God?" (Job 40:8-9).

But what good would it do? These men were in no state of soul to submit to the Scriptures. But they would be found out. They would be arraigned and condemned. They would find themselves in stony places. The time would come when they would be ready to hear God's Word.

The story is told that when the saintly Oswald Chambers was a young man, he was out for a walk with a well-taught Scottish minister. A shepherd appeared around the mountain track and was about to pass the two men with a courteous nod. Young Oswald Chambers stepped forward and pointedly asked the shepherd if he was saved. He returned to his companion thinking he had seized a good opportunity to witness for Christ. He was brought up short, however, by his companion, who asked him: "Did you have the Holy Spirit's permission to speak to that man about his soul?" It was a point well made. Not all persons are ready.

David realized that the people about whom he was praying were not ready to hear from God. But the time would come. *Then* they would hear his words.

It was thus with Saul of Tarsus. Stephen's testimony only infuriated him. As he said later to King Agrippa, describing his attitude toward the Christians, he was "exceedingly mad against them" (Acts 26:11). It would have been of no use to "witness" to Saul of Tarsus when he was in that frame of mind. But after he had seen the heavenly vision—then talk to him about Jesus and you would be talking to a different man.

IV. DAVID'S DISMAY (141:7)

"Our bones are scattered at the grave's mouth, as when one cutteth and cleaveth wood upon the earth." Some atrocity had taken place which brought David up short. Rotherham thinks it was the massacre of the priests of Nob by Doeg the Edomite, at the command of Saul. He pictures the victims being hastily buried in a mass grave and a farmer, at a later date, plowing up the bones—thus recalling the dark tragedy. Whether that incident lies in back of this verse is hard to say (probably it took place at a later date than this psalm). Some such discovery of a mass grave, however, might well have sparked David's words. And he knew enough about Saul's erratic violence to know that mass murder was not beyond him.

Rotherham has an interesting rendering of this verse: "As a rock which one cleaves and shatters on the land, so shall their bones be strewn at the mouth of Sheol." It is thus that David saw the end of these wicked men. Their position looked secure enough. They looked as immovable as rock, but a rock can be shattered. Given time and persistence, iron can shatter rock. Rock can be reduced to rubble. God's hammer can shatter the biggest rocks. Where now are the Alexanders, Neros, Napoleons, Hitlers, and Stalins of history? God has shattered them. They are dead now and their bones are strewn at the mouth of Sheol.

In spite of his dismay at the violence of Saul, at the treachery of Saul's advisors, at the malice of those who would direct Saul's hatred against himself, and at those who falsely befriended him, David took courage. In time God would level them to the dust. Time was not on their side, but on his.

After this brief glance at his powerful and treacherous foes, David brought his eyes back to God. That was the sensible thing to do. It gave him back a sense of proportion.

V. DAVID'S DEFENSE (141:8-10)

David throws himself on God.

A. Lord, My Soul Is Destitute (141:8)

"But mine eyes are unto Thee, O GOD the LORD; in Thee is my trust; leave not my soul destitute." There must have been many a time when David felt defenseless before the unremitting enmity of Saul, perhaps never more so than when he discovered that people in high places were wanting to use him to further their own nefarious ends.

But David's eye was no longer on Saul, no longer on the conspirators. His eye was on the Lord. He was no longer trusting his own cleverness or his own courage; he was looking to the Lord.

It is an interesting, an easily demonstrable fact, that when we are walking, where we look is the direction in which we go. If we keep our eyes steadily fixed to the right, our footsteps will wander to the right; if we look steadfastly to the left, we will wander to the left. If we look straight ahead, we will walk straight ahead. When I was a boy, farmers still used horses to plow their fields in some parts of Britain. In some of the country villages annual plowing competitions were held. The challenge was to see who could plow the straightest furrow across a wide field. We had a number of farmer friends who always entered the competition. They told us that the secret of plowing a straight line across that field was to fix the eye resolutely on an object on the other side of the field, start up the horses, and never once take the eye off that object as long as that furrow was being plowed. They would drive a straight line right to it—just so long as their eye never wavered. David's soul was destitute, but he had a good solution to finding an honorable way out: keep his eye resolutely on the Lord.

B. Lord, My Situation Is Desperate (141:9-10)

"Keep me from the snares which they have laid for me, and the gins [traps] of the workers of iniquity. Let the wicked fall into their own nets, whilst that I withal escape." The word for *snares* is in the singular, suggesting a specific plot of which David knew; the word for *gins* actually means "engines," or an ingenious contrivance. David could now see clearly the machinations of his foes. Their minds were at work inventing a scheme to trap him. "Keep me!" he prayed. The expression comes from the same root as the word *watch* in verse three. David wanted the Lord to watch out for him.

Further, with the righteous indignation of an Old Testament saint, he asked the Lord to work in poetic justice and catch these unscrupulous men in their own schemes. The long record of history shows us that God has a way of doing that. Men and nations lay down with their own hands the paving stones along which retribution travels. It is one of God's ways of showing us that He is still on the throne and that His moral government of human affairs is indeed a power to be reckoned with on earth.

Psalm 142

DOWN IN THE VALLEY

I. THE DISTRESSED MAN (142:1-2)
   A. His Spoken Request (142:1)
   B. His Specific Request (142:2)
      1. The Complaint on His Lips (142:2a)
      2. The Complication in His Life (142:2b)
II. THE DESPERATE MAN (142:3-4)
   A. He Was Fearful (142:3)
      1. Pressures Within (142:3a)
      2. Problems Without (142:3b)
   B. He Was Friendless (142:4)
      1. Treated with Social Indifference (142:4a)
      2. Treated with Spiritual Indifference (142:4b)
III. THE DISCERNING MAN (142:5-6)
   He found in God:
   A. A Satisfying Portion (142:5)
   B. A Secure Protection (142:6)
IV. THE DELIVERED MAN (142:7)
   He was brought into the prospect of:
   A. Freedom (142:7a)
   B. Fellowship (142:7b)
   C. Fullness (142:7c)

THE TITLE TELLS US that this is a psalm of David, written when he was in the cave. It does not tell us which cave, whether the one at Adullam or Engedi. Let us review David's experiences.

David's troubles as a young man came swiftly to a head at King Saul's court. After Saul had tried to have him murdered in his bed, he fled to Naioth. He had a secret meeting with his loyal friend Jonathan who promised to find out if it was safe for him to return home. Shortly afterward Jonathan returned for a clandestine meeting with David and warned him that his life was in danger. By this time King Saul was under the tormenting influence of a demon. Nine times in two chapters he tried to have David murdered (1 Samuel 19 and 20).

Thoroughly frightened, David fled to Philistia for political asylum. It was a disastrous move and he escaped from Gath only by feigning to be insane himself. Back in Israel, he sought refuge in the cave of Adullam, a big cave not far from the famous "valley of the shadow." It was a natural refuge for the beleaguered outlaw and for those who were allied to him. David's own family came to the cave about this time, it evidently being no longer safe for them to stay on in Bethlehem. A growing band of desperadoes, refugees from Saul's excesses and injustices, found a natural leader in David. The frightened priest Abiathar also joined David after Saul's slaughter of his family and the priests of Nob. There was treachery everywhere at that time, even from the men of Keilah whose town David had rescued from the invaders.

Shortly after this particular act of treachery David made use of another cave in the wild wastes of Engedi. Saul, with some three thousand chosen men who were selected from all Israel, scoured the countryside in search of David. The hunt for David blossomed into a national crusade. Saul's whole life became one mad obsession—get David! While David and his men were hiding in the recesses of the cave at Engedi, Saul came into it, apparently alone, threw himself down, and fell asleep. He was now in David's power. David crept up to him but, instead of killing his enemy, contented himself with cutting off a piece of his robe. After Saul left the cave to take up a position with his men some little distance away, David showed himself. He exhibited the piece of cloth to Saul, to show the demented king that his crusade against him was unjust.

It is against this stormy background that David wrote this psalm. The psalm can be attributed to David's desperate situation in either of the two caves. The probability is that it was written when David was first in Adullam. He was alone; his fellow outlaws had not yet heard of his escape from Gath. Nor had he yet become a guerrilla chief with a force of several hundred tough and determined men at his command.

The psalm is a *maschil* psalm, a psalm written for instruction. David felt that the lessons he had learned in his troubles should be recorded to help and encourage others. For some reason this psalm did not find its way into the Hebrew hymnbook for a very long time. It was given its place probably by Hezekiah, who could appreciate David's experiences, having gone through troubles enough of his own.

I. The Distressed Man (142:1-2)

David was keenly aware of his distressing circumstances. He was the object of a persistent manhunt at home, he had been refused asylum in Philistia, he had no home and few friends. His flight to Gath had caused the murder of an entire family of priests. No wonder he was distressed. We note:

A. His Spoken Request (142:1)

"I cried unto the LORD with my voice; with my voice unto the LORD did I make my supplication." There is more than one way to cry unto the Lord. There is, for instance, that groaning of spirit which cannot find outlet in words. This, however, was a spoken request. Twice in this verse David mentions his voice.

There is something to be said for audible, spoken prayer. When something is actually spoken, it articulates a thought and converts it from a vague longing into something concrete. Our thoughts tend to wander, drifting here, there, and everywhere, dissipating themselves into abstract vagaries. Our minds rebel against unarticulated thoughts. They go off woolgathering, leaving the original thought abandoned and soon forgotten altogether.

Speaking puts thoughts into words. It calls for exactness, which often eludes us when we content ourselves with unvoiced prayers. Praying out loud, with the voice, is an antidote to wandering thoughts in prayer.

So David prayed out loud. His request was a spoken request. He put his concerns into words, a sensible thing to do.

B. His Specific Request (142:2)

First, there is:

1. The Complaint on His Lips (142:2a).

"I poured out my complaint before Him," he says. How much of what we call praying is really complaining. We would not like to admit that, perhaps, but David does.

How wonderful God is: He listens even to our complaints. There He sits on high, surrounded by scenes of splendor no mind can conceive and no pen can describe. Every whirling atom, every blazing star, proclaims His wisdom, love, and power. He is attended by shining seraphim who sing His praise. There, too, the chanting cherubim ceaselessly proclaim His holiness. Angel choirs singing His praise awake the echoes of the everlasting hills. The spirits of just men made perfect add their anthems, celebrating on high the wonders of the redemption He has wrought. Yet He listens to our complaints.

Our loving God is forever planning for us, looking out for us, and implementing ways to make us eternally happy. He sovereignly overrules the factors of time and space so that all things work together for our good. He is determined that we shall be heirs together with His Son, joint heirs with Jesus Christ, seated with Him in heavenly places, far above principalities and powers and every name that is named, not only in this world but also in the world to come. He intends us to be more glorious than the shining ones who walk the golden streets of heaven.

How dare we complain! Should we not rather sing:

> All the way my Saviour leads me,
>   What have I to ask beside?
> Can I doubt His tender mercy
>   Who through life has been my guide?
> Heavenly peace, divinest comfort,
>   Here by faith in Him to dwell,
> For I know whate'er befall me
>   Jesus doeth all things well.

David also records:

2. The Complication in His Life (142:2b)

"I showed before Him my trouble," he says. As if He did not already know! How wonderful that God has revealed Himself, supremely, to be a Father: "As a father pitieth his children, so the LORD pitieth them that fear Him" (Psalm 103:13). We come to God knowing that He is big enough, loving enough, and kind enough to lend a sympathetic ear to our troubles, knowing they are very big to us. He knows and understands.

Our children come running to us with a scratched knee, a broken toy, or some childish complaint, confident we can make everything well again. Busy as we might be with what we are doing, perhaps beyond the ability of the child to comprehend, we feel a sudden surge of warmth at the little one's tearful plea. We stop, gather the toddler into our arms, whisper words of comfort and hope, and either take care of the problem or promise that it will be fixed in just a little while. Off the tiny one goes, confident that all will be well, leaving behind a warm glow in the parent's heart. "I showed Him my trouble," says David. And, wonder of wonders, God heard and cared.

II. THE DESPERATE MAN (142:3-4)

The situation in which David found himself was a desperate one.

A. He Was Fearful (142:3)

He mentions:

1. Pressures Within (142:3a)

"When my spirit was overwhelmed within me, then Thou knewest my path," he said. The word for *overwhelmed* is literally "darkened." It carries the idea of fainting. "He blacked out" is the way we would put it today. David's troubles were not imaginary, but real. They had created so much inner tension and stress that even his buoyant spirit could not rise above them. He was overwhelmed. There was however, a safety valve: "Thou knewest my path." That is what enabled David to retain his sanity. God knew all about it. God knew his path, knew the route he had taken from Gath to Adullam, knew the road ahead, knew the pitfalls. David did not need to pour out his troubles to a human counselor; he took them to the Lord. The inward pressures could be relieved on his knees, in the presence of God.

2. Problems Without (142:3b)

"In the way wherein I walked have they privily laid a snare for me." This is the third in a trilogy of Davidic psalms mentioning that his enemies were out to trap him, to snare him like a beast (140:5; 141:9). It was this problem without that caused the pressure within. Surely there can be nothing more trying than to know that those in power are deliberately setting traps in which to snare one.

B. He Was Friendless (142:4)

Those first few days alone at Adullam, after his esape from Gath, must have been particularly trying to David. The nights were long and lonely, the days full of lurking peril. At any moment Saul might pick up his trail and corner him in that cave. But he had nowhere else to go.

He tells us he was:

1. Treated with Social Indifference (142:4a)

"I looked on my right hand, and beheld, but there was no man that would know me." All his one-time friends had put discretionary distance between themselves and him. It was not safe to know David. Where was Jonathan now? Even he had seemingly abandoned him and made his peace with Saul. All his former companions at court had proved to be fair-weather friends.

When he had killed Goliath, the whole nation had shouted his praise. Suddenly he was a somebody. He was court musician with the ear of the king, captain of the guard, the king's son-in-law. He had plenty of friends. But when Saul turned against him, his "friends" did not know him any more. David, a companionable man, found this social indifference hard to accept.

2. Treated with Spiritual Indifference (142:4b)

"Refuge failed me; no man cared for my soul." Not a man in all the land thought enough of David to seek him out, to point him to a verse or two of Scripture, to encourage him in his hour of trial. Nobody cared sufficiently for him to look him up and say, "David, I know there's not much I can do for you, but I should like to take a few minutes and pray with you."

"No man cared for my soul." This must be one of the most powerful missionary texts in the Bible. Think of the untold millions still untold. Think of the Hindu with his millions of gods. He prays to elephants and snakes, resorts to sacred prostitutes in his temples, thinks he can wash away his sins in the waters of a river. He must not kill a malarial mosquito because it might be his reincarnated uncle. He must not kill a rat or a flea, even though it carries bubonic plague, because it might be his cousin. He lives without Christ, he dies without God, he goes into the grave without hope, having never heard John 3:16 or Romans 10:9. When he stands before the judgment of God his only plea is: "No one cared for my soul."

Here is a Russian commissar. He has been brought up on Marx and Lenin. Since he was a boy it has been drilled into him that there is no God, that religion is an opiate. He is taught to ridicule the Bible, that Christianity is a great blot on the history of mankind. He lives for this present evil world, dies, and goes into a lost eternity. He is without God, without Christ, and without hope. Does any one of us care for his soul?

And what about our neighbors, relatives, and friends? Can they say, dare we let them be able to say, "No one cared for my soul"?

Where was Jonathan when David wrote that, Jonathan who once had come out to "strengthen his hand in God"? Where was Samuel? Dead, perhaps, or too busy on his circuit preaching here and there. David felt that nobody cared for his spiritual welfare at all.

But then he cheered up. Maybe no human being cared for his soul, but God did.

III. THE DISCERNING MAN (142:5-6)

David looked away to that "friend that sticketh closer than a brother." He found in God:

A. A Satisfying Portion (142:5)

"I cried unto Thee, O LORD: I said, 'Thou art my refuge and my portion in the land of the living.'" David still had God.

The expression, "the land of the living," occurs eleven times in the Bible. It has to do with being alive on earth in contrast to being alive in the eternal state. David had come to realize that, though his present circumstances left much to be desired, it was still good to be alive. He had a satisfying portion.

Some time ago I was having meetings in Scotland and my host asked me if I should like to visit Blantyre where David Livingstone was born. I was eager to go. I discovered that the great doctor, missionary, and explorer was born and raised, along with his brothers and sisters, in a home that consisted of a single room. There were twenty-four such one-room homes in the building. The room contained two beds, a fireplace, a table, some chairs, a cupboard, and a few utensils. That was all. To help make ends meet, David had to work from six o'clock in the morning until eight o'clock at night. To prepare himself for his life work he had to pinch and save his meager pennies. He had to study until the early hours of the morning.

I stood in that one-room house wondering where everyone slept and how they managed to get along with so little. The hard training stood David Livingstone in good stead for the hard life he was to live.

Eventually Livingstone went to Africa and his life became a legend. A number of dioramas in the museum at Blantyre depict various scenes from Livingstone's adventures in Africa. One of them gripped me especially. It portrayed Livingstone's farewell to his benefactor, H. M. Stanley, who, after numerous adventures of his own, found the missionary deep in the interior of the dark continent. Livingstone was in desperate straits when Stanley found him. The well-equipped Stanley ministered generously to the missionary's needs and stayed with him for a considerable time. At last, however, he turned homeward and urged Livingstone to come with him. He gave all kinds of reasons why he should avail himself of this opportunity for a furlough. The old warrior refused to go—his work in Africa was not yet done, the gospel had still to be preached in the regions beyond. The sources of the Nile were not yet found. The running sore of the African slave trade had not yet been staunched. Time was running out.

And so they said farewell. The scene in the little museum depicts Stanley with his bearers around him about to leave. There they stand, an impressive group, ready to plunge back into the bush, but pausing for one last look at Livingstone. And there stands the missionary—alone. When the last noise of the Stanley expedition had died away in the jungle, Livingstone went back to his hut, lonelier than ever now after the departure of the man who had come to him out of the long grass to be his friend. Back in his hut he took down his diary. After a few minutes he wrote again his vow of dedication to his Lord, and that was that. The Lord was his portion.

B. A Secure Protection (142:6)

"Attend unto my cry; for I am brought very low: deliver me from my persecutors; for they are stronger than I." Somehow, strength always seems to be in the hand of the enemy. The reason is that the enemy is always willing to use physical force. God rarely does. King Saul had the power of the government on his side. He had a subservient court, he had the armed forces of Israel, he had spies only too willing to curry favor and to inform.

David had God. That cancelled out all Saul's seeming advantages.

David could not see the end of the story as he lay there alone in Adullam, but he saw it later: Saul dead on the battlefield of Gilboa; Saul's body hacked and mutilated, nailed to a wall in Bethshan. So much for Saul. He never did succeed in getting his hands on David. Instead David sat enthroned in Jerusalem as Israel's greatest king, founding a dynasty that would last until the coming of Christ. It was no vain thing for David to see in God a secure protection.

Last of all we see in David:

IV. The Delivered Man (142:7)

David had no doubt that God would see him through. By faith he staked his claim in all that he believed God would do for him.

Now he strikes a threefold note of deliverance, long before that deliverance actually came. He confidently looked forward to:

A. Freedom (1427a)

"Bring my soul out of prison, that I may praise Thy name." David's soul was in prison. The freedom he desired was to be obtained, therefore, only on spiritual terms. David realized that. God must set him free. Fear will put a person in bondage; so will anger or a spirit of retaliation. Sin makes captives of us all. Sin robs us of liberty in prayer, of freedom to witness, of joy and peace. There is no bondage worse than soul bondage. David asked the Lord to bring his soul out of prison. He wanted the Lord to restore to him the joy of his salvation.

B. Fellowship (142:7b)

"The righteous shall compasss me about," he says. Note the word *shall*. He was free already. He was on the victory side. All doubts were dissolved. He was looking forward already to gathering again with God's people, the righteous, his kind of people. It was not long before Adullam rang with the shouts of David's men, gathered back into the cave, and to whom David imparted the benefit of his experiences in Gath (Psalm 34).

C. Fullness (142:7c)

"For Thou shalt deal bountifully with me." There is nothing stingy about God. David's life, so impoverished at the moment, would soon be filled to overflowing with bountiful blessings. He staked his claim on that, doing so because he knew in what kind of God he trusted.

Thus the psalm ends. David is still in the valley, but he is no longer depressed. He had been brought very low, as he says (142:6), but now he is looking up.

Psalm 143

DEPRESSION

THIS IS ANOTHER PSALM of David, the last of the penitential psalms. In all probability it was written during the time of the Absalom rebellion. Its prophetic overtones, however, carry us forward to the time of the great tribulation when the Hebrew people, in their extremity, will use such psalms to express their sense of need.

The psalm is in three parts.

629

I. DAVID'S APPEAL (143:1-4)

In his distress David does what comes naturally to him; he turns to God. He says:

A. Lord, Answer Me (143:1)

"Hear my prayer, O LORD, give ear to my supplication: in Thy faithfulness answer me, and in Thy righteousness." Not even the dangers David had to face in his outlaw years when he fled from Saul could be compared with those he faced when he fled from Absalom. In his former fugitive days he at least had the knowledge that he was being persecuted unjustly. He knew, too, that he had the secret sympathy of many in the nation who remembered his victory over Goliath. He was a hero in the eyes of the youth.

But with the Absalom rebellion it was different. Absalom had stolen the hearts of the men of Israel. David was plagued by a bad conscience. Although his sin with Bathsheba had been put away, he had Nathan's word for it that he would never outlive the consequences of that sin. Now he had lost the sympathy of many in the nation, and the youth had turned against him. The tribe of Benjamin and most of the northern tribes nursed jealous resentments. Where could he go but to the Lord?

He appealed to God—but with some trepidation, it would seem; he was not too sure that the Lord would hear him. He could remember only too well the time when God had refused to hear Saul. In the end God's silence had driven Saul to distraction. He had gone down to Endor to consult a witch. When he did that, God opened that dark door at which Saul knocked, and Saul walked straight through into a lost eternity.

David did not appeal to God's mercy. He had a surer ground than that, vast though he knew God's mercy to be. He appealed to God's faithfulness and righteousness. God was too faithful to forget the covenant He had made with him long years ago, too righteous to allow a man like Absalom to push David off that throne. For with all his charm, Absalom was a scoundrel, and with all his faults, David was a saint. So David asked God to hear him. "Lord, answer me," he says.

B. Lord, Aid Me (143:2-4)

David asked God to aid him along three lines. Aid me, he says, because:

1. My Soul Is Doomed (143:2)

"And enter not into judgment with Thy servant: for in Thy sight shall no man living be justified." David took his stand on solid ground. It was God Himself who first called David His servant. We read that the word of the Lord came to Nathan: "Go and tell My servant . . ." (2 Samuel 7:5). That was in the good old days, right after David had opened his heart to Nathan about his desire to build God a temple in Jerusalem. As soon as David had listened to God's word through Nathan, he took his position before God as God's servant: "And what can David say more unto Thee? for Thou, Lord GOD, knowest Thy servant . . ." (2 Samuel 7:20-21). Then, warming up in his prayer of thanksgiving, David had used that new title, "servant," seven more times in swift succession (2 Samuel 7:25-29).

Now in his difficulty he goes back and claims that title again on the ground of faith. He has failed, failed miserably. But God could not fail. David had learned that no one can stand before God and plead his own merits. He knew his soul was doomed, let alone his kingdom, if he had to plead his own merits. Instead, he acknowledged his guilt and asked God once more, as he had asked Him in the past, not to impute sin to him (Psalm 32:1-2).

Aid me, he continues, because:

2. My Safety Is Destroyed (143:3).

"For the enemy hath persecuted my soul; he hath smitten my life down to the ground; he hath made me to dwell in darkness, as those that have been long dead." Such was David's condition. And to make matters worse, "the enemy" was his own favorite son. The word *persecuted* here can be rendered "pursued." The word for *soul* can be rendered "me," an emphatic me. David is saying, "The enemy [Absalom] has pursued me." Absalom was pursuing his own father, determined to kill him.

So exuberant were Absalom's supporters, so sure that within days David would be caught and put out of the way, it was as though David were already dead. Not recently dead, but long dead—dead and buried and forgotten, as if he had never lived at all. That is how thoroughly the mass of Israel had forgotten David. All his achievements, his good, kindly, kingly deeds, his generosity—all forgotten. That sad obliteration of David from the memory of the majority of his subjects made his present perils a thousand times more serious. His safety was thoroughly in doubt. If he hoped that the mass of his subjects would spare him a kindly thought and take his side, if only in their secret souls, he was doomed to disappointment. He was as good as dead.

Aid me, he continues, because:

3. My Spirit Is Desolate (143:4)

"Therefore is my spirit overwhelmed within me; my heart within me is desolate." What a terrible experience, to have a loved son turn against one in callous disdain. What an awful experience, to be betrayed by a close friend in the way Ahithophel betrayed David. What a desolating experience, to be treated with indifference by former colleagues. Add all those together and it amounted to a rejection so overwhelming that the resulting devastation of spirit overwhelmed David's soul.

David had nowhere to go but to the Lord, and now he turned his tearful face toward Him. He was broken, lonely, afraid, overwhelmed, desolate. Nor did he seek the Lord in vain.

II. DAVID'S ATTITUDE (143:5-6)

Looking the Lord full in the face, David now makes two profound observations.

A. Lord, I Am Awed by Your Power—I Long to Apprehend You More Completely (143:5)

"I remember the days of old; I meditate on all Thy works; I muse on the work of Thy hands." A sensible thing to do. Instead of moping, David began musing; instead of groveling in guilt, he looked to God; instead of thinking about what he had done, he began thinking about what God has done; instead of worrying over the present with its troubles, he went back to the past with its truths. He thought about the God of yesterday— and behold, He is "the same yesterday, and today and forever."

The word *muse* here means "to talk with oneself." Some say to do that is the first sign of insanity. Really it is often the first sign of sanity. It certainly was with the prodigal son (Luke 15). It was so, too, with this Old Testament prodigal. David began to talk to himself—about God.

Perhaps he looked up at the stars. Perhaps he picked a flower from the hedgerow. Perhaps he took out his Bible and began to read again how God stretched out His capable hands to those who trusted in Him. He mused on the work of God's hands.

He thought perhaps how God's hand had protected him as a shepherd boy from lions and bears. He hadn't thought about that for years. He thought how God's hand had been on him in the valley of Elah. What was it he had said to Saul? "The Lord that delivered me out of the paw of the lion, and out of the paw of the bear, He will deliver me out of the hand of the Philistine" (1 Samuel 17:37). What an immense fierce hand that Philistine had. He could brandish a spear the size of a weaver's beam. So what! God had a bigger hand than that.

When David talked to himself, it did his troubled soul a world of good.

B. Lord, I Am Aware of Your Presence—I Long to Approach You More Closely (143:6)

"I stretch forth my hands unto Thee: my soul thirsteth after Thee, as a thirsty land. Selah." Thinking about God had cheered David up immensely. Aware now not only of God's power but also of His presence, David reached out to Him. It was a wonderful gesture, the gesture of a child putting out its arms to its daddy to be picked up and hugged. Such a gesture of love and trust brings an immediate response.

We can be sure that the God who planted paternal and maternal instincts in the human breast (love was His idea) knows just what a tug such a gesture gives to the heart.

David now abandoned logic; he had a much more eloquent appeal—the invincible language of love: "Lord, I am aware of Your presence. I long to approach You more closely. I stretch out my hands to You. My soul thirsts for You like thirsty soil yearns for rain." Here was David, cut off from all, overwhelmed in soul, turning instinctively to God, the One who, while He never lets us off, never lets us down, and never lets us go.

III. David's Aspirations (143:7-12)

David had three aspirations, which occupy the last half of the psalm. First he wanted the Lord to:

A. Discern Him (143:7)

"Hear me speedily, O Lord: my spirit faileth: hide not Thy face from me, lest I be like unto them that go down into the pit." Such flights of ecstasy as David has just expressed are often followed by a sudden return to the cold, hard facts of present circumstance. Soaring prayers and praise, however, are not just flights of fancy. They are motivated, usually, and in the first instance, by very present needs. So David came down to earth again.

He told the Lord again how depressed he was, how fearful he was in this latest trouble which had come into his life. He asked God not to hide His face from him. David knew what had happened to Saul: Saul went down into the pit (the word literally means the grave). What could be worse than to die in one's sins with God's face resolutely turned away? David pleaded that the Lord would not let that happen to him. He wanted God to discern him, to keep His eye on him, to keep His face turned toward him.

He also wanted the Lord to:

B. Direct Him (143:8-10)

Here again he had a threefold petition. He says, first: Lord, help me to know something of:

1. Your Way (143:8)

"Cause me to hear Thy lovingkindness in the morning; for in Thee do I trust: cause me to know the way wherein I should walk; for I lift up my soul unto Thee." Lord, he said, I am ready to listen—cause me to hear; I am ready to learn—cause me to know. He wanted to know the right steps to take in this life crisis.

The Lord gave him the wisdom he needed. We see David acting like a king in exile up there in Gilead near Mahanaim. First came Ittai the Gittite, a seasoned warrior, along with his noble six hundred from Gath. Ittai was a skilled swordsman, so David sent him off to Joab to take his place in the front line. Then came Zadok the priest, bringing the ark, a man versed in handling holy things. He would be of no use in the front line, so David sent him back with the ark to Jerusalem. There he was to continue in the presence of God on David's behalf, and to keep in touch with David as events unfolded. Then came Hushai the Archite, David's friend. David sent him back too, to put in a word for David in the counsel chambers of the foe. His job was to defeat the clever counsel of Ahithophel, to bring all his suggestions to nothing by quietly reminding Absalom of what David was really like.

Thus step by step David followed the Lord's inner leading in all these pragmatic matters. Every decision he made was the right decision. Absalom's rebellion crumbled into dust and was blown away into oblivion.

David relied on the Lord to direct him in these things. Lord, he said, help me to know something of Your way.

Next, he said, Lord, let me know something of:

2. Your Welcome (143:9)

"Deliver me, O LORD, from mine enemies: I flee unto Thee to hide me." It was the only place to which David could flee to hide from his foes. He had found a welcome in God before; he was confident he would find a welcome there again. He ran to God as a child would run to a parent to escape a barking dog, as chicks run to the mother hen when danger looms, as a man runs to the cleft in the rock to escape the violence of the storm.

Then, David added, Lord, let me know something of:

3. Your Will (143:10)

"Teach me to do Thy will; for Thou art my God: Thy spirit is good; lead me into the land of uprightness." Mature believer that he was, David felt he still had a great deal to learn about God. He had spiritual insight enough to know that he could know God better only if his life was conformed to God's will. So he surrendered unconditionally to God's will, knowing that will always to be good, acceptable, and perfect (Romans 12:2).

How reluctant we are to surrender unconditionally to the will of God. Satan deceives us. He says, "If you let God have His way, He'll send you to serve in a leper colony," or "You'll have to give up your boyfriend," or "You'll never have any more fun." Satan, liar that he is, persuades us in our subconscious minds that God's will is bad, unacceptable, and irksome.

So David surrendered to God's will—be it victory and vindication, or defeat, disgrace, and death. God's will be done. Whatever it was, David felt sure he would get to know God better if he did His will. He would know more of His *nearness* ("Thou art my God"), more of His *nature* ("Thy Spirit is good"), more of His *name* ("for Thy name's sake").

Finally, David wanted the Lord to:

C. Deliver Him (146:11-12)

Though he was ready for God's will at any cost, David had a deep inner feeling that the present situation in Jerusalem could not possibly be God's will. Nor could he see that his death, at this juncture, could be God's will. There was too much at stake for the theocratic kingdom.

He prayed therefore that the Lord would:

1. Give Him Life (143:11)

"Quicken me, O LORD, for Thy name's sake: for Thy righteousness' sake bring my soul out of trouble." The word *quicken* simply means "to make alive." David doubtless knew through his spies that Ahithophel was counseling Absalom to have David put to death at all costs. "Give me life!" he prayed. His work was not yet finished. The site for the temple had not yet been chosen. Arrangements needed to be made for the orderly transfer of power in the kingdom to the heir whom God Himself would choose.

"For Thy name's sake." There can be no greater argument in prayer than that. God is always going to protect the honor of His name. David could not see how his dying at the hands of a vain young rebel like Absalom could bring honor to God's name.

Finally he prayed that the Lord would:

2. Give Him Liberty (143:12)

"And of Thy mercy cut off mine enemies, and destroy all them that afflict my soul: for I am Thy servant." Back he came again to the original covenant.

God's mercy is the basis of David's plea that his enemies might be cut off. Surely it was a mercy for the future good of Israel that Absalom did not triumph. It was a mercy that so vile and violent a man as Absalom be cut off, that so vindictive and vicious a man as Ahithophel hanged himself, that a man like David, who truly loved the Lord and who desired God's best for His people, should triumph. It was a mercy to David. And it was a mercy to Israel. It is always a mercy when God puts an end to the power and oppression of evil people.

Much in this prayer of David can be applied to our own lives when we are called to face trying circumstances. May we all have the grace to do it.

Psalm 144

A HAPPY PEOPLE

I. DAVID'S SOURCE OF VITALITY (144:102)
His fame as:
A. A Soldier (144:1)
B. A Sovereign (144:2)
II. DAVID'S SENSE OF VANITY (144:3-8)
A. The Vanity of Man's Person (144:3-4)
1. How Insignificant Is Our Existence (144:3)
2. How Inconsequential Is Our Experience (144:4)
B. The Vanity of Man's Plans (144:5-8)
1. Apprehending the Power of God (144:5-6)
2. Appropriating the Power of God (144:7-8)
III. DAVID'S SONG OF VICTORY (144:9-15)
A. His Determination (144:9)
B. His Discernment (144:10-11)
God delivers kings from those who would:
1. Destroy Them (144:10)
2. Defame Them (144:11)
C. His Desire (144:12-15)
1. For a Magnificent Population (144:12)
2. For a Manifest Prosperity (144:13-14a)
3. For a Meaningful Peace (144:14b, c)
4. For a Mirthful People (144:15)

WHEN SEVENTY Hebrew scholars of Alexandria, some three or four centuries before the birth of Christ, translated the Hebrew Bible into the Greek Septuagint version, they added a note to the title of this psalm. It reads: "A psalm of David concerning Goliath." The more one studies the psalm, however, those words hardly seem to fit. The psalm obviously does not concern David's early days: his days of boyish exuberance, or even his days of exhilaration after killing Goliath. The suggestion by those scholars may be attributed,

637

perhaps, to the fact that two of the verses in this psalm echo verses in Psalm 8—clearly a Goliath psalm. Psalm 144:3 is the same as Psalm 8:4. Also, Psalm 144:10 refers to David's deliverance from "the hurtful sword," which some have taken to be a reference to the sword of Goliath. Nonetheless, however tempting the Septuagint phrasing is, it simply isn't an accurate assessment of the situation. If anything, Psalm 144 is a sequel to Psalm 143. In Psalm 143 David prayed for deliverance from his foes, seemingly in reference to the time of the Absalom rebellion. Psalm 144 is a paean of praise, best suiting the time when David was back on the throne in answer to his prayer in Psalm 143.

The psalm divides into three parts.

I. David's Source of Vitality (144:1-2)

David had no hesitation whatever in attributing all to God. There was, for instance, his fame as:

A. A Soldier (144:1)

"Blessed be the LORD my strength, which teacheth my hands to war, and my fingers to fight." That sounds like a strange beatitude. It is a long cry from this beatitude to the phrase, "Blessed are the peacemakers," from the Sermon on the Mount. But blessed indeed, at times, are those who know how to battle a nation's foes. Many a time in Britain, during the dark days of World War II, the embattled nation gave thanks to God for a man like Winston Churchill.

There can be no doubt that David's fame as a fighter weighed heavily on Absalom, even though he had the bulk of the army with him. It weighed heavily, too, on the mind of Ahithophel the traitor, who urged Absalom not to dilly-dally with delay. "Let me now choose out twelve thousand men, and I will arise and pursue after David this night: and I will come upon him while he is weary and weak handed, and will make him afraid: and the People that are with him shall flee; and I will smite the king only," he said (2 Samuel 17:1-2). But then came Hushai the Archite, David's friend and secret agent at Absalom's court. He preached caution and delay, his secret plan being to gain time for David so that he might consolidate his position and collect his forces. "Thou knowest thy father," he said to Absalom, "and his men, that they be mighty men, and they be chafed in their minds, as a bear robbed of her whelps in the field: and thy father is a man of war, and will not lodge with the People" (2

Samuel 17:8). The counsel of the crafty Hushai was to put the fear of David into Absalom. We know how well he succeeded. Absalom chose to wait until his army was even stronger than it already was, and Ahithophel, realizing that his game was lost, went out and hanged himself.

Back on the throne David took all his victories and put them reverently at the feet of the Lord. "It wasn't me," said David, "it was the Lord."

Then David attributes to the Lord any fame he might have as:

B. A Sovereign (144:2)

"My goodness, and my fortress; my high tower, and my deliverer; my shield, and He in whom I trust; who subdueth my People under me." David was back on the throne. His people were once again subdued under him. He again swayed the scepter as their rightful king. Other peoples, too (as the text perhaps suggests), were hastening to make their peace with him.

David attributed it all to God. The source of his vitality was God. Without God he was nothing. It was God who had been his high tower and fortress. It was God who had swept away the threatening clouds of the Absalom rebellion. It was in God he had trusted in those desperate hours, not in his own prowess, not in his skill as a warrior. His trust had not been in his veterans nor in Joab's toughness and tactical skill.

David would have us all learn not to trust in our own skills and abilities, but to acknowledge that they all come from God. Any successes we achieve in life come from Him.

II. David's Sense of Vanity (144:3-8)

When David climbed back on his throne he was still deeply shaken by recent events, still somewhat unsure of himself. Humanly speaking, it had been touch and go, his future had hung by a hair. He had to be careful even yet of the touchiness of the tribes, the jealousy of Ephraim, the resentfulness of Benjamin. One attack had been repelled. Others might easily be brewing in the boiling cauldron of the times (we know from the historical text that other insurrections were in the air). David had to take firm measures, but an iron hand had to be covered with a velvet glove.

Ascending his throne again, he had a fresh sense of the vanity, the transience of things—something he had already expressed in Psalm 39. He must have brooded over his failure to win the affections of the younger generation. There was a strong reaction against the establishment, an impatience at any mention of past glories. The repression of the Absalom rebellion had not mollified the feelings of the young generation. They were not old enough to appreciate how much the nation owed to David. They were tired of hearing about Goliath, and all the rest of it. They wanted change, any change; even Absalom was a change.

So David brooded over the vanity of things.

A. The Vanity of Man's Person (144:3-4)

1. How Insignificant Is Our Existence (144:3)

"LORD, what is man, that Thou takest knowledge of him! Or the son of man, that Thou makest account of him!" There are two words for *man* in this verse. The first is *adam*, which denotes mankind in general. Why should God take knowledge of mankind? After all, there are ranks and orders in the universe far greater and much more splendid than the human race.

The second word is *enosh*. This word first occurs in Scripture in the story of the flood, in connection with the "sons of God" having illicit liaison with "the daughters of man" so that a progeny was born which became famous on earth: "men of renown" or "men of the name," as the expression suggests. *Enosh* is always used in a bad sense in Scripture. Morally, it stands for man in his frailty and weakness. It comes from a root that means "to be sick" or "to be wretched or weak." It denotes man's inability. It shows that man has neither physical strength nor the capacity for moral goodness. So why should God take account of man?

Yet He does. In spite of our insignificance, in spite of our fallen condition, God does take us into account. It must be a matter of ceaseless wonder to the angels. C. S. Lewis brings that out in his *Screwtape Letters*. He pictures Screwtape describing human beings as "disgusting vermin" and has this senior devil express not only amazement but also shuddering abhorrence at the astounding fact that God likes people.

David was awed by it himself. He was forever haunted by his own fearful moral lapse. As many of the psalms hint, he had only recently come through a terrible illness which had brought him down to the gates of the grave. Back on the throne, he expresses a healthy respect for the terrible weakness of the human race. He is aware of the vanity and emptiness of all the things for which men struggle and strive in the light of the fact that man is *enosh* after all.

2. How Inconsequential Is Our Experience (144:4)

"Man is like to vanity: his days are as a shadow that passeth away." David reviews his own life with its accumulated experiences. He thinks back over the great events in which he played a part. He thinks of the ups and downs of life: one moment a national hero, the next an object of official suspicion and hate; one moment a king, the next a fugitive; one moment a saint writing psalms, the next a seducer of another man's wife. He thinks of his days as a shepherd in the country, of his days as a singer at court, his days as a soldier in the camp, his days as a sojourner in the cave. It all seems like a dream. His days have been as a shadow cast on the wall. It is hard to believe that they have all come and gone so swiftly.

He thinks of his years on the throne. Three times he was anointed, he remembers, before he had all the tribes in hand. He thinks of his *victories* and how glorious they were. Nation after nation had been forced to make peace with him—on his terms.

He thinks of the good things he has done, of his *virtues*, of the times when divine inspiration welled up in his heart and psalms flowed from his pen. He thinks of his decision to build God a house—what an inspiration that was. He thinks of his organization of the priests into twenty-four orderly courses, of his contribution to the sacred hymnology of his people, of the treasure he has accumulated so that his son might build the temple. He thinks of his kindness to Mephibosheth, of his forgiveness of Abner. He thanks God for many such virtuous deeds.

He thinks, too, of his *vices*. Few, perhaps, but those he had indulged had been terrible. Will he ever be able to forget the earnest face of his faithful guardsman Uriah? Will he ever get out of his mind Bathsheba's despair when she heard of the suicide of her grandfather Ahithophel? He thinks of Michal, his first love. He thinks of spiritually-minded Abigail. Why did he ever have to be such a fool as to sin with Bathsheba? He thinks of his sons and of the pandemonium of disorder in his own family. Vanity of vanities! Like the wise man, Solomon, his son, he could write those words as a text over it all. It was his vanity that had led him into his affair with Bathsheba—what with his good looks, personality, power, wealth, and position as Israel's hero—it had all gone to his head. And what a high price he had paid for it all: Amnon dead; Tamar shamed; Absalom dead and damned; a score of his own wives publicly shamed by Absalom; Ahithophel his best friend, dead by suicide and accursed of God.

And was he mistaken? Or could he detect a hidden streak of

this same vanity even in Solomon, the best of all his boys? And could he be sure he had rooted all the noxious weed out of his own soul? What were these thoughts he had been having lately about getting a headcount of the tribes? Had his experience taught him nothing at all?

"Truly man is like to vanity: his days are as a shadow that passeth away," he wrote. And for a long time he must have simply stared at that potent passage on the page before him. The vanity of man's person! If his experience had taught him nothing at all, how inconsequential that experience was, after all. Why did God bother with man?

Next, David turns his attention to:

B. The Vanity of Man's Plans (144:5-8)

He turns his eyes away from himself to God so that he might better be able to appreciate how puny were all his plans and schemes and ambitions, not to mention all the plottings of men. What are man's plans when confronted with the sovereign will of an omnipotent and omniscient God? The recent civil war, brought on by an egotistical young man's sinful ambitions, were the background for David's musings. Months of careful planning had gone into that rebellion. With infinite caution and consummate skill Absalom had laid the foundations of it all, systematically and subtly stealing the hearts of the men of Israel. Now he was dead and damned and David was back on the throne.

First we see David:

1. Apprehending the Power of God (144:5-6)

"Bow Thy heavens, O LORD, and come down: touch the mountains, and they shall smoke. Cast forth lightning, and scatter them: shoot out Thine arrows, and destroy them." Crushing the Absalom rebellion by no means solved all David's problems. There was, for instance, that "man of Belial whose name was Sheba, the son of Bichri, a Benjamite," who blew a trumpet and said, "We have no part in David, neither have we inheritance in the son of Jesse: every man to his tents, O Israel" (2 Samuel 20:1). This insurrection threatened to be even more disastrous than the Absalom rebellion, as David rightly assessed: "Now shall Sheba the son of Bichri do us more harm than did Absalom," he said (2 Samuel 20:6). David felt the throne wobbling beneath him even before he was securely seated on it again.

Worse still was Joab's cold-blooded execution of Absalom. It was the sensible and political thing to do but it had touched a raw nerve in David's soul. He had suffered long under Joab's insolence. "Tool turned tyrant" was Joab, ever since the affair with Uriah. David had always been somewhat intimidated by his capable, ruthless, and ambitious nephew Joab. With his soul still smarting under Joab's rough but timely words at David's inordinate grief over Absalom's death, David did a hasty and foolish thing. He chose this inopportune time to depose Joab from his post as commander-in-chief. Worse still, he promoted an incompetent officer, Amasa, to the position. Both Joab and Amasa were nephews of David: Joab the son of David's sister Zeruiah and Amasa the son of David's other sister Abigail. So, with this new rebellion brewing, David found himself deprived of Joab's competent generalship. Amasa's bungling almost cost David his throne a second time.

No wonder David, in this new crisis, appealed to God to bow the heavens and come down and thus once more demonstrate to vain and ambitious men His almighty power. God had given the throne to David. David staked everything on that, in thus appealing to heaven for an immediate response. And God, indeed, did answer David's prayer, but not by supernatural means—God is always sparing of miracles.

We next see David:

2. Appropriating the Power of God (144:7-8)

"Send Thine hand from above; rid me, and deliver me out of great waters, from the hand of strange children; whose mouth speaketh vanity, and their right hand is a right hand of falsehood." This time the danger threatened to blossom into full-scale civil war: states' rights against federal rights, the tribes of the north against the tribes of the south. Like the American Civil War, this new threat promised to tear the nation apart. Old rivalries and jealousies of north and south threatened to reduce Israel to warring factions, undo all the good David had done, weaken the nation, and make it a prey to foreign powers. Moreover, David had other sons eyeing the throne, notably Adonijah. What would happen if Joab, sore at his dismissal as general, should fan the ambitions of that young man?

Then, too, Amasa quickly displayed his ineffectiveness as a general. So where could David go but to the Lord? Nor did he appeal in vain. God answered, and it was Joab who again saved the day. He seized his opportunity the moment he saw the inefficiency of Amasa and the despair of David. After callously murdering his cousin and rival Amasa to get him out of the way once and for all, Joab took charge. He soon crushed the incipient rebellion and once more restored the kingdom to David.

He did so with minimum effort, with barely a ripple of war.

The king was now in Joab's power. David made no further attempt to get rid of Joab, and in the end he handed the Joab problem over to Solomon. Nevertheless he felt keenly the defection of Absalom and the murder of Amasa. "Deliver me . . . from the hand of strange children," he said. The expression literally means "sons of the foreigner." From now on, David wrote Joab down as a stranger. He committed his case to God. Absalom was dead and David's heart was broken. Joab, who had killed him, was all-powerful with the troops. David's plan to get rid of him had failed and now he was stronger and more daring than ever. In the end Joab would try his own hand at being king-maker, when David was enfeebled with his last illness.

What was the use of it all? It was all vanity, even life's successes. But the psalm does not end on that depressing note.

III. David's Song of Victory (144:9-15)

We sense at once:

A. His Determination (144:9)

"I will sing a new song unto Thee, O God: upon a psaltery and an instrument of ten strings will I sing praises unto Thee." David now strikes a new note in the book of psalms which, from here on to the end of the book, wells louder and louder until we reach the tremendous crescendo of the closing psalm. From now on, David lives above his troubles. He takes his stand on the highlands of faith. His determination to sing a new song is picked up by the Holy Spirit and carried through by Him to the end of the book. The next psalm is called "David's Psalm of Praise" and the last five psalms are all doxologies of praise. We note also:

B. His Discernment (144:10-11)

David sees now, more clearly than ever, that God is the one who is really enthroned. It is He who delivers kings from those who would:

1. Destroy Them (144:10)

"It is He that giveth salvation unto kings: who delivereth David His servant from the hurtful sword." Whether it was the terrible sword of Goliath, or the murderous sword of King Saul, or the treacherous sword of Absalom, or the hurtful sword of

Sheba the Benjamite, or the waiting sword of some foreign foe, God was the one from whom deliverance came. Many a battle had David been in, yet he had every assurance he would die in bed. He had been in the thick of battle most of his life, but God had always delivered him from the hurtful sword.

Moreover it is God who delivers kings from those who would:

2. Defame Them (144:11)

"Rid me, and deliver me from the hand of strange children, whose mouth speaketh vanity, and their right hand is a right hand of falsehood."

The murder of Amasa by Joab seems still to be on David's mind. The story is recorded in all its sordid detail. Joab, with his sword in his left hand, had gone up to his cousin with a cheerful hail: "Art thou in health, my brother?" he said. Then "Joab took Amasa by the beard with the right hand to kiss him." It was an affectionate gesture, a Judas kiss, and Amasa suspected nothing. We read that he "took no heed to the sword that was in Joab's hand: So he smote him therewith in the fifth rib . . . and he died" (2 Samuel 20:8-10). Such a man was Joab. The cold-bloodedness of the murder greatly troubled David (he mentions it twice in the psalm, here and in verse 8) as well as did his own inability to avenge this innocent blood. He now handed Joab over to God as later he handed him over to Solomon. We note also:

C. His Desire (144:12-15)

David now begins to soar. His concept of the kingdom is greatly enlarged. Despite the civil wars, he sees "one nation under God with liberty and justice for all." He begins to pray for such a kingdom to be established in Israel. He prays:

1. For a Magnificent Population (144:12)

"That our sons may be as plants grown up in their youth; that our daughters may be as corner stones, polished after the similitude of a palace." David envisions a nation of healthy young men, virile, straight, and tall, drawing their strength from their native soil, strangers to everything decadent and diseased. He envisions young women, future mothers of Israel, as cornerstones of the nation, polished and cultured, strong and stable, beautiful and upright as fluted columns, fitted to grace the palace of a king. Happy indeed is a nation that has such sons and daughters. Well might America write these verses over the portals of every school, college, and university. Well might we pursue such a national goal, ridding our land of those who would debase our youth with drink, drugs, sex, and atheism.

David prays, too:

2. For a Manifest Prosperity (144:13-14a)

"That our garners may be full, affording all manner of store: that our sheep may bring forth thousands and ten thousands in our streets: that our oxen may be strong to labor." He envisions a nation with a healthy economy, where prosperity is the rule, where production is high and the gross national product beyond all normal expectation, where the flow of goods is steady and sustained. Such material blessings are the byproduct of a nation's right relationship with God.

He prays also:

3. For a Meaningful Peace (144:14b, c)

"That there be no breaking in, nor going out; that there be no complaining in our streets." He prays, in other words, for the country's wellbeing *internationally:* "that there be no breaking in," that is, that there be no invasions of the country by a foreign foe; "that there be no going out," that is, that there be no deportations, no captivity to a foreign power. In other words, he prays for peace. No nation can have such peace apart from a right relationship with God.

He prays, too, for the country's well-being *internally:* "that there be no complaining in our streets." That had been at the heart of the Absalom rebellion. Absalom had capitalized on that, fanned it, fomented it. That, too, had given credence to the Sheba rebellion. It is that which gives every power-seeker his chance. The antidote for all that is to bring the nation back to right relationship with God.

Finally, David prays:

4. For a Mirthful People (144:15)

"Happy is that people, that is in such a case: yea, happy is that People, whose God is the LORD." David's national goal was that his people be free from complaints and full of contentment. He realized that there was only one way for such national goals to be realized. They cannot be attained by political acumen nor by the pursuit of peace and prosperity in themselves. No humanistic policies will produce the national happiness envisioned by David—policies that leave God out.

True political stability and national well-being must be related to God. Any nation that departs from God sows the seeds of its own disunity, discontent, and dissolution.

HAPPY IS THAT PEOPLE WHOSE GOD IS THE LORD. It should be written in the halls of Congress and in the houses of parliament of the nations. It should be written over the Senate and in the chambers of the Supreme Court. It should be written in the council chamber of the United Nations. It should be at the core of the curriculum in our schools. It should be the first essential and inviolate plank in every political platform. It should be the conviction of every politician and statesman. It should be the motto of every king, president, and prime minister. It should be drilled into the consciousness of every citizen. It should be written on the table of every human heart. HAPPY IS THAT PEOPLE WHOSE GOD IS THE LORD.

Psalm 145

A WONDERFUL GOD

I. GOD'S GREATNESS (145:1-6)
   A. The Thoroughness of David's Praise (145:1-2)
      1. Why He Wanted to Praise God (145:1)
         a. God's Personal Relationship to Him (145:1a)
         b. God's Permanent Rule over Him (145:1b)
      2. When He Wanted to Praise God (145:2)
   B. The Theme of David's Praise (145:3-6)
      1. The Awesome Mystery of God's Person (145:3)
      2. The Awesome Might of God's Power (145:4)
      3. The Awesome Majesty of God's Purpose (145:5)
      4. The Awesome Meaning of God's Providence (145:6)
II. GOD'S GOODNESS (145:7-10)
   A. The Moral Goodness of God (145:7)
   B. The Merciful Goodness of God (145:8)
   C. The Manifold Goodness of God (145:9)
   D. The Meaningful Goodness of God (145:10)
III. GOD'S GLORY (145:11-13)
   A. God's Inspiring Kingdom (145:11-12)
   B. God's Invincible Kingdom (145:13)
IV. GOD'S GOVERNMENT (145:14-17)
   A. Based on True Kindness (145:14)
   B. Based on True Kingliness (145:15-17)
      1. Absolute Impartiality (145:15-16)
      2. Absolute Impeccability (145:17)
V. GOD'S GRACE (145:18-21)
   A. How God's Grace Is Reviewed (145:18-20a)
      1. How Approachable God Is (145:18)
      2. How Appealing God Is (145:19-20a)
   B. How God's Grace Is Revoked (145:20b)
   C. How God's Grace Is Rhapsodized (145:21)

CALLED "DAVID'S PSALM OF PRAISE," this is the only psalm thus inscribed. It is a psalm of pure worship, a fitting end to the Davidic psalms. It brings all of David's other hymns to a climax. It forms an end, too, to the main body of the book of Psalms itself. The remaining five psalms are an appropriate appendix of appreciation for God, a supplementary doxology.

This psalm is also the last of the acrostic psalms. All the letters of the Hebrew alphabet are present, with the exception of the letter *nun*, the fourteenth letter of the alphabet. The alphabetical arrangement suggests that the confusion of language which began at Babel will be reversed when all people learn to praise the Lord, when all unite in mind and purpose around the throne of the Lord Jesus. Then Jew, Gentile, and the church of God will unite in true praise. Heaven above and earth beneath will ring with the praises of God.

This psalm is about God. It begins with:

I. GOD'S GREATNESS (145:1-6)

A. The Thoroughness of David's Praise (145:1-2)

David mentions, first:

1. Why He Wanted to Praise God (145:1)

David wanted to praise God for two reasons.

a. God's Personal Relationship to Him (145:1a)

"I will extol Thee, *my* God." Nobody can praise God apart from this personal relationship. To try to worship God in the abstract is unsatisfactory. Such concepts as "providence" or "nature" do not touch the chords of our hearts. But to think that the God of suns and stars, the God of singing seraphim and adoring angels, is *my* God. If that does not tune up the heart, what will?

b. God's Permanent Rule over Him (145:1b)

"I will extol Thee, my God, O king; and I will bless Thy name for ever and ever." David had long since surrendered his sovereignty to God. God was his king. He was a man *under* authority and was therefore fit to be a man *in* authority

Nor did David contemplate any end to this lordship in his life. It was "for ever and ever." That is why he wanted to praise Him.

He had learned by experience the blessedness of obedience and the bitterness of self-will.

Next he tells us:

2. When He Wanted to Praise God (145:2)

"Every day will I bless Thee; and I will praise Thy name for ever and ever." David takes both an everyday view of things and an everlasting view of things. His time was made up of days— not a day would pass without praise. He might write in his diary: "Today I praise God for sending old Barzillai to me with all those generous provisions for me and my men." Or "Today I praise God for bringing to nought the counsel of Ahithophel." Or "Today I praise God for such a competent general as Joab." Or "Today I praise God that Absalom is dead, even though my heart is broken. At least I did not have to sign his death warrant." Or "Today I praise God that He put it into my heart to grant that wicked man Shimei a stay of execution."

David determined never to let a day go by without discovering some way to freight it down with praise. What a noble ambition for us to emulate—and all because David was looking forward to praising God forever and ever in yonder bright regions of joy. He wanted to be in practice. When he arrived on the golden sands beyond the shining river, he did not want to have to start out in the kindergarten of praise and learn how it was done. He wanted to graduate from earth with high honors in the subject of praise and arrive in heaven able to take his place at once with the worthies on the other shore.

B. The Theme of David's Praise (145:3-6)

Here we see a fourfold theme. David wanted to be taken up with:

1. The Awesome Mystery of God's Person (145:3)

"Great is the LORD, and greatly to be praised; and His greatness is unsearchable." David is talking about the great I AM, the God whose name is ineffable and unpronounceable, the God who met Moses at the burning bush with the demand that he remove his shoes from off his feet because he stood on holy ground. He is a God so unsearchable that no human mind can comprehend Him. He is so vast we can touch but the fringes of His garment. He is a God who has revealed Himself in three persons as Father, Son, and Holy Spirit, three in one and one in three. He is a God who is without beginning or ending of days, eternal, uncreated, self-existing. We go back before the dawn of time, before the first star glimmered in the sky, before the rustle of an angel's wing disturbed the silence of eternity, back into the dateless, timeless past, into the void of nothingness—and lo! God was there and had been there, glorious, sublime, needing nothing. Surely, with David, we must fall down and worship at His feet.

2. The Awesome Might of God's Power (145:4)

"One generation shall praise Thy works to another, and shall declare Thy mighty acts." To create an atom. What a mighty work! To pack within the confines of a speck of matter, so small the eye can never see it, enough power to annihilate a city. What a mighty act. To create a galaxy. To people it with suns and stars, novas and supernovas, quasars and black holes, to toss millions upon millions of stars into space like fireworks. What an act. Or to pick up a planet and raise mighty mountains on its face, and mantle them with the sea, to swathe it in clouds and give it seasons, and plant it with rolling meadows and far-flung forests, to fill it with minerals and to populate it with thousands upon thousands of different sorts and kinds of living things, and then to make a man in His own image and after His own likeness. What a mighty work.

Truly, "One generation shall praise Thy works to another, and shall declare Thy mighty acts." It is the sane and sensible thing to do. It is the intelligent thing to do. The insulting thing to do is to say that it all happened by chance, that it is a "fortuitous concourse of atoms," to invent theories to argue God out of His own creation. But no amount of manmade theory, however cleverly presented, however persistently trumpeted, will stop the devout from praising God.

3. The Awesome Majesty of God's Purpose (145:5)

"I will speak of the glorious honor of Thy majesty, and of Thy wondrous works." Let some be skeptical, if they will, but David is awed by the wonder of God's ways. There are so many instances of God's direct intervention in human affairs that unbelief is a species of inexcusable folly.

In Old Testament times, God's "wondrous works" were frequently manifested in judgment—as they will be again during the Apocalypse. He intervened in the judgment of the flood. He intervened at the overthrow of Babel. He intervened in the overthrow of Sodom. He intervened to emancipate the Hebrews from Egypt. He intervened to clear their way into Canaan.

The greatest act of divine intervention, however, took place, in New Testament times, at Calvary. God's wondrous works were manifested by Jesus throughout His life, in mighty acts of mercy. They were manifested at Calvary when He shook creation's rocks and plunged the sun into darkness. They were manifested when He rose from the dead. Above all, they were manifested in the marvelous exhibits of His grace and love in turning the cross of Calvary into a symbol of salvation from sin.

4. The Awesome Meaning of God's Providence (145:6)

"And men shall speak of the might of Thy terrible acts: and I will declare Thy greatness." The word translated "terrible" is rendered in various ways in the Old Testament. In Psalm 119 it is used for God's name: "Holy and reverend [terrible] is His name." The word comes from a root meaning "to be afraid." Well might human beings be afraid. In his own experience, David had seen God's providence at work. Time and time again God had providentially delivered him from his enemies.

He thinks, perhaps, of the most notable occasion of all, the time when Saul had him trapped. The Ziphites had betrayed him and were cooperating with Saul in a final effort to take him. "And Saul went on this side of the mountain, and David and his men on that side of the mountain: and David made haste to get away for fear of Saul; for Saul and his men compassed David and his men round about to take them" (1 Samuel 23:26). David was trapped. Saul had him in the net at last. Or did he? The next verse says: "But [and that *but* is the Holy Spirit's way of drawing our attention to the providence of God] there came a messenger unto Saul, saying, 'Haste thee, and come; for the Philistines have invaded the land.'" David saw an awesome meaning in God's providential acts—to the unsaved those acts should be a source of terror: to the child of God, a source of testimony.

David now moves on to his second major theme:

II. GOD'S GOODNESS (145:7-10)

Again David has a fourfold emphasis.

A. The Moral Goodness of God (145:7)

"They shall abundantly utter the memory of Thy great goodness, and shall sing of Thy righteousness." David links the goodness of God and the righteousness of God. God is a good God, morally good. It is impossible for Him to be anything but good. God is not the author of sin—sin did not begin with God; it began with Lucifer. God always does good things, things consistent with His righteousness. Because He is good, God has to punish sin. But because He is good, He never does so vindictive ly or capriciously. He is good and righteous. Therefore He always does what is right. When sinful people call God's good ness into question, it is because they are blinded by sin. When all the facts are in, at the judgment seat of Christ and at the great white throne, everyone will be forced to acknowledge, and that for all eternity, the fact of God's moral goodness, even if they are in a lost eternity.

B. The Merciful Goodness of God (145:8)

"The LORD is gracious, and full of compassion; slow to anger, and of great mercy." His goodness is not just a cold, impassive rectitude. It is a goodness that reaches out warmly in mercy and compassion to the lost, the erring, and the fallen. It is a goodness that holds back God's righteous anger as long as it may.

David had experienced this. All the long years he fled from Saul he must have wondered why God allowed his troubles to continue so long. Now he could see that it was part of God's merciful goodness to Saul, giving an envious and misguided man year after year to repent.

David could think, too, of his own great sin and at how long God had held back the smiting sword. And even when judgment could no longer be delayed, instead of acting arbitrarily, He had sent Nathan with his parable and given David room for repentance. God's goodness was a merciful goodness.

C. The Manifold Goodness of God (145:9)

"The LORD is good to all: and His tender mercies are over all His works." He is good to all. He makes His sun to shine on the bad as well as on the good. He metes out His tender mercy to the stubborn elder brother as well as to the repentant prodigal son. He loves the vilest sinner just as much as He loves the most virtuous saint. The greatest manifestation of that mercy was at Calvary when Jesus prayed for those who nailed Him to the tree: "Father, forgive them; for they know not what they do" (Luke 23:24). Surely the thunderbolts of God's wrath would have been unloosed without that prayer. But He spreads the rainbow against the blackness of the storm. "His tender mercies are over all His works." Not just His mercies, but His tender mercies.

We see that exhibited in the story of the prodigal son. Mercy would have found a place for the penitent with the hired servants; tender mercy seated him again as a son, tender mercy called for the ring and the robe, the feast and the fun, the music and dancing in the hall. Tender mercy is what set the father on his watchtower day after day while the wretched boy was in the far country wasting his substance with riotous living; tender mercy is what made the old man run to meet the halting, hesitant boy on the faltering footpath for home; tender mercy is what stifled all suggestion by the prodigal that he be found a home in the barn and be given a servant's place in the kitchen.

D. The Meaningful Goodness of God (145:10)

"All Thy works shall praise Thee, O LORD, and Thy saints shall bless Thee." All God's works in *creation* will sing His praise; all His works in *redemption* will sing His praise.

That is what we have in the book of Revelation. In Revelation 4:11 we see Him worshiped as *the Lord of Creation:* "Thou art worthy . . . for Thou hast created all things." In Revelation 5:8 we see Him worshiped as *the Lamb of Calvary:* "Thou art worthy . . . for Thou wast slain." The seraphim sing creation's song. The saints lift the anthems an octave higher and sing redemption's song. So meaningful are these two themes that they occupy the minds of the highest of all created, unfallen intelligences in the universe on the one hand and the rapturous songs of the redeemed in heaven on the other.

III. GOD'S GLORY (145:11-13)

David sees God's glory centered in the kingdom of which, in his day, he was the earthly viceregent. He sees:

A. God's Inspiring Kingdom (145:11-12)

"They shall speak of the glory of Thy kingdom, and talk of Thy power; to make known to the sons of men His mighty acts, and the glorious majesty of His kingdom." The kingdom age is the millennial age, the glory age. The world has never yet seen anything remotely like it. Many an Old Testament Scripture anticipates it with the keenest delight. The Lord Jesus taught us to pray for its coming: "Thy kingdom come. Thy will be done on earth, as it is in heaven."

As David foresees here, the kingdom will be established in power. From other Scriptures we know it will be preceded by the battle of Armageddon and by the judgment of the nations in the valley of Jehoshaphat. It will be accompanied by a complete renovation of the earth and a restoration of Eden's pristine splendor.

The glory of this world's kingdoms is soon tarnished. Earth's empires wax and wane until all that is left of them are exhibits in museums. But the power and glory of the kingdom of Christ will be talked of to earth's remotest bounds. The power of every other kingdom crests, and then the decline comes, sometimes swiftly, sometimes slowly. Gone are the pomp and power of Pharaoh's Egypt. Gone is the imperial might of Nineveh. Gone is the glory of Greece, the power of imperial Rome. All that is left of Britain's worldwide empire is a piecemeal Commonwealth, the mere ghost of a lost imperial might upon which the sun never set. Gone soon will be the American dream. Gone will be Russia's hope of conquering the world. We find little today to inspire us in Spain's former splendor or in Napoleon's fallen empire. But the coming kingdom will inspire awe until time shall be no more.

B. God's Invincible Kingdom (145:13)

"Thy kingdom is an everlasting kingdom, and Thy dominion endureth throughout all generations." The expression, "an everlasting kingdom," is literally, " a kingdom for all ages."

That kingdom was here on earth in *modesty* in David's day. David's kingdom was a modest portrayal of God's kingdom. God is one day going to give Jesus "the throne of His father David." David was a true shepherd-king, a sovereign pastor of the people of God, a man with a heart for the flock, and, despite all his faults and failings, a man after God's own heart. David's modest portrayal of the kingdom was given even greater portrayal in the days of Solomon. Thus it is that both David and Solomon are types of Christ. When Jesus comes He will reign first as David to subdue all His foes, and then as Solomon as the prince of peace.

The kingdom was here in *ministry* in the days of the Lord Jesus. When His enemies offered Him the supreme insult, suggesting that His power was that of Beelzebub, He replied, "If I by Beelzebub cast out devils, by whom do your children cast them out? . . . But if I cast out devils by the spirit of God, then the kingdom of God is come unto you" (Matthew 12:27-28). The King was rejected, however, and the tangible kingdom postponed.

The kingdom is here in *mystery* today as the so-called "mystery parables" of Matthew 13 make clear. Truth concerning the kingdom was concealed from the unsaved at the same time it was revealed to the disciples. Jesus said, "It is given unto you to know the mysteries of the kingdom of heaven, but to them it is not known." All attempts to bring in the kingdom by law and legislation will fail. It is not to be established that way. It will not be visibly established at all in this age. It is in mystery.

The kingdom will be here in *majesty* when Christ comes back. It will then be set up in power and great glory. It is a kingdom for all ages. Eventually it will be transferred from earth to heaven and will then run on for all eternity "a kingdom for all ages."

David now picks up his fourth theme:

IV. God's Government (145:14-17)

What a marvelous government the government of God will be. It will have two great foundation stones. It will be:

A. Based on True Kindness (145:14)

"The Lord upholdeth all that fall, and raiseth up all those that be bowed down." David knew all about that. Few people have ever fallen so badly as he. Few have ever been so bowed down by a greater burden of guilt, contrition, and shame. Yet God had picked him up.

What a great day it will be for suffering humanity when at last there is set up on earth a kingdom based on kindness, the kindness Jesus never wearied of showing to the fallen.

B. Based on True Kingliness (145:15-17)

It will be marked by:

1. Absolute Impartiality (145:15-16)

"The eyes of all wait upon Thee; and Thou givest them meat in due season. Thou openest Thine hand, and satisfiest the desire of every living thing." There will be no respect of persons. Everyone will be treated in the same way. As the Old Testament prophet puts it, every man will sit under his own fig tree and his own vine. There will be bread enough and to spare. All people will be wealthy and have need of nothing. Not a single person will be neglected in the daily ministration. Those living near the palace of the King in Jerusalem and those living on the remotest ranges of the high Andes will be treated in the same just way. The Lord will satisfy the desire of every living thing. No longer will people drink from muddy streams and broken cisterns. No longer will there be poverty and want. Everybody will find everything in Him.

2. Absolute Impeccability (145:17)

"The LORD is righteous in all His ways, and holy in His works." It will be the same with the administration of justice as with the apportionment of resources: God will have no favorites. In His government there will no longer be one law for the rich, another for the poor; one set of standards for the rulers, another for the ruled. There will be no executive privilege or diplomatic immunity. There will be no loopholes in the law. Everything will be impeccable.

David concludes by singing of:

V. GOD'S GRACE (145:18-21)

A. How God's Grace Is Reviewed (145:18-20a)

1. How Approachable God Is (145:18)

"The LORD is nigh unto all them that call upon Him . . . in truth." So often this world's false religions portray God as remote and unapproachable. Or, if He is to be approached at all, it must be through a privileged priestly caste that has some special knowledge, sanctity, or office. "Nonsense!" says David. "God is approachable." Thus, when Jesus came as God manifest in flesh, He was the most approachable of men. Even in the Old Testament, when God enthroned Himself behind the veil, it was not so that He could not be approached at all but that He might be approached on His terms.

Now we have an open invitation to "come boldly unto the throne of grace" (Hebrews 4:16). The New Testament ends with the ringing of the changes on that great word *come!*

2. How Appealing God Is (145:19-20a)

"He will fulfil the desire of them that fear Him [that is, He *satisfies*]; He will hear their cry, and will save them [that is, He *saves*]; the LORD preserveth all them that love Him [that is, He *secures*]." What more could we want than that? Where else can be found such a God as this? What an appealing God He is! What terrible lies false religions tell about Him.

B. How God's Grace Is Revoked (145:20b)

"But all the wicked will He destroy." God's marvelous grace is not to be trifled with. Those who "do despite to the Spirit of grace" will find that there is a reverse side to the coin. If God's grace is inscribed magnificently on the one side, His holiness is inscribed on the other. God never allows His grace to interfere with His government, any more than He allows His government to interfere with His grace. He holds the two in perfect balance. Noah "found grace" in the eyes of the Lord; he and his family found salvation and security in the ark. Those who despised God's grace died in their sins, the inevitable result of their rejection of that grace.

The end of the millennial age will be reminiscent of that. Grace will give way to flaming fire upon all those who thought they could trifle with grace.

C. How God's Grace Is Rhapsodized (145:21)

"My mouth shall speak the praise of the LORD: and let all flesh bless His holy name for ever and ever." David sees his own enthusiasm for God's greatness, goodness, glory, government, and grace spreading out at last to all humankind.

Thus the psalm fittingly ends with everyone praising the Lord. This is the theme toward which all David's hymns have been tending. He invokes all living flesh to praise the Lord. That is to be our occupation throughout eternity. We might just as well get in tune now! The secret is simple. Just think about *Him.*

Psalm 146

GOD CARES

I. TRIUMPH (146:1-2)
  A. Praise Deliberately Provoked (146:1)
  B. Praise Distinctly Promised (146:2)
II. TRUST (146:3-7)
  A. Misplaced Trust (146:3-4)
    1. Subtle Enticement (146:3)
    2. Simple Error (146:4)
  B. Meaningful Trust (146:5-7)
    1. Our Song (146:5)
    2. His Strength (146:6-7)
      a. Strength to Create a Universe (146:6)
      b. Strength to Control a Universe (146:7)
III. TRUTH (146:8-10)
  A. God's Infinite Mercy (146:8a)
  B. God's Inflexible Morality (146:8b-9)
  C. God's Invincible Majesty (146:10)

FIVE HALLELUJAH PSALMS, five great doxologies, bring the Hebrew hymnbook to its close. The organ booms, cymbals clang, trumpets sound, the people sing. Waves of sound roll toward the throne of God. Deep calls unto deep. The silent planet, as C. S. Lewis calls the planet earth, is silent no more.

These five psalms were probably written about the time of the completion of the second temple, completion of the walls of Jerusalem, and reconstitution of the body politic of the newborn nation of Israel. The Septuagint attributes the authorship of Psalms 146 and 147 to the prophets Haggai and Zechariah. If this is so, then these two beginning doxologies would have been sung at the dedication of the new temple.

Before we begin our study of these doxologies it will be helpful to review the sequence of events connected with the rebirth of the state of Israel in post-exile times:

539 On October 29 Cyrus the Persian entered Babylon.
538 Zerubbabel, a prince of the house of Judah, led a contingent of Jews back to the promised land. He was accompanied by Joshua the priest, some Levites, and the heads of the tribes of Judah and Benjamin.
536 In April or May the foundations of the new temple were laid, aided by a grant from Cyrus. The Samaritans asked to help and were rebuffed, whereupon they began to harass the builders. They hired lawyers to misrepresent the Jews at the Persian court. So for sixteen years nothing further was done on the temple. The reigns of the Persian kings Cyrus, Cambyses, and Smerdis came and went, while this sad neglect of the temple continued.
520 Haggai began to exhort the Jews to get on with the temple on August 29. On September 20 work began again. On October 17 Haggai gave further encouragement to the workers. On December 18, in the second year of Darius Hystapses, the prophet gave his final message. In October or November the prophet Zechariah added his voice, encouraging the builders to keep up the good work and enlarging their vision of the future.
519 Tattenai, a Persian governor, wrote to Darius I to challenge what the Jews were doing. Joshua the high priest was symbolically crowned by Zechariah to illustrate the coming of Messiah as a priest-king.
518 The temple was completed and dedicated with pomp and ceremony amid general rejoicing (Ezra 6:14-22), bringing to an end a special captivity of seventy years (Zechariah 1:12; 7:5).

The fact that five doxology psalms close the five books of Psalms and the fact that these five books more or less parallel the five books of Moses lead to the suggestion that each of these five books relates to a book of the Pentateuch. If such a parallel can be drawn, then Psalms 146 and 147 relate to Genesis and to Exodus and the remaining three psalms to Leviticus, Numbers, and Deuteronomy. We can, perhaps, detect a general undercurrent in these psalms to justify the suggestion but it cannot be pressed too far.

Prophetically these psalms anticipate the enthronement of the Lord Jesus amid the praises of all humankind at the beginning of the millennium.

Psalm 146 divides into three parts.

I. TRIUMPH (146:1-2)

A. Praise Deliberately Provoked (146:1)

"Praise ye the LORD. Praise the LORD, O my soul." As has been noted, the expression, "Praise the Lord," is the word *Hallelujah!* These last five psalms have been called double Hallelujah psalms because they begin and end with this note of praise.

The psalmist calls on his soul to *"hallelu* Jah!" *Jah* is an abbreviation of the name Jehovah [Yahweh]. It stands for God as the one who has become our salvation. The first occurrence of the name is in the first song in Scripture (Exodus 15:2). God had just overthrown Pharaoh's regiments in the falling waters of the Red Sea and Moses burst into song: "Jah is my strength and song," he cried out. Jah is the eternal one who inhabits eternity. The first mention of the name links it with redemption and salvation. It occurs forty-nine times in the Old Testament (a significant number, the product of 7 x 7, which suggests the utmost perfection of being).

B. Praise Distinctly Promised (146:2)

"While I live will I praise the LORD [Jehovah]: I will sing praises unto my God [Elohim] while I have any being." A sensible thing to do. The psalmist, having urged us to sing, promises that he will sing himself.

With the completing of the second temple, the repatriated Jews had much to sing about. That temple, as we know, was not so magnificent as the one Solomon had built, but it was to be blessed in a way Solomon's never was. The incarnate Son of the living God would come to that temple, first as a boy of twelve, later as a man with His disciples.

The psalm thus begins on a note of triumph. The singer has things in proper perspective. He knows now what is his supreme task in life: to dedicate himself to praising God.

Next we have:

II. TRUST (146:3-7)

The psalmist thinks of two kinds of trust.

A. Misplaced Trust (146:3)

Millions of people have misplaced trust—trust deposited (often sincerely enough) in the wrong person, the wrong institution, the wrong object. We sometimes hear well-meaning people say, "Just have faith." That is a foolish exhortation.

Faith in what? Faith in whom? Some put their faith in money, but banks fail and there are many things money cannot buy (including happiness and holiness). Some put their faith in politics, but political systems break down because of the limitations of the people who run them or the wrong philosophies they espouse. Some put their faith in religion, but religion apart from Christ is a satanic delusion and leads to a lost eternity. Some put their faith in education, but persons of equal education often differ radically on important issues. Two doctors can examine the the same patient and diagnose different illnesses; two statesmen can weigh the same international situation and recommend opposite policies; two judges can listen to the same evidence and pronounce different verdicts.

Nor can we put our faith implicitly in conscience. When John Huss was burned at the stake, a poor widow brought a faggot of sticks and gave them to the priest in charge of the pyre. She said, "Put them up close, holy father." John Huss said to her, "You must hate me a great deal. What have I done to you or yours that you hate me so?" She said, "You are a heretic. Wood is expensive and I am poor. I cannot afford this bundle of sticks, but to burn a heretic is a good work so I have made the sacrifice." Conscience said to John Huss, "Give your body to be burned." Conscience said to the widow, "Give your bundle to burn him." Conscience alone is a poor thing in which to trust.

Simply to say, "Just have faith," is folly. The psalmist, then, draws our attention to misplaced trust.

1. Subtle Enticement (146:3)

"Put not your trust in princes, nor in the son of man, in whom there is no help." When the repatriated Jews went marching to Zion in the days of Cyrus the Persian, how they must have rejoiced in the patronage and protection of such a powerful king. All was well. Cyrus was on the throne. None could dare to make them afraid. They had the weight of a great world empire to back their cause. What more could they want than that?

By the time the singer wrote this hymn, times had changed. It was not long before the Samaritans were writing insinuating letters to the Persian kings: "Beware of these Jews! They are a troublesome crowd. They intend to fortify Jerusalem so as to raise insurrection against the throne. That is their history. Search the archives and see. Let your history books tell you how much trouble Nebuchadnezzar had with these Jews." Before long the Persians had second thoughts about letting the Jews continue with any more building, and orders were issued for the work to stop (Ezra 4).

So much for putting one's trust in princes. Modern Jews had a similar experience with Great Britain. During World War I, a grateful British government (deeply indebted to a Jewish chemist, Chaim Weizmann, for aid which saved the empire from certain defeat) issued the famous Balfour Declaration. It pledged itself to aid the Jews in establishing a national home in Palestine once the war was over. Britain cleared the land of the Turks, brought their disastrous misrule to a well-deserved end, received a mandate from the League of Nations, and began to fulfill her pledge.

Zionists rejoiced. All was well. They had the backing of a great world power. But things went wrong. Britain had other interests in the Middle East: interests in Arab oil, interests in maintaining a strong and determined presence in this strategic area of the world. Those interests soon ran counter to British interest in aiding the Jews to build again the walls of Zion. When Arab protests began to escalate, Britain changed her mind. Idealism was all very well, but Britain needed oil and she needed to keep the lines of empire open. Those lines ran down through the Suez Canal, embraced the Gulf of Aden, the Persian Gulf, and half a dozen Arab emirates. So, after an initial influx of Jews into the promised land, the mandate broke down. Great Britain, in the end, became an obstacle to the Jews.

The temptation to lean on the arm of princes is always there: to trust in the one at the top, the one with the money, the one who makes decisions, the one who makes promises, the one with the right connections. We are all guilty of it. So stubborn is our native unbelief that we find it hard to trust in God alone.

In Jeremiah's drawn-out wail over the destruction and desolation of Jerusalem, he cried, "Our eyes as yet failed for our vain help: in our watching we have watched for a nation that could not save us" (Lamentations 4:17). The situation in Judah was desperate. Nebuchadnezzar's armies were on the march. The prophet Jeremiah urged those in authority to surrender because the Babylonian invasion was of God. Instead, high policy dictated trusting in Egypt. Egypt looked so strong, such a dependable ally. But such trust was in vain. God was not in alliance with Egypt.

2. Simple Error (146:4)

"His breath goeth forth, he returneth to his earth; in that very day his thoughts perish." That is why it is vain to put one's trust in "princes." The word *earth* here is *adamah,* not the usual word for earth, but one that directs our thoughts back to Adam. No wonder there is no help in man. Man is made of the earth, a creation of clay. He has no enduring strength; his thoughts and plans perish with him.

God, indeed, may direct us at times to man, but that is quite a different matter. Then we will be looking to man, not instead of to God but because of God.

Having discussed misplaced trust, the psalmist describes:

B. Meaningful Trust (146:5-7)

1. Our Song (146:5)

"Happy is he that hath the God [El] of Jacob for his help, whose hope is in the LORD his God." The name *El* denotes God in all His strength and power, God the almighty. The psalmist describes Him here as "the God of Jacob." He is the God who met Jacob at Bethel when he was a fugitive from Esau, when he deserved nothing but God's judgment for his sin and unprincipled behavior. Now Jacob was going to pin his hopes on his Uncle Laban, in whom indeed there was no help. God met him there at Bethel and promised him everything. That is the kind of God He is. With El, the God of Jacob in whom to trust, no wonder we should be happy.

Haggai stirred up the people to get busy with the building of the temple, using a plea similar to that of the psalmist: "Ye looked for much, and lo, it came to little; and when ye brought it home, I did blow upon it" (Haggai 1:9). God will not let us look elsewhere for our help. Haggai sought to get the people to look to the Lord: "For thus saith the LORD of hosts, 'Yet once, it is a little while, and I will shake the heavens, and the earth, and the sea, and the dry land; and I will shake all nations and the desire of all nations shall come' " (Haggai 2:6-7).

Our attention is drawn also to:

2. His Strength (146:6-7)

a. God has strength to *create a universe:* "Which made heaven, and earth, the sea, and all that therein is." Imagine the folly of trusting to some puny man, when we are invited to trust such a God as this. We have a God who can orbit galaxies, a God who can make or move mountains with equal ease, a God who can swirl seas in their basins as though they were a few pints of water in a pail. We have a God who can do the impossible, a God who can make galactic empires out of nothing.

When Pasteur conducted his famous experiment to prove to

his peers the law of biogenesis—that there is no life without antecedent life—he held up a sterile test tube and said, "I beg life to appear, I implore it to rise from nothing, life however humble or minute. What do I get? Nothing!" The Bible does not begin with the statement, "In the beginning nothing"; it begins with the statement, "In the beginning God." That makes all the difference.

When we pray, we are not addressing our prayers to empty space, to nothing; we are addressing our prayers to God. Just because He is invisible and inaudible does not mean He is not there. He *is* there. And He is there in omnipotent power and infinite love.

b. Then, too, we have a God with the strength to *control a universe:* "Which executeth judgment for the oppressed: which giveth food to the hungry. The Lord looseth the prisoners" (146:7). God allows nothing to get out of hand. God can control heavenly bodies and human beings with equal ease. He can curb the power of princes.

Israel had recently seen that fact demonstrated to the full. True, the Babylonians had sacked Jerusalem, burned the temple, reduced the walls to rubble, and deported God's people— but that was of God, God's punishment for persistent apostasy and rebellion. If the Jews had abided by the terms of God's covenants no invader could have crossed their frontiers. But God knew where to draw the line with empires. Decades before the first Medo-Persian storm troops donned their armor to invade Chaldea, God had said, "Yet seventy years and Babylon shall be overthrown."

God knew how to control the Persians too. When He wanted His temple rebuilt He had a Cyrus ready to issue the decree. Nor could any Persian potentate, no matter how powerful he looked, prevent that temple being built. The nations are a drop in the bucket to God, something worth thinking about in a world menaced by the superpowers' military arsenals.

So, then, the psalmist sets before us a contrast, misplaced trust and meaningful trust, and urges us to put our trust in God.

III. Truth (146:8-10)

We are given three final glimpses of God. We are shown:

A. God's Infinite Mercy (146:8a)

"The Lord openeth the eyes of the blind: the Lord raiseth them that are bowed down." God is not so preoccupied with such concerns as creating nebulae and curbing nations to be too busy for us. Does He care if I am sick? Does it matter to Him if I am hungry? Of course! His wisdom and power are not divorced from His compassion and love. He loves people. That was dem onstrated in the life of the Lord Jesus, who came to seek the lost, to heal the sick, to raise the dead, and, above all, to die, that heaven's gates might be opened for all humankind. We have a God of infinite mercy.

B. God's Inflexible Morality (146:8b-9)

"The LORD loveth the righteous: the LORD preserveth the strangers [the alien]; He relieveth the fatherless and widow: but the way of the wicked He turneth upside down." We are living in a lawless world where sin and death reign. All too often wickedness and injustice, oppression and crime, have their way—so that it is not always easy to trace God's overruling providence. We have to trust Him where we cannot trace Him. In the end, however, right always triumphs and wrong reaps the due reward of its deeds. The final settling of mankind's moral accounts is not always in our history books. The fact remains that God loves the righteous and turns the way of the wicked upside down.

C. God's Invincible Majesty (146:10)

"The LORD shall reign for ever, even thy God, O Zion, unto all generations. Praise ye the LORD." This last stanza of the psalm transports the feeble Jewish remnant, clapping their hands and singing at the dedication of their new temple, from the setting of their own day and age and sets them down in the millennial age, in Zion, the beautiful city of God. We see them amid scenes of splendor in the courtyard of that temple of which the exiled prophet Ezekiel wrote, a temple far more splendid than Solomon's. "Praise ye the Lord!" the psalmist urges. The temple recently built by the repatriated minority of Jews in a desolate city, surrounded by jealous foes, was a reminder that God is still on the throne and that His purposes can never fail.

Psalm 147

THE GOODNESS OF GOD

L IKE THE PRECEDING ONE, this psalm seems to be linked to the ministry of Haggai and Zechariah. It appears to have been used in the dedication of the second temple. This psalm seems to echo the prophet Zechariah, whose visions were of much greater scope and were much more apocalyptic than those of his colleague. It also echoes the Exodus. We can detect in it reminiscences of God's mastery over the elements which devastated Egypt in the days of Moses. We hear echoes of God's scorn of horses and chariots, the super-weapons of the pharaoh and of the warrior nations of the ancient world.

The psalmist strikes eight notes in this psalm, an octave of praise.

I. God and His Praise (147:1)

A. The Psalmist's Appeal (147:1a)

"Praise ye the Lord." We have so much for which to be thankful that our lives should be an anthem of praise. It is when we get our eyes off the Lord and get taken up with our own petty problems, when we neglect prayer and praise, that our lives lose their luster and our souls lose their song.

B. The Psalmist's Appreciation (147:1b)

Praise never arises from a vacuum. The singer says we are to praise, "for it is good to sing praises unto our God; for it is pleasant; and praise is comely." The psalmist appreciated the fact that praise of God is the appropriate response of intelligent people toward the might, majesty, and mercy of God. Some time ago I took part in a conference with a pastor from North Carolina, a man of some repute in his area as a preacher. It was a delight to preach with this brother because he so obviously and thoroughly enjoyed not only his own preaching, but everyone else's too. He would sit on the front row beaming when someone else was preaching. Every once in awhile he would jump to his feet, point an enthusiastic finger at the preacher, and say, "I like that, Doc! I like that!" His enthusiasm was infectious. Praise, says the psalmist, is good! It is pleasant! It is comely!

II. God and His Pity (147:2-3)

Again the psalmist strikes two notes. He thinks of:

A. Israel's Broken Home Being Rebuilt (147:2)

"The Lord doth build up Jerusalem: He gathereth together the outcasts of Israel." Haggai's great complaint was that the people were too busy building their own homes to be bothered about rebuilding the temple. Now that the temple had been rebuilt, this psalmist saw what Zechariah saw: Jerusalem being rebuilt, this time by the Lord. The outcasts of Israel had come home—at least, some of them had. The psalmist believed that completion of the temple would prompt a greater ingathering of the exiles.

It is here, of course, that Zechariah's apocalyptic visions come in. Zechariah saw the angel of the Lord (the Lord in one of His pre-incarnate forms) standing amid the myrtle trees to receive the reports of four horsemen. He was told that the nations were at rest. The fact that Jerusalem and the Jewish people were in distress did not trouble them at all. Zechariah then saw four horns, symbolic of the four world powers (perhaps Assyria, Babylon, Greece, and Rome) responsible for scattering the Jewish people. Then four carpenters appeared. These were God's agents employed by Him to whittle the arrogant Gentile super powers down to size and to frighten the complacent nations into a realization that there could be no peace for the world until there was peace for Israel and Jerusalem. Next Zechariah saw a man with a measuring rod preparing to size up Jerusalem. The man was told, however, that the Jerusalem of the future would not be circumscribed by walls, nor would the city need protec tion from its foes. Finally Zechariah heard the Lord challenge those Jews who had settled down comfortably in the lands of their dispersion (Zechariah 1–2).

Zechariah's prophecies skillfully touched on the state of affairs in his day, but they were also apocalyptic. They looked forward to just such days as those in which we live. Again the Jews have gone back; again their temple remains unbuilt; again the majority of Jews prefer the comforts of the far-flung lands of their adoption to the rigors of the war-threatened land of Israel; again the nations have scant sympathy for Israel's needs or little concern to see that the Jews are settled in the promised land, and even less interest in seeing Jerusalem established as Israel's capital. Zechariah's vision of the enlargement of Jerusalem is already a fact today. The world superpowers will one day be whittled down to size in the apocalyptic judgments following the rapture of the church. Zechariah was a true prophet. The nations, so careless of Isarel's welfare, will be punished. Here the psalmist echoes the prophecies of Zechariah.

B. Israel's Broken Heart Being Revived (147:3)

"He healeth the broken in heart, and bindeth up their wounds." Go back in thought again to those distant days when the singer lived. When the foundations of the second temple were laid, the older Jews wept. They thought of the vanished splendors of Solomon's temple, splendors they could never hope to emulate (Ezra 3:10-13). Balm poured into their wounded hearts, however, when the prophet Haggai promised that the glory of this second temple would greatly exceed the glory of Solomon's. His temple had to make do with the symbolic Shekinah presence; the second temple would be graced by the person of the Christ Himself (Haggai 2:3-4, 7).

III. God and His Power (147:4-6)

The psalmist now turns his thoughts to God's ability and willingness to act on behalf of His own. He contemplates:

A. The Greatness of God's Comprehension (147:4-5)

1. Its Exactness (147:4)

We have a God who *numbers the stars*: "He telleth the number of the stars" (147:4a). That is something we human beings cannot do. The word *telleth* is the Old English word for counting (still used in banking circles; the person who counts money at the counter is called a teller). Only God can count the stars. The best we can do is make estimates—and these vary and are constantly being revised. Astronomers tell us there are a hundred billion stars in our galaxy, that there are a hundred million galaxies in known space, and that known space is only one billionth of theoretical space.

Estimates like those make our heads whirl. But God has an exact count. He knows how many there are, where they are, where they came from, and where they are bound. There is not a speck of dust in cosmic space for which He does not know its full history. A star is born. It grows old and explodes. He knows. That is omniscience, God's mind.

We have a God who *names the stars:* "He calleth them all by their names." We do have names for some of them. But we are far too finite to name them all, so we end up giving them numbers. God, however, names them each one.

2. Its Extent (147:5)

"Great is our Lord, and of great power: His understanding is infinite." God understands all about us and our circumstances, feelings, hopes, yearnings, ambitions. He understands us better than we understand ourselves. Better still, His omniscient perception is linked to His omnipotent power. The word for "Lord" is *Adonim,* which has to do with God as Lord and ruler of earth, God as the one who blesses His people. This thought is emphasized by the use of the pronoun *our*—"Great is our Lord." God makes use of His infinite knowledge to look out for His own, as the next verse emphasizes.

B. The Greatness of God's Compassion (147:6)

"The LORD lifteth up the meek: He casteth the wicked down to the ground." Jesus said, "The meek shall inherit the earth," and so they will. This verse is thus not only pragmatic, it is prophetic. We tend to equate meekness with weakness, whereas in fact it is strength expressed in self-control. Often people take advantage of meekness, as the children of Israel did of the meekness of Moses. God, however, vindicates the meek in the end. His heart goes out to them. He will rescue them from the tyranny of the wicked.

IV. GOD AND HIS PROVIDENCE (147:7-9)

The singer expands on this idea of God using His wisdom and power in love for His own. He says that God's providential dealings:

A. Should Make Us Thankful (146:7)

"Sing unto the LORD with thanksgiving: sing praise upon the harp unto our God." We should summon song and skill to praise God. Our vocal expressions of joy can be amplified with instrumental accompaniment. This is the first hint, in these closing doxologies, of the use of musical instruments to add an extra dimension to praise. By the time we reach the last psalm the whole orchestra will be involved. In the meantime, accompaniment on one instrument was quite acceptable to God.

Also thoughts of God's providence:

B. Should Make Us Thoughtful (147:8-9)

"Who covereth the heaven with clouds, who prepareth rain for the earth, who maketh grass to grow upon the mountains. He giveth to the beast his food, and to the young ravens which cry." How much we depend on rain. Without it grass does not grow, crops do not germinate. Nor can we do much, even with all our scientific knowledge, to make it rain. We can seed the clouds, but what if there are no clouds? Enormous amounts of water are drawn up into the sky every day from the world's oceans. Mighty currents and winds move these cloudy masses northward and southward toward the continents. With invariable laws to govern it all, the clouds discharge their contents on the thirsty farms and forests below. And these vast engineering works of God move so smoothly, so efficiently, that we scarcely notice them.

Indeed there is nothing we grumble more about than the weather, which should be one of our greatest themes of praise. We scarcely think of the celestial machinery that underlies the laws of evaporation and precipitation. We scarcely give God a thought in all of this until He sends a drought to remind us how vulnerable we are. As the psalmist says, this should make us very thoughtful.

V. GOD AND HIS PLEASURE (147:10-11)

The psalmist now turns to discuss what pleases (and displeases) God. He shows us first the negative, then the positive. He speaks of:

A. What Disinterests God (147:10)

"He delighteth not in the strength of the horse: He taketh not pleasure in the legs of a man." God takes no delight in military might (as symbolized by the strength of a horse) or in marching armies (as symbolized by the legs of a man). God is not impressed by big battalions. Egypt had its famed horses and its mobilized troops, but God ambushed them all in the Red Sea. He knocked off the wheels of the stylish, swift-moving war chariots (we can well imagine that the bed of that sea was no smooth highway) and then summoned the thundering seas to return to their proper bed.

God takes no delight in war. He will use it as a scourge to whip wicked nations, but He takes no pleasure in it. So much of human history is taken up with the pomp and pageantry of parading warriors and the proud display of weapons of war. God is not impressed.

The armed might of Babylon and Persia could not keep Israel captive when God's clock struck the hour for its emancipation. When God's prophet said to the repatriated Jews, "Build!" the Persians could not mobilize sufficient men to enforce its countermanding decree, "Don't build!" God simply ignored Persia. He is not impressed at all by the might of the world's superpowers. He needs neither weaponry nor men to enforce His will.

B. What Delights God (147:11)

"The LORD taketh pleasure in them that fear Him, in those that hope in His mercy." The Lord would rather sit down with a small company of His own and listen to a handful of people singing a psalm, however untunefully, than assemble with the princes of this world in their banqueting halls and listen to their boasts and the playing of their bands. He took more pleasure in the company of that little group of His own, gathered in the courts of their rebuilt temple in Jerusalem, than in all the gatherings of the great in Babylon and Persepolis.

Ezra the scribe fills in the details. The repatriated remnant offered seven hundred sacrifices of varying kinds. Then, token company that they were, with many of the northern tribes still scattered and hardly represented, they offered *twelve* he-goats for a sin offering "for all Israel." And, for good measure, they kept the Passover along with the fourteen-day feast of unleavened bread. And it was all done "with joy," as the scribe records (Ezra 6:15-22).

"The Lord taketh pleasure in them," the psalmist adds. They were a company of nobodies. Their service was of no interest to the great world outside. "But the LORD made them joyful," says Ezra. They made Him joyful, too, adds the psalmist. God finds pleasure in the likes of them, and in the likes of us. He comes to our meetings, attends our services, listens to our hynms, delights in our prayers, finds joy in our expressions of praise.

VI. GOD AND HIS PROTECTION (147:12-14)

Just the same, they were a feeble flock, a tiny remnant, and there were plenty of fierce wolves prowling around their fold. The psalmist now takes note of that. He speaks of:

A. The Bulwarks of the Almighty (147:12-13a)

"Praise the LORD, O Jerusalem, praise thy God, O Zion. For He hath strengthened the bars of they gates." If this psalm was written at the dedication of the temple, as some believe, the walls of Jerusalem were still in total disrepair. It was not until Nehemiah came that anything was done about that. So the temple was standing amid a sea of rubble. But God Himself was Israel's protector. He threw Himself, so to speak, as a rampart around His own, around the city where He had put His name. Better than walls of stone were the encircling arms of the living God. His hand, held up at the fallen gates, would keep out any foe better than bars of iron.

B. The Blessing of the Almighty (147:13b-14)

"He hath blessed thy children within thee. He maketh peace in thy borders, and filleth thee with the finest of the wheat." We see the Lord securing *the people* of Jerusalem so that the little ones could grow up under His smile and blessing. We see Him securing *the peace* of Jerusalem so that walls and gates would be little more than a decorative flourish. We see Him securing *the prosperity* of Jerusalem so that barns were filled to overflowing with the produce of the land.

Although all this doubtless applied to those far-off days, these verses also anticipate the coming millennial reign of Christ. We catch here, too, the tones of Zechariah's farsighted words about the future of Jerusalem: "Jerusalem shall be inhabited as towns without walls . . . I . . . will be unto her a wall of fire round about" (Zechariah 2:4-5). That is certainly not the case today, but it will be during the millennium. When, at the end of the millennial age, the massed armies of Satan-deceived men mobilize against Jerusalem, the literal truth of Zechariah's words will be evident as the Lord dissolves the planet in an atomic holocaust, as Peter later describes.

VII. God and His Purposes (147:15-18)

The psalmist turns again to the evidence of nature. He wants us to see God in control of all the factors that make up daily life on earth. For instance, at God's word:

A. Winter Starts (147:15-17)

God acts *swiftly*: "He sendeth forth His commandment upon earth: His word runneth very swiftly" (147:15). He acts *surely:* "He giveth snow like wool: he scattereth the hoarfrost like ashes. He casteth forth His ice like morsels; who can stand before His cold?" (147:16-17). We could well ask that question of Napoleon and of Hitler, both of whom lost whole armies to God's cold on the frozen Russian plains. Winter starts at God's command. He has complete sovereignty over the forces of nature. He uses them for human good and He uses them as weapons of war.

B. Winter Stops (147:18)

"He sendeth out His word, and melteth them: He causeth His wind to blow, and the waters flow." It is *His* word, *His* wind, *His* ice, *His* cold. Let us remember that. If God so desires, He can plunge the planet into another ice age or swathe the world in a blanket of flame. He can hang a rainbow in the sky and command the seasons to come and go in blessing to humankind. We can no more prevent God from working out His purposes than we can change the march of the seasons.

VIII. GOD AND HIS PRECEPTS (147:19-20)

This same God, whose word controls the wind, weather, and waves of the sea, has given His word to His people. The psalmist shows that the possession of that Word is:

A. Israel's Exalted Privilege (147:19)

"He showeth His word unto Jacob, His statutes and His judgments unto Israel." Israel was marked off from other nations by its possession of God's Word, with its precepts and principles, revelations and responsibilities. God gave His Word uniquely to Israel. With no other nation has God made the kind of contractual arrangements He has with Israel. It is true that, during this gospel age, Japheth is dwelling in the tents of Shem, and the Gentiles have entered into the fatness and fullness of the olive tree, but this age of Gentile privilege is to expire soon and Israel will again come into her own. Israel alone has basked in the blessing of an unconditional, constitutional, special-nation status with God.

All this was fresh in the minds of the repatriated exiles of Judah, since Haggai had conveyed God's word to them: "According to the word that I covenanted with you when ye came out of Egypt, so My Spirit remaineth among you" (Haggai 2:5). And again, "Consider now from this day and upward, from the four and twentieth day of the ninth month, even from the day that the foundation of the LORD's temple was laid, consider it . . . from this day will I bless you" (Haggai 2:18-19).

The psalmist says that God gave His word to Jacob, His statutes and judgments to Israel. Jacob is the nation in its feebleness and failure; Israel is the nation in its princely power.

B. Israel's Exclusive Privilege (147:20)

"He hath not dealt so with any other nation: and as for His judgments, they have not known them. Praise ye the LORD." The word *judgments* here is "ordinances." It is true that today God is visiting the nations, but He is doing so to call out a people for His name (Acts 15:14). It is also true that any nation with a large number of Christians is bound to be blessed for their sakes. But Christians themselves are part of a different entity in God's dealings with humankind; they are members of the church, the mystical body of Christ. Their citizenship is in heaven.

For a *nation*, however, to be bound to heaven by a solemn treaty, given by the living God—such is Israel's privilege alone. God has instituted no such treaty with the United States, nor with Great Britain, nor with Germany, France, or Spain. God does not have an embassy in Washington, nor does He have one at Rome. God does not guarantee the defense of our country or any country—except Israel. Nor has God promised to make any city His capital, except Jerusalem. For all that, the psalmist shouted, "Hallelujah!"

Psalm 148

PRAISE HIM ALL CREATURES
GREAT AND SMALL

THIS PSALM IS pure praise. It contains not a single prayer, plea, or petition, only praise. The psalmist warms to his theme. His vision is expanded, his soul soars skyward, he mounts up on eagle's wings. He calls on all those high in glory to praise the Lord. He calls on all those here on earth to praise

Him. Animate and inanimate, pure spirit and human being, all alike are summoned to sing.

I. PRAISE HIM! HIGH IN THE GLORY (148:1-6)

The psalmist's thoughts first wing their way upward to the courts of bliss. He tells us:

A. Where God Should Be Praised (148:1-4)

Understandably, the psalmist feels that praise ought to begin where God is pleased to make His home. Praise should begin with the realms:

1. Where the Spirits Reside (148:1-2)

"Praise ye the LORD. Praise ye the LORD from the heavens: praise Him in the heights. Praise ye Him, all His angels; praise ye Him, all His hosts." It seems almost impertinent of the psalmist to summon the seraphim to sing, for a mortal man to tell the hosts of heaven their duty. How dare he command to sing those high and lofty ones who surround the throne of God, who dwell forever in His presence, who awake the echoes of the everlasting hills? It would be the height of impertinence, too, if it were merely a man so admonishing the angelic hosts. But this is a man filled with the Spirit of God. This is not just a Hebrew harpist speaking; this is the Holy Spirit speaking.

If only we could borrow Jacob's ladder. If only we could climb that shining staircase and scale those awesome heights. If only we could tread the streets of gold. If only we could stand before the throne of God. Then we would see how gloriously the seraphim sing. They sing with faces aglow, with happy hearts, with tireless zeal, in perfect harmony, in endless song. All heaven resounds with the music of the hosts on high. "Praise Him, all ye angels!" They do. Hasn't Job told us that when God laid the foundations of the earth, mapped its measurements, stretched His line upon it, and put down its cornerstones, "the morning stars sang together, and all the sons of God shouted for joy" (Job 38:7)? God's wisdom and power, manifested in the creating of the universe and in the making of our planet, furnished the angels of God with ample themes for praise.

They saw a shapeless void swirling through the darkness. They saw sullen seas washing this planet from pole to pole. Then light burst upon it and the thick clouds rolled away. The sun shone. Continents and archipelagoes and islands by the score emerged from beneath the billows, rolling back the seas, raising lofty peaks, burying snow-capped heads in swirling masses of cloud.

Then life came. Green grass, fragrant herbs, and all kinds of bushes and trees appeared to mantle the earth with green. In the deep seas, life arose in myriad forms, in unimaginable prodigality. All kinds of fish and marine creatures flung themselves through the surging seas. On the earth other creatures arose, to fly and swarm and multiply and fill the earth with music from the treetops to the clouds. Land animals appeared to roam the virgin forests, to bound across the pristine plains. And last of all man was made, in the image and likeness of God, lord of creation, king of the earth.

The angels saw it all and sang around the throne of God: "Thou art worthy, O LORD, for Thou hast created all things" (Revelation 4:11). And still they sing, making merry music of it all, celebrating in celestial anthems God's omniscient genius and omnipotent power. How often has the beauty of a sunset or the splendor of the sea wakened our own wonder and praise. How much more then the praise of those who saw it all begin.

"Praise ye Him, *all* His hosts!" the psalmist says. The angelic throngs are not the only ones who crowd the mansions in the sky. God has already begun to populate heaven with the redeemed. They, too, have a song to sing.

God's wisdom and power are the theme of angels' song, a magnificent theme, illustrated in flaming suns and endless galaxies carpeting the blackness of the sky. Theirs indeed is a great song, but our song is greater far. Our song celebrates not just God's wisdom and power, but the amazing mysteries of His grace, the fathomless oceans of His love.

To display His wisdom and power God merely had to *create;* to manifest His love He had to *redeem.* To do the one He simply had to *speak;* to do the other He had to *suffer.* So, on the other side of Jordan, God has a redeemed people. They, too, are summoned to sing. Over there the "spirits of just men made perfect" see Him as He is and praise Him as they ought.

God is to be praised where the spirits reside. He is also to be praised:

2. Where the Stars Revolve (148:3)

"Praise ye Him, sun and moon: praise Him, all ye stars of light." The sun praises Him simply by shining in the sky, a reminder to those on earth of the blinding glory of God. It praises Him with such a shining face that we cannot look at it with the naked eye. It praises Him with such warmth that its smile melts winter snows. It praises Him with such infectious delight that a family of planets whirls and dances about it in rhythmic patterns of orbital bliss.

The moon praises Him. Astronomers tell us that the moon is dead. But dead or alive, it praises God. It praises Him by reflecting the light of the sun. Since it has no light of its own, it borrows the light of another and flashes that to earth to brighten the dark corners of our planet. It praises Him by waxing and waning, by tugging on the tides, by awakening poetic thoughts in people's hearts.

The stars praise Him. He stokes their enormous fires with reservoirs of energy. They praise Him for that. They praise Him for giving them such freedom of movement, freedom to pursue journeys through intangible space, through distances that stagger and bewilder human thought. They praise Him because, vast as their freedom is, they are not left to wander on aimless journeys; their paths are ordained for them. They praise Him because in their inimitable way they can testify, "The hand that made us is divine."

So, God is to be praised where the stars revolve. Coming closer to home, the psalmist says that God is to be praised:

3. Where the Sky Reigns (148:4)

"Praise Him, ye heavens of heavens, and ye waters that be above the heavens." High above our heads, suspended in space, are vast oceans of water that roll majestically across the sky in ever-changing patterns. Now their billows are congregated together in vast battalions; now they bring up their artillery and thunder and roar out their praise; now the lightnings flash, blazing out their message of splendor. The lightning flash, the thunder's roar—these are nature's way of praising God in the skies. Then the clouds open up and down comes the rain to bless the parched regions of the earth as the sky weeps for joy and paints the rainbow arch across the heavens to remind us that it has not forgotten its creator's decrees.

The heavens praise Him for the fact that once they were permitted to wrap themselves around His form when He, the ascending Son of God, set His face toward the New Jerusalem. They rejoice too at the thought that one day they will do that at His return. "Behold, He cometh with clouds!" cried John in commencing the apocalypse.

So the psalmist tells us where God should be praised, He should be praised everywhere and by everything. Next he tells us:

B. Why God Should Be Praised (148:5-6)

The psalmist gives two reasons why God should be praised in all places and at all times.

1. He Originated All Things (148:5)

"Let them praise the name of the LORD: for He commanded, and they were created" (148:5). The word *them* refers to spirits, stars, and skies. He created all of them, each in its order and time, each for its purpose and place, each created to hymn His praise.

The highest archangel in glory did not make himself. The most splendid seraph that sings, the chief of the cherubim, the lordliest of the sons of light, did not make himself. God made him. To praise Him is the highest end and joy of all the angel hosts. It is their highest security as well.

One of their number once forgot to praise. He took his eyes off the creator and became infatuated with himself. He had been given splendor greater than all others in the celestial hierarchy. He had been endowed with vast gifts and abilities. When he stopped praising God he sealed his doom; when he stopped praising he started plotting. Then he involved others of his glorious kind and they stopped singing too. Soon the standards of rebellion were unfurled. It was not long before Lucifer, son of the morning, the bright and morning star, the choirmaster of heaven, was hurled headlong from the heights and transformed into Satan, a serpent, the great dragon, a fallen fiend.

The psalmist summons the heavenly orders to praise God because He is their creator. They should praise Him as a reminder to themselves that between Him and them a great gulf is fixed, the gulf that divides the creature from the creator, the finite from the infinite. Praising Him serves to remind them that their powers are limited; His are limitless. They are creatures of time. He is eternal, uncreated, self-existing, God over all, blessed forevermore.

They should praise God also because:

2. He Ordains All Things (148:6)

"He hath also stablished them for ever and ever: He hath made a decree which shall not pass." He has set the bounds of their being. He has set the bounds of the *skies,* which have their function in relation to earth as long as time lasts in accordance with the decrees of the Noahic covenant (Genesis 9:9-17). He has set the bounds of the *stars* which, He has said, shall in the end wax old like a worn-out garment (Psalm 102:25-26). He has set the bounds of the *spirits* which, though almost deathless in their nature, are ordained their place in the order of things and are His servants sent to minister to those who are the heirs of salvation.

The reference to "the decree" here carries with it an echo from the experiences of the returned remnant of Israel. Cyrus the Persian had issued a decree. Under its provisions the Jews were given freedom to return to the promised land. There they were to rebuild a temple for their God (Ezra 1:1-4; 6:3). Then Darius made a decree to stop the building of that temple (Ezra 4:17-24). The Jews, however, referred him to the decree of Cyrus (Ezra 5:13-15), a decree he was bound to honor according to the laws of the Medes and Persians which allowed no alteration (Daniel 6:8). Thereupon the Persian king made another decree and a search was to be made of the Persian records (Ezra 6:1). When the original decree was discovered, the Persian emperor reversed his own wrongful decree and issued yet another one commanding the enemies of the Jews to stop hindering them and he himself diverted funds from the imperial treasury to their aid (Ezra 6:8).

So much for human decrees. God's decrees, by contrast, are beyond question or challenge. Such, then, is the psalmist's opening theme; God is to be praised high in the glory. All the heavenly realms are to unite in praising Him. In cloudland, in starland, and in gloryland, all His works must praise Him. The psalmist now comes down to earth.

II. PRAISE HIM! HERE ON THIS GLOBE (148:7-14)

A. The Psalmist Views Our Planet (14:7-10)

He looks here, there, and everywhere, summoning all things to unite in praising the living God. His eye takes in:

1. The Restless Sea (148:7)

"Praise the LORD from the earth, ye dragons, and all deeps." The word *dragons* can better be translated "sea monsters." The denizens of the deep are to praise Him, the strange creatures that haunt the subterranean caves in the recesses of the sea. Scientists say that marine life is the oldest life on earth. Certainly the last frontier man has attempted to subdue is the sea. Its depths are so dark, its pressures so enormous, its perils so awesome, that it has defied us until now. All we know for sure is that down there, where man could not survive for a moment, strange forms of life live and move and have their being in a world alien to man. There are giant squid, man-eating sharks, enormous whales, and creatures whose lifestyles are as remote from us as though they lived in some science-fiction world.

Can the denizens of the deep praise Him? We have to think only of that creature that arrested Jonah, the disobedient prophet, and held him captive in "the belly of hell" until such time as God commanded it to restore the chastened human to the world of living human beings.

We think, too, of the little fish that found and kept a coin, just sufficient to pay the Lord's taxes, and Peter's—and which, at a word from its creator, took hold of Peter's line and delivered the money to him. Or we think of those multitudes of fish which hurled themselves headlong into Simon Peter's nets at a word from their Lord. Obedience to His slightest wish was their way of expressing their praise to Him.

2. The Raging Storm (148:8)

"Fire, and hail; snow, and vapors; stormy wind fulfilling His word." The summer storm with its lightning and hail, the winter storm with its fog and snow: both fulfill His word and thus offer Him praise. The stormy wind fulfills His will. The cyclone that whips the waves into a fury, the tornado that marches in terrible power across the summer plains, the hurricane and the gale howling across land and sea: all are giving voice to their creator's praise.

So the raging storm praises Him. The elements that make what we call bad weather are simply praising God by obeying the laws of nature which He, in infinite wisdom, has decreed. They obey His voice. Thus it was that when a mighty rushing wind swept down from the hills to turn a placid lake into a storm-tossed sea, when He arose and said, "Be still!"—instantly there was a great calm. Heaving wave and howling wind subsided at a word from Him. That storm was intended simply to demonstrate the incarnate creator's absolute power even over nature's fiercest forces. "Even the winds and the sea obey Him!" said the disciples as they gazed on Him in awe (Matthew 8:27).

3. The Rocky Steeps (148:9a)

"Mountains, and all hills." They are to praise Him too. The Himalayas, Rocky Mountains, and Alps raise their heads and point skyward in eloquent praise. The architects of the world's greatest cathedrals copied them and devised the spire as a silent finger to catch the eye and turn it away from earth, away from the gorgeous cathedral itself, away from the mundane things of time and sense, up and up until, leaving behind even the point of the spire itself, the eye continues upward to God's home on high. Hills and mountains likewise draw the eye of the beholder up their crags and awesome heights to the heavens above.

4. The Rural Scene (148:9b-10)

a. The psalmist looks at earth's *flora:* "Fruitful trees, and all cedars." They are to praise Him: the fruit trees with bowed heads, heavy with produce, praising God for loading them down with so many benefits; the stately cedars, king of the trees of the wood, waving far-flung branches in an ecstasy of praise. The one kind of tree praises God by producing fruit fit for a prince; the other praises God by producing wood fit for a palace.

b. The psalmist looks at earth's *fauna:* "Beasts, and all cattle; creeping things, and flying fowl." The brute creation is to praise God, wild animal and domesticated beast, the serpent gliding through the grass, the eagle soaring upward or hurtling from the heights. The lion is to praise Him, stalking with majesty through the scrub; the cattle on a thousand hills are to praise Him. Even the creeping things are to praise Him, the insect creation in their millions of kinds. The cricket chirping on the hearth, the ant colonizing the earth, the bee storing up its golden treasures in the hive, the spider taking hold in king's palaces—all are to praise Him according to the limits of their varied lives. All have a place in the scheme of things. All have a voice with which to praise.

B. The Psalmist Views All Peoples (148:11-14)

1. The Heathen (148:11-14)

All the world's Gentile tribes are to praise the living God. We notice:

a. The Call to Praise (148:11-12)

First and foremost, *this world's sovereigns* are to praise God: "Kings of the earth, . . . princes, and all judges of the earth" (148:11). Everyone in authority is commanded to praise Him because, as Paul reminds us, "the powers that be are ordained of God" (Romans 13:1). He is the one who sets up this king or puts down that ruler. The last lesson this world's princes and politicians want to learn is that all authority is delegated authority, held in trust from God, with accountability ultimately being to God. The highest function of those in power is to lead people in the praise and worship of the living God and to set an example of godliness in character, conduct, and career.

God had to teach Nebuchadnezzar that lesson. After his humiliating experience of insanity, the proud Babylonian king came to a realization of the divine responsibility of kings. He said, "Now I Nebuchadnezzar praise and extol and honor the King of heaven, all whose works are truth . . ." (Daniel 4:37). It is a good thing for a nation when it has leaders who take the lead in praising God.

Then all *this world's subjects* are to praise the Lord: "Both young men and maidens; old men, and children." Men and woman, old and young, all should praise Him: little ones, with warm, open, responsive hearts, should learn to sing His praise; young people with all the strength of their zeal and idealism should praise Him; old people, with all the wealth of their maturity, experience, and knowledge should praise Him.

Such is the call to praise. All peoples in all lands are called on to unite heart and mind and voice in giving praise to God.

b. The Cause for Praise (148:13)

"Let them praise the name of the LORD: for His name alone is excellent; His glory is above the earth and heaven." God is not content when people make vague reference to "providence." Prayers in state legislatures and parliaments are inadequate if made merely to "God." Compromises that accommodate the world's false religions will not do. God has a name. In the Old Testament He was known as Jehovah; in the New Testament He is to be addressed in the name of Jesus. The psalmist insists that prayer be made to the name of the Lord. In other words, the prayers of the nations are not to be made to Allah or Buddha, but to the true and living God of the Bible and in the saving name of Jesus. There is no avoiding this. Anything less is not praise, but compromise.

Finally, the psalm focuses on:

2. The Hebrews (148:14)

In the psalmist's day, the Hebrews, of all people, had the supreme knowledge of God and enjoyed a unique relationship with Him. They, of all people, should praise Him. The psalmist, then, calls on the Hebrews to praise the Lord for:

a. The Power They Enjoy (148:14a)

"He also exalteth the horn of His People." A horn, in Scripture, symbolizes power. In the book of Daniel and in the book of Revelation, Gentile world rulers are symbolized as wild animals with horns. "The horn" of God's people Israel is the Lord Jesus Himself, the one they presently despise but who will appear, at the end of the battle of Armageddon, with mighty power to rescue them from all their foes.

b. The Privilege They Enjoy (148:14b)

The psalmist speaks of "the praise of all His saints; even of the children of Israel." The word *saints* means "favored ones" or "beloved ones." God has addressed no other nation in such endearing terms.

Last, the psalmist calls on his own people to praise God for:

c. The Position They Enjoy (148:14c)

"A People near unto him. Praise ye the LORD." Although they had wandered far from Him, He had never forsaken them. The rebirth of the nation after the Babylonian captivity was proof of that. Israel held a place close to the heart of God; it still does. The regathering of Israel from the nations in our day, the rebirth of their national life, proclaims God's good hand on this people in all their wanderings down through the long ages of time.

Psalm 149

THE SONG OF THE SWORD

I. THE SONG (149:1-3)
   A. The Theme (149:1a)
   B. The Throng (149:1b-3)
      1. The Great Congregation of Israel Is Assembled (149:1b)
      2. The Great Creator of Israel Is Acclaimed (149:2-3)
         a. O! What a King! (149:2)
         b. O! How We Sing! (149:3)
II. THE SAINTS (149:4-5)
   A. Their Blessing (149:4a)
   B. Their Beauty (149:4b)
   C. Their Bliss (149:5)
III. THE SWORD (149:6-9)
   A. Trusting in That Sword (149:6)
      1. What Must First Be in Our Heart (149:6a)
      2. What May Then Be in Our Hand (149:6b)
   B. Thrusting with That Sword (149:7-9)
      1. In Vengeance (149:7-8)
      2. As Viceroys (149:9)

C HRIST'S SECOND COMING is clearly anticipated in this psalm. We might call it "The Song of the Sword." The first song in Scripture was composed by Lamech, seventh from Adam in the godless line of Cain. Lamech was the great rebel of the antedeluvian world, a man who shook his fist in the face of God and told God to stay out of his life. Moreover, he threatened with dire and swift vengeance anyone who opposed him. He was the world's first polygamist, a man who gloried in his self-will. Lamech embodied the spirit of permissiveness that permeated the days of Noah. Lamech first gave tongue to the anti-God spirit of the age before the flood.

After the flood, God took the sword of the murderer and

687

converted it into the sword of the magistrate. He delivered it into the hands of Noah, proclaiming the principle of capital punishment for the crime of murder: "Whoso sheddeth man's blood, by man shall his blood be shed" (Genesis 9:6). The principle remains in force. The Holy Spirit says of the magistrate that "he beareth not the sword in vain" (Romans 13:4).

Not long after the time of Noah, Nimrod seized the sword of the magistrate and turned it into the sword of the monarch, the sword of the empire-builder, the conqueror, the imperialist, the world ruler (Genesis 10).

The sword symbolizes power. It speaks of war. The rider on the red horse, in the apocalypse, carries a great sword in his hand. One of these days the sword is to be wrested from Gentile hands, from those who have abused the power of which it speaks. It will be given to God's beloved Son, who will wear it on His thigh as the symbol of His right to reign (as we learn from Psalm 45). When John saw the Lord Jesus descending from the sky he saw a great sword coming out of His mouth to destroy all His foes. On His thigh were emblazoned the words KING OF KINGS AND LORD OF LORDS (Revelation 19:16).

This psalm looks forward to that day. We notice:

I. THE SONG (149:1-3)

The song of which the psalmist first speaks draws two things to our attention.

A. The Theme (149:1a)

"Praise ye the LORD. Sing unto the LORD a new song." This is the last of half a dozen "new songs" in the book of Psalms (33:3; 40:3; 96:1; 98:1; 144:9; 149:1). Two of these new songs were written by David; the others are anonymous. Looking elsewhere in the Bible we find that another new song was commanded by God (Isaiah 42:10) and that two new future songs will be sung (in the book of Revelation). One of these is sung by the four and twenty elders to celebrate the taking of the scroll, the title deeds of earth, by the Lord into His capable hands. The last new song will be sung by the 144,000 witnesses in heaven to celebrate their victory over the beast. Invariably the new songs of Scripture anticipate the millennial reign of Christ. This then is the underlying theme of this song.

B. The Throng (149:1b-3)

"And [sing] His praise in the congregation of saints."

1. The Great Congregation of Israel Is Assembled (149:1b)

The word for *congregation* here suggests "a military assembly of favored or beloved ones." Our thoughts go back to that assembly of the Jewish remnant which gathered to celebrate the Passover and to dedicate the new temple with sacrifices and joy after the return from Babylon. A little flock, yet they stood there surrounded by hostile Israel-watchers, Gentile nations. Satan was more afraid of that little gathering of God's dear people than of any other company in the universe. God was on their side.

Ezra records, "And . . . the LORD had made them joyful, and turned the heart of the king of Assyria unto them, to strengthen their hands in the work of the house of God, the God of Israel" (Ezra 6:22). Assyria had once deported them. But where was mighty Assyria now with its fearsome armies and wide domains? Gone. Assyria was now a province in the realm of another Gentile king, one whose heart was as wax in the hands of God.

Our thoughts go back to the days of Nehemiah. He had rebuilt the walls of Jerusalem in a record-breaking fifty-two days. "Now the city was large," says the Holy Spirit, "but the People were few therein" (Nehemiah 7:4). This fact troubled farsighted Nehemiah, who knew that a city, no matter how strong its walls, could not be held against a determined foe if there were not enough men within to fortify its walls. Taking a census, he found that in all the land there were only a scant 42,360 people (Nehemiah 7:66). Truly they were a feeble folk.

But then came Ezra with the book of the law. As God's Word was read to the remnant, there followed a time of heart-searching, confession, and rededication. Out of this came a pledge, or a covenant with God, sealed by the leaders of the little nation: they would repopulate Jerusalem. The walls were then dedicated "with singing, with cymbals, psalteries, and with harps" (Nehemiah 12:27).

Satan feared that little flock, above all because of its resolve, signed and sealed by its leaders, to be true to the book. Satan was strategist enough to know that this little company of believers was the greatest obstacle on earth to his plans. Since he could not conquer these "feeble Jews" (Nehemiah 4:2) he set about corrupting them. He attacked them at their greatest point of strength, their new-found attachment to the Word of God.

According to Talmudic writings and early tradition, "those that sealed" the new covenant became the great synagogue (Nehemiah 10:1-24). This important Jewish institution originally comprised 120 members (afterward reduced to 70) from representative national groups: the scribes, chief priests, Levites, and chiefs of the people and of the cities. The duties of this synagogue included collecting and preserving the Scriptures, safeguarding the purity of the nation by forbidding intermarriage with pagans, preservation of the Sabbath, commemoration of the feasts, and so on. The great synagogue lasted for over a century, when it became known as the Sanhedrin, the supreme governing body of the Jewish nation. By that time it had departed so far from the simple truth of the Word of God, had become so wrapped up in rabbinical traditions, that it was a ready tool in Satan's hand to bring about the crucifixion of Christ.

In the psalmist's day, however, it was a small but notable assembly. It was this assembly of beloved little flock which the psalmist summons to sing. It was as thus that the Lord Jesus addressed His disciples: "Fear not, little flock; for it is your Father's good pleasure to give you the kingdom" (Luke 12:32).

Our thoughts go to the scattered assemblies of God's people in the world today. "Where two or three are gathered together in My name, there am I in the midst of them," our Lord says (Matthew 18:20). With such a one in their midst they cease to be a collection of this world's nobodies, but become assemblies of His favored ones. "Upon this rock I will build My church; and the gates of hell shall not prevail against it," our Lord has declared (Matthew 16:18).

We note next that:

2. The Great Creator of Israel Is Acclaimed (149:2-3)

The psalmist gives voice to two exclamations as he contemplates this wonderful God who has so generously adopted the nation of Israel as His own. He exclaims:

a. O! What a King! (149:2)

"Let Israel rejoice in Him that made him: let the children of Zion be joyful in their King." In the great confession that preceded the sealing of the covenant in the days of Nehemiah, the Levites prayed on behalf of the nation: "Now therefore, our God, the great, the mighty, and the terrible GOD, who keepest covenant and mercy, let not all the trouble seem little before Thee, that hath come upon us, on our kings, on our princes, and on our priests, and on our prophets, and on our fathers, and on all Thy People, since the time of the kings of Assyria unto this day. . . . Behold, we are servants this day, and for the land . . . it yieldeth much increase unto the kings whom Thou hast set over us because of our sins: also they have dominion over our bodies, and over our cattle, at their pleasure, and we are in great distress" (Nehemiah 9:32-37).

The psalmist wanted to lift the eyes of the remnant to the *real* King. Zion was the poetical name for Jerusalem and the prophetical name for the city as the center of all political power in the coming millennial age. The singer urged the children of Zion to acknowledge what a King they really had, not some Persian potentate but one who sat enthroned high and lifted up above any earthly prince.

b. O! How We Sing! (149:3)

"Let them praise His name in the dance: let them sing praises unto Him with the timbrel and harp." The psalmist wanted to see God's people happy in the Lord, so happy that it livened their steps, came out of their fingers, and came sounding out of their mouths. It was thus that David danced before the Lord with all his might when he brought up the ark to Jerusalem in his day. It is thus that God's people will sing and dance in a coming millennial morn when dancing is cleansed of its present impurities and is restored to spiritual men and women as a legitimate way of expressing the overflow of their love for the Lord.

The focus of the psalm now turns to:

II. THE SAINTS (149:4-5)

The psalmist has three things to say about God's beloved ones.

A. Their Blessing (149:4a)

"For the LORD taketh pleasure in His People." We soon get tired of pleasures centered in things or in entertainment. But we never get tired of the pleasure we derive from the company of those we love. After all, what pleasure does God get out of stars? He dismisses the creation of all the suns and stars of space in five words in the story of creation: "He made the stars also." He devotes twenty-five percent of the book of Genesis, however, to tell us of a man called Abraham; another twenty-five percent of the book to tell us about a man called Jacob; and another twenty-five percent tells about a man called Joseph. That is the Holy Spirit's way of showing us that God finds pleasure in His people. God is more interested in making saints than He is in making stars.

But how astonishing it is, just the same, that God should take pleasure in people, that He should take pleasure in stumbling Abraham, in sinning Jacob, and in suffering Joseph. To think that God derives His pleasure in the likes of us. What an astonishing fact.

B. Their Beauty (149:4b)

"He will beautify the meek with salvation." The salvation referred to here is not salvation from sin; it is deliverance. God loves the meek. Jesus said that the meek will inherit the earth: "Blessed [happy] are the meek." A lot of people today do not admire meekness because they equate meekness with weakness. They applaud the man who answers back, who gives blow for blow, not the man who replies with a soft word to one spoken in anger or who turns the other cheek.

Our forebears used to speak of "an affair of honor." In the circles of high society it was expected, as a matter of honor, that if a man was insulted he would respond immediately in kind. The result was a duel, usually fought with pistols or swords and usually ending in the death of one or other of the estranged parties. To refuse to respond to an insult or challenge branded a man a coward and led to his exclusion from aristocratic society and from the company of his peers. When a man refused to fight a duel, his honor was tarnished. In point of fact, however, to refuse to fight a duel took more courage than to fight one. A man of a meek and quiet spirit, in declining to defend his honor by the world's code, might actually be displaying the very highest kind of courage: moral courage. His contemporaries, however, would find it difficult to appreciate that. Meekness was not a quality they admired.

It is a quality, however, that God prizes. It was a quality of character of the bravest man who ever lived on earth. Nobody could accuse the Son of God of cowardice. He had the courage to face scoffing and scorn, the Roman scourge, and the cross. For,

> By meekness and defeat
> He won the throne, the crown;
> Trod all His foes beneath His feet
> By being trodden down.

God has pledged Himself to beautify the meek with deliverance. This world may trample on them, but this world never has the last say. Look again at the Lord Jesus. See Him standing there before Pilate with His lips sealed, ("as a sheep before her shearers is dumb, so He opened not His mouth"). See Him give His back to the smiters, His cheeks to those that plucked off the hair (Isaiah 50:6). At His call were twelve legions of angels straining over the battlements of heaven, waiting for a single word from the Son of God. One word from Him and they would have swept this world clean of evil men in a moment. They would have ushered in Armageddon two thousand years before its time. He had not come down here to fight, however, to answer blow for blow; He had come to exhibit meekness.

God says that He will beautify the meek with deliverance. And so, God rent the tomb, raised Jesus from the dead, lifted Him to the highest halls of heaven, seated Him at His right hand, crowned Him with glory and honor, and set Him forth as the most beautiful man in the universe.

C. Their Bliss (149:5)

"Let the saints be joyful in glory: let them sing aloud upon their beds." The psalmist thinks God's people should be a happy people. They should sing as they go to bed, when they awaken in the dark watches of the night, when they awake in the morning. So often bed is a place where people worry and fret. Trouble comes, things go wrong, and bed becomes an instrument of torture. The saints of God are to turn those hours when sleep flees into hours when the soul gets in touch with God and sings.

The phrase "in glory" used by the psalmist can be rendered "with [ascriptions] of glory." In other words we are to glorify God. When we cannot sleep, we can sing!

The thought of the glory of God, the glory of the heavens where God lives, the glory of the coming millennial reign, the glory the Lord Jesus had with the Father before the worlds began and which He laid aside for the years of His sojourn on earth, the glory He has assumed again but manifested now in a glorified body, the glory that outshines the sun and outlives the stars—thoughts of this glory (which we shall one day share) should banish sobs and sighs and tune our hearts to song. Such thoughts will turn night into day in the soul's darkest hour. As we have seen in a whole segment of the psalms, the Lord Jesus, in the upper room, faced Gethsemane, Abbatha, Golgotha, and the grave with song.

Now comes the final movement of the psalm. The final subject is:

III. THE SWORD (149:6-9)

The psalmist points the way to victory for the saints of God. He has two things to say about "the sword of the Spirit, the word of God" (Ephesians 6:17).

A. Trusting in That Sword (149:6)

God has entrusted to His saints a powerful weapon, one feared by Satan; we can have implicit trust in its power, the power of the Word of God.

1. What Must First Be in Our Heart (149:6a)

"Let the high praises of GOD be in their mouth." God is not going to entrust His mighty sword to everyone. It is the praising person who is the prevailing person. Believers have the high praise of God in their mouths because they have the high praise of God in their hearts.

How worthy God is to be praised: eternal, uncreated, self-existing; omnipotent, omniscient, omnipresent; holy, just, true; tender and loving, gracious and kind. He is Father, Son, and Holy Spirit. He is and was and is to be. He is Elohim, Adonai, and Jehovah.

We praise Him for what He is and for what He does. We praise Him that He is too loving to be unkind, too wise to make mistakes, too powerful to be thwarted in His good and acceptable and perfect will.

No wonder we are called on to occupy ourselves with the high praises of God. Those who will thus extol and exalt the living God in their hearts will have a song in their mouths. Tears will be transformed into rainbows. When we learn what must be first in our hearts we are ready for the next thing.

2. What May Then Be in Our Hand (149:6b)

"And a twoedged sword in their hand." The two-edged sword is "quick, and powerful," able to pierce through to the inner man. It is "a discerner of the thoughts and intents of the heart" (Hebrews 4:12). It is the one great weapon with which we can meet all attacks, whether from men or from the evil one. We are not to rely on our own cleverness or wisdom, but on God's Word.

The word translated "discerner" in Hebrews 4, *kritikos* (critic), is used only once in the New Testament. The Word of God is to be man's ultimate judge (John 12:48). What folly it is for anyone to set themselves up as a "higher critic" of God's Word. What folly for men to bring their human powers of reasoning, darkened by sin, deceived by Satan, and to sit in judgment on God's Word. God has ordained that the Scriptures, which they arrogantly dismiss as full of errors and contradictions, as unreliable and uninspired, will be their doom in the end.

God's Word can divide between soul and spirit. It can separate between that which is born of the flesh and that which is born of the spirit. It can differentiate between the natural man (*psuchikos*) and the spiritual (*pneumatikos*) man (1 Corinthians 2:13-15), something it is virtually impossible for us to do.

God's Word is the weapon we use in our battle with Satan. In the list of the Christian's armor it is the only weapon for attack; note that all the others are for defense (Ephesians 6:17). When Satan first attacked the human race in the garden of Eden, his primary goal was to persuade Eve to discard the sword of the Spirit, the Word of God. As long as she relied on what God had said, Satan could get nowhere.

God's Word was the only weapon Jesus used in His hour of temptation. To every suggestion of Satan He simply said "It is written. . . ."

B. Thrusting with That Sword (149:7-9)

The scene in these closing verses is almost certainly millennial, although it can apply to us today as we use God's Word, the Spirit's mighty sword, in our spiritual warfare. When the Lord descends out of the sky to engage the enemy at Megiddon, the sword comes out of His mouth to destroy His foes (Revelation 19:15). He uses that sword to deal with Satan, with the beast, with the false prophet, and with millions of men massed to oppose His return to earth. It seems the psalmist has this in mind as he speaks of the way the saints will use the sword. The Lord will leave "mopping up operations" to His saints once He has dealt with their principal foes. They will use the sword:

1. In Vengeance (149:7-8)

"To execute judgment upon the heathen, and punishments upon the people; to bind their kings with chains, and their nobles with fetters of iron." Thus, with God's Word as their authority, the saints will round up the remaining Gentiles and bring them, bound, to Jerusalem to stand trial in the valley of Jehoshaphat.

2. As Viceroys (149:9)

"To execute upon them the judgment written: This honor have all His saints. Praise ye the LORD." The sword of the magistrate will be wielded on earth, during the millennial age, by the restored, redeemed, and rejoicing Hebrew people. The sword of supreme justice will be wielded by the saints of the church age, dwelling in heavenly places, those who have trampled on the serpent himself (Romans 16:20) and judged angels (1 Corinthians 6:3). They will judge the world throughout the millennial age (1 Corinthians 6:2). But, high over all, reigning in glory, will be the Lord Himself. "Praise ye the LORD!"

This, then, is the song of the sword. The world places its confidence in the secular sword, the sword of the conqueror, the empire builder. The world settles its disputes with the sword. The sword will become more and more prominent in world affairs as the end of the age of grace draws near and the judgment age begins.

The people of God place their confidence in the spiritual sword, the sword of the Spirit, the Word of God. The world may despise that weapon but the world will learn to fear it, as Satan does, with a terror that defies description.

Psalm 150

THE HALLELUJAH CHORUS

WE COME FINALLY to the last psalm, the climax of the great doxology, the "Hallelujah Chorus" of the Hebrew hymn book. The sobs and sighs of many a previous psalm are now changed into shouts and songs. The wistful longings, triumphant hopes, and soaring faith of so many of the Hebrew hymns are now caught up in rapture and made to reverberate around the throne of God. We stand now at faith's Niagara, entranced by its resistless flow of praise, dazzled by its rainbow-tinted spray, awestruck by its thundering sound. Nowhere, not even in the vastness of the book of Psalms itself, is there anything to compare with this last resounding doxology of praise.

The book of Psalms begins with God blessing man: "Blessed is the man that walketh not in the counsel of the ungodly, nor standeth in the way of sinners, nor sitteth in the seat of the scornful. . . ." The book of Psalms ends with man blessing God. In this last psalm praise to God springs up like a fountain. It spreads out in all directions. It plunges down again only to soar once more skyward in an endless round of song.

We note four things in this psalm.

I. The Proper Auditorium (150:1)

The psalmist mentions two spheres where God is to be praised, one below, the other above; one on earth and one in heaven. The golden thread uniting both worlds is praise to God. The auditorium above and the auditorium below are much the same. The one is a copy of the other (Hebrews 8:5; 9:23; 1 Chronicles 28:11,13,19). The heavenly hosts above and the human hosts below blend their voices in harmony. The deep bass notes, learned in many a sorrowful hour down here below, join with the high treble notes of those who have known nothing, since the morn of their creation, but the bliss and beauty of heaven's enchanted halls.

Like a modern musician at some grand piano keyboard this ancient singer uses both his hands to bring out the two-part harmony. His right hand races up the keyboard to its highest, most rarified notes. His other hand moves down to the booming notes of the bass. He brings together the two worlds of the piano keyboard, the notes above middle C, the notes below. The music of the two spheres comes together in harmonious blending of sound.

A. The Sacred Auditorium Below (150:1a)

"Praise ye the LORD. Praise God in His sanctuary." That's the auditorium below. It had just been rebuilt in the psalmist's day. From the ruins and rubble of Solomon's temple had been raised a second temple, not so magnificent as the first, but still suitable as an arena of praise. This new auditorium had been dedicated with a mixture of sadness and sentiment, solemnity and song. Compared with Solomon's magnificent temple it was a humble edifice. Compared, too, with the temple rebuilt by Herod, the temple of the repatriated Jews from Babylon was none too grand. Solomon had lavished upon his temple the wealth of a nation made rich by the conquests of David. Upon Herod's temple, too, would be poured the labor of a generation and the genius of a king who, however wicked, knew how to build.

The repatriated Jew, in the days of Persian power, could praise God in His sanctuary nevertheless. Such as it was, it served and God accepted it. He who one day would come down to sojourn on earth as a carpenter, who was content to enter into human life in a cattle shed, and who lived and died in poverty, was not too proud to accept, as His temple, a sanctuary which, though far from splendid, was the best an impoverished, struggling people could do. They could praise God there. It was His. He accepted it as His. That was enough.

The *people* could praise Him in the outer courts. They could praise Him in the sin and trespass offerings for sins forgiven. They could praise Him in the meal offering for the glorious perfection, purity, and evenness of His person. They could praise Him in the peace offering for His grace in condescending to sit down with them to a meal. In an overflow of gratitude, they could praise Him in the burnt offering—lavishly with an ox or in a lowly way with a dove.

The *priests* could praise Him at the laver, which not only revealed the incidental defilement of their walk through the wilderness of this world, but which also made provision for that defilement to be removed. They could praise Him in the holy place, giving thanks for the lampstand which shed a golden light on their ministry. They could praise Him for the table which brought them into even closer weekly communion with Himself. They could praise Him at the golden altar where their praise could ascend Godward in clouds of fragrant incense.

The high priest, once a year, could praise God inside the veil, in the holiest place of all. He could praise Him standing before the sacred ark and the mercy seat. He could praise Him that the cherubim, those glittering guardians of God's creatorial and redemptive rights on earth, were forever occupied, gazing inward and downward, with the blood. They could praise Him in the beauty of holiness.

We should, of course, learn to praise God everywhere and anywhere. But there is such a thing as praising Him in His sanctuary, in the gathering place of His people, with those, many or few, who gather in His name and where He has promised to be.

B. The Spacious Auditorium Above (150:1b)

"Praise Him in the firmament of His power." The word *firmament* is literally "expanse." Rotherham puts it like this: "Praise ye Him for the spreading out of His strength." That rendering conjures up for us an impressive picture of God. It sets before us the upper sanctuary where He sits enthroned in a limitless expanse and from which His power reaches out beyond the confines of time and space. The spacious auditorium above seems to be designed on similar lines with the Hebrew temple which was a model on human terms of the temple above. That temple comes into view from time to time in the apocalypse. We find the Lord, in that book, taking up His position in relation to the cherubim in the inner holy of holies. We see the crystal stream of which the laver, perhaps, was a mirror. We see the Lord at the golden altar with the golden censer in His hand. We see Him at the brazen altar.

The end-time events of the apocalypse are introduced by an awe-inspiring vision of the upper sanctuary, the place of "the spreading out of His strength." We hear the four living creatures, the cherubim, praising Him with their ceaseless chant: "Holy! Holy! Holy!"—Holy Father, Holy Son, Holy Spirit. We see the four and twenty elders praising Him in acts of deepest obeisance, casting down their golden crowns before the glassy sea. We see the countless multitude of the heavenly host broadcasting His praise until the courts of heaven ring. We see too "the spirits of just men made perfect," those of every kindred, people, nation, and tongue, who have been ransomed, healed, restored, forgiven, joining their voices with the celestial sons of light. At the focal center of things, close to the throne, the bright spirits who throng the courts of bliss, and there, too, at the farthest circumference of things, where dread darkness reigns, all praise Him. We are on our way yonder. Then we who have tuned our harps in the auditorium below will blend our voices in the auditorium above:

> At the name of Jesus bowing,
>   Falling prostrate at His feet;
> King of Kings in Heaven we'll crown Him
>   When our journey is complete.

For every knee *shall* bow and every tongue *shall* "confess that Jesus Christ is Lord, to the glory of God the Father" (Philippians 2:10).

He is to be praised eternally, in all places, at all times, world without end, in the spacious auditorium above. The thunder of that praise will find answering echoes in the deep, lonely caverns of the lost. "Worthy is the Lamb that was slain!"

Some of us have loved ones in that spacious auditorium in the skies. Their worship blends with ours. We can join our hallelujahs with those who sing out around the throne. And this indeed we do, everytime in private or in public worship we praise the Lord.

II. THE PEALING ANTHEM (150:2)

"Praise Him for His mighty acts: praise Him according to His excellent greatness." One of His mighty acts, in the psalmist's day, was to sweep Babylon off the map and replace it on the world stage by Persia. One of His mighty acts was to put on the throne of the world a man by the name of Cyrus, whose coming and name He had foretold a hundred years before, who issued a decree of emancipation ending the captivity for the Jewish people. That was a mighty act, evidence of His excellent greatness, indication that a giant step forward had been taken in human history toward the coming of the Christ.

What had happened so dramatically in the psalmist's day has happened again in ours. God picked up a great world power with an empire on which the sun never set and used it to settle Israel back in the land. Moreover, as He did in the days of the psalmist, He has preserved the reborn nation against the bitter and unrelenting attacks of its foes. In so doing, He has heralded to our age that a move has been made in world history toward the second coming of Christ. Hardly a day goes by without Israel making the headlines. God is speaking to a generation, which has set aside the Bible, from the pages of the newspaper and newscasts on the television screen. Time and again in history God has acted to bring glory to His name. The book still awaits a writer who will explore the onward march of history and chronicle all the events that mark God's hand in human affairs. Such a book, when written, will give us the greatest apologetic of all: humankind will then learn that history is *His story*.

What a movement was made in history when Jesus was born. What a heart-stopping moment of time it was when Jesus died, the just for us the unjust, to bring us to God. What a monumental moment it was when He arose from the dead. What a moment it was in history when the Holy Spirit of God swept into that crowded upper room in Jerusalem and gave birth to the Christian church, the mystical body of Christ. What a moment it was when the New Testament was completed and when the world had, for its own, God's final revelation of Himself. What a moment it was when Saul of Tarsus was converted. What a moment when He obeyed the Spirit's call, and crossed over to Europe with the gospel. What a moment it was when Roman missionaries brought the gospel to the shores of Britain to set a tremendous seal on the English speaking world. What a moment it was when the translation of the Bible into English was completed. Who will ever be able to evaluate the impact the English Bible has had on the world?

These are some of God's mighty acts that demonstrate His excellent greatness. These are some of the things that fill out the anthems of our praise.

III. THE PERFECT ACCOMPLISHMENT (150:3-5)

The psalmist tells us how this melody of praise is to be made.

A. The Trumpet Call (150:3a)

"Praise Him with the sound of the trumpet." This instrument is the *shophar,* the curved ram's horn used by the watchman on the city wall; used too by warriors on the march; and also used by the worshipers in the temple. The use of the trumpet goes back to Mosaic times.

The music here, then, begins with the sound of the trumpet, designed to arouse the sleeper. It reminds us that with the sound of the trumpet Jesus is coming again. It reminds us of the annual feast of trumpets among the Jews, reminds us that with seven trumpet blasts the end-time events of the Apocalypse will be hurried on to their climax. It was with a great sound of a trumpet that the walls of Jericho fell down. Those mighty walls of that impregnable Canaanite fortress fell flat on the ground.

A trumpet blast clears away wandering thoughts and wins our instant and total attention. It banishes rebellious thoughts, commands us to gird up the loins of the mind, prepares us for the great work of praising the Lord. Away with sloth and sleep. Away with idle daydreams. Away with all that would hinder worship. Let the clarion call of the trumpet, then, alert us, quicken us, ring out like a summons in our souls.

B. The Triumphant Chords (150:3b-4)

Here we have the stringed instruments. "Praise Him with the psaltery and harp"—the lute and the lyre. The lute was a kind of portable guitar; the harp was larger with deeper tones, better able to bring in the bass. The ability to compose music and to play complicated scores on multiple instruments must surely be numbered among the greatest human accomplishments. Music, as such, seems to have been invented by Jubal, one of the sons of Cain. He it was who first filled a sad world with the sound of song.

The first recorded song in Scripture, the first real hymn, shows that music was adopted by the people of God and converted by them into an instrument for praise (Exodus 15).

The composition of music calls for considerable expertise. A composer must have a grasp of music theory and the ability to produce the desired sounds and harmonies in a written score. Composing music also demands a high degree of inspiration, natural talent, imagination, and inventiveness. The ability to play an instrument calls for companion skills. There must be diligence in mastering the mechanical techniques as well as a certain natural flair.

A well-played piece of music has a magic all its own. It can stir the emotions and set the soul aflame. Each composition makes its own appeal whether it be a martial air, a sentimental ballad, a national anthem, a great old hymn of the faith, a rousing chorus, a popular ditty, a splendid symphony, or a childish lullaby. And, while we admire the skill of the composer and the conductor, the talent of the instrumentalist, soloist, or choir, the real appeal of music is to the emotions. Music can put courage into a platoon of marching men, melting away the miles beneath their weary feet. Music can evoke shouts and applause, it can produce mass hysteria, it can reduce a man to tears or inflame him with rage. But its greatest use is to evoke worship in the human heart.

It is by no means an accident that, next to our Bibles, we cherish our hymnbooks. Every great spiritual revival in history has produced its own additions to the vast collection of sacred hymns of the faith. Where would John Wesley have been without his brother Charles? Where would D. L. Moody have been without his friend and colleague Ira Sankey?

The psalmist then calls for the percussion instruments: "Praise Him with the timbrel and dance." The timbrel is the tambourine, a hand drum, an instrument for emphasizing the rhythm, for beating out the time. If lute and lyre get the fingers flying, the timbrel gets music and praise into the feet. It is an instrument naturally linked by the psalmist with dance.

Then the psalmist calls for more strings as well as for a new segment of the orchestra, the wind instruments. "Praise Him with stringed instruments and organs." The strings, here a generic term, comprise a basic section in any orchestra: the humming notes of the violin, the deep notes of the bass fiddle.

In the psalmist's day the pipe (here translated organs) would have been a simple wind instrument made up of a number of reeds into which the musician blew, as we today would blow into a mouth organ. In time this simple pipe developed into the organ as we know it. Even in Talmudic times it had become a considerable instrument, capable of producing a hundred sounds.

C. The Tremendous Crescendo (150:5)

"Praise Him upon the loud cymbals: praise Him upon the high sounding cymbals." The psalmist now has his orchestra almost complete. The trumpets are sounding long and loud. The stringed instruments are adding warmth to the swelling song. The timbrels are beating out the time. The pipes are adding body to the whole. Hands and feet are aiding mouth and lungs as the music swells. Then, as a final climax, the psalmist calls for the cymbals.

There were two kinds of cymbals. There was "the cymbal of clear tone" which added a ringing emphasis to the beat. There was "the cymbal of loud clang" which was used from time to time to overpower all other sound and call for silence. At its loud summons all sound would cease. A sudden cessation of all sound is impressive. The swelling volume of sound, overpowered by the cymbal of loud clang, stopped. Like that "silence in heaven about the space of half an hour" of which John speaks, the silence must have been deafening. The loud clang of that lordly cymbal added to the music a kind of musical "*Selah!*"

Then, in the sudden silence, perhaps the voice of a soloist would be heard, his words penetrating into the depths of the human soul. And then, perhaps, the choir would pick up the strain and again the orchestra would join in.

IV. The Participating Audience (150:6)

"Let everything that hath breath praise the LORD. Praise ye the LORD." The orchestra is in full voice. The choir sings out with all its might. The grand conductor himself, the chief Musician, turns to the enraptured assembled crowds. He beckons to them. He calls upon everyone to sing. Now, heart and mind, hands and feet, lungs and breath, all the orchestra, all the choir, all the people, unite in a volume of sound fitting to the worship of a God of majesty, mercy, and might.

Then, would it be too much, to visualize the chief Musician Himself, the Lord Jesus Christ, beckoning to *us*, the heaven-born, heaven-bound church, living in an age of grace, with the invitation, *"Praise ye the Lord"*? With that the Hebrew hymnbook ends.

> Crown Him with many crowns, the Lamb upon
>   His throne;
> Hark! how the heavenly anthem drowns all
>   music but its own.
> Awake, my soul, and sing of Him who died
>   for thee,
> And hail Him as thy matchless King
>   through all eternity.